The Professional Make-up *Artist*
Volume III

Motion Pictures • Television • Print • Theatre

The Professional Make-up *Artist*

Motion Pictures • Television • Print • Theatre

VOLUME III
Laboratory Procedures

Joe Blasco   Vincent J-R Kehoe

Library of Congress Control Number: 2006905073 July , 2011

© 2008 by Joe Blasco.

ISBN 0-9771580-1-2

10 9 8 7 6 5 4 3 2 1

Published by Joe Blasco

To those who were, are, and will be Professional Make-up Artists, this work is gratefully and sincerely dedicated.

The contents of this book represent the art, skills, and useful current methods of many knowledgeable and working professional make-up artists, including the writings of the two authors, who have carefully compiled the procedures and regimens currently being employed in professional studio work.

This book is intended to be used not only as a text for make-up artist schools, but also as an up-to-date reference guide for both studio and laboratory procedures and methodology.

The most current technical data from laboratory results have been included to provide the student and aspirant to the profession with the latest information possible. All aspects from the simplest to the most complex are covered to present many choices for creating all variations from basic to complex procedures for character and laboratory work.

The authors recommend Volume I of this work as required study prior to commencing with Volume II. The complete understanding and mastering of the information and techniques found in the first volume will provide the reader with the profound education necessary for becoming a more consummate artist of character make-up and special make-up effects.

The future is created through your inspired and passionate imagination.

Contents

AUTHORS' BIOGRAPHIES   xii

FOREWORD   xvi

ACKNOWLEDGMENTS   xix

PREFACE   xxxiii

INTERLUDE   xxxv

INTRODUCTION I, VOL III   xxxvii

INTRODUCTION II, VOL III, JOE BLASCO   xxxix

INTRODUCTION III, VOL III, JOE BLASCO   3

INTRODUCTION IV, VOL III, VINCENT J-R KEHOE   7

CHAPTER 1: BASIC PROSTHESES   9

LAB TECHNIQUES   11

   Sculpture Materials   11

   Molds   14

LATEX AND PLASTIC MATERIALS   24

   Natural Rubber Materials   24

   Plastic Materials   38

CHAPTER 2: PROSTHETIC MAKE-UP MATERIALS   95

**CHAPTER 3: NATURAL AND FOAM RUBBER
HISTORY AND TECHNIQUES**   119

FOAM USE   123

    The Beginning of Foam Use in Motion Pictures   123

    Early Foam Use   124

MODERN FOAM   126

    Chemistry of Modern Foam   128

    Types of Mixers and Their Uses   129

    Mold Filling   131

    Types of Mold Materials   134

    Demolding, Washing, Storage   136

    Seaming and Patching   138

    Tips for Running Foam Latex   137

    Gil Mosko Application   144

CHAPTER 4: SCULPTING AGE   149

    Mark Alfrey Application   151

    Kazuhiro Tsuji Applications   156

CHAPTER 5: CREATING A BALD CAP   161

    Ed French Application   163

CHAPTER 6: DENTAL VENEERS   171

    Casting Teeth   173

    Making a Silicone Master of Dental Casts   180

    Making Dentures   184

    Making Vacuum-formed Veneers   193

    Making Vacuum-formed Veneers with Acrylic Tooth Added   198

CHAPTER 7: BLADDERS   201

    Making Bladders   203

CHAPTER 8: ARTISTS WORKING WITH SILICONE   215

    Silicone Appliances (Justin Raleigh)   217

    Environmental Conditions and Mold Acceptability   222

    Encapsulates   223

Pigmentation of Silicone   224

Preparation, Application, and Adhesion of Silicone Appliances   228

Step-by-step Condensation Cure Silicone
    Gel-filled Appliances with a Balloon Rubber Encapsulate   228

Application   246

Removal   266

Interview: Greg Cannom   269

CHAPTER 9: CASTING   289

Interview: Matthew Mungle   291

PROCEDURES   299

Alginate   299

Ply-O-Life   337

Digital Renderings   370

Additional Technique   372

CHAPTER 10: MOLDS   387

Positive and Negative Molds   387

CHAPTER 11: GELATIN   489

Gelatin   489

CONCLUSION   581

APPENDIX A   583

THE MAKE-UP SCHOOL   583

How to Select a Make-up School   585

Attending a Make-up School   603

After Graduation and Starting Out in Business   604

When You Are Working   605

What Makes Joe Blasco Make-up Artist Training Unique   607

Hollywood Supply House History and Legends the True Story   627

APPENDIX B   613

CURRENT SUPPLIERS AND MANUFACTURERS   613

DEDICATIONS   627

VINCENT J-R KEHOE
Biography

This is his 15th book on the art of make-up, the first being published in 1958. His career started in 1940 with the Lowell Light Opera Guild when he designed the make-up for Gilbert and Sullivan's *Iolanthe* and *The Gondoliers*. Shortly after he joined the U.S. Signal Corps, he then transferred to the Mountain Troops as a ski instructor, another of his civilian professions. After being discharged in 1945, he went back to the city of his birth, New York City, and by 1948 became the first make-up artist for the CBS-TV network, designing all the Ford Theatre and Studio One productions. The following year, he commenced doing make-up for films and then moved back to television, where he became Head of Make-up for all the original Hallmark Hall of Fame productions for two years. He then worked on the following films: *Giant, The Court-Martial of Billy Mitchell, The Thomas Crown Affair,* and finally, *Charly,* which won its star, Cliff Robertson, the Academy Award®. In 1962 he started the Research Council of Make-up Artists, a firm that produces specialized make-up for the studios, and he has been both Director of Research and President ever since. His further biography can be found in *Who's Who in America, Who's Who in the World,* and *Who's Who in Entertainment.*

With a BFA in motion picture and television production from Columbia University in 1957, he went on to become the pioneer of make-up artistry instruction through his historic first book, *The Technique of Film and Television Make-up.* For five years, from 1962 through 1966, he directed all make-up for the International Beauty Show in New York City. In the film *On the Waterfront,* Mr. Kehoe researched the make-up which was done for Marlon Brando and worked on two motion pictures with Steve McQueen on location in Boston and Pennsylvania. The Pennsylvania film was none other than the historic *The Blob!* Mr. Kehoe designed and applied all of the make-up for the film and worked closely with the special visual effects artists by providing them his learned input.

Aside from his many triumphs in make-up artistry, Mr. Kehoe has written two award-winning books on the art of Los Toros, as well as eight books on American Revolutionary War history.

Now with all of these accomplishments behind him, he and Joe Blasco have joined forces to create what they feel will be the most definitive book on the art of make-up—in full color—ever written.

JOE BLASCO
Biography

The name Joe Blasco, which is rapidly becoming as well-known to the general public as it already is in the make-up industry, is synonymous with glamorous celebrity make-up, high quality cosmetics products, and cutting-edge make-up artistry education.

Born in a small suburb of Pittsburgh, Pennsylvania, Joe Blasco began his study of the art of make-up at the early age of 7. He was awarded a scholarship to cosmetology school, and after graduating in 1964 at the age of 18, he arrived in Hollywood to work for the Max Factor Cosmetics Company as a traveling make-up artist representative. After receiving their training, he discovered he was to be sent to Pittsburgh to represent the company in various department stores. Unhappy with the situation, he left the Factor Company with $50 in his pocket to pursue a career in Hollywood as a make-up artist.

In 1967 he took a job as an instructor with a small, obscure society make-up school in Westwood, California. Recognizing the need for a course that taught motion picture and television make-up artistry, Blasco created a new curriculum for the school. The school, under Blasco's direction, became the first to teach full-time courses in professional make-up artistry. For three years, while working for various production companies, Blasco also apprenticed with major professional cosmetics manufacturing firms as a cosmetics chemist and compounder. As a make-up artist working in film and television, he experienced first-hand what made a cosmetic product ideal for use in these mediums.

His career progressed rapidly. Blasco worked at all the major television networks in Hollywood as his reputation grew. He became renowned for his work in the development of new and unique techniques for special make-up effects, especially as an innovator of the "bladder technique" utilized in films depicting horror/monster transformations showing bulging and bubbling skin effects. He became personal make-up artist to scores of personalities including Rona Barrett, Bette Midler, Olivia Newton-John, Lauren Bacall, Carol Burnett, Donnie and Marie Osmond, Dick Clark, Hal Linden, Carmen Zapata, Dorothy Lamour, the late Orson Welles, and scores of others too numerous to mention.

In 1976, he opened the doors of the first of two Make-up Training Centers, which have since received international acclaim. In 1984, Blasco introduced his cosmetics line to professionals in Hollywood. Today, Joe Blasco Cosmetics can be found in fine retail outlets worldwide.

In 2004, Mr. Blasco received a distinguished Lifetime Achievement Award from the USITT (United States Institute of Theatre Technology). The Award in Make-up Artistry, Make-up Manufacturing, and for pioneering professional make-up schools was the first of its kind ever bestowed by the prestigious organization.

Mr. Blasco is currently embarking on establishing a broadband broadcast system for teaching make-up that would enable students from around the world to interact with teachers from his domestic make-up schools. The project, which is the first of its kind, is the next step in the evolution of make-up education, and has become part of the new Joe Blasco Make-up School curriculum in Hollywood, Orlando, Amsterdam, Helsinki, and through several Joe Blasco seminar centers in New York City.

Joe Blasco remains a consultant to many celebrities and continues to set higher standards in the cosmetics industry with his many new and unique products. Mr. Blasco, aside from being listed in *Who's Who in Business*, also appears in over 64,000 web listings. His make-up schools continue to dominate make-up education worldwide through the use of not only his most up-to-date techniques, but also from the collaborative efforts and contributions of the most highly respected working veteran professional make-up artists from Local 706 I.A.T.S.E. Hollywood and Local 798 I.A.T.S.E. New York, as well as from those of the most elite European union and independent make-up artists alike. This book represents only a small portion of the detailed knowledge that is offered to students of his make-up schools.

Foreword

BY JOE BLASCO

Make-up artistry is a fine art form that originated centuries ago. Scientists have recently discovered a 2.4 × 2 inch tin canister dating back to the mid-second century AD. The small pot was found in an excavated Roman temple in London, deep within thick layers of mud beneath a waterlogged ditch. The cream contained within the canister was white and was probably intended to be worn by fashionable Roman women, for a fair complexion was popular during Roman times, according to historians. The scientists who unearthed this incredible discovery have speculated that the material, which consists of approximately 40 percent animal fat, probably from cattle or sheep, and 60 percent starch and zinc oxide, was a foundation cream. The fat comprised the creamy base vehicle, while the starch acted as a thickening agent. The zinc oxide was the pigment that provided the mixture with its white color and opacity. This formula does not differ much from ones created by today's cosmetics technologies. In fact, the inert quality of the zinc oxide would alleviate any dermatological problems. It is amazing that throughout history, cosmetics, in terms of formulation, have actually changed very little.

Innovative systems of high-quality make-up and precise color coordination principles help the modern-day professional make-up artist meet the demands and technical standards of film, television, stage, and fashion photography.

Professional make-up manufacturers are continually improving their lines, as well as developing new products in order to remain on the cutting edge of this ever-changing industry. With great advances in film, video, lighting, and processing chemistry, today's photographic systems can easily detect critical variations in skin color, texture, reflectivity, and contrast, which makes it more important than ever before to furnish the professional make-up artist with the finest materials available, as well as to educate the artist in state-of-the-art techniques and applications.

An additional purpose of this book is to provide you—the aspiring and the professional make-up artist—with the accurate information needed to remain up-to-date and advised of the professional materials and application techniques used in this wonderful field. As a reference guide, this book will also aid you in selecting proper colors and products to create the polished, professional image that best suits the needs of each client upon whom your wondrous work is performed.

It is my opinion that a make-up artist must fully understand the fact that he or she is truly a *sculptor of light*. By that, I mean that as artists, we apply color, texture, and form to the human face, which by reflecting, absorbing, and/or refracting light will create the illusion of either beauty or character. This methodology is often only thought of as being related to character make-up, however, despite the fact that it is paramount, and sometimes more vital, for the execution of an undetectable, yet flawless beauty and/or corrective make-up procedure that appears entirely natural.

From early in my career, I had longed to one day produce a book that would show the many outstanding and creative character make-up and special make-up effects techniques that I learned from my past teachers, and which I have also been blessed with the ability to innovate. This volume is the physical manifestation of that longtime desire. For many years, I have taught the intricate make-up procedures which you will see in this book at my Hollywood and Orlando Make-up Schools. It is now my privilege and pleasure to make this knowledge available to you—our most valued readers.

Prior to embarking on any make-up procedure, the make-up artist studies the face and figure, touching on character analysis and perhaps physiognomy as a basis for artistic departure, lest the artistic endeavor leave unconvincing, unnatural, or "made-up" results.

I was very fortunate to learn many of these important basic theories and principles of the art during my youth when, at the age of seven, I first stumbled upon a small book on stage make-up by Richard Corson (the second edition of *Stage Makeup*), which I immediately read from cover to cover, and the seed was planted. My fascination in the fine art of make-up was born. Shortly thereafter, on another elementary school library shelf, I found the book that would change my life: *The Technique of Film and Television Make-up* by Vincent J-R Kehoe. This fine book nurtured my interest in make-up artistry and enabled my fascination to grow to a level at which my passion to become a part of this awe-inspiring field would consume my every thought.

As a first-time reader, you will welcome and appreciate this book as the current standard text that defines the fine art and science of today's professional make-up artist. Others, who are familiar with the past writing of Vincent J-R Kehoe, will recognize Mr. Kehoe's inimitable style and intense effort to make this book his best.

As a make-up artist, educator, and cosmetics manufacturer, there have been many events that have greatly inspired, enriched, and validated my personal passion for the art of make-up. Now, after forty years in the field, I have experienced an event that has overshadowed all other events, both professionally and personally: collaborating with my teacher, Mr. Vincent J-R Kehoe. Those of you who are familiar with my history will know that I have been permitted to count among my friends and instructors many legendary make-up masters. However, my first instruction, prior to arriving in Hollywood, was received primarily from reading make-up textbooks and comparing my newly found knowledge to the work I closely observed on motion picture and television screens. The most technically correct and influential of those books were the early works of my teacher, Vincent J-R Kehoe.

My pride in collaborating in the writing of this book is only superceded by the immeasurable honor and rich opportunity I had been given when finally meeting and getting to know the man whose written words have guided me and innumerable others to success in this wonderful field.

I am confident in believing that I do speak for my current students and thousands of graduates and colleagues in saying, "Thank you, Vincent, for all the knowledge that you have so generously imparted to all involved in make-up artistry worldwide."

Together, Vincent J-R Kehoe and I, through this book, will introduce the knowledge that constitutes, dictates, and advances today's and tomorrow's state-of-the-art techniques of the studied and true professional make-up artist.

It has been my pleasure to personally apply many of the make-ups throughout this volume, in addition to providing the reader with a vast array of work from professional make-up artist contributors, who in my opinion, and in the opinion of Mr. Kehoe, represent some of the most outstanding and highly talented professional make-up artists of our time. You will note that the text throughout this book, although completely comprehensive, is in many ways enhanced by each photo caption's intricate details, which punctuate and often elaborate information that previously appears.

This book—through its copy and detailed photo captions—is ideally suited for use as a textbook in all schools that wish to teach the finest and most state-of-the-art techniques of professional make-up artistry. Although this book is the actual text used at the Joe Blasco Professional Make-up Schools, I have chosen to make this book available to *all* schools that wish to offer the techniques which have made many of today's best known make-up artists successful in their fields. The instruction herein represents many classic techniques, which have been taught to me by the great masters of the past, as well as techniques which I have refined and created specifically throughout my career, both for practical on-set purposes and for my students.

You now have, within your reach, the knowledge to excel. It has been a joy and a labor of love to work with Mr. Vincent J-R Kehoe in the production of this book, and he and I are certain that the benefits you will derive from its contents will be invaluable.

Acknowledgments

We wish to acknowledge the following for their contributions to the making of this book:

Edward Cuny Miller
Associate to Joe Blasco

John Cameron Cox
Chief Photographer and Digital Image Consultant
for Joe Blasco Hollywood, California and Orlando, Florida

The Eastman Kodak Company

Alan Masson, Technical Manager
and
Jay Beehner, Senior Process E-6 Specialist

The authors wish to thank the following individuals whose creative, artistic, and technical contributions have given form and flow to this work:

Chuck Alessio
Senior Production Advisor

Jason Pires
Creative and Production Director

Marioly Molina Pires
Key Production Artist

Michele Lingre
Senior Editor

Modern Visual Communication, Inc.
Etc. Graphics, Inc.
9205 Alabama Avenue, Suite E
Chatsworth, CA 91311
(818) 718-2005
www.modernvisual.com

The authors thank the following individual and company for specific digital photography of guest artists shot primarily in Los Angeles, California:

Jim Richer
Photographer

Thexposure Studio Incorporated
741 North Cahuenga Blvd.
Los Angeles, CA 90038-3701
323-460-4528
www.thexposurestudio.com

The authors wish to thank the following for providing information, inspiration, and/or life experiences, which have generously contributed to the success of our careers and the making of this book:

A & S Case

ABC-TV/Disney

A. Carlson Industries

Larry and Kathy Abbot

F. Murray Abraham

Forrest J. Ackerman

Acuvue

Alex Agupitan

Alan Gordon Enterprises, Inc.

Darla Albright

Alcone Company/Vincent Mallardi

Chuck Alessio

Henry Alfaro

Mark Alfrey

Steve Allen

American International Industries/
Peggy Beste and Terri Cooper

American International Pictures

Fred Anderson

Richard Anderson

Dorothy Andre

Julie Andrews

Art Anthony

John M. Appelroth

Stanley Arenberg

Samuel Z. Arkoff

Del Armstrong

James Arness

Danny Arnold

Bob Arrollo

Bea Arthur

The Artisan Magazine (Local 706)

Roy Ashton

Atlas Beauty Supply

Lauren Bacall and Humphrey Bogart

Miss Marilyn Bailey

Abe Balaban

Charles Balazs/Cinema Beauty Secrets,
Budapest, Hungary

Ball Beauty Supply

Holly Bane

Miss Rona Barrett

Jack Barron

George Bau

Gordon Bau

Mark Bautista

Les Baxter

Gene Beach

Ron Beaton

Ralph Bellamy

Steve Binder

Dr. Michael Bjornbak

Harry Blake

Joe Blasco, Sr.

Caesar Blasco

Knish Blasco

Malcolm Blasco

Rudy Blasco

Sunny Blasco

Fred Blau/Reel Creations

Frank Boch III

Frank Bolkovac

Larry Bones

Francis Bonfigli

Sonny Bono

Chuck Boswell

Shirley Botsford

Becky Bowen

Andrea Boyd

Robert Boyd

Adam Brandy

Ryan Brigman

Brioschi

Tia Britt

Brian Brown

Todd Browning

Jim Burchum & Co.

Bobby Burgess

Burman Industries

Barney Burman

Carol Burnett

Stephanie Cozart Burton

Doris Butler

Raffaella Butler

Ed Butterworth

John Byner

Tom Byner

Susan Cabral-Ebert

Sid Caesar

California Aviation

Ashlee Petersen Callahan

Beth Calliwag

Don Cambern

Greg Cannom

Captive Audience Productions, Inc./
    Michal Gregus

Bill Cardille

George Carey

Rod Carey

Ed Carlin

Richard Carlson

Don Carmody

Jim Carrey

Carter Sexton Art Supply

Marietta Carter-Narcisse

Bill Castleman

CBS-TV

Danny Celaya

Jim Centi

Louis Centi

Nancy Centi

Joe Cervantes

John Chambers

Charo

Lon Chaney, Jr.

Lon Chaney, Sr.

Ron Chaney

Francis Cheplik

Sarah Churchill

CIBA Vision/Amanda Cancel

Cinovation Studios

Dick Clark

Colin Clive

Helen Cohen

Tommy Cole

The Color Wheel Company

Ted Coodley

John Cooper

Roger Corman

Bill Corso

Richard Corson

Joseph Cotten

Jack Counts, Jr.

John Cox

David Cronenberg

Jordan S. Cronenweth

Scott Cunningham

Peter Cushing

Jim Cussmen

Allan Cutrow, Esq.

Larry Darr

John Davidson

Embeth Davidtz

Phil Davis, Esq.

Bob Dawn

Jack Dawn

Jeff Dawn

Glenn Dayton

Landy Dean

Vincent Dee

David DeLeon

Ivette Delestre

John Dennis

Alberto De Rossi

Ralph Desidario

Gregory Devlin

Ken Diaz

George Spiro Dibie

Rose Dinh

Joseph DiStefano

David Dittmar

Sam Dodge

Doris (Columbia Cosmetics)

Dick Drago

Joe Drago

Bari Dreiband-Burman

The DuMont Television Network

Jerry Dumphy

Sandra Dumphy

Tim Dunn

John Dunning

Jim Kelly Durgin

Duro-Test

Harold Dwyer

Eco-House

The Ed Sullivan Show

Don Edmonds

George Edwards

John Elliot

Jimmy Emerson, Karen Raider, and the

entire cast of *An Evening at La Cage* at the Riviera Hotel and Casino in Las Vegas, Nevada

Kris Evans

Peter Falk

Al Fama

Famous Monsters of Filmland magazine

Fangoria magazine

Farrell Hair Replacement/Richard Farrell and Michael Garcia

Bill Fife

Ron Figuly

Larry Fine

P.J. Finster

Terence Fisher

Ella Fitzgerald

Flax Art Supply

Flight East

Myron Floren

Forest Lawn Mortuary (Glendale)

Forest Lawn Mortuary (Hollywood Hills)

Hal Foster

FOX-TV

Tyson Fountaine

George Fragos

Ed French

Frends Beauty Supply/Emad Esper and Nigel Dare

Kelcey Fry

Dwight Frye, Sr.

Dwayne Fulcher

Bren Futura

Toni G

G.A. Enterprises/Gary Archer and Steven Anderson

Gable's Beauty Supply

Morgan Gaffney

Katherine Gavatorta

Michael Gavatorta

Jeanne Gerson

Estelle Getty

Alice Ghostly

Giles Gilbert

Ron Glass

James Glavan

Donald F. Glut

Michael Godfrey

Kelly Golden

Graftobian/Eric Coffman

Peter Graves

Dave Grayson

Dr. Mort Greenspoon

Lee Greenway

James Gregory

Aida Grey

Deborah Grieger

Lee Grimes

Ralph Guerriero

Sydney Guilaroff

Raf Guiterrez

Ralph Gulko

H. Kohnstamm Co.

Abe Haberman

Gene Hackman

Joe Hadley

Joe Hailey

Linda Haines

Stuart Haines

Monty Hall

Hallmark Hall of Fame

Margaret Hamilton

Scott Hamilton

Kevin Haney

Art Harding

Ray Harryhausen

John Hartford

Alexandra Hay

Zoe Hay

Billie Hayes

Don Henderson

Chuck Henry

Bernard Herman

Marilyn Hernandez

Julie Hewett

Gene Hibbs

Tyler Hillman

Al Hodges and Tobor

Kiva Hoffman

Cecil Holland

Fred Holliday

Hollywood Chamber of Commerce

Hollywood Forever Mortuary

Hollywood Star Video

Esther Horvatich

Rudy Horvatich

Curly Howard

Moe Howard

Shemp Howard

Jill Hudson

Ken Hurst

Bruce Hutchinson

Don Hutchenson

Image Exclusives/Monet and
 Dee Mansano

Dr. Robert Improta

Rick Ingersol

John Inzerella

Frank Ippolito

Betty Iverson

The Jack Benny Show

John Jackson

Japonesque

Bob Jermain

Ann Jillian

Steve Johnson

Morgan Jones

Rocky Jones S.R.

J.S. Graphics, Hollywood

Earl Kage

Gabe Kaplan

Steve Karkus

Boris Karloff

Lars Karlsson/Leslie Cosmetics, Vietnam

Marty Katz

Steven Kay

KDKA-TV

Mary Keats

Gena Kehoe

Tyler Kehoe

Mr. and Mrs. Kehoe
  (parents of Vincent Kehoe)

Richard Keil

Sean Kenney

KIEV Radio

Hal King

Sissy King

Kinoflo/Scott Stueckle

Kitchel Theatre

Kris Kobzina

Allan Kolman

Elisabeth Koningstein, Lelystad,
  The Netherlands

Koontz Hardware

Barry Koper

Martin Kosleck

Ernie Kovacs

Eryn Krueger

Krylon

Kryolan Corp./Claudia Longo

Erwin Kupitz

La Femme Cosmetics/Gary Balaban

James Lacey

Dorothy Lamour

Elsa Lanchester

Michael Landon

Ben Lane

Lou Lane

Dave Langford

Angela Lansbury

Ken Larsen

Last Chance for Animals

Charles Laughton

Mark Leabo

Philip Leakey

Christopher Lee

Peggy Lee

Lee's Drugs

Eileen Leonard

Les Nouvelles Esthetiques/
  Monica Schuloff Smith

Hal Linden

Harold Lipton

Rich Little

Christopher Lloyd

David Lockwood

Sharon Lockwood

Steven Lockwood

Susan Lockwood

Carmela Logusto

Louis Logusto

Paul Lohman

Phil and Shelly London

Ellyne Lonergan

Brad Look

Peter Lorre

Peter Lorre, Jr.

Leo Lotito

Bela Lugosi

Christine Lund

John J. Lyman

Bob Mackie

Make-up Artists and Hairstylists
Local 706 I.A.T.S.E. Hollywood

Make-up Artists and Hairstylists
Local 798 I.A.T.S.E. New York

Priscilla Mandolin

Manos Theatre

Ralph Manza

Emil Maralit

John Maranville

Noah Mariano

Dennis Marsh

Jos Michael Martin

Todd Masters

Richard Matheson

Raymond Massey

Jacklin Masteran

Rodd Matsui

Max Factor Company

Kevin May

Patricia Mayer, Esq.

Gene Maze

Karen Maze

Peggy Maze

Randi Maze

Randy Maze

Mitzi McCall

Dr. Michael McCann

Rod McCary

Rue McClanahan

Bill McCoy

Malcolm McDowell

Todd McIntosh

Emily McLaughlir

Media 8/Audrey Delaney

Dr. William Meditz

Mehron, Inc./Martin Melik

Ronald Mennano

Lee Meriwether

Donna Messina-Armogida

Kenny Meyers

Michael Davy Film & T.V. Makeup

Michaels Art Supply

Keith Michelle

Bette Midler

June Miggins

Alan Migicovsky

Dale Miller

Edward Miller

Carrie Milligan

Mitchell, Silberberg, & Knupp LLP

Sally Montijo

Clayton Moore

Barney Morris

Kathryn Morris

Gil Mosko/GM Foam

Mr. Blackwell

Gary Mumper

Matthew Mungle

Paul Muni

Musso & Frank Grill

John Myers

NABET

Naimie's Beauty Center/Naimie Ojeil
and Samuel Bekerian

Dick Narr

Charles Nash

NBC-TV/Universal

Ve Neill/Ve's Favorite Brushes

Steve Newburn

Anthony Newland

Olivia Newton-John

James H. Nicholson

Douglas Noe

Barry Nolan

Negar Noori-Khorasani

Ritva and Alti Norris

Dennis Nudine

Barbara Nye

Ben Nye, Sr.

Ben Nye, Jr.

Bob O'Bradovich

Willis O'Brien

Mari Okumura

Gary Oldman

Orlando Chamber of Commerce

Marie Osmond

Bob Osterman

Don Otis

Pete Otto

Valerie O'Tuohy

Bill Ozzello

Paasche

George Pal

Ronald Jason Palmieri, Esq.

Panavision

Edie Panda

Charles Parker

Frank Patrill

Paramount Pictures

Travis Pates

Lisa Pharren

Carl O. Peterson

Robert E. Peterson

Regis Philbin

Dr. Joe Philipson, USN

Lou Phillippi

Fred Phillips

Saul Pick

Jack Pierce

Pierce Brothers Mortuary

Irene Pinn

Jason Pires

Steve Polinsky

Katherine Popiel

Marion E. Popeil

Charles Portier

Don Post, Sr.

Dr. Irving Posalski

Premiere Products, Inc./Scott Heinly

Ruby Prevost

Vincent Price

Dr. Dale Prokupek

Sheryl Ptak

Dr. Oksana Puuste/Puuste Cosmetics,
  Tallinn, Estonia

R & D Latex Co.

Claude Rains

Justin Raleigh

Basil Rathbone

Rebecca Rachael Designs/
  Rebecca Rachael Frye

Red Book magazine

Lynn Redgrave

Lynn Reynolds

Phil Rhodes

Richard A. Rivas

Joan Rivers

John Rizzo

Doris Roberts

Edward G. Robinson

Kim Robinson

Robinson's Beautilities

Jill Rockow

Ylianna Rodriguez

Bob Romero

Miklos Rozsa

Don Rutherford

Gail Ryan

Bob Ryan

Dahlias Salinas

Bob Salvatore

Charles Sampas

George Sanders

Katrin Sangla

Trisha Sawyer

Peter Saxby

Richard Scarso

Red Schaffer

Bob Schiffer

Don Schoenfeld

Linda Schoonover, Esq.

Charles Schram

Avery Schreiber

Dr. Robert H. Schuller

Elaina Schulman

Phil Schulman

Schwab's Pharmacy (the original)

Screenface/John Danvers and J. Pellin

Al Searcy

Jay Sebring

Dr. George Semel

Ira and Eddie Senz

Rod Serling

Setwear/Lance Coury

John Severino

Paul Shannon

Philip Shear

Martin Sheen

Shields & Yarnell

Shotgun Britton

Doug Shotts

Karl Silvera

Sirona Dental Systems/Michael Dunn

Sister Esther

Howard J. Smit

Bill Smith

Christina Smith

Dick Smith

Eric and Aki Smith

Janie Smithrow

Smooth-On

Richard Snell

Jack Soo

Ronnie Specter

Spectrum

Jack Sperling

James Stagnitta

Florence Stanley

Stan Winston Studios

Barbara Steele

Ray Steele

Jean Stein

Jay Stewart

Hank Stohl and Knish

Studio One

Sugano

Richard Sugi

Barry Sullivan

Richard E. Sulprizio

Dr. Stacey Sumner

Jeremy Swan

Bud Sweeney

Amy Tafurt

Jan and Ray Taketaya

Adele Taylor

Ted Tetzlaff

Thomas Theis

Charlize Theron

Harry Thomas

Claude Thompson

Diane Thorne

Christien Tinsley/Tinsley Transfers

Lily Tomlin

Spencer Tracy

Ralph Travis

Mike Tristano

Kazuhiro Tsuji

Christopher Tucker

William Tuttle

Twentieth Century Fox Pictures

Michele Tyminski

USITT (United States Institute for Theatre Technology)

Hank Valardo

Donni Vango

Boris Vanoff

Nick Vanoff

Vapon

Viacom/Larry McCallister

Abe Vigoda

Vistakon/Dr. Christina Schnider

Albert Viziola

Margaret Viziola

Nancy Ann Viziola

Alexis Vogel

The Voice of Firestone Show

W.M. Creations/Eddie Vargas,
   Clinton Wayne, Kris Kobzina,
   Chris Burgoyne, and Ryan McDowell

Alan Waite

Niea Walker

Vivienne Walker

Clyde Ware

Warner Brothers/Laura Sharp

David Wainer

Lee Wainer

Ray Walston

James Wast

Pete Wast

Way Out

Damon Wayans

Andrew Lloyd Webber

Janet Weber

Christopher Weeks

Rabbi Weinberg

Orson Welles

Ron West

The Westinghouse Broadcasting System

Bud Westmore

Ern Westmore

Frank Westmore

Marvin Westmore

Mike Westmore

Perc Westmore

James Whale

Dr. Wes Wheadon

Dona Whelan

Don Wheeler

Betty White

Melodie Whitney

Robert Wigle

Ralph Wilcox

Phyllis Williams

Robert Wilson

Jim Withrow

Katriina Wuoristo/
   The Norris Company, Helsinki, Finland

Mary Ann Wymore

Paul and Millie Yamashiro

John Zak

Dr. Millard Zisser

All Joe Blasco Students from Joe Blasco
   Make-up Centers West, East, and
   Europe, Past and Present

All Models who greatly assisted in
   the creation of this book

Preface

BY VINCENT J-R KEHOE

There is a vast difference today between those who practice the profession of make-up artistry in the commercial or public consumer area as estheticians, cosmeticians, or cosmetologists, and those who work in the venue of the professional motion picture, the television studio, the Broadway-level stage production, or even in the world of fashion magazines. The former are licensed by state cosmetology boards to perform many varieties of personal service in beauty salons for the public—often having passed limited level examinations for all their designated areas of work. Their qualifications are primarily based on a certain number of school practice hours (normally about 1,500) at a state-licensed beauty school. Actual license examinations are often perfunctory, while school hours take precedence in the final judgment of a student's qualification.

Conversely, studio-employed make-up artists have never been state-licensed (and frankly never wish to be). They apply make-up services for performers at the studios that produce entertainment features on film, television, and the stage, where excellence is the ultimate criterion of both their employers and the viewers themselves. As such, the results of their particular work must be nearly faultless. While cosmeticians and the like are mainly responsible for applying and producing straight fashion or beauty make-ups for their clients, the professional make-up artist, in addition to doing this work, must be able to employ various feature-altering make-up products to create age levels, duplicates of historical figures, and changes in ethnicity, race, or time period in accordance with a script. The professional make-up artist must also be familiar with various laboratory procedures in order to make appliances or prostheses to achieve these ends, and on some occasions, must also rely on imagination and innate talent to create images of fantasy creatures. The professional make-up artist must be both knowledgeable in many areas of endeavor and able to apply such knowledge in an effective and believable manner.

Although recent changes in the laws and rules of the California Make-up Artists' Union, Local 706 I.A.T.S.E., do not require applicants to perform a talent examination for their membership, the East Coast Local 798 I.A.T.S.E. Union still holds basic membership examinations that are judged by peers in the industry.

Because of the burgeoning need for make-up personnel in the constantly expanding film and television industries, there are vastly increased opportunities for people seeking work in the field. Unfortunately, the true talent level of professional make-up artistry has suffered from the appointment of unqualified people to head make-up positions by producers. These people often do beauty make-up for the star of a show but do not have the knowledge—or talent—to do much else. These sometimes limited individuals must employ other, more knowledgeable make-up artists to perform specific procedures such as beard, moustache, or hairpiece application, aging and character work, or prostheses application for anyone else in the cast.

Years ago, when the film and television studios had true make-up departments run by a charge man or Head of Make-up for production, there was an established apprentice system under which acolytes could train and work with journeymen make-up personnel to study and learn the profession from the bottom up. With the demise of the major film studio as a production entity (most are now simply rental facilities) and the passing of the live television shows in the New York networks, this apprentice system faded into history. Now, at the television studios (both network and independent), make-up artists are employed for newscasters, their guests (such as politicians), soap operas, and game shows. All of the above need straight beauty make-ups that are quite simple to apply. There is little opportunity, therefore, for the aspiring artist to really learn the details of corrective and character make-up.

This is not to suggest that formerly, stars did not have personal preferences or employ their own personal make-up artists as part of their entourage. But these artists had usually risen in the profession as a result of their particular talents and were quite proficient in their work. They had passed stringent examinations and proven their ability before an examining committee.

So how can we, today, raise the standards of the make-up profession and gain the respect of the entertainment industry in doing so? We must begin a return to more stringent training and a clearer and better certification process for those who wish to enter the profession. To do this, we must now look to the make-up artist training schools that have proliferated on both the East and West Coasts of the United States, as well as around the world. It is up to them to set a new level of standards for both their teachers and their graduates, as they are now the only sources we have for the improvement in the quality of professional make-up artists.

As such, the practice of make-up artistry really has no common denominator, but is instead subject to interpretation in methodology of design and the means employed to achieve an end. Personal expression is always paramount in its result. Individuality is part of the talent of true make-up artists, who must always seek innovation in favor of the repetition of common or even established modes of expression and design. The best in the field are those who can conceive and design an overall pictorial effect and result that is outstanding for the subject matter.

With this in mind, the talents, special aptitudes, and skills of many working professional make-up artists have been featured in this book. All of these artists display an excellence that must be shown by the studio professional and to which students or apprentices to the art must aspire in order to excel in this unique field of endeavor.

Therefore, we shall show that there is always more than just one manner, aspect, or method to achieving any beauty, or even any character make-up effect; in fact, there is often a variety of ways and means to complete the finished look. Creativity and new directions in approach should be all-important to the inventive mind of any professional make-up artist.

Interlude

There must always be a separation between basic and advanced techniques in any field, but few other areas of endeavor feature this line so clearly drawn as it is in professional make-up. Those with the talent needed for continuing the study from beauty make-up into character make-up are obviously demarcated.

Many people who enter the field of make-up learn to do a beauty make-up with a certain degree of facility and success. Oftentimes, they do so with considerably innovative and fashionable results. However, when continuing their studies and efforts in the direction of character make-up, many lack the necessary interest or drive, or they display little talent or patience. It is not a realm for the diffident, the dabbling, or the artist who lacks confidence in his or her skill. The climate is one of competition—with challenges at each turn—but with the sharing of knowledge amongst peers.

Today, the old paint-and-powder styles are still important, but the application of increasingly common three-dimensional make-up with the employment of appliances or prostheses requires considerably more diverse study than the old stage methods of utilizing nose putty, cotton and collodion, muslin, and so on. Molded plastics and lattices, waxes, foam materials, gelatins, silicones, and many other products and means are part of the principles of character make-up. Proficiency in the laying and cutting of facial hair for men, for example, is requisite.

This book aims to impart necessary character make-up knowledge—from paint-and-powder techniques, to mold making and appliance manufacturing, to a sound expertise in hair goods, among others.

Make-up artists with a full range of capacities in such character make-ups will always be more in demand for challenging jobs and will therefore gain more respect in the profession. In addition, they will learn that any created effect is never the last word on the subject; further research will always show the way to an improved method. All those who excel in character make-up are constantly researching and testing new ways to recreate the old or discover the new and exciting. It is insufficient to consider oneself fully knowledgeable after making one beard, one cast, one appliance, or one effect. Constant practice and repetition will ensure proficiency and facilitate the learning of something new or different each time the exercise is performed.

~~~~~~~~~

This Interlude, written some twenty years ago by Vincent J-R Kehoe, in every way expresses his attitude and respect for his chosen profession. From the late 1930s, he desired to learn everything that he possibly could about the art of make-up, to apply make-ups in a realistic and believable manner, and to advance his knowledge of the art.

His practicing at home after school at a young age was paralleled some almost twenty-five years later by Joe Blasco, who shared the same avidness and deep interest, so that when their paths finally crossed, they had much in common, with topics to discuss and experiences to share with one another. The final results will be found throughout the two volumes of this work on professional make-up principles and methods, the contents of which both authors hope will serve to guide and train others who wish to make a career in the field and excel in all areas of the art.

Introduction I

VOLUME III

Today, the category of character make-up represents many advances in materials, methods, procedures, and uses, the majority of which were not previously available. In short, character make-up entails the use of these special materials to change the appearance of a person as to age level, race, and various characteristics of facial or body form. Such changes may be simple or complicated and are intended to aid the performer in the portrayal of a role by producing a facial and/or body form conducive to the character being played on screen or stage.

From the basic Jack Pierce Frankenstein's Monster character, which rather began the basic monster trend in films during the early thirties, to the monumental John Chambers ape make-up for *Planet of the Apes*, to the work of the current day (as illustrated in many examples of superior make-ups that we explore in this work), the degree and quality of character make-up can be illustrated in order to show the continued advances in this phase of professional make-up artistry.

The background history of character make-up starts with the professional stage before moving to its adaptation in motion pictures, where varying camera lenses and distinct camera placement (in relation to the performer) allowed different aspects of viewing. Whereas the stage only permitted a viewer to see the entire production from a specific seat in the audience, motion pictures could produce a range of perspectives—from far in the distance to extremely close—resulting in make-ups that required more realistic application, and thereby placing the work in the hands of the studio make-up artist and away from the actors themselves. The development of television make-up followed a similar path as technical improvements in cameras and lighting continue to this day with Hi-Definition Television (HDTV), which produces results that are extraordinarily clear and sharp. Therefore, make-ups done for film and television now always require close inspection before they can be shot—a reality which must be considered by modern make-up artists in the application of their character work.

Whereas years ago, the television system (or the movie camera, to a lesser degree) allowed some diffusion, such is not the case with today's HDTV advances, in addition to the newly improved Eastmancolor Negative films. All blends must be smooth, all lines definite, and all aspects of the make-up—as seen in close-up by the human eye—must exhibit a suitable level of perfection regardless of medium.

As the camera's eye is often more critical and difficult to please than our own, each character make-up should be carefully checked both in the reflected image of the make-up setup mirror and directly by the eye of the artist.

Of particular importance are the variety and scope of the materials—be they new or adaptations of past products—available to today's make-up personnel. In the 1940s, make-up artists were experimenting with liquid gum latex for the composition of various facial features and learning techniques for molding and casting. The introduction of foam latex prostheses, which were lighter in weight and could produce more intricate appliances with more effective edges (and better adherence to the skin), followed. From there, experimentation with silicone, gelatin, and other materials ultimately produced better appliances and more natural skin surfaces than heretofore, allowing the make-up artist to create more realism.

New careers (and subsequent respect) were accorded to make-up artists who could produce such specialized character make-ups. Herein, we present some of their intricate work and share with you their talents and accomplishments.

Today, there are no locked make-up doors; all artists are quite willing to share and disseminate information, as well as to improve their respective auras of change. The first book to impart such wisdom was Vincent J-R Kehoe's *The Technique of Film & Television Make-up* (1958), which introduced all the materials and methods available during its day. Now, we update our readers with the latest information and products available to current make-up artists.

Introduction II

VOLUME III
BY JOE BLASCO

So many of today's most talented artists embarked on a career in the professional make-up industry as a result of being greatly influenced by make-up application which dramatically alters the physical countenance of an actor and thus enables a realistic character portrayal. This type of make-up is known as *character make-up*. Oftentimes an actor will become known as a character actor; names from the past, such as Paul Muni, Paul Winchell, Charles Laughton, Agnes Morehead, and Elsa Lanchester set the standard for those recognized today: Gary Oldman, Christopher Walken, and Christopher Lloyd, among many others.

Certainly there exist many actors who accomplish their performances by simply adapting their acting style without the assistance of significant make-up. Spencer Tracy's magnificent portrayal of the transformed Dr. Jekyll into the evil Mr. Hyde is an excellent example of a performer relying on acting skills—with only the aid of simple, yet defined highlights and shading—to realistically embody a character. But others, whose effective performance depends heavily upon realistic physical recreation, require varying degrees of make-up application that are dictated by the script. Years before Tracy's Hyde, John Barrymore portrayed the character through the use of much more dramatic make-up application, which included a domed cranium piece with wig, extremely accentuated and protruding teeth, and stark facial highlights and shading. Barrymore even wore finger extensions—perhaps the first occasion of such devices in motion pictures—designed by the famous Westmores.

Another Westmore-supervised make-up (said to have actually been applied by George Bau during his apprenticeship at Paramount) was Charles Laughton's portrayal of Quasimodo, the Hunchback of Notre Dame—again, a very extensive design that permitted Mr. Laughton tremendous latitude in executing his historic performance. This make-up—according to Dick Smith, as told to me during dinner after a recent annual Make-up Artist Tradeshow in Pasadena—was the one that influenced him more than any other in wanting to become a make-up artist. Interestingly, many years later it was this same make-up which also caught my attention as a young man of five years old when I watched reruns of this wonderful film on television.

Sometimes historical characters are portrayed by actors who closely resemble them. Raymond Massey, who portrayed Abe Lincoln with only the simple addition of a beard, a more aquiline foam latex nose, the appropriate mole, highlights and shading, and proper costume is one such case. Another example is Hal Holbrook as Mark Twain. His famous stage portrayal utilized a make-up—albeit designed for stage use—which was so perfectly executed that it was able to also satisfy the stringent technical requirements of television during that time period.

Aside from actors being known specifically for their work as *character actors*, there are also make-up artists who are known for their ability to perform such specific character work.

Oftentimes make-up artists who choose to work strictly in the realm of beauty make-up underestimate their ability to utilize their extensive knowledge of highlighting and shading and consequently do not enter the character make-up field. This is unfortunate, because there are many extremely talented artists who are only known for their beauty work but who, I believe, could quite easily excel in the field of character make-up with an understanding that the basis for character make-up is strongly rooted in the realm of light reflection through the proper use of highlighting and shading, in which they are already well-versed, as well as of three-dimensional applications which raise and/or depress areas of the face and add texture.

Other artists enter the field of professional make-up with only the desire to create character make-ups, particularly ones which involve prosthesis application. Oftentimes I have seen such artists execute a beautifully applied character and/or prosthetic make-up, but because they lack a basic knowledge of highlighting and shading as a result of eschewing a thorough exploration of beauty and corrective make-up techniques, their results sometimes fail in terms of a loss of detail. In my observation, the artists who understand the full range of make-up application techniques—from beauty through prosthetics—are best able to not only create realistic character make-ups, but are also able to work quite rapidly.

Additionally, in efforts to create appropriate naturalness, such artists without comprehensive training require a great deal of time—which is often not afforded on the set, especially for television work—for the completion of their work. Make-up artists who are schooled in television make-up techniques—especially those artists who worked in the era of live television—are customarily able to work very quickly while, in most cases, having the ability to accomplish necessary detail in their work. Such artists were trained to work so efficiently in order to satisfy the stringent time requirements of live television and were not afforded the opportunity to work at a slower pace as permitted on most motion picture sets. Make-up artists who have made the transition from film to television seem to eventually possess the benefits derived from both mediums. Having acquired sufficient enough experience and expertise in the realm of film in order to create very realistic and anatomically correct character make-ups, these artists adapt to television's time constraints and work in record-breaking time.

Today, efficiency in application is superseded by the need for perfection, as today's film and SHDTV (Super Hi-Definition Television) processes reveal all shortcomings, however minute. Today's technologies call for make-up artists to be much more exacting and deliberate throughout the entire process of character development—from concept to completed application. Never before in the history of film and television has such fastidiousness been requisite. Today's make-up artists, unlike artists of the past, must never rely on the inherent camera diffusion that was at one time of assistance to the illusion. The people who create character make-ups for today's digital film and SHDTV processes are among the most talented of all artisans who comprise the crew of motion picture and television productions.

It is so interesting to observe the history of character make-up from the early silent films through today's extremely accurate digital mediums; albeit crude by today's standards, the character make-ups of Lon Chaney, Sr., who is rumored to have also been aided by the veteran make-up artist of the day, Cecil Holland, are astounding to behold. In my opinion, it is so incredibly important that the serious student of make-up study the art from its earliest period in order to acquire an understanding and appreciation for the talents of the past and to see how technical advances have so greatly affected the evolution of professional make-up. Lon Chaney, Sr., known as "the man of 1,000 faces" because of his scores of character portrayals through the use of make-up specifically designed to recreate such startling characters as the original Phantom of the Opera, the original Quasimodo (the Hunchback of Notre Dame), and so many others too numerous to mention; Boris Karloff, made-up by Jack Pierce during the 1930s as the Frankenstein Monster; Bela Lugosi, also made-up by

Pierce to portray Igor in *The Son of Frankenstein*; and Lon Chaney, Jr., who, following in his father's footsteps (although not applying the make-up himself), portrayed the Wolfman made-up again by Jack Pierce are only a few examples of actors wearing early, historically important character-type make-ups, some of which could be categorized as realistically grotesque human-type designs, while others fall distinctly into the realm of horrific monster-style make-ups that contain yet an element of human anatomy. It is a common belief among most make-up artists that the most effective monster make-ups are in fact those which contain a great degree of human element within their structures. I believe it was Dick Smith who said: "No make-up artist can improve upon the horrors of nature." Although this is quite true, if one is fortunate enough to obtain crime scene investigation photos or photos of human deformities and facial abnormalities for study, a make-up artist can make a valiant attempt to mimic nature and oftentimes, as was the case with Greg Cannom's brilliant make-up on Gary Oldman in *Hannibal* (*see Part II, Chapter 15*), triumphantly succeed in doing so.

Character make-ups which require paint and powder and/or three-dimensional wrinkles, the illusion of balding, or the addition of various wigs and hairpieces to affect degrees of aging, style, and period requirements are among the most popular and difficult to execute realistically. The silicone appliances so beautifully done by Greg Cannom in the motion picture, *The Bicentennial Man*, are tremendous examples of expert aging simulation, while a more simple hand-applied stretch and stipple technique, as was done on Marlon Brando in *The Godfather*, is also extremely effective and impressive. Closely observing the character work in these aforementioned films—including *Once Upon a Time in America*, which I admire greatly for its aging make-up continuity—and so many others should be part of every make-up artist's curriculum. Students will find that studying the techniques used to transform the age of characters so dramatically is akin to taking a college course in anatomy and gerontology. All make-up artists should train to study the faces of everyone around them as unobtrusively as possible. It is by having a full understanding of how a facial surface structure reflects light—and in doing so, creates the illusion of character make-ups of a million and more types—that true expertise is acquired.

The script is the first dictate of what is required from both the actor and the make-up artist when creating any and all forms of character make-up. Again, historical characters, whose faces are known to us, leave little to our imagination and creativity aside from the need to absolutely duplicate the appropriate physical appearance as effectively as possible. It is aging make-ups to known actors, however, in addition to the creation of various deformities and explicit horror and science fiction characters which require much more thought prior to execution. These make-ups are often quite satisfying from an artist's point of view to the extent that one is not simply copying "a look" of sorts but is actually creating something new and original.

My belief is that every artist in this field should strive to have as complete an understanding of every aspect of make-up artistry—from beauty through character and prosthetics—as possible. Laboratory work, which encompasses the knowledge of the actual fabrication of facial appliances—be they foam rubber, gelatin, silicone, et al.—is in my opinion the only area of the art that can be eliminated from a make-up artist's bag of tricks, unless of course he or she wishes to be schooled through and through.

With all of the above being said, both Vincent and I, as well as all of the extremely talented artists who have been so generous in providing us with their valued talents (and often quite secret techniques) are offering you, within this volume, what we feel is today's state-of-the-art information for the application of what you will soon appreciate—when finished reading this work—as one of the more particularly demanding aspects of make-up artistry . . . character make-up.

Volume III

Laboratory Procedures

Introduction III

VOLUME III,
BY JOE BLASCO

In 1955, as the lights dimmed each week at the Kitchel Theatre in Jeanette, Pennsylvania every Saturday morning at 10 A.M., and the American International Pictures logo (The U.S. Capitol Building floating among clouds in mid-air) appeared on the screen followed by the words, "James H. Nicholson and Samuel Z. Arkoff Present," I knew that I was about to experience another brief but significant moment in my life as a child that would ultimately lead me into the world of professional make-up artistry.

The memories of such wonderful, and often comedic films such as *The Raven, The Pit and the Pendulum, The House of Usher, Tales of Terror, The Comedy of Terrors, Black Sunday, Voodoo Woman, It! The Terror from Beyond Space, It Conquered the World, Night of the Blood Beast, The Neanderthal Man, The Amazing Colossal Man, Konga, Reptilicus, This Island Earth, Creature from the Black Lagoon, Revenge of the Creature, The Creature Walks Among Us, Plan 9 from Outer Space, Bride of the Monster, Frankenstein 1970* (made in 1958), *The 7th Voyage of Sinbad, The Golden Voyage of Sinbad, Jason and the Argonauts, Jason and the Eye of the Tiger, 20 Million Miles to Earth, It Came from Beneath the Sea, The Curse of Frankenstein, The Revenge of Frankenstein, Horror of Dracula, Creature with the Atom Brain, Man with the X-Ray Eyes, The Crawling Eye, The Brides of Dracula, The Mummy* (Christopher Lee), *The Curse of the Werewolf* (Oliver Reed), and so many others too numerous to mention continuously solidified my desire to become part of this fascinating world which I observed on the silver screen each anticipated weekend.

I was approximately eight years of age when I began attending Saturday and Sunday movie matinees. Prior to my movie going experiences, I was fortunate to be permitted every Friday night to watch Bill Cardill's *Chiller Theater* on WIIC-TV NBC in Pittsburgh. Later, Bill Cardill and I were to become fast friends. He would invite me to the studio, where I would bring my many friends, and after I turned them into monsters, they would proceed to menace Mr. Cardill during his on-camera segments prior to each commercial. I recall being asked by NBC to create a monster for the *Chiller Theater* float during a Halloween parade in downtown Pittsburgh. I worked for weeks to make a full body suit which covered my poor subject from head to toe with foam latex, cotton, liquid latex, and a myriad of prosthetic make-ups and greasepaints of every color, shape, and form! It was at that parade that I can recall being approached by a very young and eager Tom Savini, who was extremely fascinated with my work and who would also go on to become one of the most talented of the Pittsburgh clan of monster makers.

From the age of five until I was permitted to attend the local films at the Kitchel Theatre, I was completely captivated by the horror films shown on NBC's *Chiller Theater*, which were predominately Universal Pictures classics such as *Dracula* with Bela Lugosi

(1931), *Frankenstein* with Boris Karloff (1931), *The Bride of Frankenstein* with Karloff and Elsa Lanchester (1935), *The Son of Frankenstein* (1939), and various others: *The House of Frankenstein, The Ghost of Frankenstein, The Werewolf, Frankenstein Meets the Werewolf, The Old Dark House, The Black Cat* with Lugosi and Karloff, *Bedlam* with Karloff, *Murders in the Rue Morgue* with Lugosi, *Doctor X, The Daughter of Dracula*, and *The Son of Dracula* with Lon Chaney, Jr. These horror films, which I originally watched on television in the quiet dark of my Aunt Kay's living room while she slept and snored with her mouth agape, were my first introduction to the world of monster and special make-up effects. I was hooked!

After that point, when I was permitted to go to the theatre, my fascination with motion pictures began to grow beyond make-up artistry, and I became completely enamored with the entire filmmaking process. In fact, at the age of eleven, my friend Frank Bolkovack (who went on to become a most successful motion picture projectionist) and I worked diligently with an eight-millimeter Kodak Brownie motion picture camera his parents bought him for Christmas, and with small fifty-foot rolls of eight-millimeter film we purchased with money earned by cutting neighborhood lawns and washing cars, we began our film careers. I personally wrote directed, and edited two films—in addition to starring in them, doing the make-up, and aligning the camera (for which Frank was the operator)—between the ages of eleven and sixteen. The classic film *Citizen Kane* served as my textbook for the art of film editing. Next to doing make-up, working as a cinematographer or editor would have definitely been my career of choice. In fact, there were moments while working on our two amateur films that I actually began contemplating moving into the realm of film editing and cinematography rather than make-up. I am so happy, however, as I am certain thousands of make-up artists who have graduated from my schools are as well, that I decided to remain in make-up artistry.

The only thing that was left for me to discover was Forrest J. Ackerman's wonderful magazine, *Famous Monsters of Filmland*. I can fondly recall not having enough money to purchase the magazine, which at that time cost fifty cents per issue, and being suddenly confronted by my Aunt Nancy, who approached me after seeing the saddened look on my face as I headed back toward my fifth grade schoolyard after lunch period. After hearing my story, she understood that all I needed were twenty-five cents more to purchase a magazine about monsters. She reached into her purse and handed me that all-important quarter, which completely changed my life forever. I immediately ran back to the store, purchased the magazine, and after arriving at my fifth grade homeroom class, proceeded to show the magazine to everyone. That's when I got to know Frank, as he seemed much more interested in the photos of monsters and the make-up artists creating them than did anyone else in the class.

Later that year, another piece of my make-up career puzzle would be found in the form of Richard Corson's Second Edition of his fine book, *Stage Makeup*. All through fifth, sixth, and seventh grade, his book never left my side. I memorized it from cover to cover. Then, in eighth grade, I discovered the ultimate book that would fine-tune my make-up knowledge: Vincent J-R Kehoe's First Edition of *The Technique of Film and Television Make-up*. This book picked up where Richard Corson's left off.

I wrote numerous letters to the Max Factor Company, which was kind enough to provide me with hundreds of products, either complimentary or for next to nothing. And finally, my decision was firmly locked into place: I would become a make-up artist. From that moment on, every class I selected and every experience that I had would in some way help me along a path to success in make-up artistry.

Those were the early years, and I owe my successful career to the fact that I was completely enthralled with the world of early construction make-up, prosthetics, and special make-up effects. Beauty make-up would not come into the picture till much later, but at that time, I found that it, too, would play a vital part in filling the gaps between times when I would be called upon to do what I loved most: monster, character, and special make-up effects.

So, I believe I have now come full circle after having enjoyed a long and fruitful career in Hollywood as a make-up artist, having created make-up schools and a cosmetics company, and now, with Vincent J-R Kehoe, having written this book, which, through its pages, will fulfill my legacy to push the envelope continuously in all aspects of the make-up profession. Within Volumes II and III, I have endeavored to present as complete a picture of not only the most current and up-to-date techniques, but also to feature some of the most current and talented generation of make-up artists who are already successful and have become today's—as well as tomorrow's—stars of professional make-up. I now invite you into what most make-up artists will consider the most interesting aspect of make-up artistry: the creation of characters through the use of paint, powder, plastic, rubber, gelatin, and silicone. Enjoy.

JOE BLASCO

Introduction IV

VOLUME III,
BY VINCENT J-R KEHOE

My initial interest in make-up was an offshoot of my sincere interest in chemistry. I often visited at the Lowell Textile School—now Lowell University—with Dr. Beattie, who was Head of Organic Chemistry. I was first taken with developing a ski lacquer for wooden skis. (I did come up with a good formula that was sold at Lull and Hartford Sporting Goods Store in Lowell, Massachusetts.) In thus dealing with various waxes and volatile solvents, I tried making some greasepaint make-ups. My first direction was to purchase a Miner's flesh and a stick of nose putty from the local costume shop. I was hooked!

My first make-up efforts were, of course, tried on myself. I wrote to Hal King at the Max Factor Company for some promotional pamphlets and saw the different make-ups that Paul Muni, a star at Warner Brothers Studio in Hollywood, had done on himself. I would spend any money I had (which was not much!) to purchase wool crepe hair, various foundations, rouges, etc., which fascinated me, and I would rush home after school to make myself up. My mother never knew what she would see as I progressed through character make-ups. Spirit gums, putties, and foundation shades were all I thought of my last year in high school. Such was my start in make-up. Straight make-up was of little interest to me, but character make-up was challenging, and I was obsessed with it!

At that time (in the late 1930s), most make-up was created for the stage, as screen make-up for films was still evolving, and television had yet to exist. The Lowell City Library had a few make-up books, but they only covered stage make-up, which was customarily applied by the performer without the assistance of an artist. Very few newer products were available. I found that almost all build-ups on the face were done with nose putty that came in a very hard waxy stick; it required manipulation with the fingers in order for it to work properly. With the distance between audience member and stage actor not requiring detailed make-up work in most instances to create and maintain the necessary illusion, skin texture was of little importance or concern. It was the motion picture close-up that prompted make-up artists to seek more effective means and products.

I next tried a waxy, soft product that undertakers employed at times to cover and restore traumatic facial loss. It was, however, not made for warm, living persons and was a bit too pliable. It proved difficult to create the desired texture, and the product failed to retain its shape. Bob O'Bradovich, a make-up artist of some note, whom I met at NBC-TV, tried a half-and-half mixture of nose putty and mortician's wax to create a more stable working product; it was rather difficult to use, however, and again failed when one tried to texture the surface of the appliance. Ultimately, when working with these rather crude materials, the best method was to coat the area to which the mortician's wax was to be applied with a non-shining matte resin adhesive, dry it, and then apply the wax on top. This provided a better bond to the skin.

After sculpting the area, the surface of the wax was then coated with RCMA Matte Plastic Sealer—a non-shining, polyvinyl butryal material. Two coats, which dried very fast, were sufficient to cover the build-up; they could be "textured" to appear more like skin pores after they dried and were receptive to the application of a cream-style make-up. The resulting build-up yielded more realistic work for the purposes of close-ups in film or television, but for effective daily matching of the application, the skills of a highly trained artist were required.

The first step to improve on such was to experiment with various lattices (sold at most good artist's supply stores). At first, one could find a pure gum latex, which featured no fillers, dried with some amount of shine, and would not build up in a plaster mold. Next appeared a fillered latex, which featured the addition of varying amounts of zinc oxide slurry. This variety was a more "friendly" product, for it began to thicken when poured into a negative plaster mold. By using cheap Chinese-type brushes and painting the casting latex into the mold, one could lessen the application on the edges in order to create a better fit to the face. Most of these paint-in styles worked best for any nasal changes and could be applied to the face with RCMA Matte Plasticized Adhesive, which contained the regular Matte Adhesive and an amount of Matte Plastic Sealer to give the adhesive better flexibility for any facial movement.

This was the beginning of lightweight, realistic appliances—medically referred to as prostheses—for facial build-ups when changes to the performer's face were needed. The finished make-up appliance would be hollow inside and could therefore fit a variety of faces; however, this did not serve well when used in jaw line prostheses, the neck area, or for eye bags that required the utmost realism.

In *The Wizard of Oz*, we saw the first major use of a new form of latex material which required a special mix of products to allow a two-part mold to be made of dental stone (which was harder than plaster); the latex was mixed with other ingredients to form a foam latex appliance or piece (in its finished product) that fit a single person exactly and was superior in lasting attachment to the human skin.

The major change in methodology came about upon the discovery that the foundation bases (customarily regular types of cream make-ups) employed with latex pieces did not work very well; the mineral oil present in most manufacturer's products prevented effective coverage between skin and appliance, and the make-up often whitened on the appliance's surface. A new form of foundation was therefore required. Max Factor answered the call with Rubber Mask Greasepaint—the first type of very thick, oily foundation compatible with latex appliances.

A vast improvement of this product was later designed by RCMA. It was more solid in the container, easier to use, and was produced in colors and shades that matched the regular Color Process Foundation (CPF) of RCMA. Incidentally, all RCMA foundation products can also be used on any latex piece, as RCMA CPF does not contain any mineral oil—the aforementioned culprit in effective latex application failure. They can be powdered with RCMA No-Color Powder. For a flatter effect, the RCMA A.F. (Appliance Foundation) series, which has fillers that produce a more matte result on both the exposed skin area and the appliance, can be used.

Today, make-up artists employ paint-in latex pieces for crowd scenes and foam latex pieces for fine work. There are even newer materials utilized, such as gelatins, silicones, and others that will be discussed in detail later in this volume.

Chapter 1

BASIC PROSTHESES

Chapter 1

LAB TECHNIQUES

Sculpture Materials

Molds

LATEX AND PLASTIC APPLIANCES

Natural Rubber Materials

Plastic Materials

MOLDING AND CASTING

Basic Introduction

History

Materials

Overlapping Appliances

CLASSIC FACIAL IMPRESSION AND FACIAL STONE POSITIVE CAST FABRICATION TECHNIQUE

Alginate Impression Theory

The Positive Cast

Historical Curing Information and Post-curing

Sculpting Materials

Summary

The Misnomer, "Rubber Mask Greasepaint"

Chapter 1

BASIC PROSTHESES

The first two sections of this chapter (Lab Techniques and Latex and Plastic Appliances) are comprised strictly of excerpts from Vincent J-R Kehoe's last book, The Technique of the Professional Make-up Artist, *and show the progression of basic molds and appliance pieces utilized before the advent of current foam latex, gelatin, silicone, and other more advanced techniques that were not available at the time of the book's publication in 1985.*

Much of these simplified techniques serve as the basics of prosthetic application with materials made for today's improved screen clarity and definition as seen in the mediums of Hi-Definition Television (HDTV) and the newest Kodak color negative films.

Many make-up artists will find that some of the useful techniques for crowd make-up scenes do not require the same finesse as work for principal close-ups; and in some cases, they can provide a background of progression in the world of appliance make-up.

LAB TECHNIQUES

SCULPTURE MATERIALS

The term *modeling clay* encompasses two types of clay-like materials. One is a water-based clay that is purchased as a powder and mixed with water to the desired consistency for use as a modeling material. Sculptures made of this material must be kept damp so they will not dry out and crack. It finds some use in the make-up lab but is not the best sculpturing material. Make-up artists find that the oil-based *plastalene* or *plasticine* serves their purposes better. It comes in 2-pound blocks of many grades, from a very soft #1 to a hard #4. It can be obtained in the normal dark green shades or in white. Opinions vary considerably as to the most useful variety, but most technicians use the dark green in either the #2 or the #4 hardness.

The tools for use with plastalene modeling are usually small and wooden (generally much smaller than the clay sculpture tools fine artists use), and the smallest wire tools are used as well. This is mainly because the make-up lab technician starts with a face casting gypsum material and adds the plastalene to achieve the sculpture, as opposed to starting with a large roughly shaped head of plastalene and carving it to shape with tools. When adding clay to a plaster or stone positive, always apply only a small amount at a time until the desired shape is built up. The wooden tools with the flat ends can do this work, while the fine wire tools can be used to diminish the sculpture gradually. The surface can also be

Fig. 1-1

The open weave burlap recommended by Dick Smith for strengthening molds and casts.

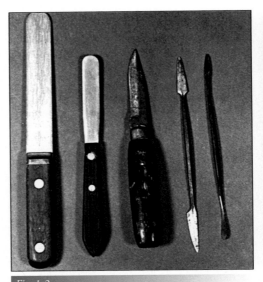

Fig. 1-2

Metal tools. **Left to Right:** *Stiff and flexible spatulas; a plaster knife; two metal plaster carving tools.*

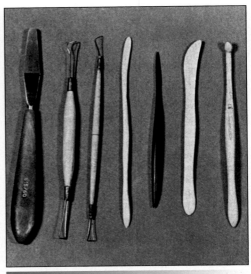

Fig. 1-3

Sculpture tools. **Left to Right:** *A small spatula; two wire tools for nostrils, lines, wrinkles; three wooden carving tools for plastalene (the smallest are most useful); a pointed ball-head wooden tool for making pores.*

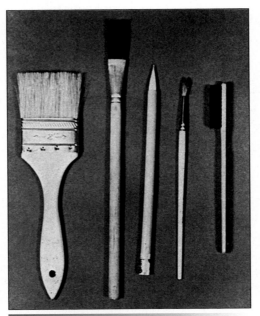

Fig. 1-4

Brushes. **Left to Right:** *Soft bristle brush for cap material or other uses; long-handled bristle brush for use with plaster; Chinese bristle brush for paint-in latex work; #10R sable brush for many applications; bamboo-handled bristle brush for cleaning plastalene from castings.*

scraped with a piece of coarse burlap to remove a thin layer of clay.

Texturing the surface to make it appear to have pores can be accomplished with a small knobbed-end wooden tool; a plastic stipple sponge; or a grapefruit tool made by coating the surface of various citrus fruits with a few coats of casting latex, drying this with a hand hairdryer, and then peeling off the latex after powdering it. This will take an impression of the surface of the orange or grapefruit (hence, the name of the tool), which has a great similarity to the human skin.

To smooth plastalene, a brush dipped in isopropyl alcohol will serve for small areas. For a larger expanse, some petrolatum jelly or mineral oil can be rubbed sparingly on the surface with the hands or a wide brush. Take care not to use too much of the latter two materials, as they will soften the surface of the sculpture. Some workers will coat a finished sculpture in plastalene with three coats of RCMA Plastic Cap Material (clear type) to provide a surface that will still require some tool and texture markings to refine the sculpture.

If one uses the sponge method, it will be discovered that the various grades of polyurethane stipple sponges work better than the red rubber ones, for the latter often leave bits of rubber imbedded in the plastalene. More often than not, a combination of the grapefruit, the sponge, and the knob tool will produce the best results for the varying skin pore textures.

Another method is to make latex stamps of skin texture areas. This can be done from the life mask cast of an older person who has good forehead wrinkles, for example. Simply apply a number of coats of casting latex to the original positive (depending upon the thickness of the stamp desired), dry, and then remove. This negative impression can then be used to press into a forehead plastalene area in order to obtain a reasonably good sculpture of forehead wrinkles. This method cannot be used too success-

Fig. 1-5

Two black rubber dental bowls for mixing small batches of alginate or gypsum materials and two small polyethylene measuring cups for weighing various foam ingredients.

fully on the soft parts of the face, such as the eye area, but it is suitable on bonier regions.

Because of the shrinkage of latex pieces, some size allowances can be made on appliances that cover a large area. This is one reason why many technicians make multiple appliances, rather than one large face piece.

In addition to wooden tools for plastalene, various metal tools with cutting edges for trimming plaster and stone, rasps, and Surform tools for removing more material are in use. Some labs even have machine tools with coarse wheels for rapidly cutting and shaping gypsum casts.

Two kinds of spatulas are used in the lab: The regular flexible type that is used for the measurement of small amounts of material for weighing, for the application of alginate to the face, and for other uses; and a stiff metal type that is obtained from a dental supply house for mixing alginate or plaster. A strong bladed knife is needed for trimming, and a heavy screwdriver is useful for prying two-piece molds apart.

Plastic bristle 1″ paint brushes, some with regular short handles and others with long handles (for more easily getting into castings) will find much use, as will some #10 round sable hair brushes, in addition to cheaper Chinese bristle brushes (for paint-in latex application). A few wig-cleaning bristle brushes are handy for scrubbing plastalene out of plaster and stone molds, as are some bristle stipple brushes of small sizes.

Sculptor's calipers for measuring head size and shape are useful when making large castings, as is a hand or electric drill with a $1/4''$ and $3/8''$ bit when drilling escape holes in positive casts for foam latex or urethane, and a $3/4''$ half-round coarse reamer or rasp bit when cutting keys.

Dental sculpture tools such as dental spatulas, curved tip tools used for handling dental amalgam for filling teeth, and others will be found useful for tooth sculpture.

Fig. 1.6

Rotary files (½ to ¾″) for use in cutting keys in gypsum materials. They work best in a good drill press or, if need be, in a handheld electric drill.

MOLDS

FLAT PLATE MOLDS

The simplest of the two-piece molds is the flat plate type. With this basic casting, one can make scars, cuts, bruises, moles, and other small appliances that do not require specific facial contours. When the prostheses made on the flat plate are adhered to the skin, they take on the natural curve of the area without any trouble in most cases.

To make a flat plate mold, form a rectangle with inside measurements of about 6″ × 10″, with four pieces of 1″ × 2″ wooden blocks. These can be held in place on a glass surface with four lumps of plastalene at the corners. The inside surface of the wood, as well as the glass, should be coated with petroleum jelly as a separator. Make some clay keys by rounding 1″ balls of plastalene in the palms of the hands, and then cutting them in half with a strand of thread. Place them about ½″ from the corners of the enclosure. Make a thin coat of stone or Ultracal 30, and blow it in to remove the bubbles. (A sculptors' trick is to use sharp breaths of air blown in on a thin liquid plaster mix surface in order to remove all the small surface bubbles.) Then fill up the enclosure with the remaining mixture. A strip of burlap can be used as a strengthener if desired, but the basic thickness of the plate is normally sufficient for most uses.

When the stone or Ultracal 30 has set, remove the blocks and slide the cast off the glass plate. The plastalene in the keys can be pried out with a wooden modeling tool. The keys can then be sanded with medium followed by fine sandpaper in order to prevent undercuts. For use, items can be modeled on the plate with plastalene, with a ¼″ gutter left

Fig. 1-7

Various tools and clamps that are useful in the prosthetics lab.

around each of the items modeled and the remainder of the plate clayed in to a depth of about ¼″. Then apply petroleum jelly to the exposed stone areas in the gutter and keys, surround the plate with another set of greased wooden blocks (1″ × 4″), and secure with plastalene at the corners to form a box around the plate. Stone or Ultracal 30 can then be mixed and added in the usual way to fill the cavity. Each of the plates, when completed, should be about 1¼″ thick.

When the stone or Ultracal 30 has set, remove the retaining wall, and separate the mold. The keys may then be lightly sanded after the plastalene has been thoroughly cleaned off both sides of the mold. Acetone or TCTFE (trichlorotrifluoroethane) can be used for this cleaning. (Prosthetic Adhesive A Thinner is this variety of solvent.) The mold is then ready for use with foam latex or foam urethane. The sculpted side of this type of mold can also be employed for paint-in plastic molding material. In the case of the latter, the smooth surface side upon which the original sculpture was done is not required, as the plastic molding material uses an open-face mold.

SLUSH AND PAINT-IN MOLDS

The basic casting latex molds are those taken as negatives in casting plaster of a plastalene sculpture on a facial cast. Noses are probably the most commonly used prostheses in make-up work, as the change of a nasal structure can delineate a character more quickly than any other transformation. Many make-up artists take a full cast of the face to acquire its correct proportions when modeling a new nose, chin, cheek, eye bag, and so on and make all their casts and molds directly from the original positive. Others take an additional cast only of the area desired (such as the nose) for use in making the necessary prosthetic mold.

This individual mold can be taken in PGC alginate, or even directly in dental plaster. The nostrils should be blocked with cotton batting and covered with petroleum jelly, leaving sufficient clearance for a clear impression of the nostril areas. During the casting operation, the subject may breathe through the mouth, as it will be free of plaster. Paint the plaster on the face with a 1" bristle paintbrush while being careful not to get any material in the nostrils or the mouth. Cover about half the eye sockets and cheeks with plaster in order to get sufficient edges for the final positive. Remember to put petroleum jelly on the eyebrows and lashes for ease in separation.

When the plaster is set, remove the cast, and pour up the positive with Ultracal 30 or stone while using either petroleum jelly or the soap method in a thin coat for separation. Another good separator for plaster to stone is made of stearic acid and kerosene. When the stone has set, the dental plaster negative can be easily cracked away, leaving the stone positive ready for use.

The Nose

To make a slush or brush application mold from this section mold of the nose (or using a full face cast), model the desired shape in plastalene on this positive, making certain that the blending edges are smooth so they will be imperceptible in the finished appliance. Take care that the nostrils are sufficiently filled on the positive with plastalene so they will not have any undercut that will prevent the removal of the negative cast to be taken. However, sculpt the nostrils so they will look natural and fit closely to the nose in the finished appliance.

The nose exhibits one of the more varied skin pore areas of the body. Sometimes the pores are small and almost imperceptible on someone with fine skin, and at other times the pores are large and the surface of the skin quite rough. Generally, a slight over-poring is normally called for during sculpture, as some of the fine details are lost in the casting of the negative on the surface of the appliance. Only by experience can the technician know the correct depth and extent of making pores.

For a clown nose (which is generally slush-cast), no pores are needed. Thus, the surface should be made as slick as possible by dipping the fingers in water (or mineral oil) and rubbing them on the surface of the plastalene.

It should also be noted that sometimes only a nose bridge or tip need be made; thus, the sculpture need not be over-extensive. However, the undercuts on the nostrils, as well as the outer curve of the alae must be filled with plastalene in order to avoid undercuts.

When the modeling is completed, coat the remainder of the exposed positive with petroleum jelly as a separator. The sculpture should then be surrounded with a clay wall about ¾″ higher than the tip of the sculptured nose and at least ¾″ from the sculpture all around. As the casting latex builds up by absorption into the plaster negative, this amount of thickness is minimal. Larger casts should be thicker (1″ to 2″) to allow for an absorptive surface.

Some technicians spray the surface of the sculpture with aerosol solution or Kodak Photo Flo (1 cubic centimeter in 200 cubic centimeters of water) to reduce the possibility of surface bubbles in the plaster. First paint in and then blow in a mix of casting plaster to cover all the sculpture and surroundings, and carefully spatulate and pour in the remainder of the mix to fill the cavity of the plastalene retaining wall. Some workers use a vibrator table to hasten the removal of all bubbles, while others tap the mold on the table top to force any bubbles to the surface of the plaster.

As soon as the plaster heats up and cools, the two sides can be pried apart with the blade of a screwdriver. Any plastalene remaining in the negative should be carefully removed with a wooden modeling tool; avoid scratching the surface of the negative. Allow the negative cast to dry out for about an hour, after which it can be cleaned of any remaining plastalene with a small bristle brush dipped in acetone or TCTFE. Rinse the negative in water before each use, and the latex appliance made in the cast will separate easily when it is completed and dried.

If the negative is to be used for brush application, no further preparation is needed, but if a slush-molded appliance is to be made, the negative requires that a plaster wall be built up in the area of the upper lip on the mold so that an even level will be achieved when the casting latex is poured into the mold.

The advantage of any slush- or brush-applied latex piece is that it will fit many faces; the inner surface is not made to fit any particular face the way in which foam latex appliances are. However, one cannot achieve the more skin-like quality on the outer surface of any slush or paint-in appliance that a foam one will display.

Whenever any additional plaster is to be added to a mold or cast, the surface should be thoroughly wetted with water before the new plaster is applied. Such additions work much better with a freshly made negative, as it has a greater water content than one that has been left to dry out—even overnight.

Any repairs on the negative, such as holes left by errant surface bubbles that may not have been dissipated when the cast was vibrated, can be easily made by scraping the underside of the negative with a metal tool to remove some plaster, as opposed to making a new mix. Dental tooth-filling tools are best for reaching into small places for such repairs.

Asian Eyelids, or the Epicanthic Eye Fold

For these, either a cast of the upper face (from the nose to the hairline) can be taken, or the full face cast used. Very little poring is needed on the lids themselves. If one wishes to make a series of stock Asian eyelids, it is advisable to vary the eyelid curves so they can be adjusted to fit a number of non-Asian eyes. Again, the negative should be taken in casting plaster and made about 1″ thick.

Bald Caps

Latex bald caps can be made in a negative plaster mold or painted on a positive one. To make a negative-type mold, get a small-sized balsa wood head form from a hat supply house, and slice it into nine fairly equal sections as follows: Create two cuts in one direction, and then turn the head 90° to make two additional cuts. Put the sides together, and hold them in place along the neck portion of the head with heavy elastic bands. Coat the entire head with a #1 or #2 plastalene, smoothing out the surface to form a bald head sculpture. The surface can be lightly pored to give it some texture. A retaining wall of plastalene is added to the desired shape of the mold, and then it can be sprayed with Photo Flo solution.

A good spray gadget, such as the PreVal Sprayer by the Precision Valve Corporation (available in many paint stores), is one made for spray-painting small objects. It consists of a bottle for the liquid and a removable unit with propellant and spray tip. The tip screws onto the bottle and can be used to spray many liquids. Buy several, and keep one with Photo Flo solution ready for use.

The retaining wall should be about 1½″ high, and the casting plaster negative taken of the plastalene positive must have that thickness all around. When the plaster is beginning to set, cover it with cheesecloth, and brush over a bit more casting plaster to strengthen the mold. When the plaster has fully set and cooled, remove the elastic bands from the balsa wood head, and carefully draw out the center section of the cut head. This can be facilitated by passing a piece of coat hanger wire through this section before putting it together to make the mold. Once this center section is out, the others will remove easily without cracking the negative. Remove the excess clay, and the mold is ready for use.

The same basic method can be used for making positive stone or Ultracal heads for plastic caps. However, do not make the casting plaster negative over ½″ thick, and do not use any cheesecloth reinforcement. When the plastalene has been cleaned out of the negative, coat the inside with petroleum jelly, and fill the cavity with a stone or Ultracal mix. The mix should be spatulated up and around the negative so that the finished cast is about ½ to ¾″ thick all around in a hollow shell. When the stone or Ultracal 30 has set, the plaster can be cracked away, and a positive cast which can be painted or sprayed remains. As previously mentioned, casting latex can also be used on a positive head, but the head positive should be made of plaster. Because of the separating medium (silicone grease type) used on the head molds for plastic cap material, molds so treated will not work with painted-on casting latex.

Generally, if the surface of the plastalene positive original has been pored sufficiently, the positive gypsum head will have a proper surface for receiving plastic cap material or latex, as the finished cap will then be reversed for use.

To make a head mold for spraying, where the adjustment of the spray on the final coating can be made to provide a more textured coat, some technicians make the head mold as slick as possible for ease in removal, and of course, the bald cap is not reversed. Make-up artist John Chambers had some head molds that were chrome-plated, while Bob Schiffer, another

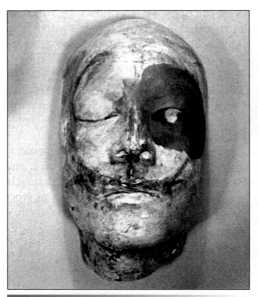

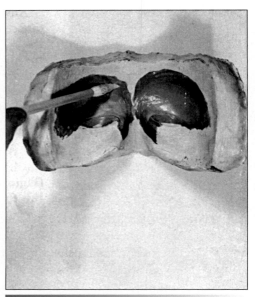

Fig. 1-8

A face cast with an epicanthic eye fold (one side is sculpted in plastalene.)

Fig. 1-9

The finished negative mold made from plaster being painted in with casting latex to form a large appliance that will cover the brows as well. A smaller piece may be painted in that will just cover the eyelid area with the same material. Such appliances can also be made of foam urethane or latex.

make-up artist of note, has made some from fiberglass, both of which are very smooth and work quite efficiently for spraying.

If one can borrow a positive head mold and wishes to make a copy, there are a number of ways that a duplicate mold can be taken. One of the basic ways is to use a flexible duplicating material such as PMC-724 or Perma Flex's Gra-Tufy CMC. Another way is to make a three-piece duplicating mold of stone or Ultracal 30. This type of mold is the same as would be made to serve as a mother mold for the flexible impression material as well.

Basically, one would divide the head mold down the center with a plastalene wall about $1\frac{1}{2}''$ high, with the division line on side one (so that when the wall is removed, the line remains on the center line of the head). A stone or Ultracal mix is then brushed and spatulated onto side one to a thickness of about $1''$ and allowed to set and cool. (Always remember that where any gypsum product meets another in casting, a separating medium is necessary.) The clay wall is then removed and keys are cut into the sides of the mold (three are sufficient), and the sides are covered with a thin coat of petroleum jelly as a separator. Side two is then taken to match the thickness of side one. When this has set and cooled, two angle keys can be cut to a depth of about $\frac{1}{4}''$ to $\frac{1}{2}''$, about $1''$ apart. A cap cavity is then formed out of plastalene of the top area of the head mold and taken in the same material. (Remember to use a separator.) This third cast should have a flat top, so the plastalene wall should be higher on two sides, and the surface can be flattened with a board that has been lacquered and then covered with petroleum jelly. When this part has set and cooled, the three pieces can be separated and the original removed. The mold is then reassembled and is ready for use.

If a flexible material were used in making the mold, the procedures would be approximately the same for making the three-piece mother mold. Then in the disassembly, the flexible mold is removed from the original and replaced in the mother mold for the sake of the negative's

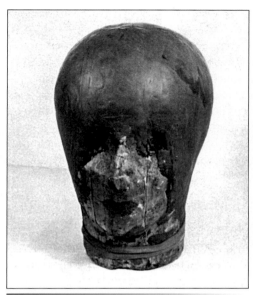

Fig. 1-10

A balsa wood head (which has been previously section-cut in nine parts and held with an elastic band at the base) is covered with a coating of plastalene.

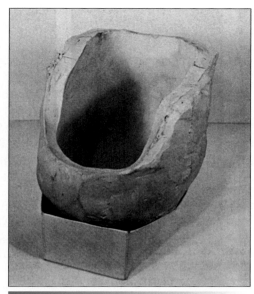

Fig. 1-11

A 1"-thick plaster mold made of this form (with the form removed.) This mold is used for slush-casting quick latex bald caps.

preparation. The negative is filled with stone or Ultracal, and a duplicate is made in the usual way. This type of duplicating mold will allow one to make a number of reproductions of the original. Check the basic shelf life of any duplicating material in the plastic varieties if the mold will be saved for future use. Of course, a stone or Ultracal 30 duplicating mold will last indefinitely with care taken in its separation from the duplicates.

Full Head Castings

Full, slip-over casting latex heads can be made with a slush cast of either one- or three-piece construction. These must be made of casting plaster and be about 2″ thick. Such molds should be reinforced with burlap strips for strength. A mix of 20-percent Ultracal 30 with casting plaster will also add strength and not diminish the slush molding time excessively.

For use, these large molds must be securely tied together with heavy cord or rope. Take care in using clamps on plaster molds, as the extra pressure exerted by the clamp may crack the mold.

Many other areas of the face and body can be cast, and slush or paint-in appliances can be produced. However, for the best fit, as well as the most natural appearance, foam latex or urethane prostheses are far superior, especially for the sake of movement.

THE TWO-PIECE MOLD

The two-piece, or positive-negative mold is required for foam appliances or for any that are pressure-molded. In theory, the positive cast is modeled upon, with the desired shape of the appliance to be made in plastalene. A negative is made of this; the clay is removed; the mold is filled with the appliance material, placed together, cured, and separated; and the appliance is ready for use. The procedure is similar to that given for the two-part flat plate mold explained previously.

To make a mold for a foam latex or foam urethane small piece—say, a nose—from a full-face cast, a plastalene wall is built around the nose of the cast to a height of about ¼″ to ½″ above the nose's tip. This cavity is then filled with PGC alginate and allowed to set. The clay wall is removed and the alginate separated from the face cast. This will produce a section negative into which an Ultracal 30 or stone mix is poured in order to make a positive. When set, this positive is then imbedded in another rather heavy mix of the same gypsum material. Generally, a surrounding round wall is made to hold the stone or Ultracal 30 mix out of 3″-wide linoleum, rubber floor mat, sheet lead, or even 6″ plastic pipe. As the positive still retains a great amount of moisture, it will incorporate itself into the new gypsum mix readily. Carefully place the positive in the center of the cavity, and with a dental spatula, seal the edges in so that the blend is perfect.

A good way to prepare the surface of a Formica-covered table for performing this procedure is to rub on a thin coat of petroleum jelly. Some workers prefer to use a glass plate or even a board with a Formica top. The linoleum or other material wall can be secured with cloth adhesive tape in order to keep its shape.

Although there is less chance of breakage with small molds, many lab technicians use fiber, fiberglass cloth, or burlap in the mold. Others prefer to use a circle of wire cloth around the positive section mold, taking care to imbed this fully within the mold.

When the stone or Ultracal starts to heat up in the set, remove the retaining wall, and while the material is not yet hard, scoop out three or four circular keys with the round end of a spatula or knife blade. Clean up the edges, and fill any defects. The desired shape of the appliance can now be sculpted on this built-up positive form in plastalene and gutters formed for an overflow area. Clean the key areas, and apply a separator on them and the overflow where the stone or Ultracal 30 can be seen. The surface can then be sprayed with Kodak Photo Flo solution and the form enclosed in a 6″ to 8″ circle (depending upon the height of the sculpture) of linoleum or such. Heavy elastic bands or cloth adhesive tape can be used to hold the form in shape. A stone or Ultracal 30 mix is then added in the usual manner to fill the cavity, and reinforcement material is added if desired.

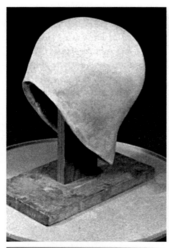  

Fig. 1-12a   Fig. 1-12b   Fig. 1-12c

(A) Positive stone or Ultracal head on a stand and turntable (for ease in spraying or painting the caps). (B) Showing one side of a section cast made to duplicate this head mold. Keys are cut (C), and the other side is made (note keys cut on top).

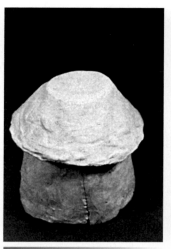
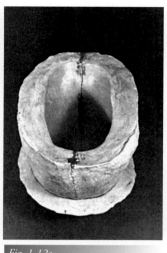

Fig. 1-12d   Fig. 1-12e   Fig. 1-12f

(D) Then a cap is cast to hold them together. (E) The completed three-piece mold put together. It is a good idea to coat the inside of the mold and the rim with two coats of lacquer to seal the surface. Small chipped areas can be filled with plastalene and then the mold given a coat of petroleum jelly as a separator. Ultracal 30 can then be used to make positive heads in this mold. (F) A head mold or full head mold can also be made of polysulfide duplicating material for a seamless flexible mold, as shown here by Tom Burman.

When the stone or Ultracal 30 is completely set and almost cool, remove the wall, and separate the two sides of the mold. The plastalene is then removed and cleaned off of the mold, and the keys can be lightly sanded to remove any burrs. The mold is now ready for use.

Molds made for foam latex prostheses should not be more than 1½" thick to allow good heat penetration for curing the latex. Also, if the appliance is large or deep, it is a good idea to have a vent hold for overflow as well. On large noses this hole can be drilled through the positive on the nose tip with a ¼" to 5⁄16" drill.

Two-piece molds for foam polyurethanes are quite similar to those for foam latex, except that the urethane molds can be heavier, as no baking is required.

Large molds that might be for extensive forehead pieces or for full heads can entail a positive core head and a two-piece negative. The vent of these molds may also be employed as filling holes for a gun filled with foam latex that is forced into the mold. Large molds must often be clamped together as the mold is being filled, and flanges must be made to give a purchase point for these clamps. Of course, the larger the mold, the more strengthening it must have a product such as Acryl 60 cement hardener and additional burlap or fiber. It is also a good idea to mark one side of the molds with a heavy marking pen or to scratch a line down the sides of both of the molds to easily see how to put the molds together during use.

Some lab technicians coat the sculpted plastalene with RCMA Plastic Cap Material when making two-piece molds so that when separated after making the negative, no plastalene will stick to it, facilitating the cleaning process. This coating should be removed from the plastalene with acetone for reuse of the clay material. There are many methods employed for making the positive-negative types of molds, and books relative to these methods may be found in the bibliography.

Incidentally, all molds used for foam procedures must be thoroughly dried out before use. One good way to do so is to put them in an oven at low heat (100 to 150°F) and leave them overnight.

Fig. 1-13a   Fig. 1-13b   Fig. 1-13c

Two-piece mold. (A) and (B) Two angles of an embedded nose that has been sculpted in plastalene and the gutters made. Note that the nostrils have been employed as a run-off for the excess material when the nose is being made, rather than the usual hold drilled through the positive on the tip of the nose. (C) The positive has been circled with a piece of inlaid linoleum and held together with rubber bands cut from an old auto inner tube. The inside of the linoleum has been greased with petroleum jelly. Sheet lead or rubber can also be used for this.

Fig. 1-13d   Fig. 1-13e   Fig. 1-13f

(D) The negative portion poured with Ultracal 30. (E) The rubber bands and linoleum removed. A plaster knife is used to clean up any flash and to round the edges of the mold. The markings are made in pencil just before the Ultracal has set, giving the type of appliance, date, and, if desired, number for cataloging. (F) The finished two-part mold with the plastalene removed and the surface given two coats of clear lacquer to seal it. This mold will be used for casting foam urethane noses.

Plastalene Transfers

Make-up artist Dick Smith often sculpts a facial transformation on the life mask, removes sections of plastalene intact, and then transfers them to an individual section positive for making the two-piece molds. Using a clean, fresh dental stone life mask, he brushes on two coats of alginate dental separator and dries the surface with a hairdryer. He sculpts his appliances with #2 plastalene as usual on the life mask, finishing the detail and the edge and then coats the plastalene with a layer of clear plastic cap material.

The entire life mask and sculpture is then submerged in cold water for about an hour, at which time some of the plastalene sections may loosen from the life mask, while others can be easily pried away. Large areas like the forehead may have to be cut in half for easy removal. These sections of plastalene are then carefully transferred to section positives. He recommends coating the section positive with petroleum jelly and then pressing on the sculpture and smoothing down the edges. The texture, edges, and minor repairs needed after the transfer can then be done, as can the plastalene flashing for casting and the negatives poured up. In this manner one can get a better perspective of how the sculptured pieces will appear on the full face, as opposed to a mere estimate on a section positive. RCMA makes a special heavy grade of alginate separator that is excellent for this use, as well as for making acrylic teeth.

Fig. 1-14

A smaller foam latex-type nose mold for just a nose tip, showing the conventional escape hole bored into the tip of the positive. (Molds by Werner Keppler.)

Fig. 1-15

Another Keppler mold for foam latex for a nose tip but with channels (or holes) cut for the excess (as opposed to the hole in the previous figure).

Molds for Teeth

Plastic teeth and caps that are pressure or heat-cured are made in special metal flasks. However, for most make-up purposes, two-piece dental stone molds will suffice.

The first step in casting the mouth is to cast the upper or lower teeth (or both) in order to create a basic cast on which to work. A dental supply house can furnish all the necessary materials and tools for this step, as well as the materials to make the teeth. A set of impression plates for both the upper and lower teeth can be obtained in a number of sizes that will fit inside the mouth. They are available in plastic or metal. Also, it is a good idea to buy a set of rubber dental base molds to make neat finished castings with which to work.

For a cast of the upper teeth, a mix of quick-set dental alginate can be made and placed in the tray. This is inserted in the mouth and pressed up to cast the upper teeth. This type of alginate sets quite rapidly (2 to 3 minutes), so the cast can be removed as soon as the alginate is firm. A mix of dental stone should then be brushed into the negative alginate mold A (while still in the tray), followed by additional stone to fill the cast. Many dental technicians employ a vibrator to ensure that the mold is well filled and packed with the stone and to dissipate any bubbles that might be formed. The rest of the stone mix should be poured into a rubber dental base mold. When the stone is of a plastic consistency, the tray is inverted onto the stone in the base mold and the join smoothed out.

When the stone has completely set, the tray with the alginate can be removed, with the alginate attached and the casting removed from the base mold. The edges can be trimmed with metal tools to form a neat casting. The lower teeth can be cast in the same manner using the lower teeth trays and the same rubber forms. As there are a number of methods for making acrylic teeth, the special molds for these are discussed in the section on tooth plastics (later in this chapter). *(See Chapter 5 for information about dental veneers.)*

LATEX AND PLASTIC APPLIANCES

An increasing number of compounds and materials is being used by make-up artists to produce appliances. The criterion is always that the prosthesis look and behave as naturally as possible for the use intended and designed. Today artists have casting latex to make slush or paint-in appliances, foam latex products, foam urethanes, gelatins, solid molded plastics, and waxes for constructions at their disposal.

NATURAL RUBBER MATERIALS

Of all the compounds utilized for appliances, natural rubber is by far the most popular and useful. Commencing in the late 1930s, make-up artists began experimenting with various forms of these products, starting with the brush-applied method into a plaster mold, and later with the use of the two-piece foam latex materials.

Beyond the making of the molds and casts, the make-up artist now had to learn a bit of chemistry to make the mixes necessary for use and had to understand the variety of solvents, polymers, colorants, and so forth that were part of the vocabulary of the make-up laboratory technician. Telephone calls to manufacturers, visits to the prosthetics clinics of the Veterans Administration, discussions with chemists, and finally note comparisons with other make-up artists interested in these new and exciting directions were all part of the education of those who wanted to learn and master these challenging techniques. Times may change, but avidity for learning should never diminish.

LATEX

Latex is a milky white fluid that is produced by the cells of various seed plants (such as milkweed, spurge, and poppy families) and is the source of rubber, gutta-percha, chicle, and balata. Most *natural rubber* today, which is a polymer of isoprene, comes from coagulating this juice.

Synthetic rubber-like substances can be obtained by polymerization of some plastic materials and may also be called *synthetic rubber* or *synthetic latex*. The term elastomer means "rubber-like," and there are many categories to which this term can be applied.

Natural rubber latex as employed by the make-up professional usually refers to a pure gum latex that has no fillers and is of varying density. Some are thinner for use as balloon-type rubber (for making bladders and so forth), while others are thicker (such as those employed for some foam latex formulas). When rubber latex has fillers, like zinc oxide, it can be used for *casting*, as it will build in thickness when left in a slush mold or can be added on with paint-in methods. Some natural rubber lattices are *pre-vulcanized*—that is, they are pre-treated and do not require a heat cure—while others require such heat treatment for curing.

Synthetic rubbers and lattices can be polysulfides, polyurethanes, acrylics, and so on. One should therefore take care in defining a material as *liquid latex* without explaining which type or grade it might be.

The hardness of the finished product can be determined with a Shore durometer. While a reading of 40 refers to the approximate hardness of automobile tire rubber, a reading of 10 is a much softer finished product, and more along the lines of what a make-up artist might wish to employ as a soft duplicating material.

For make-up purposes, three types of latex molding methods are employed: the slush molding method, the paint-in (or paint-on) manner, and the foam latex procedure.

Grades of Lattices

Many grades of latex compounds are available from a multitude of sources and can be employed for slush, paint-in, duplicating, or foam latex.

Natural rubber lattices that have no fillers dry with a yellowish translucency and an elastic resiliency such as might be found in elastic bands or balloons. The General Latex Corporation makes 1-V-10, which can be used for dipping or for the creation of thin pieces. RCMA also supplies a pure gum latex that is excellent for bladder effects. These natural rubber lattices are pre-vulcanized and have good stability, fast drying rates, good water resistance, and excellent aging properties and flexibility.

Slush molding lattices have higher solids (because of the fillers) and higher viscosities. They can be easily colored with dyes or colloidal colors and are pre-vulcanized. RCMA supplies a casting latex for slush molding and brush coating. RCMA also supplies a casting filler that can be stirred into the casting latex to hasten the build-up in slush casting and to provide more viscosity for brush application. *(For foam lattices and their components, see the section on Foam Latex later in this chapter.)*

Coloration

Coloration of appliances made with lattices can be done intrinsically—that is, with color added to the initial formulation before curing—or extrinsically, with color added over the finished appliance. Intrinsic coloration is best done with universal colors like those supplied by RCMA or paint stores, and a drop or so of burnt sienna color is usually sufficient to color a pint of latex as a light flesh tone. Other colors such as reds, ochres, and blues can be added for coloration, but it should be kept in mind that the color of the finished material is usually quite darker than the liquid's appearance before curing. Testing on a plaster plate will show the end color before adding too much.

Dyes may also be used for coloration of water-based lattices, and a 10-percent solution, added drop by drop, is usually sufficient in order to achieve the best color. Unfilled lattices will deepen in coloration considerably more than the filled types of slush or paint-in lattices. Some workers use 30-percent dye solutions for intrinsically coloring a foam latex so that the higher concentration of dye in water will not affect the water balance of the mix. Colloidal colors such as universal colors, however, are considered to be more manageable and more versatile than dyes for coloring most latex products.

Extrinsic coloration of appliances requires special vehicles for the color, as some affect natural rubber or synthetic rubber appliances. Cake make-up foundations, cream-stick foundations, and a number of the cream-cake foundations in general use for make-up foundations on the skin do not work as a prosthetic base, just as the old greasepaints did not. The main reason is that they contain mineral oil, which has a tendency either to attack the rubber or to whiten out after application. (Note: All RCMA Color Process Foundations can be used with latex appliances.) Max Factor formerly made a product called Rubber Mask Greasepaint that was essentially a castor oil vehicle base that did not attack the rubber. Other theatrical make-up companies have copied this foundation, so it is readily available. Also, RCMA has devised a new variety of foundation, Appliance Foundation (A.F.), which is superior to the old rubber mask greasepaint types. The company also makes an A.F. Powder that has more coverage than the regular RCMA No-Color Powder for use with these foundations. Powdering A.F. Foundations with A.F. Powder will produce a more matte surface on an appliance than a No-Color Powder, so sometimes a light stipple of glycerin will restore a better surface halation to an appliance.

The RCMA A.F. series has replaced the RCMA PB (Prosthetic Base) materials, as the newer A.F. series features a thicker form of foundation from which the oils do not separate, as is prevalent with most of the rubber mask greasepaint types, and it is neither sticky nor hard to blend, as are some of the firmer ones.

The A.F. series is obtainable in the basic color wheel primary colors of red, yellow, and blue, which can be combined to form any of the other in-between or secondary colors. Additionally, it comes in white, black, brown (KN-5 shade), and the earth colors of Ochre-1624, Warm Ochre-3279, Burnet Sienna-2817, and Red Oxide-6205, which are some of the main basic color ingredients that are components of the majority of skin color foundation shades. RCMA also makes a number of shades matched to its regular Color Process Foundations, such as KW-2 and KM-2. Other useful shades are constantly being added to the line as a result of the wide acceptance of the A.F. type of make-up for high coverage use.

The A.F. series comes in various sizes and also in kit form of six colors per tray, thus providing great convenience for transport in the make-up kit. The products can be applied with brushes or sponges and provides a super-coverage of both skin and appliances made of foam latex or plastic, as well as for slush or paint-in molded rubber.

The mixing of earth colors with the bright colors and the dilution with white will produce almost any shade of foundation. As most make-up artists who employ appliances in their work prefer to mix their own shades for the particular intended use, this provides an excellent basic method. The colors are easily spatulated together on a glass or plastic plate into the required shade. It is a good idea to mix more than is required so that one does not run out of a special color during the job at hand. The extra can be stored in a container for future use. It is also advisable to keep track of the mix by marking down the amounts of the basic materials used (such as spatula tips or spoonfuls) in the event that additional material must be mixed.

The A.F. kits are numbered as #1, #2, etc. Kit #1 features 1624 (Ochre), 2817 (Burnt Sienna), 3279 (Warm Ochre), 6205 (Red Oxide), KW-2, and KM-2. Kit #2 contains Red, Yellow, Blue, Black, White, and Brown-KN-5. Other kits with regularly matched Color Process shades are also being made. Special kits are available to order for specific use.

Although the viscosity of the A.F. series is high, its blendability and coverage is superior for any type of appliance.

A new concept of extrinsic coloration is being done with acrylic emulsion colors. Dick Smith devised a mixture of RCMA Prosthetic Adhesive B and acrylic paints that coats a foam latex appliance with an excellent surface material. His basic formula is an equal mix of PA-B and Liquidtex tube colors. This he stipples on the appliance with urethane stipple sponges after giving the appliance a stipple coat of PA-B and powdering. To lessen the halation, he might stipple on a coat of Liquidtex Matte Medium.

Some firms make a paint for latex castings with xylol as the solvent. The latter seems to incorporate the color quite well into the latex but does not give as much of a flesh-like look as the Dick Smith mixture (which he calls PAX).

RCMA also makes a special line of flexible acrylic foam latex or foam urethane paint colors for make-up use similar to the PAX material. The colors can be painted or stippled onto the appliances. There are matting agents that can be added to produce a less shiny coating as well. A new series with FDA-certified colors has also been developed by RCMA; this Appliance Paint (A.P.) series is available in colors matching the Appliance Foundation (A.F.) series.

pH Value

Natural rubber lattices are suspensions in ammoniacal water, and the correct pH value for most systems is between 10 and 11. pH test papers can be obtained from chemical supply houses. *(See Appendix B)*. The excess ammonia loss of natural rubber lattices can be corrected with a 2-percent solution of ammonium hydroxide in water, with tests conducted as one adds the solution to obtain the proper pH.

Fillers

Lattices used for slush or paint-in casting can be adjusted for various degrees of stiffness or hardness of finished product with the addition of a filler. This filler can be prepared by adding 25 grams of zinc oxide to 100 cubic centimeters of distilled water, or it can be purchased from RCMA as Casting Filler. Depending upon the degree of opacity and stiffness required, anywhere from 1 to 10-percent of filler can be added by stirring into any pre-vulcanized latex for slush use.

Softeners

To make softer latex pieces, any latex compound can have a plasticizer, which consists of the addition of 400 grams of stearic acid, 500 grams of distilled water, 100 grams of oleic acid, 12 grams of potassium hydroxide, and 12 grams of ammonium hydroxide (28-percent). This mixture can be added 5 cubic centimeters (to 100 cubic centimeters of latex compound) at a time, while testing a finished piece in between in order to achieve the degree of softness required. Such products also affect the drying time of the latex, as well as its durability.

Thickeners

Most natural and synthetic lattices can be thickened to a soft, buttery consistency in a few minutes by stirring in Acrysol GS. This product is the sodium salt of an acrylic polymer and is supplied at 12- to 13-percent solids in water solution. For most applications, the use of 0.10- to 2-percent Acrysol GS (solids on latex solids) is adequate. Natural rubber has approximately 60-percent solids, and thus, 5 to 10 cubic centimeters of Acrysol GS added to 100 cubic centimeters of latex will thicken it considerably. This mix can then be spatulated into a mold in order to add bulk to a particular section for paint-in or slush molding. Note that thickeners retard the drying time of any latex compound.

As the Acrysol GS is a very heavy, viscous liquid, a diluted solution in water will work better for additions to lattices. Therefore, if the Acrysol GS is diluted 50/50 in water, it will have half the strength of the stock solution and should be used accordingly. Tincture of green soap can also be employed as a latex compound thickener for some applications.

LATEX APPLIANCES

Slush or Slip Casting

Casting latex is poured into a slush-type mold and allowed to set for a period of 10 to 30 minutes, depending upon the thickness of the desired appliance. The excess latex is then poured back into the container and the mold turned upside down to drain. It can be blow-dried with a handheld hairdryer, set underneath a large hairdryer, or placed in a low-heat oven. Drying time varies with the thickness of the prosthesis, but separation from the mold is relatively simple because of latex shrinkage. It should be noted that the appliance will have rather heavy edges and is unsuitable for blending into the face during application.

A slush-cast nose is generally made for clowns, as the piece will last longer than the delicate paint-in or foam version. Full heads often found in joke and costume shops are made in this manner, as well as full or partial appliances for extras in a production where special make-ups are required but do not require any facial movement.

 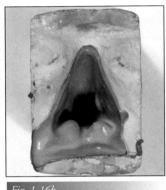 

Fig. 1-16a   *Fig. 1-16b*   *Fig. 1-16c*

Slush casting. (A) A nose mold is filled with casting latex and allowed to set until the build-up is about 1/16 to 1/8". (B) The latex is poured out of the mold and the surface of the latex dried with a handheld hairdryer. Unless over-cured in a low heat for about 1 hour, the mold should be left to air-cure for about 8 hours after the latex has been thoroughly dried. (C) The nose is then removed and trimmed for use. Clown noses are usually made with this method, as their edges do not require thinness for blending into the skin. As with all slush- or paint-in-type molds, they should be rinsed in clean water if they are to be used when dry, especially after oven-curing. This restores some of the moisture in the mold and prevents the latex from adhering strongly to the plaster when the appliance is removed. Otherwise, no separating medium is required for latex-to-gypsum castings.

Paint-in or Brush Application Molding

This method consists of painting casting latex into the mold in successive overlapping coats, the thinnest of which is closest to the edge of the prosthesis. While a slush molded piece has a heavy ungraduated edge, the brush application method will allow the blending edge to be carefully controlled. This is quite necessary, because a casting latex edge cannot be dissolved into the skin area, as can many of the plastic types. Another advantage of a painted-in piece is that it can be built up more heavily where necessary. For example, the alae and the bridge of the nose will require extra coats in the production of an appliance that will hold the proper shape.

Sometimes workers add in small pieces of paper toweling to strengthen a piece. The toweling should always be torn into shape, rather than cleanly cut, in order to produce more graduated edges. It is then placed where desired with a brush, and additional casting latex is coated over the paper in order to make it a part of the prosthesis.

Medium-sized Chinese bristle brushes are used for this work by many technicians because of their size, configuration, and low cost. Always work up a good lather of soapsuds on a cake of Ivory soap with the brush, and wipe it lightly before putting it into the casting latex. This procedure prevents the latex from solidifying or building up on the bristles of the brush and facilitates its cleaning in cold running water after use. It is a good practice to pour some casting latex in a 16-ounce wide-mouth jar for painting use. The brush should always be left in the latex when not in use between coats so that it will not dry out. Leaving the latex-covered brush on a counter top for just a few minutes can ruin it for further use. Sometimes a coated brush can be salvaged by soaking it in RCMA Studio Brush Cleaner overnight.

Some appliances require special attention and painting—for example, Asian eyelids, where the lid area must be painted heavily enough to hold the proper shape, while the upper portion that is attached to the skin must blend off in a thin coat. It is a good idea to have a series of eyelid molds and to paint up a sample of each for try-ons when a number of them are required. Then the eyelids can be individually fitted and the area to be painted in casting latex noted. (As eyes tend to vary, some lids may be attached higher or lower on the frontal bone for the best effect).

Another case is the making of latex bald caps for extras or large casts. This method consists of pouring some casting latex into the mold cavity and turning the mold back and forth, with the latex being carried higher and higher each time and forming an edge. This procedure should be performed carefully so that the leading edge around the forehead line of the hair receives only one or two such coatings of casting latex. Do not allow the latex to sit in the mold without this turning agitation, because it will build in rings that might be apparent when the piece is dried out for use. Experience will show how long this procedure must be kept up in order to obtain a bald cap effect that is both fine at the edges and heavy enough in the crown to hold its shape.

Pour off the excess out of the back portion of the mold, and drain fully before drying the surface with a handheld hairdryer. 30 minutes of drying is generally required before the mold can be set aside for another hour or so to cure fully. The cap can then be peeled off the mold, and to ensure that it will retain its shape, it should be placed over a head form for about another hour so that the surface can fully dry out. It is then ready for use.

Inflatable Bladder Effects

Many special effects transformations or illusions employ the use of some form of inflatable bladder, the effect of which is to ripple the surface of the skin to indicate violent changes taking place systematically. In essence, these bladders are inflatable plastic or latex balloons that can be controlled in size and flexibility by the introduction of air into them through fine plastic tubing. Such bladders may be concealed under surface appliances made of foam latex, urethane, or plastic molding material so that when they are inflated and/or deflated, it appears that the surface of the skin is expanding as air is introduced into the bladder or contracting as air is released. As such, a rippling effect can be created (as visible on William Hurt's arm in Dick Smiths' make-up for *Altered States* [Warners, 1980], for example).

For a simple bladder, pure gum latex can be used. Make a plaster flat plate (a good size would be 6 × 12″, or about 1″ thick for a permanent stock plate) with a smooth surface.

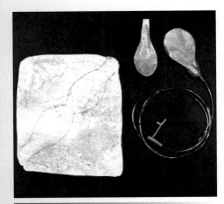

Fig. 1.17

Various inflatable bladder effects are often seen in transformations. These can be made of PMC-724 or in pure gum latex. This is a plaster flat plate with an outline inscribed in pencil. A finished bladder is shown after having been attached to the tubing with Dermicel tape and a coat of pure gum latex (as a sealer). In the center is the cutout wax paper used to keep the sides of the bladder from one another when it is folded over.

Sketch an outline with a #2 lead pencil of the two sides of the bladder, and paint on three even coats of RCMA Pure Gum Latex, right to the edges of the outline, drying each coat thoroughly with a handheld hairdryer. This will normally give a sufficient thickness for the walls of the bladder, but larger-sized bladders can be made with additional coats for more strength.

Cut out a piece of heavy waxed paper, allowing about $1/2''$ clearance to the edge of the outline. On larger bladders, allow at least $3/4''$ (for an adhering edge). This waxed paper will delineate the inside dimension of the bladder, which of course can be made in many shapes.

Dust this waxed paper cutout with RCMA No-Color Powder on both sides, and lay it down on the latex-painted shape on one side. Take care not to powder the surface of the latex. Carefully peel up the other side of the bladder, and fold it over to exactly fit the outline of the other side. Press the edges together firmly so that the latex will adhere to itself and form the two sides of the bladder. Strip off the other side of the bladder form the plaster, and trim the latex nozzle end to within about $1/8''$ from the waxed paper end.

To remove the waxed paper, push in a small rounded wooden modeling tool in order to first force an entrance, and then take it out. In its place, insert a drinking straw with an end dipped in No-Color Powder. Blow the powder into the bladder cavity on each side. Then the waxed paper insert can be teased out with a pair of dental college pliers or tweezers. The bladder with a nozzle end is now complete. Clear plastic tubing can be obtained from a medical or chemical supply house and inserted into the nozzle of the bladder. This can be sealed in with Johnson & Johnson $1/2''$ Dermicel Clear Tape and then coated over with pure gum latex. The bladder is then ready to be attached and used.

Although the illustrated bladder has no excess edge for attachment to the skin, the $1/2''$ to $3/4''$ excess previously described during manufacture can be used for the adhesion area. RCMA Prosthetic Adhesive A is best for these bladders, as it has excellent retention.

FOAM LATEX

The present-day* ultimate in prosthetic appliance use for make-up purposes is foam latex. It is unsurpassed for the best possible effects, as well as for skin adhesion. Since MGM's classic, *The Wizard of Oz* (1939), when Jack Dawn, then Head of Make-up, employed foam appliances for the unforgettable characters of the Cowardly Lion, the Tin Man, and the Scarecrow, as well as for many others in the film, foam latex has been the mainstay of three-dimensional character work in motion pictures. In the early days of television in New York (the 1940s and 1950s), studios relied mainly on painted-in casting latex appliances because of their low cost and ability to be made rapidly, which were especially important factors considering the lack of preparation time afforded make-up artists for work in television. Today, foam latex has become the standard for most appliances for professional make-up work.

Like many laboratory procedures that have been developed strictly in the make-up field, the parameters of the chemistry and mixing of foam latex have been found to extend beyond the seeming restrictions of the expensive scientific or special equipment so that easily obtainable results are possible. At first, special handmade beaters, bowls, and laboratory ovens were considered requisite, but many labs today use kitchen-type Sunbeam Mixmasters with regular beaters and bowls, along with either standard electric kitchen ovens or the newer air-convection tabletop types. Only when full heads and bodies must be made are larger ovens required and restaurant-type Hobart mixers employed.

Fig. 1-18a

Fig. 1-18b

Fig. 1-18c

*Mixing foam latex. (Lab work by Werner Keppler.) (**A**) Paper cups used to measure ingredients by weight. (**B**) Beating foam in a kitchen mixer with regular beaters. (**C**) The latex mix beat to correct volume and refined.*

However, some conditions still do not vary much, and general room temperature and humidity do affect foaming procedures. The optimum is 68 to 72°F with a midrange of humidity. It is not difficult to maintain such with air conditioning and heating today. Higher temperatures will cause faster gelling and setting, while lower temperatures will extend the time. Successful foaming operations are impractical below 60°F.

Small quantities of ingredients can be weighed in plastic cups and the standard bowls of the Mixmaster used. Some artists mark the foaming volume on these bowls. (Five volumes is approximately correct for most appliances). All measurements given are for wet unfoamed ingredients, and a basic mix can often create quite a few small pieces. As it is rather impractical to mix very small amounts, most workers fill the molds that they are presently working on and, with the remaining material, fill some stock molds for extra pieces. Otherwise, much foam product is wasted.

Wholesalers of foam latex ingredients normally sell 5 gallons as a basic lot, but 1-quart sizes of both the three-part latex and the four-part Burman formula are available through RCMA. Some other suppliers will furnish 1-gallon lots. It should be noted that a lot consists of the measured amount of the basic latex material, plus all the necessary chemicals for the foaming operation, although they are also available separately from most sources. European users will find a very soft and excellent foam available through Christopher Tucker in England. *(See Appendix B for other suppliers.)*

The Three-part Foam Latex

1. Mix Parts A, B, and C thoroughly to be sure there is no material separated and caked on the bottom of the containers.

2. Combine 170 grams (6 ounces, or ¾ cup) of Part A and 22 grams (1 tablespoon) of Part B in a mixing bowl.

3. Mix with an electric mixer to three to six times the original volume, depending on the firmness desired.

4. Add 6 grams (½ teaspoon) of Part C, and mix until uniform (about 1 minute).

5. Pour or inject into the mold, and allow to stand undisturbed until gelled. Place in oven and cure (bake) at 200°F for 4 to 5 hours. If the material gels (sets up) too fast, gradually reduce the amount of Part C used until the proper amount of working time is acquired. Normally it is not desirable to exceed 10 minutes after the addition of Part C.

Fig. 1-19a   *Fig. 1-19b*   *Fig. 1-19c*

Mixing foam latex. (Lab work by Werner Keppler.) (A) Paper cups used to measure ingredients by weight. (B) Beating foam in a kitchen mixer with regular beaters. (C) After baking, the mold is separated. Gloves are used to hold the still-hot mold.

Fig. 1-19d   *Fig. 1-19e*

(D) The appliance removed. Flash, or run-off can be seen. (E) Comparison with a file photo upon which the nose was based for duplication.

One of the most knowledgeable lab technicians in California, Werner Keppler, who formerly headed the Universal Studio Laboratory and is now at TBS in Burbank, has modified and simplified the foaming procedures, making small to large appliances with a minimum of difficulty. He prefers to use the three-part material and makes minor adjustments for each run if need be.

Using the regular Mixmaster bowls, Keppler's overall mixing time is 10 minutes, and his measurements are made in plastic cups. One cup of Part A (the latex) in the small bowl is about the minimum, and this will be enough for half a dozen noses, while four cups in the large bowl will suffice for a full head.

His molds are prepared by coating a fully dried-out cool mold with two coats of thinned-out clear lacquer. After this has dried, he coats with a thin brushing of castor oil and then applies Mold Release prior to use. He also prefers the Kerr Toolstone (about 2″ thick) with fiber hemp casting reinforcement for making his molds.

To prepare for a run, Keppler lays out his molds, coated with Mold Release, side by side. The foam ingredients are measured on a scale and poured into the mixing bowl along with a few drops of burnt sienna universal color in order to make slightly flesh-tinted appliances. If he decides that he wants softer-than-usual foam, he adds two drops of glycerin per cup of Part A. He then hand-mixes the ingredients and places them under the mixer, starting at a slow speed and gradually turning the speed wheel up. Timing begins as desired with the onset of mixing by machine.

Fig. 1-20a

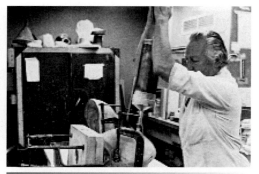

Fig. 1-20b

A full head made for foam latex. (A) Coating the negative with separator. (B) For a large mold with many surfaces, a special gun is filled with the foam latex mix and injected into a hole drilled into the mold surface for this purpose. This particular mold is a three-piece affair with a front, back, and core all held securely together for casting with large screw clamps.

Fig. 1-20c

Fig. 1-20d

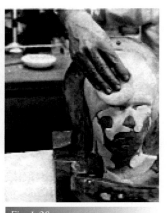

Fig. 1-20e

(C) As the mold fills, two exit holes for the excess material are seen. As the foam bubbles through the one closest to the injection hole, it is stopped up with plastalene. The second hole has just been plugged with the clay material before removing the injection gun. (D) The injected molds are placed in the large oven for baking at the proper temperature and timing. (E) The cured appliance is removed from the oven, and the front half of the mold is opened and powdered.

With the small bowl, at a speed of 7, he mixes the measured ingredients Part A (latex) and Part B (curing agents), and with a large bowl, the speed is 12 for 4½ minutes. He then tests the mix by dipping a kitchen knife into the mass. If the mix does not fall off the blade readily, he estimates that it is ready. He then turns the mixer to speed 1 in order to refine the foam for 3½ to 4 minutes. He adds Part C (gelling agent) and beats for the remaining time (about 1 minute), stirring down to the bottom of the bowl with his knife blade to ensure that the gelling agent is thoroughly mixed in. He also hand-reverses the motion of the spinning bowl to aid in removing all the excess or large bubbles that might have formed. If the piece is a large one, he often adds the same amount of water to the gelling agent in order to slow down the gel time.

He then pours into his molds immediately and holds them shut until the excess material gels to the touch. Large molds are filled with an injection gun and are clamped shut during this procedure as they are filled.

Keppler bakes the molds in a 200°F oven for 2½ hours for a small piece and 5½ to 6 hours for full heads or large molds. On completion of bake time, the molds are removed from the oven with welder's gloves and taken apart. Small molds are opened, and the pieces

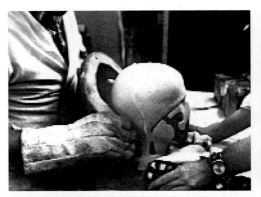

Fig. 1-21a

Fig. 1-21b

(F) The back half of the mold is removed as the latex head remains on the core section of the mold. Note that as the piece is a head and forehead appliance only, the core face portion has been cut away to remove any undercuts. Note also the excess foam latex that has flowed into the prepared channels away from the front blending edge of the appliance. (G) Leo Lotito, Make-up Department Head at TBS Studios, views the completed appliance with Terry Smith, the make-up designer for the production (The Last Star Fighter, Lorimar Productions, 1984). Note also the two approximately ½" projections that are the injection point and one of the excess flow holes of the mold. These will be removed, and the hair portion of the appliance will cover them. For a large piece like this, Werner often paints the inside of the mold with a coating of the latex used for the foaming procedure in order to give a skin to the surface of the appliance. Werner (center) is seen re-coating the molds with castor oil prior to allowing them to cool off slowly before another use. Large molds are covered with towels or blankets to slow the cooling process. These molds were made of Kerr Toolstone.

are left out to air-dry, while larger appliances are left on the positive side of the mold after being taken apart and replaced in the oven for about ½ hour so that their more extensive surfaces can fully dry out.

He then coats the molds, while hot, with some castor oil from a paintbrush and sets them aside to cool off. Large molds are covered with towels to slowly dissipate the heat. The molds must cool off completely before another use.

He fills small holes in a finished foam appliance with a mixture of pure gum latex into which Cabosil M-5 has been stirred for thickening. Sometimes, when the head is a large one, he will coat the negative mold surface with a brush coat of Part A before pouring in the foam mixture, especially if the modeling is intricate and detailed on the finished piece. This "skins" the mold and becomes part of the appliance during the baking.

Some additional notes on the three-part foam late come from Dick Smith, who uses it only occasionally, since he seems to prefer the four-part latex mix. He does not recommend the use of the castor oil separator but does lacquer-coat his molds and uses a stearic acid-type mold release. When beating the foam, he sets his mixer on the highest speed for about 2 minutes so that the volume of the mix will be increased to about four volumes. Three volumes will make a firm foam, four volumes a soft foam, and five volumes a very soft piece. He then turns the machine down to a speed of about 3 and refines the foam for 3 minutes. In this way, the volume remains about the same, but the foam cell structure becomes finer.

He measures out the gelling agent with a spoon that has been waxed—for the gelling agent will not stick to a waxed surface—or a small receptacle, such as a cut-off paper cup that has been coated with a paste wax. A level teaspoon of gelling agent is about 8 grams, which he normally uses. If the foam mixture fails to gel within 15 minutes after the mix is stopped, it will start to break down and collapse the foam. A good average time is between 5 and 10 minutes for gelation, when the room temperature is in the mid-70s.

He also mixes his color in the gelling agent, using casein artist tube colors slightly thinned with water. A light flesh tone is provided with a teaspoon of color and ¼ teaspoon of water for a standard mix (using burnt sienna as the colorant).

Like Keppler, Smith uses a spoon to scoop out the foam from the mixing bowl and pours it carefully into the mold, taking care not to entrap any bubbles. If the negative has deep texture or pits, the foam mix should be poked into these with a pointed wooden modeling tool. Special care should be taken with nose tips.

Smith cautions that too much foam should not be placed in a small mold, as it will make it too difficult to press completely closed. He recommends a preheated oven of 210°F. With a mold about 4″ high, 3 hours of baking time should be sufficient. When the foam is believed to be cured, the mold should be removed from the oven and gently pried open. The foam should be poked in an inconspicuous spot (such as an overflow area). If it stays indented, it is not baked enough. Leave the piece on the positive half of the mold, and return it to the oven for another 30 minutes. Test it again before removing completely. He also recommends that all molds be wrapped or covered in old bath towels to prevent rapid cooling or cracking.

Foam can be made softer to the touch by adding 3 grams of Nopco 1444-B from Diamond Shamrock Chemical Company to 2 grams of Part B, and then adding this contribution to Part A. If you want to beat to volume 5, also add 10 grams of water to the ingredients prior to beating.

As once can readily see, foam latex mixtures can be varied by different technicians to achieve what they consider to be the most efficient or simplest method of use. Certainly there is little contradiction in the methods, and they show the versatility of the material, as well as slightly different approaches to achieving the same end result.

Most lab technicians who employ dental or tool stone molds will coat them when hot with castor oil, but this method should not be employed for Ultracal molds, as it often leaves the edges of the appliances gummy. Use only the Mold Separator with the latter after the mold has cooled off and prior to the next use.

The Four-part Foam Latex

Some basic differences between the three-part and the four-part foam latex procedures are noted here.

Sponge rubber will cure properly only in a thoroughly dry mold. When one mixes gypsum products, a large amount of water is used. Some of this water goes into the molecular change when the gypsum sets up, but the rest has to be removed from the mold before it is suitable for molding sponge rubber. Separate the two halves of the mold, and bake at 200°F for 4 to 6 hours for a small mold or from 10 to 12 hours if larger.

Once the mold is dry, it should not be heated above 200°F, as the water of crystallization will leave, and the mold material will break down. Mold separator should be applied in a *thin* coat to both halves of the dry mold only where the modeling occurred. Do not allow this material to get into the keys. When the mold is thoroughly cold and the separator has dried, the sponge can be poured in.

Room temperature and humidity have a great bearing on the operations and results. With an optimum room temperate of 68 to 72°F, it may be necessary to vary the amount of gelling agent from between 9 and 16 grams to have the foam gel in about 10 minutes.

Using the deluxe model of the Mixmaster with the small bowl, the beater speeds and times should be carefully noted for each batch. (Note that some other kitchen mixer models usually beat too fast at their slowest speeds and are therefore unsuitable.) As the latex is stabilized with ammonia, the recommended speeds will assure that a sufficient amount remain in the mix so that it will gel with 14 grams of gelling agent. If it is beaten faster, at too high a volume, or if the temperature of the latex or air is too warm, the mix will gel too quickly—even during the mixing process. Conversely, if the latex or air is too cold, 15 minutes of beating time will not remove enough ammonia, and the foam will not gel in 30 or more minutes. If during the final refining process of slow beating, the speed of the beaters is too fast, a nice fine foam cannot result, and the mix will set up too quickly. Also, with some other beaters that do not fit the contours of the bowl correctly, poor mixing of ingredients will result.

To ensure a very slow low speed, one can connect a light dimmer fixture (or studio light dimmer) in series with the Mixmaster. The controls of the Mixmaster are then set at 12 (the highest speed), and all the speeds set up with the dimmer. One must carefully calibrate the dimmer switch with markings to indicate the speeds of 1, 5, and 6 for correct operations; the Mixmaster will then run much cooler and quieter, and infinite speed control is possible.

Although the latex is simply stirred carefully to remove any lumps, the three other components—curing agent, foaming agent, and gelling agent—should be thoroughly shaken up just before weighing them; otherwise, the heavier ingredients will settle to the bottom, while the lighter ones will be poured off first. Thus, the first and last batch mixed will have the same mix if they are properly shaken. Otherwise, the formula will vary considerably—and so will the foaming operation. The four-part latex is considerably thicker than the three-part one, so turning the containers every 2 weeks on the shelf is quite important to avoid settling and to extend shelf life.

To prepare the foam mix, pour 12 grams of curing agent into the mixing bowl, add 30 grams of foaming agent and 150 grams of the latex, and mix thoroughly with a rubber spatula. Adjust the beaters so they fit to the sides of the bowl.

Begin the mixing and foaming cycle as follows:

- 1 minute at speed #2 (mixing)
- 7 minutes at speed #8 (whipping)
- 4 minutes at speed #4 (refining)
- 2 minutes at speed #2 (ultra refining)

Then add 14 grams of gelling agent (shake the bottle first!) over a period of 30 seconds while staying at speed #2. Finally, continue mixing at speed #2 for 1 more minute, turning the bowl back against the beating action to ensure a complete mix. This gives a total beating time of 15½ minutes. (Timings are for 70°F.)

The mix can then be poured into the prepared molds. Roll the molds around to cover the necessary surfaces, and then slowly set on the other half of the mold, while adding weights to close it tightly. The remaining foam can be poured on a glass or Formica sheet, where it should set to a solid mass in 10 to 30 minutes. When you can press it down with a finger and a permanent indentation is formed, you may put the molds in the preheated oven and bake for 5½ hours at 200°F. When the time has elapsed, the now-vulcanized piece can be removed from the molds and the molds put back into the oven to cool slowly. Do not forget to turn off the oven! To prolong the shelf life of the latex, it should be kept as close to 70°F as possible.

Those who have used this formula and material for some years note that a new mold should be prepared for use by first spreading castor oil on both sides to clean it and prevent the latex chemicals from attacking the mold. A new mold should be given a good soaking coat of castor oil, and after each use, while the mold is still warm after being removed from the oven, it should again be coated with oil and then wiped with a clean towel. These latter directions preclude leaving the molds in the still-hot, turned-off oven to cool. Instead, after coating the hot molds with the oil, set them aside wrapped in towels to cool. After the mold has thoroughly cooled, and before the next use, both sides of the mold should be covered with the recommended mold separator for foam latex.

Another suggestion is to add the color directly to the latex, tinting a gallon at a time, and then storing the latex in ½-gallon, brown glass wide-mouth bottles until ready for use.

Most workers agree that over-curing in an oven of no more than 200°F will neither ruin the appliance nor the mold, but careful watch should still be paid to all timings for foam products. Large-sized batches might require double the beating time—for example, batches that cannot be handled in the large Mixmaster bowl and require the large restaurant kitchen-type Hobart mixers.

Regarding the injection by gun of large molds, breathing holes or exit holes placed along the line of the injection flow are necessary, and as the foam begins to escape from each successively, they can be plugged with a blob of plastalene until the mold is filled and the material has gelled. These blobs of clay be can removed before the mold is placed in the hot oven.

Carl Fullerton, who often works with Dick Smith, considers the four-part foam to be superior and experiments constantly with it to get better results. In a move to save the molds from calcining as a result of excessive heat, as well as from the shock of going to and from a hot oven, he does not preheat his oven, but turns it on just before putting his filled molds inside. In this way, the cold mold enters a relatively cold oven. He turns the oven up to 200°F (or slightly lower on occasion) and bakes for only 1 to 1½ hours. He then turns off the oven and leaves the mold to cool for about 3 hours. At that time both the oven and the mold should be cooled off. He then takes the mold out and separates it. His theory is that the shorter baking time not only saves the mold, but also yields a stronger appliance. Again, personal experimentation will allow the lab technician to devise individual methods and techniques based on the experiences of others, as well as to research new ideas.

Some of the main differences between the three- and four-part formulas are as follows: the lacquer sealing of the molds for the three-part foam (which is not recommended for the four-part method); the amount of beating time—for example, only 10 minutes for the three-part formula but 15½ minutes for the four-part one; the speed recommendations for each; the baking timings; and, of course, the basic chemistry of each formulation. Additionally, the three-part materials carry a somewhat greater latitude for storage, as well as for use temperature.

Nevertheless, in all cases, the final product is the ultimate criterion, and whichever method the make-up artist chooses, it may be wise to test the other as well for the sake of comparison. Also, although simplification of any manufacturing process leads to faster and less complicated procedures, the final outcome should not suffer unless the compromise will accomplish the same result.

In this vein, the newer flexible polyurethane foams might be considered. Certainly, with more experimentation and possibly even more improved products, these materials will gain more favor with make-up artist technicians, as the two-part formula does not require any beating with a machine or baking in an oven, and the piece can be completed in less than an hour from the start of the entire operation.

Repairing and Cleaning Foam Latex Appliances

When an appliance first comes out of a mold, it may have small defects (especially in a large section or a full headpiece). These can be repaired by mixing some pure gum latex with Cabosil M-5, or the inside can sometimes be strengthened by brush coating in a thin piece of netting or nylon stocking.

Rips or tears made when the mask or large piece is removed from the performer can sometimes be repaired by using Prosthetic Adhesive A on each side of the tear, allowing the application to dry for a few minutes, and then contacting the sides so that adhesion takes place. Both surfaces (inner and outer) can be stippled lightly with some pure gum latex to disguise the line.

Normally any foam latex appliance can be cleaned of most adhesives and make-up coloration by immersing it in acetone and squeezing the solvent through the foam. Two baths will normally remove all the color and adhesion, but the piece will shrink. Shrinkage can be somewhat controlled by a method recommended by Dick Smith in which he adds 1 part light mineral oil to 6 parts of Ivory Liquid or Joy detergent in a bowl large enough to immerse the piece. The liquid should be squeezed through the foam (for about 2 minutes) until it is saturated. Then rinse out the detergent from the appliance with about 10 to 20 rinses of cold water. The foam should have expanded about 10-percent. If the mix is decreased to roughly 4:1 detergent to mineral oil, this results in about a 20-percent enlargement. The appliance can then be placed in a warm oven to dry. He also states that this procedure is not exact; therefore, make tests before trying it on a valuable appliance. Generally, such methods may be employed when a fresh prosthesis is not available but are not normally practiced.

BASIC PROCEDURES FOR HANDLING LATEX APPLIANCES

As both natural and synthetic lattices will stick to each other, and the edges may curl and be difficult to straighten out, it is standard procedure to powder any appliance before removing it from any mold. This also can be said for plastic caps, plastic molding materials, and the like. RCMA No-Color Powder or non-perfumed talc can be used because it will not impart any color to the appliance. Also, when the prosthesis is removed from the mold, it is a good practice to powder its outside or face, as well as its back.

PLASTIC MATERIALS

Plastics are widely used by make-up lab technicians in a number of appliance types. A distinction can be drawn among the following: foam urethanes, solid urethanes, cap materials, molding materials, tooth plastics, special construction plastics, and gelatin materials.

FOAM URETHANES

A number of these products see increasing employment in the lab. The semi-flexible types can be used for filling or supporting certain molds or constructions, while the flexible types can replace some foam latex applications.

Fig. 1-22a   *Fig. 1-22b*

(A) A commercial plastisol full head form (left) from a beauty supply firm that is suitable for some applications. It fits on a standard adjustable wig block stand that can be clamped to a tabletop. On the right is a latex head filled with foam as made by Werner Keppler for beard laying. (B) A self-skinning type of urethane foam head made by Gary Boham with a plastic PVC pipe insert that will also fit on the wig block stand.

Semi-flexible Types

What industrial chemists think is a flexible type of urethane may not be flexible enough for the make-up artist. Rigid urethanes, in the strict sense, are those with little or no flexible qualities, but the semi-flexible types may still not be as resilient to the touch as what a make-up artist might classify as foam or sponge rubber appliances. There are, however, some new skin-like urethanes which will be covered later.

One product that could be considered semi-flexible is made by the Hastings Plastics Company and is excellent as a filler product when a slush-molded item must be made that will hold its shape. Werner Keppler has made some heads using this technique that are suitable for laying on pre-made beards. Using a face cast in casting plaster, he removed all the undercuts around the nose and took away part of the forehead area, keeping only the area of the face where the beard normally grows intact. The ears were also cut down, leaving only an indication so that sideburns could be laid in the correct area. He then made a negative mold of this face in casting plaster (about 2″ thick). In separating the two, he acquired a negative of the face. Into this he poured a lightly filled casting latex and let it build up to about $\frac{1}{8}$″ in thickness. He then poured out the latex and almost dried the slush piece (so that it would not shrink too much). At this point, he made a mix of the Hathane Polyurethane 1640C-54 and filled the cavity. As it foamed up, he laid a silicone-greased board and weight over the top of the mold so that the foam would not spread (but would remain confined). It is necessary to determine exactly how much foam mixture to add, as it does expand. Also, the mold must be made so that it has a flat top for accommodating the board.

When the foam has set, the head can be removed and a hole drilled up through the bottom and fitted with a plastic tube so that the form can be set on a head form support. This particular polyurethane comes in a range of densities from 4 to 16 pounds per cubic foot. Many companies make numerous varieties of this type of foaming product. *(See Appendix B.)*

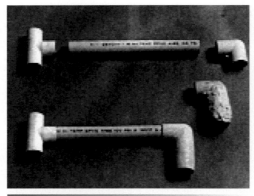

Fig. 1-23a

Fig. 1-23b

The making of a foam urethane face block. (Photos and lab work courtesy of Gary Boham.) **(A) Top:** *The pipe sections are shown.* **Middle:** *The elbow covered with fiberglass material.* **Bottom:** *The finished support with the extended elbow finished to fit a wig block stand.* **(B)** *A plywood board with the gasket channels cut and the holes drilled for the support rod (and for pouring).*

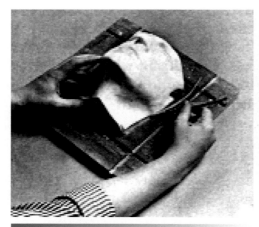

Fig. 1-23c

Fig. 1-23d

(C) *The plaster mold sealed to the board with plastalene.* **(D)** *RTV 700 flexible mold is made. The keys shown at the sides were made of cut foam urethane and sealed into the flexible mold with the material.*

Fig. 1-23e

Fig. 1-23f

(E) *The base of the plaster mother mold must be flat so that it will set straight upon inversion to make the heads. Rigidity is maintained with the particle board box.* **(F)** *Placement of the support rod.*

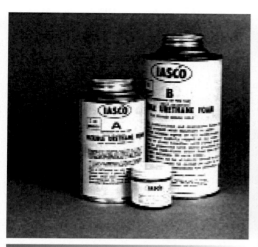

Fig. 1-23g   Fig. 1-23h

(G) IASCO two-part self-skinning flexible urethane foam and the flesh colorant material. (H) The mixed foam material is poured into the closed mold. Note the positioning of the clamped pipe support and the stage weights.

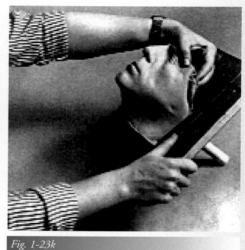

Fig. 1-23i   Fig. 1-23j   Fig. 1-23k

(I) The foam having set, the mold is opened. (J) The flexible duplicating mold is stripped from the foam head still attached to the board. (K) The foam head pulled away from the board. (The finished head can be seen in the previous set of figures.)

Gary Boham makes his beard block, as well as full heads for ventilation hair with a flexible self-skinning urethane foam that has a 5-pound density and sets rapidly. The support rod is made of ¾″ PVC tubing. A T-connector is cemented to one end of the pipe and imbedded in the foam during manufacture of the head. A special elbow joint is made by using a regular PVC join covered with fiberglass resin. The tapered portion of a wig clamp is covered with masking tape to serve as a release agent and then inserted into the open end of the 90°, ¾″ elbow joint. A thin layer of fiberglass resin is applied and then wrapped with fiberglass cloth or tape. The continuous-strand type gives slightly more strength than the cloth. After curing, the wig stand can be removed by twisting and pulling, and the completed fiberglass connector sanded as necessary.

The head form can be any ear-to-ear cast of a male head of average size that is either cut to shape or flattened on the top and bottom portions to form a block of the desired size. Although the one illustrated does not include the forehead, it is a good idea to do so if the block is to be used to make any eyebrows. Another method is to make a section mold of a face cast using alginate for duplication (if one does not wish to ruin a good original face casting).

A wooden base is made, as illustrated, with plywood or ¾″ particle board that is at least 3″ longer and wider than the plaster mold. Center the mold on the board, and trace its outline. Using a router or table saw, cut gasket channels all around the four sides of the mold, 1″ away from the widest portions. These channels should be about ¼″ wide and ¼″ deep. 1″ below the center of where the mold will fit on the board, drill a hole about ¼″ larger than the outside dimension of the plastic pipe to serve as a support rod for the head form. Then 1″ up from this hole, drill a 1½″ hole that will receive the foam and allow an exit for the excess during the foaming procedure. Seal both sides of the board with two coats of a polyurethane lacquer. Then center the head on the board, and seal down with plastalene.

To make a flexible duplicating mold, a number of products can be used, but the one recommended here is GE's RTV 700 with Beta 2 curing agent. The surface of the original plaster mold should be sealed with lacquer before use in most cases. This is a high elongation and tear strength material with a variety of curing agents available for room temperature use. No heating is required. An amount of 10 parts of base to 1 part of curing agent is recommended, and mixing is done by hand using a spatula or paint stirrer. Avoid rapid stirring so as not to induce bubbles into the mass, and mix for about a minute; then apply to the mold with a spatula. Any bubbles should be broken by passing the spatula over the surface. The pour time is about 30 minutes, and the work time about an hour more.

Allow to stand at room temperature until the mass has completely set, but with this curing agent, a minimum of 3 hours is required. Take care that the molding material extends just beyond the gasket channel. A minimum thickness of about ¼″ is desirable, so add layers as required. The edges may be reinforced with gauze to prevent any tearing during removal from the mold. Make certain to shake the curing agent well before mixing it into the base. The finished mold has a Shore A Durometer reading of 30 and an elongation of about 400-percent. Shrinkage for this use is minimal. A three-piece mother mold of plaster is recommended, and it can be confined in a box made of particle board. The flexible mold is stripped from the plaster head, the mother mold is inverted, and the flexible mold is set in. Keys can be made to ensure proper fitting. The wooden portions of the mother mold, the base board, and all tools as well as the surface of the flexible duplicating mold can be coated with paste wax which will serve as a separating medium. Trewax is a good product for this.

The support rod is placed inside the negative flexible mold and passed through the board, which is carefully fitted into the gasket portion of the mold. The correct height of the plastic pipe can be maintained with a spring clamp as shown, lifting it up about 1″ from the surface of the flexible mold to be embedded there. Stage weights (wrapped in plastic wrap as a separator) can be employed to hold down the spring clamp and board during the foaming procedure, or a clamp arrangement can be devised.

The foam material used was IASCO's two-part self-skinning flexible urethane foam with 240 grams of Part B to 80 grams of Part A. This can be tinted with fleshtone plastisol pigment if desired by mixing it into Part B before adding Part A. Mixing time is about 20 seconds before the foam will start to rise, at which point the material should be poured into the large hole of the cast. Expansion and exothermic action start immediately, so steady the support pipe and apply some body weight to the mold.

The foam will set in about 1 minute, and the mold can be opened in 5. The flexible mold can be removed and the head stripped from the base board. The excess can be trimmed with a sharp knife or shears. The block can be cleaned with acetone to remove any excess wax, and the special elbow joint can be glued with PVC cement to the end of the pipe support. The length of this pipe support can be varied to suit, but 6″ to 8″ is normally long enough.

With experimentation, full heads, prosthetic arms or legs, and other items can be made with this same self-skinning foam. Imbedding wire forms in it is also possible for the governing of the position of appendages. A burnt sienna shade of colorant will be found useful for most appliances for light skin, while darker-colored skin can be simulated with the addition of a burnt umber for ochre shades, as an example. This foam has excellent solvent resistance for normal usage and is rather easy to manipulate overall.

Flexible Polyurethane Foam

A unique material made by BJB Enterprises, TC-274 A/B, is a two-component flexible foam system specifically developed for low-density molding, and as with most of these polyurethane foams, a simple matter of mixing A with B; noting how much time is allowed to mix; determining how long it takes to foam; and finally accounting for how long the cure time is for completion are all that is necessary. This particular material has a density range of about 3.5 to 4 pounds per cubic foot, but it is very soft. It has a cream time of 90 seconds at 75°F and a cure time of 15 to 20 minutes at room temperature, depending upon part size and cross-section. It offers low oral, skin, and eye toxicity; low vapor pressure; and good storage stability. Shelf life is six months at room temperature, but the product may last considerably longer.

For molding, a regular two-piece mold similar to that employed for sponge rubber is used, although one can make it a trifle heavier for the sake of more endurance. The mold should be prepared by coating it with a polyurethane lacquer to seal the gypsum material. It should then be warmed slightly and coated two or three times with BJB Mold Release #86 or RCMA MR-8 (which is a wax in solvent), while allowing it to dry between coats. A single nose will take about 8 grams of Part B and 2 grams of Part A mixed and then poured into the negative. The positive is pressed on and the mold clamped for about 20 minutes. Test the overflow foam with the finger, and keep clamped until the foam is no longer tacky. The molds can then be separated and the piece removed for immediate use.

Considerable research has been done on this product by Werner Keppler and David Quashnick of California, and it has been used for some very fine foam work thus far. Part B can be intrinsically colored with universal colors or RCMA Color Tint Light (1 drop per 10 grams of mixture) before mixing. The manufacturer recommends a 4:1 (B to A) mix, while experimentation may prove that a 5:1 mix will produce a softer product more suitable for make-up use.

Werner Keppler makes gang nose molds for the TC-274 mix with five different noses. It takes a 30-gram B and 6-gram A mixture just to fill the cavities and give sufficient over-

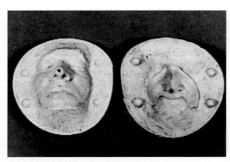 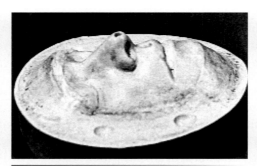 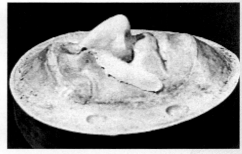

Fig. 1-24a   *Fig. 1-24b*   *Fig. 1-234c*

(A) Flexible urethane appliance. (A) A two-part mold for making flexible urethane appliances. Note that it is constructed in a heavier form than the normal foam latex molds for a similarly sized appliance. (B) The male portion of the mold. (C) A finished piece, exemplifying the fine edges possible with this versatile material.

flow. These appliances can be attached and made up like any other. The TC-274 A/B polyurethane foam material are available from RCMA, as is the MR-86 and MR-8 Mold Release.

SOLID POLYURETHANE ELASTOMERS

It is sometimes convenient to make a core mold or an item in a more solid compound with some elastomeric qualities. BJB makes a multipurpose elastomer numbered TC-430 A/B that is suitable for a variety of applications (and available from RCMA in small quantities). This material has a high tear strength; an ability to accept coloration; and being odorless, a high acceptance in the medical prosthetics industry. It can be used to make both positive casts and negative molds, and most thermoset liquid plastics and gypsums can be readily cast in its molds.

TC-430 A/B is available in two versions: TC-430 A/B for casting and TC-430 A/B-10 as a brushable grade. The standard versions of these are white, but they also come in clear (which yellows with aging).

Fig. 1-25a   Fig. 1-25b   Fig. 1-25c

A gang mold for noses. (A) Werner Keppler pours flexible urethane into a gang mold. (B) The mold is clamped shut. Note the excess coming out of the overflow holes, which were made in the nostril area of the noses. (C) The separated mold with noses in a row still in the negative portion of the mold.

Equal weights of the two parts are mixed together and have a work life of 30 minutes at 75°F in a 100-gram mass. Cure time is 24 hours at room temperature and 48 hours for full properties. A heat cure of 200°F only accelerates de-mold time, which is 4 hours at room temperature and 2 hours at 200°F. Again, good ventilation is recommended during use, and avoid skin contact with the liquid materials.

To increase the hardness, use 60-percent Part A and 40-percent Part B. To make the end product softer, use 40-percent Part A and 60-percent Part B. This will make a difference of ± 10 durometer hardness.

When TC-430 A/B is used to reproduce molds from gypsum or other porous materials, a silicone release #1711 is recommended. Shrinkage is very low, and the material has good tensile strength and elongation. Additionally, with a 50/50 mix, the durometer A hardness is 50 to 55. A note about this durometer A reading: This is a means of comparing the relative hardness of a mass with a scale of 0 to 100. Soft, very flexible materials will be 6 to 10, while a stiffer product (such as auto tire) would be 40 to 50.

Some general basic notes on urethanes of all varieties will help those who handle these materials. Storage in an area between 70° and 90°F is best. During colder weather the resin should be inspected to ensure that there is no crystallization. If the resin appears cloudy or the hardener becomes gummy, the component should be heated to a temperature between 120° and 160°F and stirred until the material returns to its proper smooth liquid consistency.

Use only metal or plastic mixing containers and spatulas, as paper cups and wood stir sticks have been known to contaminate the ingredients, which are porous and can absorb moisture in storage. Weigh all parts accurately, and always mix thoroughly. Polyethylene mixing containers are good because the cured urethane will not adhere to them.

Molds should always be quite dry and made non-porous. A lightly warmed mold is preferred. The sealing process must be done with a material that will withstand the exotherm generated when the urethane cures, and it must not melt at the peak temperature. There will be some shrinkage, as in all rubber or urethane materials, but this depends greatly upon the thickness (cross-section) and configuration of the casting.

Always use any urethane with adequate ventilation, and avoid skin contact with the uncured ingredients. Protective barrier creams are recommended for the hands, and brushes and equipment may be cleaned with MEK (Methyl Ethyl Ketone) if the solid urethanes are being mixed and have not hardened. General cleaning can be done with soap and water or a 1:1 mixture of toluene and isopropyl alcohol.

RCMA can furnish 8-ounce quantities of both foam and solid urethane materials for laboratory work.

CAP MATERIAL

Bald front wigs and fully bald head appliances have been made with a number of materials and in a variety of ways, but the only really good bald cap material is made from a vinyl resin of the Union Carbide Corporation called VYNS. There are a number of formulas in use employing MEK or acetone (or a mixture of the two) as a solvent plus a plasticizer to control the degree of desired softness. A basic formulation is 25 grams of VYNS to 75 grams of MEK, with the addition of 10 to 25 grams of plasticizer.

There are many plasticizers on the market, with dibutylphathalate (DBP) and dioctylphathalate (DOP) among them. The Monsanto Company also makes a series of plasticizers called Santicizers; their #160 is used where DBP is appropriate, and #711 for DOP. The DOP will retain the soft quality of a cap material and be less affected by ultraviolet than DBP.

After dissolving the entire solid in the liquids, cap material can be tinted by shaking in some of the RCMA PB Foundation. To make a bald cap, one requires a positive mold made from plaster, stone, metal, or even fiberglass. One of the production methods to make thin caps is to spray the cap material with a Paasche L head airbrush with a medium (#3) nozzle. John Chambers sprays about five heads at a time, one after the other, with about six coats of spray. In this way, the first head sprayed will have basically set before the second coating is applied after spraying head number 5 in the sequence. Careful guiding of the spray, plus a rather rough final coating spray is best, as the caps, when removed from the molds, will not be reversed. As such, head forms for spraying are made quite smooth for ease in removal of the plastic cap from the form.

A more tedious method, but one that allows full control over the thinness of the blending edge wherever desired and a heavier weight of material on the hairline or the pate is accomplished by painting the plastic cap material on a head form that has a slight pore effect on the surface. When completed, this cap will be reversed to show this aspect.

The best way to make caps is to make use of a ventilated spray hood for either the spraying or the painting in order to protect against the fumes of the solvents. Otherwise, this operation should be carried out in the open air on a calm day or with a fan blowing the fumes out a window. The cap plastic can be brushed on with a 2½″ ox hair or sable hair brush in a flowing manner, rather than brushed back and forth the way one would paint. The brush should always be significantly wet with material, as it will evaporate very rapidly. Most metal molds do not require any separating medium, but others should be lightly rubbed with a silicone mold release and wiped almost dry for ease in separation. Head molds can be lightly marked in pencil in the general shape of the hairline so that a reference point is available when graduating the coats to make a fine blending edge on the cap.

For a full cap of regular thickness, brush on 5 coats over the entire head form. Then brush on an additional 25 coats just up to the hairline marking, graduating the coats in order to form a thin edge. Finish off with a few more coats over the entire head. Allow 10 minutes of drying time between coats. To reiterate, it is efficient to work on several heads at once.

Always immediately remove any stray brush hairs if they fall out while the cap is painted onto the mold. (A small sable brush is best for this type of work.) The same precautions should be observed for dust and dirt in the air when painting caps, as when using any fine varnish or lacquer. Never sweep the room or in other ways disturb any settled dust while caps are being sprayed or painted, as dirt specks will ruin the caps.

Allow the cap to remain on the mold overnight to air-cure. Caps can also be cured (and much shrinkage prevented) by placing finished ones on the molds in an oven at 150°F for 5 minutes.

To remove the cap from the mold, cut a line with a sharp knife or razor blade around the base of the head mold through the plastic material, and carefully strip the cap from the mold. To prevent edge turnover (or the cap from sticking to itself), a thorough powdering prior to cap removal (and on its other side after removal) is best. (No-Color Powder is recommended.) Some very shiny (chrome-plated metal) molds only require the beginnings of work on the edge before the cap can be easily rolled off.

Another way of making a partial bald cap is to use a try-on cap on the performer and carefully mark out the hairline that must be covered, in addition to where the hairpiece is to be added on top of the bald cap area. As the cap will be made quite heavy, it is often unnecessary to make a blending edge in the back of the neck area, as it will not be adhered there. The top or pate area can be made quite heavy with 45-60 coats, depending upon the desired weight. Also, when the cap is made for one particular performer, the edge can be painted with a finely graduated painting process that becomes heavier and thicker more quickly than on a stock cap.

Cap material can also be used to make thin sections that will be used to cover eyebrows. Generally these can be made by painting cap material on a flat plate and building edges and sufficient weight for covering the hairs. Some brows will require heavier buildups than others to cover the coarse hairs.

Clear cap material is also employed by some sculptors to cover their plastalene modeling. Additional sculpture can still be done over the coating, or fine lines can be refined. RCMA supplies two grades of cap material: one tinted for cap use, and the other clear for sculpture. These are fast-drying and can be thinned with acetone if they thicken during use. For slower setting time, thin with MEK. *(See Chapter 4 for more information about the creation of bald caps.)*

MOLDING PLASTICS

Molding plastics can be divided into two categories: those that are simply painted into a negative mold in layers to form a piece, and those that are pressure-molded in a two-piece mold.

Paint-in Plastic Molding Material

RCMA furnishes a Molding Material in Light (KW shade), Deep (KM shade), and Dark (KN shade) that can be painted into a negative mold in successive coats for the building of an appliance. This Molding Material is also available in a thicker, quicker-drying form in a tube under the name of Scar or Blister Making Material by RCMA. Essentially, these products are methacrylates in a solvent with plasticizer and are excellent for temporary appliances. As a result of the manner in which they are made and their basic qualities, appliances should be produced only a day or so before use when these products are involved. Otherwise there is a tendency (of all such molded plastics) to lose some of the sculptured surface during long storage periods. However, appliances made with this material are soft and flexible and are easily adhered to the skin with Prosthetic Adhesive A.

Negative molds should be coated with RCMA Silicone Mold Release or silicone grease before use, with care taken to avoid brushing too much into the fine sculpturing. This type of material is especially good for making eye bags when time and budget do not allow for foam versions. The liquid Molding Material should be put in a small wide-mouth jar with an easily cleaned stopper or cap and thinned out somewhat with acetone. Make certain to stir the stock bottle in order to disperse all the coloration that might have settled to the bottom during storage.

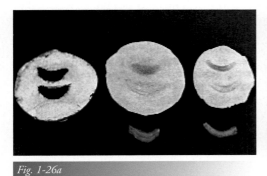
Fig. 1-26a

Fig. 1-26b

*Plastic molding material. (A) A set of eye bags sculpted in plastalene on a plaster flat plate. **Left: Middle and Right:** Finished plastic molding material appliances. (B) The appliances painted into the mold before powdering and removal.*

Eye bags can be sculpted on a flat plate along with the creation of a negative mold of stone or Ultracal 30. After the silicone separator has been applied, give the bags 10 coats of thinned-out Molding Material (while not over-painting the blending edge), and allow them to air-dry between coats. (The use of a hairdryer will bubble the material.) Slightly heavier coats can then be applied as the cavity of the sculpted eye bags begins to fill up. Dry between coats. Finally, lay in a heavy coat of material so that the level of the eye bag is built up higher than the mold surface, and set aside to dry overnight. As the solvent evaporates completely, the level of the built-up portion will shrink down to slightly below the surface level of the mold so that the appliance can be attached flat to the skin. For removal, powder the surface, use a sharp tool to gently tease up an edge, and then peel out the appliance. It is then ready for immediate use.

This material can also be used to make interesting forehead pieces for gunshot wounds, veins that pulsate, and such. For example, for a gunshot wound, take a negative cast of the forehead area in salt-accelerated casting plaster. The surface can be sealed with RCMA Silicone Mold Release agent and the coatings built up by brushing the Molding Material into the form in order to cover the entire forehead area, resulting in a good blending edge just above the eyebrows and at the point where the nose meets the forehead, as well as all around the hairline edge. The thickness of the appliance can be increased near the center of the hairline where either the performer's own hair or a small hairpiece will cover this edge.

After painting on about 15 coats of thinned Molding Material, a small-diameter polyethylene plastic tube can be imbedded with its end roughly in the middle of the forehead. This tubing should be about 4 feet long so that the other end will remain off camera with a blood syringe attached. Hold the tube in position, and carefully paint in a few coats of material to imbed it into the surface of the appliance. Adhesive tape can be used to position and hold the tubing where it should remain. Then add more coatings of Molding Material over the tape in order to fully seal and cover the tubing. Graduate the coatings away from the tubing to prevent it from resembling a bulge when the appliance is attached to the face. Thicker coats can be applied until the desired amount is reached.

Fig. 1.27

Top: A plaster cast of a forehead with a bullet hole cut into the center to show where the tubing must end. Bottom: After painting into a negative mold, an appliance with a tube imbedded into the material. The hole is cut with sharpened metal tube and the plug saved for later insertion.

Let the appliance dry on the mold overnight, and then strip it off, taking care that the tube remains firmly imbedded in the appliance. Always select a color of Molding Material that will be closest to the skin coloration of the performer so that little foundation will be required for coverage. Next, with a sharp, round punch about the size of the bullet hole, cut out a circle just below the end of the imbedded tube. The hole in the tube can then be cleared with a sharp instrument. A needle about the size of the tube can be imbedded in a wooden dowel point first. (The protruding head portion serves as a good tool for this purpose.) Save the cutout portion of the plastic, as this will be used as a plug. Attached to a length of clear filament, this plug can be pulled out as part of bullet-hit sequence before the blood flows through the tubing.

Dick Smith imbeds removable strips cut in the shape of veins in this material and, in use, fills the spaces with a fluctuating air stream to simulate the pulsation of forehead veins. Small bruises, cuts, scars, moles, burn tissue, and many other marks can be made similarly with this type of Plastic Molding Material. One of the main advantages of the Molding Material is that its blending edges are soluble in acetone. It can therefore be washed in to the point of imperceptibility. *(See Volume II, Chapter 6 for more information about injury simulation.)*

Press-molding Material

This polyvinyl butyral plastic is employed to make appliances with a method devised by Gustaf Norin a number of years ago. Although it is employed relatively seldom, the procedure is an interesting one that produces an appliance with edges that are soluble in isopropyl alcohol.

The original formulation consists of 4½ fluid ounces (by measure) of Vinylite XYSG (a white powder, polyvinyl butyral) dissolved in 32 fluid ounces of isopropyl alcohol. Then add a plasticizer mixture of 25 cubic centimeters (cc) of castor oil, 25 cc of DBP, and 50 cc of isopropyl alcohol. If a harder appliance is desired, use 10 cc of castor oil, 10 cc of DBP, and 25 cc of alcohol. Mix well, and keep tightly capped until use.

To prepare the plastic for molding, pour some of the compound into clean, cold water, and with sanitized, well-scrubbed hands, knead the then-coagulated mass until it stiffens into a ball. This squeezing will press out all of the solvent alcohol into the water after roughly 3 minutes of work (for a piece large enough to form a nose). Remove the plastic from the water, and the result will be a semi-translucent white mass. Stretch a clean, lint-less dishtowel, often called a *huck towel*, over the knee, and carefully roll the plastic back and forth for about 15 minutes in order to remove all of the water. When ready to color and place the plastic in the mold, it is important that no water content remain in the plastic, as this will cause shrinkage.

When the mass is dry to the touch, dip the roll of material into some dry calcium carbonate in order to give it some opacity, and knead this well into the material. A slight coloration can be imparted by rubbing the material lightly on a cake of a pale shade of dry cheek color and kneading the color into the material. To hasten the drying-out period, a stream of warm air from a handheld hairdryer may be used, while being careful that the material does not stick to the fingers because of the heat. It is advisable to continue dipping the fingers into No-Color Powder in order to prevent sticking during this part of the operation. Provide any type of coloration gradually, and never color deeply, as the plastic has a propensity to deepen in shade as it cures, and again, a pale shade is easier to cover with make-up than a dark one.

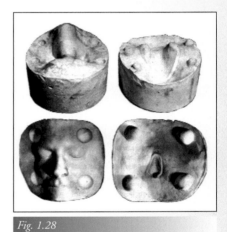

Fig. 1.28

Comparative casts. **Top:** *A foam latex nose mold.* **Bottom:** *A pressure casting or foam urethane-sized mold.*

The material is then ready to place in the mold, which is a pressure type made of dental stone. Grease the female side with petroleum jelly, and lightly wipe the male side with the same separating medium. Place the material on the negative female side—spreading it out into the general shape of the desired prosthesis—and put the two sides of the mold carefully together. Place about 200 pounds of pressure on the mold for approximately 15 minutes. Large sections may require up to 400 pounds of pressure in order to create a fine blending edge and correct construction of the material. 25-pound iron stage weights are very good for applying such pressure. Build them up by crossing two over two at a right angle until the correct weight is achieved. Sitting on the built-up weight platform will increase the pressure if necessary.

After the required pressing time, remove the weights, and open the mold carefully. The negative side, which was greased, should release quite easily and leave the completed prosthesis on the positive male side. If the appliance is well made without bubbles or defects, let it stand overnight on the open mold. However, if the appliance has defects such as thick edges or a lack of completeness, add molding material where necessary and re-press the material for about 10 minutes. Separate, and check once more. If perfect, leave the mold

Fig. 1-29a

Fig. 1-29b

Fig. 1-29c

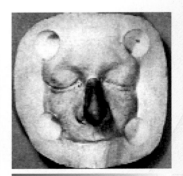

Fig. 1-29d

Press molding. (A) Plastic poured into water and coagulated. (B) Opacity and color kneaded into plastic. (C) Stage weights used for pressure on mold. (D) Finished appliance on the male side of the mold after pressing and trimming edges.

open overnight, but if still defective, repair in the same manner. Sometimes rearranging or replacing the material is necessary to get a perfect pressing.

The prosthesis can be removed from the mold the next day by lightly brushing under the edge of the appliance with a small flat brush covered in No-Color Powder or very fine talc. Then the overflow excess plastic material that forms in the gutters during the pressing can be cut away from the appliance, leaving just enough of the thin blending edge to adhere the appliance to the skin. This blending edge can be thinned out to a very fine result against the positive mold with a flat sable brush that has been dipped in isopropyl alcohol. It is best to keep the appliance on the male mold or another positive cast of the same until ready for use. It is also a good idea to make up plaster duplicates of the male side of the mold for this purpose so as to leave the actual mold free for another pressing if necessary.

For adhesion of this type of appliance to the skin, cover the area where the prosthesis is to be placed with a coating of the liquid plastic molding compound, and dry thoroughly. Powder this area with No-Color Powder, and center the appliance in place. With a small brush, carefully touch under the appliance with isopropyl alcohol. This will immediately dissolve the appliance into the adhesive coat of molding compound, attaching the prosthesis firmly to the skin. Carefully wash the edges of the appliance into the skin with the alcohol, and powder the appliance and the edges with No-Color Powder or very fine talc. Do not use the so-called "translucent" or "neutral" powders for this type of appliance, as these powders do have color and fillers that will affect the coloration of the piece. Extrinsic coloration can be done with a high-pigment cream-type foundation, such as RCMA Color Process Foundation.

TOOTH PLASTICS

Dental acrylic resins of methyl or ethyl methacrylates are supplied as a *monomer* (a colorless liquid) and a *polymer* (a fine powder that comes in a number of shades). For additional coloration, there are liquid stains that can be painted over any finished denture material.

When the monomer and the polymer are mixed together, the polymer is partially dissolved so that the mixture becomes a dough-like plastic mass. The monomer in the mixture is then polymerized to form the solid acrylic resin. Two types of acrylic resins are used by dental technicians and dentists: In one, the polymerization is activated by heating the mixture; in the other, polymerization is activated chemically. The latter type is self-curing and is generally the variety employed by make-up lab technicians for teeth. One of the best textbooks on oral anatomy and techniques, entitled *Dental Technician, Prosthetic* (1965), is published for training prosthetic dental technicians in the U.S. Navy and is available through the U.S. Government Printing Office (NAVPERS 10685-C).

The Lang Company makes a number of materials for dental use that can be adapted by make-up lab technicians:

- **Jet Tooth Shade Acrylic**   A very fast-setting, self-curing powder and liquid combination available in shades 59, 60, 61, 62, 65, 66, 67, 68, 69, 77, 81, 87, and Light and Dark Incisal.

- **Jet Denture Repair Acrylic**   Strong and fast setting, this self-curing acrylic is colorfast in Pink, Fibred Pink, Translux, and Clear and is used for simulating gum tissue.

- **Colored Jet Acrylic**   Self-curing resins that set hard in less than 10 minutes. Available in colored powders with clear liquid monomer or with clear powder and colored liquids. Tans, greens, reds, blues, yellows, violets, and blacks are available in sets.

- **Flexacryl-Soft Rebase Acrylic**   An ethyl methacrylate formulation that is plasticized to remain resilient in a cushion-like consistency for a number of months. This material is nonirritating and dimensionally stable.

Warm weather and humidity will affect these self-curing polymers during mixing. Working time can be extended with chilled mixing containers for large batches.

In most cases, the polymer powder is wetted with the monomer to make the casting. Many workers coat the negative cast with a brushing of monomer and then add a bit of powder to start before dropping powder and liquid a little at a time in order to form the mass. As long as it appears glossy, it can be worked and brushed into a form.

To make teeth, one can employ a number of techniques. Each one is a bit different and better designed for make-up use than regular dental application. The simplest way to make flat-form teeth for imbedding in gum material is to fill preformed plastic crown forms with tooth shade acrylic and allow them to set. Odd-shaped or special teeth can be made by spatulating additional material on these formed teeth. One can also obtain various preformed teeth from supply houses that serve dentists in order to identify tooth shades and shapes. Sometimes dentists have a set of discontinued artificial teeth that they will provide upon request.

One method is described by Lee Baygan in his book on prostheses for make-up, *The Techniques of Three-Dimensional Make-up* (Watson Guptill, 1982), in which he sculpts the desired teeth in plastalene on the positive dental stone cast. Using petroleum jelly as a separator on the gypsum portion of the cast, he takes a negative of the sculpted teeth in alginate in the dental tray. When the alginate is set, he removes it, and since the next step may take some time, he immerses the alginate negative in water to prevent any shrinkage from air-drying. The plastalene is removed from the positive (or negative, if any becomes imbedded), and the positive is given a coating of petroleum jelly. The negative is then removed from the water and the surface quickly dried. (Do not use heat.) Self-curing tooth-shade acrylic polymer powder is added to the tooth cavities. The liquid monomer is added with an eyedropper, and the mass is mixed with a small narrow tool. Adding a bit of each at a time will fill the teeth and allow some extra for flash over the gums (which he has allowed for in the plastalene modeling). The positive is then placed carefully over the negative and the two pressed together and held for a minute or two until set. This is put aside for about 30 minutes so that the acrylic will fully harden.

The two sides can then be separated and the teeth pried from the positive cast. The casting of the teeth is then trimmed with a Mototool and polished so that no rough edges are felt. The teeth may be colored (or discolored) with acrylics and then given a coat of 5-minute epoxy. This can be yellowed for some effects. The epoxy will gloss the teeth to a natural shine. Baygan then recommends that a bit of flesh pink be added to an epoxy mix and painted on the gum section of the acrylic to simulate the gums.

Tom Savini's *Grande Illusions* (1983), a book about special make-up effects, shows a method of making a set of vampire teeth by building up a wax covering over the teeth in the stone cast and then imbedding some artificial teeth into this wax in front of the teeth on the cast. He also makes some long incisors by mixing the polymer-monomer into a heavy paste and, while wearing surgical gloves, rolls the material to get the shape of the desired tooth. Filing and grinding produce the finished teeth. Using a medicine dropper, monomer is used to wet the area above the teeth, and some pink gum shade polymer powder is sprinkled on. The process is repeated until the proper amount is built up to surround the teeth in front. The wax is removed after the acrylic is set (for about 10 minutes), and the back of the teeth are treated in the same manner to form around them. Small dental tools can be used to sculpt around the gums and teeth.

When the material is set, it can be removed from the positive form, and the result is a dental plate that fits directly over the subject's own teeth. They can be finished with acrylic lacquer if need be to restore the shine. Dental powder or cream can be used to hold the teeth in for use in the mouth.

If someone has space between the teeth, a set of snap-on tooth caps can be made from a cast of the front teeth which is imbedded in a heavy stone-reinforced mold or a dentist's flask. Make a mix of the proper tooth shade, and after coating the positive side with an alginate release agent, apply a layer of the mix, and place a sheet of cellophane separator on top of the plastic. Close the mold, and put it in a dental press for 1 or 2 minutes. Remove the mold from the press; separate the two halves; lift the cellophane separator sheet; and with light pressure, use a sharp scalpel to trim off the excess flash material from the appliance before re-pressing the appliance in the mold press for a minute or so. Repeat this until no excess extrudes from the prosthesis. Replace the cellophane sheet with a new one each time a re-press is made. When the appliance is complete and perfect, leave the mold halves separated until the material sets. Then ease the appliance off the positive cast, and

Fig. 1-30a

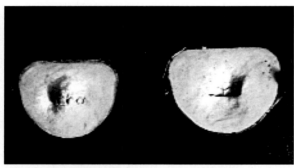

Fig. 1-30b

Fig. 1-30c

Tooth caps. (A) Flasked male mold of actual teeth. (B) Male and female mold before pressing. (C) The finished caps on the male mold.

clean and polish it with burrs, abrasive paper discs, rubber cups, and felt wheels (with a paste of chalk, or with tin oxide and water), in that order. These very thin caps should then clip onto the real teeth and look perfectly natural. Note: These teeth are not made for eating and are rather fragile, so keep them in a small plastic box when not in use.

Variations of these methods include sculpting the teeth in an inlay wax material, rather than in plastalene, or using a Flexacryl-Soft Rebase Acrylic for making the pink gum material for teeth, which may be easier on the wearer. Colored acrylics can be used to make teeth of any shade for certain effects, while the Flexacryl-Soft material can be used alone to make an appliance that would cover all the teeth for a toothless gum effect.

It is not a good idea to apply any of the polymer-monomer mixture directly into the mouth in order to form teeth, as it may firmly attach itself to the subject's real teeth. Work only from a tooth cast, and always trim the finished plate so that the performer's speech will not be impaired—unless that is the desired effect. If too much acrylic is formed on the inside portion of a tooth prosthesis, it may produce lispy speech patterns. *(See Volume 1, Chapter 9 for more information about dental proceedure.)*

SPECIAL CONSTRUCTION PLASTICS

Certain special effects require construction plastics such as epoxies, fiberglass, polyester resins, and other such industrial materials often employed by auto repair shops. Most of these are rigid materials, although some technicians are also using flexible urethanes and polysulfide products as well. None of these are for application to the skin, and they represent mostly substances that are being adapted to make the dummies, figures, puppets, and simulations of humans or animals that are usually mechanically operated and serve to replace a living thing in order to achieve situations that might either be physically impossible or that might prove dangerous to a living person or animal.

Sometimes these materials are used as part of an overall make-up effect and the finished piece attached to the body. In general, the special construction plastics and other materials serve as stimulation to new make-up effects, and in the future, more industrial products designed for other uses will find their way into the laboratories of the creative lab technicians/make-up artists.

Again, great care should be taken with researching not only the finished qualities and restrictions that might affect the human skin for all these products, but also whether or not any dangers exist in the use of the raw materials to laboratory personnel. None of these materials are classified for cosmetic use, so great care should be taken whenever their use is contemplated.

Two-part epoxy may be used for glossing over latex or plastic in the development of false eyes. One method is to paint ping-pong balls with artists' enamels in the shape and color of eyes, and then give them a coating of the epoxy. This material comes in a handy two-barreled ejector type of dispenser that can be purchased in hardware stores. This fast-drying epoxy can also be used to put a gloss on teeth in latex masks.

Polyester resin used by auto repair shops with fiberglass cloth comes with a can of resin and a tube of curing agent, plus some open fiber or mesh cloth to soak in the compounded resin. Also available from the same source are the fillered polyester resins that are used as auto body fillers. Both types set hard and can be worked with files and sandpaper in the development of various constructions.

GELATIN MATERIALS

In addition to synthetic processed materials, one can also include animal gelatin for the manufacture of special constructions. A basic formula recommended by Tom Burman is as follows:

- 20 grams of gelatin powder
- 12 cc of distilled water
- 100 cc of glycerin

Set this mixture aside to saturate for 45 minutes. First, heat to 140°F in a water bath in order to melt the mass, and then pour this into a plastic Ziploc-type bag and flatten it out for cooling. For use, this gelatin compound can be made opaque with talc and titanium

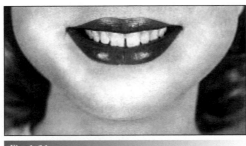
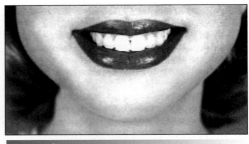

Fig. 1-31a   *Fig. 1-31b*

Tooth caps. (A) The natural teeth without caps. (B) Appearance after adding temporary caps. Bonding can produce the same effect on a more permanent basis.

dioxide, and water-soluble vegetable colors can be used for various shades. Dry colors can also be ground into the dry mixture of talc and titanium dioxide, while kaolin can be used as a filler if required. Tom Burman uses this formula gelatin with a red coloration for blood effects on certain projects.

Softer constructions can be made with 15 grams of gelatin, while 25 grams are appropriate for ones that are harder. Another formula calls for 50 cc of Sorbitol and 50 cc of glycerin, with 1 gram of salicylic acid as a preservative (or a few drops of wintergreen oil).

The molds used are similar to any type of pressure mold that is well greased with petroleum jelly as a separating medium. In use, the gelatin material is melted, fillered, and colored; it is then poured into the negative (female) mold. The positive is placed on and weights or clamps applied to hold the molds together. When the material is cold, the molds are separated and the appliance powdered and removed.

Note: The remaining sections of this chapter feature the latest information about prosthesis materials and application techniques.

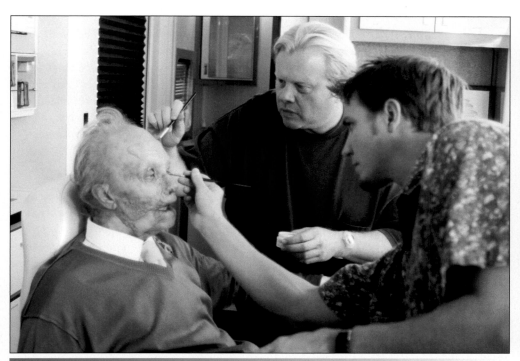

Fig. 1-32

Fig. 1-33

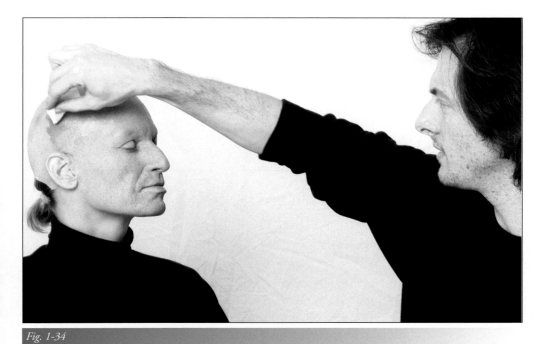

Fig. 1-34

The terms molding and casting, in relation to the professional make-up industry, have a history that dates back to the fine arts methods of body part preservation. Faces and hands of famous people were captured in life and death masks (taken before and after death, respectively) with the use of Plaster of Paris molds as negatives from which positive castings were then made.

Throughout the years, both fine artists and make-up artists have sought to improve the methodology of the process in terms of speed by virtue of doing the negative mold on the subject, and in terms of accuracy with the positive cast that follows. A somewhat pliable, solid agar-agar material (trade name, Negacol), which required heating, was applied to the body part to be molded. It was then necessary to apply a mother, or retaining mold over the basic mold in order to retain the original's shape before removing it from the body part being duplicated for the creation of a positive casting. The application of this mold required a certain skill and timing so as not to burn the skin of the subject with the hot molding material. The frailty of the two-part mold's soft material necessitated careful handling. It was also quite weighty, as the primary molding material, as well as the plaster mother mold, required at least a one-inch thickness. On a very delicate or soft facial feature, such weight could create distortion.

The next method, which came from the dental profession, involved the use of an alginate product in powder form that was mixed with cold water and had a setting time of about three minutes. This could be applied in a far thinner coat for a facial cast, as it had considerably more tensile strength. The use of a three-minute-setting-time dental plaster as a mother mold proved to be much quicker, and usually, a make-up artist with help from an assistant who did the mixing could perform a mold on the face in about ten minutes before removal. One had to work very efficiently and rapidly, as both the alginate material and the three-minute plaster would set rather quickly.

Experimentation and advances in this new technology led to improvements such as a slower-setting alginate product, plus the adoption of plaster bandage in the formation of the mother mold. As additional make-up materials and prosthetics products were developed for such character work as transforming the faces of subjects into those of historical characters, as well as for the burgeoning genre of horror and imaginative films featuring extra-terrestrial creatures, more and more actors were asked to have molds and casts made as a basis for such required changes in appearance.

In recent years, it is the studio make-up industry that has come to the forefront in this artistic direction and has even surpassed the medical world, from which so many ideas originally emerged and so many products came into use. The following methods are those currently in use by professional make-up personnel.

MOLDING AND CASTING

BASIC INTRODUCTION

Prosthetic make-up involves the application of handmade artificial pieces that are molded from a human face. The pieces themselves are usually made of foam latex or rubber, and sometimes even urethane rubber or gelatin. They show surface detail (skin texture, for example) that would normally be applied with construction make-up.

The cast is customarily produced in Hydrocal or stone. After the creation of the first cast, which is called a positive cast (and reproduces the performer's features or body parts), clay can be used for sculpting new features on top of it. The clay comes in an oil-based version, such as Plastilina, and a water-based version. After the features have been constructed, a mold of what was sculpted—which is also usually comprised of Hydrocal or stone and is known as a negative cast—is then taken.

Fig. 1-35

The original negative cast made in 1971 by Mr. Blasco to create the Frankenstein Monster head piece used in a Shasta Cola commercial.

Fig. 1-36

A mold for a nose piece worn by Ricardo Montalban.

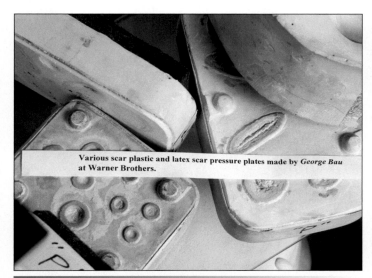

Fig. 1-37

Various latex and plastic scar pressure plates made by George Bau at Warner Brothers.

Fig. 1-38

The original positive and negative mold created by George Bau for the Warner Brother's film The Illustrated Man, *starring Rod Steiger. This mold produced the effect of Mr. Steiger's crushed face in the final scene of the film.*

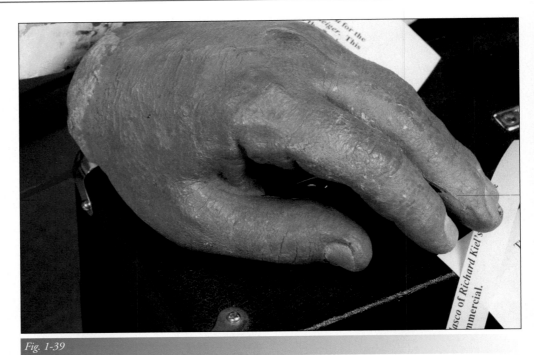

Fig. 1-39

An original mold made by Mr. Blasco of Richard Kiel's hand for the giant in the first Eggo Waffles commercial.

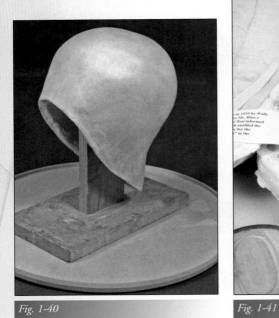

Fig. 1-40

A bald cap form.

Fig. 1-41

Mr. Blasco's original negative mold for the hands of the creature from Track of the Moonbeast.

The process begins with *conceptualizing* the project. Work in conjunction with the director, actor, writer, etc. in order to determine what types of pieces are desired. Before taking a facial impression of the subject, first speak with the subject, and explain the procedure to alleviate apprehension. The subject should be free of claustrophobia—otherwise, a special kind of casting, which involves the separate creation of individual facial sections, may need to be taken. Provide soothing music during the process, and develop a method of communication (prior to application) that can be used while the subject's face is restricted.

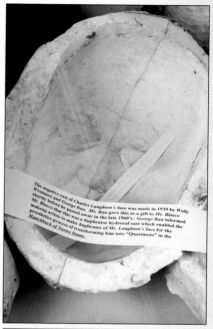

Fig. 1-42

This negative cast of Charles Laughton's face was made in 1939 by Wally Westmore and George Bau. Mr. Bau gave this to Mr. Blasco as a gift shortly before he passed away in the late 1960s. Mr. Bau informed Mr. Blasco that this was a duplicator Hydrocal cast which enabled the make-up artists to create duplicates of Mr. Laughton's face for the prosthetics process of transforming him into Quasimodo for The Hunchback of Notre Dame.

Fig. 1-43

An eye bag appliance used on James Dean in Giant.

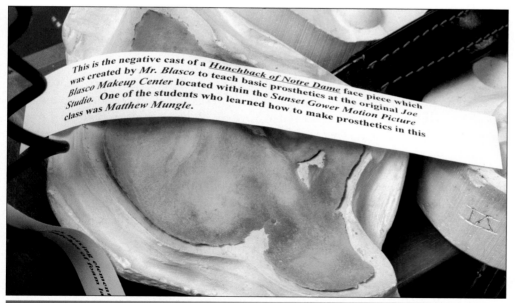

Fig. 1-43

The negative cast of a Hunchback of Notre Dame *face piece created by Mr. Blasco for teaching basic prosthetics at the original Joe Blasco Make-up Center located within the Sunset-Gower Motion Picture Studio. One of the students who learned to make prosthetics in this class was Matthew Mungle (featured heavily in this volume.)*

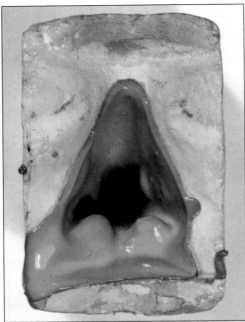

Fig. 1-46

Fig. 1-47

Fig. 1-48

The creation of a nose mold.

A material known as *alginate*, which comes in several grades, is normally used. A dental version used by dentists for making casts of teeth is inappropriate for facial impressions; ice cubes or ice water is necessary for keeping this material cold, but neither will cool it sufficiently to allow a long setting time, which is needed in order for the artist to properly smooth the material over the face. A prosthetic-grade version, on the other hand, can provide fifteen minutes of setup time, depending upon the water temperature. The hotter the room, the faster the material will set; therefore, cool the room as needed. It may be advisable to experiment with the alginate in different room and water temperatures, as well as with different alginate-to-water ratios, in order to determine a suitable mixture.

HISTORY

In days past, a *moulage*, which was essentially a melted gelatinous agar material, was used for facial impressions. It was initially heated, and after it became cool enough to touch, it was applied with a stiff-bristle brush and allowed to solidify. A mother mold (or a retaining mold) made of plaster or plaster bandages would be put over the moulage to remove the entire construction from the face. The mold was needed to provide reinforcement in order to prevent the moulage from falling apart. During the application, straws would be put into the nostrils through which the subject could breathe. But two problems existed with this old method: As the actor leaned back, the skin was pulled, resulting in a slight distortion of the cast; and the straws themselves would distort the nostril areas.

The moulage itself could be reused. After running it through a meat grinder, the material was stored in a jar and could be melted down in preparation for application.

MATERIALS

Today, the following materials are used to create basic prosthetic pieces:

- Bald Cap (a good, high-quality rubber or vinyl version with thin edges)
- Rubber Spatula for Mixing (or various knives)
- Alginate (prosthetic-grade)
- Flexible Rubber Bucket (with spout)
- Plastic Bowls (for mixing alginate)
- Rubber Bowl (intended for stone plaster mixes; the bowl can be bent, and the material, once hardened, is easily removed)
- Castor Oil (for conditioning molds)
- Alcohol (for removing clay, sterilizing, etc.)
- Acetone (same as above)
- Respirator or Thick Particle Mask (for protection when working with alcohol, acetone, or other volatile chemicals and inhalable materials; always work outdoors or in a well-ventilated area)

Fig. 1-48

- Safety Glasses (for eye protection from lye, which can cause blindness)

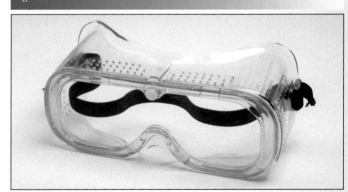

Fig. 1-49

- Wooden Dowels (imbedded into the back of the positive cast as handles to facilitate the positive's removal from the negative)

Fig. 1-50

- Plaster bandages (cut into different lengths to accommodate different areas of the facial impression exterior; the pieces are quickly wetted in salty hot water immediately prior to application in order to help accelerate the setting time, and once hardened [set], are used to support the alginate)

- Krazy Glue (used to hold the alginate—should it fall away—against the sides of the plaster while the positive cast is fabricated within the alginate negative impression)

- Hair Gel or Gafquat

- Tissues

- Silicone Releasing Agent

- Hemp, Burlap, or Fiberglass Rovings (used within the stone as reinforcing materials [a George Bau technique]; the hemp and burlap may rot after a period of time and could be unsuitable depending upon the number of times the cast and molds are run, while the rovings do not shrink or dry out)

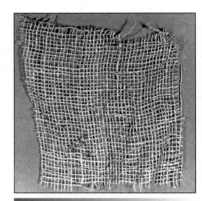

Fig. 1-51

- Pair of Vinyl Gloves (which fit close to the skin)

- Duct Tape (for help in preparing the model for the impression; it can be wrapped around a wooden dowel for convenience when measuring the exact length needed for specific jobs and for saving space in the facial impression kit)

- Stanley Surform Pocket Plane (for refining the finished cast by sanding away various portions)

- Roma Plastilina (sulfur-based oil clay for the casting; other clays, which are not sulfur-based, are required for processes that are adversely affected by sulfur; the non-sulfur clay is described further in this volume)

- Water-based Clay

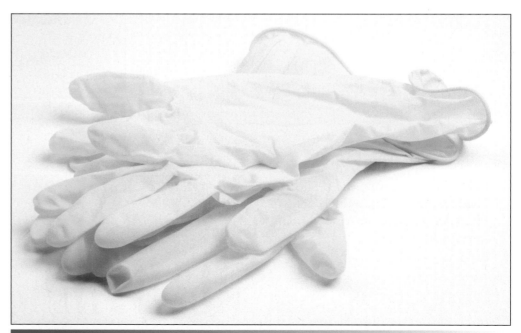

Fig. 1-52

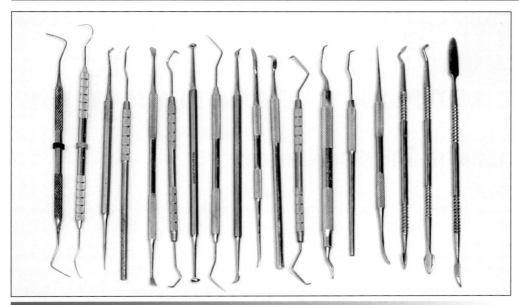

Fig. 1-54

Fig. 1-53

- Various Modeling Tools (wooden and metal, for clay sculpting)
- Brush (with a ½ or 1-inch diameter for painting in the first layers of Ultracal 30 or Hydrocal B-11)
- Sculpting Toolbox
- Wooden Rod (for prying open the mold without damaging it)
- Clay-pounding Tool (for softening clay)
- Several Large and Small Hypodermic Syringes (from which the needle should be removed and discarded appropriately before use for blood tubing, or purchase the syringe without the needle; also used for dispersing the gelling agent during the foaming procedure)
- Cellulose Smoothing Sponges and Sea Sponges (for smoothing the surface when curing [setting] stone casts)
- Long-handled Brush (for applying talc down in the mold)
- PM (Pro Mascara) Bristle Fan Brush (for lifting the latex piece away from the mold)
- Dental Cups (used for various liquids, most frequently when working with teeth)
- Cotton Swabs
- Dental Vibrator (which helps to remove bubbles from the liquid stone as follows: Rest the bowl on top of its vibrating platform, and blow on the bubbles to break them as they come to the surface of the mix; or use a small paper cup to pick up the material containing air bubbles after first rotating the bowl to make the bubbles gravitate toward the center; to avoid weakness in the stone once cured, never pour stone mixes into the mold when air bubbles exist)
- Joe Blasco P.M. (Prosthetic Make-up) or RCMA A.F. (Appliance Foundation) (for use on rubber)

The above is only a basic list of materials for beginning the study of prosthesis fabrication. More items can be included as needed.

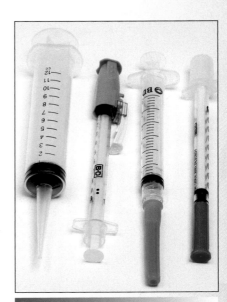

Fig. 1-55

CLASSIC FACIAL IMPRESSION AND FACIAL STONE POSITIVE CAST FABRICATION TECHNIQUE

ALGINATE IMPRESSION THEORY

The following theory is presented as preliminary information that is derived from classic techniques and should be thoroughly understood prior to reading the following chapters, which actually show the impressions and positive cast-making process.

Apply the bald cap. Prepare the hair prior to applying the cap with Gafquat, hair gel, etc., and comb it back off of the face as flat against the head as possible. Remove portions of the cap around the ear. Show as much of the forehead skin surface as possible. Use just enough adhesive under the edge of the cap in order to keep it adhered to the skin. If desired, the ears do not need to be entirely uncovered, and the alginate need not be applied over them. If an impression of the ears is required, however, press cotton into them to prevent the alginate from entering. Bald cap edge lines that appear on the dried cast may be sanded down.

Use a cotton swab to work Vaseline through the eyebrows and eyelashes, all the way down to the roots. Be sure that the hairs are well lubricated. Comb through the brows in order to return them to their original direction. Put a pillow at the lumbar area of the back to keep the subject completely erect in the seat. The face needs to remain unwrinkled throughout the entire process, so the head needs to be in the same position as if the subject were standing. A pillow or other type of support can be placed behind the head if the chair headrest is too far from the subject.

Before working with the alginate, determine a method of communication with the subject (be it sounds or hand signals), because the subject will be unable to speak during the process. Provide a pencil and a piece of paper in the event the subject needs to express more detailed information.

Begin by opening the alginate bag and folding down its edges. Keep the bag of alginate closed when not in use to prevent water from accidentally dripping into it, resulting in large pieces that will solidify and potentially ruin future impressions. Pour cold water into a bowl to a depth of 1″. Determine how much of the face will be cast, and sprinkle alginate onto the water's surface. While working the material with a spatula, have an assistant add more water or alginate as needed. Create a creamy consistency. Do not leave any jewelry on during this process (or when applying alginate), for the material can potentially become imbedded in it. Use tight-fitting surgical gloves of either latex or vinyl prior to starting and throughout the entire process.

The fingers are used to work the alginate onto the face. Push the material into the corners of the eyes, around the sides of the nose, and onto the mouth. Allow the excess to drip back into the bowl. Ask the subject to inhale deeply and then exhale through the nose while the alginate is applied around the nostrils. Continue with the sides of the face and underneath the chin. Be certain at all times that the nostrils are clear of the material.

Work the alginate back onto the sides of the neck and the top of the chest. Pour an additional amount on top of the head. Catch the material as it continues to drip off the bottom of the face, and place it back on top of the head. Make sure all of the edges are consistently thick. Continue pushing it into the corners of the eyes to ensure proper application with no air pockets. (Detailed application of alginate around the nostrils is best done three-quarters of the way through the process.)

Continue building around the nose, and wipe down areas where excess material still hangs. As the impression material solidifies, cut away unneeded areas, and fill in gaps in order to prevent holes. Within a short time, the material begins to set up. A thicker mixture will have an even quicker setup time. The material hardens on the hands, but it peels off quite easily. Alternatively, simply remove and quickly replace your surgical gloves. The impression material may be cut, once solidified, at its outer borders with a dull wooden sculpting tool for the removal of excess areas of dripped material.

With a wooden stick, carve the appropriate line around the face, beyond which the material can be removed. Be cautious around the ear area. Allow the material to stay attached to the shoulder. Begin then to cut around the chest portion in order to remove outer edge excess.

Start applying plaster bandages that have been immersed in water. First cut them into appropriate sizes. Allow the edge of the first one to overlap the edge of the alginate on top of the head. Lay a second, longer piece over the top of the first one. This bandage, which should hang down below the ears on both sides, can be worked in front of the ears and attached down the sides of the neck. Again be certain that the bandage folds over the alginate.

At this point, cut a piece of duct tape, fold it in half width-wise, wrap it around the neck (on top of the bandages), and attach it at the back of the neck with a clothespin or any other type of clip that is fast and easy to use. As the bandages harden, the tape will help to keep them firmly in place against the alginate.

Communicate with the subject to learn of any possible discomfort. Continue applying smaller pieces of bandage down from the top of the head. Each new bandage should overlap the previous one. Work the bandages to fit into any potential depressions in the alginate. Some of the bandage pieces can be rolled into a ball and fitted into spaces for extra support. *(This entire plaster bandaging process will be described and shown in great detail in subsequent chapters of this volume.)*

Breathing may become a little more difficult at this point—so forewarn the subject—but the nostril passages will not be blocked. Usually no more than two rolls of plaster bandage are used for a single mold.

Be certain the sides are reinforced. If a portion of the chest needs to be retained in the mold, add extra support to the neck and chest area. Make sure the edges of the bandage application are very substantial.

Replace the surgical gloves as needed. While the bandages harden, trim away excess alginate beyond the bandage area with a wooden tool, if necessary. The tape tied behind the neck will hold the bandages in place (optional).

Use a towel or sea sponge soaked in warm water to sponge off material from the shoulders. At this point, the alginate should be completely solidified, so the movement should not create distortion of any kind. Clean the ears as well.

Lightly tap the cast surface with the fingers or a wooden tool in order to determine whether the alginate has hardened sufficiently. Then prepare a cradle for the cast. A cardboard box or a plastic bin lined with towels works suitably, as does a plastic bag filled with Styrofoam peanuts or a bean bag pillow.

Release the clothespin or clip, and cut off the excess support tape. Gently squeeze the model's skin at the back of the neck while holding the front of the cast along the jaw with the other hand. Openings will start to form between the skin and cast. Pull the ears back gently. Massage the top of the exposed head (the visible cap may be removed at this point to acquire access to the model's actual hair and scalp), and stretch the skin on the chest down away from the cast. Ask the subject to move the eyebrows, eyes, and mouth to create even more separation.

Carefully and slowly remove the cast. A perfect impression has been made. Lay the cast into the cradle.

Note: As long as the alginate is kept cold with a wet towel and cold water, and the mold is completely enclosed in a plastic bag, it can maintain its form for quite some time. If it becomes exposed to the air, the alginate will eventually shrink.

THE POSITIVE CAST

In the past, clothespins were used along the entire perimeter of the outermost or top join of the alginate to the edges of the plaster bandages (mother mold) in order to keep the bandages attached to the mother mold, thereby preventing the sides of the alginate from collapsing into it. Today, Eastman 910 Adhesive (or Krazy Glue), a gel form of glue, can be run along the edges of the alginate to ensure proper adhesion. With a stick, work away the excess adhesive, and press the two surfaces together. If there are cracks in the mold, the glue can be used to seal these as well. If no adhesive is available, squeeze denture cream into the gap, and press the alginate back into place against the dry plaster mother mold.

With cotton swabs or tissues, wipe excess pieces of material from the inside (negative) of the impression. Pieces that are attached to the mouth area can be removed with tweezers or cuticle scissors. Blot the alginate, and push the tissue down into the nostril areas to remove any moisture.

Return the mold to the cradle. Place a towel underneath it for extra support.

Plug the nostrils with clay (#1, or preferably, #2 grade). First knead the material, and then apply it as a cap over the nostrils on the outside bandage. Do not actually stick the clay down into the holes, because it will distort the alginate. Smooth it out so that both outside nostril holes are covered completely, which will prevent the liquid stone mixture from extruding through them.

Lay the mold into the cradle, bandage-side first. In a cup, mix dental alginate, which sets quickly, with water. Create thin slurry with the spatula, and then pour it into a small hypodermic syringe (with a curved applicator tip). Turn the syringe over, and push the plunger until the material comes out of its curved nozzle. Wipe off the end, and point it down into the nostril hole. Fill the hole with alginate. With a cotton swab or small dental spatula, remove the excess before it hardens. Then reapply alginate to build up the nostril hole just slightly (resembling a stalagmite). This elevation will create a deeper nostril hole for the positive cast (optional). The holes that exist in the alginate will become bumps that can be slightly sanded down on the finished cast. Return the mold to the cradle.

Always work with surgical gloves when dealing with stone materials. Wear a particle mask as long as the materials are still in powder form, and never breathe the dust. Wear goggles under all circumstances.

Pour between 1″ and 1½″ of water into a bowl. Sprinkle Hydrocal down into it. A sifter can be used for neatness. Ultracal 30 can in fact be used for *both* the positive and negative cast, but it works more effectively for the negative because of its supposedly better surface detail pickup. (**Note:** As previously stated, the term *casts* normally refers to positives, while the term *molds* refers to negatives.)

With an inexpensive disposable tongue depressor or spray-coated (with Pam, for example) rubber spatula, spread out the material, and push it down into the water. Remove pieces of debris that may be floating inadvertently in the mixture. Palette knives or wooden sticks can be used for mixing.

Immerse hands into the material, and squeeze it through the fingertips so that all large lumps and bubbles are removed. Clean the gloved hands in water, or replace the gloves as needed throughout the process.

Place the bowl on top of the dental vibrator. Shake and rotate the bowl to help move any existing bubbles that migrate towards the center of the mixture. Remove the particle mask, and blow on the surface. Dot the surface with a tissue. With a small cup, skim the bubbles off the top. Once again, cover the mouth and nose with a particle mask for safety.

With the $1/2''$ bristle brush, try to remove any remaining bubbles from the mixture. Then start painting the undercuts (around the nostrils, near the eyebrows, etc.). Work the mixture down into the wrinkles. The first layer must have no bubbles. Paint it very smoothly onto the surface of the alginate, right up to the very edge of the mold. Then apply a second, heavier coat.

When a substantial amount of material exists—at which point fiberglass rovings, hemp, or burlap can be placed upon the mold without actually touching the alginate—proceed. Normally about $1/4''$ will suffice, and at the very most, $3/4''$. Do not apply any undue pressure against the mold. Avoid working beyond the area where the alginate lies in order to avoid locking the stone and the plaster mother mold.

Begin laying the reinforcement material of your choice onto the stone (in the mixing bowl) in order to thoroughly saturate it and/or coat it with stone mixture prior to application to the negative wall. Keep the reinforcement within the confines of the mold. For a thin mold, avoid adding too much reinforcement, as the stone may be overwhelmed, and the mold will weaken. There should be no less than $1/4''$ of stone build-up in the negative prior to the introduction of the reinforcing material.

As the stone mixture thickens, the second layer of reinforcement can be applied. Again, drop the reinforcement first into the liquid stone, saturate it thoroughly with mixture, and then lay it along the sides of the mold to add substance and internal reinforcement. Work the reinforcement material along the edge of the mold and around the neck area. Be sure there is plenty of strength between the neck extension and the facial negative to prevent the neck join from weakening, which could result in cracking.

With a tissue and cotton swabs, absorb any water resting in the mold. Use the remaining stone mixture to add thickness. (**Note:** Explanations in this section will be depicted in following chapters.)

Add extra pieces of mixture onto the sides of the facial cavity onto which the wooden dowel can be attached. Work the material around the ends of the dowel in order to fix it in place. Wrap some extra fiberglass rovings or other reinforcement material around the dowel, and saturate it within the stone mixture prior to applying the material to the inner backside of the negative mold.

Add a small amount of water into the mold, and move it around with the fingers. Pour out the excess, and use a cellulose smoothing sponge (available from Joe Blasco Cosmetics) or a mold makers sponge to smooth out the mold's surface. Remove (cut away) stray reinforcement, which may extend from the edges of the hardening stone. With the fingers, continue the smoothing process, and add more stone where necessary to conceal reinforcement and to make the curing stone as smooth and symmetrical as possible.

As the stone material heats up during the curing process, steam will appear on the surface. Steam usually rises from the bandages during the creation of the mother mold.

With the sponge, clean excess material off the now-imbedded wooden dowel. Continue smoothing and cleaning the entire inner backside with the mold makers sponge.

If the positive cast has been made incorrectly, the rubber appliances will not properly fit. Pay close attention to detail. Also, when working with alginate and stone materials, never allow these to go down the sink drain. (Special metal mesh or a plaster catch can be purchased from a plumbing supply company in order to prevent this from happening.)

Next, peel back the mother mold (plaster bandages) very carefully, and discard. Then peel off the alginate layer. Use a small Stanley planer and/or various sizes of rasps to remove uneven areas of the cast bottom edges and surface, followed by sandpaper to smooth and refine the outside of the cast.

A small, rounded, beveled chisel or dental spatula and/or any number of appropriately sized metal and wooden sculpting tools can be used to remove lumps from the face of the cast. Use a small hammer and chisel to chip off the larger pieces. With an even smaller chisel and/or dental tool, wooden sculpting tool, or metal spatula, refine along the lips to remove excess remaining imbedded alginate. Refine around the eyebrow areas, and use a soft brush to dust away the material. The cast at this stage still contains quite a bit of moisture that will be removed during the curing process. If it were hardened at this point, the stone would not break apart as smoothly, and the carving process would prove more difficult.

Mix up a small amount of gypsum stone (which is not porous compared to plaster) in order to fill in any remaining small holes along the edges of the cast. Refine the mold to be as aesthetically perfect as possible while the positive cast is still warm.

In order to get the edges of the appliances to reach perfectly around the nostril region, after curing the cast, the nostrils must be filled with clay so that an undercut is avoided; otherwise, when the negative is made, the plaster applied on top of this positive will grab onto the inner portions of the nostril, as well as the undersides, and prevent the negative from being removed. Similarly, the eyelids and lips need to be filled in so that locking is prevented. (This undercut prevention process, as well as the creation of retaining walls around the completed clay appliance sculpture, will be shown in following chapters.)

HISTORICAL CURING INFORMATION AND POST-CURING

After the cast is wrapped in a towel and cured in an oven preheated to approximately 150°F for three to six hours, allow it to cool in the oven with the oven turned off. Permit air into the oven by cracking the door just slightly. Note that the color of the cast lightens slightly from the baking process.

Pour a small amount of castor oil in a dish, and use a brush to apply it to the cast. Castor oil should not be painted on the cast before curing. The surface, once conditioned, will more readily accept the addition of clay. Condition the underside as well. Allow the oil to soak for an hour. (Some artists will pickle their casts by allowing them to be completely immersed in a large bucket of castor oil for several hours after oven curing. Normally, four to eight hours is sufficient. This process is thought of as unnecessary by some artists, however.) Use a dry towel to rub down the mold.

SCULPTING MATERIALS

For use when sculpturing the new features upon the positive cast:

- Various Rubber Fruit/Vegetable Skin Surface Transfers (casaba, grapefruit, orange, and avocado, all of which work effectively for the creation of texture and wrinkles when pressed into clay sculptures)
- Brushes, Metal Tools, Metal Plate, etc.
- Orange Stipple Sponge
- Castor Oil
- Acetone
- Alcohol
- Tissues

Note: When using liquid latex (de-ammoniated, such as Joe Blasco Datex), follow these safety suggestions:

- Avoid eye contact.
- Use with adequate ventilation.
- Keep it away from children.
- Do not get it onto hair and/or fabric—it will dry and become difficult to remove.
- Datex contains a small amount of ammonia that acts as a preservative. Avoid prolonged, repeated breathing of vapors.

SUMMARY

The preceding information serves as a brief introduction to the facial impression process (with alginate) and the preparation of the stone (Hydrocal/Ultracal 30) positive facial cast. A more detailed explanation with photographs will follow later in this volume. This theory section should be analyzed thoroughly and well understood prior to continuing with the following chapters.

THE MISNOMER, "RUBBER MASK GREASEPAINT"

This material is a rather archaic form of make-up product—with a somewhat unrefined grade of castor oil as a vehicle—designed by the Max Factor Company in the 1940s. At that time, it was found that any type of make-up foundation that contained any animal or mineral products (such as mineral oil or petrolatum) was incompatible with the lattices employed to make appliances, be they slush or painted-in types, or later, foam latex pieces or prostheses.

Today's latex appliance foundation base make-up is better described as a type of Appliance Foundation, or A.F., and is a much improved version from RCMA of the old material. It is compounded to be less oily and does not separate, nor does it require stirring before use. It employs a very new, refined grade of castor oil as the vehicle, plus, like any RCMA C.P.F. (Color Process Foundation) or Joe Blasco P.M. (Prosthetic Make-up) product, it does not contain any mineral oil, lanolin, Vaseline, or other similar materials. As such, A.F. and

P.M. colors do not require the heavy colored powders that old RMG (Rubber Mask Greasepaint) products did. The natural skin halation can be obtained with RCMA or Joe Blasco No-Color Powder, while a matte finish can be achieved with RCMA A.F. Powder. These varieties of powder contain no coloration and thus cannot change the shade of the finished application of an A.F. or P.M. shade.

It should also be noted that any RCMA C.P.F. color or shade can also be applied over any latex appliance without affecting it, but these colors or shades do not have the covering power of the RCMA A.F. materials. Therefore, delineations with any C.P.F. color can be applied over an application of any RCMA A.F. shade without being detrimental to the latex prostheses.

RCMA also furnishes special A.F. Palettes to enable the make-up artist to carry this product in a compact container of six or sixteen different shades and colors.

All Joe Blasco products that are preceded by the initials P.M. (Prosthetic Make-up) are suitable for use on skin and all forms of artificial appliance fabricated of slip or shell latex, foam latex, gelatin, and silicone. Just like RCMA A.F. colors, Joe Blasco P.M. appliance colors have a very extensive color range—from fleshtones to primary pigments—and are available in jars or palettes.

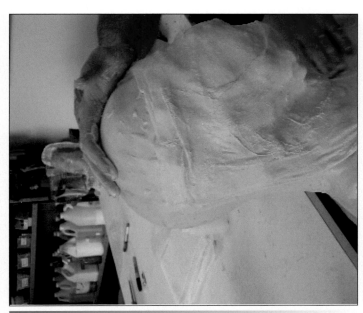

Fig. 1-83

Plaster bandage application to the face cast is completed. Let it cure.

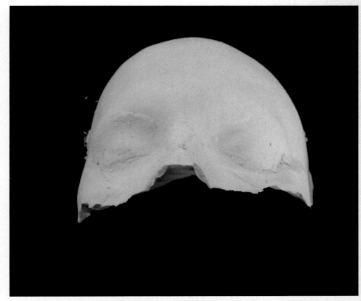

Fig. 1-84

While the face cast cures, the other two pieces are demolded. Here is the Hydrocal positive of the forehead.

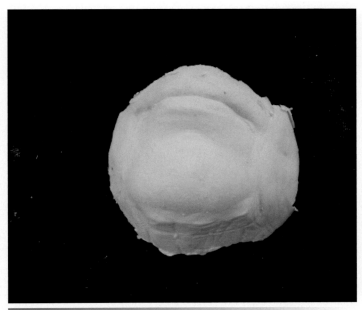

Fig. 1-85

The Hydrocal positive of the chin.

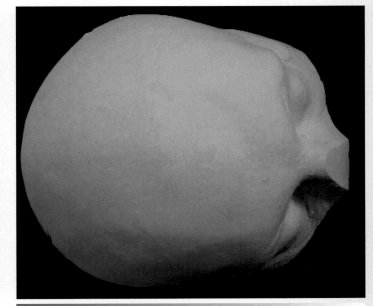

Fig. 1-86

The positive must be cleaned up. Rasp or sand the edges smooth and straight. Carefully remove and surface air bubbles.

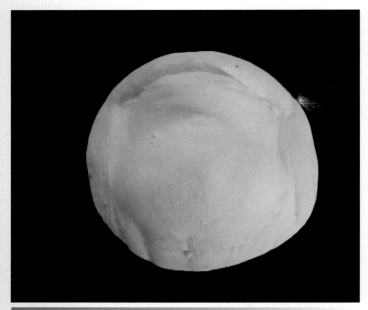

Fig. 1-87

The chin is cleaned up and rasped into a small cylindrical shape.

Fig. 1-88

The Hydrocal positive must be torn into a "corrected" positive. The open end must therefore be filled in, and undercuts must be corrected.

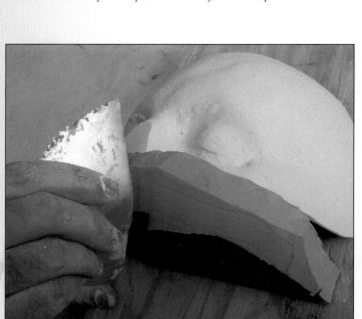

Fig. 1-89

The open end is filled in or drafted. A thick slab of water-based clay (EM-210) is cut and gently pressed into the stone. Use a serrated kidney tool to shape the clay into a 45° angle.

Fig. 1-90

A small amount of clay is used to correct any small undercuts, or contours or depressions such as the temples, jaw line, and nostrils. If these undercuts are not corrected, the artist will have difficulty separating the mold.

Fig. 1-91

The large alginate mold is removed from the life cast. The alginate is glued to the bandage.

Fig. 1-92

Continue to refine and smooth the clay. A soft sponge makes the clay as smooth as possible.

Fig. 1-93

The finished corrected positive. Now the mold can be sealed. Two coats of Krylon Crystal Clear are sprayed onto the clay followed by the application of a light coat of Vaseline to the Hydrocal.

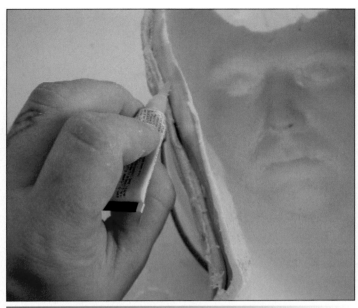

Fig. 1-94

Mix up some alginate, and cover the entire positive. Apply the alginate slowly in order to avoid trapping air bubbles.

Fig. 1-95

Once the alginate gels, begin adding bandages.

Fig. 1-96

Add enough bandages to ensure a sturdy mold.

Fig. 1-97

The large face mold with the cured Hydrocal inside.

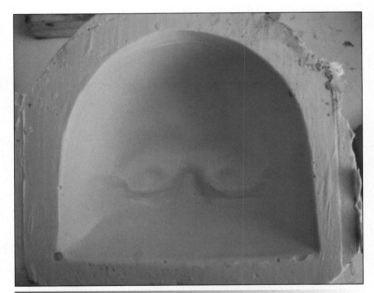

Fig. 1-98

Once the bandages cure, pry the mold off the table, and clean it out.

Fig. 1-99

The corrected positive is cast with Ultracal 30, a much stronger material than Hydrocal. Since all of the molds will be placed in a hot oven (for cooking the foam), the material must be able to withstand the conditions.

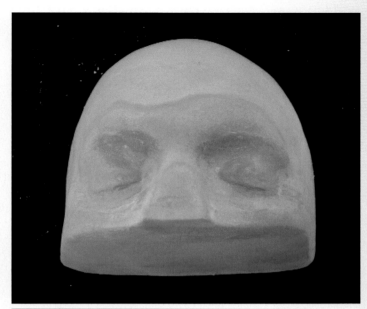

Fig. 1-100

The finished Ultracal 30 positive. Remove any imperfections, and sand the outside edge. The positive is ready for clay.

Fig. 1-101

The clay forehead is retrieved and used for a test fitting on the new Ultracal positive. It fits incorrectly because of the edges that were blended down prior to making the mold. To correct the problem, shave down the backside of the clay appliance.

Fig. 1-102

The shaving process may need to be repeated.

Fig. 1-103

The chin cast is placed on a ball of water clay and then pressed down. BE certain the cast is flat and level. The total thickness from the table to the top of the chin is about 1½" to 2".

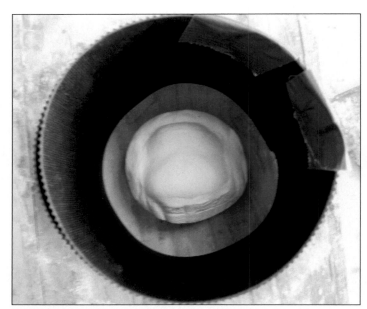

Fig. 1-104

Rubber floor (matte) is used to create a round wall surrounding the cast. Leave approximately 1½" all the way around the cast in order to provide space for drilling keys. Use duct tape to hold the floor in place.

Fig. 1-105

Hot glue or water clay can be used to seal the bottom of the floor, which should be kept as round as possible, to the counter. Make sure there are no leaks.

Fig. 1-106

Mix up a runny batch of Hydrocal, and pour it in on the side. Continue pouring until the stone is flush with the top edge of the cast.

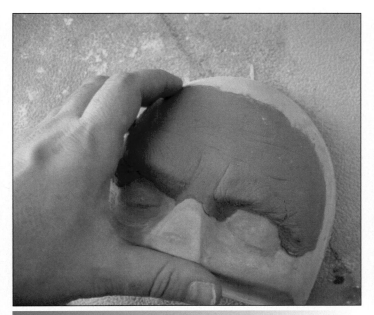

Fig. 1-107

With the forehead piece finally in place, it is time to blend the edges down and finish the sculpture.

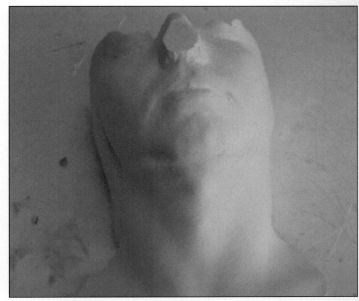

Fig. 1-108

The large Hydrocal positive before any corrections have been made.

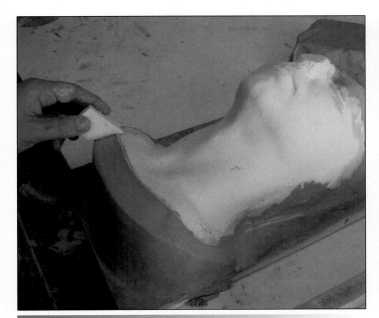

Fig. 1-109

The clay should be made as smooth as possible before it is sealed.

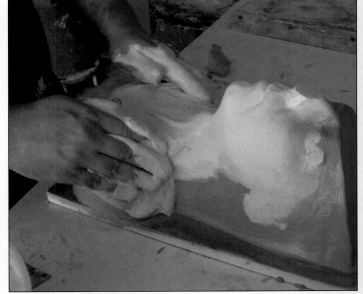

Fig. 1-110

Once everything is sealed and released, apply alginate over the entire positive.

Fig. 1-111

The demolded Hydrocal chin positive.

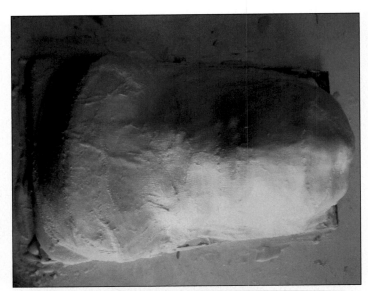

Fig. 1-112

Plaster bandages applied over alginate. It is in the mold where the corrected Ultracal 30 positive will be cast.

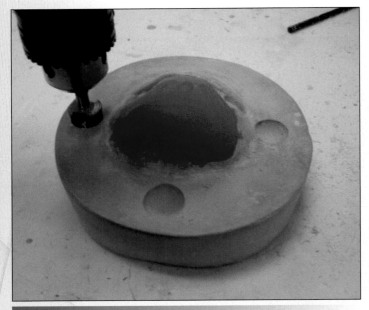

Fig. 1-113

Once all of the positives in Ultracal 30 are made, the edges are sanded smooth before keys are drilled. Keys are depressions made in the stone that allow the negative half of the mold to sit where needed. Here three keys a drilled with a ¾" router bit.

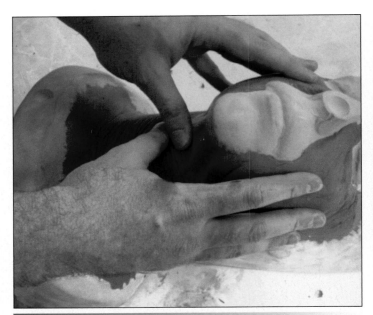

Fig. 1-114

The clay is fitted onto the corrected positive.

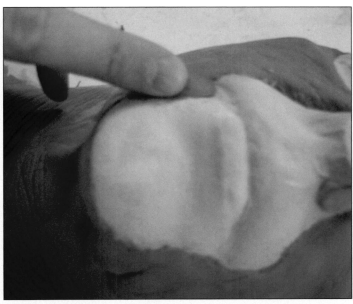

Fig. 1-115

Be certain to blend all of the edges seamlessly into the stone..

Fig. 1-116

Once the pieces are blended down and finished, it is time to add the flash and establish the cutting edge. First make a pencil line, ⅛" away from the edge of the appliance model, on the plaster. This narrow gap is to remain uncovered. Over the remainder (except for the keys), model a smooth layer of clay about ³⁄₁₆" thick. Try to make the flash as smooth as possible. Push the clay slightly over the pencil line, and then use a sharp tool to cut it back to the line at about a 60° bevel. This narrow strip of exposed Ultracal surrounding the appliance model is the cutting edge. Some contact points, which help the negative half to fit more accurately, are added to the flash in between the keys.

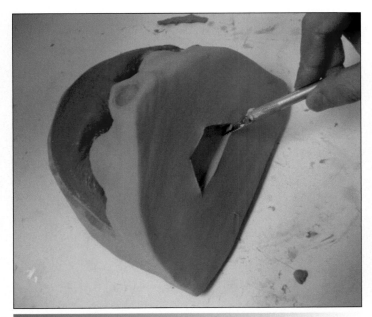

Fig. 1-117

Contact points are added to the forehead model.

Fig. 1-118

Start with the chin for the negative mold. Prior to adding any stone, the clay is sealed with Crystal Clear. First, make sure the cutting edge, keys, and contact points are clean. Use a cotton swab with alcohol to gently scrub the cutting edge. Cleanliness here is essential. Next, roll out a long worm of clay, and gently lay it over the entire cutting edge. This worm is designed to protect the edge from any chemical buildup caused by sealing the piece. Add one liberally spraying of Crystal Clear, and then quickly remove the worm before it dries. Allow the Crystal Clear to dry. Add a small amount of Vaseline to the keys and contact points. Since the chin piece is a cylindrical mold, simply rewrap it in rubber floor (matte), and begin adding Ultracal 30.

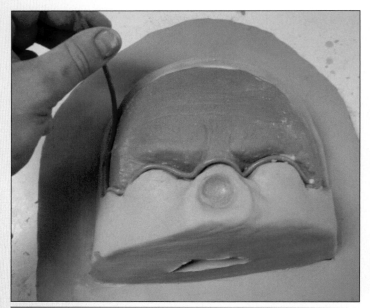

Fig. 1-119

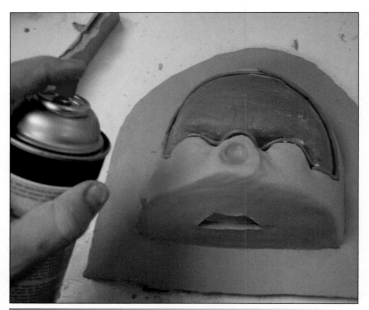

Fig. 1-120

For odd-shaped molds, a base flange must be added. Use ½" water clay slabs around the base. Blend and smooth the top. The clay only needs to be about 1½" wide. This base flange will make the negative mold ½" shorter all around and provide room for prying open the mold. The base flange is finished, and the worm is added..

The entire piece is sealed with Crystal Clear. Don't forget to remove the worm immediately after spraying.

Fig. 1-121

Fig. 1-122

When layering the mold, use burlap or fiberglass matte. Here fiberglass matte is used to strengthen the molds. The finished molds should only be about 1" thick.

Saturate the burlap or fiberglass matte in Ultracal 30. Make sure there are no dry spots.

Fig. 1-123

Only after the first layer of stone has firmed up is the fiberglass added. Two layer of two (or four layers total) add strength.

Fig. 1-124

The last and largest piece is begun. Because the sculpture comes so close to the bottom of the positive, it must be raised in order to make room for the base flange. Make sure it is level before proceeding.

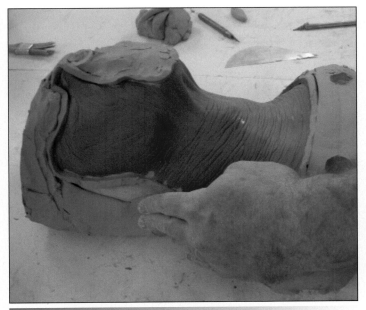

Fig. 1-125

The flash is added.

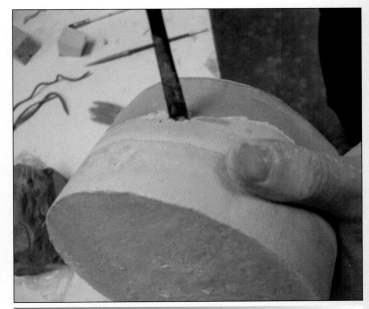

Fig. 1-126

Before working with the last piece, the other two are opened. Use a screwdriver to gently pry. Work around slowly to avoid chipping.

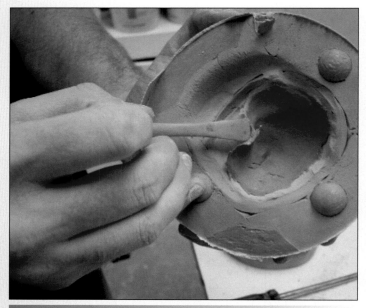

Fig. 1-127

Once the mold is opened, remove any clay with a plastic or wooden tool. Never use a metal tool—the stone may be scratched.

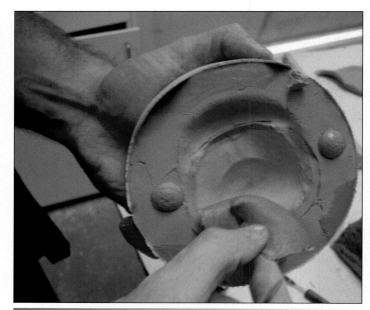

Fig. 1-128

After all the clay is removed, rasp or sand down the sharp edges, and scrub the mold clean with 99 percent alcohol.

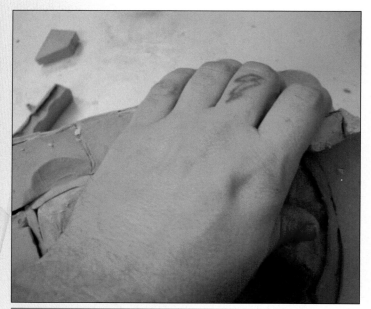

Fig. 1-129

Move on to the forehead mold. Flip it over, and remove the base flange from the stone. This exposes the ½" lip that is used to pry out the positive.

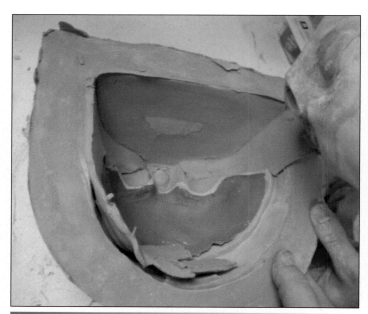

Fig. 1-130

The positive is pried free. Remove all clay, sand all sharp edges, and scrub the positive and negative with alcohol.

Fig. 1-131

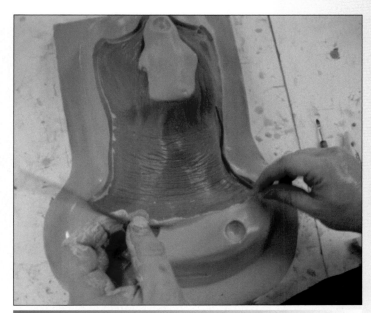

Fig. 1-132

On the last mold, the ends have been drafted, the cutting edge and flash established, and the base flange finished.

The worm and Crystal Clear are added.

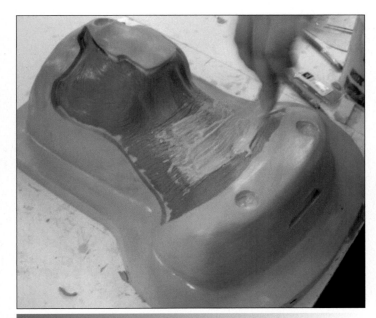

Fig. 1-133

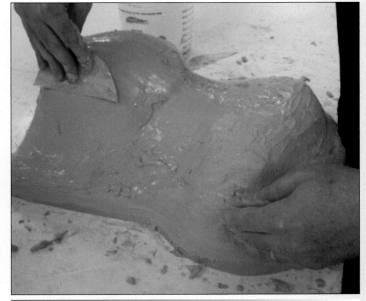

Fig. 1-134

When making negative molds, always begin by adding stone to the sculpture first. Brush it on slowly to avoid trapping air bubbles. When finished, move on to the keys and contact points, and finally the flash. Wait for the splash coat to turn matte or dull before using burlap or fiberglass matte.

Application of the finish coat. Use a kidney tool to shape the stone.

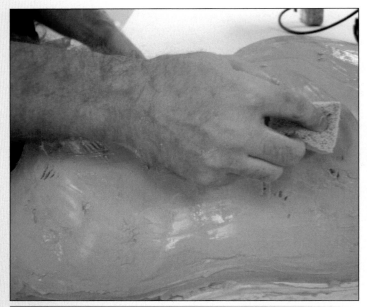

Fig. 1-135

Use a sponge to further refine and smooth the stone.

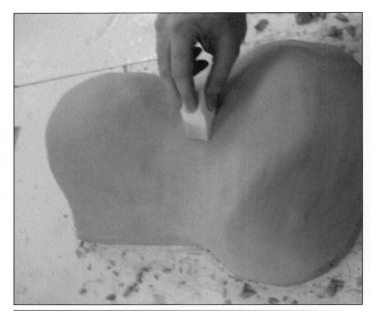

Fig. 1-136

As the stone begins to cure, switch to a fine sponge in order to smooth the surface as much as possible.

Fig. 1-137

When the mold is cured, flip it over, and remove the base flange.

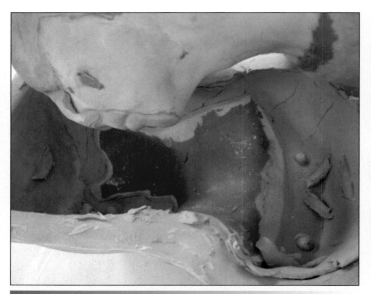

Fig. 1-138

The mold is pried open.

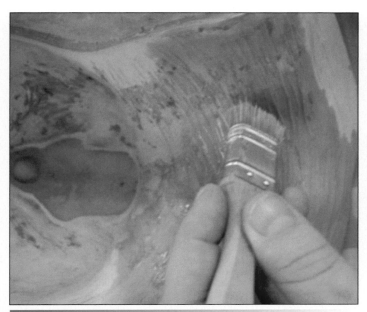

Fig. 1-139

All the clay is cleaned out prior to scrubbing the mold clean with alcohol.

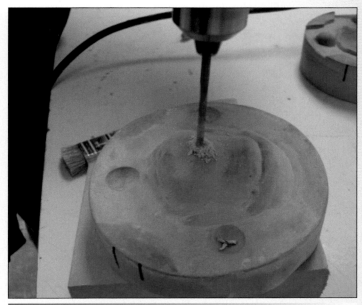

Fig. 1-140

After all the molds are cleaned, vent holes must be drilled. Without them, the foam latex between the molds in that area can provide so much hydraulic resistance that the mold will not close tightly enough for the creation of thin edges. A ⅜" drill bit is used on all three positives.

Fig. 1-141

The center of the forehead is drilled.

Fig. 1-142

The center of the neck is also drilled.

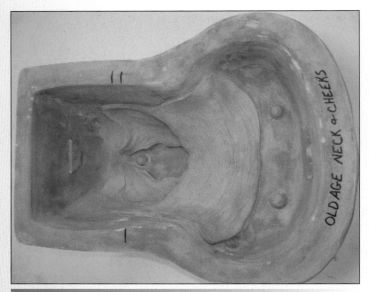

Fig. 1-143

The molds must be released. First mix up some "alco-wax," which is simply paste wax broken down with 99-percent alcohol. Brush the mixture on, let the alcohol evaporate, and then buff with a lint-free cloth.

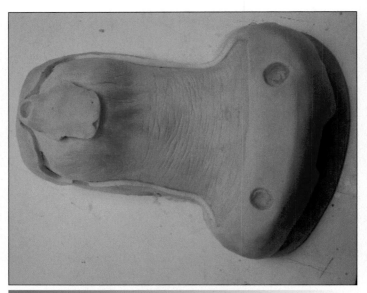

Fig. 1-144

Finally, a small amount of stearic acid mold release (included in the foam latex kit) is added. A little goes a long way, so avoid using too much. Cover all molds, and run the foam.

Fig. 1-145

While the foam is mixing, registration lines are added, and the molds are labeled.

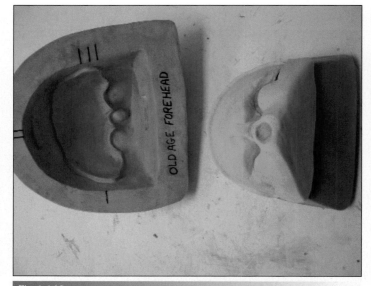

Fig. 1-146

The foam latex prosthesis rests on the positive.

Fig. 1-147

The finished chin prosthesis and mold.

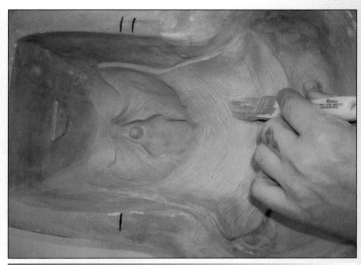

Fig. 1-148

The finished forehead prosthesis and mold.

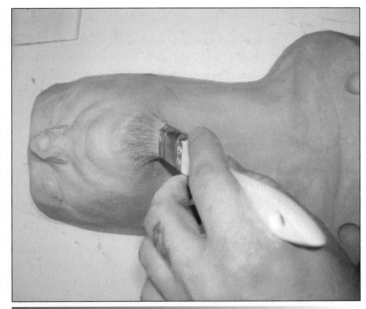

Fig. 1-149

The finished pieces. (Sculpture and make-up by Bill McCoy, molds by Bill McCoy and Kelly Golden.)

CLASSIC FACIAL IMPRESSION AND FACIAL STONE POSITIVE CAST FABRICATION TECHNIQUE

ALGINATE IMPRESSION THEORY

The following theory is presented as preliminary information that is derived from classic techniques and should be thoroughly understood prior to reading the following chapters, which actually show the impressions and positive cast-making process.

Apply the bald cap. Prepare the hair prior to applying the cap with Gafquat, hair gel, etc., and comb it back off of the face as flat against the head as possible. Remove portions of the cap around the ear. Show as much of the forehead skin surface as possible. Use just enough adhesive under the edge of the cap in order to keep it adhered to the skin. If desired, the ears do not need to be entirely uncovered, and the alginate need not be applied over them. If an impression of the ears is required, however, press cotton into them to prevent the alginate from entering. Bald cap edge lines that appear on the dried cast may be sanded down.

Use a cotton swab to work Vaseline through the eyebrows and eyelashes, all the way down to the roots. Be sure that the hairs are well lubricated. Comb through the brows in order to return them to their original direction. Put a pillow at the lumbar area of the back to keep the subject completely erect in the seat. The face needs to remain unwrinkled throughout the entire process, so the head needs to be in the same position as if the subject were standing. A pillow or other type of support can be placed behind the head if the chair headrest is too far from the subject.

Before working with the alginate, determine a method of communication with the subject (be it sounds or hand signals), because the subject will be unable to speak during the process. Provide a pencil and a piece of paper in the event the subject needs to express more detailed information.

Begin by opening the alginate bag and folding down its edges. Keep the bag of alginate closed when not in use to prevent water from accidentally dripping into it, resulting in large pieces that will solidify and potentially ruin future impressions. Pour cold water into a bowl to a depth of 1″. Determine how much of the face will be cast, and sprinkle alginate onto the water's surface. While working the material with a spatula, have an assistant add more water or alginate as needed. Create a creamy consistency. Do not leave any jewelry on during this process (or when applying alginate), for the material can potentially become imbedded in it. Use tight-fitting surgical gloves of either latex or vinyl prior to starting and throughout the entire process.

The fingers are used to work the alginate onto the face. Push the material into the corners of the eyes, around the sides of the nose, and onto the mouth. Allow the excess to drip back into the bowl. Ask the subject to inhale deeply and then exhale through the nose while the alginate is applied around the nostrils. Continue with the sides of the face and underneath the chin. Be certain at all times that the nostrils are clear of the material.

Work the alginate back onto the sides of the neck and the top of the chest. Pour an additional amount on top of the head. Catch the material as it continues to drip off the bottom of the face, and place it back on top of the head. Make sure all of the edges are consistently thick. Continue pushing it into the corners of the eyes to ensure proper application with no air pockets. (Detailed application of alginate around the nostrils is best done three-quarters of the way through the process.)

Continue building around the nose, and wipe down areas where excess material still hangs. As the impression material solidifies, cut away unneeded areas, and fill in gaps in order to prevent holes. Within a short time, the material begins to set up. A thicker mixture will have an even quicker setup time. The material hardens on the hands, but it peels off quite easily. Alternatively, simply remove and quickly replace your surgical gloves. The impression material may be cut, once solidified, at its outer borders with a dull wooden sculpting tool for the removal of excess areas of dripped material.

With a wooden stick, carve the appropriate line around the face, beyond which the material can be removed. Be cautious around the ear area. Allow the material to stay attached to the shoulder. Begin then to cut around the chest portion in order to remove outer edge excess.

Start applying plaster bandages that have been immersed in water. First cut them into appropriate sizes. Allow the edge of the first one to overlap the edge of the alginate on top of the head. Lay a second, longer piece over the top of the first one. This bandage, which should hang down below the ears on both sides, can be worked in front of the ears and attached down the sides of the neck. Again be certain that the bandage folds over the alginate.

At this point, cut a piece of duct tape, fold it in half width-wise, wrap it around the neck (on top of the bandages), and attach it at the back of the neck with a clothespin or any other type of clip that is fast and easy to use. As the bandages harden, the tape will help to keep them firmly in place against the alginate.

Communicate with the subject to learn of any possible discomfort. Continue applying smaller pieces of bandage down from the top of the head. Each new bandage should overlap the previous one. Work the bandages to fit into any potential depressions in the alginate. Some of the bandage pieces can be rolled into a ball and fitted into spaces for extra support. *(This entire plaster bandaging process will be described and shown in great detail in subsequent chapters of this volume.)*

Breathing may become a little more difficult at this point—so forewarn the subject—but the nostril passages will not be blocked. Usually no more than two rolls of plaster bandage are used for a single mold.

Be certain the sides are reinforced. If a portion of the chest needs to be retained in the mold, add extra support to the neck and chest area. Make sure the edges of the bandage application are very substantial.

Replace the surgical gloves as needed. While the bandages harden, trim away excess alginate beyond the bandage area with a wooden tool, if necessary. The tape tied behind the neck will hold the bandages in place (optional).

Use a towel or sea sponge soaked in warm water to sponge off material from the shoulders. At this point, the alginate should be completely solidified, so the movement should not create distortion of any kind. Clean the ears as well.

Lightly tap the cast surface with the fingers or a wooden tool in order to determine whether the alginate has hardened sufficiently. Then prepare a cradle for the cast. A cardboard box or a plastic bin lined with towels works suitably, as does a plastic bag filled with Styrofoam peanuts or a bean bag pillow.

Release the clothespin or clip, and cut off the excess support tape. Gently squeeze the model's skin at the back of the neck while holding the front of the cast along the jaw with the other hand. Openings will start to form between the skin and cast. Pull the ears back gently. Massage the top of the exposed head (the visible cap may be removed at this point to acquire access to the model's actual hair and scalp), and stretch the skin on the chest down away from the cast. Ask the subject to move the eyebrows, eyes, and mouth to create even more separation.

Carefully and slowly remove the cast. A perfect impression has been made. Lay the cast into the cradle.

Note: As long as the alginate is kept cold with a wet towel and cold water, and the mold is completely enclosed in a plastic bag, it can maintain its form for quite some time. If it becomes exposed to the air, the alginate will eventually shrink.

THE POSITIVE CAST

In the past, clothespins were used along the entire perimeter of the outermost or top join of the alginate to the edges of the plaster bandages (mother mold) in order to keep the bandages attached to the mother mold, thereby preventing the sides of the alginate from collapsing into it. Today, Eastman 910 Adhesive (or Krazy Glue), a gel form of glue, can be run along the edges of the alginate to ensure proper adhesion. With a stick, work away the excess adhesive, and press the two surfaces together. If there are cracks in the mold, the glue can be used to seal these as well. If no adhesive is available, squeeze denture cream into the gap, and press the alginate back into place against the dry plaster mother mold.

With cotton swabs or tissues, wipe excess pieces of material from the inside (negative) of the impression. Pieces that are attached to the mouth area can be removed with tweezers or cuticle scissors. Blot the alginate, and push the tissue down into the nostril areas to remove any moisture.

Return the mold to the cradle. Place a towel underneath it for extra support.

Plug the nostrils with clay (#1, or preferably, #2 grade). First knead the material, and then apply it as a cap over the nostrils on the outside bandage. Do not actually stick the clay down into the holes, because it will distort the alginate. Smooth it out so that both outside nostril holes are covered completely, which will prevent the liquid stone mixture from extruding through them.

Lay the mold into the cradle, bandage-side first. In a cup, mix dental alginate, which sets quickly, with water. Create thin slurry with the spatula, and then pour it into a small hypodermic syringe (with a curved applicator tip). Turn the syringe over, and push the plunger until the material comes out of its curved nozzle. Wipe off the end, and point it down into the nostril hole. Fill the hole with alginate. With a cotton swab or small dental spatula, remove the excess before it hardens. Then reapply alginate to build up the nostril hole just slightly (resembling a stalagmite). This elevation will create a deeper nostril hole for the positive cast (optional). The holes that exist in the alginate will become bumps that can be slightly sanded down on the finished cast. Return the mold to the cradle.

Always work with surgical gloves when dealing with stone materials. Wear a particle mask as long as the materials are still in powder form, and never breathe the dust. Wear goggles under all circumstances.

Pour between 1″ and 1½″ of water into a bowl. Sprinkle Hydrocal down into it. A sifter can be used for neatness. Ultracal 30 can in fact be used for *both* the positive and negative cast, but it works more effectively for the negative because of its supposedly better surface detail pickup. (**Note:** As previously stated, the term *casts* normally refers to positives, while the term *molds* refers to negatives.)

With an inexpensive disposable tongue depressor or spray-coated (with Pam, for example) rubber spatula, spread out the material, and push it down into the water. Remove pieces of debris that may be floating inadvertently in the mixture. Palette knives or wooden sticks can be used for mixing.

Immerse hands into the material, and squeeze it through the fingertips so that all large lumps and bubbles are removed. Clean the gloved hands in water, or replace the gloves as needed throughout the process.

Place the bowl on top of the dental vibrator. Shake and rotate the bowl to help move any existing bubbles that migrate towards the center of the mixture. Remove the particle mask, and blow on the surface. Dot the surface with a tissue. With a small cup, skim the bubbles off the top. Once again, cover the mouth and nose with a particle mask for safety.

With the $\frac{1}{2}''$ bristle brush, try to remove any remaining bubbles from the mixture. Then start painting the undercuts (around the nostrils, near the eyebrows, etc.). Work the mixture down into the wrinkles. The first layer must have no bubbles. Paint it very smoothly onto the surface of the alginate, right up to the very edge of the mold. Then apply a second, heavier coat.

When a substantial amount of material exists—at which point fiberglass rovings, hemp, or burlap can be placed upon the mold without actually touching the alginate—proceed. Normally about $\frac{1}{4}''$ will suffice, and at the very most, $\frac{3}{4}''$. Do not apply any undue pressure against the mold. Avoid working beyond the area where the alginate lies in order to avoid locking the stone and the plaster mother mold.

Begin laying the reinforcement material of your choice onto the stone (in the mixing bowl) in order to thoroughly saturate it and/or coat it with stone mixture prior to application to the negative wall. Keep the reinforcement within the confines of the mold. For a thin mold, avoid adding too much reinforcement, as the stone may be overwhelmed, and the mold will weaken. There should be no less than $\frac{1}{4}''$ of stone build-up in the negative prior to the introduction of the reinforcing material.

As the stone mixture thickens, the second layer of reinforcement can be applied. Again, drop the reinforcement first into the liquid stone, saturate it thoroughly with mixture, and then lay it along the sides of the mold to add substance and internal reinforcement. Work the reinforcement material along the edge of the mold and around the neck area. Be sure there is plenty of strength between the neck extension and the facial negative to prevent the neck join from weakening, which could result in cracking.

With a tissue and cotton swabs, absorb any water resting in the mold. Use the remaining stone mixture to add thickness. (**Note:** Explanations in this section will be depicted in following chapters.)

Add extra pieces of mixture onto the sides of the facial cavity onto which the wooden dowel can be attached. Work the material around the ends of the dowel in order to fix it in place. Wrap some extra fiberglass rovings or other reinforcement material around the dowel, and saturate it within the stone mixture prior to applying the material to the inner backside of the negative mold.

Add a small amount of water into the mold, and move it around with the fingers. Pour out the excess, and use a cellulose smoothing sponge (available from Joe Blasco Cosmetics) or a mold makers sponge to smooth out the mold's surface. Remove (cut away) stray reinforcement, which may extend from the edges of the hardening stone. With the fingers, continue the smoothing process, and add more stone where necessary to conceal reinforcement and to make the curing stone as smooth and symmetrical as possible.

As the stone material heats up during the curing process, steam will appear on the surface. Steam usually rises from the bandages during the creation of the mother mold.

With the sponge, clean excess material off the now-imbedded wooden dowel. Continue smoothing and cleaning the entire inner backside with the mold makers sponge.

If the positive cast has been made incorrectly, the rubber appliances will not properly fit. Pay close attention to detail. Also, when working with alginate and stone materials, never allow these to go down the sink drain. (Special metal mesh or a plaster catch can be purchased from a plumbing supply company in order to prevent this from happening.)

Next, peel back the mother mold (plaster bandages) very carefully, and discard. Then peel off the alginate layer. Use a small Stanley planer and/or various sizes of rasps to remove uneven areas of the cast bottom edges and surface, followed by sandpaper to smooth and refine the outside of the cast.

A small, rounded, beveled chisel or dental spatula and/or any number of appropriately sized metal and wooden sculpting tools can be used to remove lumps from the face of the cast. Use a small hammer and chisel to chip off the larger pieces. With an even smaller chisel and/or dental tool, wooden sculpting tool, or metal spatula, refine along the lips to remove excess remaining imbedded alginate. Refine around the eyebrow areas, and use a soft brush to dust away the material. The cast at this stage still contains quite a bit of moisture that will be removed during the curing process. If it were hardened at this point, the stone would not break apart as smoothly, and the carving process would prove more difficult.

Mix up a small amount of gypsum stone (which is not porous compared to plaster) in order to fill in any remaining small holes along the edges of the cast. Refine the mold to be as aesthetically perfect as possible while the positive cast is still warm.

In order to get the edges of the appliances to reach perfectly around the nostril region, after curing the cast, the nostrils must be filled with clay so that an undercut is avoided; otherwise, when the negative is made, the plaster applied on top of this positive will grab onto the inner portions of the nostril, as well as the undersides, and prevent the negative from being removed. Similarly, the eyelids and lips need to be filled in so that locking is prevented. (This undercut prevention process, as well as the creation of retaining walls around the completed clay appliance sculpture, will be shown in following chapters.)

HISTORICAL CURING INFORMATION AND POST-CURING

After the cast is wrapped in a towel and cured in an oven preheated to approximately 150ºF for three to six hours, allow it to cool in the oven with the oven turned off. Permit air into the oven by cracking the door just slightly. Note that the color of the cast lightens slightly from the baking process.

Pour a small amount of castor oil in a dish, and use a brush to apply it to the cast. Castor oil should not be painted on the cast before curing. The surface, once conditioned, will more readily accept the addition of clay. Condition the underside as well. Allow the oil to soak for an hour. (Some artists will pickle their casts by allowing them to be completely immersed in a large bucket of castor oil for several hours after oven curing. Normally, four to eight hours is sufficient. This process is thought of as unnecessary by some artists, however.) Use a dry towel to rub down the mold.

SCULPTING MATERIALS

For use when sculpturing the new features upon the positive cast:

- Various Rubber Fruit/Vegetable Skin Surface Transfers (casaba, grapefruit, orange, and avocado, all of which work effectively for the creation of texture and wrinkles when pressed into clay sculptures)
- Brushes, Metal Tools, Metal Plate, etc.
- Orange Stipple Sponge
- Castor Oil
- Acetone
- Alcohol
- Tissues

Note: When using liquid latex (de-ammoniated, such as Joe Blasco Datex), follow these safety suggestions:

- Avoid eye contact.
- Use with adequate ventilation.
- Keep it away from children.
- Do not get it onto hair and/or fabric—it will dry and become difficult to remove.
- Datex contains a small amount of ammonia that acts as a preservative. Avoid prolonged, repeated breathing of vapors.

SUMMARY

The preceding information serves as a brief introduction to the facial impression process (with alginate) and the preparation of the stone (Hydrocal/Ultracal 30) positive facial cast. A more detailed explanation with photographs will follow later in this volume. This theory section should be analyzed thoroughly and well understood prior to continuing with the following chapters.

THE MISNOMER, "RUBBER MASK GREASEPAINT"

This material is a rather archaic form of make-up product—with a somewhat unrefined grade of castor oil as a vehicle—designed by the Max Factor Company in the 1940s. At that time, it was found that any type of make-up foundation that contained any animal or mineral products (such as mineral oil or petrolatum) was incompatible with the lattices employed to make appliances, be they slush or painted-in types, or later, foam latex pieces or prostheses.

Today's latex appliance foundation base make-up is better described as a type of Appliance Foundation, or A.F., and is a much improved version from RCMA of the old material. It is compounded to be less oily and does not separate, nor does it require stirring before use. It employs a very new, refined grade of castor oil as the vehicle, plus, like any RCMA C.P.F.

(Color Process Foundation) or Joe Blasco P.M. (Prosthetic Make-up) product, it does not contain any mineral oil, lanolin, Vaseline, or other similar materials. As such, A.F. and P.M. colors do not require the heavy colored powders that old RMG (Rubber Mask Greasepaint) products did. The natural skin halation can be obtained with RCMA or Joe Blasco No-Color Powder, while a matte finish can be achieved with RCMA A.F. Powder. These varieties of powder contain no coloration and thus cannot change the shade of the finished application of an A.F. or P.M. shade.

It should also be noted that any RCMA C.P.F. color or shade can also be applied over any latex appliance without affecting it, but these colors or shades do not have the covering power of the RCMA A.F. materials. Therefore, delineations with any C.P.F. color can be applied over an application of any RCMA A.F. shade without being detrimental to the latex prostheses.

RCMA also furnishes special A.F. Palettes to enable the make-up artist to carry this product in a compact container of six or sixteen different shades and colors.

All Joe Blasco products that are preceded by the initials P.M. (Prosthetic Make-up) are suitable for use on skin and all forms of artificial appliance fabricated of slip or shell latex, foam latex, gelatin, and silicone. Just like RCMA A.F. colors, Joe Blasco P.M. appliance colors have a very extensive color range—from fleshtones to primary pigments—and are available in jars or palettes.

Chapter 2

PROSTHETIC MAKE-UP MATERIALS

Chapter 2

JOE BLASCO AND RCMA FOUNDATIONS AND PIGMENTS

Special Foundations

Joe Blasco P. M. Foundation Base (Prosthetic Make-up Base)

RCMA Effects and Specialty Colors

Joe Blasco Effects Bases

Joe Blasco Additive Pigments (Powder Form)

JOE BLASCO AND RCMA ADHESIVES, SEALERS, AND ADDITIONAL PRODUCTS

A History of Adhesives and Sealers for Professional Make-up Use

Products

Buyer Beware

Chapter 2

PROSTHETIC MAKE-UP MATERIALS

For consumer cosmetics products (those sold to the public in commercial venues, like drug and department stores, and designated as such by the Federal Drug & Cosmetic Agency (FD&C), there are a number of stringent restrictions relating to labeling, ingredient listings, and the ingredients themselves. Theatrical and professional make-up materials are, in general, not as restricted, provided they are solely employed by professionally trained personnel. As such, make-up artists sometimes carry materials that people working with commercial cosmetics cannot.

*For example, many of the **adhesives** utilized by professional make-up artists are specialized **sealers**, **old-age stipples**, **prosthetic pieces**, and other substances and staples of the make-up kit that are never seen by the general public, nor by cosmeticians, beauty salon make-up artists, cosmetologists, or other licensed beauty salon personnel.*

The professional make-up artist's kit materials must include products that are employed for prosthetic and/or character make-up that changes the appearance of a performer's race, age, facial or body structure, or creates various effects which might include cuts, bruises, or other injuries, plus tattoos, hair growth, wrinkles, and other facial abnormalities. There is, of course, the possibility that a certain performer may be allergic to or affected by the use of some of these unusual items; great care must therefore be taken to perform various tests in order to determine whether certain items should be used in moderation (or perhaps avoided altogether). Sometimes, the quick evaporation on the skin of the solvents in some adhesives or sealers will produce a temporary irritation on skin that is sensitive, while other performers will react from the blockage of the pores by prosthetic pieces. In such cases, some roles may have to be recast. Tests must always be made prior to commencement of a production for such unusual make-ups. Liability can become an issue in such cases if proper testing is not done.

Please note that the following products do not comprise the entire kit of the make-up artist embarking on a prosthetic make-up application by any means; the following chapters in this volume will serve to elaborate on the subject of make-up materials as they pertain to specific make-up procedures.

For full company listings and contact information, please see Appendix B. For detailed information about beauty and character make-up materials, please see Volumes I and II, respectively.

JOE BLASCO AND RCMA FOUNDATIONS AND PIGMENTS

SPECIAL FOUNDATIONS

RCMA makes an **A.F. (Appliance Foundation)** series—in the same colors and shades as its regular Color Process Foundations—which is compounded with a higher degree of pigmentation in order to provide the coverage necessary for prostheses made of slush or foam latex, gelatin, or other plastic varieties. The products are available in one- and six-ounce sizes, and in palettes of six and sixteen colors.

Although the regular CP shades of RCMA foundation may be utilized for latex pieces (as they do not contain mineral oil), the A.F. shades provide more coverage and spread easier

Fig. 2-1

on prostheses. They can be powdered with either RCMA No-Color Powder or with the matte form of A.F. Powder.

Joe Blasco manufactures an extremely large array of Special Foundations, Death Colors, Creative Colors, and Prosthetic Foundations (P.M.) suitable for all types of character make-up. Both Joe Blasco and RCMA will also produce custom colors and specialty products on special order.

JOE BLASCO P.M. FOUNDATION BASE (PROSTHETIC MAKE-UP BASE)

Foundations #1–18 are formulated specifically to be compatible with human skin and for application upon the surface of prosthetic appliances. Although primarily designed for use as extrinsic coloration for foam latex prostheses, they may also be used to color gelatin and silicone appliances. The colors (#1–18), which identically match the Joe Blasco Studio Base colors, may be ordered from the Studio Base Olive Series, Studio Base Neutral Series, and/or Studio Base Ruddy Series. Also, special mixes for custom colors are available upon request. (Note: "P.M." is an acronym for prosthetic make-up.)

Fig. 2-2

P.M. Studio Base #1	(Extra Light #1)
P.M. Studio Base #2	(Extra Light #2)
P.M. Studio Base #3	(Extra Light #3)
P.M. Studio Base #4	(Light #1)
P.M. Studio Base #5	(Light #2)
P.M. Studio Base #6	(Light #3)
P.M. Studio Base #7	(Medium #1)
P.M. Studio Base #8	(Medium #2)
P.M. Studio Base #9	(Medium #3)
P.M. Studio Base #10	(Dark #1)
P.M. Studio Base #11	(Dark #2)
P.M. Studio Base #12	(Dark #3)
P.M. Studio Base #13	(Extra Dark #1)
P.M. Studio Base #14	(Extra Dark #2)
P.M. Studio Base #15	(Extra Dark #3)
P.M. Studio Base #16	(Darkest #1)
P.M. Studio Base #17	(Darkest #2)
P.M. Studio Base #18	(Darkest #3)

PROSTHETIC EFFECTS AND COLOR ADDITIVES
(To be used alone or mixed with P.M. bases)

P.M. CREAM ADDITIVE COLORS (used to alter undertone and/or value when mixed into any of the P.M. Studio Base colors)

P.M. #6205	(adds richer red undertone)
P.M. #2817	(adds burnt sienna undertone)
P.M. #8534	(adds umber [rich, deep brown] undertone)
P.M. #1624	(adds deep yellow-ochre undertone)
P.M. #1654	(adds reddish brown for lowering value/altering undertone)
P.M. #2962	(adds dark coral brown for lowering value/altering undertone)
P.M. #2673	(adds sienna undertone)
P.M. #1667	(adds light yellow-ochre undertone)
P.M. #35060	(adds light yellow-green undertone)

P.M. SPECIAL ADDITIVE COLORS

P.M. #45750	[Ultramarine Blue] (adds royal, dark blue undertone)
P.M. #C-7111	[Chromium Hydroxide Green] (adds rich, dark blue-green undertone)
P.M. #82140	[Black] (deepens/darkens value and adds grayness [lowering intensity])
P.M. #09990	[White-TiO$_2$] (increases/lightens value and decreases grayness [raising intensity])

ADDITIONAL P.M. COLORS

P.M.-White (P.M.-W)

P.M.-Black (P.M.-Bk)

P.M.-Red (P.M.-R)

P.M.-Blue (P.M.-Be)

P.M.-Yellow (P.M.-Y)

P.M.-Green (P.M.-G)

P.M.-Green Gray #3 (P.M.-GG #3)

P.M.-Purple (P.M.-P)

P.M.-Gold Olive (P.M.-GO)

P.M.-Suntan Stipple (P.M.-SS)

P.M.-Blondeen (P.M.-BL)

P.M.-Russet (P.M.-RU)

P.M.-Lilac (P.M.-LI)

P.M.-Cocoa (P.M.-CO)

P.M.-Death Straw (P.M.-DS)

P.M.-Death Green (P.M.-DG)

P.M.-Death Blue-Gray (P.M.-DBG)

P.M.-Death Gray (P.M.-DG)

P.M.-Death Purple (P.M.-DP)

P.M.-Death Flesh (P.M.-DF)

P.M.-Frankenstein (P.M.-F.Stein)

P.M.-Halloween (P.M.-Hallo)

P.M.-Vampire Pale (P.M.-Vamp)

Fig. 2-3

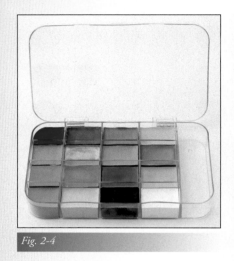

Fig. 2-4

SPECIAL MIXES OF BASIC EARTH COLORS	
1624	Warm Ochre mixture
1624W	Lighter Warm Ochre
1667	Pale Ochre (Minus-Red tone for adding to any RCMA Foundation)
6205	A Russet shade (Plus-Red tone for adding to any RCMA Foundation)
YO-1	Yellow Ochre
YO-2	Deep Yellow Ochre
Dark Skin Toner	

RCMA EFFECTS AND SPECIALTY COLORS

RCMA makes four-color kits of many shade combinations and some sixteen-color palettes for professionals who prefer to carry the colors in this new format. All of the colors and shades are standard for RCMA and were never discontinued, unlike those of many commercial companies that simply follow fashion trends or change their packaging for promotional purposes. One last note: RCMA professional make-up products are never sold in drug or department stores, or through house-to-house sales, but strictly through distributors of professional make-up materials.

In addition, RCMA also has a **Rainbow Color Wheel Series** that covers the most useful range of bright colors: **Red, Maroon, Orange, Bruise Yellow, Yellow, Lime, Green, Midnight Green, Opal, Turquoise, Blue, Ultrablue, Navy Blue, Lilac, Violet, Purple, Black** and **Super-White**.

Others include **Beard Covers** for men: **BC-1** (Pink), **BC-2** (Orange), and **BC-3** (Tan-Orange). Additionally, **Beard Stipple** and four special Beard Stipples devised by Marvin Westmore: **MW-1** (Deep Greenish undertone), **MW-2** (Green undertone), **MW-3** (Blue-Green undertone), and **MB-4** (Green-Black undertone).

JOE BLASCO EFFECTS BASES (not in the P.M. formula)

DEATH COLORS

To simulate various stages of flesh color after death. Intended to be applied as skin stains but can be applied more heavily for opaque coverage. Also for creating ghosts, ghouls, vampires, zombies, gnomes, and other fantasy characters.

Death Green	(drab, grayed, medium yellow-green)
Death Blue Gray	(drab, medium blue-gray)
Death Flesh	(drab, sallow, light grayed yellow)
Death Straw	(dull, grayed straw yellow)
Death Gray	(light, sallow gray)
Death Purple	(dark, grayed purple)
Frankenstein Green	(medium, grayed mint green)
Werewolf Brown	(dark, rich, yet vibrant red-brown)
Beetle Juice	(light, grayed, beige yellow-green)
Vampire Pale	(light, sallow, grayed off-white [dark eggshell])
Ghostly	(darker version of Vampire Pale)
Sallow	(drab, grayed medium beige to simulate sallow skin or illness)
Lilac	(light lilac-purple to create unusual fashion fleshtones)
Milk	(a light cream-yellow for highlighting, counter-shading, or simulating extremely pale skin for illness)
Sahara	(medium, yellow-brown beige used as blue neutralizer and bruise cover)
Cocoa	(dark, ruddy-chocolate for ruddy dark skin; may be used as an additive for the Dark Skin Studio Base colors to add warmth and remove unwanted gray undertone)
Black Base	(very vibrant blue-black that is neither dull nor grayed)
White Base	(all-purpose pure white base)

JOE BLASCO ADDITIVE PIGMENTS (Powder form)

For use as color additives for custom fantasy face powder; for make-up effects products, such as film-forming sealers, lattices (liquid latex), and liquid foam rubber compounds (primary dispersions); and for extrinsic and intrinsic coloration for all forms of prosthetic appliances and devices (including gelatin and silicone).

JB Pigment #6205   (to add richer red undertone)

JB Pigment #2817   (to add burnt sienna undertone)

JB Pigment #8534   (to add umber [rich, deep brown] undertone)

JB Pigment #1624   (to add deep yellow-ochre undertone)

JB Pigment #1654   (to add reddish brown for lowering value/altering undertone)

JB Pigment #2962   (to add dark coral brown for lowering value/altering undertone)

JB Pigment #2673   (to add sienna undertone)

JB Pigment #1667   (to add light yellow-ochre undertone)

JB Pigment #35060   (to add light yellow-green undertone)

JOE BLASCO SPECIAL ADDITIVE PIGMENTS (POWDER FORM)

JB Pigment #45750
[Ultramarine Blue] (to add dark, royal blue undertone)

JB Pigment #C-7111
[Chromium Hydroxide Green] (to add a rich, dark blue-green undertone)

JB Pigment #82140
[Black] (to deepen/darken value and add grayness [lowering intensity])

JB Pigment #09990
[White-TiO_2] (to increase/lighten value and decrease grayness [raising intensity])

Joe Blasco Additive Pigments (in powder form) can, in certain instances, be added directly into liquid, film-forming plastic sealer, liquid latex, foam latex base compound (dispersion A), liquefied gelatin, and fluid silicone preparations. In some instances—as in the case of water-soluble liquid latex, foam latex base compound (dispersion A), and liquid gelatin—it may be advantageous to pre-wet these powdered pigment additives into a small, predetermined amount (by weight) of the actual liquid into which the pigment can be added to create a fluid vehicle, which will permit the color to emulsify more easily into the preparation as a colorant. In the case of lattices (liquid latex/foam latex base compound [dispersion A]), distilled water may be used as the vehicle, and it is usually necessary to also add one or two drops of ammonia per ounce of liquid mixed. The ammonia acts as an emulsifier and as a preservative, permitting the mixture to be more compatible with the liquid latex preparations. Obviously, experimentation is vital to this process.

Dry Joe Blasco Pigments can also be used as powder colorant applied directly over make-up with a powder puff and/or various sizes of professional brushes appropriate for that use.

When using extrinsic powder colorant, colors may be mixed with talc or No-Color Powder to subdue their intensity. This process can be done by hand or through the use of a very small, electric, home kitchen-type (pepper grinder) mixing device, which has a lid to prevent the powder from permeating the atmosphere.

JOE BLASCO AND RCMA ADHESIVES, SEALERS, AND ADDITIONAL PRODUCTS

A HISTORY OF ADHESIVES AND SEALERS FOR PROFESSIONAL MAKE-UP USE

Since actors began using make-up materials to change or delineate characters, they have required some form of facial adhesive for attaching beards, wigs, and various items to change facial structure. The original adhesive, **spirit gum**, is named after its key ingredient or spirit, be it rosin, sandarac, balsam, or other. The gum readily dissolved in the solvent and evaporated when brushed on the face, leaving a very sticky coating onto which hair could be laid or an appliance could be attached. This product had been the standard for many years until the new breed of make-up artist, who began doing the make-up for actors in the film studios, began to experiment and design improvements in adhesive products for studio use.

The first such improvement was the removal of the objectionable, constant shine that spirit gum emitted when it set upon the human skin. The Max Factor Company tackled this problem by introducing a **Matte Adhesive** that featured the addition of some of the new finely powdered silica materials developed by paint manufacturers for dulling the shine of their paint products. The early silicas were not entirely efficient, and therefore much tacking of the application with the fingers was necessary, but the product was certainly an improvement over the old varieties.

Later, RCMA developed a two-stage, two-product addition of silica, which served as a vast improvement over the Max Factor version. At first, the silica was added to the resins with hi-shear equipment. Later, with improved silica products, the manufacture was simplified.

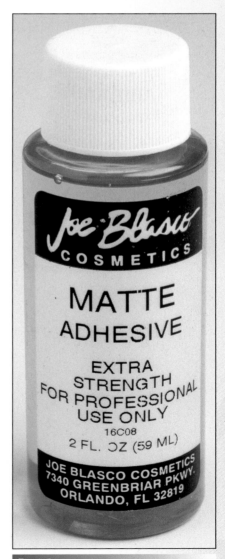

Next, a polyvinyl butryal product was added to some grades of this new Matte Adhesive to provide better track and flexibility for use with latex prostheses. Also, a slightly heavier resin and plastic material were added to provide a Matte Adhesive #16 (on the experimental list!). An adhesive was then developed with all-natural materials and solvents for those with allergenic or environmental concerns. With this, the resin-based adhesives reached their peak and remain preeminent even today.

One of the main objections to the use of resin/solvent adhesives was the inability of the artist to place any foundation base nearby, for the areas would then darken, and the lace edge of the hairpiece would stain. This posed difficulties when the foundation was of a dark shade, as required for some character make-ups, such as in the case of a light-skinned actor portraying a Native American or a dark-skinned person of Middle Eastern descent. Although artists experimented with the addition of products such as kaolin or Attapulgus clay, the resin stained nonetheless.

This problem was solved when a new series of plastic/polyvinyl-based materials came into use. These materials, water-white in color, were usually painted over the lace on the edge of a hairpiece. When dry, the resulting film could then be made-up along with the rest of the facial skin. Most make-up artists trimmed back the edge lace nearly to the hairline as well. In essence, therefore, these adhesives acted in the manner of **sealers**.

Fig. 2-5

Both polyvinyl butryrals and polyvinyl acetates/chlorides were employed in these adhesives/sealers, which became very useful to the make-up profession.

The next step in the progression occurred after 1975, when medical adhesives were introduced. The first was a fluorocarbon solvent style produced by the Dow Corning Company called **355 Medical Adhesive**, which was a pressure-sensitive, non-curing clear liquid especially suitable for adhering non-permanent materials to the body surface. It retained adhesive qualities in the presence of moisture and was unaffected by normal temperature variations and/or time. It became the adhesive of choice for many make-up applications.

The next variety, which was introduced a few years later in a water-based formula, was called **Pros-Aide**, which could be employed both as a pressure-sensitive adhesive and as a contact one. It was whitish in appearance, but dried clear. Dick Smith also developed some colors in combination with art store materials, which were deemed **Liquitex**, in order to make a paintable material, known as **PAX**, which could be employed for extrinsic coloration for prosthetic appliances. However, by the end of 1994, the Environmental Protection Agency negated the further use of fluorocarbons for being detrimental to the atmosphere, and this product was discontinued.

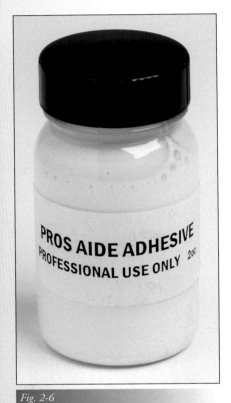

Fig. 2-6

Premiere Products, Inc. commenced research to replace the solvent on the still-available silicone base of this popular adhesive. Ethyl acetate was experimented with at first, but this solvent had a very strong and objectionable odor. The company finally came up with a suitable solvent, and we list its available products for make-up use below:

- Telesis 5 Silicone Adhesive

The most popular of the Telesis Silicone Adhesive line and the most similar to the original Dow Corning 355.

- Telesis 5 Silicone Matte Lace Adhesive

The ideal adhesive for adhering lace hair goods. The matting agents are mixed intrinsically during the manufacturing process, which ensures a fluid consistency so that the adhesive never hardens or cracks. It dries matte, is non-flammable, and is non-toxic.

- Telesis 6 Silicone Adhesive

The fastest drying of the Telesis Silicone Adhesives, but not quite as strong as Telesis 5.

- Thinners for both Telesis 5 and 6
- Beta Bond

A polymer acrylic formulation similar to Pros-Aide or RCMA "B" Adhesive. *Beta Bond Plus* is tackier and more pliable than the original Beta Bond. *Beta Solve*, which may be thinned with water, removes these products.

RCMA styled DC-355 as Prosthetic Adhesive "A" and Pros-Aide as Prosthetic Adhesive "B" in order to differentiate between the two.

PRODUCTS

RCMA MATTE ADHESIVES

The material featured in these products was introduced in 1965 and is made by combining *microsilica* materials of various micron sizes with the resin mix under high shear. In this way, the smaller-sized silica particles hold the larger ones in solution (the latter provide better matting) and, at the same time, add considerably more adhesion to the final mix because of the molecular structure of the finished material. **RCMA Matte Adhesive** can be employed both as an adhesive for hair goods and lace to the skin, as well as a skin sealer with residual tack.

Matte Adhesive #16

A superstick adhesive (for hair goods) that contains additional solids, plus a plastic material to aid adhesion, even when a subject perspires more than usual.

Matte Plasticized Adhesive

An adhesive designed for use with latex appliances. Provides more "all-ways" stretch capability and the tackiness required for holding cast or foam appliances to the skin.

Matte Adhesive Naturale

A specially compounded beard adhesive made with all-natural ingredients. No preservatives, animal products, or ketones. Dries matte when tacked with the finger for hair application.

Special Adhesive #1

Specifically designed to adhere any lace goods or hair to plastic bald caps. Normally, the plastic bald cap or front is attached to the subject with RCMA Matte Plasticized Adhesive or one of RCMA's Prosthetic Adhesives before the hair goods are attached. Special Adhesive #1 is a very fast-drying, heavily matted adhesive/sealer that will form a film that incorporates itself into the plastic bald cap while adhering the hair or lace to it. The product must be thoroughly shaken before use and applied over the lace as the hairpiece is held in place. Foundation make-up may be applied directly over RCMA Special Adhesive #1 without darkening the surface of the lace.

Fig. 2-7

Special Adhesive #2

A neoprene-based adhesive for attaching Velcro or other items to appliances, or for repairing foam pieces. Not for skin use!

Matte Lace Adhesive

Dries matte on application. Utilized for toupees and other lace-fronted pieces. Make-up can then be applied over the edge without any staining or discoloration.

Toupee Tape

A number of varieties are available, but a product called **Secure** is a colorless, two-sided, very sticky tape that is excellent for holding down toupee tops. These often find use in the wardrobe department for holding together low-cut gowns!

Fig. 2-8

RCMA PROSTHETIC ADHESIVES

These adhesives from the medical profession have various uses in make-up artistry:

Prosthetic Adhesive "B"

A water-based milky white (but clear-drying) acrylic emulsion adhesive that has a low irritant factor because it does not contain any strong solvents. Although the dried film is insoluble in water, the liquid can be diluted with a few drops of a mixture of isopropyl alcohol and water.

(A word of caution: Take great care in testing or using some of the new superadhesives made for industrial use, as they are extremely difficult to remove from the human skin without serious damage.)

Premiere Products makes a non-flammable, non-toxic, medical-grade silicone adhesive "A" called **Telesis** (5 and 6), as mentioned previously.

JOE BLASCO ADHESIVES FOR HAIR WORK, LIFTS, AND PROSTHESIS ATTACHMENT

Formulated to give the artist ample working time; extremely strong tack; adhesion; and matte, non-discoloring, long-lasting results:

Matte Finish Adhesive (Regular Strength)

The latest in the evolution of advanced matte adhesive or matte spirit gum products. It has been accepted by make-up artists worldwide as the ultimate replacement for the original, exceptional Max Factor *Mat Finish Adhesive*, which Factor produced from the 1940s through the 1970s before it was eventually discontinued. *(See Volume I.)*

Matte Finish Adhesive (Extra Strength)

Primarily used to attach fine lace hairpieces, but also successful with bald caps and prosthetic appliances. As an alcohol-based product (as opposed to silicone) it displays surprisingly secure longevity and is easily removed and cleaned from lace and reusable appliances. Joe Blasco Matte Finish Adhesives are available in two-ounce pints and gallons only.

ADHESIVE REMOVER

RCMA makes a cleanser that will dissolve and remove any type of plastic sealer, adhesive, or scar material for make-up use from the skin, which will remain soft and lubricated. It is not to be employed for cleaning adhesives from lace goods or in cleansing the face before applying hair goods, for it contains a moisturizing agent that prevents proper adhesion. A new variety of remover in a cream form, called **ADKLEN**, is made for cleansing adhesives from the skin. If it is applied underneath and to the edges of appliances with a brush, it will loosen and then cleanse the adhesive from the skin in a very gentle manner.

Alcohol

Ordinary drugstore rubbing alcohol is only a 70-percent type and is not a suitable solvent for make-up use. A 99-percent isopropyl alcohol should be stocked, because many adhesives and sealers contain a solvent mixture of 60-percent acetone and 40-percent isopropyl alcohol. Alcohol is also a good sterilizing agent for cleaning tools and tabletops.

LATEX

There are many grades of latex for specific professional make-up usage:

Pure Gum Latex

An un-filled pure gum rubber that air-dries to a tough elastic coating. It is not suitable for casting, as it does not build in slush molds, but is excellent for making inflatable bladders.

Casting Latex

A latex compound employed for slush or paint-in appliance making. Can be tinted to any shade with colors. **Casting Filler** can be added to this product to control buildup density and stiffness of the finished item or to work as pure gum for flexibility.

Foam Latex

A three- or four-part combination of various materials used to produce foam latex appliances (the actual latex portion being a heavy gum mixture).

Joe Blasco produces an excellent de-ammoniated liquid latex called **Datex** that is durable, transparent, non-fillered, and suitable for all high-quality liquid latex applications. It is easily removed with the application of medium compresses followed by gentle peeling with plain soap and water.

Fig. 2-9

SEALERS

Some of the first sealers used by make-up artists were **flexible collodion**, **filmstock**, or **guncotton** dissolved in ether with castor oil as a plasticizer. Make-up artist Jack Pierce employed such buildups on the face with successive layers of spirit gum, cotton batting, and a cover of flexible collodion when doing the first Frankenstein Monster on Boris Karloff. This was a laborious, time-consuming method and did not guarantee a fully controllable surface or buildup. Many theatrical make-up books employed this procedure for many years, and unfortunately, some actors still thought it was the only way to change features. The resultant film over the cotton lacked flexibility and hardened as the day passed. The surface could also be easily marred if pressed or dented.

Joe Blasco Sealer

Available in two types: **Clear** and **Flesh**. Both are matte and are used for all make-ups which require sealer. They can be used in place of liquid latex and painted over stretchable skin to pre-form naturally appearing stretch and stipple aging. The process can successfully be accomplished over already powdered "paint-powder" aging effects. Available in pints and gallons only.

RCMA Matte Plastic Sealer

Can be employed both as a surface sealer for wax buildups or as an adhesive for lifts. It can also be used in conjunction with other materials to cover eyebrows and seal latex pieces wherever a film former is required.

RCMA Clear Plastic Sealer

A fast-drying paintable or sprayable coating used to seal a specific area.

Fig. 2-10

WAXES

Dental Waxes

Black Carding Wax For blocking out teeth (toothless effect).

Red   For simulating gum tissue.

Ivory   A hard wax for forming temporary teeth.

Molding Waxes

Although some grades of mortician's wax may be used in make-ups, old nose putty is seldom used today. A new type of micro-synthetic wax material made by RCMA comes in various shades and is less affected by body warmth than the mortician variety.

P.M.A.* Plastic Wax Material

No-Color   A clear wax that can be tinted with RCMA Color Process Foundations.

White

Light   F-4 shade

Women   KW-3 color

Men   KT-3 color

Dark Skin   KN-5 color

Violet   Matches RCMA Color Process Violet and is used to make raised bruises.

Fig. 2-11

ARTIFICIAL BLOODS

The search for realistic-appearing human blood has led to the use of many products—from casein paints to food-colored syrups.

RCMA Bloods

Color Process Type A A water-washable material that is very realistic in appearance and flow. It is nontoxic, does not cake or dry, and looks fresh for some time.

Color Process Type B A resin plastic formulation designed for use where a blood effect must remain in place and not run during a long scene. It is solvent-based and sets quickly, remaining shiny and fresh-flowing in appearance. It is removed with RCMA Adhesive Remover or **ADKLEN**.

Color Process Type D A rapid-drying liquid suspension of a brownish tone employed to simulate dried blood on bandages. Not for any fresh blood effect or skin use.

Fig. 2-12

Joe Blasco Bloods

Joe Blasco produces two varieties of realistic-appearing artificial human blood for motion picture, television, and stage use. Both blood types are non-staining and may be safely used in the mouth. Because they have no artificial flavor, they are not distracting to the actor during serious performance, unlike some other theatrical bloods, which are available in a variety of candy and fruit flavors. Joe Blasco blood products may be thinned with distilled water for use in plastic tubing for various bleeding effects. They may also be thickened with corn syrup, Cabosil, and/or liquid gelatin to produce a blood gel. These bloods may be used alone or mixed together to produce varying shades to suit the requirements of the film stock or television electronic process.

JB-Classic Artificial Blood Clear, realistic venous (unoxygenated) blood for general purposes. Simulates blood from a punctured, cut, or lacerated vein.

JB-Bright Blood Bright orange-red opaque blood. Simulates blood from an arterial injury. The blood of choice for low-light photography or for use on dark skin.

Joe Blasco Bloods are particularly effective, as they do not stain like some other varieties of artificial blood liquids.

Joe Blasco Cosmetics also creates special **Gel-Blood** products in the above types, as well as glittered and iridescent **Alien Blood** in green, blue, and custom colors.

There are a number of releases that can be applied to plaster, stone, and other mold materials that aid in separating the manufactured appliance:

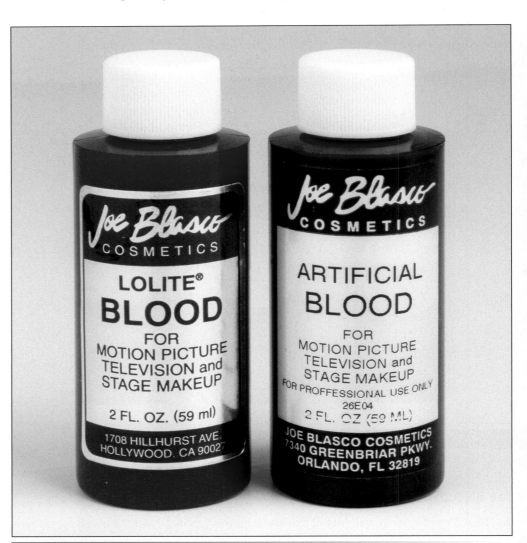

Fig. 2-13

Alginate Separator

Utilized as a water-soluble material for sculpture and mold-making procedures.

P.M.A. Silicone Mold Release

A silicone grease product used to ease separation of an appliance from a stone mold (such as RCMA P.M.A. Molding Material or Plastic Cap Material).

OTHER PRODUCTS

RCMA Artificial Tears and Perspiration

A clear liquid that can be used to simulate tears when placed below the lower edge of the tear duct. It can also be stippled or sprayed on the skin to simulate perspiration. Avoid eye contact.

RCMA Beard-setting Spray

A solvent-based artificial latex material that is used to set pre-made laid hair beards on forms. Not for facial use as a spray.

Color Tints

Fig. 2-14

Colloidal colors utilized for intrinsic coloration when manufacturing latex prostheses. (The color pigments are not for skin use.) A few drops in latex will tint the material. Available in a variety of shades.

Gelatin Capsules

Obtainable in various sizes from most drugstores. They can be filled with RCMA Color Process Type "A" Blood and then crushed with the fingers or in the mouth for blood flow effects. Do not pre-fill these for future use, because the artificial bloods will soften them too much.

Hair Whiteners

RCMA makes four shades of cream-style hair whiteners: **HW-1**, **Grayed White**; **HW-2**, **Pinked White**; **HW-3**, **Ochre White**; and **HW-4**, **Yellow White**. In addition, a **Super-white** can be used for highlighting. These are for small areas of whitening only, and full head graying or whitening should be done with liquid sprays.

The Lamaur Company makes the following shades of liquid sprays in cans: White, Beige, Silver, and Gray. It also makes other hair colors such as Brown, Black, Blonde, Auburn, Light Brown, and Gold, as well as Pink and Green for special effects. Very realistic hair changes can be made with these sprays.

Joe Blasco **Liquid** and **Cream Hair White** are available as follows: **Orange** for whitening black hair; **Pink** for brown hair; **Off-White** for blonde hair; and **Yellow** for red hair.

Eyelash Adhesive

A special low-ammonia latex form that has excellent adhesive qualities for attaching strip and individual lashes. It can be used as an edge stipple for latex appliances.

Old Age Stipple

A compound containing latex made specifically for wrinkling the skin. Not just any latex material will act in the same manner. RCMA Old Age Stipple is made in four regular shades: **KW-2**, **KW-4**, **KM-2**, and **KN-5**. Other colors are available on special order.

P.M.A. Molding Material

P.M.A. materials are made by RCMA for professional use and encompass some interesting new special products. P.M.A. Molding Material is a paint-in type of plastic for making small or flat appliances. It dries rapidly and builds up well. It is supplied in four shades: **Light (KW)**, **Deep (KM)**, and **Dark (KN)** colors, as well as **Clear**.

Plastic Cap Material

The lightly tinted variety is used for making plastic bald caps and fronts. It is also available in **Clear** for coating plastalene sculpture.

P.M.A. Press Molding Material

A clear, heavy liquid employed to make press-molded appliances. Also comes in different shades.

Scar Material

Fig. 2-15

A slightly tinted material with a tinge of pink color that dries semi-matte upon application to form realistic incised scars. Can be removed from the skin with RCMA Adhesive Remover or ADKLEN. Because it irritates some sensitive skin as a result of its fast-drying quality, it should be tested on each individual.

Scar or Blister-making Material

A molding plastic type that can be formed into keloid scar tissue or dropped on the skin with a spatula to simulate second degree blister burns or other effects.

SPECIAL TOOLS

The following medical, dental, and hair tools are used by make-up artists:

College Pliers

Six-inch stainless steel curved tip dental pliers (large tweezers) are best for handling false lashes, small prostheses, and other items.

Dental Spatulas

The stainless steel 2½-inch blade spatula is excellent for mixing colors, stirring liquids (such as stipples), and removing make-up to be placed on a plastic tray or disposable butter chip for individual portions of lip color from a container, etc.

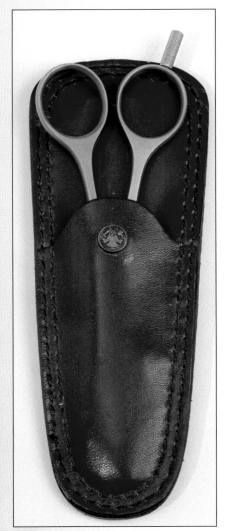

Fig. 2-16

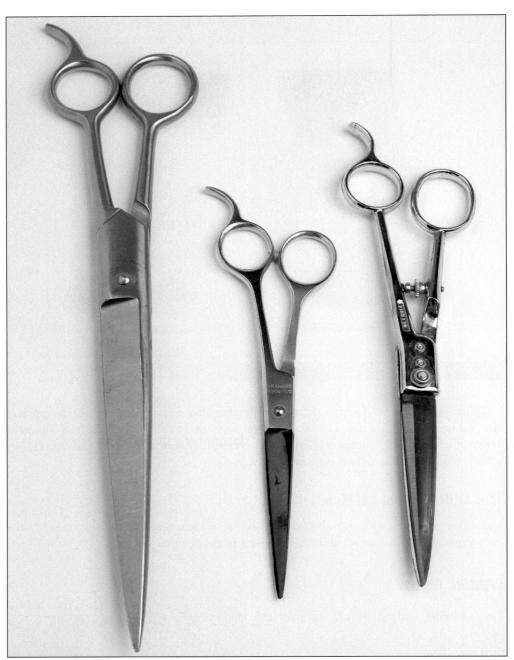

Fig. 2-17

Scissors

Hair Scissors Get the best available, keep them sharp, and only use them to cut hair. The 3-inch barber's style is most useful on brows, sideburns, nape hair, and for trimming artificial eyelashes.

Straight Scissors A good pair with short blades for cutting all other materials, such as plastic and fabric, is best.

Curved Scissors Surgical, stainless steel with a 1½-inch blade length are best for cutting curves on latex or plastic appliance trimming, artificial lashes, brows, and ear and nose hair.

Pinking Shears A small pair of these for trimming lace on prepared hair goods should be part of a make-up artist's hair kit. They are also useful for trimming lifts (if a pinked edge is desired) and for cutting templates for fantasy airbrush make-ups.

Comb

An aluminum rat-tail comb with widespread, unserrated teeth for hair work.

Acetone

A highly volatile liquid that is one of the main solvents in adhesives, sealers, and prosthetic plastics. Also used for cleaning the lace portion of hair goods after use, as well as reusable lifts.

Fig. 2-18

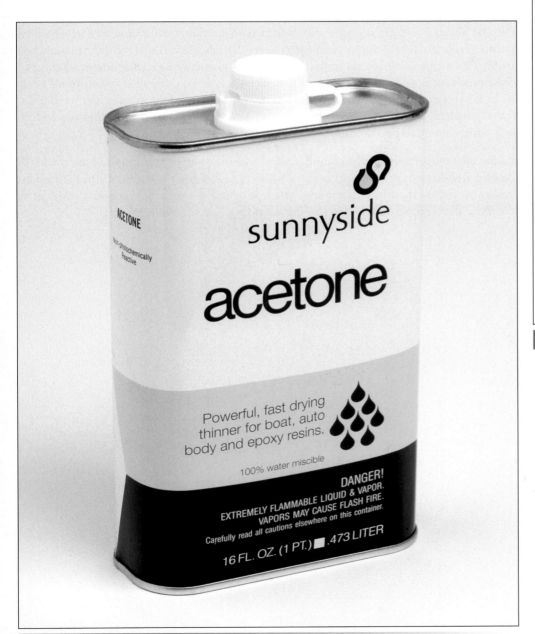

Fig. 2-19

Adhesive Tape

Some new varieties of this old material are translucent and porous with excellent adhesion. The 1-inch width is best. Very useful in making fast handmade lifts.

BUYER BEWARE

Today, there is a growing tendency for beauty suppliers, salons, and make-up boutiques to design generic, proprietary make-up products that tout the name of the store in which they appear. These private labels and brand names are produced by cosmetics manufacturing laboratories that specialize in creating personalized brands of make-up. In most cases, their products are much less expensive and lower in quality than the superior professional-grade products, which are manufactured to precise specifications by companies that understand the needs of the professional make-up artist. These house names can even be found in beauty supply stores, which tend to offer a wide variety of professional products that are simply augmented with the private label brand bearing the name of their store. The astute professional make-up artist will normally recognize the marketing of these products as a ploy developed by the store owners attempting to reap additional profits by selling a substandard substitute. These products are often not limited to foundations, powders, or lip and eye colors; often professional products such as adhesives, sealers, and other such materials are subject as well.

Unfortunately, some store owners and professional make-up distributors will use the high-quality, well-known professional brand cosmetics to lure their customers into their establishments, while their sales personnel attempt to sell as much of the house product as possible. The authors simply defer to the old adage, *Let the buyer beware.*

Chapter 3

NATURAL AND FOAM RUBBER
HISTORY AND TECHNIQUE

Chapter 3

FOAM USE

The Beginning of Foam Use in Motion Pictures

Early Foam Use

MODERN FOAM

Chemistry of Modern Foam

Types of Mixers and Their Uses

Mold-filling

Types of Mold Materials

Demolding, Washing, and Storage

Seaming and Patching

Tips for Running Foam Latex

Gil Mosko Application

Chapter 3

NATURAL AND FOAM RUBBER HISTORY AND TECHNIQUE

Drafted by the authors from information generously submitted by Gil Mosko.

Natural gum latex, or rubber, has been known to mankind since prehistoric times. Central and South American natives would coat the bladder of a goat with sap from the South American rubber tree, or *Hevea brasiliensis*. When dried over a smoky fire, this coating made a resilient and springy skin, and imparted a bounce to the bladder. The resulting early soccer ball was used in serious tribal games, which were played over a period of days. The losing team was put to death. In the 1600s, Spanish explorers learned how to cut into the trunks of certain trees to make the milky sap ooze out. They coated their capes with sap in order to make them waterproof, but the Spaniards found the same disadvantage as had the natives: This untreated rubber would become sticky with heat, brittle with cold, and eventually would rot.

By the late 1700s, the English had become interested in this unusual material. In 1770, the English chemist, Priestley, gave this material the name rubber, since it would rub off pencil marks. In 1791, a patent was issued to Samuel Peal for the adhesive he acquired by putting dried rubber into turpentine. At this time, only dried rubber was available to Europeans, since there was no known method of preserving the raw latex for shipment from the New World to Europe. This dried rubber had been subjected to smoke as a means of partially preserving it for the trip overseas. The smoked sheet could be placed between strong rollers and masticated in a process developed by Thomas Hancock in England. Through mastication, the rubber would become soft and pliable and could then be molded into shapes. Thomas Hancock also cut rubber into long strips and invented the rubber band in 1823. Up until this point, there had been no satisfactory process to give the finished pieces long life. In time, they would become brittle, losing both strength and resiliency.

It is an American, Charles Goodyear, who is credited with inventing the process of vulcanization. In 1839, he found that rubber in the presence of sulfur and heat would cure into a more desirable material. The newly vulcanized rubber would become neither sticky with heat nor brittle with cold. His patent was granted in 1855 and shared with Thomas Hancock.

The English were not only world explorers—they also had an eye for commerce. Realizing the potential for this new material, they set out to develop rubber plantations. This was accomplished over a period of decades and is testimony to the tenacity of the English spirit. On a sailing ship in 1876, Sir Henry Wickham carried 70,000 seeds of the *Hevea brasiliensis* tree from the forests of Brazil back to England. These seeds were taken to Kew

Gardens in London, where only a few germinated. These sprouts were grown, potted, and carried aboard a freighter to Ceylon (now known as Sri Lanka), where they grew vigorously. From there, twenty-two cuttings were carried to Singapore.

By 1888, over a thousand adult trees were growing on the Malay Peninsula. At that time, Henry Ridley took over the Singapore Gardens. It was Ridley's idea to replace coffee, the major agricultural crop, with the slow-growing rubber trees. This earned him the name of Mad Ridley. The reason Ridley opted for rubber crops was because of his insight into the success of the pneumatic tire, newly invented by John Dunlop in England. Ridley felt that this invention would create a huge market. He, of course, was right, and this would mark the beginning of a worldwide industry supplied by the rubber plantations. England's colonies in the tropics became fertile ground for the propagation of rubber trees, and eventually plantations spread through Malaysia, Indonesia, Thailand, Sri Lanka, and all of Indochina. Colonies in Africa were also established, the largest being in Liberia.

Throughout the remainder of the nineteenth century, dried smoked sheet was the only type of rubber being commercially imported into Europe and the United States. Even after the discovery in 1857 of ammonia as a preservative, liquid latex was too expensive to transport as a result of the low solids content (only 36-percent) of the tree sap. It was not until the twentieth century that two methods of concentrating the latex were developed.

The first was **creaming**. Because the tree sap consists of rubber particles suspended in a **serum** layer of mostly water, given enough time the rubber will separate toward the top of the container. To accelerate this process, a natural gum, Irish moss, which made the rubber particles float to the surface much faster, was added. The serum layer could be drained from the bottom of the container, and a latex was produced with 67- to 68-percent solids content. The ammonia preservative in this latex gave a pH of 10.6 to 10.8. Even today, this process is done by the batch and remains time-consuming.

The second method of concentrating the latex is by **centrifuging**, whereby the latex flows into a chamber that has many hollow vanes. When the chamber is operated at high speed, the denser serum is forced to the perimeter, where it flows out openings in the vanes. The less dense rubber is forced to the center, where it flows into a center outlet tube. By concentrating in this way, latex can be produced with a solids content of 60-percent. Furthermore, this is a continuous-feed process, which makes it particularly efficient.

Because there was now a greatly improved concentration of rubber in the latex, it became commercially viable, and a worldwide industry came into being. Dipped goods, such as rubber gloves, used thousands of tons of latex every year. New applications were developed, and plantations flourished.

Current production techniques do not vary much from the original methods. To gather the latex, a cut is made into the bark of the tree. Under this slanted incision is placed a metal or earthenware cup. Sap slowly drips out from the cut and into the collection cup. A total of about four ounces is collected per tree, every other day. One can see that millions of trees are needed to obtain quantities of latex for shipping. Tapping is done in the morning. The contents of the cups are collected into bulk containers and then brought to the collection station, where ammonia is added. Without this addition of ammonia, the latex would become a medium for bacterial growth and would be rendered useless in less than 12 hours. The collection stations have 1,000-gallon tanks. Tanker trucks then carry the latex to the central plant. More ammonia is added, and the latex becomes ready for concentrating. The creaming process yields latex with a solids content of 68-percent, while the centrifuging process yields latex with a solids content of 60-percent.

Today the largest producers of natural rubber are Malaysia, Indonesia, Thailand, and Liberia. About 95-percent of all the rubber produced is centrifuged latex, primarily used for dipped goods such as gloves and condoms. Only about five-percent or less of all the production is creamed latex, and the majority of this is used in the elastic thread industry.

FOAM USE

THE BEGINNING OF FOAM USE IN MOTION PICTURES

Theatrical actors, in addition to actors in the very first films, customarily did their own make-up work, including crepe wool application for facial hair and the application of greasepaints that came from Europe. Many actors became quite adept at these arts and often traded techniques with each other. Still, these techniques were guarded from the outside world as trade secrets.

In 1935, Charles Schram started working at MGM Studios. He was hired by MGM's Make-up Department Head, Jack Dawn. At that time, any appliance work was done by constructing pieces on the actor's face with collodion, liquid latex, and/or LePage glue, which was then colored with greasepaints. Jack Pierce's masterful make-up on Boris Karloff for the Frankenstein Monster was done this way. The only other way to create an appliance was by using mortician's wax, commonly called **nose putty**, and carefully stippling greasepaint onto the wax. Both methods had their drawbacks. The collodion and cotton constructions were inflexible, took a long time to build, and were difficult to remove. Nose putty, alternately, was an impermanent choice, as it never hardened.

Max Factor was the only supplier, and the company's products consisted of greasepaints, spirit gum, and collodion, both flexible (for scars) and non-flexible (for cotton constructions). The head of Factor's lab was Max Fierstein, and he would talk with Jack Dawn about the development of products.

For *The Good Earth* in 1938, MGM needed to create hordes of bald Chinese-looking characters. The early bald caps were made by dissolving nitrate film stock in acetone and plasticizing this mixture with a little castor oil. The caps had a shelf life of only about half a day before they would dry and crack. MGM employed some young men to make these bald caps at night for the next day's filming. The make-up artists would apply the fresh caps in the morning, and by afternoon most had become brittle and had broken down. When there were too few characters remaining to continue filming, the set would wrap for the day.

There was a need for a flexible material that could be used to fabricate appliances. The development of early flexible appliances was begun with glue. A particular type of mucilage* came in small cakes. These cakes could be heated in a double boiler and softened, then spooned into a mold, where the positive and negative were clamped together and held tightly. When the glue had cooled, the mold could be opened, and a reasonably good appliance was demolded. These appliances remained flexible and were adhered to the skin with spirit gum. Because of the proteinaceous composition of the glue, the appliances behaved much like our modern day gelatin appliances. Sweat, rain, or any source of moisture would ruin the pieces, and they often needed replacement throughout the day. This glue went by the name of **eye material** and was used in the fabrication of pieces that would resemble Chinese-looking eyelids for the characters.

*A thick, glue-like substance often produced by plants.

After *The Good Earth*, the next improvement marked a technological breakthrough of sorts. By that time, Max Factor had developed a product called **cap material**, which consisted of vinyl resin dissolved in solvent, with the addition of some plasticizer. It was used as a sealer to blend the edges of the nitrate film bald caps. Josef Norin, a sculptor at MGM, accidentally poured some of this cap material into a bucket of water. The cap material congealed into a mass. After picking the blob out of the water, Mr. Norin discovered that by kneading it, the cap material would thicken to the consistency of chewing gum. He also found that by putting this thickened cap material into a mold and clamping, he could create flexible plastic appliances. These were the first vinyl appliances, and they worked very well for small thin pieces, such as ears and eyelids. They were adhered with spirit gum, and the edges were melted away with acetone. Thick pieces would not work, because the solvent was unable to escape them, leaving the interior soft, gummy, and dangerously filled with solvent.

EARLY FOAM USE

In the 1930s, two major processes of manufacturing foam rubber were developed. The **Talalay Process** used the catalytic decomposition of hydrogen peroxide as a means of foaming the rubber. The rubber was then frozen, gelled with carbon dioxide, and heated in order to **vulcanize**. The **Dunlop Process** was patented in 1929, and by 1931, the first bulk shipment of centrifuged latex arrived in England. This process was done by the batch in large bakery-type mixers with 120-quart bowls and wire whisks, which would whip air into the mix. Late in the mix cycle, gelling agent was added, and the foam was poured into molds. When the molds were closed and the **gelation** complete, heat was applied to vulcanize the foam. This method was eventually updated to use continuous-feed machinery. Mattresses, car seats, pillows, and the like were made this way. A modernized version of the Dunlop Process is what we use today in make-up labs.

In the same decade, MGM's prop shop needed to make dummy horses. At that time, all the process shots of actors riding horses in close-up were done using fake horses. Jack Dawn, always on the lookout, had the prop department contact Firestone Rubber in order to acquire some Dunlop Process type of foam latex compound. They were sent a two-component kit, which consisted of a pail of liquid latex and a smaller container of cure paste. Employees of the prop shop found that by using liquid hand soap in the mixture, they could whip the latex into froth. This froth was then poured into molds, and after some time, it gelled into a solid. The molds were then put into a brick-lined oven from the plaster shop and heated for several hours. To everyone's great delight, flexible foam parts were removed from the molds. This material was not easy to manipulate. According to Charles Schram, it contained enough ammonia for initial stability, and then boom!, it would gel.

The timing of the batches was imprecise, and the mold filling was hectic, but for a good while, satisfactory foam pieces were produced. The lifespan of the finished foam was not long, and after a few weeks, it would turn to powder. Still, the prop shop had sculpted individual muscles of the horses, and these foam pieces were used to cover the mechanical moving parts. Then paint and hair were applied to the surface, and a very believable horse, which moved realistically under the actor riding it, could be produced. Since there were many Westerns made during this period, there was a constant need for this kind of foam. No attempt was made to soften it. It was flexible, but too stiff for facial appliances.

After *The Good Earth*, Charles Schram spent a lot of time in the lab at MGM. A film was coming up that required midgets to wear fur-covered foam ears that were supposed to move. He devised a system whereby telescoping brass tubing built into the ears was connected to plastic tubes running to squeeze-bulbs in the actor's pockets. When squeezed by the actor, the bulbs created air pressure that controlled the movement of the brass tubing, and thus the forward motion of the ears. This is one of the earliest examples of mechanized appliance work in film.

While Charles Schram was working at MGM, a gentleman named George Bau was at Warner Brothers. Perc Westmore, Make-up Department Head at Warner Brothers, had hired George to develop a foam for the prop shop. By 1939, when MGM was making *The Good Earth*, George was beginning work on *The Hunchback of Notre Dame*, which was actually produced by RKO. The foam used was probably the same as the foam used in the MGM prop shop for horse dummies. Charles Laughton's hump was made with this foam, but some artists say that the facial appliances were fabricated using silk and collodion. According to these old stories, the eye was actually painted onto this silk construction, and eyelashes were added. One of the authors disagrees, however, as the face, according to Bau in a private conversation just before his death, consisted of foam latex with an inserted glass eye.

By this time, Firestone had improved its commercial foam and called it Lo-Tol 531. Also available were foams from B.F. Goodrich, Naugatuck, and Uniroyal. These were all three-component foams available by the gallon. The three-component system featured latex mixed with potassium oleate soap, separate components of curing agent, and gelling agent. This type of system was far superior to the foam used in the prop shop for the horses. The timing could be worked out so that results could be duplicated; a softer, more flexible foam resulted from the increased frothing action and higher foam volume. The cell structure was slightly coarse, and the flexibility was less than that of modern foams, but quite acceptable pieces could be produced.

Uniroyal's successor became a company called R&D Latex, which produced foam that was widely used. When the character of Mr. Spock came along, Fred Phillips from Paramount asked Charles Schram to make the ears. Charlie enjoyed his side job of manufacturing the Spock ears and selling them to Fred. The R&D foam was in extensive use by then. During later shows, John Chambers also fabricated ears for the Spock character.

Experimentation to soften the foam was conducted at MGM and at Warner Brothers. A known technique was to add mineral oil to the foam as a plasticizer. According to Charlie, the resulting foam had very fine cells and was quite soft. Unfortunately, the mineral oil attacked the rubber, making it rot in two or three days. If pieces were kept tightly sealed in jars, they would only last for about a week before becoming diseased-looking and gummy. The grayish color could be masked with castor oil greases, but after a while, the pieces became too rotted.

Another softening method involved the use of **mold separator**. A common one consisted of stearic acid dissolved in kerosene. Charlie experimented with this by adding mold separator—kerosene and all—into the foam. The resulting foam became finer, but it was thick and very hard to pour. Too much of the stearate mixture could not be included, for the resulting foam would be so thick that it proved unusable.

During this period, George Bau was working with foam. He was a brilliant innovator and was able to overcome the rotting problem. Through talks with the R.T. Vanderbilt Company, George was able to learn which other kinds of oil would be compatible with the foam. Castor oil—a vegetable oil with high viscosity as it is—was the choice. In reality, castor oil is not really an oil—it is a fatty acid that plasticizes rubber without rotting it. George developed a way to emulsify castor oil with water and other fatty acids in order to make soap. This soap was the foaming agent used to whip the foam into froth. It not only produced fine cells, but it also imparted a soft, silky feel to the finished pieces. This foam cured in a reasonable amount of time and was relatively easy to use. George was not a man

Fig. 3-1

The Bau Flask and Bau Screw.

to take notes, probably driven by his intense need to protect his formulas. There were thus no written instructions for using this foam, which George implemented for many films throughout the 1950s.

George had a unique method of mixing foam. Sunbeam Mixmasters were essentially the same then as they are now, featuring two sets of flat blades that rotate in opposite directions and fit closely with the contour of the Sunbeam bowl. George opted for the use of a special spiral whisk. He had the prop shop cut the flat blades off the Sunbeam mixer assembly, leaving the bare axle that fit into the mixer motor. Then, a set of bent spiral wires was welded onto this axle. This intriguing device is commonly known as the **Bau Screw**.

This whisk was inserted into the Sunbeam mixer motor but was used alone—there were not two opposing whisks. For a bowl, George used a tall, cylindrical stainless steel flask, which rotated on the Sunbeam bowl platform. The whisk had less beating action than the Sunbeam's own mixing blades, and the narrower flask had less surface area than the Sunbeam bowl. In this way, George reasoned, he could more accurately control the rate of ammonia evaporation. At that time, the foam was whipped to a volume of 3 to 3½, which is less than today's typical 4 to 5 volumes used by most labs.

By the 1960s, George had begun to sell his foam commercially. It was more expensive than the Uniroyal foam. It was not until the 1970s that the Bau foam became popular. Stuart Freeborn imported George's foam to England for use on *2001: A Space Odyssey*. Hollywood artists then began using it.

By that time, George had retired from Warner Brothers. On a fateful day in 1974, Charlie Schram went to George's house to pick up a gallon of foam for a current project, only to find that George had piled all of his lab equipment and supplies in a heap in the middle of the floor. George informed Charlie that he was stopping production. George had sold his house and was moving away. In the middle of a film and desperate, Charlie asked if he could buy the remains of the foam components and the formula. George refused. Still desperate, Charlie continued to plead his case, and after two or three hours, George agreed to sell the formula and the rest of his supplies for a few hundred dollars! Because no written formula existed, George dictated information, and Charlie took notes. The formula and manufacturing procedure were sketchy, but Charlie was able to get enough information to begin testing of his own.

An unsung hero of the foam world, Charlie Schram did a great amount of testing to regenerate a good foam formula. His work yielded a very good product, which he called Windsor Hills Foam. Charlie manufactured his fine product for about ten years, until he retired from the business.

MODERN FOAM

The current foam industry is led by a company founded by Gil Mosko. GM Foam, Inc. is a leader in the innovation of the modern foam system. In 1984, Mosko began testing formulations that would perform to meet the requirements of the make-up labs in Los Angeles. After extensive research, he developed foam with all of the good qualities of Bau's and Schram's foams. In addition, it was much easier to use. Up until then, foam latex always maintained an air of unpredictability—sometimes it would gel properly, and other times it would not. The new GM Foam offered the advantage of working dependably all the time. During the late 1980s and into the 1990s, this foam became (and remains) the standard of the industry.

Concurrent with this development arose a huge global demand for more latex in the medical industry. AIDS had become epidemic, resulting in greater degrees of precaution by medical practitioners. Doctors, dentists, nurses, police officers, and many others began wearing latex gloves. In addition, the use of condoms to prevent sexually transmitted diseases became necessary. A worldwide need for latex ensued. The discrepancy between available centrifuged and creamed latex grew even more. Stresses on the rubber trees and increased production demands in the fields caused the quality and availability of good, fresh creamed latex to diminish. Almost all of the latex was being centrifuged, and the quality of the creamed latex was suffering. Malaysian rubber processing plants, in an effort to speed production, began adding more and more creaming agent in order to speed the production time. This practice, although insignificant to the elastic thread industry, had profound consequences for the foam latex industry. The Irish moss creaming agent in the latex had been replaced with ammonium alginate, which in too great an amount caused finished foam pieces to have an inherent tackiness; when the individual cells in the foam were squeezed together, they would slightly stick to each other, causing a slow return (cell tack). In addition, any raw liquid latex in containers would continue the accelerated creaming process. Foam users had to constantly shake the containers in order to prevent the latex from separating.

During this period there were additional problems with which the foam industry had to cope. Rubber trees, long stressed to increase production, were experiencing more variation in the composition of the sap. Producers were shipping latex that possessed tremendous variation in composition. Logistical problems caused latex to become old before it was shipped.

In 1998, something revolutionary transpired. Having experienced problems with the rubber companies for years, Mosko made a radical departure in formulation. Centrifuged latex—with a solids content that was too low for use in foam—had always been overlooked as a means of formulation. Mosko discovered a method for concentrating fresh centrifuged latex—without the addition of any creaming agents—to a solids content of 68-percent. When stabilized with a blend of soaps, pH-adjusted, and KOH-adjusted, this centrifuged latex could be blended with creamed latex to yield a product that possessed never-before-seen advantages. This blend contained far less sodium alginate, hence fewer separation problems and longer shelf life. The centrifuged latex had a rejuvenating effect on the creamed latex, giving it increased mechanical stability. The resulting foam cells (the little bubbles that comprise foam) were smaller and more regular. Resulting foam pieces had more realistic wrinkling when actors moved their faces. Seeing the potential for greater quality, Mosko worked with a major rubber bureau office in London and the plantation importers to ensure that the latex arriving in the United States was of good quality. There was finally a voice in the industry that demanded higher quality for this segment of the industry.

This new GM Foam marked a milestone in development. A tireless experimenter, Mosko tuned his curing agent to be as fast as possible without risk of overcuring. He created helpful adjuncts to the foam system, most notably a flow increaser that would allow very high volume foams to remain pourable. This can be of crucial importance in the avoidance of trapped air bubbles in a foam piece. The foam system became so dependable that even first-time users had only to read and follow the instructions to obtain excellent results. At the present time, most feature films and television shows that require foam utilize GM Foam.

CHEMISTRY OF MODERN FOAM

Natural Hevea latex has a typical composition of the following:

Contents	Percentage
Total solids	36 (including a dry rubber content of 33-percent)
Proteins	1 to 1.5
Resins	1 to 1.5
Ash	Less than 1
Sugars	1
Water	About 60

The rubber molecule consists of cis-1, 4-polyisoprene. This is a long chain molecule, or **polymer**, consisting of up to a million repeating units. The actual molecule looks like a long, loosely coiled strand, with loops and curves occurring in a random fashion. This long coiled shape is what gives the material—even when uncured—its elasticity.

In its liquid environment, the rubber molecules are isolated from their neighbors by a thin layer of soap-like material, or **stabilizer**. Molecules of the much smaller soap are attracted to the surface of the rubber, with their **hydrophobic** ends facing inward toward the rubber, and their **hydrophilic** ends facing outward, toward the water. This tiny **micelle** can almost be thought of as a dandelion flower, with the rubber in the center and the soap molecules radiating outward like the dandelion seeds.

Without this stabilizer, the rubber particles would become stuck to one another, and eventually the rubber would coagulate into a hard lump. The stabilizer allows tiny particles of rubber to be isolated from their neighbors, producing a homogeneous, free-flowing fluid. This affects all phases of the rubber's behavior in whatever processing method will follow.

The free flow of air between the cells gives the cured foam the ability to immediately return to shape after it is pressed. This property is called **rubber memory**.

Controlling the gelation process is of primary importance to the foam technician. The foam must gel slowly enough for molds to be filled, yet it must gel fast enough so that the cells do not break down. To complicate matters further, the process is sensitive to temperature and humidity. Higher temperatures and higher humidity cause faster gelling. *(For an explanation of this phenomenon, see the Advanced Notes at the end of this chapter.)* The foam technician, with a little bit of experience, can adapt to changing atmospheric conditions. Instruction sheets for foam products often list schedules for a wide range of temperatures.

After the molds have been filled and the foam has gelled, the molds are replaced in an oven and heated to 185°F for approximately three hours. During this time the curing agent turns into a vapor and vulcanizes the rubber. If finished pieces are springy, the foam is cured. Undercured pieces will have a slow return when pressed. Overcured pieces will lack tear strength. Cure times can be adjusted accordingly to compensate for under- or overcured pieces.

The curing process is a chemical reaction that produces **crosslinking**. As we learned earlier, the rubber molecule is a long chain **polymer** that has a carbon backbone. The chain-like shapes of these molecules allow free movement of the strands, resulting in the stretchiness of dried rubber. Without the crosslinking, however, the rubber will have no memory. The sulfur in the curing agent is activated by **accelerators** and seeks out the carbons in the rubber. A sulfur bond is formed between two carbon atoms and acts as a crosslink between two rubber chains. It is this link that causes the rubber to have memory and return to its shape when pressed. Another benefit is that the rubber is now far less susceptible to oxidation and degradation from air, light, and ozone.

There is no scientific way to predict the amount of cure time a mold will need. Experience will help in estimating the cure time. Usually, small molds will take 2½ to 3 hours at 185ºF. If the foam is cured fully, it will spring back to shape immediately after pressing it. A sluggish return means that the next run will require additional time in curing. Start by adding an extra half-hour.

Convection ovens are the preferred types to use, since circulating air heats the molds much more efficiently than still air. Many labs use commercial ovens. The small studio can often be sufficiently equipped with only a small household convection oven, such as a Farberware. These ovens hold a full face-size mold or several small molds and can be purchased at appliance stores. Microwave ovens are inappropriate for curing foam, since their temperatures are impossible to regulate. Any stone mold that had water in it could be heated to greater than steam temperature and cause an explosion. For full head molds, a larger oven will be needed.

CAUTION: Your home oven should never be used for foam curing. At oven temperatures, the curing agent creates a vapor, which cures the foam. This vapor is toxic and will contaminate the interior of the oven. Future heatings will re-volatize the residue, and this vapor could poison food. Some people have reported success with Easy-Off Oven Cleaner when home ovens have been contaminated, but it is far safer to avoid home oven usage altogether.

Gary Boham is an oven specialist. He has published a book on oven design and is an authority on the subject. His book, *Foam Latex Ovens*, which is published by Alchemy Press (4100A Madison Street NE, Minneapolis, MN 55421-2811), covers heat, insulation, oven adaptation, and oven building, including wiring and all other specifications.

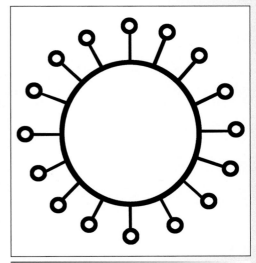

Fig. 3-2

Cis-1, 4, polyisoprene. Repeating units, where n=100,000 or more.

Fig. 3-3

The rubber micelle, consisting of a rubber particle surrounded by stabilized molecules.

TYPES OF MIXERS AND THEIR USES

By far the most popular mixers for foam use are the Sunbeam Deluxe Mixmaster and the Hobart KitchenAid. The Sunbeam uses two sets of flat blades, which turn in opposing directions, and the KitchenAid uses a wire whisk, which rotates in a planetary motion.

The basic unit of foam use is the 150-gram batch, or small Sunbeam bowlful.

Into the bowl are added 150 grams of latex base, 30 grams of foaming agent, and 15 grams of curing agent. 14 grams of gelling agent are weighed into a small cup and then set aside. The bowl is placed on the mixer, and the foam is processed according to the schedule supplied by the manufacturer. (Use a stopwatch to keep track of the time.) The blades whip the foam and also cause the bowl to turn in a clockwise direction. Usually, when the foam rises to about 1" from the rim of the bowl, the mixer's speed is decreased, and the foam is refined. When the time is right, the gelling agent is slowly dripped into the mix. The mixer bowl automatically turns clockwise.

When all the gelling agent has been added, the bowl is turned backwards, or counterclockwise, by hand for thirty seconds. This helps the gelling agent disperse evenly throughout the entire batch. Finally, the bowl is allowed to turn in its normal clockwise direction for another half-minute. The mixer is turned off, and the mixing head is raised to an upright position above the bowl. The foam adhering to the mixing blades is allowed to drain into the bowl, and the foam is ready for filling into molds. Later, when the foam has gelled, it easily pulls away from the mixer blades for cleaning.

The large Sunbeam bowl is used for larger batches. It can handle about 500 grams of latex base, but the usual batch is 375 to 450 grams. The procedure is the same as that used for the small bowl, except the mixing times are different. The instructions will include schedules for this type of bowl. The addition of gelling agent follows the same procedure—it is slowly dripped into the mix. The large bowl is also turned backwards by hand (*backbowled*)—in order to disperse the gelling agent—and is then allowed to run another half-minute or so. When the foam is ready, the mold-filling procedure is exactly the same as that used with the small bowl.

KitchenAid mixers work differently. The 5-quart mixer has a bowl that locks onto the pins of a forked receptacle, which holds the bowl and can be moved up and down with a handle on the mixer body. The whisk locks in place. The bowl and whisk must be attached and removed together; there is not enough space to slip the whisk off unless the bowl is also removed. This takes a bit of practice to accomplish comfortably. When it is time to add the gelling agent, it is slowly dripped down the perimeter of the bowl as the whisk is turning.

There is no way to backbowl this mixer, since the bowl is stationary. To disperse gelling agent into the dead spot in the center of the whisk, it is necessary to lower the bowl position several times while the mixer is turning at low speed. By doing this, foam drains out of the whisk and can be blended with the gelling agent in the bowl. With the careful lowering and raising of the blow, the gelling agent can be well dispersed.

In England, the Kenwood Mixer is often used. Its motion is the same as that of a Hobart Mixer: a planetary rotation of a single whisk. Also available are large Hobart Mixers. The most often used size is the 20-quart mixer, which allows batches of almost 5 gallons of whipped foam to be processed. Larger, restaurant-size mixers, with up to hundreds of gallons in capacity, are not widely used for foam.

Fig. 3-4

The small Sunbeam bowl.

Fig. 3-5

The large Sunbeam bowl.

Fig. 3-6

The Hobart 5-quart KitchenAid.

Fig.3-7

The Hobart 20-quart Bench Model Mixer.

MOLD FILLING

The most basic types of molds are two-piece appliance versions, which are used for small individual pieces: noses, foreheads, cuts, bruises, and any appliance that only partially covers the face. There exists both a mold positive, or **core**, and a mold negative, or **cap**. The basic 150-gram batch of foam will often fill several of these molds, so it is most efficient to have at least a few of them lined up and ready for filling. Both the positive and negative mold pieces have had mold release thinly painted onto them, which is allowed to dry. When the foam batch is ready, one can fill molds by either pouring directly form the bowl into the negative or by spooning an amount into the mold negative. The mold positive is then held directly over where it will fit onto the negative and slowly lowered into place. Care is taken to prevent the pieces from clapping shut. When the negative is allowed to close slowly, excess foam can easily flow out of the mold, often carrying stray air bubbles with it. When the negative does come into contact with the positive, the two pieces are pressed together firmly for a few seconds or held together with mold straps. The pressing together of the two mold pieces causes them to pinch the edge of the appliance, creating a very thin membrane. This type of filling is called **squash molding**.

Often the artist will have to fill a mold that has more than two pieces. In this case, there needs to be an **injection port**, or hole through one side of the mold (usually the positive) that will allow foam to enter the assembled mold.

It is useful to also have one or more bleeder holes for air venting. When the foam batch is ready, it is poured into a foam injector (often called an **injector gun**), and the tip of the

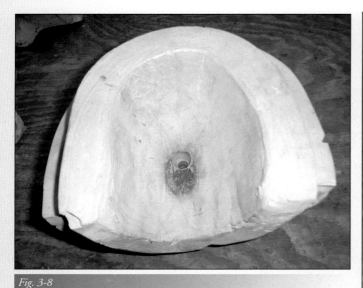

Fig. 3-8

Mold injection port.

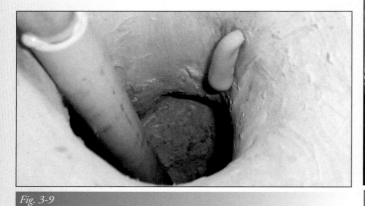

Fig. 3-9

Foam venting through bleeder holes.

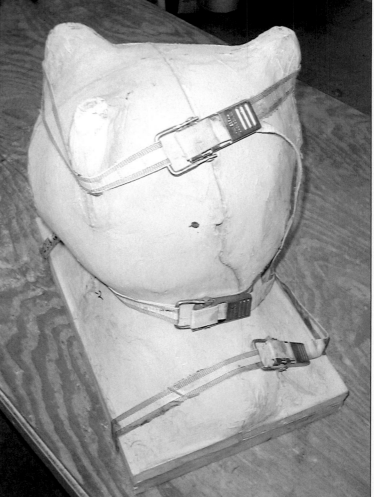

Fig. 3-10

Mold feet.

injector is placed onto the pre-drilled injection port. Foam is then injected into the interior of the mold by depressing the injector's plunger. As the foam fills the mold, air is allowed to escape through the bleeder holes. When the mold is filled, it is wise to shoot a little excess foam into the mold and allow some of this foam to ooze out through the bleeder holes. Many times, air bubbles, which are undesirable because they appear as holes in the finished piece, will be carried away with this excess foam bleeding.

Full head masks are best filled by drilling a ¾" hole through the top of the head on the positive mold piece. From the inside of the head, a section of PVC plastic pipe (½" inside diameter) can be mounted into the drilled hole with gentle tapping. Bleeder holes are usually drilled at the bottom of the neck, near the lower edge of the appliance. When the negative pieces are assembled and strapped or clamped in place, the whole mold can be inverted and stood on its head. Molds that have been designed with lugs at the top of the head can stand on these lug feet, while rounded head molds will need to be placed into a 5-gallon bucket or other device to keep them in place for injecting purposes.

When the foam batch is ready, it is poured into an injector, and the injector tip is inserted into the pre-mounted PVC pipe. Foam can then be shot into the mold, entering at the low point (the top of the head) and filling upwards. By looking into the interior of the mold core, one can watch the bleeder holes. When foam begins oozing out of the bleeder holes, the mold is filled.

If there are only a few bleeders, it is good to continue holding backpressure on the injector and bleeding foam for at least ten seconds to help flush out stray air bubbles. If there are many bleeder holes, it is good to use wet clay balls to plug the lower holes, leaving a few upper holes open for further venting of foam.

With any multi-piece mold, it is best to have the foam enter the mold at the lowest possible point and fill upwards. The bleeder holes should be at the uppermost point of the mold, and also in any protruding dead-end areas. The clever moldmaker will design the mold's parting line to cut across protrusions, such as fingertips. Scratches, which act as air vents, can then be cut through the case line.

If it is impossible to design the parting line across a protrusion, and a dead-end recess is created in the mold, it is still possible to fill this type of area. A $\frac{1}{16}$" diameter hole can be drilled through the deepest part of the interior with the use of a long aircraft drill bit. These bits are at least 6" long and can reach into many deep areas. The small hole will allow trapped air to exit the mold as foam fills the area. In the most extreme case, when it is impossible to drill any holes, deep recesses can be pre-filled with foam in the open mold and allowed to gel. The mold can then be closed, followed by running a new batch of foam and filling the mold as usual. The fresh batch of foam will completely bond to the pre-gelled foam and when cured, will be indistinguishable as a separate batch.

Often there will be a huge amount of detail in the interior of a mold. Some details are so irregular that foam flowing over the interior surface as it is injected will never properly fill them. The solution to this predicament is to fill the mold in separate batches. The first batch, which is usually small, is painted into the mold interior with a brush. It helps to first saturate the bristles of the brush with liquid dishwashing detergent before partially rinsing the soap out of the bristles with water. Only a thin film of soap remains, and the bristles are squeezed between the fingers to remove most of the water. The brush is left damp. This soaped brush prevents clumping of foam onto the bristles (which will occur for a dry, untreated brush) and allows the brush to be cleaned and reused. When the small batch of foam is ready, it is thinly painted onto the mold's interior surface with care to prevent any foam from slopping over the edge of the parting line.

This thin coating is allowed to gel before the mold is assembled as usual. The larger batch of foam is then mixed and injected. The fresh foam will completely bond to the already gelled skin. When the fresh batch of foam has gelled, the mold is placed in the oven and cured as normal. In the final cured piece, it is impossible to distinguish any demarcation between the two layers.

Sometimes, it is useful to have a tough skin, such as on the soles of the feet, on a portion of the finished piece. Foam latex base is stippled or painted into the area of the mold that needs it and allowed to dry. Second and even third coats can be used if needed, but it requires care to avoid lifting the existing film away from the mold surface when applying newer layers. When the skin is dry, the mold can be filled as usual. The foam will bond to the latex base skin. In the oven, the curing agent becomes volatile, and vapors will cure the latex skin, which alone contains no curing agent.

Fig. 3-11

Scratches through the case line for venting air.

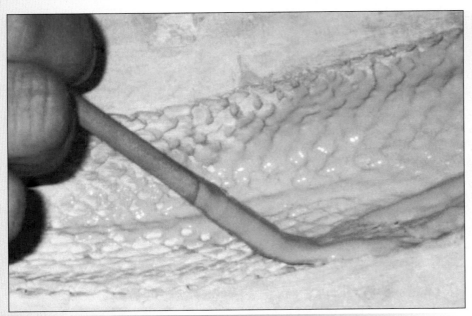

Fig. 3-12

Foam being painted into detail.

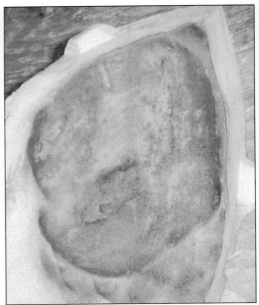

Fig. 3-13

Residue buildup.

Animatronic figures are subjected to tremendous movement. Often, they benefit from being reinforced with fabric. Full-head masks, which are taken on and off repeatedly, also benefit from reinforcement. The simplest and most effective way to accomplish this is to use the foot portion of nylon stockings or pantyhose, which when stretched over a head positive, completely cover it. The face area is usually cut away, and the perimeter of the cut can be adhered to the mold with latex base. There will be certain areas where the nylon is under tension and does not touch the mold, such as the throat area. These areas should be attached to the core. The former adhesive of choice was Dow Corning 355 Medical Adhesive, now replaced by several similar adhesives from Premiere Products. Joe Blasco Extra Strength Matte Adhesive or RCMA Matte Plasticized Adhesive works effectively but should be kept thin. Periodically, it will need to be cleaned from the mold core. Once the nylon fabric has been thoroughly attached to the mold core where needed, the mold can be assembled and filled with foam as usual. The liquid foam permeates the porous fabric and creates an unbelievably strong bond. The final tear strength of the cured foam bonded to the fabric is many times stronger than bare foam.

Another good material for reinforcing foam is **power net**, which is an elastic mesh used inside swimsuits. It has excellent elasticity and conforms well to curvatures because of its mesh construction. It can be found at many fabric stores.

TYPES OF MOLD MATERIALS

The most common molding material is Ultracal 30, manufactured by United States Gypsum (USG). It has excellent strength and accuracy when setting. Most foam molds are made using Ultracal and hemp or burlap for fiber. (George Bau used fiberglass rovings.)

Before using a new Ultracal mold, both the interiors of positive and negative mold pieces are treated. First, a light sealer is used. This can be prepared with paste wax (such as one produced by S.C. Johnson), which is thinned with 99-percent isopropyl alcohol. A useful ratio is as follows: one part wax to four or five parts alcohol. The resulting fluid is quite thin and can be brushed liberally onto the interior mold surfaces of positive and negative. When the alcohol has evaporated, the mold surface is brushed out with a dry brush, and a sheen develops. The mold is then put into the oven and baked out for several hours at 150° to 180°F. When the mold has cooled, another coat of **alcowax** is applied, dried, and brushed out. The mold is then ready for use.

A thin coat of mold release, furnished with the foam kit, is painted into the mold and allowed to dry before the mold is ready to be filled with foam. Sometimes the first foam piece will not be perfect as a result of the new mold's residual moisture, which can be limited with further alcowax applications. Moisture in new molds can cause an irregular pocked surface on the foam. As soon as the mold is dry and sealed, this will stop.

After repeated uses, Ultracal molds develop a buildup of brown residue. This residue is broken-down foaming agent, hardened by curing agent fumes. Molds can be cleaned with 99-percent alcohol and a short bristle brush. Disposable chip brushes can have their bristles cut with scissors to about ¾" for this purpose. Care should be taken not to press too hard or scrub too vigorously, as sculpting detail may be lost. When the mold is clean and all the alcohol has evaporated, the mold can be alcowaxed, and it is again ready for use.

Larger molds are sometimes made from fiberglass. This kind of mold presents problems for the foam user. The gel coat of the interior is non-porous. Furthermore, the polyester resin outgasses for weeks after the mold has been made. This type of mold interior creates the hazard of **steam laking** and does not allow the foam to stay in contact with it. During the curing process, pockets of steam can develop between the foam and the mold. These steam pockets push the foam away from the mold surface, making it cure in an odd shape. The finished piece will have a depressed area, which is lower than the rest of the piece, and the foam in this area will be denser than the rest of the piece.

Fig. 9-14

Steam laking.

There are several ways to prevent steam laking. The first and simplest way is to decrease the oven's cure temperature, but extra time will have to be added to the curing schedule to compensate for the lower temperature. If a typical mold cures in 3½ hours at 185°F, a fiberglass version of the same mold could take five or six hours at 165°F.

Sometimes lowering the cure temperature is not enough. Full bodysuit fiberglass molds can stubbornly continue to steam lake, even at lower cure temperatures. The solution is to pre-cure a skin of foam in the mold negatives. The mold negatives are usually filled with a thin skin of foam by painting it into the mold. After this skin has gelled, the mold negatives are placed in the oven open and cured at a low temperature. In some instances, a temperature as low as 125°F is used. Such low temperature cures may require ten hours. After the foam skin has been cured and the mold has been cooled, the mold is assembled and filled with foam, as usual. It is advisable to cure this fresh foam at a somewhat low temperature to prevent the first cured layer of foam from being overcured. A secondary cure temperature of 165° to 175°F is acceptable.

Mold release should not be used with fiberglass molds. An initial coating of alcowax is advisable, since it helps to seal the interior from the outgassing of the polyester resin. This plastic outgassing (*styrene monomer*) is believed to provide sites for steam accumulation, so one can see the value of an interior wax coating.

United States Gypsum also manufactures an epoxy system for use with Ultracal. Epoxical 415 Surface Coat Resin is a wonderful material to use for increasing the longevity of molds. This epoxy is an A + B system that is painted onto the sculpture as a face coat.

Second and third layers are used to build up thickness between ⅛″ and ¼″. The beauty of this epoxy system is its ability to cure against wet stone. After the last resin layer is painted, it is allowed to get tacky. Then hemp or burlap that is saturated with wet Ultracal is carefully pressed into the tacky resin. A mechanical bond develops when the epoxy cures. These molds are like any other Ultracal mold, except for the fact that they have a very durable plastic lining. The virgin surface of the epoxical interior is painted with alcowax, dried, and buffed with a brush or cloth. No further release is needed for this surface, although stone cores will require the usual mold release. Epoxical molds can steam lake and thus require curing at lower temperatures, although the occasional mold of this type can be cured at the normal 185°F with no ill effects.

Syntactic dough is an aerospace mold material often used for large molds. This is an epoxy system that has a face coat much like Epoxical 415. Onto the face coat is painted an epoxy laminating resin. Fiberglass cloth can be used with this resin in the same manner as polyester resins. For the bulk of the mold, however, an epoxy dough is used. This material is an A + B epoxy that has been filled with fibers and microballoons. The two parts are kneaded together (while the artist wears gloves), and when a uniform color is achieved, the dough can be patted into place onto the laminating resin layer. A buildup of ¼″ to ½″ is enough for most molds. When the dough has stiffened sufficiently, a cover coat of laminating resin is brushed on. These molds benefit from the use of strengthening ribs, which are built into the dough coating. The finished mold is slightly flexible at room temperature, and more so at curing temperatures. It helps to design some ribs to stiffen the shape. Even with the strengthening ribs, this type of mold needs to be well strapped or clamped in order to keep the flexing to a minimum. The lifespan of these molds is almost indefinite.

DEMOLDING, WASHING, AND STORAGE

Demolding foam pieces after curing is an important procedure. This is a stage where an otherwise perfect piece can be ruined by carelessness. It is of vital importance to be patient and focused.

After curing, molds are allowed to cool somewhat prior to opening. Never allow molds to cool to room temperature, because foam does not release when cool. A good target temperature is when the mold is just cool enough to handle without gloves. Molds are slowly opened by using a tool to pry the halves apart. A flat screwdriver is the simplest tool, but **mold-opening pliers** are better.

These pliers are essentially snap ring pliers, which are obtained from auto parts stores. As you squeeze the handles, the jaws of the pliers open. These jaws are inserted between mold halves, and the handles are squeezed to separate the mold.

As the mold halves are pried apart, it is common for areas of the appliance to stick to one side of the mold, while other parts of the appliance stick to the opposite side. With the use of a thin wooden sculpting stick, gently pull the entire appliance to one side of the mold. By freeing the foam from one side of the mold, the piece can be powdered and then carefully peeled away from the second part of the mold. It is often desirable to leave the flash attached to the finished piece. By having the flash intact, the thin edge of the appliance can remain flat and unfolded. The bulk of the flash can be cut away with scissors, while leaving just a small amount to hold the edge intact.

Demolded pieces should never be placed into Ziploc bags or other airtight containers until they have dried completely. A sulfurous, rotten egg odor develops from storing wet

Fig. 3-15

Mold-opening pliers.

foam this way as a result of residual curing agent in the foam, which outgases over time. Anyone who has ever done this once will never do it again! This vapor can be trapped in a Ziploc bag, and the resulting stench can be terrible. At the very least, foam pieces should be allowed to dry thoroughly before placement into containers. While drying, it is advisable to drape the foam over a surface that matches the appliance's contour. This will allow the piece to sit naturally while it dries and not create any wrinkles, which would become permanent if allowed to dry in place.

The best treatment for finished foam pieces is washing. A small amount of baby shampoo, dishwashing liquid, or other soap is added to a container of warm water. Foam pieces are immersed and then gently squeezed or pressed to work the soapy water into the foam. Next, the piece is rinsed in clear water in the same way. Gentle pressing is sufficient. Never wring the foam, or it may tear. Continue rinsing until no soap residue remains. This may require changing the rinse water a few times. Clean foam pieces are pressed (and not wrung) onto dry towels in order to remove as much water as possible and then draped over forms to dry. A convenient form for draping is a rolled towel. If face forms are available, they can be used. Any form is acceptable, as long as the foam piece can retain some of its own curvature while drying. It helps to turn on a fan in the vicinity of the drying pieces so that gently moving air can help to dry the foam without blowing the pieces away.

When entirely dry, pieces are best stored away from air and light. It is oxidation, catalyzed by ultraviolet light, which accounts for the degradation of foam over time. This is easily avoided by placing washed and dried pieces either into Ziploc bags that are then sealed, or into airtight plastic kitchen containers. The bags or containers should then be stored in a cabinet, box, drawer, or other place that does not admit light. When stored this way, pieces can last several years without showing any signs of aging. There are even fanatics who store their finished pieces in Ziploc bags in the freezer. The shelf life appears to be indefinite.

Large items, such as full-head masks, can be stored (after washing and drying) inside of black plastic trash bags, which are sealed shut. It helps to put some cushioning material inside of the heads to help retain the shape. Never leave anything sitting on top of stored foam pieces; a permanent indentation will develop, and the pieces will be ruined.

SEAMING AND PATCHING

When multiple-piece molds are used, the resulting foam pieces always have seam lines where the mold pieces join each other. If the mold pieces fit well, this seam line will be very narrow; if the mold pieces do not fit well, the resulting seam line can be quite thick. In any case, it must be removed. The first step is to carefully cut the foam seam away with a good pair of cuticle or medical scissors. Some people like to do this work under a magnifying lens to achieve the best results.

The remaining bit of seam line is melted away with the use of a **foam seamer**. To make one, start with a 25-watt soldering iron. The tip can be unscrewed and held with a pair of pliers, and the end can be pounded into a flat paddle shape by using a hammer. This flat shape can be rounded and refined with a file and sandpaper. It is recommended to add a slight bend in the tip of the flat area. When shaped satisfactorily, the tip is screwed back onto the soldering iron and is ready for use.

A 25-watt soldering iron heats to a recommended temperature for melting rubber. The iron requires several minutes of time to become hot but holds the heat indefinitely. By carefully touching this hot copper tip to the foam seam, rubber is melted away. It is important to use a fan that blows across the user in order to remove the subsequent small amount of smoke and strong smell of burning rubber. Adequate ventilation is also necessary for the removal of these noxious fumes. A light touch is crucial, as the hot iron can create gouges if used too heavily. Rubber that melts and sticks to the iron becomes burned, and a dark scale develops, which should be periodically removed with a wadded paper towel.

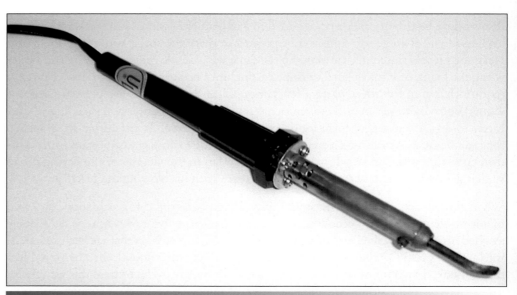

Fig. 3-16

Foam seamer.

Even the most careful seamer leaves some gouge marks in the foam. These are easily filled by first applying a stipple of Pros-Aide. When the Pros-Aide has dried, a dental spatula is used to trowel in thickened Pros-Aide, or Bondo, which is thick putty that can be made by adding Cab-O-Sil to Pros-Aide. When the Bondo dries, it is usually much smoother than the surrounding areas. Texture can be added by stippling a final layer of Pros-Aide with a red stipple sponge. When this layer is dry, the piece is ready for painting.

TIPS FOR RUNNING FOAM LATEX

Courtesy of GM Foam, Inc.

MOLD PREPARATION FOR ULTRACAL OR OTHER STONES

1. If your mold is new and wet, you can *seal the surface* with wax before applying release. Failure to do so usually results in pocked surfaces on the finished foam and loose skin. An effective wax sealer can be made by thinning paste wax (carnauba wax) with 99-percent isopropyl alcohol. This thin wax sealer is painted into the mold and then dried by baking the mold at 150°F for at least one hour until all the alcohol fumes and much of the water are gone. Thick molds can take many hours to dry properly. The dried wax surface is then buffed with a lint-free rag. (Nylon pantyhose material works well.)

2. On the sealed, buffed mold surface, paint a thin layer of *GM Mold Release*, and allow it to dry. Whisk away any excess dried release with a dry brush. The mold is now ready for use.

3. For those who prefer *silicone release*, be certain to brush it on thinly, and leave no puddles. When the silicone is thin and even, shake in some baby powder, and whisk it out with a dry brush. The surface will then be extremely slick and ready for use.

FOAM TIPS

1. Please read the instructions prior to starting the foam job. Your supplier can also provide you with *Materials Safety Data Sheets*, which should be examined, for the foam components.

2. *If your foams gel too fast*, cut a minute or two off your refining time. That means you will pour the gelling agent a minute or two sooner. In extreme cases, as in a hot garage with high humidity, you may need to not only cut down the refining time, but also use two or three grams less gelling agent (per 150 grams of base).

3. *If your foams gel too slowly*, add minutes to the refining time. In extreme cases, such as an unheated room in the winter, it is wise to put mold(s) in the oven and heat to 85–90°F before using them. You may need to add several minutes to the refining time, and you can increase the gelling agent to as much as 20gm/150gm of base. If you have a case where the foam fails to gel after fifteen minutes, increase both the refining time and the gelling agent.

4. *Sluggish or undercured foam* can be remedied with a longer cure time. If the oven is tightly packed with molds, allow extra time for heat-up, and also leave enough space between molds to ensure that all of them receive the same amount of heat. *Overcured foam* loses tear strength and stretch. Cure for less time to avoid such problems.

5. *Pigmentation* is best accomplished by using *GM Foam Water Base Pigments*. These are very concentrated and will not over-plasticize the foam, as Universal Tints will do.

DEMOLDING

1. Demolding should be done when the molds have cooled to 120–130°F. You can demold at 200°F, but it is very hard on the molds and causes cracking. It helps to have a thin wooden stick for insertion between the mold halves as they open. This wooden stick can be used to carefully pull the foam away from one side of the mold, leaving it intact on the other side. The foam is then powdered and removed from the second mold half.

2. *It is very important to wash the foam pieces.* They should be placed in a container of warm water with the addition of a couple of drops of liquid dish soap. Do not use too much soap. Gently squeeze the wash water into and through the pieces. Rinse in clear water until no trace of soap is left. Press water out of the pieces on top of cloth or paper towels. Do not wring. Dry pieces flat or on forms that match their natural curvature to avoid wrinkles. IT IS IMPERATIVE TO DRY THE PIECES BEFORE STORING. Otherwise, a severe sulfur smell will result. When dry, powder the pieces.

3. When molds are used repeatedly, a brown residue builds up on the mold surfaces. This buildup should be scrubbed out with solvent and a short-bristled brush. The safest solvent to use is 99-percent alcohol, although you may also use acetone or trichloroethane. Remember to reapply mold release when finished.

STORAGE OF PIECES

When foam pieces have been washed, dried, and powdered, they should be stored in the dark in airtight containers. It is convenient to use either Ziploc plastic bags or plastic refrigerator containers with airtight lids. The baggies or plastic containers are then stored in a cardboard box or any other opaque container that can keep out the light. If stored in this way, pieces can be kept for years without any deterioration.

SAFETY INFORMATION

1. *Read the instructions* before starting.
2. Maintain adequate ventilation for the removal of ammonia fumes.
3. Wear safety goggles and gloves when working with foam.
4. *DO NOT let foam components come into contact with skin.* If this accidentally happens, wash with soap and water as soon as possible.
5. Wash your hands after working with foam. Never eat, drink, or smoke without washing first.

An instructional video from GM Foam is available for purchase. See Appendix B for information.

INSTRUCTIONS FOR A SMALL SUNBEAM MIXING BOWL

Before starting, prepare the molds. A thin coating of GM Mold Release should be brushed onto interior mold surfaces of both positive and negative and then allowed to dry thoroughly. (GM Foam uses a *triple beam balance* for all gram weights.)

1. Shake the bottles of components before using them.

2. Into the small Mixmaster bowl, add the following together:

    A. 150 grams FOAM LATEX BASE

B. 30 grams FOAMING AGENT

C. 15 grams CURING AGENT

3. Into a small cup, weigh out 14 grams of GELLING AGENT. Set aside.

4. Begin the foaming process according to one of the schedules detailed ahead.

5. When the processing is completed, pour or inject the foam into cool molds. Work quickly.

6. Pour the remaining foam onto a smooth surface, where it should set to a solid mass in 5 to 20 minutes. When you can press it with a finger and form a permanent indentation, the foam has gelled. Place the molds in the oven and cure at 200°F for approximately 3 hours. Small thin molds may take as little as 2 hours, while huge thick molds may take up to 5 hours.

7. Let the molds cool in the oven for at least 30 minutes after curing, and then slightly open the oven door for additional cooling. Removing very hot molds from the oven will crack them.

8. Demold the foam pieces from warm molds. DO NOT LET THE MOLDS COOL TO ROOM TEMPERATURE BEFORE DEMOLDING. If they do cool, the demolding process will prove more difficult.

COLD ROOM SCHEDULE (65–69°F), 16½ Minutes Total Time

Speed #1 for 1 minute (mixing)

Speed #7 for 6 minutes (whipping)

Speed #4 for 4 minutes (refining)

Speed #1 for 4 minutes (ultra refining)

Speed #1 for 30 seconds: Add GELLING AGENT

Speed #1 for 30 seconds: Turn bowl backwards to mix GEL

Speed #1 for 30 seconds

Turn mixer OFF

NORMAL ROOM SCHEDULE (70–75°F), 14½ Minutes Total Time

Speed #1 for 1 minute

Speed #7 for 6 minutes

Speed #4 for 3 minutes

Speed #1 for 3 minutes

Speed #1 for 30 seconds: Add GELLING AGENT

Speed #1 for 30 seconds: Turn bowl backwards to mix GEL

Speed #1 for 30 seconds

Turn mixer OFF

WARM ROOM SCHEDULE (76–80°F), 13½ Minutes Total Time

Speed #1 for 1 minute

Speed #7 for 6 minutes

Speed #4 for 2 minutes

Speed #1 for 2 minutes

Speed #1 for 30 seconds: Add GELLING AGENT

Speed #1 for 30 seconds: Turn bowl backwards to mix GEL

Speed #1 for 30 seconds

Turn mixer OFF

- If your foam gels too fast, cut a minute off your refining time, or use slightly less gelling agent (11 or 12 grams).
- If your foam gels too slowly, add a minute to your refining time. You can place molds in a pre-heated oven to hasten the gelling in such cases.
- Larger batches require different schedules.
- Wet molds cause pocked surfaces on the foam and loose skin. Undercured foam will spring back too slowly.
- The latex base needs to be shaken once a week in order to prevent the serum layer from settling on the bottom.

INSTRUCTIONS FOR A LARGE SUNBEAM MIXING BOWL

2½ BATCH MIX (very soft, 6 to 6½ volumes) at 68–70°F. Humidity: 50- 65-percent.

1. Into the large bowl, weigh the following:

    A. LATEX BASE   375 grams

    B. FOAMING AGENT   90 grams

    C. CURING AGENT   38 grams

2. Into a small cup, weigh 28 grams of GELLING AGENT. Set this aside.

3. Run the following schedule:

    Speed #2 for 1 minute (mix ingredients)

    Speed #12 for 7 minutes (whipping) [will rise to less than 1" from the rim]

    Speed #8 for 2 minutes (rising slightly) [height to ¾" from the rim]

    Speed #4 for 3 minutes (begin refining)

    Speed #2 for 4 minutes (finish refining)

    Speed #2 for 30 seconds: Use 30 seconds to pour GEL

Speed #2 for 30 seconds: Backbowl (slowly turn bowl backwards by hand)

Speed #1 for 30 seconds

Turn mixer OFF

Backbowling is the most effective way to disperse the GELLING AGENT. Do this slowly to prevent mixture with air.

Variations in the above schedule are unavoidable, because weather conditions vary so widely. Differing room conditions of temperature and humidity affect the working time of the foam.

The main principles to remember are as follows:

- Higher Temperature Shortens Working Time
- Higher Humidity Shortens Working Time

To correct these conditions, use these tips:

- When the Humidity is 70-80 percent, cut the GELLING AGENT to 30–40 grams.
- When the Temperature is 75–80°F, cut the GELLING AGENT to 30–32 grams.

If conditions are hot and muggy, you can reduce the refining time and decrease the GELLING AGENT. Try pouring the GELLING AGENT at 15 minutes, and use 28–30 grams, or even less if the room is extremely hot and damp.

- In cold rooms (64–67°F), *add* two or three minutes to your refining time.

HIGH-RISE FOAMING AGENT may be substituted for *part* of the FOAMING AGENT. Resulting foam can be whipped to the top of the bowl if desired (7½ volumes), or any height less than that. Remember: The higher you whip the foam, the softer it will be, but it becomes more difficult to refine and pour since foam is thicker at higher volume.

When using HIGH-RISE FOAMING AGENT, increase the amount of CURING AGENT to 42 grams per bowl (17 grams per 150 grams of base).

GIL MOSKO APPLICATION

Fig. 3-17

The model.

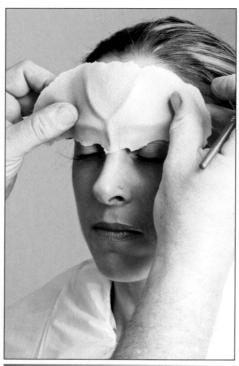

Fig. 3-18

Positioning the appliance prior to attachment.

Fig. 3-19

After the center is tacked, the appliance is folded away from the skin to allow gluing.

Fig. 3-20

Working from the center, out toward the edge, the foam is glued to the skin.

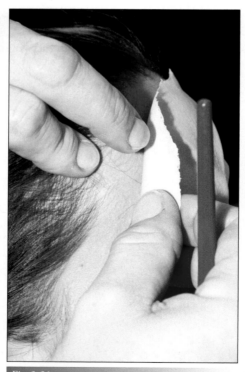

Fig. 3-21

Detail of gluing near the edge.

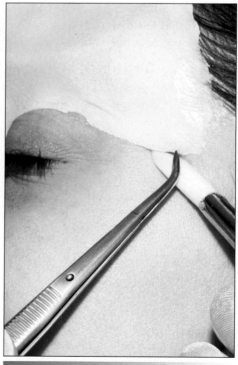

Fig. 3-22

Forceps are used to lift delicate edges, enabling a glue brush to get under the foam.

Fig. 3-23

After gluing, edges are pressed using powdered fingertips.

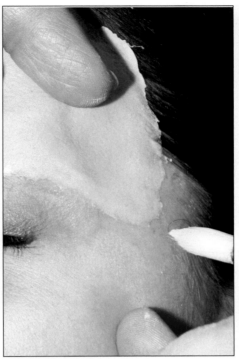

Fig. 3-24

The well-glued edge blends invisibly with the skin.

Fig. 3-25

Detail of the top edge.

Fig. 3-26

A chin piece is added.

Fig. 3-27

After covering the entire foam piece with a layer of PAX paint, rubber mask greasepaints are used to create highlights and shadows, as well as to add color and warmth.

Fig. 3-28

We must not forget make-up for the eyes, cheeks, and lips.

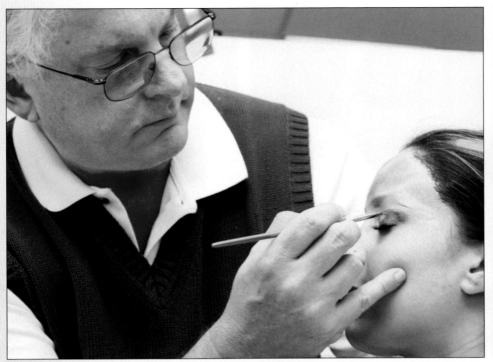

Fig. 3-29

When working around the eyes, the artist has stabilized the hand for safety and accuracy.

Fig. 3-30

Letting the hair down covers the top edge.

Fig. 3-31

Make-up artist Gil Mosko with his beautiful alien.

Fig. 3-32

Before

Fig. 3-33

After

Chapter 4

SCULPTING AGE

Chapter 4

Mark Alfrey Application

Kazuhiro Tsuji Applications

Chapter 4

SCULPTING AGE

Drafted by the authors from information generously submitted by Mark Alfrey.

With the continual advances being made in computer technology, it may come as no surprise in the future if movie sculpture becomes as antiquated as silver nitrate film, or film altogether. But today sculpture is still an integral part of make-up effects.

MARK ALFREY APPLICATION

PREPARATIONS

The lifecast for this demonstration is of a thirty-year-old woman. Before placing a single piece of clay onto the plaster bust, gather some reference materials, predominately photographs of women at the appropriate age. These can be found in various magazines, especially those that make no obvious attempt to enhance the appearance of their subjects (such as news magazines, as opposed to fashion publications). *Time* magazine features many useful shots of mature politicians and other older figures.

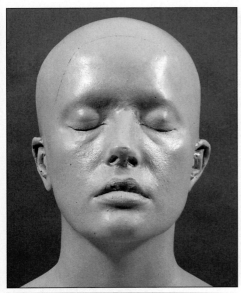

Fig. 4-1

Fig. 4-2

Once the material has been collected, begin to conceptualize the project by asking the following questions:

- How much older should the subject appear?
- How much sun exposure should be reflected in the skin?

Sun damage, for instance, would make the skin more cracked than wrinkled.

This particular demonstration will add approximately twenty-five years to the subject. The more years that need to be added to the subject, the more challenging the work will be. Facial structure changes considerably over the years. Very old people tend to have wrinkles, eye sockets, temples, and cheeks with much more depth. To create the illusion of depth, build up the face's high points. The risk of overdoing this procedure is making the subject look as if he or she is wearing a thick mask.

Lighting is a very important consideration. The lighting setup should bring out the form and detail of the artist's work. The lights themselves need to be moved fairly often to reveal every detail and flaw, for certain wrinkles are only visible from particular angles, as are some unfinished areas. If the lights cannot be moved, then reposition the sculpture. Turn it sideways and spend time working in this new position. Then, continue from several other angles, which enables the artist to see every detail of the sculpting surface.

PROCEDURE

Begin by applying clay to the jowls and nasolabial folds. The actual starting point may be chosen at random. As more clay is added, try to avoid building more than ¼" of thickness at any place on the subject. A thick sculpture will produce an undesirably thick appliance with limited mobility. Add only ⅛" of thickness to the areas that will remain shallow, and emphasize the bone structure to nearly ¼". Thicken the soft tissue under the eyes and the nasolabial folds.

Use a small wooden spatula from Kemper Tools to smear the clay and shape general forms. With regard to choosing tools, there are no strict rules. Do not be resigned to the use of

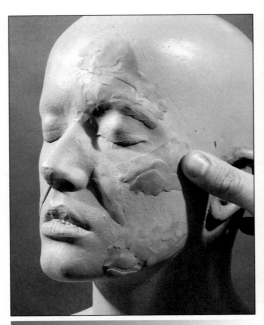

Fig. 4-3

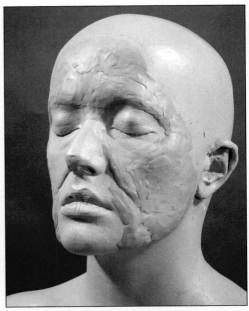

Fig. 4-4

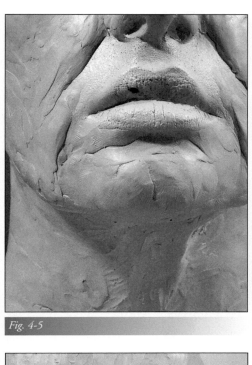

Fig. 4-5

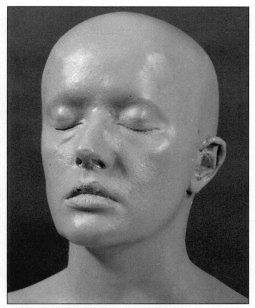

Fig. 4-6

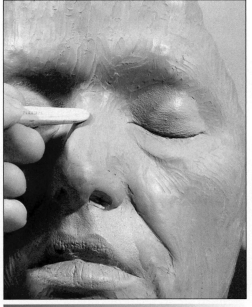

Fig. 4-7

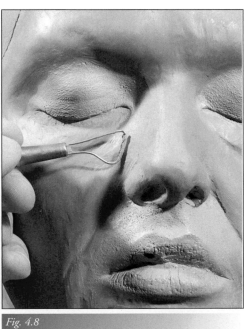

Fig. 4-8

implements that are suggested by a supposedly knowledgeable sculptor. The artist should experiment to find tools that may better suit the individual's style.

Before progressing too much with the facial work, move down to the neck, and make this portion of the anatomy more apparent. The neck tends to lose roundness with age. The muscles and tendons show through better, and years of gravity pull some loose skin down under the chin, and sometimes as far down as the clavicle. Knowledge of anatomy is obviously very useful. Make a habit of studying faces on a daily basis. Friends, relatives, and random encounters on the street provide a variety of interesting looks. Life's experiences tend to show on people's faces. By applying this philosophy to sculpting, the artist will undoubtedly enhance the reality of the results.

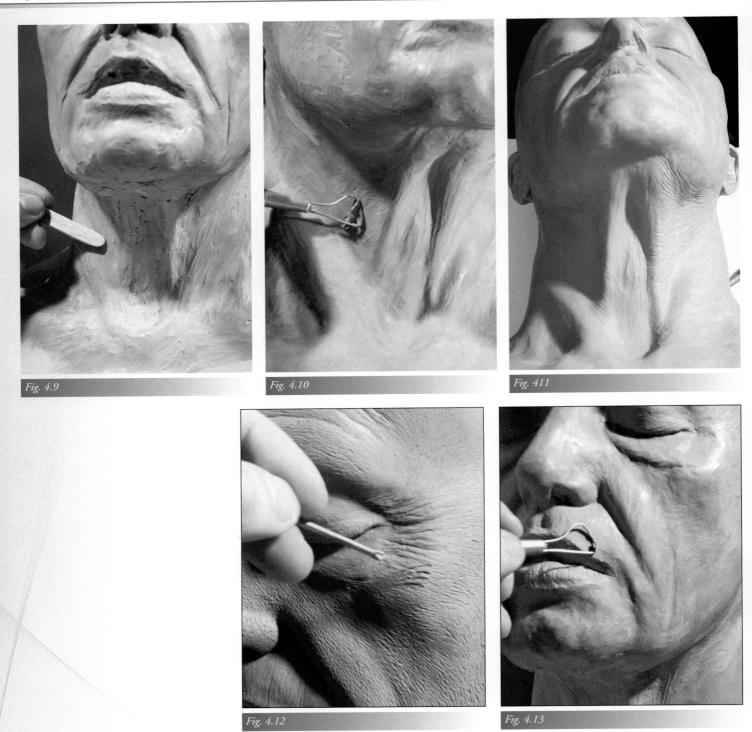

Fig. 4.9

Fig. 4.10

Fig. 411

Fig. 4.12

Fig. 4.13

When sculpting near the eyes, it is advisable to end around the eyeball area. Never sculpt onto the eyes, because if the prosthesis is glued to the eyelids, the subject wearing the make-up will not be able to open them.

It is recommended to keep the clay very thin at the corners of the mouth. Resist sculpting right into the corners, and leave some space at each side to allow for expected wear and tear. Utilize a Kemper loop tool for sculpting up to the edge of the lips. If the artist plans to cover them completely, preparations must be made to cut the lip pieces off and place them on separate snap molds.

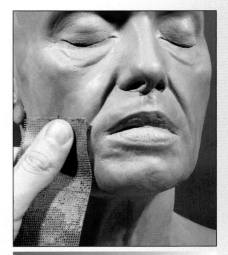

Fig. 4.14

Use a piece of metal screen to roughly polish the clay. This type of screen, unlike one used for a screen door, is actually a brittle sanding screen that can be purchased in a hardware store. It comes coated with a rough, gravel-like surface that must be scraped off with a coarse wire brush. The artist may also use sanding wood to wear it down. Once it is used for sculpting, it will collect clay and require cleaning accomplished by pressing it against a block of clay and peeling off the remnants. Most of the clay tends to stick to the block.

Once the basic forms exist, begin shaping wrinkles. They may simply look like lines to the untrained eye, but in fact, each individual wrinkle is an array of forms. If the wrinkle is very deep, this quality is easier to behold. Each wrinkle tends to cut in with an upward angle. Gravity affects wrinkles to the extent that each fold tends to have a slight downward droop, especially the deep ones around the corners of the eyes. A clear example of this effect can be seen when examining the nasolabial fold, which is more than just a facial line. The fold consists of a little pouch that droops over the groove at places where the pouch is thick. Gaining a thorough understanding of wrinkles requires diligent study. Reference photographs can certainly help in this direction.

When satisfied with the wrinkles (or if the allotted time has elapsed), begin the process of texturing. Sculpting texture is the artistic equivalent of polishing furniture. It is necessary to give the clay a similar sheen to human skin in order to provide appropriate light reflection. A Kemper loop tool with a pointed tip can be used to create the texture of pores, which should be sculpted in the proper directions (a requisite for realism). A stipple sponge can also be used for texturing, either before or after use of the Kemper tool. Press it into the clay, or drag it in a slight wiggling manner. Delicate prong tools, made by James Conrad, can be used to create fine lines of texture, while a prong tool with harder prongs can be used to lay directional pores with overlapping lines. Additionally, cat and dog hairbrushes will create fine texture in a crosshatching manner. The red-handled tool made by James Conrad works well for pore texture on the nose and, if used directionally, on just about any other part of the sculpture.

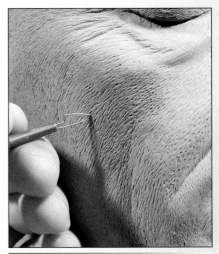

Fig. 4.15

Little flakes of clay will collect on the tools and on the sculpture itself. A wet chip brush works effectively to wipe them away. The water helps to prevent the bits of clay from smearing back onto the sculpture. Before laying fine lines, it is optional to brush some talcum powder onto the sculpture to prevent clay bits from collecting on the surface. Then, place plastic wrap, through which the details can be formed, over the powdered clay. The powder will prevent the plastic from sticking to the clay.

Before finishing, check the quality of the edges by shining a lamp against the sculpture from various angles, the result of which will particularly emphasize the blending effectiveness. Ultimately, the clay edges should blend seamlessly into the bust.

SUMMARY

When sculpting at a leisurely pace, the artist can make as many changes as necessary. But deadlines rarely allow for such liberties, especially in the world of television make-up, in which only a few days (if not even less time) are normally allotted for the sculpting process. Speed is therefore very important if the artist hopes to work on a regular basis. For shows with ample time and a good budget, a week may be allowed.

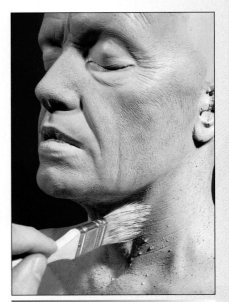

Fig. 416

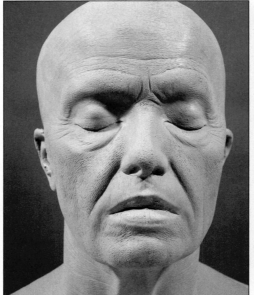

Fig. 4.17

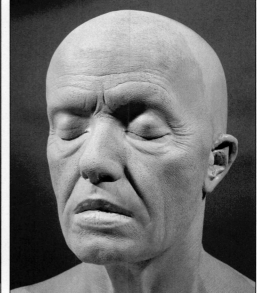

Fig. 4.18

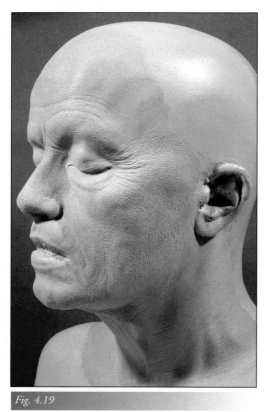

Fig. 4.19

KAZUHIRO TSUJI APPLICATIONS

Fig. 4-20

A Closeup of the finished work

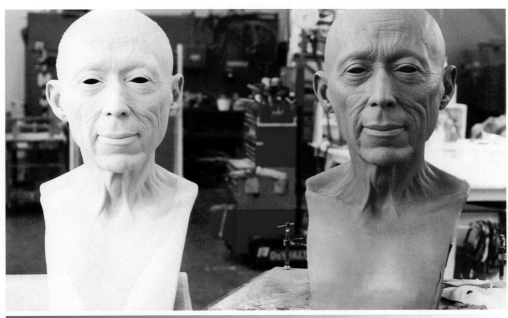

Fig. 4.21

Demolded sculpture and skin.

Fig. 4-22

Dressing the hair.

Fig. 4-23

Kazuhiro Tsuji continues working with the hair.

Fig. 4-24

A finished portrait of the work.

Fig. 4-25

The head in profile.

Fig. 4-26

A closeup view.

Fig. 4-27

The real Dick Smith with the finished work.

Fig. 4-28

A display of General Thade from Planet of the Apes
(2001, 20th Century Fox).

Fig. 4-29

A display of The Grinch from How the Grinch Stole
Christmas *(Universal).*

Chapter 5

CREATING A BALD CAP

Chapter 5

Ed French Application

Chapter 5

CREATING A BALD CAP

Drafted by the authors from information generously submitted by Ed French.

ED FRENCH APPLICATION

PREPARATIONS

To create a rubber cap, begin with the following items:

- Rubber
- Pliatex Molding Rubber
- Krylon Crystal Clear Spray
- Epoxy Parfilm Spray
- Slip Latex
- Baby Powder
- Pieces of Upholstery Sponge
- Red Marker
- Pencil and Notepad
- Red Food Coloring
- Powder Brush
- Respiratory Mask
- Scissors
- Hairdryer

The head form is made of Ultracal plaster in this example. It is secured to a base with wood glue on top of an adjustable sculpture stand with a lazy Susan.

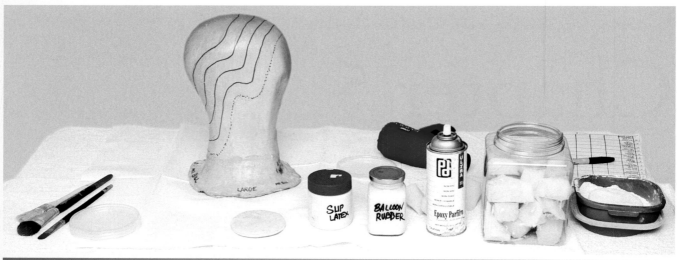

Fig. 5-1

Materials for creating a custom-designed rubber bald cap. All work is done in a well-ventilated area.

PROCEDURE

Begin by drawing five separate lines in pencil that stretch across the head form from base to base. The lines should be equidistant from one another and will serve as guides when applying the latex mixture. The first line should cross near the intended edge of the bald cap. Draw a separate dotted line in front of this first line that will actually serve as the bald cap edge. Once these lines have been properly placed, trace over them with red marker.

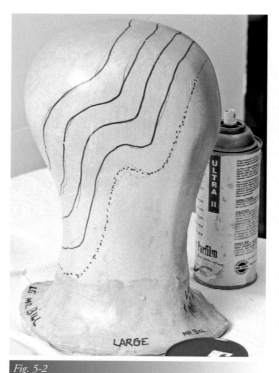

Fig. 5-2

Ten layers of liquid rubber will be applied and individually dried. The dotted line is where the edge of the bald cap appliance will be.

Fig. 5-3

Plaster form is marked with an indelible marker. The four solid lines and one dotted line are sealed along with the porous surface by applying three light coats of polyurethane spray. Allow it to dry completely. Before applying the liquid balloon rubber, spray Epoxy Parfilm release on the form.

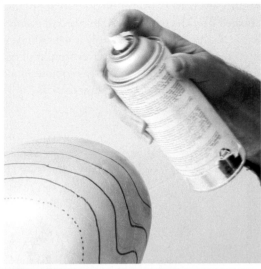

Fig. 5-4

Spray a light coat of release agent (Parfilm is wax) over the entire form, and allow it to dry for 30 seconds. Apply a second light, quick coating.

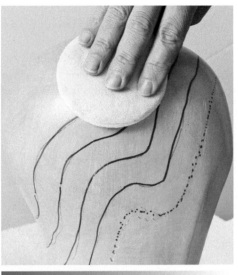

Fig. 5-5

Polish the entire surface using a new powder puff.

Use Crystal Clear Spray over the entire form; it will both seal the ink and protect the surface of the form from becoming pitted after repeated usage. After the first coat dries, spray a second coat. Then, spray Epoxy Parfilm on the form, which allows for easy removal of the cap (or apply carnauba wax, allow it to dry, and then buff).

When creating the latex mixture, utilize water-soluble pigments with only a slight tint of color. Add three drops of red food coloring to three ounces of balloon rubber, and mix. (Pliatex Molding Rubber can also be used.)

Fig. 5-6

Because of the ammonia content in liquid latex, I recommend working from a small container. This balloon rubber is uncolored.

Fig. 5-7

Keep your rubber source from drying out by pouring out a small quantity onto a plastic lid or dish and keeping the jar sealed until more is needed.

An upholstery sponge that has been separated into seven sections can be used to apply the mixture to the cap. The first layer should be brushed over the entire form, thinly and evenly. Paint one half of the form at a time. Once dry, in a stippling motion, apply a second layer from the first solid line back, the results of which should prevent the first layer from pulling up prematurely. Use a hairdryer on the form to accelerate the drying process. (Keep notes during this process as to which layers have been applied, for it is quite easy to lose track.)

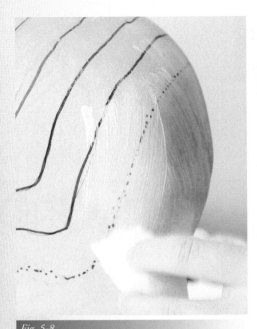

Fig. 5-8

Use cut-up upholstery sponge to brush a light, even coat over the entire form.

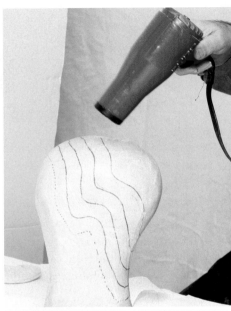

Fig. 5-9

The balloon latex is completely dry when the pale whitish color of wet rubber appears clear and shiny.

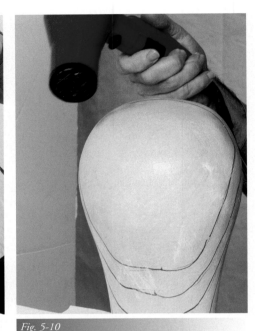

Fig. 5-10

Note the whitish areas. Make sure these completely disappear by using the heat setting on the hairdryer.

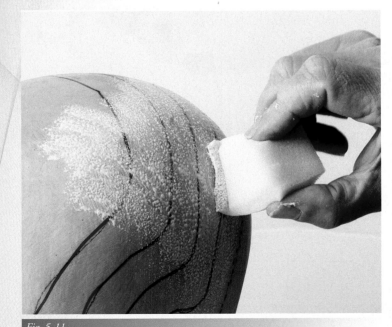

Fig. 5-11

Apply layer two by stippling or patting up and down and filling in balloon rubber up to the dotted line.

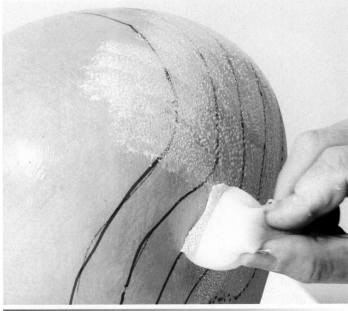

Fig. 5-12

Work quickly when patting up and down. Stippling—as opposed to brushing—will prevent the first layer from being separated or dragged off the surface of the form.

Brush on a third layer more liberally, but avoid leaving puddles. Each successive layer (seven in all) should begin from the next line. The cap will therefore become thicker away from the blending edge. The penultimate layer can be carried down the nape of the neck. Finish by applying the final layer over the entire designated cap area.

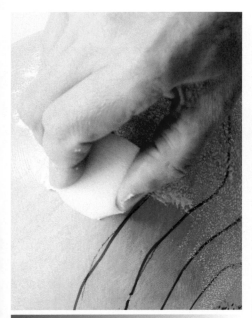

Fig. 5-13

This activity also creates the feathered membrane/thin edge. Dry completely.

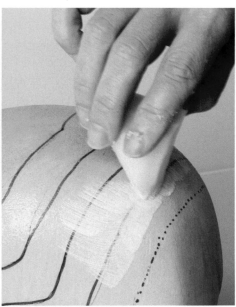

Fig. 5-14

The third layer of balloon rubber is brushed onto the point between the dotted line and the first solid line. The third layer must then dry completely.

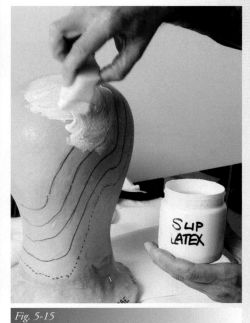

Fig. 5-15

Paint slip latex or ordinary latex rubber (the fourth layer) up to the second solid line.

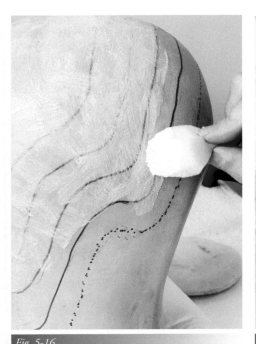

Fig. 5-16

Work continues on the fourth layer.

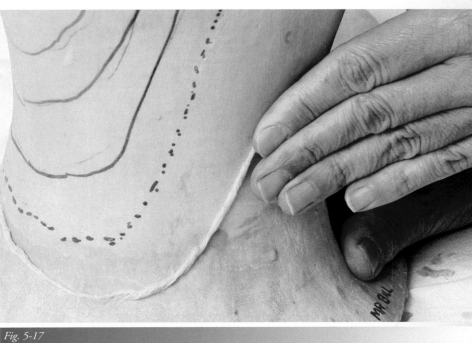

Fig. 5-17

To remove the cap, start rolling the edge in a uniform manner up to the dotted line.

Locate the blending edge, and roll it back towards the dotted line. (The edge should reach just beyond it.) Fill a dish with baby powder, and brush it over the entire surface. Use a 1" chip brush to dust powder on the inner surface of the cap while slowly peeling it from the form. Continually reload the brush with powder. Continue pushing back the cap, and once a large portion becomes loose, utilize a powder puff instead of the brush. Examine the cap for holes and imperfections.

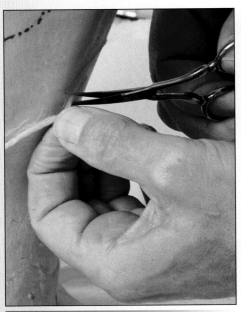

Fig. 5-18

The tacky latex surface sticks to itself, forming a rubber band. You may need to snip this as you roll.

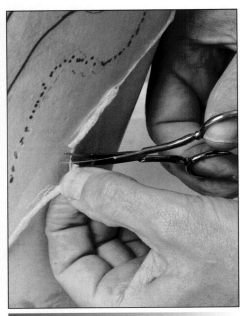

Fig. 5-19

An occasional cut will keep the edge aligned with the dotted line.

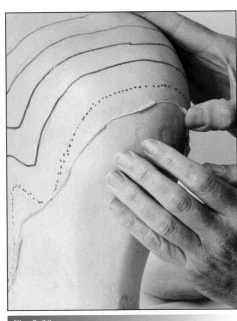

Fig. 5-20

Roll the edge up evenly.

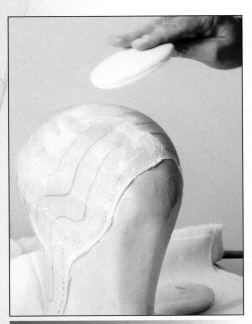

Fig. 5-21

When the dotted line is reached, powder the cap liberally with baby powder.

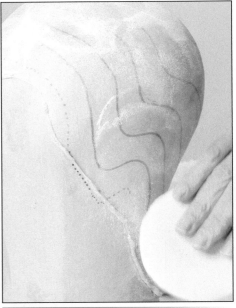

Fig. 5-22

Continue powdering.

Fig. 5-23

Load the large powder brush.

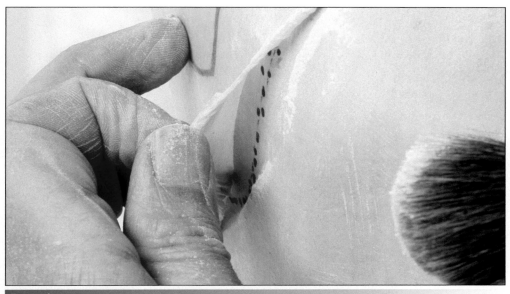

Fig. 5-24

Start peeling back the latex about ½", and thoroughly coat any exposed inner surface with powder.

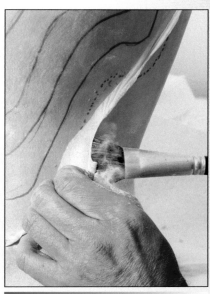

Fig. 5-25

Immediately powder the fresh inner surface as it is pulled up.

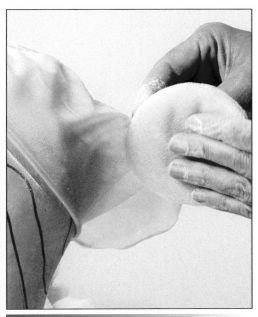

Fig. 5-26

Any unpowdered surface will stick to itself. You can use a powder puff at this point.

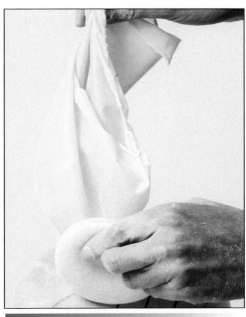

Fig. 5-27

Once the entire inner and outer surfaces are powdered, you may use the cap or store it for future use.

SUMMARY

Caps can also be designed that feature simulated hair growth. Apply adhesive to a cap that has already been removed from the form, allow it to become tacky, and apply chopped hair through a piece of netting. Gradations of hair growth can be achieved by sprinkling hair into the bristles of a large toothbrush (or brush of similar shape) and running the fingers through it to spatter the hairs onto the cap.

Please see Part I, Chapter 3 for more information about bald caps.

Fig. 5-28

Over long periods of time, store the cap in a Ziploc bag or preferably on a bald cap form covered with a plastic bag.

Chapter 6

DENTAL VENEERS

Chapter 6

Casting Teeth

Making a Silicone Master of Dental Casts

Making Dentures

Making Vacuum-formed Veneers

Making Vacuum-formed Veneers with Acrylic Tooth Added

Chapter 6

DENTAL VENEERS

Drafted by the authors from information generously submitted by Matthew Mungle.

CASTING TEETH

MATERIALS NEEDED

- Dental Alginate (Hollywood Impression by Art Molds)
- Rubber Gloves
- Rubber Dental Mixing Bowls
- Dental Impression Trays
- Die-Keen Blue Stone
- Dental Vibrator
- Dremel Moto-Tool

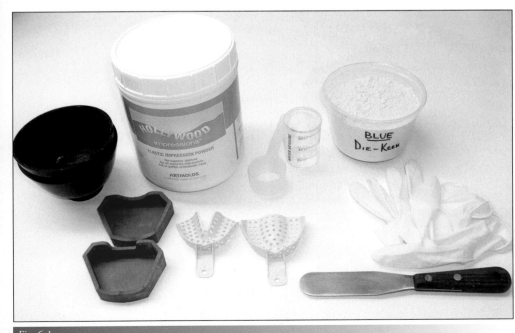

Fig. 6-1

- Measuring Containers (usually included with alginate)
- Water
- Metal Spatula
- Dental Molding Forms
- Can of Compressed Air
- Stanley Planer

PROCEDURE

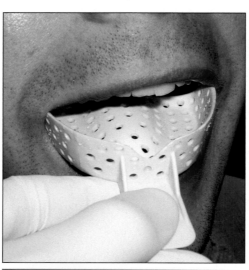

Fig. 6-2

1. Fit the upper and lower dental impression tray into the subject's mouth. (Be certain the tray fits loosely.)

Fig. 6-3

2. Pour 60 cc of water into a rubber dental mixing bowl.

3. Place three scoops of dental impression alginate into the bowl of water, and stir until thoroughly mixed. The mixture is extremely thick and will not run out of the dental impression trays.

Fig. 6-4

Fig. 6-5

4. Spatulate thick alginate into the upper dental tray, and smooth out the surface under cold water with a finger. This step prepares the surface of the alginate to accept the impression of the gums and teeth. (Wear rubber gloves when working the following steps.)

Fig. 6-6

Fig. 6-7

5. Place the tray into the mouth, and have the subject bite down slightly into the alginate. Push the material from the front of the tray up between lip and gums, ensuring the upper gums are in the impression.

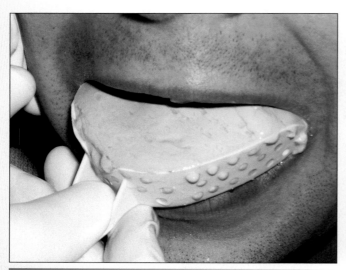

Fig. 6-8

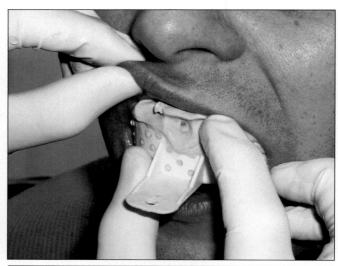

Fig. 6-9

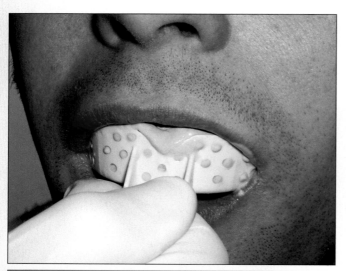

Fig. 6-10

6. Press the tray up until it touches the teeth, and then pull the tray down ever so slightly. Hold in place until the alginate sets (about one minute).

7. Once the alginate sets, have the subject close the lips around the tray, and blow. This action breaks the vacuum between the teeth/gums and alginate material. Remove the tray and place it into a bowl of water in order to keep the alginate moist and reduce the chance of shrinkage. The lower denture cast can be taken at this time.

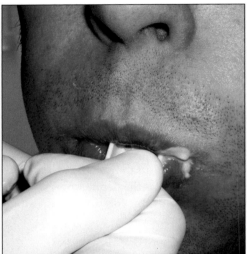

Fig. 6-11

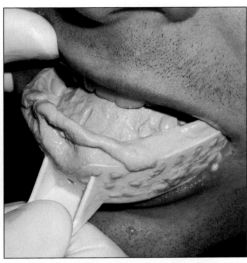

Fig. 6-12

Fig. 6-13

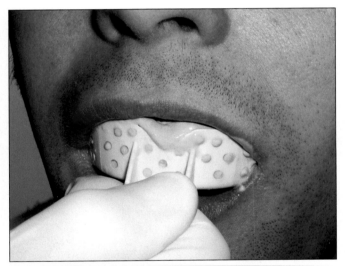

Fig. 6-14

8. When ready to cast the teeth and/or gums in stone (which should be done as soon as possible to avoid shrinkage of the alginate), blow out all the water from the casting with a can of compressed air.

Fig. 6-15

9. Pour at least 60 cc of water into a clean rubber mixing bowl, and sift Die-Keen Blue Stone onto the water until fully saturated.

Fig. 6-16

10. Stir with a metal spatula until thoroughly mixed. The result should look as thick as the dental impression alginate was previously. This thickness makes the stone extremely hard.

11. Place the impression onto a dental vibrator plate, if available, and slowly spatulate the stone into the back of the cast, letting it run into all the teeth cavities. A finger may be used to gently nudge the stone into the teeth. If a dental vibrator is not available, the casting should be gently tapped onto a tabletop as the stone is introduced into the casting.

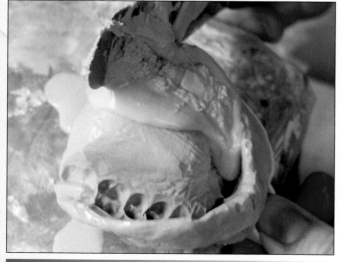

Fig. 6-17

Fig. 6-18

12. While the stone is still fluid, spatulate the material into the dental molding forms, and gently press the impression into the form. Clean up the excess overflow with a spatula or a finger. Let the stone set for approximately 90 minutes.

Fig. 6-19

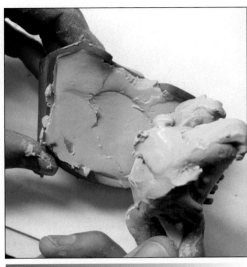

Fig. 6-20

Fig. 6-21

13. Remove the upper and lower alginate impressions from the stone casting, as well as the casting from the rubber dental form.

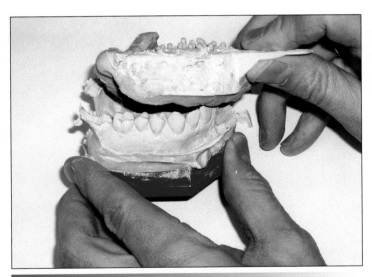

Fig. 6-22

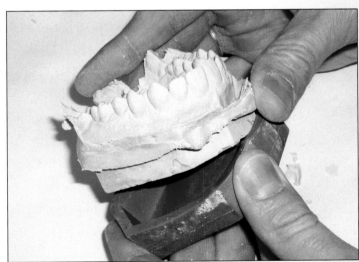

Fig. 623

14. Clean up the casts with a planer and Dremel Moto-Tool. Be careful not to alter the teeth and gum area, as this will not allow the veneers or dentures to fit properly.

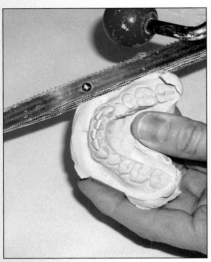

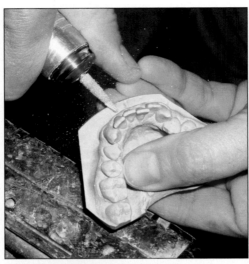

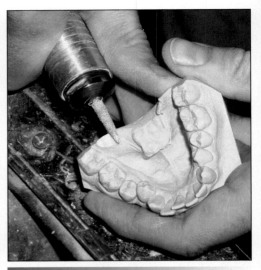

Fig. 6-24

Fig. 6-25

Fig. 6-26

MAKING A SILICONE MASTER OF DENTAL CASTS

MATERIALS NEEDED

- Vi-Sil Silicone 1065 (base and catalyst)
- Rubber Gloves
- Hot Glue Gun
- Project Board
- Measuring Containers
- Metal Spatula
- Plastic Deli Cups
- Gram Scale
- Cynoacrylate Glue
- Kleen Klay
- Scissors

Because the teeth on dental casts are very delicate, a silicone master of the casts should be made, especially if multiple dentures are to be produced. The following steps show how this is accomplished with Vi-Sil Silicone; however, other mold-making silicones may be used.

PROCEDURE

1. Fill in the back part (where the tongue lays) with Kleen Klay.

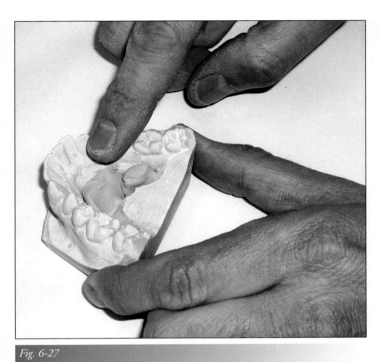

Fig. 6-27

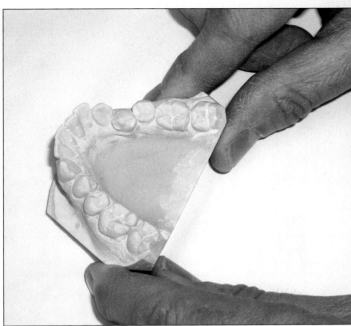

Fig. 6-28

2. Apply a small amount of cynoacrylate glue to the back of both upper and lower casts, and glue them to a project board.

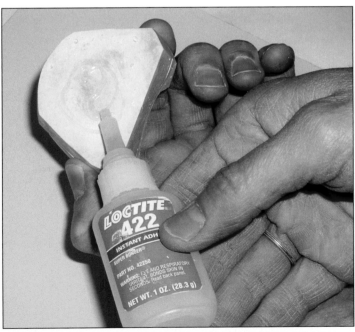

Fig. 6-29

Fig. 6-30

Fig. 6-31

3. Spray the impressions with a light coat of Krylon Crystal Clear.

Fig. 6-32

4. Cut the bottom out of a short deli cup, and center it on the teeth cast. Glue it down to the project board with hot glue.

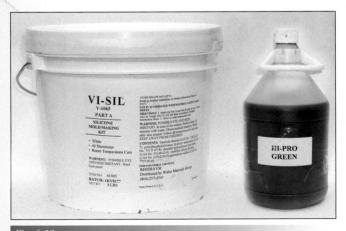

Fig. 6-33

5. Mix Vi-Sil 1065 Silicone as directed in the instructions (10 parts base to 1 part catalyst). Mix 400 grams of base to 40 grams of catalyst. If available, de-gas (removing the air from the mixture) before pouring.

6. Pour silicone at the back of the teeth casts, and let the material run slowly onto the teeth. Let set overnight.

Fig. 6-34

Fig. 6-35

7. When silicone is set, cut the plastic deli cup with scissors, and remove from silicone mold.

Fig. 6-36

Fig. 6-37

8. Remove mold from project board and dental casts. Set aside the original dental casts.

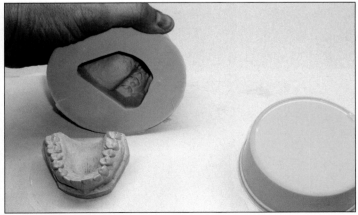

Fig. 6-38

Fig. 6-39

9. Remake new upper and lower dental casts from the silicone masters with Die-Keen Blue Stone, mixed and poured in the same fashion as casting from alginate impressions.

Fig. 6-40

MAKING DENTURES

MATERIALS NEEDED

- Pre-made Acrylic Teeth
- Lang Jet Adjuster Kit
- New Stone Dental Cast
- Wooden Tongue Depressors
- Rubber Gloves
- Veined Tissue Shade Gum
- Colored and Clear Dental Cold Cure Polymer
- Small Metal Spatula
- Fine Fiberglass Cloth (available at hobby stores)
- Dremel Tool with Grinding Bit and Polishing Bit
- Kleen Klay
- Petroleum Jelly
- Plastic Medical Mixing Cups
- Methyl Methacrylate Monomer
- ½" Disposable Brush
- Pumice
- Dental Pressure Pot

PROCEDURE

1. Grind down pre-made acrylic teeth (purchased at a dental supply company). Various tooth sizes and shades may be used, mixed, and matched within one set of dentures (upper and lower) to create a character effect.

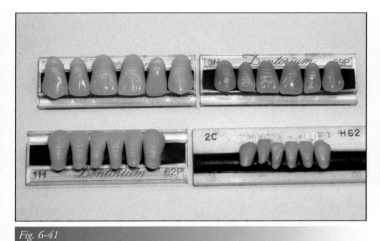

Fig. 6-41

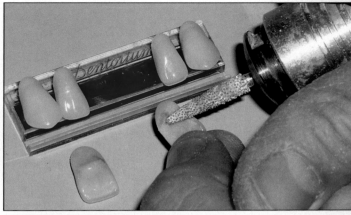

Fig. 6-42

2. Each tooth must be a very thin veneer shell. When the acrylic teeth are placed onto the original stone dental cast, the result should not be that the teeth are built out too far, thus making the upper and lower lips protrude (unless that is the desired effect). The teeth may be placed temporarily onto the original dental casts with Kleen Klay.

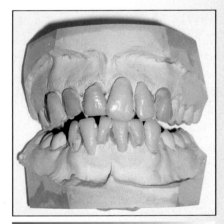

Fig. 6-43

3. Cut a small (½" × 4") strip of fine fiberglass cloth, and place it on the cast. This will eventually be embedded into the dental acrylic, adding strength to the dentures. Use the dental casts made from the new silicone master.

Fig. 6-44

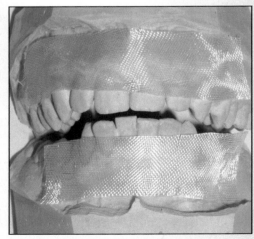

Fig. 6-45

Fig. 6-46

4. Remove the strips of fiberglass cloth, and apply two coats of Alcote, which must then be dried, to the dental casts.

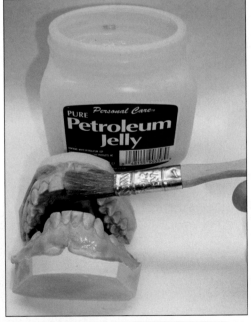

Fig. 6-47

5. Coat the dry dental casts with a very light coating of petroleum jelly.

6. Mix ½ ounce clear cold cure polymer with ½ ounce veined tissue shade cold cure polymer. Any shade of coral gum color may be used. (Clear polymer, which gives the gums a translucent quality, may or may not be used.)

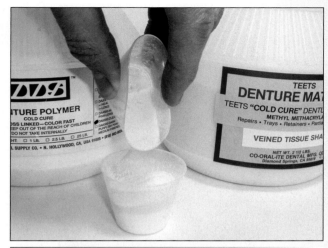

Fig. 6-48

7. Remove teeth veneers from the cast, and place them in a row for easy access, while noting the particular arrangement. Dip the fiberglass cloth into the liquid dental monomer, and place it over the teeth and gum area on the pre-released dental cast.

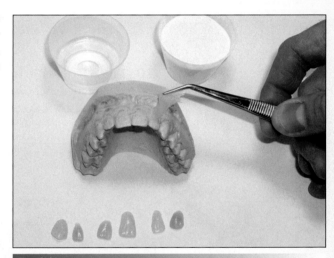

Fig. 6-49

8. The following step should be done rapidly once the polymer and monomer are mixed, for the mixture sets quickly: Mix ¼ ounce liquid monomer with ½ ounce pre-mixed polymer, and stir until thoroughly mixed. Keep a separate container of liquid monomer nearby.

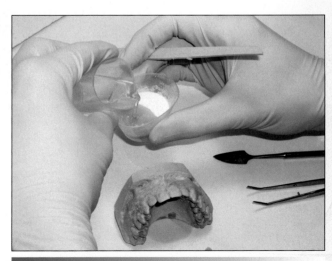

Fig. 6-50

9. Spatulate the dental mixture onto the cloth, gum, and teeth area of the cast, while building the gums up as the mixture thickens.

Fig. 6-51

10. Dip the center tooth into the liquid monomer, and press it into the acrylic, pushing the material back and over the tooth to create the gum area. Continue the process until all of the teeth are imbedded into the acrylic gums and positioned correctly.

Fig. 6-52

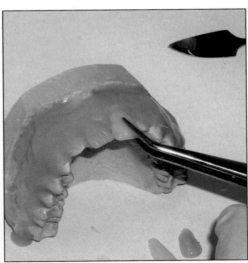

Fig. 6-53

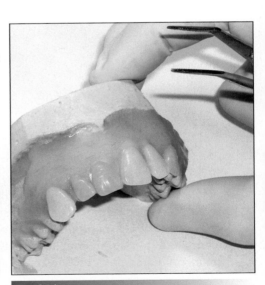

Fig. 6-54

11. Before the acrylic sets, dip a metal spatula into the liquid monomer, and cut back the excess gums. At this time, the gum can be sculpted around the teeth by pushing the acrylic with the moistened spatula.

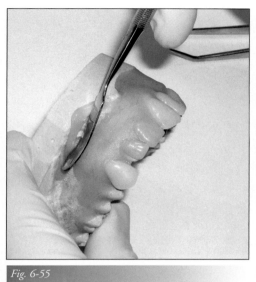

Fig. 6-55

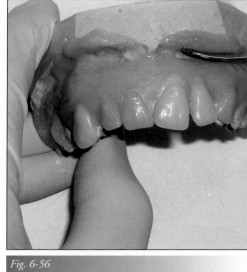

Fig. 6-56

Fig. 6-57

12. The acrylic may also be used to fill in between the acrylic teeth and the dental cast.

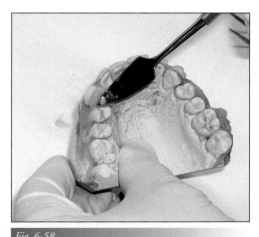

Fig. 6-58

13. The whole dental cast may be placed into a dental pressure pot filled with hot water and pressurized. If this equipment is not available, the cast may be placed into a bowl of hot water to strengthen and set the acrylic more quickly.

Fig. 6-59

14. Repeat the same process with the bottom dentures.

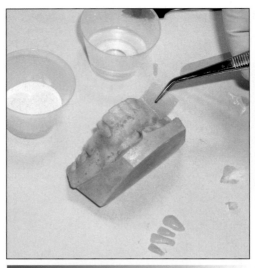

Fig. 6-60

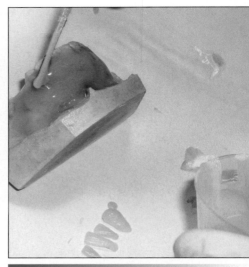

Fig. 6-61

15. The gum area should be pressed back over the exposed real teeth before the acrylic sets.

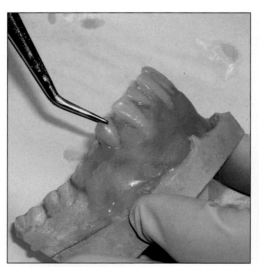

Fig. 6-62

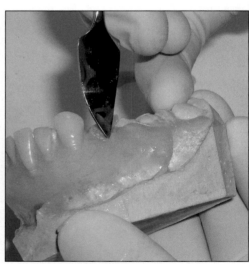

Fig. 6-63

16. After the acrylic has set (approximately 20 minutes), remove it from the water, and carefully pry the dentures off of the dental casts. Place it back on the cast in order to let the acrylic set properly for at least one hour. Also remove the upper acrylic set.

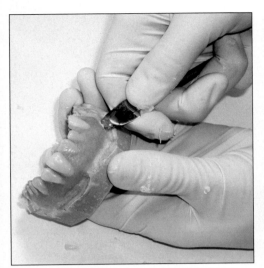

Fig. 6-64

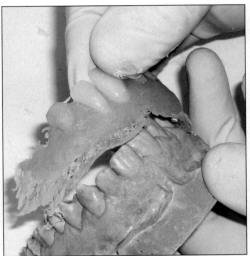

Fig. 6-65

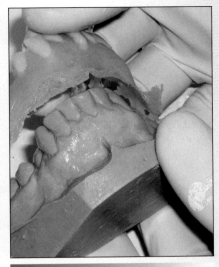

Fig. 6-66

17. Grind the excess acrylic off the dentures with a Dremel tool and bit. Avoid grinding on the back side of the dentures, the result of which would prevent them from fitting correctly on the subject's teeth and gums.

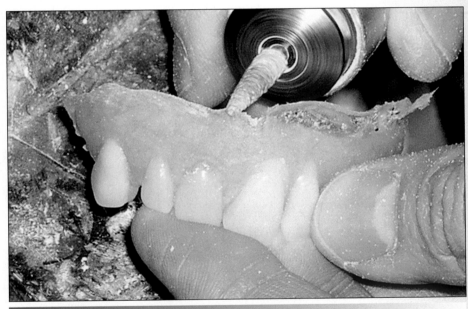

Fig. 6.67

18. Polish the dentures with pumice and a polishing wheel (available from Dremel Tools).

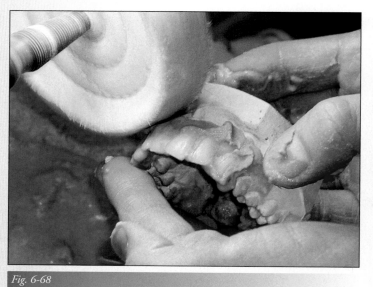

Fig. 6-68

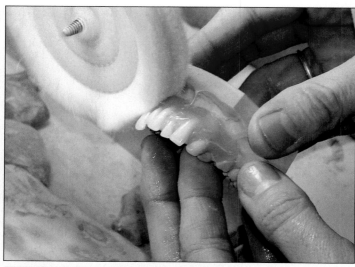

Fig. 6-69

19. Stain the teeth with various shades available in a Lang Jet Adjuster Kit. Gray, violet, yellow, and brown are the most commonly used staina.

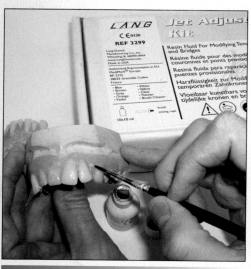

Fig. 6-70

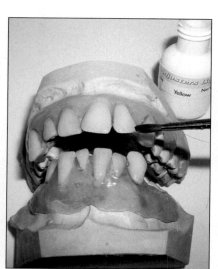

Fig. 6-71

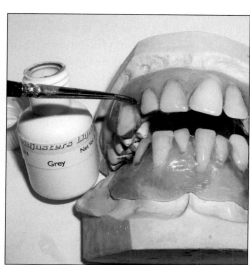

Fig. 6-72

20. Teeth should be fitted to the subject's mouth before use. File down any rough or sharp areas.

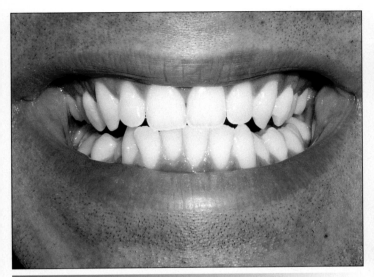

Fig. 6-73

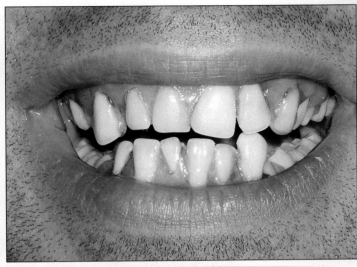

Fig. 6-74

MAKING VACUUM-FORMED VENEERS

MATERIALS NEEDED

- Dental Vacuum-forming Machine
- Dental Stone Casts
- Lang Jet Adjuster Kit
- Small Pair of Scissors
- Plastic Vacuum-forming Sheets
- Epoxy Parfilm Release

PROCEDURE

1. A dental vacuum-forming machine (available at dental supply stores) made for vacuum-forming bite guards and thin veneers.

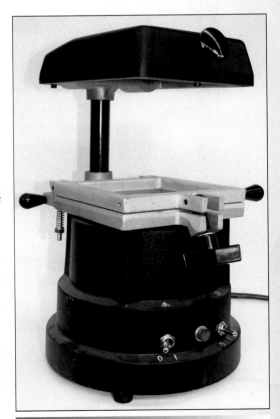

Fig. 6-75

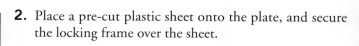

2. Place a pre-cut plastic sheet onto the plate, and secure the locking frame over the sheet.

Fig. 6-76

3. Raise the frame with plastic sheet in place, and set pre-released (previously sprayed) dental stone cast onto the vacuum-forming plate.

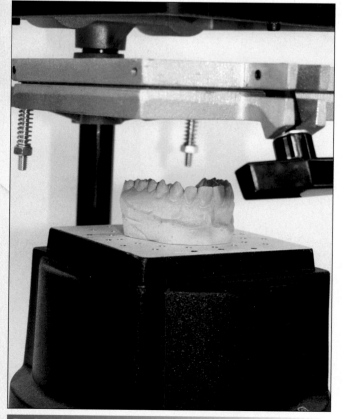

Fig. 6-77

4. Heat plastic under the heating element. Lower the plastic onto the dental cast, and turn on the vacuum system, which will pull the plastic down over the cast, forming it to the teeth and gums.

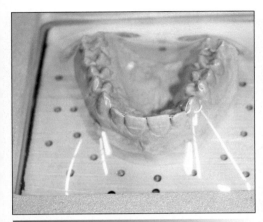

Fig. 6-78

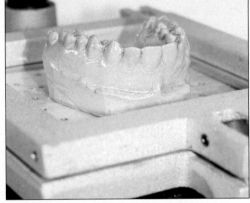

Fig. 6-79

5. Remove the plastic from the dental cast, and repeat the process with the lower dental casts.

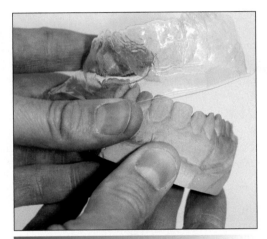

Fig. 6-80

6. Trim the plastic to the gum area with a small pair of scissors.

Fig. 6-81

Fig. 6-82

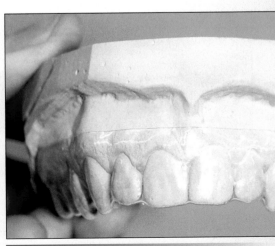

Fig. 6-83

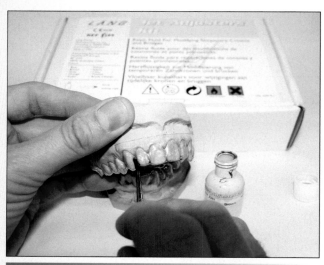

Fig. 6-84

7. Detail the plastic veneers on the outside or inside with various colors included in a Lang Jet Adjuster Kit. Start with brown.

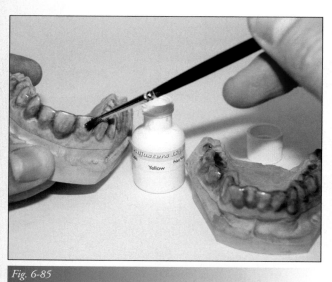

Fig. 6-85

8. Continue with yellow color in order to age the teeth.

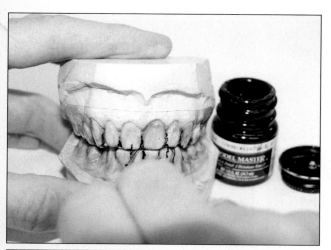

Fig. 6-86

9. Black enamel paint may be used to create cracks and deeper gaps between the teeth. Painting the cracks and gaps with a single bristle of a throwaway chip brush will create a very fine line.

10. The plastic veneers may be stored on the dental casts until ready for use.

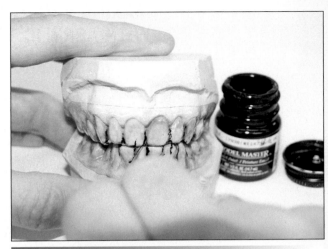

Fig. 6-87

11. Finished plastic veneers.

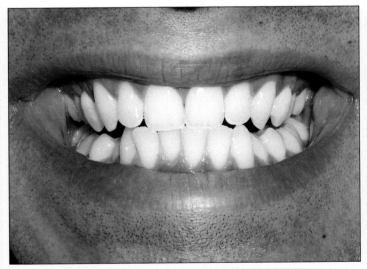

Fig. 6-88

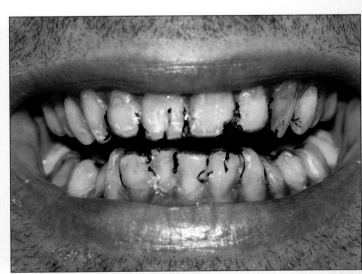

Fig. 6-89

MAKING VACUUM-FORMED VENEERS WITH ACRYLIC TOOTH ADDED

MATERIALS NEEDED

- Dental Vacuum-forming Machine
- Dental Stone Casts
- Lang Jet Adjuster Kit
- Wooden Tongue Depressors
- Clear Dental Polymer and Monomer
- Dremel Moto-Tool
- Plastic Vacuum-forming Sheets
- Spray Release
- Acrylic Stock Teeth
- Plastic Medical Mixing Cups
- Grinding Bit

Stock acrylic teeth (or a single tooth) may be adhered to a vacuum-formed plastic veneer to create crooked or distorted teeth.

PROCEDURE

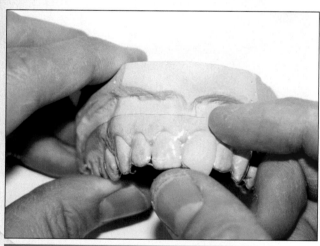

Fig. 6-90

1. File down a stock acrylic tooth, and fit it onto a pre-vacuum-formed plastic veneer.

2. Mix a small batch of clear dental acrylic, and paint onto the area where the tooth is to be secured.

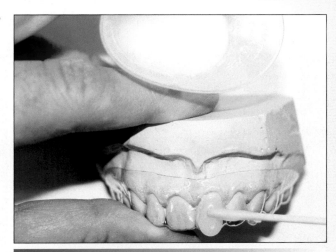

Fig. 6-91

3. Immediately set the acrylic tooth into place, and remove any excess acrylic from around it.

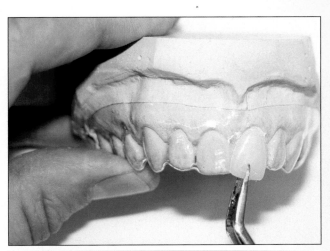

Fig. 6-92

4. Paint the acrylic tooth and the surrounding plastic veneer with a Lang Jet Adjuster Kit as explained previously.

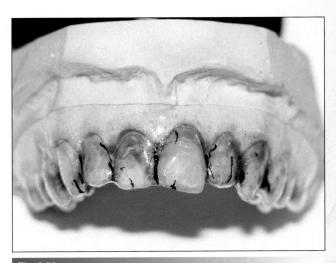

Fig. 6-93

5. Finished plastic veneers with acrylic tooth.

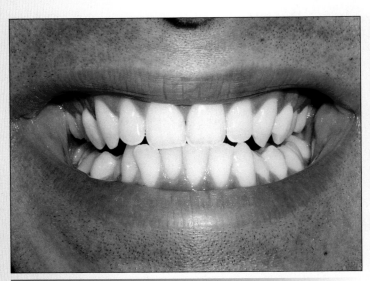

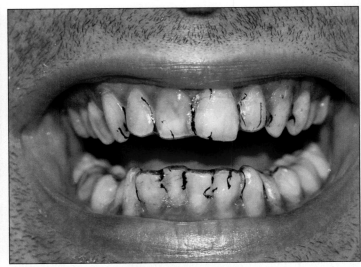

Fig. 6-95

Chapter 7

BLADDERS

Chapter 7

Making Bladders

Chapter 7

BLADDERS

Drafted by the authors from information generously submitted by Matthew Mungle.

MAKING BLADDERS

MATERIALS NEEDED

- Hairdryer
- Balloon Rubber
- Scissors
- W.M. Creations Scar Material
- Red Sharpie
- Pencil
- Powder

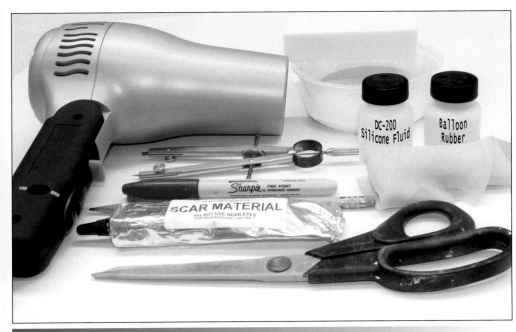

Fig. 7-1

- Powder Puff
- DC-200 (Dow Corning) Silicone Fluid
- Cut White Foam Sponges
- Silk Organza Fabric
- Dental Dam
- Drafting Compass
- Project Board (with Formica top)
- Small Cups for Rubber
- Cotton-tipped Applicator
- Acetone
- ⅛" I.D. Vinyl Tubing
- Barge Cement

PROCEDURE

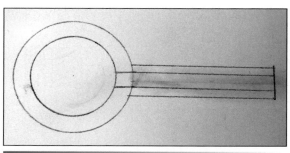

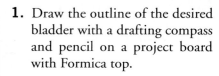
Fig. 7-2

1. Draw the outline of the desired bladder with a drafting compass and pencil on a project board with Formica top.

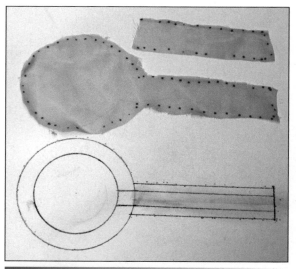
Fig. 7-3

2. Pre-cut silk organza to fit the drawing of the full bladder, and prepare an extra piece for the air passage.

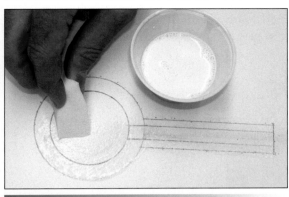

Fig. 7-4

3. Stipple balloon rubber onto the drawing of the bladder. Make sure each coat is dry before applying additional ones.

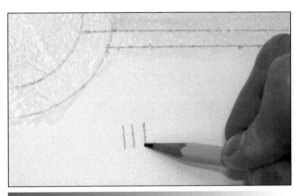

Fig. 7-5

4. Keep track of the number of coats of rubber applied by writing next to the bladder.

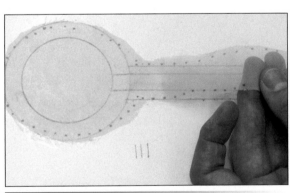

Fig. 7-6

5. After application of the third coat of rubber, carefully place the larger pre-cut piece of silk organza onto the bladder, ensuring there are no wrinkles or bubbles.

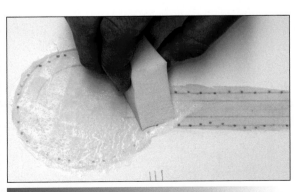

Fig. 7-7

6. Apply four additional coats of balloon rubber over the organza.

7. Deposit ¼ ounce of W.M. Scar Material into a medical plastic cup, and thin it with ¼ ounce of acetone. Apply one coat of plastic mixture into the center of the bladder, and ½" into the air passage.

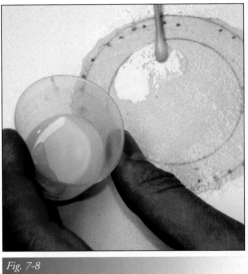

Fig. 7-8

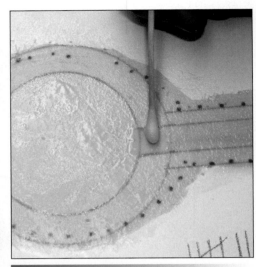

Fig. 7-9

8. Apply a very light application of DC-200 Silicone Fluid onto the same area where the scar material was applied.

Fig. 7-10

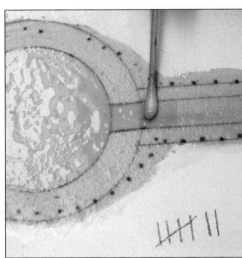

Fig. 7-11

9. Lightly coat a pre-cut piece of dental dam (sized to fit the air channel) with DC-200 Silicone Fluid.

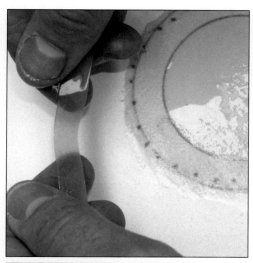
Fig. 7-12

Fig. 7-13

10. Carefully place the pre-lubed dental dam rubber piece over the air channel.

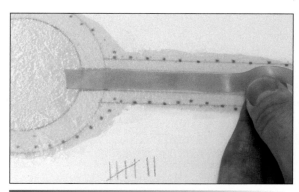
Fig. 7-14

11. Apply a thin coat of balloon rubber around the outside perimeter of the bladder.

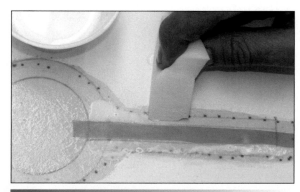
Fig. 7-15

12. Set the shorter pre-cut piece of organza over the air passage and into the wet rubber that was previously applied.

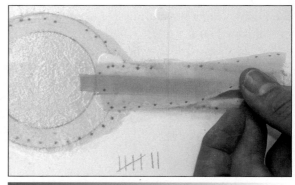

Fig. 7-16

13. Stipple one coat of rubber over the whole bladder, starting with the outside of the air passage area.

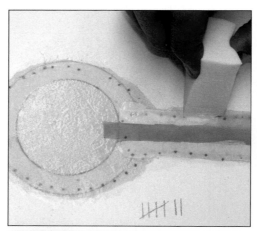

Fig. 7-17

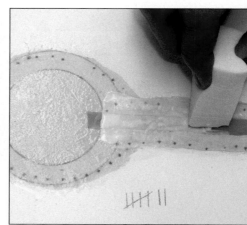

Fig. 7-18

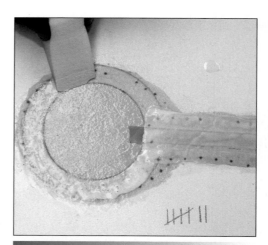

Fig. 7-19

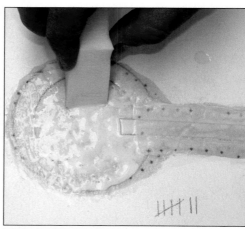

Fig. 7-20

14. Keep track of the number of coats applied.

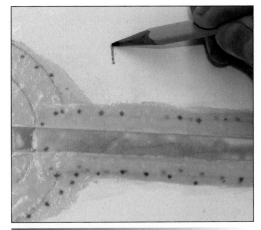

Fig. 7-21

15. After the application of the sixth coat of rubber, use a cotton-tipped applicator to apply an additional coat to the end of the dental dam rubber.

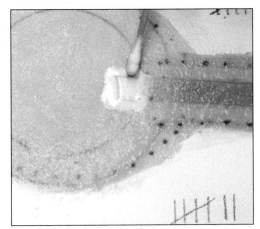

Fig. 7-22

16. Apply two more coats of rubber to the entire bladder.

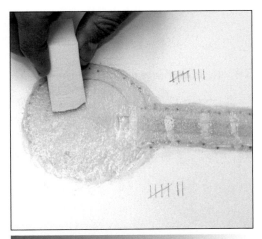

Fig. 7-23

17. Apply an additional four coats of rubber to the center of the bladder.

Fig. 7-24

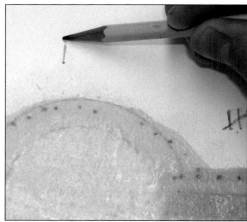

Fig. 7-25

Fig. 7-26

18. Apply powder with a powder puff to the bladder after the last coat of rubber has set.

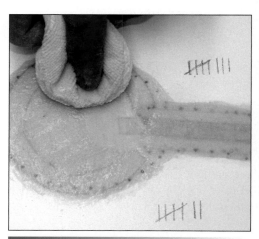

Fig. 7-27

19. Remove the bladder from the project board, and powder the backside.

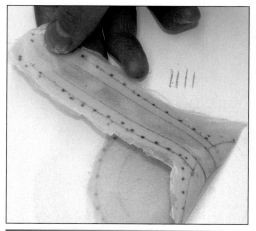

Fig. 7-28

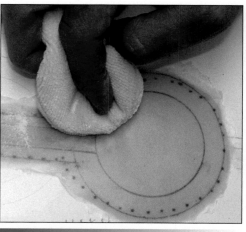

Fig. 7-29

20. Carefully trim the excess edges of the bladder with scissors.

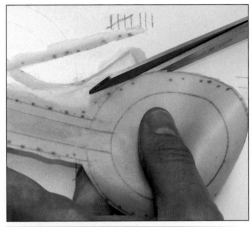

Fig. 7-30

21. Place the bladder onto a paper towel in a convection oven for 30 minutes at 150°F in order to vulcanize the rubber.

Fig. 7-31

22. Pull the dental dam air passage from the bladder.

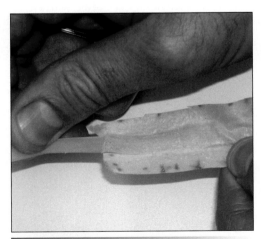

Fig. 7-32

23. Cut off the end of the bladder with scissors.

Fig. 7-33

24. Cut off the end of ⅛" inner diameter vinyl tubing at an angle.

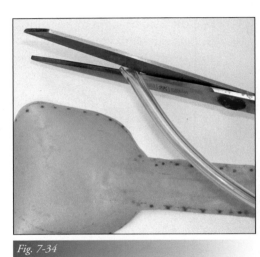

Fig. 7-34

25. Coat the end of the tubing with barge cement, and immediately insert it into the end of the bladder (approximately 1").

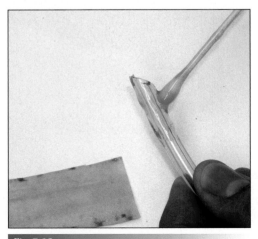

Fig. 7-35

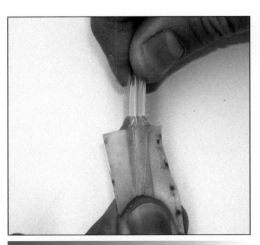

Fig. 7-36

26. The bladder may be blown up after drying for 2 hours.

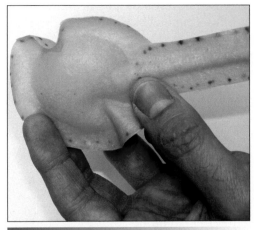

Fig. 7-37

FLAT TUBING FOR BLOOD PUMPING

1. Flat tubing may be made from heat shrink tubing purchased in any electronics store. Pulling the tubing creates a flat portion which can be applied underneath an appliance from which blood or goo may be pumped.

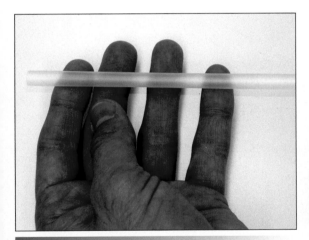

Fig. 7-38

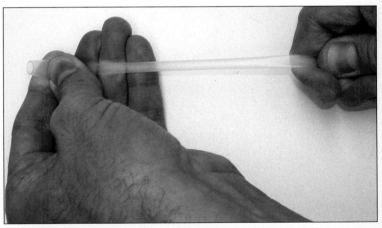

Fig. 7-39

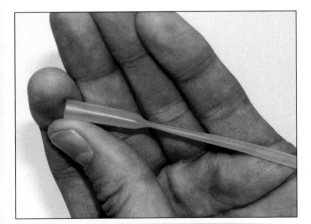

Fig. 7-40

2. Insert a vinyl tube into the round end of flattened tubing, and heat it with a heat gun, the result of which shrinks the heat shrink tubing around the vinyl tubing.

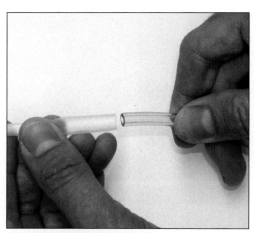

Fig. 7-41

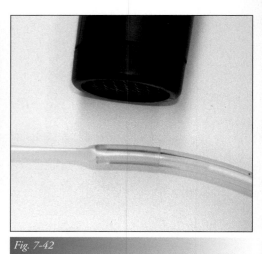

Fig. 7-42

Chapter 8

ARTISTS WORKING WITH SILICONE

Chapter 8

Silicone Appliances

Environmental Conditions and Mold Acceptability

Encapsulates

Pigmentation of Silicone

Preparation, Application, and Adhesion of Silicone Appliances

Step-by-step Condensation Cure Slicone Gel-filled Appliances with a Balloon Rubber Encapsulate

Application

Removal

Interview with Greg Cannom

Chapter 8

ARTISTS WORKING WITH SILICONE

Drafted by the authors from historic original silicone techniques. Many of which still apply today, and serve as a basic foundation for beginners in silicone work.

SILICONE APPLIANCES

SILICONE PROPERTIES AND USES

Silicones have been utilized for industrial and commercial applications since the 1960s. Every day, silicones are employed by hundreds of fields, such as medicine and dentistry, and industries, such as automobile, food, entertainment, aerospace, electronics, and military defense. Silicones are used for their heat resistance, chemical inertness, non-flammability, low surface tension, and high compressibility. These industries depend on silicones and would not work with the same speed and efficiency without them.

Silicones are synthetic polymers derived from the two most abundant elements on Earth: silicon and oxygen. Sand, clay, granite, quartz, and many other minerals contain the raw material, silicon. As a raw material, it is extremely useful. Some products are built from silicon in its elemental state. For example, small chips containing highly purified silicon are found in virtually every computer. Typically, silicon is processed in a number of ways for the manufacture of a huge family of products, including: fluids, emulsions, compounds, lubricants, resins, elastomers or rubbers, silicone sealants, and silicone adhesives, to list only a few of the varieties of silicone products.

Silicone is broken down from its raw form through a smelting process, which yields an ash-like product known as *fumed silica* (silicone dioxide). The fumed silica is then intermixed with methyl chloride to create methyl chlorosilanes. This is then distilled and hydrolyzed to create *poly* (dimethylsiloxane). At this point, *poly* (dimethylsiloxane) can be formulated into thousands of different products. In essence, the final result is flexible glass, which holds all the properties of glass without the disadvantages.

The make-up and special make-up effects industry typically only deals with poly (dimethylsiloxane) fluids, commonly known as DM fluid, silicone elastomers or rubbers, silicone adhesives, fumed silica, and silicone sealants or caulking.

HEALTH AND SAFETY

As with all chemicals, an M.S.D.S. (Materials Safety Data Sheet) should be read and followed in order to ensure safety and acquire a full understanding of the mixing procedure of your product. The M.S.D.S. should be provided with the purchased chemical. If one is not provided, request one from the manufacturer. The M.S.D.S. contains all the information for mixing your product, suggested room temperature, setting time, pot life, library life, chemical intermixing hazards, contact information for poison control centers, and necessary actions in the case of toxic interaction, among others.

At all times, all necessary steps and precautions must be taken to protect the artist, others, and the environment according to the M.S.D.S. and government regulations. This includes disposal of product waste, proper protective wear such as safety gloves, respiratory protection and ventilation, and storage of the product.

TYPES OF SILICONE APPLIANCE ELASTOMERS

Silicone appliances have been used for decades in the field of medicine for facial appliances, breast implants, and as skin for prosthetic limbs. Silicone is an excellent product for appliances and skin because of its strength, durability over time (or library life), and most of all, its realistic skin appearance and flesh-like feel. Within the last twenty years, the make-up and special make-up effects industry has begun to incorporate silicones for mold making, realistic props, mechanical skins, and prosthetic appliances.

Silicone appliances are separated into two different types: **gel-filled silicone elastomers** and **solid silicone elastomers**. The differences between the two silicone appliance types are very simple.

A gel-filled silicone appliance is based on the same technology used to create a silicone breast implant and consists of two aspects:

1. The silicone gel, which is a highly plasticized silicone elastomer that provides the flesh-like translucency and the soft, fleshy feel.

2. The envelope or encapsulating layer, which holds in the gel, creates fine blending edges, and has two major roles:

   A. To create a barrier for the silicone gel.

   B. To take a detailed impression of the sculptural surface details in the mold into which it is cast.

The envelope also moves with the silicone gel and creates its own small wrinkles, just like actual skin. For example, when you smile, your skin folds into itself, creating large and very fine surface wrinkling. A silicone gel-filled appliance will act, move, and maintain the same visual appearance as human skin. For these reasons, gel-filled silicone is the preferred method for silicone appliances.

The second type of silicone appliance is a solid silicone appliance. This method of silicone casting is typically used for props, mechanical skins, and medical prostheses. A solid silicone appliance is a cast silicone elastomer with oils added for plasticity (softness and flexibility) without additional surface layer or envelope as one would find in a gel-filled appliance. These appliances are typically used for medical appliances because of their durability and their longer shelf life, which makes them more cost-effective for long-term usage.

The disadvantage of cast silicone appliances is that they are unable to possess the same level of softness as with gel-filled varieties and inherently have a higher resistance of adhesion to skin. (which does not apply when this method is used for props and mechanical skins). The lack of adhesion is caused by the silicone oils—added to give the silicone its plasticity—which will eventually leak out of the silicone appliance. This escape of oil transpires with almost all silicone appliances, but more so with non-encapsulated silicones. The more silicone fluid, the more the appliance will leach.

SILICONE ELASTOMER CURE TYPES

All of the silicone systems are based on **vulcanization**, or how the silicone will cure. **Curing** refers to the process of how the silicone composition bonds or cross-links on a molecular level to make the silicone liquid turn into an interlocking chain of molecules or, in other words, into a solid silicone. This solid silicone will take an exact impression of any model into which it is cast. It also has memory, or the ability to compress, stretch, and return back to its original cured shape without the need for a new impression. Silicones are broken into two different cure types:

1. Addition cure
2. Condensation cure

These two types of silicones primarily cure by room temperature vulcanization (RTV). Although some silicones will only cure in the presence of heat, these silicones are high temperature vulcanization silicones (HTV). These HTV silicones will only be found in addition cure and will rarely be encountered by the make-up industry. Almost 99-percent of all the silicones utilized by the make-up industry—addition cure or condensation cure—will be RTV silicones.

Two-part Condensation Cure Silicones

Condensation cure silicones are the most commonly used of these two cure types. These silicones are by far the most user-friendly of all silicones. They will cure in practically any environment, against virtually any mold surface, and in conjunction with any mold release, except in a complete vacuum because of the required presence of air and its ambient moisture. This cure process is uninhibited by any scenario 99-percent of the time. Virtually all effects labs use these silicones for mold making, mechanical skins, and realistic props.

Condensation silicones consist of four major parts: a silicone polymer (silanol), water, a cross-linking agent, and a catalyst which contains tin. The purchased product that you will encounter will have only two parts: the silicone base, which contains the polymer and the cross-linking agent; and the catalyst (sometimes called an *activator*), which contains the tin and water. The tin initiates the cross-linking reaction and expedites the curing process. These condensation cure silicones are commonly called *tin silicones*, which refers to the tin catalyst. The cross-linking chemical reaction that takes place causes a chemical byproduct to be released. Usually, the byproduct is ethyl alcohol, which evaporates from the curing silicone. This small loss of material results in some slight shrinkage as cross-linking occurs and the ethyl alcohol evaporates.

Condensation silicones (tin) generally cure at lower temperatures than addition silicones; therefore, tin silicones should not be accelerated with additional heat. Tin silicones that have had an overabundance of heat added to them tend to swell and become brittle.

One-part Condensation Cure Silicones

There are several types of one-part condensation cure silicones, silicone caulking, silicone adhesives, and silicone sealants. These silicones are all very similar, are typically very thick and semi-translucent, and will take from several hours to several days to fully cure depending upon the thickness of the material. There are two different one-part condensation cure types:

1. Acetoxy
2. Oxime

Acetoxy is very easily distinguished. It has a very strong vinegar odor because of the acetic acid it releases as it cures. This silicone will cure at an accelerated rate in the presence of excessive moisture.

Oxime cures in a very similar way to the acetoxy one-part silicone, but with minimal odor. It cures in a very neutral fashion, releasing a very small amount of byproduct. These silicones tend to cure somewhat more slowly than acetoxy, but are much safer to work with. Oxime will also cure at a faster rate with the presence of excessive moisture.

Addition Cure Silicones

Addition cure silicone is by far the most stable silicone composition available. These silicones exhibit excellent physical properties such as library life, tear strength, and elongation. Addition cure silicones are the most commonly used elastomers in the medical field for prosthetic appliances. They are considered to be the safest for long-term contact (over years, for example) with human tissue because the silicones do not release a byproduct during the curing process.

Just as condensation cure silicone elastomers employ several elements to create the cross-linking reaction, so do addition cure silicones, which consist of three major parts: vinyl polymers, a cross-linking agent (methyl hydrogen fluid), and a catalyst (platinum). The purchased product has only two parts: the silicone base and the catalyst. The base will contain the vinyl polymers and the cross-linking agent. Note that sometimes the cross-linking agent is placed in the catalyst instead of in the base. The second part is the catalyst, which contains the platinum. The platinum is what initiates the cross-linking reaction and speeds up the curing process.

Addition cure or *platinum cure silicones*, as they are commonly known, work according to a self-contained chemical reaction. Unlike condensation cure silicones, addition cure silicones do not need air or moisture to cure, which means they can cure in a vacuum if required. Addition cure silicones also have negligible shrinkage since no byproduct is released during the cure process.

Unlike condensation cure, addition cure silicones can be accelerated by the addition of heat. There are two different addition cure types: RTV (room temperature vulcanization) and HTV (high temperature vulcanization). RTV silicones can have the curing time accelerated with heat, but HTV silicones will *only* cure with heat. Some HTV silicones can be cured in a matter of minutes without damage to the integrity of the final product.

The disadvantage of addition cure silicones is that they are easily cure-inhibited by many of the materials used by make-up effects artists. Most addition cure silicones will not cure against or in close proximity to materials that contain sulfur. Almost all forms of latex contain some amount of sulfur, such as foam latex; sulfur is one of the main ingredients in the curing agent. Many sculpting clays may also contain sulfur. Make sure to purchase sulfur-free clay when working with addition cure silicones. There are many other materials that will inhibit addition cure: tin, which is in all condensation cure silicones; the ammonia that is added to all latex products; polyester resin, among other resins (test for compatibility, not all platinum silicones have the same sensitivity); a variety of different mold releases and solvents; and a multitude of other materials. For safety, it is always recommended to test the compatibility of materials with addition cure silicones before extensively working with them. As a result of these compatibility problems, many make-up and effects artists will not use addition silicones. If proper testing and precautions are taken, however, addition silicones can be very useful.

SILICONE ADDITIVES AND CATALYSTS

There are many additives that can be used to change the properties of silicone elastomers. These additives can alter the setting time, change the viscosity from a liquid to a paste (or vise versa), and change the durometer or softness. Each cure type or addition or condensation cure will have its own list of compatible ingredients. Each silicone manufacturer will have its own additives that are designed to work with its materials. This does not mean that you can only use the additives in conjunction with their designed partner. After some amount of testing, most additives can be used with any silicone elastomer system of choice as long as they are in the same family of cure types. The rule of thumb is as follows: condensation with condensation, and addition with addition. Simply put, you would not want to mix a tin catalyst with an addition cure silicone system, nor a platinum thixotropic (thickening) agent with a condensation cure system. This mismatching of additives and silicone brands will change the product's reaction, the setting time, and the physical properties of the finished cured piece. So be certain to test before working with any new product combination.

Rapid Catalysts

Rapid catalysts are one of the most common additives. These catalysts can be used to alter the setting time of your silicone system from hours to minutes, and even seconds if necessary. In addition cure systems, they can even be used to help with cure inhibition while also accelerating the curing process. It will sometimes help to add a very thin layer of an addition cure rapid catalyst to the mold surface in order to create a barrier from inhibition.

The only downside to accelerating the setting process with rapid catalysts is the shrinkage of the silicone and ultimately, an accelerated breakdown of the material. This shrinkage will eventually cause the silicone to become brittle, and even malformed. These factors are based on the amount of rapid catalyst that is added the silicone mixture. These catalysts can be used in addition to the regular catalyst, and sometimes even used to replace the original catalyst. This all depends on how fast you need the silicone to cure.

Just as with most silicone additives, different types are manufactured by each brand and for each cure type.

SILICONE FLUIDS

Poly (dimethylsiloxane) fluids work as softening agents and thinners for silicone elastomers. They can also be referred to as DM fluids, diluents, plasticizer, or silicone oil. These fluids are measured in viscosity by centistokes (cst). The viscosity of DM fluid can range from water-thin to a very slow-moving gel. The most common fluids used are 20, 50, 100, and 1,000 centistokes. Silicone fluids can even be found in the tens of thousands of centistokes. The larger the number, the more viscous the material. The most commonly used fluids are 20 and 50 (cst). These fluids are mostly used for thinning and softening silicone elastomers. The higher-centistoke fluids can be used for softening, but their viscosity does not work for thinning elastomers. Silicone fluids are virtually odorless, and in lower centistokes are as clear as water.

When plasticizing silicone elastomers, the amount of silicone fluid is determined by percentage. For example, a silicone plasticized by 30-percent means that an additional 30-percent of oil has been added to the original amount of silicone base. The higher the number, the softer the elastomers will become with increased elongation. There are two downsides to heavily plasticized silicone elastomers (50-percent and above). First is the loss of tear strength due to the weakening of the silicone's molecular chain. This weakened molecular chain also produces the second disadvantage: the migration of the silicone fluid out of the finished cured silicone. The fluid migration or *leaching*, as it is sometimes called, causes the surface to become oily and somewhat shiny. An overabundance of fluid migration can cause the cured silicone elastomers to shrink and eventually lose some or most of their memory.

Volatile silicone fluids are similar to the previously described poly (dimethylsiloxane) fluids. These fluids will evaporate when exposed to air and are flammable. They can be used to thin silicones or can act as solvents for painting. They have virtually no odor, which make them a user-friendly solvent substitute. The evaporation rate is similar to that of isopropyl alcohol. The viscosity is much less than standard silicone fluids. Dow Corning Corporation manufactures the most common fluids: OS-10, 20, 30, 70, 80, and 90. As with other silicone fluids, the lower the number, the lower the viscosity. When using these volatile fluids, especially for airbrushing, make sure to do so in well-ventilated areas. *(For more information about airbrush techniques, see Volume I.)*

THIXOTROPIC AGENTS

Thixotropic agents or *thix*, as they are sometimes referred to, work as thickening agents for silicone elastomers. Most thixotropic agents are typically made from silicone polyether co-polymers with dioxane, ethylene oxide, and propylene oxide.

Once thixotropic agents are added to catalyzed silicone elastomers, the material will begin to thicken. The thixotropic agent is activated by pressure; the more force used to mix the material, the faster the material will thicken. Depending on the amount of thix added to the mix, the silicone can change drastically. Small percentages can force elastomers to thicken faster and shorten the work time. This works especially well when using a very thin silicone that is brushed into a mold with an abundance of detail, with the following considerations: You do not need a lot of working time; you wish to add thickness; and you do not want to weaken the silicone by adding extra catalyst or a fast-setting catalyst. You can also thicken elastomers to paste-like consistencies for building thickness quickly by using higher percentages of thix. This works very well when creating brush-up molds and castings that require minimal drips and runs.

ENVIRONMENTAL CONDITIONS AND MOLD ACCEPTABILITY

When working with silicone elastomers, consider the following: room temperature; humidity; mold type; mold release; and naturally, the silicone cure type to be used. All of these steps must be taken before casting silicone elastomers. By understanding the material and the way in which the environment will affect the material, you can predetermine the final result of the cured elastomers.

As stated before, addition cure silicones are very easily inhibited. This problem can be avoided if the proper steps are taken and a study of your working environment is done.

The rule of thumb with any new addition cure system is to test by casting a small batch into the mold you plan to use. This test will allow you to see what the final result might be. Before testing, make sure that the mold is platinum-friendly. Addition cure silicone molds are safe, but you cannot cast into condensation (tin) cure molds, since tin will inhibit addition cure. Other non-compatible molds would be polyester (Some platinum silicone may be compatible), some aromatic and aliphatic epoxies, some poly-urethanes, and any mold that has been contaminated by sulfur, or a mold in which foam latex cast has been baked.

To reiterate, test the compatibility of any molds you plan to use. If you have no other choice but to use an addition cure system, perform these tests before molding your sculpture. (Your sculpting clay should be made form a non-sulfur-based material.) If using a pre-existing mold, make sure to clean the mold completely with acetone (if it will not damage the mold's surface) or alcohol. Methyl ethyl ketone (M.E.K.) can even be used. It is sometimes beneficial to bake the mold at a temperature of 180°F for 4–6 hours in an oven that is free of sulfur.

Once a compatible molding material has been determined, you must then determine a safe mold release, such as the following: epoxy parfilm; a tin foil substitute very similar to alcote without the tin; clear poly vinyl alcohol (P.V.A.); sulfur-free wax; some soaps; and in some rare cases, petroleum jelly, which should be pre-tested before use.

Once all measures have been taken to ensure that there is complete compatibility, you can then cast your addition cure elastomers. If there are still inhibition problems, go back and double-check your steps. If the process is error-free but problems remain, try heating the mold in an oven to accelerate the cure process, slightly increasing the catalyst, or brushing a platinum rapid catalyst onto the surface of the mold.

Condensation cure silicones are much easier to use than addition cure silicones. These silicones will set up in virtually any environment, with any kind of mold release, and against almost any type of mold. Condensation silicones are primarily affected by heat and humidity. Since condensation silicones cure with the amount of moisture in the air, it is assumed that the setting rate will change based upon the amount of present moisture. For instance, on a hot, humid day, your silicone will set at a much faster rate. But, on a very cold day with low levels of humidity, your silicone could take many more hours than normal. These weather conditions can pose quite a bit of trouble if the material must set within a normal time limit as the result of a tight deadline. If the silicone needs to reach a de-moldable point quickly on a cold day with low humidity, you could do two things:

1. Find a warm area, possibly even an oven, but no warmer than 90°F. The warmth will help accelerate the process. Too much warmth will cause the material to expand.

2. Increase the catalyst by a percentage point or two to speed the process.

Overcatalyzing does come with a price, however: a very minute amount of shrinkage, and a shortened library life. On average, condensation silicones are catalyzed at 10-percent to the base (100 grams of base to 10 grams of catalyst); adding 1- or 2-percent will not make a huge amount of difference in the long run. On the other hand, if you were casting silicone on a very hot, humid day, 1- or 2-percent above the normal amount of catalyst could make a drastic difference. This would especially affect the pot life or the amount of working time. On such a day, it might be beneficial to decrease the amount of catalyst slightly by 1-or 2-percent, which will afford more working time. Lowering the catalyst should only be done in extreme conditions because of the risk of undercatalyzing the silicone. An undercatalyzed silicone would not have enough memory and could be damaged quite easily. Extreme cases of memory loss usually happen when the catalyst is under by 3 or more percent.

ENCAPSULATES

Gel-filled silicone appliances require encapsulates or a barrier between the silicone gel and the mold surface. The encapsulate serves three purposes: It acts as a container for the silicone gel; it creates superior blending edges; and it allows the surface to move with the gel, giving it the look of real skin. A simple way to visualize this is to imagine the encapsulate as a plastic bag inside which the silicone gel is permanently bonded. The silicone therefore moves according to the bag, which allows the encapsulate or membrane to create subtle surface wrinkling. But in this case, the plastic bag would be an impression of the sculpture created from negative and positive molds.

There are many different materials that can be used for the surface encapsulate. The most commonly used are one- and two-part silicone elastomers, natural latex, acrylic polymers, plastics, and urethanes. The silicone cure type you choose to use will determine the choice of encapsulate. With addition cure silicones, you must test the compatibility. As discussed before, addition cure silicones are easily cure-inhibited. With most addition cure silicone gels, you will find that there are many silicone elastomers that can be used. Some acrylic and plastics polymers can also be used as the encapsulate but must first be tested for compatibility. With condensation cure silicone gels, 99-percent of all encapsulates can be used.

Most encapsulates can be applied in a variety of different ways. Some require the use of an airbrush, while others are hand-stippled or thinly brushed into the mold. The airbrush usually creates superior results that produce a more even layer with more control for the creation of thin blending edges. This technique cannot always be used, however. Many silicone elastomers can only be brushed by hand because of the viscosity of the material and the artist's inability to dilute it without drastically altering its properties. Hand-brushed materials must be applied as thinly as possible and feathered at the edges. Most two-part silicone elastomer encapsulates must be applied very quickly as a result of the fast setting time. This must be taken into consideration when working with very large molds.

When using any of the above-mentioned methods, make sure to use clean new tools (airbrush bottles, needle and caps, solvent safe brushes, and new stipple sponges [latex or synthetic]) that are dedicated to applying the encapsulate. Any contamination could result in a damaged encapsulate layer. The risk of an encapsulate not setting as a result of contamination is especially high when working with platinum-based materials.

It is very important to understand how the encapsulate works and how many layers need to be applied to achieve the desired look. The encapsulate creates the subtle surface wrinkling that you see when the appliance moves. The amount of encapsulate applied can affect how the appliance will move. A thinner layer will produce very subtle wrinkling, while heavy layers will produce heavy or even exaggerated, animal-like wrinkles. The movement of the encapsulate is also affected by the softness of the silicone gel. Testing a combination of the two (the thickness of the encapsulate and the softness of the silicone gel) can take time. Once established, the final look and feel of the appliance can be truly shocking as a result of its realistic appearance.

PIGMENTATION OF SILICONE

Silicones can be intrinsically or extrinsically colored, or a combination of the two. Silicone gels are traditionally translucent materials. The translucent quality of silicone accounts for its realistic appearance. When choosing a silicone pigmentation process, you must first decide on the final design. The design type (human or otherwise) will determine how translucent or opaque the silicone need be. There will be times when you may need to overlay your appliance with an abundance of extrinsic color. This will require the silicone to be more translucent in order to allow the opaque extrinsic paintwork. This same rule would apply in reverse: If you were to create a more opaque silicone appliance and wished to retain its subtle translucence, you would need to make your extrinsic paintwork more translucent by applying washes of color instead of opaque layers.

Understanding translucency is very important when pigmenting silicone to resemble human skin. Skin is only somewhat translucent and absorbs a certain amount of light. If translucency were built on a scale from one to ten, with one being completely transparent and ten completely opaque, human skin would lie somewhere between a seven and an eight. To therefore resemble skin, the silicone would need to be more on the opaque side of the scale, allowing only a small amount of light to pass through it, much as light passes through the thin parts of the ears. This in turn will allow you to color extrinsically with translucent washes of color. The process of coloration allows you to match the subject's base tone intrinsically and to apply extrinsic adjusting colors subtly, such as warm red tones, blue tones, olive tones, highlights and shadows, liver spots, freckles, etc.

Some artists may prefer to achieve the final result with heavy extrinsic painting, which will work just as effectively and impart the same translucent look, but it must be approached in reverse of the previous technique. In this process, you must mix the silicone more translucently, somewhere along the lines of a five or six on the scale. This will allow more room for extrinsic painting while resulting in the same natural and realistic appearance.

INTRINSIC COLORATION

The intrinsic pigmentation process can be achieved through many different techniques. Some of the most common are as follows: cosmetic pigment dispersions, cosmetic make-up dispersions, powdered pigments, universal colorants, and flocking fibers. Note that all of the techniques and pigments must be tested with addition cure silicones for compatibility. Many minerals and metals used in cosmetic pigments and other colorants can inhibit addition cures. Remember: If unsure, it is always safer to test.

Cosmetic powdered pigments can be used to pigment silicone elastomers, although emulsifying the powdered pigment into the silicone base can be very difficult. Powdered pigment added directly into the silicone elastomer can be almost impossible to mix, depending upon the size of the pigment granules. Small pigment granules will intermix somewhat easily, but many times they will begin to separate within a matter of hours and will need to be mixed for reincorporation prior to catalyzing.

This process requires the cosmetic pigments to be pre-emulsified or dispersed into a compatible vehicle. The vehicle is most commonly a poly (dimethylsiloxane) fluid, such as 100 (cst). Hundred-centistoke fluids are used for their viscosity and will hold the pigment in place better than a fluid with a lower centistoke. Fifty-centistoke fluids can also be used, but the pigment will separate at a much faster rate. Emulsifying the pigment into the silicone fluid can be a very tenacious process. A blender works very well when started at a low speed and then accelerated until a mixture is achieved. A 60/40 (60-percent pigment, 40-percent oil) or a 50/50 ratio works well to create a thick fluid that is highly pigmented. The less of this dispersion used, the better. Too much of the dispersion will cause the silicone to become overly opaque and change the plasticity.

This dispersion concept also works very well with oil-based cosmetic make-up. Cosmetic make-up can be milled into silicone fluids by mixing it directly into a small amount of the silicone base in order to create a concentrated paste. Incorporating the make-up base into silicone fluid can be very labor-intensive, but utilizing a household blender will save a large amount of time and create a more structural emulsion. A 2/1 (2 parts oil, 1 part make-up base) ratio works well to create a concentrated, thick fluid. The same ratio works effectively for incorporating a make-up base directly into silicone elastomers. When doing so, the ratio would be 2 parts silicone elastomer to 1 part make-up base. Mix these two components until uniform. Mixing on a wax paper palette with a palette knife and aggressively milling the pigment into the silicone elastomer will save time and allow the true color to be visible on the white wax palette. This is the preferred technique.

Universal colorants are very commonly used in labs for many different reasons: They are very opaque; are much cheaper than cosmetic pigments and make-up bases; and also have a very long shelf life with minor pigment-to-vehicle separation. Universal colorants can be found at most paint stores and hardware stores. They are commonly used outside of our industry for pigmenting house paints. One downside to pigmenting silicones with universal colorants is the fact that these contain a certain amount of water. This is a problem especially when working with condensation cure silicones. The common ratio is 1-percent (or less) pigment to 99-percent silicone base for natural skin translucency.

Flocking fibers, which are very small and colored—like tiny little hairs—are very useful when pigmenting silicones. They are commonly made from rayon or cotton. The rayon fibers disperse more evenly and hold true to their color. Cotton fibers tend to swell and change color as a result of the amount of oil in the elastomer. Flocking can be used as an adjusting color and can provide a natural modeling to a pre-pigmented silicone. Flocking can also be used to pigment silicones completely, which will give the effect of a painted, finished piece. Too much flocking can present a problem, however. On many occasions, the flocking can migrate, gather, and settle in dense groups, especially around blending edges on injected silicone appliances, bleeder holes, and low areas in the mold. The likelihood of this occurrence is based upon the amount of oil and the length of the pot life. The longer the silicone takes to set, the higher the probability that flocking migration will take place. This only applies to large amounts of flocking. 1- to 2-percent is usually enough when used as an adjusting color. Other options include manufactured silicone pigments, which are preferred with platinum silicones. These pigments come at a premium cost, but are safe and highly emulsified. Artist' oil paint may also be used for intrinsic colorization but should be tested with addition cure silicones for compatibility.

EXTRINSIC COLORATION

Now that we have covered some of the most common methods for intrinsic coloration, let us examine some of the common techniques for extrinsic coloration. Extrinsic coloration is very important when detailing and adding elaborate patterns to the finished appliance. Intrinsic coloration can only give a certain amount of detail, such as a base tone on top of which the paintwork can begin. Note that there are certain techniques that can be used to color silicones completely intrinsically. This would require many different colors of silicone to be painted into the negative mold and a thixotropic agent to be added to the mix in order to hold the colors in place. This technique only works well with solid silicones elastomers for skins or non-gel-filled appliances.

Extrinsic coloration can be achieved by hand-painting, airbrushing, or even spattering colors to achieve a pointillism effect. A combination of techniques will give extreme depth and realism, especially with skin-like effects. Most coloring mediums that can be used extrinsically will be determined by the material from which the encapsulate is made. Only certain materials can be used to color certain encapsulates. Some of the most common coloring mediums are as follows: temporary tattoo inks, silicone paints, rubber mask grease paints, air brush acrylics diluted with 70- or 99-percent alcohol, and powder pigments.

The only problems are that certain materials will stick to silicone encapsulates, and the alcohol used in some colorants can dissolve others. Overall, extrinsic paints are very difficult to adhere to silicones, because simply from a technical standpoint, only other silicones will permanently bond to them.

With silicone encapsulates and solid silicone elastomers, it is preferable to pre-paint with silicone paints. A mixture of oxime silicone caulking and oil-based pigment, diluted with a solvent, will create a silicone-based paint. The mixing process is detailed in the next section.

SILICONE PAINT MIXTURE

The first step is to create a silicone caulking paste. It is necessary to thin the caulking slightly before adding the pigment; otherwise, the caulking will be too thick and the pigment will not intermix smoothly. Adding a solvent to the caulking will allow dilution. Common solvents are OS-10 silicone solvent, naphtha, D-limonene, or mineral spirits. (Naphtha and mineral spirits are more widely used). Add a small amount of solvent to your caulking, and mix till combined. It is easier to emulsify a small amount at a time as opposed to adding all the solvent at once. Mix until the emulsion is similar in consistency to Vaseline (not runny but smooth).

Once this paste is made, you can add your pigment. Oil-based artist pigments and oil-based cream make-up can be used to pigment the silicone caulking paste. A 2-part caulking, 1-part pigment ratio works well to create a medium opacity high-adhesion paint base. This paint base can be diluted with 4 to 8 parts solvent in order to create an airbrush consistency. The addition of more solvent would create a very thin translucent paint that will retain adhesive qualities.

This paint mixture can be airbrushed or hand-painted over the solid silicone elastomers, silicone encapsulated gel-filled appliances, some plastic and vinyl cap material encapsulates or latex encapsulated gel-filled appliances. This will provide a paint that will permanently adhere to the appliances or elastomers. Before painting it is very important to clean the silicone appliance and elastomers. Using acetone and 99-percent isopropyl alcohol to remove any residual mold release and oils leaching from the silicone will prime the material for paint. **Note:** *Many plastic, vinyl, and acrylic encapsulated appliances can not be cleaned with 99% isopropyl alcohol or acetone as it will damage the material. Soap and water or alcohol free baby wipes should be used instead. As a result of their solvent sensitivity, these materials allow a better adhesion of temporary tattoo inks than other encapsulates.*

Once painting with the silicone paint mixture is finished, it is important to seal the paintwork with a final layer of silicone caulking, which will lock the paint in place and insure proper adhesion. This final clear layer is mixed the same way as before—by adding solvent to the clear oxime silicone caulking to create a paste. Once the paste is created, TS-100 can be added to the mix to make the mixture matte. TS-100 is very similar to Cab-O-Sil (fumed silica), but it is better for matting than thickening. (Note: When working with Cab-O-Sil or TS-100, it is important to wear proper respiratory protection and work in a well-ventilated environment, preferably a filter spray booth.) Once the TS-100 has been emulsified into the mix, you can then thin the mixture further with solvent to create an airbrush consistency.

With any of these paint mixtures, it is important to pour it through a paint strainer to remove possible small particulates before putting it into your airbrush. It is also very important to clean the airbrush with the solvent you have chosen for painting immediately after you have finished painting; otherwise, your airbrush will permanently seal shut. (*For more information about airbrush techniques, see Volume I.*)

Many other types of paintwork can be sealed with a clear layer of silicone caulking paint. In case you use an acrylic-based encapsulate and paint it with temporary tattoo inks, you can seal the final paint job with a layer of clear silicone caulking paint to lock the colors in place. You can also paint your silicones with temporary tattoo inks or acrylic airbrush paint (diluted with 70-percent alcohol) and lock it all together with a layer of clear silicone caulking paint. If left unsealed, the paint will wipe off the silicone somewhat easily. The only way to ensure a paint job will stick to silicone is to use silicone paints. As mentioned previously, only silicone will stick permanently to silicone. This material is never safe for use on skin. **Note:** *As stated previously, many plastic cap materials can be used as an encapsulating material (Baldiez and Super Baldiez by Mould Life is the industry standard). These materials do not usually need any type of sealer and allow temporary tattoo inks to adhere on their own.*

PREPARATION, APPLICATION, AND ADHESION OF SILICONE APPLIANCES

Once your silicone appliance is de-molded, you must first prepare it by removing all bleeders and excess overspray on the blending edges. (Tear the fine blending edges with your fingers. Never cut with scissors.) Trim all bleeders down, flush on the back of the appliance. In some cases, it may be necessary to seal the bleeder areas with a thin layer of silicone caulking to ensure that once applied, the appliance will stick to the skin without the oil from the silicone gel inhibiting the adhesion. **Note:** *Many artists that do not inject their silicone gel instead use an open pour method such as in foam latex and gelatin casting. With this type of casting process it is preferred to retain at least 1/4 inch of flashing attached to the edge to be used as a handle while applying and blending the silicone edges.*

When applying silicone appliances, it is always important to clean them prior to sealing bleeder or painting with the appropriate solvent for the encapsulate. Once cleaned, you can then seal and pre-paint. Most silicone must be applied with silicone medical adhesives, and it is important to use a double-contact approach, which requires painting silicone medical adhesive onto the skin and the back of the appliance. Once applied, the edges can be further blended with silicone medical adhesive thinner. Final blending can be achieved by stippling with a red stipple sponge over the edge with an acrylic emulsion adhesive such as Pros-Aide or Pros-Aide thickened with Cab-O-Sil. **Note:** *In the case od plastic encapsulates (baldiez) a small amount of 99% alcohol can be used or a very dry application of acetone can be used to melt the edges in to the skin.*

With addition cure silicone appliances, depending upon how much silicone oil was used to plasticize the silicone, an acrylic emulsion adhesive such as ADM Tronics Pros-Aide (prosthetic adhesive) or Premiere Products Beta Bond, or any silicone medical adhesive can be used to apply them. The same double-contact adhesion approach should still be used.

STEP-BY-STEP CONDENSATION CURE SILICONE GEL-FILLED APPLIANCES WITH A BALLOON RUBBER ENCAPSULATE

The creation of a silicone overlapping make-up is very similar to any other overlapping process, albeit with a few new necessary steps. After the sculpture is finished and broken down into all the individual appliance parts by using a standard float and snap technique, all detailing and blending onto the new corrected positive molds must be finished. (Note: All molds should be designed so that they can be easily clamped.) Before flashing, scribe a line into the positive mold about ⅛" from the edge of the sculpture's edges.

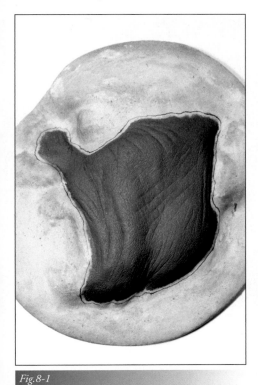

Fig. 8-1

Marked for etching.

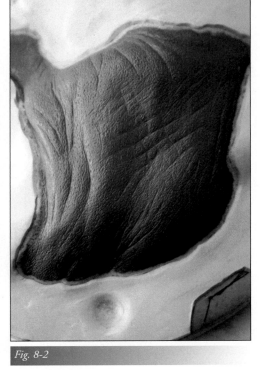

Fig. 8-2

Left cheek flashed.

This line does not need to be very deep (¹⁄₃₂" will suffice), but deep enough to make a subtle line that will be permanently visible. This line will be necessary later when the encapsulate is applied to the mold. It will give a visible reference for the end of the cutting edge. The flashing clay is then applied to the mold as would normally be done with a ⅛" thickness of clay. A 45-degree angle is then cut along the edge that was scribed.

After the molds have been completed and cleaned (preferably made from epoxical, BJB 16-30, or epoxy syntactic), it is necessary to drill and prep the molds for injection. Note that the molds I used to form this make-up were made with epoxical negatives and ⅓ Die–Keen and Ultracal 30 positive. All sculpture (not flashing) clay should be kept for use as a visual volume reference. This clay can be weighed, and 70-percent of that total can be used as the silicone amount.

The drilled injection points on the positive mold should be placed in the thickest area of the sculpture to ensure the silicone flows easily. This injection point should only be ¼" or less, depending upon the size of the appliance, and then taper up in the back of the positive to the size of the syringe that will be used. Aside from the injection point, bleeder holes are also drilled about 3/16" from the etched scribe line on the positive. For these bleeders, I used a 1/16"–6" long aircraft bit. The bleeder holes are placed every one to two inches apart and in any deep area. Note that if the mold does not bleed when injecting silicone, it may be necessary to enlarge these holes. If the area does not fill, additional bleeders may be drilled.

Fig. 8-3

Further drilling.

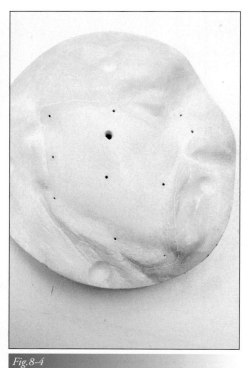

Fig.8-4

Cheek drill holes.

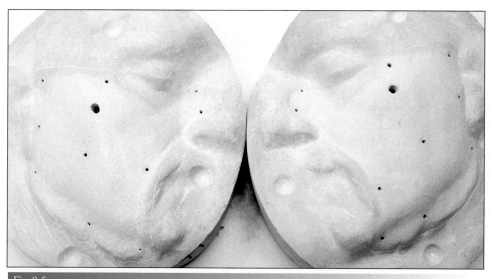

Fig. 8-5

Drill holes seen in both cheeks.

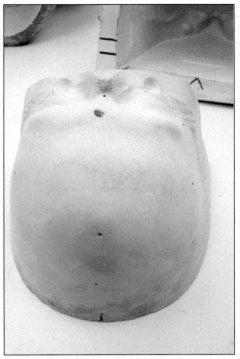

Fig. 8-6

Forehead drill holes.

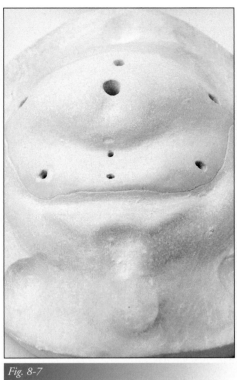

Fig. 8-7

Chin drill holes.

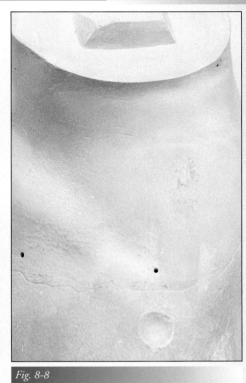

Fig. 8-8

Neck drill holes.

Fig. 8-9

Another view of drill holes in the neck.

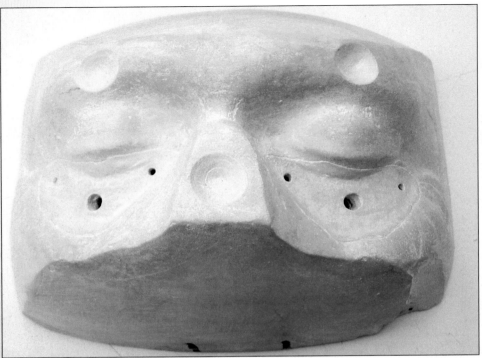

Fig. 8-10

Eye bag drill holes.

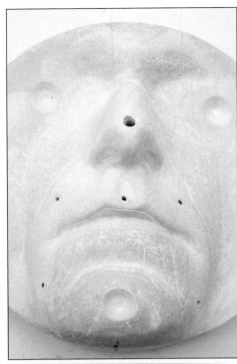

Fig. 8-11

Nose drill holes.

Once drilled and cleaned with 99-percent alcohol to remove all clay (Chavant NSP was used for this sculpture), the mold is ready for release. A dry non-petroleum release should be applied. Stearic acid, which is the white mold release found in all foam latex kits, is the perfect choice.

This will not only allow the encapsulate to be de-molded easily, but it will also break the

Fig. 8-12

Mold release.

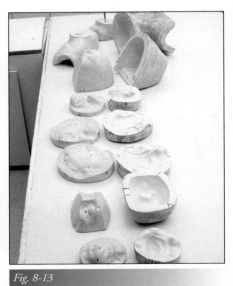

Fig. 8-13

Released molds.

surface tension when airbrushing the latex into the molds. The stearic acid should be applied thinly and evenly to all parts of the positive and negative molds and allowed to dry completely. Once dry, the molds will turn a matte, cloudy white color, which will enable you to see where the shiny encapsulate has been applied.

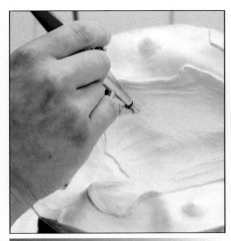

Fig. 8-14

Airbrushing the encapsulate.

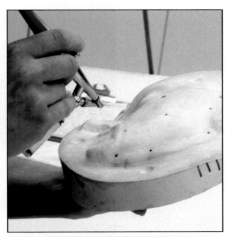

Fig. 8-15

Another view of the airbrushing process.

At this point, the encapsulate can be applied to the molds by airbrush. For this application, a low-filler, high-clarity balloon rubber that was diluted with about 5-percent household ammonia was airbrushed into the molds. One wet (but not running) even coat was airbrushed into the negative molds, covering only the sculptural parts and keeping a light touch on the cutting edge. Then, one even layer was sprayed on all the positives, just slightly past the scribe line. Once dry, a second coat was sprayed on the positive, but about ¼" away from the scribe line to ensure that the edges are not too thick. **Note:** *The natural latex encapsulate can be replaced with a plastic encapsulate such as Baldiez or Super Baldiez which is currently the industry standard.*

Once all the latex is dry, the adhesion layer is airbrushed into all the molds. This is a mixture of oxime one-part silicone caulking and DC OS-10 volatile silicone solvent. This layer will help the latex bond to the silicone gel. To mix, inject some silicone caulking into a solvent-safe mixing cup, and slowly incorporate the OS-10 solvent until thin enough to spray, but not so thin that it lacks enough silicone for bonding.

Fig. 8-16

Silicone caulking.

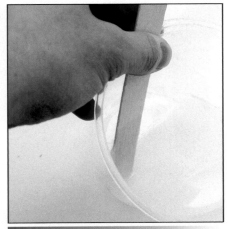

Fig. 8-17

Caulking and OS-10.

Use a paint strainer to make sure there is no debris in the mix. Spray one even coat onto the positive and negative mold within the sculptural areas. Allow five to ten minutes for full evaporation. Note that during all airbrushing, a respirator should be worn for safety.

Fig.8-18

Airbrushing the caulking.

Fig. 8-19

Closing the molds.

After the encapsulate is fully dried, it is time to close the molds. This must be done very carefully to ensure that the encapsulate does not stick to itself except where the edges come in contact at the cutting edge. Keeping even pressure at all times, clamp or strap all molds as tightly as possible, but not so tightly that you break the molds. Make sure you do not cover any of your injection points.

Fig. 8-20

Closed and clamped.

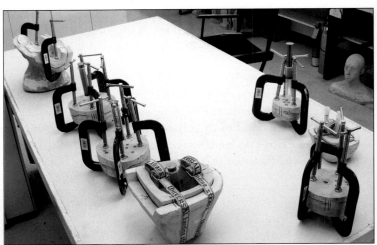

Fig. 8-21

Ready for injection.

Fig. 8-22

Addition of catalyst.

The silicone can now be mixed and catalyzed.

Fig. 8-23

Evacuating the silicone.

Fig. 8-24

The evacuation process continues.

Fig. 8-25

Evacuated silicone.

Once the silicone and catalyst are thoroughly mixed, and after scraping the bottom and sides of the cup, vacuum (evacuate) the air bubbles from the silicone. The evacuator creates suction within a chamber that draws all the excess air out of the silicone that was incorporated during the mixing process.

The evacuator will expand the silicone volume up to four times its original size, so make sure you have the necessary room in the cup.

Without the evacuator, there is a chance that you will transfer some small air bubbles into the appliance castings. Once the air bubbles have been vacuumed (evacuated), the silicone can be loaded into the syringes and carefully injected into the molds.

Fig. 8-26

Injecting the silicone.

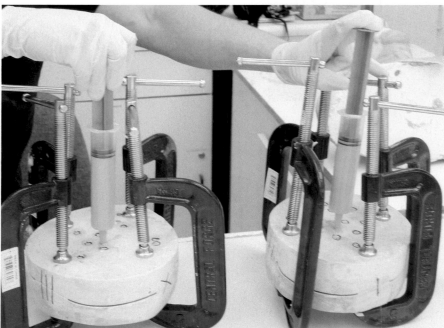

Fig.8-27

A wider angle of the same.

Fig. 8-28

A closer view of injection.

Do not force the silicone through. Keep an even, constant pressure. If there is too much force, there is a chance that the silicone will force the mold open just enough in order to break the encapsulate's bond at the cutting edge.

Make sure all of the bleeders have bled before the silicone begins to thicken. The bleeders can be sealed off with a small ball of clay or dry wall screws. The silicone can also be allowed to gel while adding minor pressure to the syringe.

I had previously colored and plasticized my silicone, so I only had to weigh and catalyze. The formulation I used was as follows:

Base

- **Silicones, Inc. GI-245**   100 grams

This can then be pigmented with up to 1-percent pigment or until the level of translucency desired is achieved. I used ProLine Universal Colorants and several colors of flocking.

Fig. 8-29

Silicone base.

Fig. 8-30

The addition of pigment.

Fig. 8-31

The addition of flocking.

Fig. 8-32

Pigment mixed.

Once pigmented, the poly (dimethylsiloxane) fluids can be added. Follow this order; otherwise, the thinned silicone may not accept the pigment, and the pigment will clump in the mix.

Silicone Fluids

Fig. 8-33

DMF-50.

• **DMF** (Poly [dimethylsiloxane] fluid) **50 centistoke**
50 grams

Fig. 8-34

A-2.

• **Silicones, Inc. A-2 Softener**
50 grams

This softener—designed to work with the GI-245 product—has a much higher viscosity than the 50-centistoke fluid and will help prevent the fluid from bleeding.

Fig. 8-35

The addition of DMF-50 to base.

Fig. 8-36

The addition of A-2 to base.

This is a very simple silicone gel that one can manufacture oneself, as opposed to purchasing a pre-made gel. It can be doubled or tripled, and so on, in order to create the desired amount of silicone gel needed. For this project, I used ten times the original measurement so that I could make multiple runs or rerun appliances if they did not turn out properly the first time.

Only catalyze to the amount of base in the mix—not the silicone fluid that is added. To find that number, take the original amount of base (100 grams), multiply this by whatever you have taken from the total mix (100 grams, for example), and then divide that number by the total mix with silicone fluids and base from the formula above (200 grams), which in this case would equal 50—the amount of base (in grams) in the 100 that you have taken from the total plasticized mix. You would catalyze 10-percent of that 50, which equals 5 grams. 5 grams of catalyst are therefore mixed into the 100 grams of plasticized silicone. (This is only an example; adjust the math according to your measurements.)

Catalysts

- **Vi-Sil Hi Pro Clear**   10-percent of base within the total mixture, as discussed before.

- **Silicones, Inc. Ultra Fast Catalyst**   Can add up to 10-percent to the main catalyst in order to accelerate the cure time.

Notes

Vi-Sil is a different brand that Silicones, Inc. and must therefore be purchased separately. I used this catalyst over the standard GI-245 catalyst because it seems to be more powerful and allows for a fast de-molding time. The standard GI-245 catalyst can be used, but it may need some help to form the Ultra Fast Catalyst in order to ensure a standard 16-hour de-molding time. The addition of the high amounts of silicone fluid will always slow the setting time, so be prepared to add some Ultra Fast.

Any other condensation cure silicone gel can be used with this same encapsulating system. Silicones, Inc. also makes another great system, GI-475, which has its own softener. This system can be softened up to 200-percent and yields excellent results. The GI-475 system is my preferred system to date because of its minimal leaching, even with extremely high levels of softener. This is a very dry silicone. The catalyst that comes with the GI-475 is extremely powerful and can usually be increased instead of adding Ultra Fast Catalyst. (This product was not available at the time this make-up was created.)

Once the silicone has fully cured, the mold can be opened.

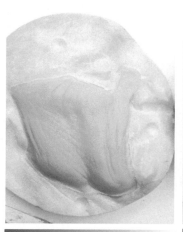

Fig. 8-37

De-molded.

Fig. 8-38

Powdering the appliance.

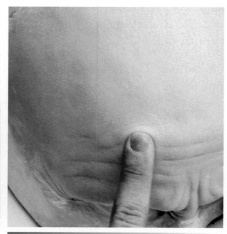

Fig. 8-39

Testing the membrane.

Fig. 8-40

All de-molded pieces.

The curing process can take anywhere from 4 to 24 hours, depending upon the amount of catalyst used, so keep a cup of the used catalyzed material on hand in order to test the cure. In order to de-mold the silicone appliances, open evenly with pliers while brushing copious amounts of powder into the mold to prevent the encapsulate from sticking to it-self. Be careful not to roll the edges when removing the appliances from the positive and negative. It is easier to de-mold if the appliances stay on their positives rather than the negatives.

After de-molding, all bleeders and injection points should be trimmed flush and stored on either a vacuform or on the positive until application.

STEP-BY-STEP ADDITIONAL CURE SILICONE GEL-FILLED APPLIANCES WITH PLASTIC CAP MATERIAL ENCAPSULATE

At the time of the writing, there has now become an industry standard for gel-filled silicone appliances. This is a process with over 15 years in the making by many open minded and talented artists. Although each artist will have his or her preferred coloring techniques, softness ratios and translucency preferences the basic principles and materials will be predominantly the same.

The sculptural process, mold making, and silicone chemistry illustrated in the previous sections of this chapter remain the same. The sculptures are broken down into multiple pieces, molds are made from addition cure safe positive and negative molds such as epoxy, BJB 16-30 urethane, polyesters and various gypsum materials (as a rule of thumb it is always best to test material compatibility). The small scribe line is added before flashing to show the end of the edge and the molds are either injected or open poured depending on the size of the appliances. The favored method is to inject any large wrap appliance or anything with complex curves and angles to minimize material waste and maximize thin edges.

For these appliances the addition cure silicone used is Polytek Platsil Gel 10 or Gel 10 (00). Gel 10 has become the industry standard for gel filled appliances due to its fast setting time, ease of use and minimal inhibition and contamination issues (a compatibility test should always be performed). Platsil Gel 10 is a 6-part system but only 4 parts are commonly used. Gel 10 is a 1:1 ratio system of a part A (activator) and a Part B (base) these two items mixed and cast by themselves create a fairly dense skin-like material. The gel comes from using a part D (deadener). The deadener is a plasticizer developed by make-up artist Gordon Smith with Polytek. The Smith's deadener creates a very soft to ultra soft plasticity with a very natural memory with minimal effect to the cure time. The three final components consist of a retarding agent to slow the rapid setting time of the material, an accelerator to speed it up, and a thixotropic agent used in open pours with a deep drafts or brush-ups.

Once a determined method of casting has been chosen (injection or open pour) you can begin to prep the mold. With epoxy, 16-30 and especially stone molds a very light layer of Vaseline is applied to surface the mold, buff away the excess to both the positive and negative molds. Only repeat this process if you have future trouble in the de-molding process. Then apply 2 generous coats of epoxy parfilm to the negative and positive and allow proper drying time.

While the mold release is left to dry, mix the encapsulating material

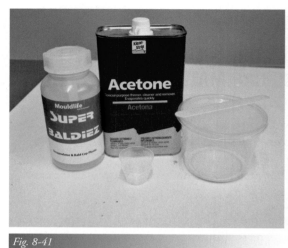

Fig. 8-41

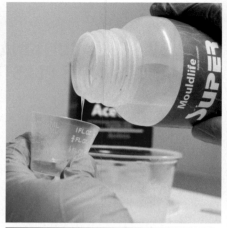

Fig. 8-42

The most commonly used encapsulate in the industry is Baldiez by Mould Life. Baldiez is a plastic bald cap material that is diluted with acetone to be airbrushed into the mold (a respirator and proper ventilation should always be used). Another option is Super Baldiez, which the edges can be blended with 99% isopropyl alcohol. The Baldiez is measured using a cc cup and mixed into a glass or solvent safe container. Mix 1 part Baldiez to 6-8 parts acetone (this mixture can be adjusted based on the type of airbrush used and temperature of the environment).

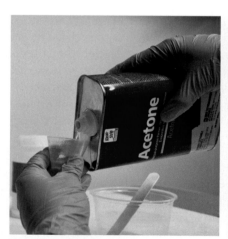

Fig. 8-43

Fig. 8-44

Spray 1 even coat onto the positive and negative mold spraying past the edge of the sculpture by at least 1 inch. This will help in the de-molding process. Repeat this process working in to feather the edge but still lightly misting over it with each pass. Up to 3-5 layers should be used depending on the mixture, desired wrinkling, and texture of the sculpture. Once these layer shave been allowed to dry for at least 5-10 minutes the silicone gel can be added to the mold. There is no need for an adhesion layer as demonstrated with the previous condensation cure technique.

Before closing the molds use a q-tip with acetone to clean all of the contact points, keys and any stray material webs before closing the molds.

Fig. 8-45

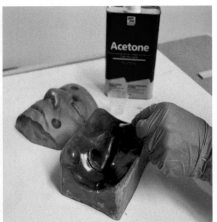

Fig. 8-46

All molds that will be injected should be closed strapped, clamped or bolted and all open pour mold should be ready with clamp and mold straps standing by

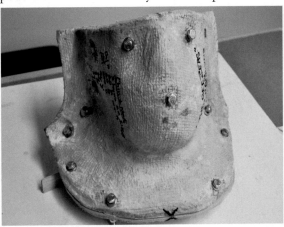

Fig. 8-47

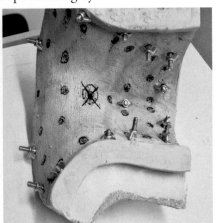

Fig. 8-48

Platsil Gel 10 Formula

Platsil Gel 10 can be deadened (plasticized) up to 250% but most appliances will be run around 120 – 180% anything beyond 200% will be almost impossible to apply and have very little memory. When finding the ratio use the total weight of part A and B to base your total percentage; i.e. 50g part A and 50g part B (1:1 ratio) equals 100g, then measure 150g Deadener to get a formula that is 150% plasticized.

When measuring the mixture try to determine how much each mold will take to fill to minimize waste. This is achieve by using the sculpture clay remove from the molds during clean up to get a visual volume or 70% of the total weight of the clay can also be used.

Once measured, label all silicone safe containers with the appropriate part and weight information so to not confuse the different components, as they are all pretty clear

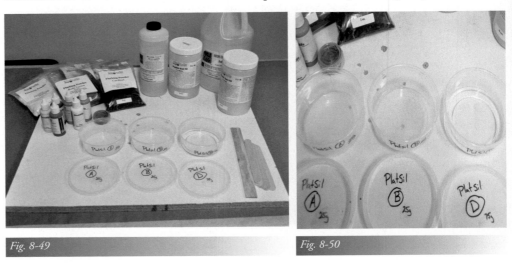

Fig. 8-49

Fig. 8-50

Each component should then be colored separately using platinum safe silicone pigments and flocking or a tested pigment and flocking of your choosing.

Fig. 8-51

Fig. 8-52

Color each part to the same shade, tone and opacity; a color log should be taken for future reference at this time. Larger quantities of each component can be mixed in advance if many castings need to be generated. Make sure to never cross contaminate any of the components as this will inhibit and damage your batch.

Base

- **Polytek Platsil Gel 10 part A**   50 grams
- **Polytek Platsil Gel 10 part B**   50 grams

Platsil base as a standard should always be measured equally.

Plasticizer

Ploytek Smith's Deadener part D   150 grams

This measurement will create a mid-level soft appliance, by increasing this up to 250% or dropping it down to 100% you can create a variety of different densities. Note: at lower densities many artists have encountered encapsulate delamination due to the lack of tackiness of the silicone. Higher percentages can almost be impossible to de-mold and required extreme care and heavy mold release.

Notes

This measurement can be increased or decreased in size depending on the amount of silicone required for your molds. This is only a sample formula. Through testing and experimentation with the formulas plasticity and encapsulate thickness you will be able to determine what you as an individual artist prefers.

Platsil Retarder and Thixotropic agents can also be added to the appropriate components at this point depending on needs, room temperature and working time needed. Please review the manufactured data sheet for recommended ratios. No more than 4 % retarder can be added to part A; a little goes a very long way, only 1-2% of the base measurement is usually used (excluding the Deadener) to get and extra 15 – 20 minutes of working time (1% Retarder added to the total of the total weight of A & B added to part A will double the working time, 2% will triple the working time).

Casting the Silicone Gel

Once you're ready to cast your appliances mix all components together completely. Evacuate the mix quickly; without retarder the material will set in about 5-10 minutes, so work quickly. Many artists have also had great success without an evacuator.

If the molds are to be injected be sure to apply even pressure, close off all bleeders as they release material and overfill the injector to retain pressure in the mold. With the injection process, all most should be tightly bolted, strapped or clamped prior to mixing the silicone. With the open pour method, a syringe can be used to fill the negative sculptural area of the mold. It is not necessary to overfill the mold and will actually create thicker edges; a visual volume should be used when filling the mold. Once the mold is filled be sure to pop any visual bubbles without disturbing the encapsulate. Gently close the positive into the negative, then strap and clamp with even pressure focusing on the mold keys (clamps create the most uniform pressure and superior edges).

De-molding the Appliances

Once the silicone is set (use a cup of left over material to test) the appliances can be demolded. Caution should be taken when opening the molds, open evenly with gentle pressure to avoid damage to the mold and the fine edges of the appliance.

Talc powder and a soft brush can be used to release the appliance from the mold. It is

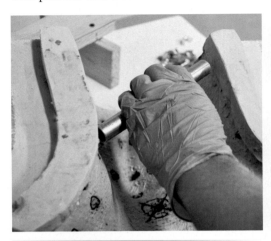

Fig. 8-53

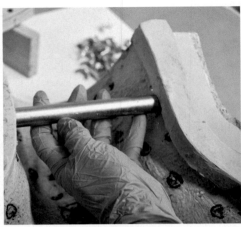

Fig. 8-54

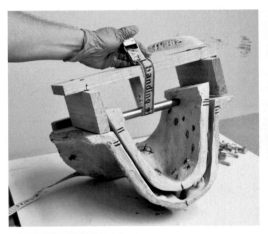

Fig. 8-55

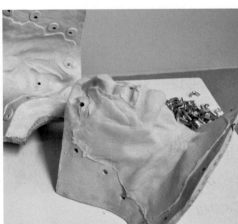

Fig. 8-56

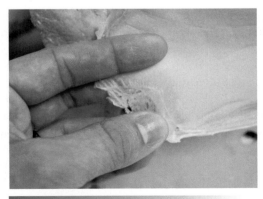

Fig. 8-57

preferable to keep the appliance in the negative or completely on the positive to avoid damage and stretching.

Once the appliances have been removed place them on a positive for so they retain their shape. Forms can be made from vauforms of your existing positives (although it is safer to have made a separate vacuform buck to generate the forms), you may also use soft poly-form forms to pin your appliances at the flashing.

Appliances should be trimmed of all bleeders and injection points and the flashing should be trimmed down to about _ inch to alleviate un-necessary weight on the fine edges.

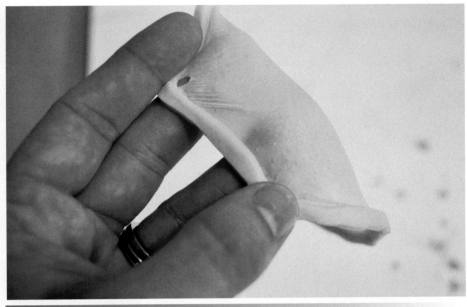

Fig. 8-58

Cleaning and Application

The appliances should be cleaned before they are applied to your talent. Regular Baldiez can be cleaned with 99% isopropyl alcohol with caution around the edges, Super Baldiez should only be cleaned with soap and water or alcohol free baby wipes without moisturizers.

Once the appliances have been cleaned and your talents skin has been prepared with an astringent you are ready for application. The preferred adhesive for these appliances is PPI Telesis 5 and PPI Telesis 5 thinner; also PPI Telesis 7 may be used around edges. Appliances are glued like any other appliance application taking care not to stretch the appliance as the appliance does not shrink like foam latex. If you have flashing at the edge, you can use it as a handle to smoothly place into the adhesive. Once the whole appliance is glued, the edge can be blended with acetone on Baldiez and 99% alcohol with Super Baldiez.

Any bad edges can be blended with some thickened pros-aide or simply using a red sponge and PPI Beta Bond to texture the edge.

Painting can be achieved with temporary tattoo inks, RMGP, and silicone make-up; the first two being the most common. Temporary tattoo inks adhere very well with very minimal touch ups.

Removal is achieved as before with Super Solve Plus or simple isopropyl myristate.

BASIC BEGINNERS APPLICATION TECHNIQUES

Before application, the appliances must be cleaned with a compatible cleaner determined by the type of encapsulate used in order to remove all mold release. If possible, it is highly recommended to do a test make-up. If a test make-up is not available, at least perform a paint test, as I have done here.

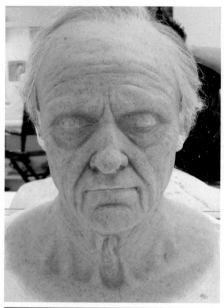

Fig. 8-59

Test paint.

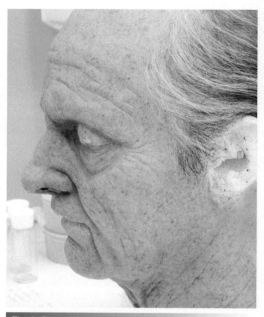

Fig. 8-60

A side view.

A paint test or test make-up will allow you to get a feel for how the appliances will glue down. Mix the colors you plan to use, and iron out any of the trouble areas. From these tests, you can take photos and get an overall look at the make-up.

The appliances can be applied with silicone medical adhesives or acrylic emulsion adhesives. I prefer Telesis 5 Silicone Medical Adhesive because it seems to adhere better to the silicone than an acrylic does, and it is also much easier to remove, in my opinion.

The skin should be cleaned and prepped with an astringent for removal of all oils. At this point, I would also recommend using a topical sweat stop, since the silicone will not absorb sweat in the way a foam appliance will.

The application process is very similar to any other application. The silicone adhesive is applied to the back of the appliance and to the skin to ensure adhesion. This double-contact adhesion technique is not always necessary. In many cases, the adhesive can simply be painted onto the skin. Make sure that during application, no area is left un-adhered; otherwise, small bubbles will pucker those areas. The edges of each piece, in order of application, should be glued last. The edges can be flattened and pressed into the adhesive by using Telesis Silicone Adhesive Thinner.

After all the pieces have been applied, the edges can be blended further by stippling a mixture (50/50) of Pros-Aide or Telesis Beta Bond and Duo Surgical Adhesive with a red stipple sponge, which will give a subtle skin texture to the edges. A mixture of Pros-Aide

(75-percent) and matte varnish (25-percent) thickened with Cab-O-Sil can be used to fill the bad edges. All stippled areas should be powdered with No-Color Powder.

Coloration of the silicone gel-filled appliances can be achieved with tattoo alcohol inks, non-toxic airbrush acrylic and alcohol, and rubber mask grease paint. For this make-up, I used the following: a combination of PAX for the bald cap and overlaps; R.C.M.A. Rubber Mask Grease Paint around the eyes; and Skin Illustrator and Reel Creations Airbrush Tattoo Inks spattered with a pointillism-style technique in warm tones, browns, blues, and pale ochre tones. The finishing fine details were done with Skin Illustrator Tattoo Ink Palettes.

Once the overall coloration is complete, the final parts must be applied. The wig and eyebrows (made by Erwin Kupitz) were applied last using Telesis 5 Matte Adhesive. The contact lenses (made by Professional Vision Care) are applied to give a subtle cataract blind effect. After these finishing elements are set, all final touch-ups are made.

Fig. 8-61

The station setup.

Fig.8-62

The model before make-up application.

Fig. 8-63

Prepping the hair.

Fig. 8-64

Drying the hair prep

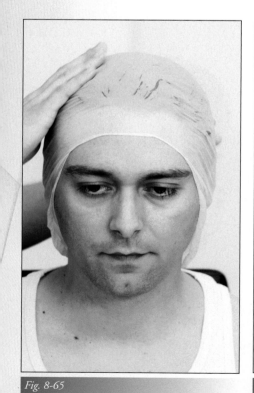

Fig. 8-65

Bald cap application.

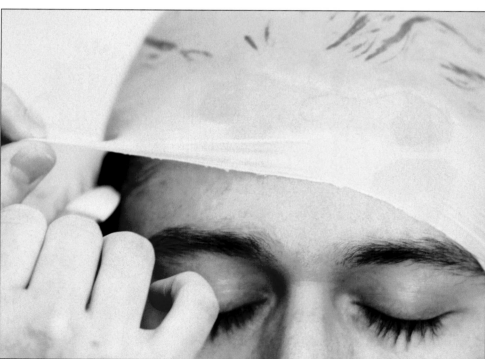

Fig. 8-66

Anchoring the cap.

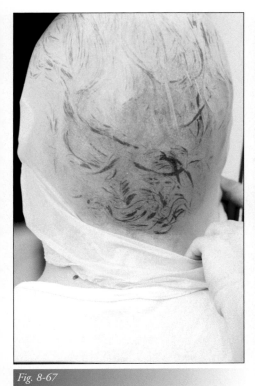

Fig. 8-67

Gluing the neck

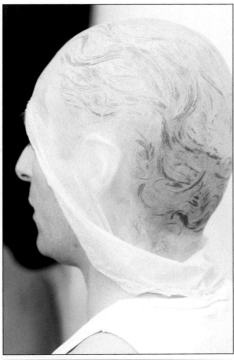

Fig. 8-68

Cont.

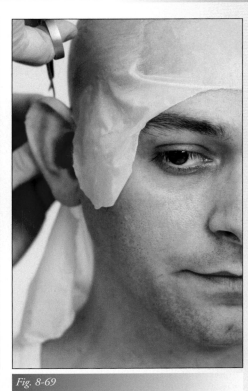

Fig. 8-69

Trimming out the ears

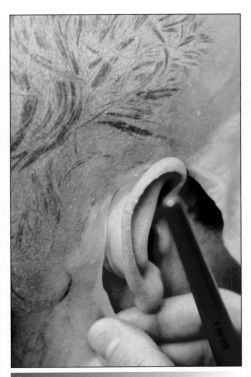

Fig. 8-70

Cont.

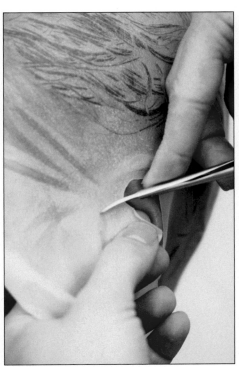

Fig. 8-71

Detail cut-out.

Fig. 8-72

Glueing the final points

Fig. 8-73

Powdering the edges.

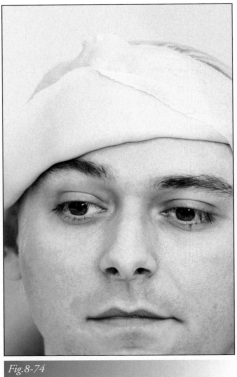

Fig. 8-74

Neck application.

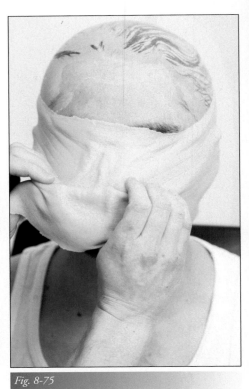

Fig. 8-75

Seemless one piece neck is pulled over the head.

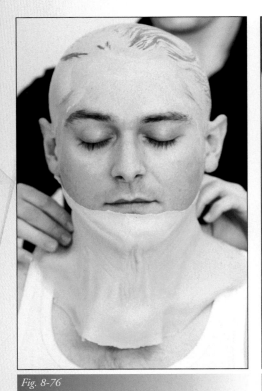

Fig. 8-76

Adjusting neck into posistion.

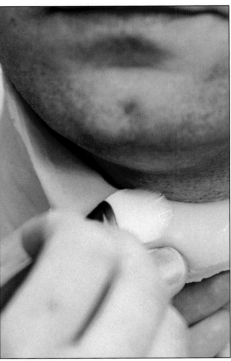

Fig. 8-77

Gluing the neck.

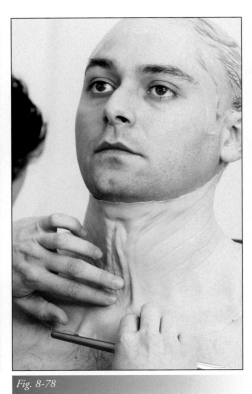

Fig. 8-78

Continued neck application.

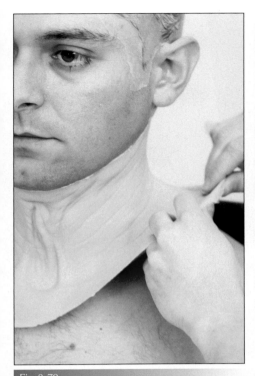

Fig. 8-79

Cont. neck application.

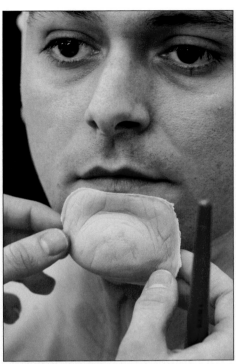

Fig. 8-80

Chin application.

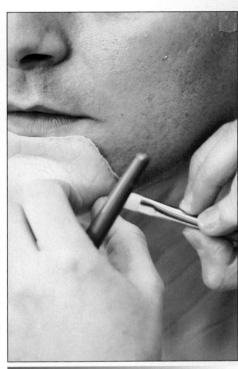

Fig. 8-81

Blending the edges.

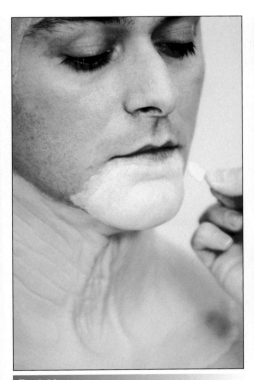

Fig. 8-82

Powdering the blended edge.

Fig. 8-83

Nose application.

Fig. 8-84

Cont.

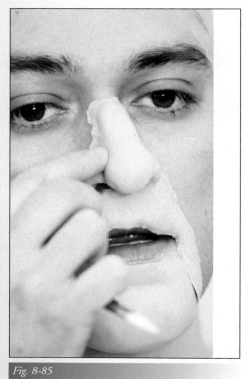

Fig. 8-85

Blending the edge.

Fig. 8-86

Cont.

Fig. 8-87

Powdering the edge.

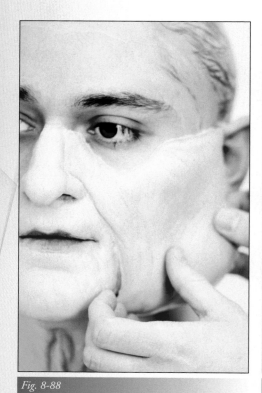

Fig. 8-88

Cheek application.

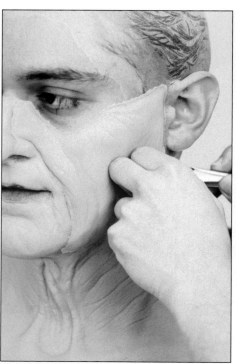

Fig. 8-89

Cont.

Fig. 8-90

Blending the cheek.

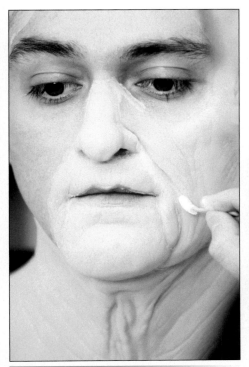

Fig. 8-91

Powdering of the edge.

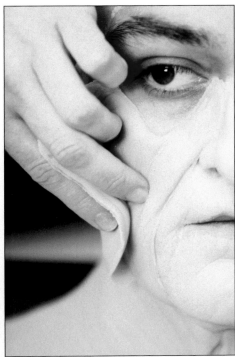

Fig. 8-92

Application of right cheek.

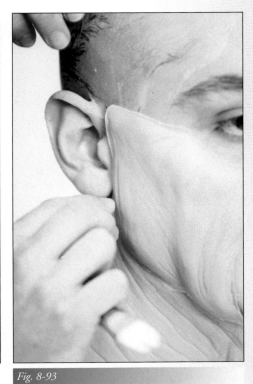

Fig. 8-93

Cont.

Fig. 8-94

Cont.

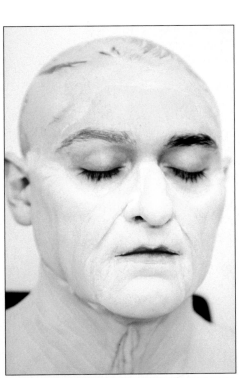

Fig. 8-95

Blended + powdered

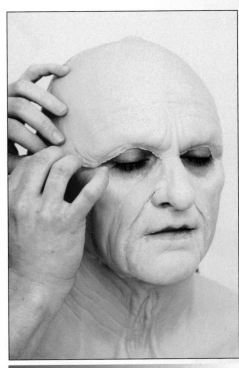

Fig. 8-96

Forehead application.

Fig. 8-97

Cont.

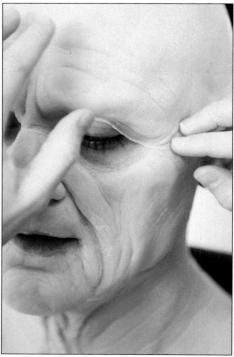

Fig. 8-98

Aligning to the eyes.

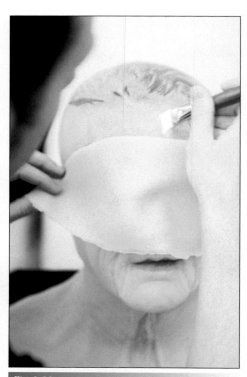

Fig. 8-99

Cont. application

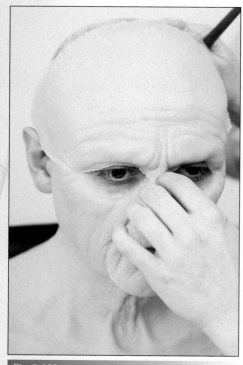

Fig. 8-100

Final placement.

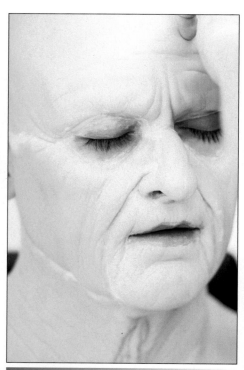

Fig. 8-101

Blending + powdering

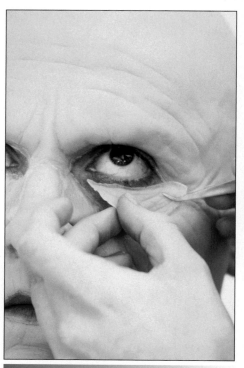

Fig. 8-102

Eye bag application.

Fig. 8-103

Blending the edges

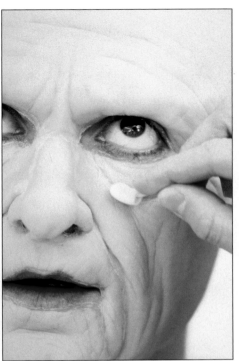

Fig. 8-104

Powdering to set.

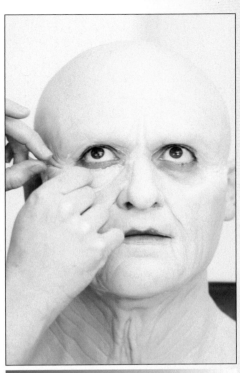

Fig. 8-105

Placing right eye bag

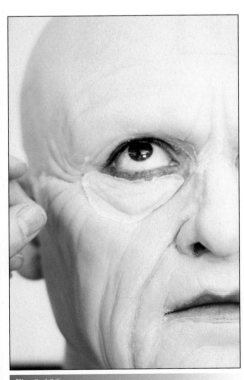

Fig. 8-106

Final placement

Fig. 8-107

Blending the edges.

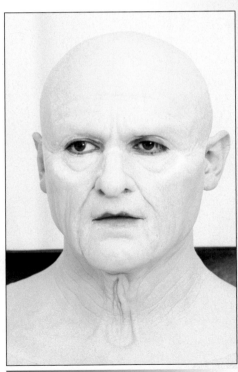

Fig. 8-108

Final application

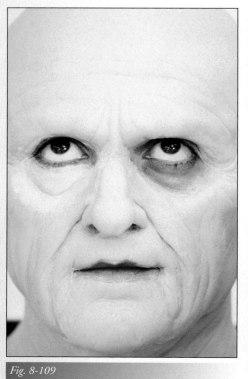

Fig. 8-109

Blended + powdered

Fig. 8-110

Stretch and stipple.

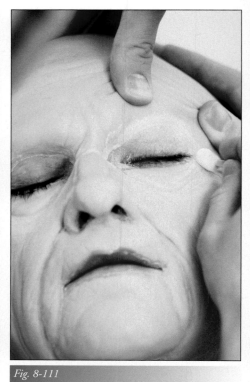

Fig. 8-111

Powdering the stipple

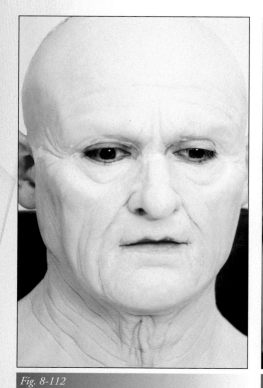

Fig. 8-112

Left eye complete

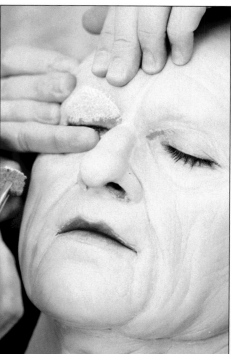

Fig. 8-113

Stretch + stipple

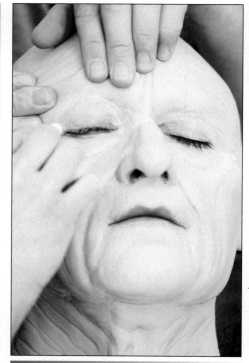

Fig. 8-114

Powdering the stipple

Fig. 8-115

Stretch + stipple applied to lips

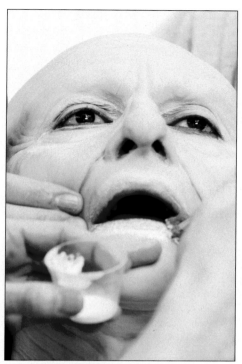

Fig. 8-116

Cont.

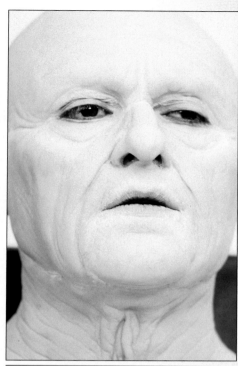

Fig. 8-117

Powdered + Finished stipple

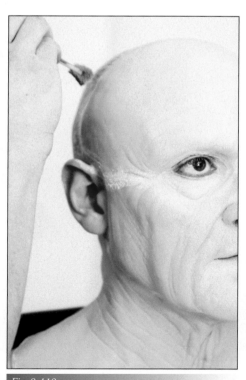

Fig. 8-118

Blending the edges.

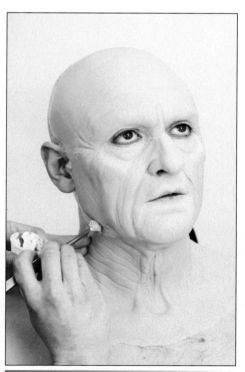

Fig. 8.119

Cont.

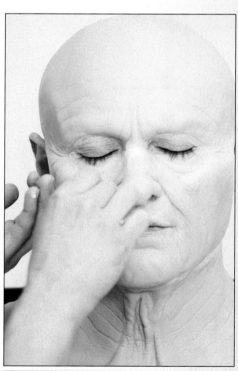

Fig. 8-120

Cont.

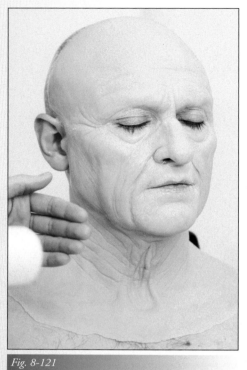

Fig. 8-121

Drying the blending

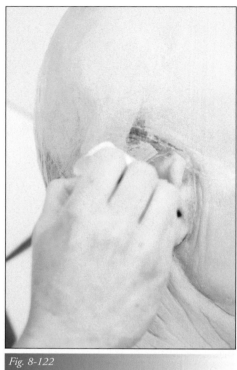

Fig. 8-122

PAX base application to bald cap.

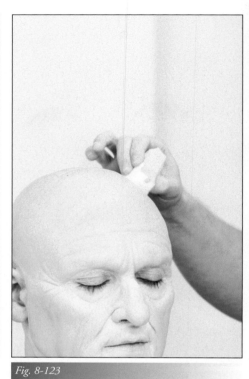

Fig. 8-123

Cont.

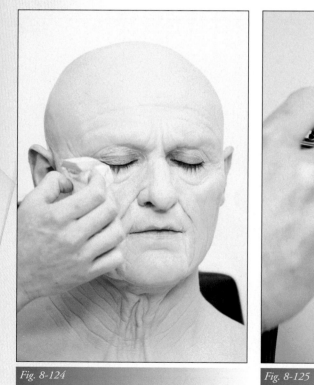

Fig. 8-124

Feathering PAX around the eyes.

Fig. 8-125

Airbrush spatter technique using a mauve and rose adjuster

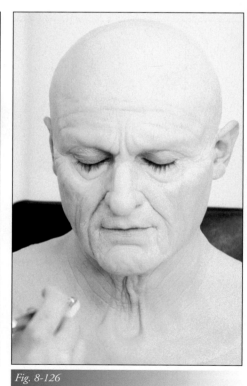

Fig. 8-126

Continued airbrush application.

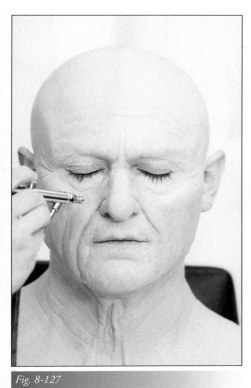

Fig. 8-127

Detailed airbrush red patterns

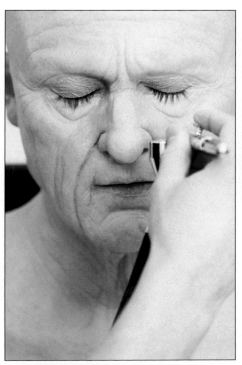

Fig. 8-128

Cont.

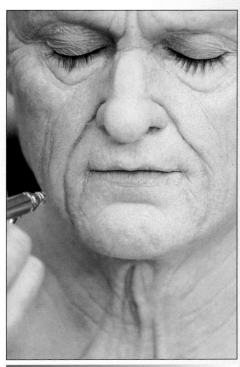

Fig. 8-129

Cont.

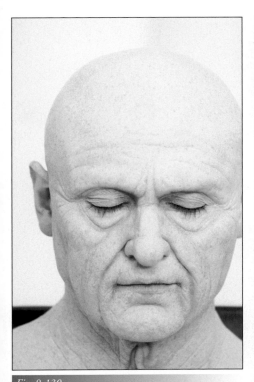

Fig. 8-130

Spatter of Brown.

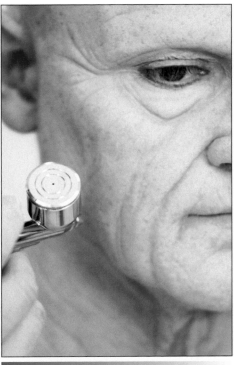

Fig. 8-131

Airbrushing vein tones.

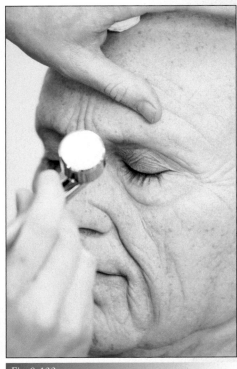

Fig. 8-132

Shadows and cool undertones.

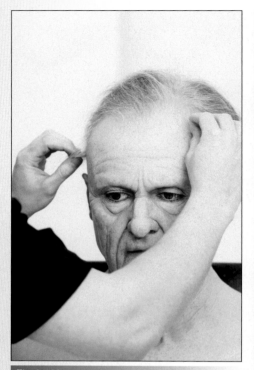

Fig. 8-133

Wig application.

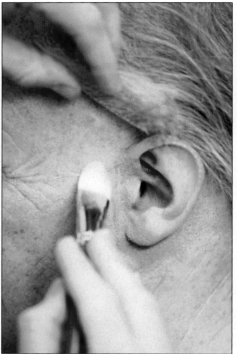

Fig. 8-134

.Wig adhered with Telesis 5 matte silicone.

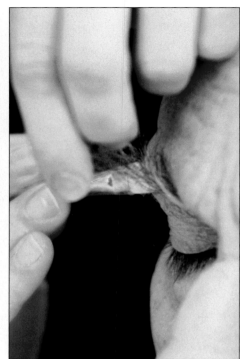

Fig. 8-135

Eyebrow application.

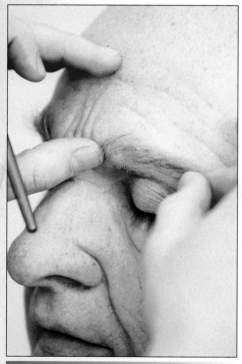

Fig. 8-136

Cont.

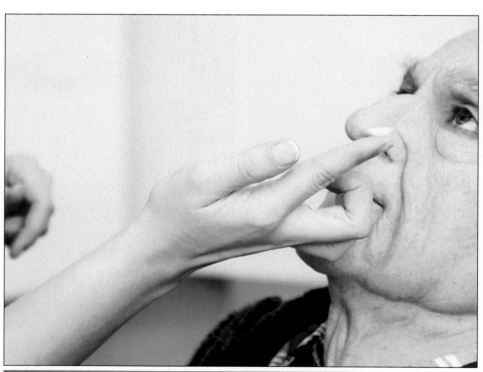

Fig. 8-137

Contact lens insertion.

Fig. 8-138

Fig. 8-139

Fig. 8-140

Finishing touches.

Fig. 8-141

Final details

Fig.8-142

Detail broken blood vessels

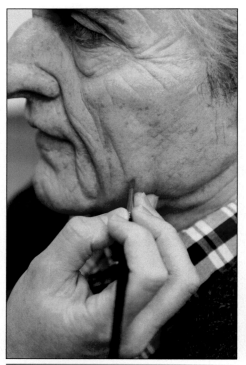

Fig. 8-143

Cont. Final details

Fig. 8-144

.

Fig. 8-145

The completed make-up.

Fig. 8-146

Fig. 8-147

Close-up detail of forehead

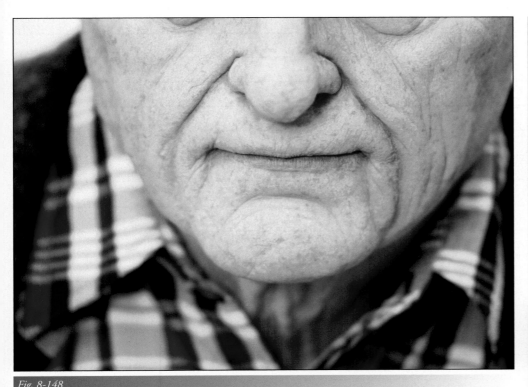

Fig. 8-148

Colse-up detail of mouth

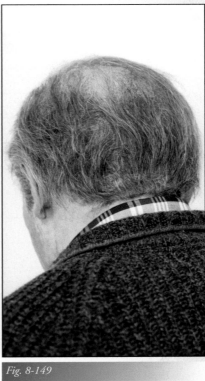

Fig. 8-149

Close-up of back of head.

REMOVAL

At the end of the day, the make-up must be removed. The wig and eyebrows were removed with 99-percent alcohol so as not to contaminate the lace with oils. The make-up itself was removed with Telesis Super Solv Plus and Telesis I.P.M. Gel on a soft brush used strictly for the removal process. After slowly removing the make-up appliances so as not to irritate the model's skin, remaining adhesive was taken off with remover from a powder puff. The final step is to steam the face with hot towels, cleanse with a gentle face soap, and moisturize to protect the skin from damage.

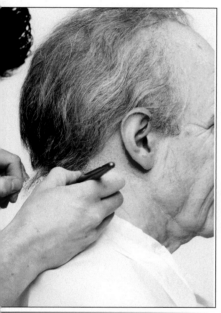

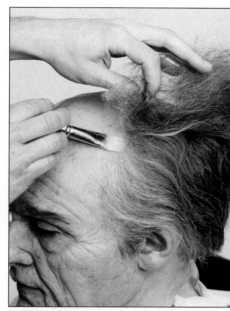

. 8-150

g removal.

Fig. 8-151

99% Alcohol to lift the wig from adhesive

Fig. 8-152

Protecting the eye.

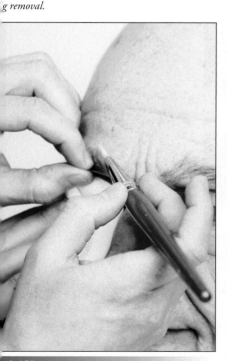

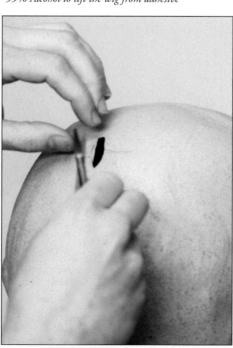

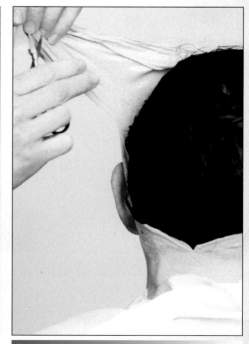

8-153

brow removal with 99% Alcohol

Fig. 8-154

Splitting the cap.

Fig. 8-155

Cap removal.

Fig. 8-156

Appliances removed w/ super soluplus

Fig. 8-157

Cont.

Fig. 8-158

Protecting the eye.

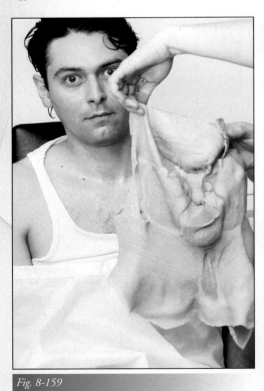

Fig. 8-159

Final face off

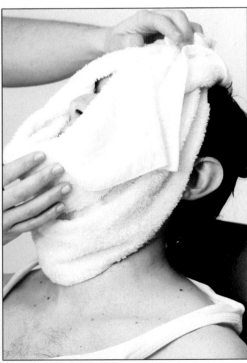

Fig. 8-160

Steaming the face.

Interview:

Greg Cannom
As Also Seen in Volume II

Joe Blasco (JB): Looking at your résumé, it is mind-boggling how one person could have done all of this work. Tell me about yourself, especially as to when you began your career in make-up. What was it that drew you to it, and how did you progress to become the successful artist you are today?

Greg Cannom (GC): I was born in L.A. and grew up in Orange County. When I was young, I was drawn to films like *The Time Machine*, *Seven Faces of Dr. Lau*, and the TV show *The Outer Limits*, which really got me interested in doing this. I played around with make-up. Dick Smith's make-up had come out. I tried doing cheesy make-ups with oatmeal and rubber, and flour and water, which didn't work very well, but then I started doing monster things from Dick Smith's magazine.

The Sixth Finger is what really got me interested in make-up, and I was just amazed at all the make-ups William Tuttle (and Charlie Schram, head of the lab at MGM) had done on Tony Randall in *Seven Faces*. When I finally went to see *The Exorcist*, that pushed me over, and at that time, I was working at Knott's Berry Farm on the log ride, right when the Halloween Haunt was starting. And of course, *Planet of the Apes* had come out before that. But *The Exorcist* pushed me over.

The first make-up I ever did on myself was of a character from *Planet of the Apes*, for which I ventilated all of the hair. It was white yak hair, so I was like an albino version. I did foam prosthetics using the old Uniroyal foam and made terrible molds that worked only somewhat. It was not the best make-up, but it was pretty amazing considering I had no idea what I was doing.

The next year, for Halloween, I did an Egyptian vampire foam make-up, and I built it out. It was interesting, because from the profile, I had no nose.

At Cyprus College, I started doing make-up for all the plays at their theatre. The work was very elaborate. I never did a slip mask of anything. I started right with foam latex, and I was aging people, doing character make-ups . . . which I'm glad I did now, because it helped me with the character aspects of make-up. I now know how to do big jowls, paint with shadows and highlights, etc., and all that really helped me later. I did about 200 shows over five years—all live stage theatrical productions—including one where I learned to do a bald cap. It fell just short of working well, but I eventually perfected it about the time when Dick Smith came up with PAX Paints. I tried all these bald caps, like the one on Robert DeNiro in *Taxi Driver*, but it just didn't work. I tried 355, and I used a rubber bald cap that always slipped. The spirit gum would split it. But on the last night that the show was still running, the bald cap was amazing, and that's when I showed Ve Neill how to do it. She started using it on *The A-Team*.

The theatre is where I really practiced and learned, and it was 1976 when I met Rick Baker and showed him my work. He was pretty amazed by it. A month later, he hired me to work on *The Fury* and *The Incredible Melting Man* with Rob Bottein, who was still working for him. Rob went on to do *The Howling*, for which I did half of the work (a lot of the make-ups, the molding and the coloring, etc.).

Then I started doing my own films. One of my first ones was a TV movie with Henry Winkler called *An American Christmas Carol*, and I was required to age him. He went through several stages, from youth to 75 years old. That was pretty scary for me, but it worked well. After that, I helped Rick Baker for about nine months on *Greystoke: Legend of Tarzan*, which is where I really learned how to do suits.

My work on *The Lost Boys* came about because the original designs, done by other artists, were unsatisfactory. As a result, I developed the famous design that features a brow piece, which everybody still uses today for all the vampire shows. I also did the cheeks. The make-up was very stylized, but subtle, with the V shape in the eyebrows.

JB: As I first recall seeing it, the make-up had a unique, bat-like appearance, which I thought was excellent.

GC: It came about because they wanted a very young, model-type look. That's why it worked so well, I think. I also did the make-up around the contact lenses, which I designed. I knew the lenses would be the most important part of the make-up, and I wanted a very subtle design around the eyes that kept the actors looking young and good-looking.

At that time in film history, contact lenses hadn't been used that much. I found a place in England that made these special lenses for *Greystoke* that were just amazing—particularly the paint jobs. I knew the whole make-up had to revolve around that.

JB: What made these lenses different from the lenses you find in Los Angeles?

GC: These lenses by Nissel were made of very hard plastic. The company laminated the paint job in between it, so that the actors could only wear them for an hour with drops. They weren't the most comfortable, like the soft ones today. Back then they couldn't do that with soft lenses. I also had to work in Kiefer Sutherland's beard—which is why the pieces were somewhat small—but it was still enough to change the cheek and the whole bone structure of the face. I had also moved the second tooth out with a little pearl drop, because I didn't want these big honking fangs in the mouths of these young people.

JB: Let's talk about motion pictures of the past that influenced you. What films intrigued you the most concerning the art of make-up?

GC: Probably the most influential was *Frankenstein*. That make-up still holds up today, and it's absolutely amazing . . . so realistic. Of course, *The Wizard of Oz* was pretty amazing.

JB: Did *The List of Adrian Messenger* influence you?

GC: I hadn't seen that film until I started working with Rick Baker. He told me about it, and I went back and saw it. When I saw *The Exorcist*, that's when I started to try and do make-up as some sort of a hobby. That make-up was so real. You couldn't believe a little girl was underneath this make-up, and it haunted me for days. That's when I decided I should try and make a go of it. After that, I did films like *Cocoon*, which I got because of Rick Baker, and eventually *Bram Stoker's Dracula*, which was probably one of my bigger films.

JB: Michèle Burke was Department Head for the regular make-up, and you were responsible for creating all of the effects and prosthetics.

GC: I was only hired to do an old age make-up on Gary Oldman, but as the film progressed, creatures were added. There was a scene where he appears as a wolf in the graveyard in this big rubber outfit and attacks Lucy. I thought we could do a beautiful half-man/half-beast—where you could see the skin through the hair while he attacked—with a face based on a bat.

For the scene with Mina, where he's in the room and needs to throw a cloak over himself so he's somewhat clothed, Gary came to me and suggested that when they break into the room, he thought it would be cool if all of a sudden he came down from the ceiling as this thing with skin hanging. Francis Ford Coppola (the director) said, "Maybe," and within a few days, I designed a maquette (a miniaturized sculpture) of what's in the film. I showed it to Coppola, and he loved it, so we wrote the scene. I had four weeks to build it, because they were tearing the set down to put in a new one on the same location. In one week we cast Gary, and then I had three weeks to build an entire foam latex suit, the make-up, spandex hand-tied hair (one by one), and punched hair in the chest. We barely made it. I would never do that again. And that was based on the fact that he was so old, and this is what he really looked like—this ancient bat creature. Of course, it had to tie in then with the suit I had done for the lake and with the old age make-up.

After that, at the end of the film, he returns to old age, and I thought that was sort of boring. So, we created something in between the bat creature and the old age, which is my favorite make-up. It's kind of an old bat creature. It was exciting when we did the suit, and Gary knew exactly how to work it, how to breathe, how to slobber . . . I couldn't believe anyone could get into a suit like that and know exactly how to make it work. That's what is so great about Gary Oldman.

JB: Prior to my having met you, I can recall sitting at home watching a film with Robin Williams I had never seen before called *Bicentennial Man*. The aging make-ups in that film were so remarkable. At that point, they were, in my opinion, the finest aging make-ups I had ever seen. I was so taken by the work that I called information for your number and was very surprised to find out that you were listed. I left a message on your machine telling you what a brilliant job you had done on that film. I believe that was some of the first silicone work done that appeared so incredibly realistic and not as though the actors were wearing pieces of any kind. Can you tell me a little about the work on that film?

GC: When we started, the main reason I wanted to do it was because we had just developed a silicone appliance which we hadn't yet perfected. I did a test on Russell Crowe for *The Insider*, and it was pretty amazing, but not perfect. Wes Wofford and I developed this new silicone appliance. I wanted it because the ones done previously were full-face single pieces that were extremely difficult to glue on and were not receptive to make-up application. We developed a silicone make-up in pieces, like foam, which was much smaller and easier to control, but which also accepted any kind of make-up. I wanted to apply five basic skin colors and make it up as I would an appliance with layers and age spots, for example. All past silicone had to be intrinsically colored (every spot within the mold).

I also wanted the movie to look like an old science fiction film, such as *This Island Earth*. Back then, artists made people up heavily with definite base. I was quite shocked that no matter how much make-up I put on this silicone, it still retained depth. The light still went through it, and that really shocked me. It was quite fun doing those make-ups with layers of blotches and blending through everything. It was quite exciting to get the edges down, especially on Embeth Davidtz, on whom we were able to blend it so that it didn't crinkle like foam on a smooth face during movement. I was able to keep the make-ups very subtle, and the necks wouldn't buckle up, as would foam rubber. The ability to age her to 130 and Robin Williams to 200 with such flesh movement would have never been the same had we only used foam.

Fig. 8-182

Actress Embeth Davidtz.

Fig. 8-183

Aging make-ups from Bicentennial Man.

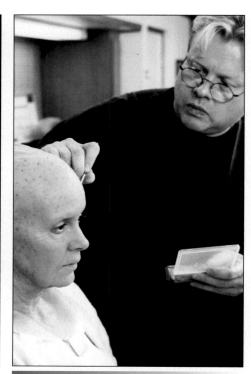

Fig. 8-184

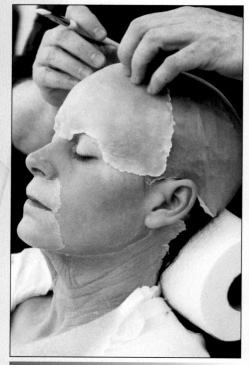

Fig. 8-185

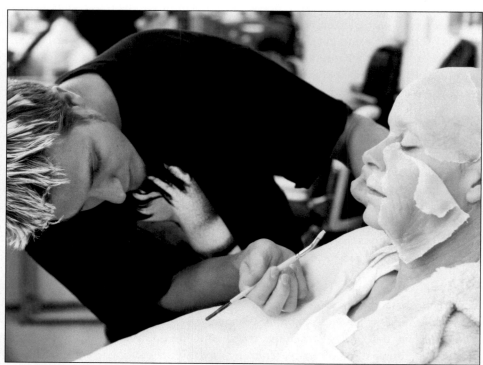

Fig. 8-186

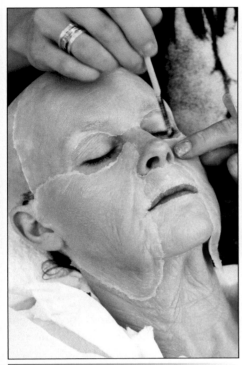

Fig. 8-187

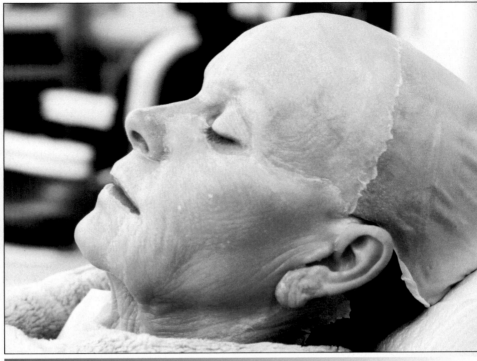

Fig. 8-188

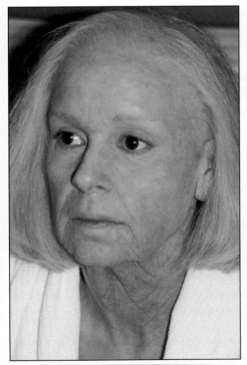

Fig. 8-189

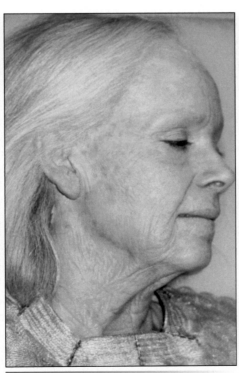

Fig. 8-190

Fig. 8-191

JB: Tell me about *Hannibal*.

GC: *Hannibal* was directed by Ridley Scott, who is absolutely brilliant and happens to be a very nice man. When we started, they hadn't cast the person who was going to play the character with the very mutilated face. But when Ridley Scott came to us, he was looking at sculptures of wax works that had been done in Italy during the 17th century of very incredible anatomical dissected faces. He wanted something similar. A specialist said that was impossible, because certain parts of the anatomy exposed like tendons wouldn't live—they would dry up and break. We designed a lot of very anatomical horror make-ups that to me all looked like zombies. When shooting started in Italy, I went down to Firenze (Florence) around the same time that Gary Oldman was hired to play the part. I thought, "Great," because I knew Gary would probably let me clamp his eye open. Gary walked into our shop and said, "Isn't there a way we can clamp my eye open?"

Pretty late in the shoot, I discussed the idea with Ridley. I brought the head with me, and I spent two weeks in Florence sculpting this new design. He wanted him to look like a diseased fetus with a little upturned nose. Gary's got a good-sized nose, so I thought it was not going to work. In one day, I designed with clay what you see in the movie. I cheated his mouth out to hide his nose. They wanted his nose to have been cut off (and they fed it to a dog in the film). I thought if I offset the nose and the whole top lip section, I could gain a successful result. It wouldn't look like a clown. We based this all on real documents, such as photographs of a man who had been attacked by two Dobermans.

To create a fisheye look on one of Gary's eyes, we designed an elaborate system of silk tabs where we actually pulled Gary's eyes wide open. The top eyelid was mixed with Duo Adhesive and made to look like a piece of damaged flesh, and it washed out very easily every night. For the bottom lash, we had a tiny overlapping silicone, and we colored the back to create clear depth. I used very little make-up on it, so it was very waxy and translucent. But under the one eye was a very tiny foam appliance—similar to an eye bag appliance—which remained unglued at the top. We pulled it out and flipped his eyelashes underneath it when we pulled his eye down. I didn't want any eyelashes to show, which would ruin the effect. The foam piece laid right on the edge, on top of his eyelashes. We used methyl cellulose material. I was always bothered by the fact that Gary wanted it tighter, so I refused. We put a huge soft lens over the eye in order to keep it moist. We'd do the make-up, which would last three-and-a-half hours, and as soon as we were ready to shoot, we would first sit for five minutes, pull his eye down (we had little flaps hidden everywhere with the wig), slip this underneath the eyelid, and shoot straight for an hour or so at a time for two weeks. We were careful to keep drops in the eye, and the contact kept it moist.

In the other eye, he wore another contact lens through which he could hardly see at all. It was still amazing to me that once again, in that make-up, he knew exactly what to do. I think it's my favorite make-up I've ever designed, because I think it's one of the most original make-ups of the last thirty years. We strapped his lips down with these little vacuformed pieces and glued the appliance right into his mouth. But we had so much happening that I thought we just didn't need it. We were trying to go for the look of no lips.

JB: I do agree that it's one of the most original make-ups that has been done in an awfully long time. The fascinating thing about this make-up to me is the fact that it seems to be a combination of construction make-up and prosthetics because of the way you've worked with the vacuform under the pieces, as well as pulling the tabs with the eyes and having to manipulate that before the take. It's quite ingenious and very unique.

GC: I also want to mention that Wes Wofford helped me on that make-up and worked out all the devices that pulled down, including all the small pieces. After I designed it in

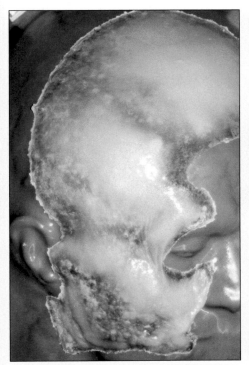

Fig. 8-192

The Hannibal *appliance.*

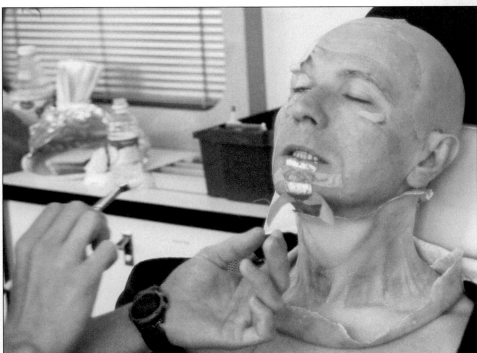

Fig. 8-193

Actor Gary Oldman.

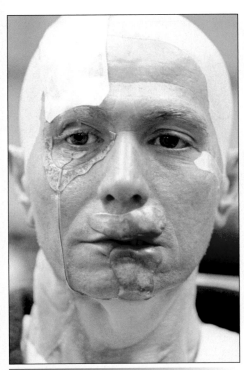

Fig. 8-194

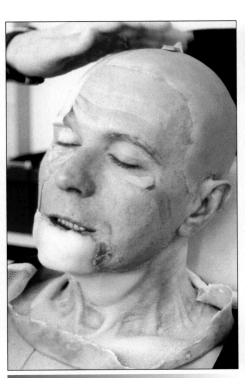

Fig. 8-195

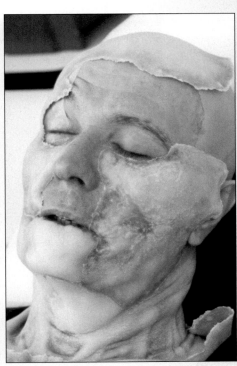

Fig. 8-196

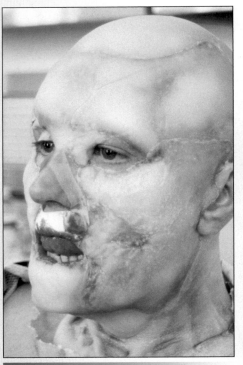

Fig. 8-197

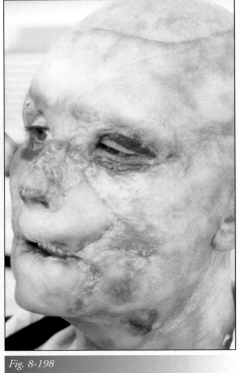

Fig. 8-198

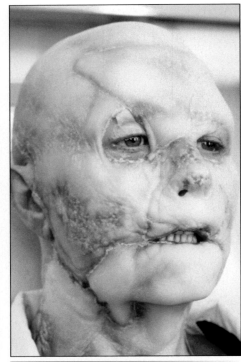

Fig. 8-199

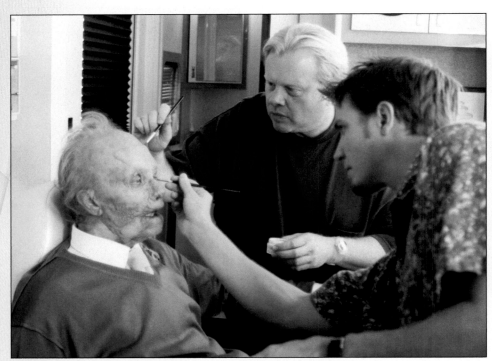

Fig. 8-200

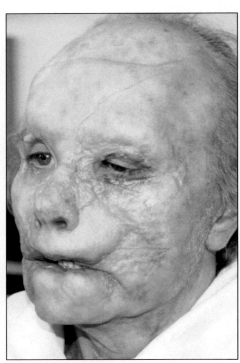

Fig. 8-201

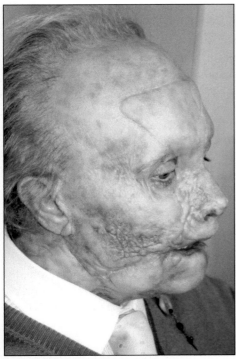

Fig. 8-202

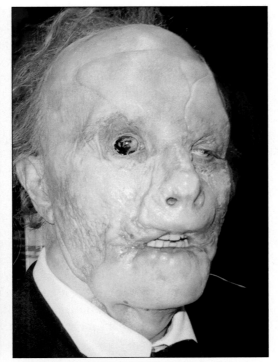

Fig. 8-203

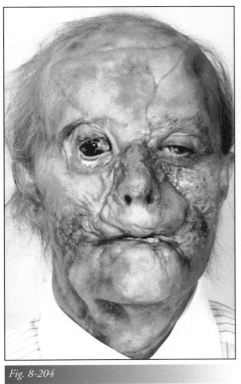

Fig. 8-204

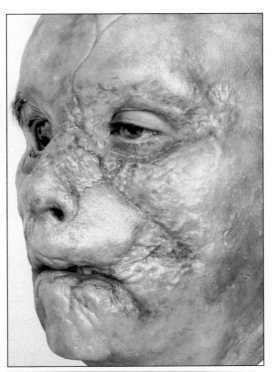

Fig. 8-205

one day, our great sculptor, Glen Hanz, worked on it another day and cleaned it up. We showed it to Ridley, and he said, "That's it." I eventually made the jaw look broken and offset, and I created a big flap of skin. At that point, it was really quite fun, because I was trying to figure out how a real grafting process would look on the scalp and the neck, where chunks of his chest would have been taken and moved up on the neck and into the face, as well as with the brow. It was actually a pretty realistic kind of make-up when it comes down to it, even though it's horrifying.

JB: Did you work with a physician as a consultant?

GC: A little bit. I researched medical books at that point to get a realistic grasp of it all.

JB: Tell us how you achieved the effect in the scene where the top of the cranium is removed from Ray Liotta.

GC: That was done in our shop with a lot of our great mechanics people. We built a full puppet body of Ray Liotta with eye movement. Everything was punched in. We shot parts of it with Liotta wearing a blue cap, and then we put the prosthesis in there. Frame by frame, we moved it exactly. We used actual pig brains in that whole scene. It worked so perfectly because of the combination of CGI (computer-generated imagery) with both him and the puppet. A lot of people thought it was entirely CGI, but we actually used our puppet the whole time.

JB: Explain a little more in depth as to how the blue cap worked for the CGI.

GC: We couldn't build up his head. If we had tried to fake it, it never would've worked. The simplest thing was to fit a really tight vacuform cap on him that went really close to his head, which we glued on (after we slicked down his hair). It was very simple, and the CGI guys created a little edge on its inside.

Whenever you build it up on the sides, it never looks right. They just created the inside of that area in the computer, and they also used our puppet to blend it. His hair went to a certain point and stopped, so they just had the top of the dummy body to work with. The scenes where you see over the side or over the shoulder feature the real top of the head with the puppet.

JB: So the scene where Anthony Hopkins actually cuts a piece of the brain, you're saying, features pig brains?

GC: We made an actual gelatin piece through which he cuts, and then we used actual pig brains that he cooks.

JB: That was incredibly effective. You also did the pigs that were puppets and the bodies they were eating.

GC: We did very elaborate silicone bodies and puppets of guys who get killed by boars. The insides of the bodies looked like the insides of a human being, and we did all these pieces of bodies, intestines, etc. and packed them with food. We did whole gelatin overlays over the bodies and faces, and even the mechanical heads were covered gelatin faces that could scream. When the real boar pigs attack them, they actually rip the faces. Everybody on set was actually getting sick. We had them up against the wall in the pen, and all our guys were behind the wall puppeteering from the back. It was pretty violent and scary.

JB: So we've gone from puppet boars to real boars.

GC: We inserted shots with a puppet head of the boar attacking the real actors for close-ups, and that was mostly used when Gary Oldman was attacked. We also built a baby in the beginning when they attack. A woman's carrying a small baby, and after she is shot, the baby is covered with blood. When the baby is hosed down, you see a mechanical baby that we made out of silicone. It's not always apparent, but there was a huge amount of work involved in that film.

JB: I was quite flattered when you asked me to attend the screening with you of *A Beautiful Mind*, for which you were the special make-up designer. Again, as in the other films, you created some incredibly realistic aging prostheses using silicone. Tell us a little about the experience.

GC: I had three weeks to do make-ups and tests, most of which were done on the day of shooting. I tried to create a smooth flow of make-up, so that as Russell Crowe aged, you would fail to really notice by the end of the film. Hopefully, you didn't see or think about the jumps. I tried to do a character make-up on him with bits of the real guy. I actually tried to put more character into him when he aged, and I think that is the closest I've come to achieving a realistic silicone age make-up with which I was really happy. Luckily it turned out really well. What amazes me is that at the end, when you see him talking, his neck is wiggling, and you'd never get that with foam latex.

JB: Tell us a little about your work on *Titanic*.

GC: I loved *Titanic*. It's my favorite experience in film because I got to do out-of-kit make-up, with no prosthetics, and I got to work with Gloria Stuart, an amazing lady with incredible stories. Jack Pierce used to do her make-up. She worked with Boris Karloff and James Whale, and she was just an amazing person. And also because of the opportunity to work with James Cameron on this film, which I knew then was going to be the biggest film of all-time.

It was a scary experience because again, I had one test for a stipple aging make-up. You can't tell when viewing the film, but Gloria's covered with make-up. It took me two hours to draw fine lines all over her face with tattoo colors using your UEM brush and create the wrinkles. She was 87 at the time but looked 70, and James wanted her to look 101. Her neck had four heavy coats of ager stipple, and every part of her face, except her nose, was covered with stipple. I learned how to control the stipple, so in certain areas it was heavier and didn't look typical.

I learned a new way of doing age make-ups, which I then perfected on the next film for Russell Crowe, *The Insider*. We planned to use appliances, and we tried one silicone and one foam. I knew there was no way in which I would get the appliances in time or get Russell to sit for two hours in Kentucky over the summer. I told them it wouldn't work. I suggested we try just using stipple and make-up to see how old I could make him appear. I thought there would be objections, but that wasn't the case. The next morning I did a stipple make-up on him—using the tattoo UEM brush—consisting of lines and very light shadowing with charcoal gray color for the aging on his chin and neck. I then used a small amount of beard stipple for accentuation. It all worked, and that afternoon, they shot the first scene where his daughter has asthma. So, how lucky was that?

I spent a week discovering how to waterproof it. In Kentucky, in the heat, the make-up stayed on all day long without coming off the skin. I used make-up from the William Tuttle line for the highlights, because it's heavier, and a rake brush for subtlety. In the make-up chair, the fine lines can be seen, but outside in the sunlight, they disappear. It really works. Where I didn't do a certain base with the ager around his face, the make-up melted off, but luckily all the stipple stayed. I had to keep touching it up constantly. I'm amazed to this day as to how well it stayed on. He was 35 and looked close to 50; it was strange to do an entire movie by trying to age a person that subtly.

My favorite make-ups in *Bicentennial Man* are on Sam Neill; I just use the silicone neck waddle, and the rest is stipple and make-up. *Titanic* opened up a whole new make-up direction for me, which I've used in every film since.

JB: Do you develop your own stipple? What type of waterproofing method did you use?

GC: I tried everything. I tried Green Marble SeLr, which also worked for stipple, but it burned my hand and didn't hold up. What worked the best was a mixture of 50-percent water and 50-percent Pros-Aide 2. I'd stipple that onto larger areas first, powder it, and then use Dick Smith's Ager Stipple. It worked great at the time, but now I use Matthew Mungle's. Dick Smith's formulas are easier around the eye area, but when you layer it, it gets too shiny and doesn't look right. I put four thick coats on Gloria's neck, and I had to paint tons of the wax dulling (anti-shine), whereas for the more recent *Bulletproof Monk*, I started using Matthew's Ager Stipple and found that it still looks real. It doesn't get shiny, even under multiple coats. The Pros-Aide coating waterproofs it.

JB: This reminds me of how we used to do construction make-ups in the past. Before I would do any buildup make-up with cotton, I would always apply a layer of latex onto the face, and that would help to prevent the moisture from coming through. When I was an apprentice to Ben Nye in 1968, I can recall him telling me that he had to do George C. Scott in *The Flimflam Man*, which he also shot in Kentucky, and he has pictures of himself with a hankie on top of his head because of the amount of perspiration while he was working. Because he felt that the rubber couldn't work, he actually took cap material (liquid), which he then bottled and sold as old age plastic, and using the same technique we use with rubber, he would stretch the skin and paint MEK (methyl ethyl ketone), XYXG (vinyl resin), and a few other odds and ends with a brush. It would dry rapidly, and you could release it; you didn't need to apply powder, because it wouldn't stick to itself. Whenever it would perspire, Ben would mop it up, stretch the skin, and paint the plastic. This would dry instantly, and you would have the wrinkles again. But it was a constant process. Now, you've created a barrier where you've actually kept the perspiration from coming out of the skin.

GC: On Russell I would first apply the tattoo color on the nasolabial folds, shadow that stuff, and then do the thin coating of the Pros-Aide 2 water mixture in order to waterproof it all. Over that I would apply the stipple. The stipple wouldn't stay on his forehead, however. I made a stipple from Pros-Aide 2 and water and mixed some Cab-O-Sil into it. I applied four or five coats that would give some wrinkles to his forehead, and I'd go in with the UEM brush for the fine lines. I raked it with the Joe Blasco P.M. (prosthetic make-up) for subtlety.

I do hands-on application. I never use airbrush techniques. For *Dracula*, I used an airbrush for veins, but I don't like it. I'd rather blotch things on. I think it looks better.

JB: Tell me about *Big Momma's House*.

GC: Martin Lawrence needed to look like a very heavy African-American woman. We had to find somebody with similar eyes, mouth, etc., because we had to do two make-ups: one on the woman and one on Martin in order to create a single character that existed somewhere between the two of them. We found a woman, Ella Mitchell, whom I'd seen as the wicked witch in *The Wiz*. We took a life cast of her and of Martin. It was amazing how identical they were during the test. The studio said they didn't see signs of Martin anymore, so we were then required to simplify his make-up. I thought it ruined the whole thing, but they were paying him a lot of money, and that's what they like. They wanted to change it even more, and I told them I would look ridiculous. . . but luckily, it turned out to be fun. The original make-up was just amazing, so the decision they made was a bit disappointing.

JB: Give us some information about *Mrs. Doubtfire*.

GC: When I went to talk about the film, the producers said they didn't want Robin Williams to wear any appliances, aside from maybe a nose. I said, "You're out of your mind if you think you'll make him look like a woman. It won't happen." I brought in a picture of a woman I found and told them I thought he should look somewhat similar. And at the same time, Ve Neill was doing a test make-up to have him resemble a woman. It looked just as he does in the film during the part when he looks ridiculous. So I did a sculpture, which is basically what ended up being used for the film, and they loved it.

Robin's face has such distinct features, and I remember thinking it was impossible to try and do something opposite (concealing a broad jaw, a distinct nose, etc.). Four hours later, I had the sculpture. I just see things in the clay, and it happened to work. I really tried to sculpt the mouth to make it look smaller, and I cheated it so close to the ends. When I did the first test with Ve's help, I applied a blotchier, more realistic make-up on him. But we also did contact lenses to change his eye color to hazel. The result looked so unlike him that we decided not to use the lenses. In the close-ups, you see his big blue eyes, and there's something left of him in there.

For *The Mask*, we tried these beautiful lime green lenses, but Jim Carrey looked so evil and demonic that we had to take them out.

JB: One of my graduates, Sheryl Ptak, was very fortunate to have worked with you on *The Mask*.

GC: That was a great film. I knew the director well. I took a head cast of Jim Carrey. I was really worried because I knew how flexible Jim's face was, and I knew if I put any foam around his mouth, it would split or do something weird. Also, the director wanted to keep the character looking like Jim. I tried to misshape his head while keeping his face very much the same as it was in real life. I stayed away from his mouth (leaving about an inch before the appliance started) and gave him a tiny chin. I put little ears on the design, but the director nixed those, and I'm glad he did. It was a bit too silly.

It was a difficult make-up to create and apply, but it worked really well. The most amazing parts were the huge piano teeth, for no one thought he would be able to speak. They thought he would have to re-dub his dialogue. We put them in the first day, and he was able to speak without fail. To this day, I don't know how it's possible.

This is another one of those films where I had three weeks to design the make-up. I did the test on Sunday afternoon, and then the movie started shooting on Monday. Luckily it worked, because we wouldn't have been able to change it.

You were the only one who made the lime green P.M. color that I used for the PAX I made. It worked absolutely perfectly.

JB: Tell me about *Man without a Face*.

GC: I had just finished aging Mel Gibson to 80 years old in *Forever Young*, and this was his first directing effort. He wanted half of his face to be burned. I wish I had the silicone then, because that would've been so perfect. He was supposed to be in a terrible car accident, and half of his face had been destroyed. It was hard because Mel was directing it, so we couldn't spend too much time on the make-up application each day. I tried to simplify it to one piece. I glued his ear down and flattened all his hair (for he didn't want to shave it) with Gafquat and spirit gum, and it worked really well for distorting his face and changing the bone structure. We had a hairpiece made that went from the top of his head back to the nape of his neck, and it blended into his regular hair and covered the whole edge of the appliance. We tried to reduce the application to about one-and-a-half or two hours so that he could spend more time directing.

The strangest make-up I ever did was on the young man who played the kid he teaches. He was about 11 or 12 years old, and in one scene at the end, he had to look 17. I did a prosthetic make-up, and it really worked pretty well, but on the very last day, they found a kid who looked just like him at the proper age, so the scene doesn't actually appear in the film.

JB: You appear in the last zombie make-up that is seen in Michael Jackson's *Thriller*.

GC: That was fun. Rick Baker asked me to help on it. I did two or three of the main make-ups on characters dancing next to Michael. Rick came up to me and said, "Here's an arm, it has to fall off a zombie, and it shoots in ten minutes, so figure it out." I created this fishing line and little pulley system with safety pins, and it worked really well.

We got to be in the film, and we all made ourselves up. I sat in the make-up all day long. I had these really cool Nissel contact lenses, and around six at night, John Landis, the director, put me in the pop dancing scene. Vincent Price laughs, and I turn and freeze in the camera. Landis told me I had to hit these marks perfectly. Fog rolls in, and I couldn't see any ground. I missed the mark, and he started screaming at me. I explained, and we did it differently. That was very exciting, because Charlie Schram applied that make-up on me in the morning.

JB: Tell me about working on *Dick Tracy* in 1990.

GC: I was not the Department Head. John Caglione and Doug Drexler did the make-up. I just came in to help. I did the one actor with a very long nose. One of the scary things was when I was asked to do a bald cap on Dustin Hoffman, and the night before he had won the Oscar for *Rain Man*. He hadn't slept all night, and I was terrified. It was very exciting the morning after.

JB: Did you do Jack Nicholson on *Hoffa*?

GC: That was interesting, because when he first came in, we did the head cast, and he didn't want a whole nose—just the tip. I noticed that most of the work was on the bridge and sides of his nose—it was very wide going towards the eyebrows. I tried everything with the tip, and instead, I did a whole bridge piece going into the eyebrows. I told Ve that I didn't care what they wanted—I thought that was how it should be done. Ve put it on him, and of course everybody loved it. Sometimes you can't go with what people tell you—you have to go with what's right. I did the old age make-ups in that film as well. That was the year I was also nominated for an Oscar for *Dracula*, so it was weird having two out of three nominations that year.

JB: One of my favorites is *Thinner*.

GC: The actor, Robert John Burke, was great. That's one of those films where I should've had more time. I had eight weeks till we started shooting. The actor went from 300 pounds down to 95, and trying to pull that off was just insane. If I had the silicone then, it would've been so amazing. It was so hard trying to do it with foam.

JB: Considering the amount of time that you had, I think the work was quite masterful. *Hook* is also an interesting film.

GC: I made little ear tips for Robin Williams and Julia Roberts. I did very extensive look-alike stunt doubles. It was really amazing how closely they resembled the actors, and they were used a lot in the movie. We made a nose for Dustin Hoffman's look-alike, and he looked just like him.

We also did Maggie Smith's make-up. As she is one of my favorite actresses, I was absolutely terrified. I was supposed to make her up for 4 days, and it ended up being 21. I was quite intimidated. I wanted about 6 weeks to do her aging make-up. They did a face cast over in England. We received it Tuesday night, I showed the sculpture to Steven Spielberg Friday morning, I molded it Saturday, and I ran the foam Sunday. Monday was a holiday, luckily, and Tuesday I did the test on her. She started shooting that Thursday.

I used a lot of stipple on her forehead and one wraparound piece. If I had more time, I probably would've done a forehead piece. Just using the wraparound piece (which covered the whole neck, jowls, and chin in one) and stipple on the rest turned out great, however. That's one of my favorite make-ups. They had a beautiful wig. I also did the bald cap on Dustin Hoffman when his wig is pulled off at the end. I think it's one of the first times we did a foam rubber bald cap with all of the hair punched into it.

JB: Tell us a little about *Flatliners*.

GC: I didn't do too much of the work on it. Ve Neill was doing the make-up. I did a contact lens that was really bloodshot, and the character's cheek had been split open. The scene in which he sews it back together worked effectively because I did a really thin foam piece that I got wet with blood. It was really wet and fleshy, and I applied a super thin vacuform piece on his cheek. He actually used a real needle, and it wouldn't go through the super thin vacuform (painted red), but would only slide across it. He actually sewed up the foam piece.

When the father blows his head up in the bathroom with the shotgun, instead of using an appliance on the character's head, Ve simply put a material in his hair and sculpted with the wax to make the final result look appropriate. It was very simple and just washed out with soap and water.

JB: Tell us about *Pirates of the Caribbean*.

GC: We met with the director, Gore Verbinski, and were thinking of doing skeletal make-ups on Geoffrey Rush, but computers took over that project. The director didn't want typical, stupid-looking pirates—he wanted ones that were realistic. We did many computer drawings with images of the actors, and he loved everything we did. So, we designed 25 of the main pirates for the film.

We made all the teeth, which worked great. We had done these typical teeth in the beginning, but we were looking at a new way of doing subtle, vacuform clear ones. We were able to add really gnarly teeth onto a vacuform and paint the ones darker that were showing through, so we didn't have to constantly color their teeth. Rush loved it, because he could really talk, and they were comfortable. The kits were given to all the make-up people on the set, and they had a guide to follow (working from a finished picture from the shop).

JB: Was the actual painting process—the layering—something you designed? Or did Ve Neill design it?

GC: We worked together.

JB: Tell us about that, because the effect is incredibly translucent, yet rugged.

GC: We came up with a new way of doing scars and transfers, which worked amazingly. We had set up little kits with tattoo colors. Ve did Johnny Depp's make-up. We had designed make-ups for Rush, but Ve changed them, still using our scars.

JB: Who invented the scar transfers that you used?

GC: Christien Tinsley. In *Master and Commander*, Russell Crowe is covered all over with burns, keloid scars, sword saber scars, etc. I don't like doing scars, because they never look right. I asked Christien Tinsley to help me on that film. He has these incredible tattoo transfers that he can age in the computer. We were using some in the beginning, and I was amazed. I asked him whether he could do that with an appliance in order to make a three-dimensional tattoo, so he worked out a way of taking this Pros-Aide material and putting it onto his special transfer base. We tried it on one guy, and the scar stayed on for a week; it looked real, moved realistically, and was transferred with water from a sponge. It's the simplest thing.

JB: The remarkable thing I see here is that it's able to be applied through a transfer process with water. How is it that water is able to work as a transfer medium and not an adhesive? The adhesive must be built into the backing, and the water activates it.

GC: It's on a non-stick form, and the water activates the adhesive and sticks it to the skin. You peel off the outer form. Once it's there, it's there for days. Christien's the one who figured it out. It's absolutely brilliant. After that, I wanted to do more scars.

From that, we did *The Passion of the Christ*. I told Christien he had to do it. I was on *Van Helsing* and was unable to be there. The make-up we had to do was so severe. Any appliances would've made the skin look too thick. It would've buckled and wrinkled. We did giant sheets of this appliance. Christien, with the help of one person, was able to get it on Jim Caviezel's whole body in one-and-a-half hours. Jim would sleep in it sometimes for the next day. It was amazing how well it held up. I don't think it could've been done as well as it was without that material.

JB: Tell us of another possible use for the transfer process.

GC: When we were doing all of this work, I told Christien I'd like to be the first one to use this on old age spots for the back of the hand, or on the forehead. Instead of trying to match the marks everyday, as they get older, we'll be able to intensify them all. Every five years (of the character's life), we can do more and more aging. You spend all the time on the face instead of a half-hour for age spot application.

JB: Let's talk a little about *White Chicks*.

GC: The producer called me up to say that Marlon and Shawn Wayans needed to be made into white girls, like the Hilton sisters. The movie would take place in the Hamptons, and Keenan Ivory Wayans was directing. I was laughing hysterically. They didn't think it could be done. So, we did a test make-up, because they didn't greenlight the film until they knew it was possible. We took about six weeks and got these poor doubles in for body make-up day after day. You think it's easy—but it isn't. We had to come up with a whole new way of doing body make-up. I came up with a bright pink/red PAX kind of paint that was first airbrushed. Then I used Revlon Colorstay, which was also airbrushed. We used tattoo colors to add freckles and various spots, or reddish areas. Margaret Beserra and Will Huff did a lot of work on that.

I was sculpting the faces, and I tried to refine a male face to a cute female one. Shawn had a very strong jaw, and it was more difficult for him to look feminine. We didn't want them to look like drag queens. A straight blonde wig got us away from that. I was shocked at how important the top lip was to the whole make-up. The hardest part was smoothing out the face, because for the first generations I did, I tried to accent the cheekbones or put a Kirk Douglas chin in there, and it was all foam. Silicone would've added weight. Foam shrinks a little bit. I would apply it like a facelift, pulling it quite tight. Any little bump or anything "character" was a disaster. The secret was in rounding everything off so there wasn't a bump or edge anywhere. Making the nose look so much smaller and upturned was unbelievable.

If you tried to put make-up on the eyes, it would never stick, and that's what I learned when I did Whoopie Goldberg for *The Associate*. By using ager stipple (one thin coat on the eyelid and under the eye), the P.M. make-up would grab it and stay all day. But without ager make-up, it would never last. That was a big secret. The contact lenses were really important. Big blue eyes made the difference. I would do a base color and then a lot of contouring with shadow colors, highlights, and cheek colors. I would say that a lot of the make-up involved heavy theatrical contouring and highlighting.

JB: What about the lighting? Was it helpful in creating the effect?

GC: It was a very hard thing to do. The lighting director tried his best to accommodate, but there were huge ballroom scenes that were hard to control. I think it works pretty well. The make-up was hard to maintain, especially on the corners of the mouth. But we didn't try to make the hands up too much. We covered as much with wardrobe as we could. Everyone knows the actors are underneath, but we got as close as we could.

JB: *Van Helsing* seems like a dream make-up picture—a lot of action and a lot of monsters. Tell me about the reality of working on the picture, because from what you've told me, there was not that much make-up per se, as far as prosthetics are concerned, except for the Frankenstein make-up. We've all been inspired by Jack Pierce's make-up for the Frankenstein monster. I'm certain that when you were asked to create a new one, it was an exciting moment in your life. How did you design it, and how did you get the make-up to mesh seamlessly with the computer-generated images of the werewolf, for example?

GC: Well, when I started, Stephen Sommers (the director) was very concerned about the creatures and computer effects. He definitely wanted Frankenstein to be the most real person in the film and very human, so he never considered that for the computer. In the beginning, he didn't know whether the werewolf and Dracula creatures would be real or computerized. We and others did a lot of creature designs. At one point, he said they may shoot the whole film, and that I might be building a werewolf suit four months from now. So we proceeded and did tests for Dracula, Igor, and the brides of Dracula. Stephen always wanted to do face replacement (a computer body with close-ups of the actor's make-up blended onto the image). He was afraid the smooth skin would look too fake.

All the creatures ended up being about 12 feet tall. There's also a Hyde make-up, and he's 14 feet tall. He wanted these big monsters, which is why we did it with computers. We did a werewolf paw for some close-ups. When they finally got the design down, they sent us a picture of what they wanted for a make-up with veins and a little bit of strange, non-realistic design. I took that and turned it into a realistic make-up. They shot for two weeks with the brides and a blue screen. The brides you see have real faces blended onto a computer body.

I was very excited of course to be able to come up with a new look for Frankenstein's monster. Stephen said he wanted a new one about 7 to 8 feet tall. He wanted a flat top to the head, perhaps made out of glass. He said that Dr. Frankenstein was not only a doctor but an inventor, so that maybe we could put some mechanical aspects into it. Parts of him were metal. He also said that he wanted a glass window over the heart.

So from that point, we acquired the actor Schuler Hensley. He gave me a lot of free range. Because of the height, we came up with very sophisticated leg extensions. It took months to perfect, where Schuler could walk around easily and not fall. It got very simple for him. We also made giant block shoes (like the ones worn by Herman Munster) for shots where you didn't see his feet, and he didn't have to wear the leg extensions.

JB: How did the leg extensions work?

GC: We worked with a specialist in leg extensions for people without legs. Finding the center of balance is quite difficult. Schuler's feet had to be pointing downward. The extensions, which were quite elaborate, ran all the way up his legs to provide strength. They were made out of a special material similar to fiberglass (but stronger). The feet featured steel coming down that could flex and bend, so he maintained some movement, as in a normal walk. Then, around that simple point at the bottom, we had to construct a giant shoe. The difficulty was amazing.

You end up having an actor with very long legs, so we therefore had to make him look bigger than a normal human. We cheated his waist down and sculpted a bigger torso. His fingers were two to three inches longer. They were very adamant about using Schuler because he's such a great actor, and they like his face. They wanted to make sure we didn't lose him in the process. I sculpted a bigger face and placed it on top of his actual face.

Then, we started adding the other aspects. I thought it would be cool if the top of his head looked like a Nautilus ship with rivets, so we acquired beautiful green glass and did the top of the head with pieces surrounding it, much like a lighthouse. We split apart the head and sculpted it to make it look like Dr. Frankenstein had pulled his head from ear to ear and shoved this lighthouse inside. Stephen would make suggestions, like the addition of the first-ever hearing aid. I thought we could add some copper work to the fingernails and teeth.

The whole make-up was done in silicone with huge overlapping pieces. I wanted it to be very translucent with no buckling on the neck, but the body was going to be made in foam, so I thought it would be too heavy. We did parts of the body in silicone. For the portion of the movie where he moved a lot with the one shoulder and pectoral, we made giant silicone pieces on the foam in order to better match with the face and head. You think of these things as you go along. By the time we were done, the whole design looked in proportion. Everything matched well. If you removed the hands, it was strange to see this giant body with his actual normal-sized ones.

JB: Is there hair work involved?

GC: Originally we were thinking of doing part of his head with hair, but it just didn't look right. The original Frankenstein (from Jack Pierce) did have hair, but the patches of hair just didn't work for us, so we went without it.

JB: How many steps were involved in the make-up, and how long did it take each day?

GC: We used a forehead piece; one whole side that included the ear, cheek, and chin; a chin piece; a neck appliance; two pieces for the right side (an upper and lower); and then a one-piece of the neck. We had to put the very thin fiberglass-type cap on him first. That had to line up perfectly so that all the pieces would properly fit. Then, we glued all the silicone to the skin. The pieces were difficult to handle because they were so big. We left the neck loose. Once he was into the suit, it was all glued down in order to prevent seams on the silicone and foam rubber suit. He stayed in it all day. I was really surprised that he could lift his arms straight up in the air.

JB: What type of adhesive did you find worked best?

GC: For this film, we used Telesis 5. Every night we would clean up the same head piece of the glass windows and the metal and reuse it. Once the silicone pieces were on, we'd paint some metal areas and add pieces like the hearing aid and the bolts on the neck. It took between three and three-and-a-half hours for the make-up.

JB: As far as the actor was concerned, how long did it take to completely get him into character with make-up, wardrobe, extensions, etc.?

GC: Once the make-up was on, then we'd do the suit and the pants, and that would take another hour-and-a-half, including these big mechanical pieces on his legs and arms. It took about five hours altogether. Then, we would go on set, and at that point, we'd slip his hands on, which was pretty simple to do. It would take 15 or 20 minutes to get the legs on, and the very last elements were contact lenses and thin veneer teeth. One of the lenses looked like a dog's eye with a very large pupil. We tried to keep it very comfortable. We actually used just one contact—the other eye was left normal.

JB: Among all the movies you have worked on, what is your favorite picture?

GC: I would probably say *Dracula*, because I was able to create amazing characters in that film and work with both Oldman and Coppola. I got to create one of the great Hollywood monsters and creature suits. Every aspect of that film was very original and fun, and it went very smoothly. It was one of the easiest films I've ever done, and that's because Coppola was so good at painting pictures of how he wanted it to look, playing music, and simply expressing what he wanted. It was so easy for me to realize these designs.

JB: To this point in your life, you have accomplished a tremendous amount. With all of the work that you've done, what could you still create that you would consider as surpassing your best to this point?

GC: I'm lucky. I feel like I've done it all. The one thing I still want to do is a movie with old age work and the time to perfect it—the ultimate age make-up film.

JB: So, perhaps a progressive aging within the film.

GC: I got close in *Bicentennial Man* and *A Beautiful Mind*. I'm happy with the work for the most part, but I feel like it could've been so much better with more time. We were still trying to figure it out. Every morning for *Bicentennial Man*, we'd do an old age make-up for shooting that day. Every afternoon we'd do a test make-up for one that was shooting next week.

JB: Correct me if I'm wrong, but what I really hear you saying is that it's the experience of having enough time that would be the epitome of what you are looking for. This would enable you to create something better, or more perfect. What I really hear coming from you is the pursuit of perfection. You are a perfectionist. I think that's one of the traits needed for success.

GC: I am a perfectionist in the sense that I'm never happy with anything, and I keep trying to perfect it. All the *Bicentennial* testing should've been done before the shooting started. I'd like to have time to design it all in the beginning, test it, sculpt it, re-sculpt it, and then shoot the film when it's all ready to go. It's hard, because I'm never happy with my work, and that helps make it better. It can always be better. That's the challenge: to find that perfect final film.

JB: Do you think perhaps in the future you may wish to be a producer of your own film so that you do maintain that kind of control?

GC: We want to do that in the shop with my business partner, Keith Vanderlaan, at Captive Audience. I have no desire to direct or produce. I have enough to do. The best thing about working on a film is designing the make-up. Sitting down with the clay and coming up with something—that's the exciting part. Going on set everyday—trying to recreate the make-up—becomes tiring.

In our shop, we're trying to get to that point where we can start doing our own movies. For *The Passion*, we opened our own visual effects. We didn't want someone else ruining our make-up. We wanted to be in control of the make-up and the computer effects that tied it all together. The next logical thing is to try and do some films we're completely in control of. I'll be working on the make-up parts and maybe have input on the rest of it.

JB: That seems to be the next logical step: proceeding from make-up to also working with computer-generated imagery that will seamlessly coexist with the make-up. That's where make-up in film is going. It must be very exciting for you to be at that frontier. In the future, do you feel individuals who pursue prosthetic make-up as a career will need to become expert in computer-generated imaging?

GC: I think so. Films are a combination now of make-ups and computers. I'm lucky that old age is still not computerized, but it's just a matter of time until it will be. I think it's great when I can slap a make-up on in an hour and not worry about edges or certain coloring to save time with the actor in shooting. It can easily be cleaned up in the computer without having to spend five or six hours in the morning.

Luckily, I think there will be a need for make-up for a long time. When I started with Rick Baker in 1976, he said that in ten years, computers would take over, and luckily they haven't. I'm really fortunate that I was there in the beginning with special make-up for *The Howling*. I was able to go through this whole time period up until now, when computers are playing such a big role. I was part of that entire time sequence.

I'm just stunned that I'm still working in the business. I thought at my age I'd be replaced by someone very young and talented, because there are so many talented people coming into this business. I thought I'd be obsolete. I'm amazed that I'm still working, and it seems to get better all the time. When I talk to directors and producers, they seem to want me to work on these films because I've done so many great make-ups, and they don't know these young people that well yet. My past obviously still helps me get these incredible films today. I'm still amazed that I'm able to create new things. It's so hard in this day and age, because so much has been done. Luckily, it still seems to work out.

I don't know where it's going to end. I think our own projects in our shop will be fun. We'll have complete control. It's hard working on films. It will be nice trying to do our own work. I can't ever imagine retiring from this. I hope I do it till very late in my life, where every once in a while I'll be able to come up with something new and exciting.

JB: I see you as a great teacher in the future, and hopefully you will be teaching at one of my make-up schools. That would certainly be a privilege to have you as an instructor. With that in mind, if there were one thing you could tell an aspiring make-up artist, what would it be?

GC: If you love doing make-up, then you have to do it. I never thought I'd be where I am today—certainly not that I would have an Oscar, let alone two. I thought of it as something exciting and as a hobby, and eventually that it would be great working in films. And then, it happened. So, you never know. You have to be in the right place at the right time, know the right people, have some talent, and it can happen.

It takes about ten years to learn special make-up and get really good at it. But you're always learning—every film I do. That's why I like doing it. Every film presents a new problem and calls for a new design. You come up with a new way of doing something, and that's what keeps it exciting.

Follow your dreams. I'm really lucky. I've had the most incredible movies one after the other. I've done everything I wanted to do. I can't imagine it having been better. I can't complain at all. If I didn't do any make-up after tomorrow, I'd still be very happy. I've been amazingly lucky.

Chapter 9

CASTING

Chapter 9

Interview: Matthew Mungle

Alginate

Ply-O-Life

Digital Renderings

Additional Techniques

Chapter 9

CASTING

Interview:

Matthew Mungle

Joe Blasco (JB): When did your interest in becoming a make-up artist first begin?

Matthew Mungle (MM): It started when I saw *7 Faces of Dr. Lao* at a very young age (probably eight or nine years old). I was fascinated by how the different characters were created on one single actor. That sparked my interest, and from there, I started doing make-up on my own. I got a hold of Dick Smith's *Monster Makeup Handbook* from *Famous Monsters of Filmland* magazine and started to recreate the monsters I saw inside.

JB: That book had a great influence on many children. I can recall reading it and particularly liked the Frankenstein monster he did with gelatin.

MM: All of those make-ups were brilliant. I especially loved the Dr. Jekyll and Mr. Hyde make-up.

JB: Yes, which involved pulling the eye down with lace. So coincidentally, you were about the same age as I when I began. What do you think is so fascinating to children about the art of make-up?

MM: I think it's the manipulation of the face. When I'm around young children, I can see them react to the strange faces I make.

JB: I've never thought of it that way, but you're right. It captivates them.

MM: I was doing that about two days ago to the granddaughter—who is only six months old—of a good friend. I was experimenting with the faces. When you frown, you get a reaction. It's similar to what happens in a horror movie. You see that type of face, and you react to the fear.

JB: Did you know you wanted to do character or horror make-ups in particular?

MM: I just wanted to do make-up, although I wasn't drawn to beauty make-ups in the beginning. I ordered products from the companies in New York, predominately Alcone, which Dick Smith had listed in his book. I remember getting everything I could. In 1980, I had to go to New York very early in my professional career, and when I visited Alcone and gave my name, a lady working there asked whether I hailed from Oklahoma and actually remembered that I had ordered years before.

JB: Prior to being the Alcone Company—and I believe it got its name from the owner, Al Cone—it was known as Paramount Theatrical Enterprises. I lived by that company as well, in addition to Max Factor.

MM: I started bringing my work to school and doing theses. My drama/speech coach in high school recognized my interest and turned me onto Richard Corson's *Stage Makeup*, which my brother purchased for me. From then on, that book was my bible. I was fascinated by Dick Smith's make-up from *Little Big Man* that was featured within.

As a freshman in 1972, one of the sequels to *Planet of the Apes* had just come out. The original, in 1968, had a strong impact on me. I wanted to emulate what I had seen. I was not familiar with sculpting on a face cast and pouring foam into the mold, so I used water-based clay to sculpt the ape look onto a Styrofoam wig form that my brother had bought me in one of the college towns. I let it dry for a couple of days and painted over it with latex several times. Then I peeled up the result and applied it to my head. While it dried, I had made a wig on a bald cap according to Dick Smith's directions, which I combed and dressed. I was then able to do a test make-up on myself.

One of my good friends, Theresa Thompson, was the daughter of the theatre owner in town. I was always taking pictures of my work or asking my sister to take them, and I showed what I had done to Theresa, who in turn showed it to her father. He called me and asked whether I would be interested in promoting one of the upcoming ape movies, to which I agreed, of course. This was a dream come true! I made myself up early on a Saturday morning by reusing the piece. I drove up in my car to the theatre, and he was astonished when he answered the door. He had made a sign that I carried around the streets of Atoka, Oklahoma (population 3,000) all day long, and nobody knew who I was. I refused to utter a sound, other than a few guttural ape noises. I wore the make-up from 8 am until at least 11 o'clock at night, and by the very end of the day, I had earned around ten dollars.

After that day, he asked me if I wanted to do more promotion, and of course I agreed. So he gave me a regular job down at the theatre, and I'd come to him with different ideas. My parents were paying for all the supplies I would use. He'd pay me a little, but being the consummate professional I've always tried to be, I put more into it than required. I'd make myself up like Frankenstein's monster, or I'd create something gross like a coffin with a dead body inside, from which I'd recycle fake blood with an aquarium pump. I also dressed up like Vincent Price in skull make-up from *Madhouse*. I constructed all of my own costumes, including the entire wolf costume from Walt Disney's *Robin Hood*. I was very proud of that.

JB: So you were able to understand the three concepts of make-up, hair, and wardrobe.

MM: Absolutely. I loved creating things and coming up with new ideas. Sometimes it wouldn't be right, but practice makes perfect.

JB: What university did you attend?

MM: I studied theatre arts at Oklahoma State University. My first semester, I went to the theatre department with my portfolio, and they were astonished that I had done this work as a kid in high school, or even before in some cases. So they immediately put me to work.

I think our first production was *The Skin of Our Teeth*, by Thornton Wilder, and whenever something special was needed, I would do the work.

JB: How did you get from Oklahoma to Hollywood? Did your parents respond well to your desire to become a make-up artist? Because you grew up very similarly to the way in which I did—quite a long way from Hollywood.

MM: After being in college for two years, I decided I wanted to work at an amusement park. I moved down to Houston and worked at Astro World in 1977, which was the summer of the big blockbuster *Star Wars*. About a week or two after it came out, the city hosted a comic book/sci-fi convention, at which Rick Baker was scheduled to speak. I was elated, because I had already been researching make-up schools in Hollywood. I knew I was just spinning my wheels at college, for my love was doing make-up. When I went to visit Rick, who was very impressed with the work I had done, he suggested I attend the Joe Blasco Make-up Center. I was amazed that I had met him and was thrilled that he had offered me encouragement. I immediately wrote to the school and received a package of the curriculum.

After meeting Rick and finishing my Astro World stint, I went back to college. My parents were always taking us to large cities when we were younger. After visiting San Francisco in 1968, we immediately went down to Los Angeles to see Disneyland and Universal City Tours. I fell in love with California and knew I wanted to be there, for that's where the business was. Two days after returning to school at O.S.U., I called my brother, Mason, and told him that I couldn't continue to attend college. I wanted to move to Hollywood and continue my dream of doing make-up. I didn't want to approach my parents, because I wasn't sure how they would react. Up until then, they thought make-up was just a hobby. But my father offered me a deal: If I finished the semester, I could move, as long as I had a school to attend. And that was perfect.

So I had written to your school and received all the information, which I took to my counselor, who was one of the theatre directors at the time. He actually called to research it as well and then spoke to my dad to tell him that it all sounded good. He stressed that I really had a talent for this and that he supported my father's decision to let me pursue my dream. Needless to say, I got D's and F's in everything I did that semester, except for scenic design, in which I got an A. My mind was already out in California.

On December 26, 1977, I loaded up the car and took off early in the morning, about five o'clock, for Hollywood. I took a detour to stay with my cousin in Santa Fe and then continued on the next day. My dad discouraged me from visiting Sunset Boulevard, which was of course the first place I went. It was scary to drive out there by myself, but exciting at the same time. I stayed at the Best Western on Highland, and the next day I introduced myself at Sunset/Gower Studios, where the school was located at that time. Within two days, Amy Tafurt, the school director, helped me to find an apartment. I remember a place I called on Cherokee, which the woman I spoke with insisted was pronounced "*Share*-o-kee." I told her I had just come from Oklahoma, so I should know how to say it!

I moved into a place on Garfield off of Hollywood Boulevard, but it was little more than a place to sleep. I spent most of my time at the school. You put me to work on various projects and showed me how to sculpt and make molds, among other things, because you recognized that I had the love and passion for the work.

JB: You did and always will.

MM: I started class in February, and I remember never before having felt the way I did about education as I did when at your school, because I was like a sponge—I was soaking up every little drop that I could. You were teaching and also just starting to record on videotape.

JB: At that time, we would use those tapes to show students what they had missed if they hadn't come to class. Many people actually thought we taught with videotapes, but that was not the case. We always had live demonstrations.

MM: But at the same time, by documenting information on tape and then later supplementing it with the human touch, I think the result was much better.

JB: I was always trying to be on the cutting edge, and it was at that point that videotapes became available to everyone. The students today have the opportunity during workshop to come in and watch any tape, some which date back to 1978, and they are actually able to see the history of make-up application.

MM: There's such a wealth of information there—you would be remiss in your education not to teach yourself the old ways of doing things in addition to learning the new methods, because there is never a wrong way of doing a make-up.

JB: Make-up is an art and always requires experimentation. You need knowledge of all aspects and techniques so you can pick and choose.

MM: When I was teaching my apprentice, John Jackson, he would always ask me to show him exactly one way to do a procedure, and I emphasized that there isn't simply one way. There may be twenty ways to start a make-up, but the end result is what counts. I envision little fingers pointing to a single end, and whether you deviate to the left or right, as long as you get there, it doesn't matter.

After I graduated from your school with honors, having won the Best Make-up Award, you were very helpful in putting me to work as a teacher. Even though I didn't really want to teach at the time, I learned how to deal with people, and I was able to reinforce what I had learned in the classes. You have to deal with people on a day-to-day basis in the entertainment industry.

JB: Teaching is the best way to re-teach yourself and confirm what you know, as well as to learn tolerance when dealing with others.

MM: You also gave me the chance to go out on shows that would call in asking for help. I really started out by working on my own, doing little independent films, as opposed to working for someone else in the industry. It wasn't until later on in my life, in 1984, that I started working with Mike McCracken, Sr. and Jr., and Tom Burman.

JB: How many Academy Awards have you won?

MM: Just one, for *Bram Stoker's Dracula*, but I've received two other Academy Award nominations for *Schindler's List* and *Ghosts of Mississippi*.

JB: And your apprentice, John Jackson, won one for *Frida*.

MM: Yes, exactly ten years after I won mine. I've also won three Emmy Awards, and John one.

JB: How does one get from working small films to receiving an Academy Award?

MM: Diligence, loving the art, and constantly working at it. I think that's the bottom line.

JB: Did you work at any of the other make-up studios or labs?

MM: Not for the first six years of my career. I just worked on my own, picking things up from books I got, and being inventive. When I did start to work with other people, they really respected me because I had gone the back way in starting my career; after work-

ing on my own, I was able to bring all of my knowledge along with me. All of those slasher and low budget films really taught me how to work with a crew and put 100-percent into every project.

JB: Tell me about the work you did on *Bram Stoker's Dracula*.

MM: Before I was called for it, I had been working as Department Head for my own shows and was asked in April of 1990 by Ve Neill to work with her on *Edward Scissorhands*, which presented a great opportunity. We ended up doing Johnny Depp's make-up together everyday, and in turn, I was introduced to Greg Cannom through either Ve or John Logan, who was working with Greg at the time. Greg had *Dracula* on the horizon, and when he offered me the opportunity to work on it, I jumped at the chance. I was in charge of doing the day-to-day application and upkeep of Gary Oldman's make-ups, except for his young look, which was handled by Michèle Burke. It was an amazing film. Up until then, I had worked on independent movies before starting on union films. It was the most amazing project I had ever been involved with to that date because of the sets, the way all of the effects were accomplished in the film, and also because of Greg's brilliant make-up designs.

JB: So you, Greg, and Michèle all won Academy Awards, but you were actually responsible for applying all of the special prosthetic pieces.

MM: Greg and I would apply them together, but there were times I would do the work by myself when Greg wasn't available. It was a great learning experience for me to be working with Gary Oldman and Stuart Artingstall, who did all of Gary's hair work. Right after that movie ended, I went on to do *Citizen Cohn* with James Woods.

JB: Let's back up a little bit. When you worked on *Edward Scissorhands*, this was obviously something that had to be a bit of an epiphany for you, because here you were working alongside Vincent Price.

MM: The project came about when I earned my union hours after having worked on *The Guardian* with William Friedkin, which became a union production after it began. I was waiting to take my test, and Ve Neill wanted me to come down to Florida for the film. Tim Burton, the director, is such a visionary, and working with Johnny Depp and Ve was great. After finishing the shoot in Florida, we returned to 20th Century Fox in Los Angeles to complete all the interiors, and that's when we worked with Vincent.

JB: I can recall working with Price at some obscure ABC show, which I'll never forget, because he was a great influence on my career. I can remember that while doing his make-up, he reached into my kit for an eyebrow pencil. He told me that he always did his own eyebrows, and he proceeded to lay it on really heavy. I wanted to grab that pencil out of his hand and brush it through, but I thought to myself, "No, I've seen those eyebrows on TV and in the films. It's exactly how they always look, and that's how they'll look this time." You don't mess with Vincent Price.

MM: You don't mess with perfection.

JB: Let's talk about *Ghosts of Mississippi*. You did a brilliant make-up not with foam latex, but with gelatin. This make-up was one of the most realistic and effective make-ups I had ever seen. Tell me a little about its creation, because until then, most make-ups were done only with foam latex. And I believe you may have been one of the first, if not the first, to use only gelatin for the complete appliance on a major star in a major motion picture.

MM: In 1993, I started playing around with gelatin, because I had used it for effects, and I thought it was a great material that could potentially be used for appliances. In 1995, I was working on *Mulholland Falls*, which featured a lot of cancer victims, so I used the material to make appliances for the face. Gelatin is semi-translucent, and I could layer it into the mold as I was making it. I then wondered whether I could use it to do an old age make-up, especially because it blends so effectively into the skin. James Woods and his make-up artist at the time, Deborah La Mia Denaver (a former student of yours), asked me to do his make-up for the film. I was really putting myself on the line, because I had never used gelatin so extensively. I was very daring with it, for it absolutely had to work. There are certainly drawbacks, which I didn't learn until I started using it, but I began to make the formula a little stronger. It was a rediscovery of sorts for me.

I did the make-up for director Rob Reiner on Jimmy (Woods), which took about 2½ hours to apply. The production was short on time, so I only had three days to sculpt it on a face cast I had made of him, mold it, and perform the test. When I learned that John Seale—the brilliant director of photography with whom I had worked on a film called *The Doctor*—was going to shoot the movie, all of my worries about lighting were alleviated. When Jimmy walked on the set, John and Rob told me that this is what an old age make-up should look like. It worked out great. There were times in Mississippi during the shooting that it would start to melt a little bit—I had to pull things out of my case to make it work—but overall, it was a great experience working with gelatin.

JB: Aside from Dick Smith, I was one of the first artists to use gelatin directly on the face. And you took it one step further into actual molds that were stripped and applied directly. I recall working on a film called *Ilsa, She Wolf of the SS,* for which I used a technique that would later become what we know today as a gelatin appliance. I would put a layer of de-ammoniated latex directly onto the face, and then I would paint the gelatin onto that layer, wait for it to become semi-solid, and drag an orangewood stick through it to create wrinkles, eye bags, nasolabial folds, etc. On occasion, I would lay in very light coats of cotton first and then paint the gelatin directly over it. Once it had dried on the surface, I would stipple latex on top of it, resulting in encapsulated gelatin that worked very much like an appliance. I can recall John Chambers coming over and seeing a picture of the work, and he paid me the greatest compliment I had received up to that point by asking whether I had sculpted the piece. I was very proud to be able to tell him that it wasn't an appliance, but rather a construction built right onto the face. You've made it more sophisticated.

MM: We actually pour the gelatin into the mold, roll it around, and put the positive into it. It's not injected.

JB: What's predominantly used as a separator?

MM: After first pickling the mold with PAM vegetable spray, we use Epoxy Parfilm as a release.

JB: In years past, we would pickle it by letting it soak in castor oil.

MM: We use the spray first because it provides the mold with a nice inside coating. The parfilm doesn't inhibit the paintability and adhesion of the piece after you pull it out of the mold. With gelatin, the artist is able to blend a small piece in the middle of the skin that proves undetectable. The drawback, on the other hand, is the gelatin's tendency to break down on a person who perspires heavily. Gelatin is also unable to be used too closely to collared shirts or suits because it will shred if not sealed effectively on the neck.

MM: Do you always encapsulate it with Pros-Aide or some form of latex- or acrylic-based material?

MM: Perspiration seems to affect it regardless. But make-up artists should keep in mind that all materials for prosthetic appliances—foam, gelatin, and silicone—have their place. Nothing is outmoded. New products may come along, but to forego the older ones and insist only upon using the latest thing is the wrong attitude. The throwbacks are always relevant. I really enjoy my work on *CSI: Crime Scene Investigation*, because I am able to use some of the old techniques: building up on the skin, doing construction make-ups, and others. We made up a girl who was supposed to have been dead for a long time, to the extent that her skin was sloughing off. We airbrushed heavy veins and painted gelatin about a quarter of an inch over the skin, which was then layered and sealed with latex, just as you did in the past. And that knowledge comes from my education at your school. I sprayed the latex with PAM so that we could push it around in certain areas. It worked so well that everybody was totally grossed out by the end result. I don't necessarily have to sculpt a new piece. I can go back to a stock piece or build one up if necessary. Never be afraid of using the old techniques.

JB: You can always interchange. You may be using a gelatin to do the nose or foam latex to do the forehead or cheeks.

The majority of this volume, as far as actual mold-making, taking facial impressions, and pouring material for use as an appliance, was done by you and your wonderful crew, which I had the privilege of photographing at your laboratory, W.M. Creations, Inc. I am pleased to be able to present information not only about foam latex and silicone, but to feature a very extensive section on gelatin that you have done. Later on in this volume, readers will be seeing the actual process from beginning to end.

MM: You photographed the portion on the impression materials, and I finished photographing everything from that point on: the mold-making, the snaps, and taking the impressions.

JB: For our readers, give me the technical definition of *snaps*.

MM: A snap is an impression of a positive that is intended to capture the positive's image. The word *snap* refers to the way in which it is removed, or snapped off. It's as simple as that.

JB: Correct me if I'm wrong, but this technique was first performed by Dick Smith, who did an entire sculpture and painted the positive first with a dental separator. The entire positive would be soaked in water and then dissolve somewhat to enable the sculpture to be cut up into sections, such as the nose piece, cheeks, etc. I actually believe it was termed *snap* because it was a snap to do. Did you use snaps for the James Woods make-up in *Ghosts of Mississippi*?

MM: I had a negative silicone of the positive of his face. I did not have time to do a full sculpture and float it off. The forehead and face were done on two separate molds, and I determined where to blend by eye.

JB: You are very busy these days with your work on a multitude of television shows. Your lab has become huge and is quite renowned. Tell me about its development.

MM: I started my career by applying bread-and-butter beauty make-ups at NBC and CBS. I got to know make-up artists who hadn't learned about special make-up effects and things of that nature, to which I would introduce them. Being an educator at heart and learning from you, I showed them different techniques. And from those experiences, work started to trickle down to me, and I discovered a niche for myself. I gained a reputation for being able to provide a stock piece or to whip something up overnight, which is often required. I think that's where our business has thrived.

I look at the make-up industry as a whole—not divided into separate little groups, as a lot of people see it. Certainly there are people who just do prosthetics or beauty make-up, but when I go onto a show, I work with the department head and never put a barrier up between us. It's all one department, and the artists are working together toward an ultimate goal of making the best project possible.

JB: So your lab has grown considerably, and you have moved in every direction. You're not just doing film and television, but even stage.

MM: Yes. For *Wicked*, we supply all the masks, the Tin Man nose and chin, and the Scarecrow cowl. It premiered in San Francisco in 2003 and then went to Broadway, where it's been set since October of that year. It recently moved to Toronto before touring throughout the United States.

JB: I hear there is talk of making a film.

MM: You never know.

JB: Tell me about the best experience you've had as a make-up artist.

MM: I would say it was working with Ve Neill on *Edward Scissorhands*, because it was the first time I worked on a high-budget film. The camaraderie among the crew was great, and there was never a dull moment. It was never stressful and always fun. I also had a great experience on *What About Bob?* with Richard Dreyfuss, for whom I did straight make-up, in addition to one of his doubles. There weren't any special make-ups, but it was fun working with him, Bill Murray, and the brilliant director Frank Oz, with whom I've worked several times since.

JB: Tell me about your worst experience.

MM: I think the worst I've had was on Oliver Stone's *Heaven and Earth*, though it had nothing to do with the people themselves. Stone is great, because he pulls things out of you that you didn't know existed. But the circumstances, particularly the location of Puket, Thailand, made it very difficult. It's a beautiful place, but it's hard to do a film there. I was again turned onto the film by Greg Cannom, and he was doing the prosthetics, but they needed a department head. I needed a right-hand man, so I picked my partner John Jackson to work with me on it.

JB: As I sit here, I feel that I'm viewing three generations of make-up artists: myself being the first, you being the second, and John, your apprentice, being the third, all of us starting from humble beginnings at my make-up school in Hollywood. I must say that John has really done well, which means that you've done a wonderful job in passing on the knowledge you've gained. That's a feather in your cap. Now that you've achieved so many of your dreams—you have your laboratory, your own product line, you've won awards, and you've moved in so many directions—what does the future hold for you professionally?

MM: I would just be thankful to continue working—to have the health to do so, and also to have the jobs continue to come in. That would be my ultimate goal.

JB: Practically every artist I've interviewed for this book has answered in much the same way, which is important, for the reader must understand that working as an artist these days is different than it was in the past, when studios employed a single department head and several dozens of artists were assigned to various films. The work is now independent, and every film is assigned its own department head. And unlike in the past, every artist working on a film is more than likely given appropriate credit in one way or another, as opposed to simply the head receiving all the notoriety. So in a way, we have progressed a great deal.

I must say that I feel a great sense of satisfaction in being able to sit in this beautiful home of yours, less than a mile from the entrance to Universal Studios, and to know that in one way or another, however small—perhaps by just opening the door, as Bill Corso kindly said to me—

some of the knowledge I imparted to you has made you successful enough to be able to live well and actually provide work to others in the field. And now we have two graduates who have won the Oscar, of which I am very proud. But mostly, I'm very proud of the fact that as a make-up artist, you have fulfilled my dreams by becoming a truly consummate artist. I'm so pleased to know that in you, I have a make-up graduate who can walk onto any set and do any make-up, and very well at that. I want to thank you for helping me realize my dreams of having someone truly follow in my footsteps as you have done so elegantly and skillfully.

MM: Thank you.

JB: I would also like to reiterate that you have contributed a great portion of this volume, as our readers will see. Gelatin application has never before been explained in such detail.

MM: I see it as the passing on of knowledge that has been kept secret in the industry for years. The more knowledge you give out, the more you get back, and of all people, you are the greatest example. I find that people are willing to share information if you do the same. I'm always willing to give advice on make-up effects through my personal website (www.matthewwmungle.com).

JB: It's always the most successful artists, in my opinion, who share. It's the yin and the yang, or the positive and the negative. I do again want to thank you for taking time on this Sunday, because I know how busy you are. Our readers will learn a great deal from what you have to offer.

PROCEDURES

Drafted by the authors from information generously submitted by Matthew Mungle.

ALGINATE

ALGINATE FACE CASTING

Alginate face casting is a slightly claustrophobic experience, especially if the subject has not been through the process before. Artists should have their own personal face casts made to be able to provide judgments during future procedures and fully understand the feeling.

It is very important for the artist to reassure the subject that the procedure will be performed with confidence. Playing classical or easy listening background music may help calm the subject's nerves. Using a comfortable chair with a headrest will help the posture of both artist and subject.

It is also imperative that each set of the face casting is achieved as fast as possible in order to minimize the subject's time under the casting.

Alginates

There are several types of alginates to use for face casting:

- Mold Gel by Art Molds
- Accu-Cast—LS 3-90, LS 6-80, and LS 8-80

- Alpha-Dent Prosthetic Grade Cream
- Imperial Body Gel Extra
- Pink House Studio Slow Set Alginate

Each of these alginates has a different viscosity and setting time. With a little experimentation, the artist will be able to find the right brand and correct measurements.

The basic mixing formula:

- 8 ounces—Alginate
- 8 ounces—Water

The temperature of the room and water will affect the setting time of alginate. Making the alginate thick to prevent it from running too much is beneficial. Alginate that is too thick, on the other hand, will result in a sagging, distorted face cast.

Materials Needed for Alginate Face Casting

- Cover Cloth or Large Trash Bag
- Paper Towels
- Bald Cap Adhesive (Pros-Aide or Beta Bond)
- Adhesive Remover
- Comb
- Masking Tape

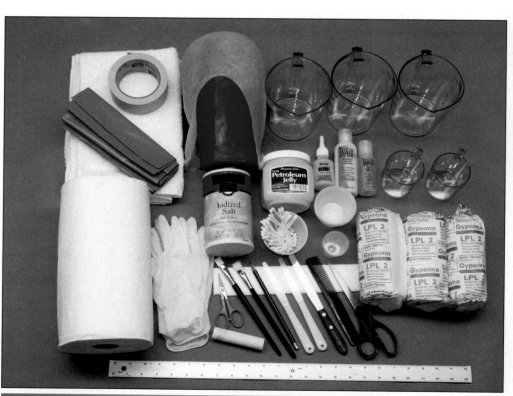

Fig. 9-1

- Indelible Ink Pencil
- Water (75°F to 80°F)
- Mixing Cups
- Cynoacrylate Glue (Krazy or Super)
- Cloth Towels
- Plaster Bandages (Gypsona Brand), 3 rolls, 6″ wide
- Cool Water (for Plaster Bandages)
- Dust Masks
- 10# White Hydrocal
- 3 to 5 Quart Mixing Buckets
- Flour Sifter
- Stanley Planer
- X-Acto Hobby Knife
- Soft Clay (Kleen Klay)
- 6 Pairs of Rubber Gloves
- Plastic or Rubber Bald Cap
- Brushes and Q-Tips (for application of adhesive)
- Cleanup Brushes (Soft Nylon Brushes)
- Large and Small Scissors
- Alginate
- Spatulas (small and large)
- Petroleum Jelly
- Zip Kicker (for Cyno Glue)
- Measuring Cups (32 oz. and 8 oz.)
- Salt (to hasten setting time of plaster bandages)
- 1″ Throwaway Brushes
- 3½″ to 4½″ PVC or Metal Tubing (for use as handle in back of face cast)
- Mold Knife or Metal Sculpting Tool
- Small Syringe

Fig. 9-2

Preparation for Alginate Face Casting

1. Lay out all tools and materials on list for casting before subject arrives.

2. Pre-weigh alginate and water.

   First Batch for Back of Ears
   2 oz.—Alginate, 1½ oz.—Warm Water

   Second Batch for Face
   32 oz.—Alginate, 34 oz.—Room-temperature Water (or slightly warmer; warmer water hastens setting time, while colder water retards setting time)

Fig. 9-3

Fig. 9-4

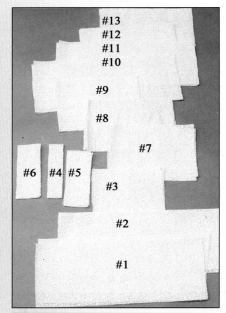
Fig. 9-5

3. Pre-cut 6″ plaster bandages,* all three layers thick. Sizes given are for an average face. (Adjust according to face size.)

Quantity	Size	Order Used
2	14″	#1 and #2
1	8″	#3
1	1″	#4
2	2″	#5 and #6
1	8″	#7
2	10″	#8 and #9
2	14″	#10 and #11
2	10″	#12 and #13

(Refer back to this list during step 8 of the Face Casting procedure.)

Procedure for Alginate Face Casting

1. Cover the subject to the neck or past the clavicle with a cover cloth or large plastic trash bag. Tape around the neck with masking tape.

Fig. 9-6

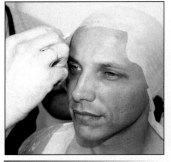
Fig. 9-7

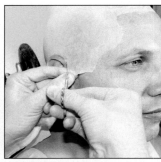
Fig. 9-8

2. Apply bald cap with ears exposed.

3. Mark hairline with indelible ink pencil.

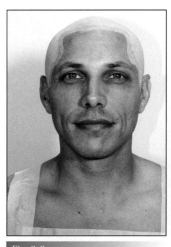
Fig. 9-9

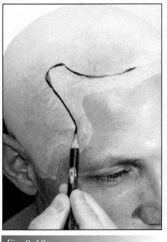
Fig. 9-10

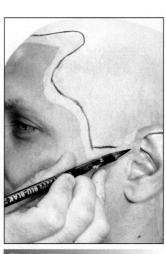
Fig. 9- 11

*Gypsona Brand plaster bandages are suggested.

4. Coat any exposed hair (eyebrows and eyelashes) and bald cap with a very light coat of petroleum jelly.

5. Mix back-of-ear alginate (thick batch).

Fig. 9-12

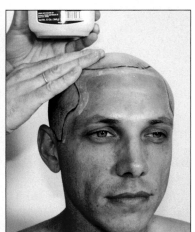

Fig. 9-13

Fig. 9-14

Fig. 9-15

Fig. 9- 16

6. Fill in the back of the ears with ear mix, apply with a spatula, and let set. This step is important in order to keep the ears from dropping during casting. This mix is very thick and will not run.

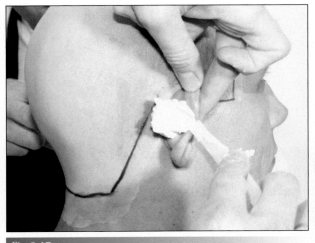

Fig. 9-17

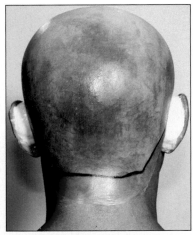

Fig. 9-18

7. Mix face batch of alginate, pouring the alginate powder into the water and mixing with the hands.

Fig. 9-19

Fig. 9-20

Fig. 9- 21

Apply to the face with gloved hands as follows, gently rubbing a small amount of alginate into the skin, back and forth, to avoid getting air pockets and bubbles. Then, add larger amounts to build up thickness. Be careful not to apply the alginate too thickly to areas of the skin that may sag, such as lips, eyelids, and neck areas.

Rubber gloves should be used to apply the alginate in order to clean hands faster and move on to the next step.

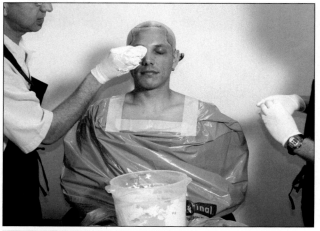

Fig. 9-22

A. Eye sockets

Fig. 9-23

B. Forehead and cheeks

Fig. 9- 24

C. Nose and lips

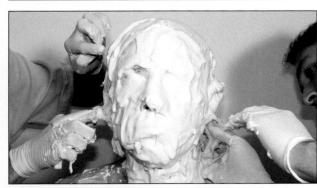

Fig. 9-25

D. Ears

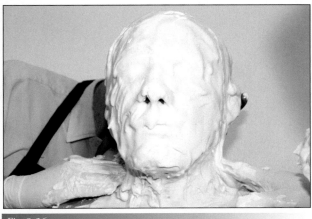

Fig. 9-26

E. Neck

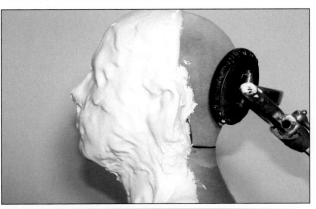

Fig. 9- 27

F. Finished alginate

*Gypsona Brand plaster bandages are suggested.

Fig. 9-28

8. After the alginate has set, mix 2 to 3 tablespoons of salt into tepid plaster bandage water.

Dip each layer into water, and apply in the following order:

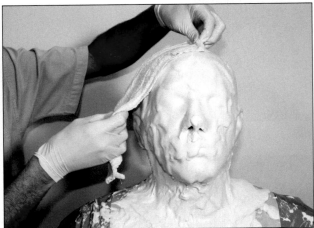

Fig. 9-29

A. #1—Triple-fold the outer edge of the bandage, and position it from the top of the head to the shoulder, over the front of the ear on the left side.

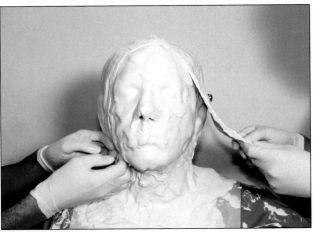

Fig. 9-30

B. #2—Triple-fold the outer edge of the bandage, and position it from the top of the head to the shoulder, over the front of the ear on the right side.

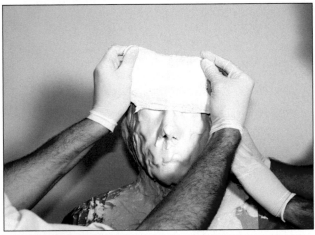

Fig. 9-31

C. #3—Over forehead.

*Gypsona Brand plaster bandages are suggested.

D. #4—On the center (septum) area of the nose.

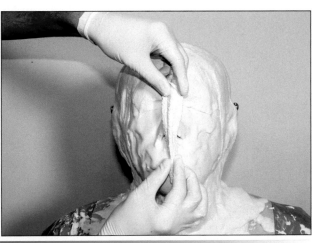

Fig. 9-32

E. #5 and #6—On the left side of the nostril.

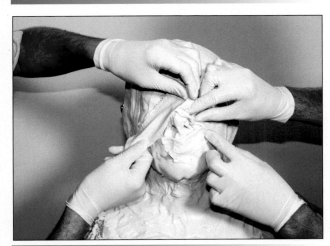

Fig. 9-33

F. #7—Over the mouth area.

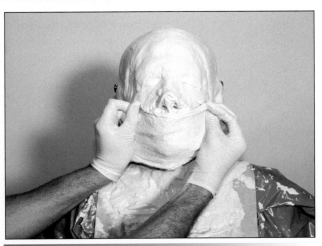

Fig. 9-34

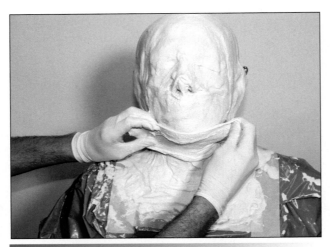

Fig. 9-35

G. #8—Under the chin area.

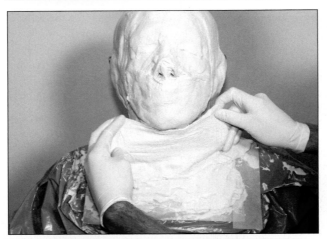

Fig. 9-36

H. #9—Over the neck area.

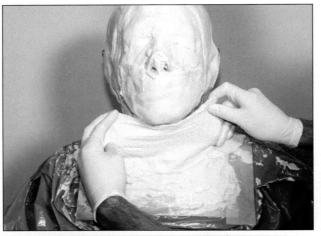

Fig. 9-37

I. #10 and #11—Triple-fold the outer edge of the bandage, and place it on the left and right side over the clavicle/neck area.

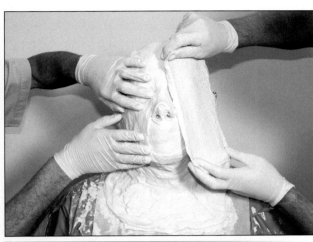

Fig. 9-38

J. #12—Over the left side of the face.

Fig. 9-39

K. #13—Over the right side of the face.

Rubber gloves should be worn when working with plaster bandages to keep hands from drying out and to facilitate cleanup.

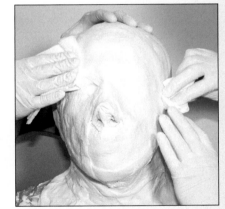

Fig. 9-40

9. Let the last piece of plaster bandage harden (1–2 minutes). Accelerate the drying process by rubbing a dry paper towel over the wet plaster bandage.

10. Ask subject to start moving the facial muscles slightly (smile, frown, and blow air out of the mouth, e.g.). Tilt the head back, which will loosen the neck area. Gently pull at the skin on the neck and the bald cap to loosen this area.

11. Carefully remove the back-of-ear plugs, which may be saved and glued back in or tossed, depending on how thick or thin the back-of-ear areas need to be on the plaster positive face cast. Plugs may be glued back in with cynoacrylate (Super Glue) after removal of the cast from the face.

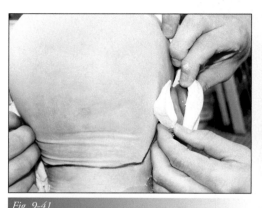

Fig. 9-41

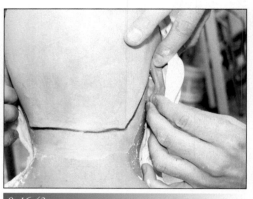

9. 16-42

12. Carefully remove alginate cast from face.

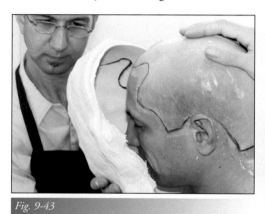

Fig. 9-43

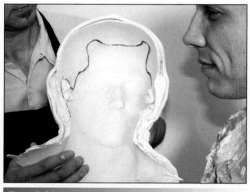

Fig. 16-44

13. Set the face casting into a cradle comprised of a towel and large bowl.

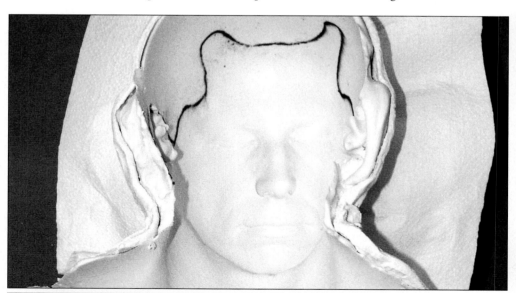

Fig. 9-45

*Gypsona Brand plaster bandages are suggested.

Fig. 9-48

14. Make sure alginate is seated properly into the plaster bandage shell in order to avoid distortions in the plaster casting. Trim any excess alginate off face casting with an X-Acto knife.

Fig. 9-49

15. Glue the alginate around edges of the plaster bandage shell (if necessary) with cynoacrylate (Super Glue), and kick the glue with Zip Kicker.

16. Nostril holes can be plugged from the outside of the plaster cast with Kleen Klay. The holes can be filled from the inside with alginate mixed with hot water that is injected into the cavity with a small syringe. Be very careful not to distort the nostril area.

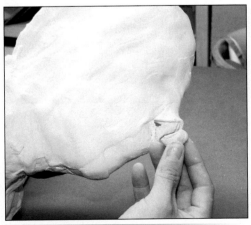

Fig. 9-50

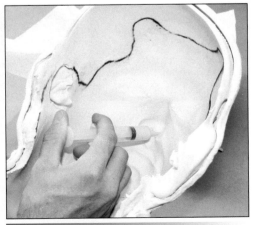

Fig. 9-51

17. Remove the bald cap with adhesive remover, and clean the subject's skin with a warm wet towel. Keep the marked bald cap for future use in marking and sizing bald caps.

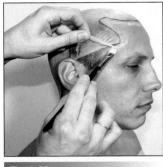

Fig. 9-52

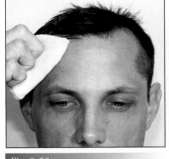

Fig. 9-53

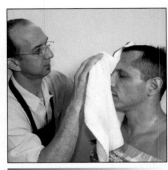

Fig. 9- 54

18. Mix and pour plaster positive immediately to avoid letting the alginate shrink. Paint the plaster in first, and then build it thicker as the plaster thickens. A handle may be inserted into the back of the cast before the plaster is completely set.

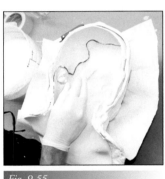

Fig. 9-55

Fig. 9-56

Fig. 9- 57

19. Carefully pull plaster face cast and alginate from plaster bandage shell. Peel alginate off of cast in pieces.

Fig. 9-57a

Fig. 9-57b

Fig. 9-57c

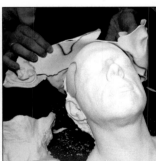

Fig. 9- 57d

20. Clean plaster positive with planer, chisel, and knife.

Fig. 9-57e

Fig. 9-57f

Fig. 9- 57g

Mixing Plaster

Fig. 9-58

1. Pour 2 quarts of cold water into a mixing bowl. This mixture is enough to fill an average face cast.

2. Sift White Hydrocal or Plaster of Paris into the water until plaster powder forms a "dry riverbed" effect on top of water. DO NOT STIR YET.

Fig. 9-59

Fig. 9-60

3. Let stand at least 3 minutes, and then mix thoroughly by hand or with paint stirrer or hand drill. Wear rubber gloves and dust mask when using plaster powders in order to prevent drying hands and to avoid inhalation.

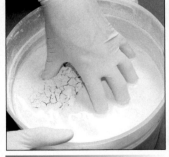

Fig. 9-60a   *Fig. 9-60b*   *Fig. 9- 60c*

Tips about Alginate Face Casting

- Apply alginate as thin as possible to prevent skin sagging while still creating a stable mold.
- To maintain easy removal, do not apply plaster bandages behind the ear area.
- Fresh alginate does not stick to set alginate. In order for alginate to bond to itself, brush or spray a mixture of one-teaspoon sodium carbonate monohydrate and 8 ounces of warm water onto the set alginate, mix a new batch of alginate, and apply. Art Molds supplies an alginate bonder/retarder and softener called *Algislo*.

ALGINATE HEAD CASTING

Head casting is a slightly more claustrophobic experience for the subject than face casting; therefore, it is extremely important to assure the subject that the procedure is safe, both beforehand and during. Playing classical or easy listening background music may help calm the subject's nerves. Using a comfortable chair will help the posture of both artist and subject.

It is also imperative that the head casting be achieved as fast as possible in order to minimize the subject's time under the mold. For head casting, two to three artists should be utilized to reduce time. The entire casting process should only last approximately 20–30 minutes.

Alginates

Refer to the section on Face Casting for types of alginates.

Materials Needed for Alginate Head Casting

- Cover Cloth or Large Trash Bag
- 6 Pairs of Rubber Gloves
- Paper Towels
- Plastic or Rubber Bald Cap
- Bald Cap Adhesive (Pros-Aide or Beta Bond)

*Gypsona Brand plaster bandages are suggested.

- Brushes and Q-Tips (for application of adhesive)
- Adhesive Remover
- Cleanup Brushes (Soft Nylon Brushes)
- Comb
- Masking Tape
- Large and Small Scissors
- Indelible Ink Pencil
- Alginate
- Water (75°F to 80°F)
- Palette Knives (Small and Large)
- Mixing Cups
- Petroleum Jelly
- Cynoacrylate Glue (Krazy or Super)
- Zip Kicker (for Cyno Glue)
- Plaster Bandages (Gypsona Brand), 8 rolls, 6″ wide
- Cool Water (for plaster bandages)
- Salt (to hasten setting time of plaster bandages)
- Cleaning Sponge
- Cloth Towels
- Measuring Cups (32 oz. and 8 oz.)
- Dust Masks
- Two 1″ Throwaway Brushes
- 10# White Hydrocal
- 3 to 5 Quart Mixing Buckets
- Flour Sifter
- Stanley Planer
- Mold Knife or Metal Sculpting Tool
- X-Acto Hobby Knife
- Soft Clay (Kleen Klay)
- Small Syringe

Preparation for Alginate Head Casting

1. Lay out all tools and materials on the list for casting before the subject arrives.
2. Pre-weigh the alginate and the water.

   First Batch for Back of Ears

   2 oz.—Alginate, 1½ oz.—Warm Water

   Second Batch for Head

   64 oz.—Alginate (alginate and water amount will vary according to head size)

   64 oz.—Room-temperature Water (or slightly warmer; warmer water hastens setting time, while colder water retards setting time)

3. Pre-cut 6" plaster bandages*, all three layers thick.

Plaster bandages, which make a better impression without distortions, will be used for the back of this head cast.

Fig. 9-61a

Back

Quantity	Size	Order Used
2	14"	#1 through #4
1	8"	#5 and #6
1	1"	#7 and #8
2	2"	#9 and #10
1	8"	#11 and #12

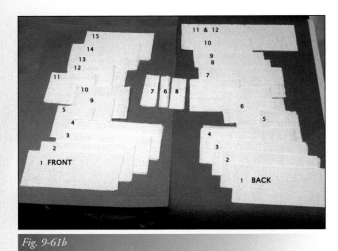

Fig. 9-61b

Front

Quantity	Size	Order Used
4	14"	#1 through #4
1	8"	#5
1	1"	#6
2	2"	#7 and #8
2	8"	#9 and #10
2	12"	#11 and #12
2	10"	#13 and #14
1	16"	#15

(Refer back to this list during step 8 of the Head Casting procedure.)

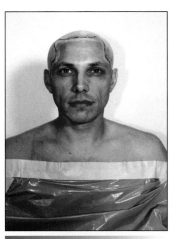

Fig. 9-62

Procedure for Alginate Head Casting

1. Cover the subject to the shoulder with a cover cloth or large plastic trash bag. Tape around the neck

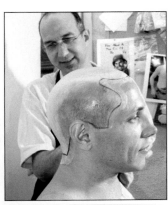

Fig. 9-63

with masking tape.

2. Apply the bald cap with ears exposed. *(Refer to the Alginate Face Casting section.)*

3. Mark the hairline with an indelible ink pencil.

Fig. 9-64

4. Coat any exposed hair (eyebrows and eyelashes), the bald cap, and the back of the neck/shoulder area with a very light coat of petroleum jelly.

5. Mix the back-of-ear alginate (thick batch), fill in the back of the ears with ear mix, apply with a spatula, and let set. This step is important in order to keep the ears from dropping during casting and to allow a larger area to be filled when making the plas-

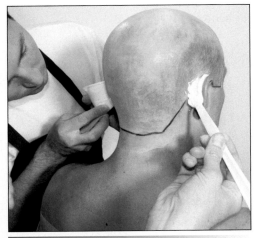

Fig. 9-65

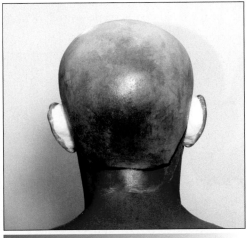

Fig. 9-66

ter positive. This mixture is very thick and will not run.

6. Make a mid-line mark starting at the top of the head to the shoulders on both sides of the head.

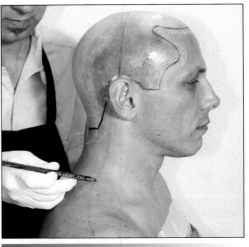

Fig. 9-67

7. Using warm water for the plaster bandages, apply as follows, smoothing the bandage

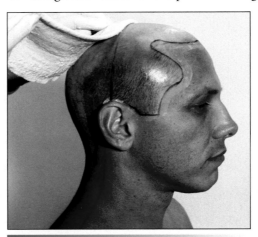

Fig. 9-68

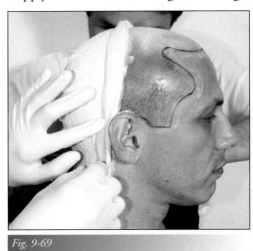

Fig. 9-69

onto the bald cap and skin surface in order not to leave too many voids. (The back of the head cast is made entirely with plaster bandages.)

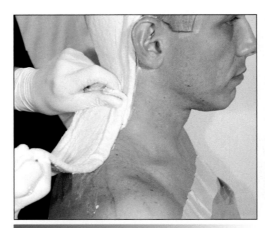

Fig. 9-70

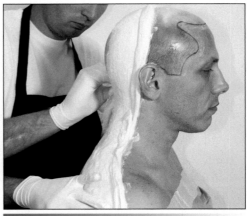

Fig. 16-71

A. #1 and #2—Triple-fold the outer edge of the bandage, and position it from the top of the head to the neck area on the right and left sides of the head.

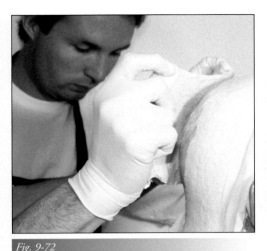

Fig. 9-72

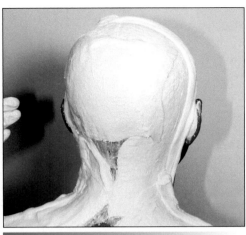

Fig. 9-73

B. #3 and #4—Triple-fold the outer edge of the bandage, and position it from

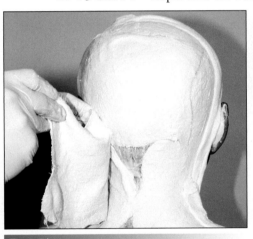

Fig. 9-74

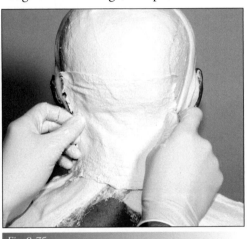

Fig. 9-75

the neck area to the shoulder area on the right and left sides of the head.

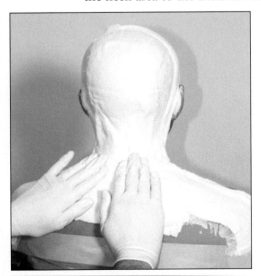

Fig. 9-76

C. #5—Back of the head.
D. #6—Nape of the neck.

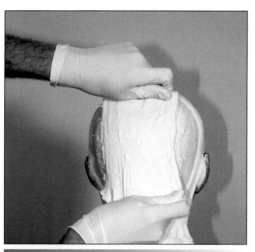

Fig. 9-77

E. #7—Across the shoulder blades.

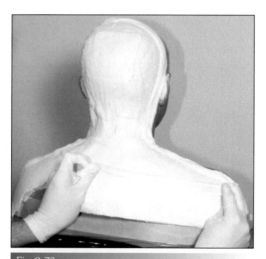

Fig. 9-78

F. #8—Back of the head.

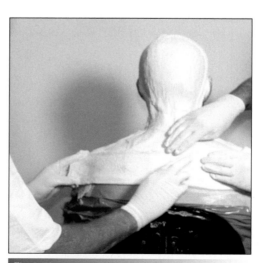

Fig. 9-79

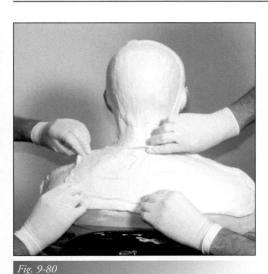

Fig. 9-80

G. #9—Triple-fold the outer edge of the bandage, and place it on the right shoulder/back area.

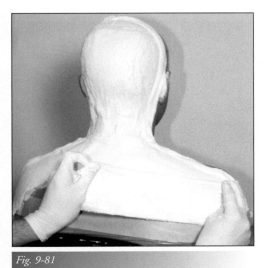

Fig. 9-81

H. #10—Triple-fold the outer edge of the bandage, and place it on the left shoulder/back area.

I. #11—Reinforce the left shoulder area.

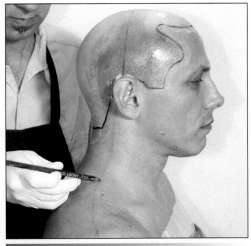

Fig. 9-82

J. #12—Reinforce the right shoulder area.

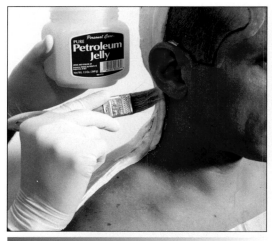

Fig. 9-83

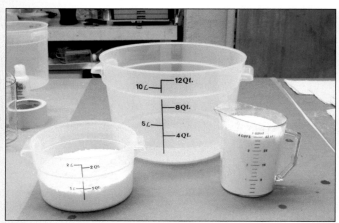

Fig. 9-84

Fig. 9-85

Fig. 9- 86

8. Clean the skin area adjacent to the plaster bandages with a wet cleaning sponge.

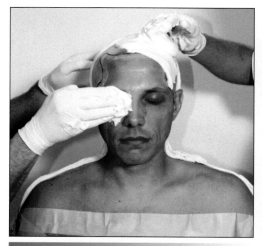

Fig. 9-87

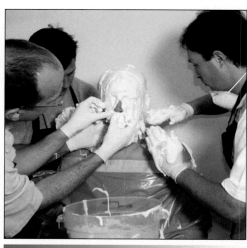

Fig. 9-88

9. Using a 1" throwaway brush, paint petroleum jelly over the plaster bandage and onto the skin area.

Fig. 9-89

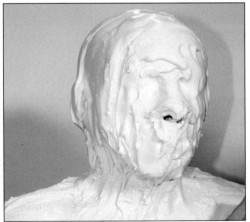

Fig. 9-90

10. Mix the front face batch of alginate, pouring the alginate powder into the water and mixing it with the hands.

11. Apply to the face with gloved hands as follows:

    A. Eye sockets

    B. Forehead

    C. Back of head

    D. Cheeks

    E. Ears

    F. Nose

    G. Lips

    H. Neck area

Gently rub a small amount of alginate back and forth into the skin to avoid getting air pockets, and then add larger amounts to build up thickness. Be careful not to apply the alginate too thickly to areas of the skin

Fig. 9-91

that may sag, such as lips, eyelids, and neck areas. Work as fast as possible without moving the subject's face around before the alginate sets.

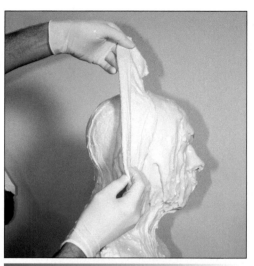

Fig. 9-92

Apply the alginate over the plaster bandage approximately 1". This will act as a bond between the front and back casts. Rubber gloves should be used to apply the alginate in order to clean the hands faster and move to the next step.

12. After the alginate has set, cut any excess alginate off of the lap over the plaster bandage area and the bottom of the cast area.

13. Release the plaster bandage/alginate area on the seam of the cast with the 1" throwaway brush and petroleum jelly.

Fig. 9-93

14. Mix 2–3 tablespoons of salt into tepid water for the plaster bandages. Dip each layer into water, and apply them in the following order:

A. #1 and #2—Triple-fold the outer edge of the bandage, and place it from the top of the head to the neck area on the right and left sides of the head over the alginate, touching the back plaster bandages.

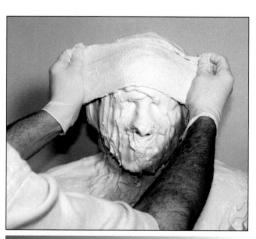

Fig. 9-93

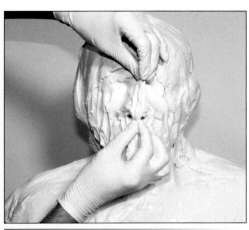

Fig. 9-95

B. #3 and #4—Triple-fold the outer edge of the bandage, and place it from the neck area to the shoulder area on the right and left sides of the head over the alginate, touching the back plaster bandages.

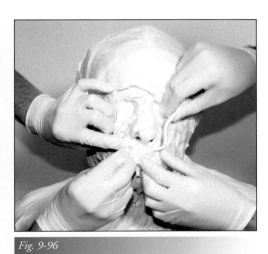

Fig. 9-96

C. #5—Over the forehead.

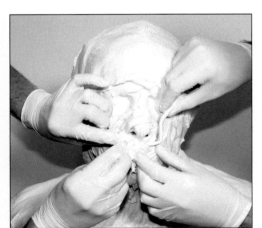

Fig. 9-97

D. #6—On the center (septum) area of the nose.

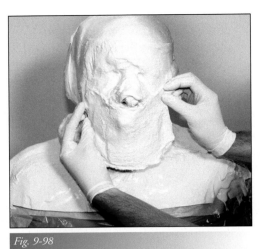

Fig. 9-98

E. #7 and #8—On the right and left sides of the nostril area.

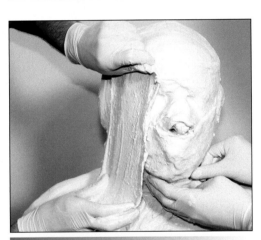

Fig. 9-99

F. #9—Over the eye, nose and cheek areas.

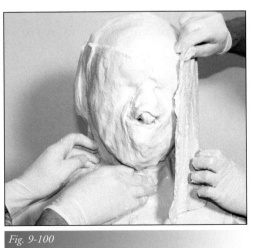

Fig. 9-100

G. #10—Under the nose and over the mouth area.

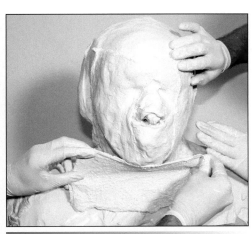

Fig. 9-101

H. #11—Right face area.

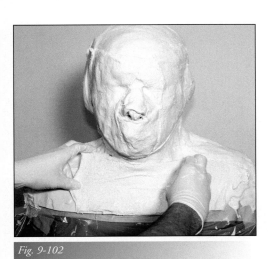

Fig. 9-102

I. #12—Left face area.

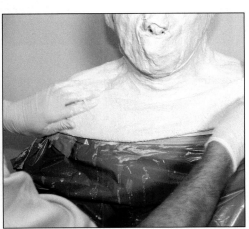

Fig. 9-103

J. #13—Under the chin and neck areas.

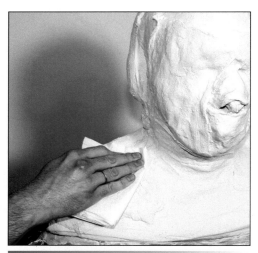

Fig. 9-104

K. #14—Center of the chest area.

L. #15—Triple-fold the outer edge of the bandage, and place it over the chest area.

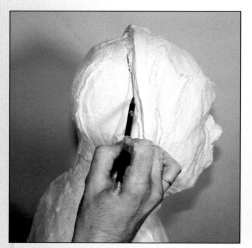

Fig. 9-105

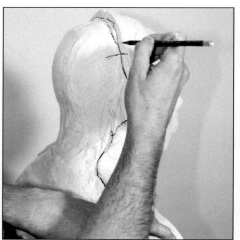

Fig. 9-106

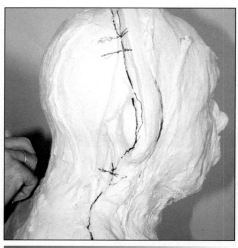

Fig. 9-107

15. Let the last piece of plaster bandage harden (1–2 minutes). By rubbing a dry paper towel over the wet plaster bandage, it will dry faster.

Fig. 9-108

16. Mark the join area between the front and back plaster bandages with an indelible ink pencil.

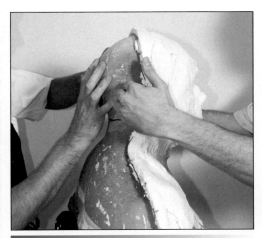

Fig. 9-109

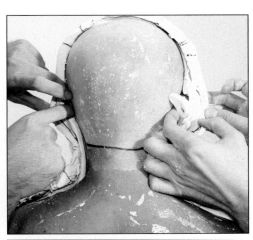

Fig. 9-110

17. Carefully loosen and remove the back plaster bandage mother mold from the alginate, and set it onto a large towel wrapped into a circle. DO NOT remove the front alginate from the face.

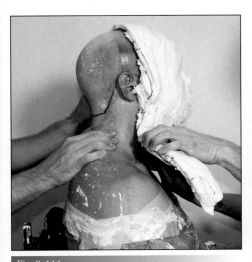

Fig. 9-111

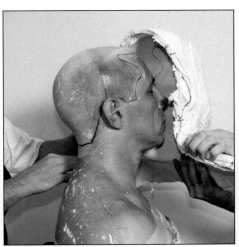

Fig. 9-112

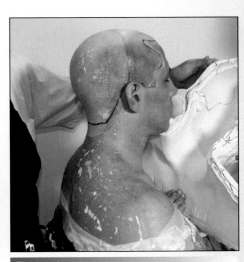

Fig. 9-113

18. Ask the subject to start slightly moving the facial muscles (smile, frown, and blow air out of the mouth, e.g.).

19. Work the hand between the alginate and the back of the ear, and remove the back-of-ear plugs, which may be saved to be glued back in or tossed depending on how thick or thin the back of the ear areas need to be on the plaster positive cast. Plugs may be glued back in with cynoacrylate (Super Glue) after removal of the cast.

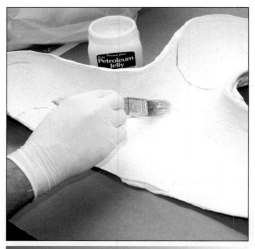

Fig. 9-114

20. Carefully loosen and peel the alginate away from the bald cap and neck area.

Fig. 9-115

21. Paint a heavy coat of petroleum jelly into the back head plaster bandage to ensure easy removal of the plaster casting.

Fig. 9-116

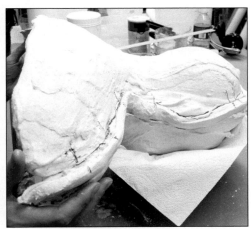

Fig. 9-117

22. Fill in the nostrils with alginate and Kleen Klay. *(See Alginate Face Casting section.)* The front alginate may need to be glued back into the plaster bandage shell with cynoacrylate (Super Glue).

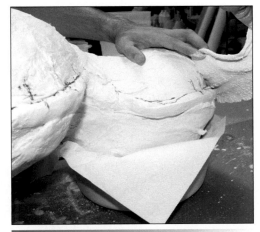

Fig. 9-118

23. Place the back plaster bandage cast

Fig. 9-118a

onto the front, making sure the alginate is seated properly into the plaster bandage shell in order to avoid distortions in the plaster casting. Glue the alginate around edges of the

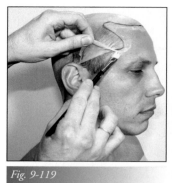

Fig. 9-119

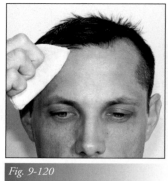

Fig. 9-120

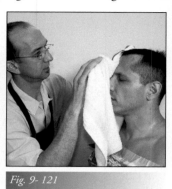

Fig. 9- 121

plaster bandage shell (if necessary) with Cynoacrylate (Super Glue).

Fig. 9-122

Fig. 9-123

24. Seal the front and back plaster bandages with a three-layer thick plaster

Fig. 9-124

bandage on the full seam.

Fig. 9-125

Fig. 9-126

25. Set the cast upside down into a large container lined with foam, and

Fig. 9-127

Fig. 9-128

be careful not to crush the top of the head and nose areas.

Fig. 9-129

26. Remove the cap and adhesive, and clean the subject's skin with a warm wet towel and adhesive remover.

Mixing Plaster

1. Sift White Hydrocal or Plaster of Paris into a mixing bowl with 3 quarts of cold water

Fig. 9-130

Fig. 9-131

until the plaster powder forms a "dry riverbed" effect on top of the water. DO NOT STIR YET. Let this stand at least 3 minutes, and then mix thoroughly by hand, paint stirrer, or hand drill. Wear rubber gloves and a dust mask when using plaster powders in order to prevent the drying of hands and the inhalation of powder.

Fig. 9-132

Fig. 9-133

2. *The following step is done as fast as possible, because White Hydrocal sets up in approx-imately 5 to 8 minutes.* Pour the plaster into the cast slowly up to the eye area. Roll

Fig. .9-134

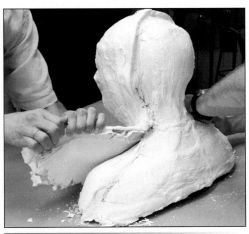

Fig. 9-135

the plaster around the inside of the cast to coat the alginate.

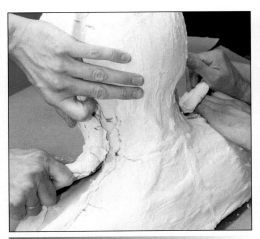

Fig. 9-136

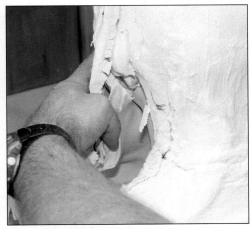

Fig. 9-137

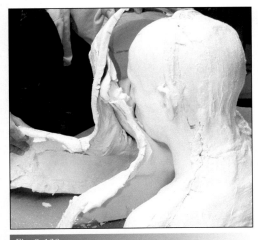

Fig. 9-138

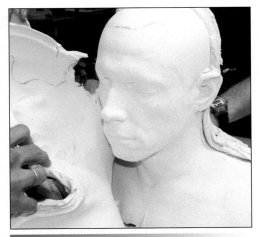

Fig. 9-139

3. Pour the remainder of plaster into the cast, and then pour it back into the bucket. (This coats the inside of the cast.)

4. Agitate the plaster inside the ear and nose area of the cast with a gloved hand to remove any bubbles. Re-pour the plaster back into the head cast.

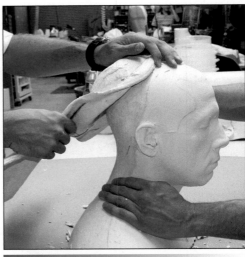

Fig. 9-140

Fig. 9-141

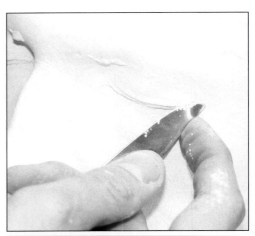

Fig. 9-142

5. As the plaster starts to thicken, scoop out the center of the head casting, and build up the edges of the shoulder area. This makes a lighter cast.

PLY-O-LIFE

PLY-O-LIFE FACE CASTING

Instructions for subject preparation under Alginate Face Casting should be followed before casting the face.

Ply-O-Life

Manufactured by Pink House Studios, Ply-O-Life is a non-toxic, odorless, platinum-based silicone impression material that may be applied directly to the skin. Hair to be included in the mold must be well-coated with a thin layer of gelatin, a hair cholesterol/castor oil mixture, and a very light coat of petroleum jelly. The advantage of Ply-O-Life molds over alginate molds is that resins, plasters, waxes, clays, and certain quick-set urethanes may be cast directly into them. Ply-O-Life does not shrink at all, unlike alginate. New mixes of Ply-O-Life may be added to freshly set batches. Ply-O-Life generally has a 6-minute working time (plus 2 minutes for a fully cured state). Refrigeration of the material for a few hours (or overnight) will slow the setting time to approximately 8 minutes.

Because Ply-O-Life is a platinum-based material, avoid contamination from rubber gloves or sulfur-based clays. Wash hands before handling material.

Ply-O-Life material adheres to hair; therefore, protect and separate/lubricate the hair for easy release.

It is highly recommended that a small amount of Ply-O-Life be applied to the subject's wrist prior to taking the cast in order to determine if any sensitivity to the material exists. Ply-O-Life is non-toxic and safe, but there may be individuals who are sensitive to almost any material, both organic and inorganic. When in doubt, use alginate for face casting.

Materials Needed for Ply-O-Life Face Casting

- Gram Scale
- Bald Cap Adhesive
- Rubber Gloves
- Masking Tape
- GM Foam Latex Pigment (Ruddy or Tantone)
- Comb
- Spatulas (Small and Large)
- Eyelash/Eyebrow Brush
- Ply-O-Life
- Plaster Bowls
- Petroleum Jelly
- Sharpie Marker (Black)
- Cloth Towels
- Paper Towels
- Cool Water for Plaster Bandages
- Plaster Bandages (Gypsona Brand), 3 rolls, 6″ wide
- Plastic Disposable Cups and Lids (2, 4, and 8 oz.)

- Salt (to hasten setting time of plaster bandages)
- Plastic Bald Cap ONLY
- Cover Cloth or Large Plastic Trash Bag
- Brushes and Q-Tips (for application of adhesive)
- Adhesive Remover
- Small and Large Scissors
- Gelatin

  > 50 grams—Sorbital
  >
  > 50 grams—Glycerin
  >
  > 10 grams—Distilled Water
  >
  > Mix the above liquids, and then add:
  >
  > 15 grams—Gelatin
  >
  > Heat in microwave until the gelatin granules have been dissolved.
  >
  > *This gelatin formula should be pre-mixed.*

- Hair Cholesterol (3 parts to 1 part Castor Oil)

Fig. 9-143

Preparation for Ply-O-Life Face Casting

1. Lay out all the tools and materials on the list for casting before the subject arrives.

2. Pre-weigh parts B and C Ply-O-Life (POL) into separate plastic disposable containers, and cap these with lids.

Fig. 9-144

First Batch for Back of Ears

10 gm.—B

10 gm.—C

Second and Third Batches for Ears

Two batches

15 gm.—B

15 gm.—C

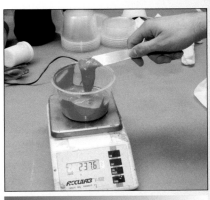

Fig. 9-145

Fourth and Fifth Batches for Face

Two batches

150 gm.—B

150 gm.—C

Mix 5 drops of GM Foam latex pigment into side B of the fifth batch of POL. This will make it easier to see if the fifth coat has sufficiently covered the fourth.

Fig. 9-146

Fig. 9-147

3. Pre-cut 6" wide plaster bandages, all three layers thick.

Quantity	Size	Order Used
2	14"	#1 and #2
1	8"	#3
1	1"	#4
2	2"	#5 and #6
1	8"	#7
2	10"	#8 and #9
2	14"	#10 and #11
2	10"	#12 and #13
1	16"	#15

(Refer back to this list during step 13 of the Face Casting procedure.)

Procedure for Ply-O-Life Face Casting

1. Cover the subject to the neck or past the clavicle with a cover cloth or large plastic trash bag. Tape around the neck with masking tape.

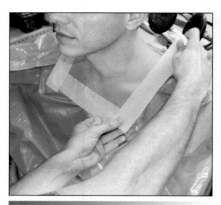

Fig. 9-148

2. Apply the bald cap with ears exposed. (Plastic cap ONLY.)

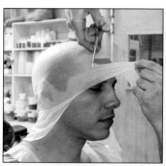 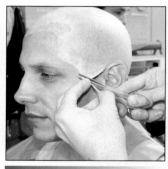 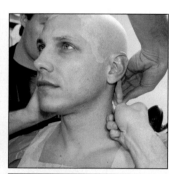

Fig. 9-149   Fig. 9-150   Fig. 9- 151

3. Mark the hairline with a black Sharpie. The line will transfer to the inside of the POL face cast negative.

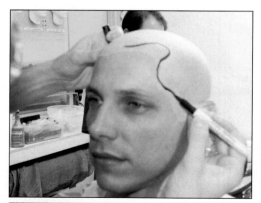 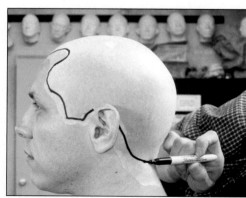

Fig. 9-152   Fig. 9-153

4. Coat any exposed hair (except eyelashes) with a warm liquid gelatin mixture, using an eyelash/eyebrow brush.

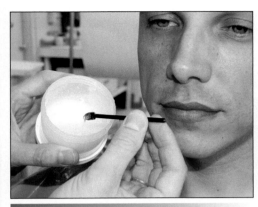

Fig. 9-154

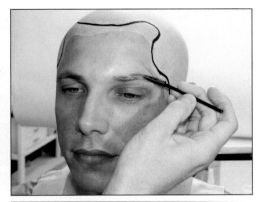

Fig. 9-155

5. Lightly coat the face (including gelatin-coated hair), eyelashes, and bald cap with cholesterol/castor oil mixture. Apply a little extra on nose area.

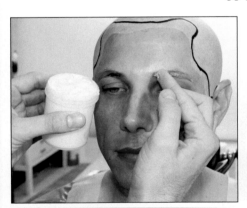

Fig. 9-156

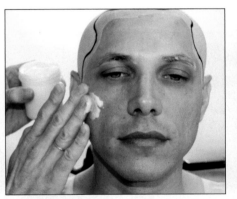

Fig. 9-157

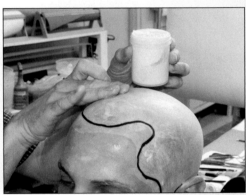

Fig. 9-158

6. Coat any lanugo hair and eyebrows/eyelashes with a very light coat of petroleum jelly.

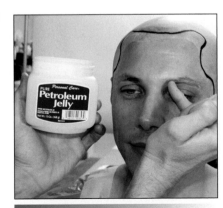

Fig. 9-159

7. Mix the first batch of POL, and fill in only the back of the ears (applied with a spatula). This step is important in order to keep the ears from dropping during casting.

Fig. 9-160

Fig. 9-161

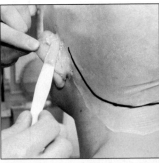
Fig. 9- 162

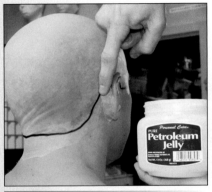
Fig. 16-163

8. Before the first batch is set, smooth it out with petroleum jelly. This will also act as a separator for future removal of the piece.

9. Mix the second batch of POL with a spatula, and apply it to the right ear, lapping over the first batch of set POL.

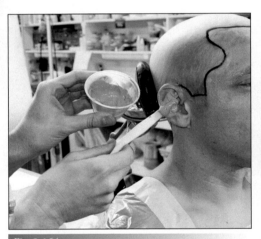
Fig. 9-164

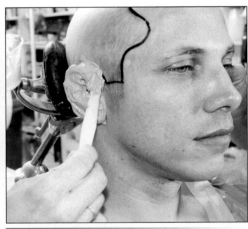
Fig. 9-165

10. Mix the third batch of POL with a spatula, and apply it to the left ear, lapping over the first batch of set POL.

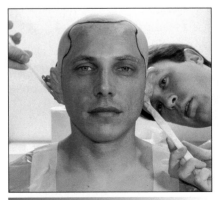
Fig. 9-166

11. Wash the hands, and apply a light coat of cholesterol/castor oil mixture to them, wiping any excess off with a paper towel.

12. Mix the fourth batch of POL, and use clean hands that have been coated with the mixture to apply it as follows (DO NOT use rubber gloves; apply POL in the direction of hair growth):

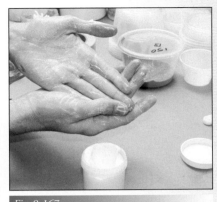

Fig. 9-167

Fig. 9-168

Fig. 9-169

Fig. 9-170

A. Eye sockets

B. Forehead

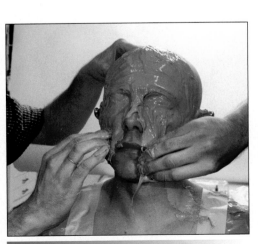

Fig. 9-171

C. Cheeks

D. Nose

E. Lips

F. Neck

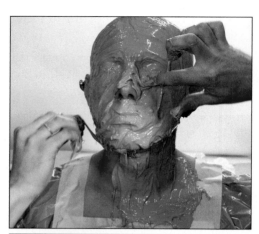

Fig. 9-172

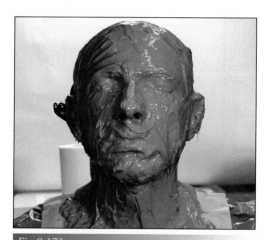

Fig. 9-173

It is very important at this point to let each coat of POL set until it is tacky to the touch; otherwise, additional coats may distort previous layers.

13. Mix the fifth batch of tinted POL, and carefully apply it over the fourth batch using a spatula in an up-and-down, side-to-side motion. Try not to disturb the first layer of POL. The finished surface should be as smooth as possible.

Fig. 9-174

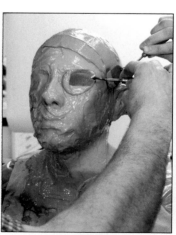

Fig. 9-175

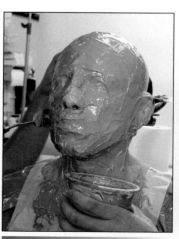

Fig. 9-176

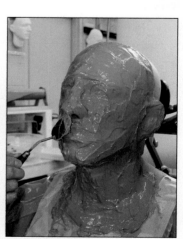

Fig. 9-177

14. After the POL has set, mix 2–3 tablespoons of salt into tepid plaster bandage water. Dip each layer into the water, and apply in the following order:

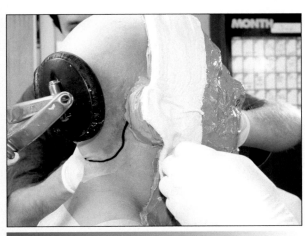

Fig. 9-178

A. #1 and #2—From the top of the head to the shoulder, over the front of the ear on the right and left sides.

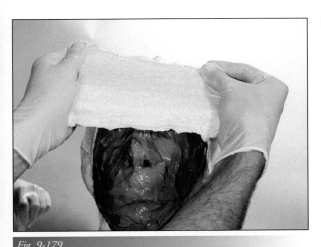

Fig. 9-179

B. #3—Over the forehead.

Fig. 9-180

C. #4—On the center (septum) area of the nose. #5 and #6—On the right and left sides of the nostril area.

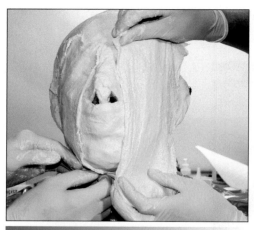

Fig. 9-181

D. #7, #8 and #9—The left and right sides of the face and over the mouth/chin area.

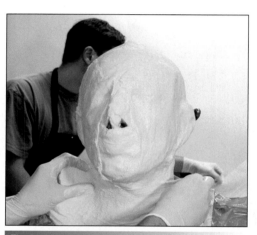

Fig. 9-182

E. #10—Over the neck area.

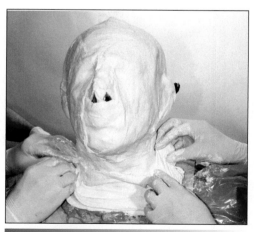

Fig. 9-183

F. #11—Below the neck area.

G. #12 and #13—The sides of the face.

Rubber gloves should be worn when working with plaster bandages to keep the hands from drying out and to facilitate cleanup.

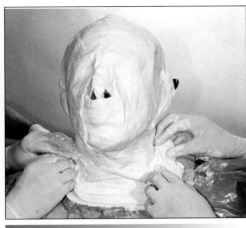

Fig. 9-184

15. Let the last piece of plaster bandage harden (1–2 minutes).

16. Ask the subject to tilt the head back slightly in order to loosen the plaster bandage shell from the POL cast at the neck area. Gently pull on the neck area to loosen the POL from the plaster bandage. Carefully remove ONLY the plaster bandage shell from the POL cast before pulling POL off the face.

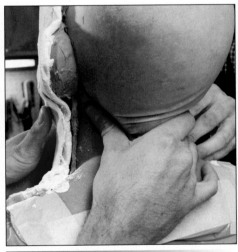

Fig. 9-185

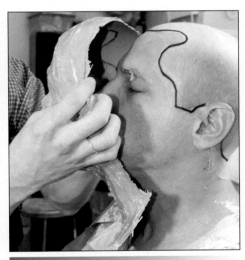

Fig. 9-186

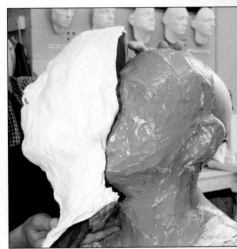

Fig. 9-187

17. Ask subject to start moving the facial muscles slightly (smile, frown, and blow air out of the mouth, e.g., but DO NOT wrinkle the nose area).

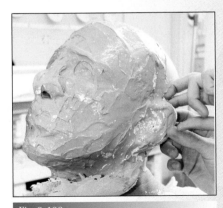

Fig. 9-188

18. Carefully remove the back-of-ear plugs, which may be saved to be glued back in or tossed depending on how thick or thin the back-of-ear areas need to be on the plaster positive face cast. Plugs may be glued back in with cynoacrylate (Super Glue) after removal of the cast.

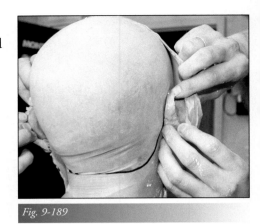
Fig. 9-189

19. As the subject moves the facial muscles, slowly and gently peel off the POL cast. POL may stick slightly to eyebrow and eyelash hair but will eventually release.

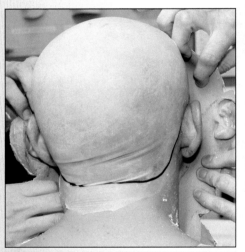
Fig. 9-190

Fig. 9-191

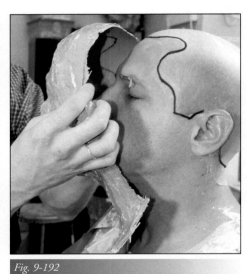
Fig. 9-192

20. Set the POL cast back into the plaster bandage shell, ensuring it is properly seated in order to avoid distortions.

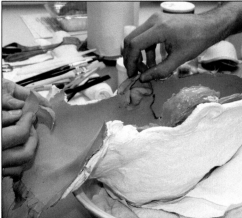
Fig. 9-193

Fig. 9-194

*Gypsona Brand plaster bandages are suggested.

21. Remove the bald cap, and clean the subject's skin with a warm wet towel. *(Refer to the Alginate Face Casting section.)*

22. Castings may be made from the negative mold at any time.

Tips About Ply-O-Life

- Do not use rubber gloves when handling POL. (POL is a platinum-based silicone impression material and is extremely sensitive to latex rubber.) To be safe, wash hands before handling POL, and coat them with a generous amount of cholesterol/castor oil mixture.

- If the artist is unsure about certain releases, he/she should try a test batch on his/her own skin.

- Always coat hair with gelatin, cholesterol mixture, and petroleum jelly. POL sticks to uncoated hair.

- Arm and body hair should be shaved before casting areas where it exists.

- For easy removal, do not apply plaster bandages behind the ear area.

Body Double, a platinum-based impression material from Smooth-On Products, is also available.

PLY-O-LIFE HEAD CASTING

Refer to the Ply-O-Life Face Casting section for details on Ply-O-Life.

Materials Needed for Ply-O-Life Head Casting

- Gram Scale
- Bald Cap Adhesive
- 6 Pairs of Rubber Gloves
- Masking Tape
- GM Foam Latex Pigment (Ruddy or Tantone)
- Comb
- Spatulas (Small and Large)
- Eyelash/Eyebrow Brush
- Ply-O-Life
- Plaster Bowls
- Petroleum Jelly
- Sharpie Marker (Black)
- Cloth Towels
- Paper Towels
- Cool Water for Plaster Bandages
- Plaster Bandages (Gypsona Brand), 3 rolls, 6" wide
- Plastic Disposable Cups and Lids (2, 4, and 8 oz.)
- Salt (to hasten setting time of plaster bandages)
- Cleanup Brushes (Soft Nylon Brushes)
- Indelible Ink Pencil

- Plaster Bandage Scissors
- Plastic Bald Cap ONLY
- Cover Cloth or Large Plastic Trash Bag
- Brushes and Q-Tips (for application of adhesive)
- Adhesive Remover
- Small and Large Scissors
- Gelatin

  50 grams—Sorbital

  50 grams—Glycerin

  10 grams—Distilled Water

  Mix the above liquids, and then add:

  15 grams—Gelatin

  Heat in microwave until the gelatin granules have been dissolved.

  This gelatin formula should be pre-mixed.

- Hair Cholesterol (3 parts to 1 part Castor Oil)
- Zip Kicker (for Cyno Glue)
- Dust Masks
- 1" Throwaway Brushes
- Cynoacrylate Glue (Krazy or Super)
- 4" × 2" Piece of Mesh Material

Preparation for Ply-O-Life Head Casting

1. Lay out all the tools and materials on the list for casting before the subject arrives.
2. Pre-weigh parts B and C Ply-O-Life (POL) into separate plastic disposable containers, and cap these with lids.

   First Batch for Back of Ears

   10 gm.—B

   10 gm.—C

   Second and Third Batches for Ears

   Two batches

   15 gm.—B

   15 gm.—C

   Fourth and Fifth Batches for Back of Head

   Two batches

   250 gm.—B

   250 gm.—C

   Sixth and Seventh Batches for Face

   Two batches

   250 gm.—B

   250 gm.—C

Mix 5 drops of GM Foam latex pigment into side B of the fifth and seventh batches of POL. This will make it easier to see if the fifth and seventh coats have sufficiently covered the fourth and sixth.

3. Pre-cut 6″ wide plaster bandages*, all three layers thick.

FRONT

Quantity	Size	Order Used
2	14″	#1 and #2
1	8″	#3
1	1″	#4
2	2″	#5 and #6
2	8″	#7 and #8
3	12″	#9, #10, and #11
2	10″	#12 and #13

BACK

Quantity	Size	Order Used
4	14″	#1 and #2
2	8″	#3 and #4
1	10″	#5
2	14″	#6 and #7
2	10″	#8 and #9

(Refer back to this list on steps 15 and 16 of the Head Casting procedure.)

Procedure for Ply-O-Life Head Casting

1. Cover the subject past the shoulder with a cover cloth or large plastic trash bag. Tape around this with masking tape.

2. Apply the bald cap with ears exposed. (Plastic cap ONLY.)

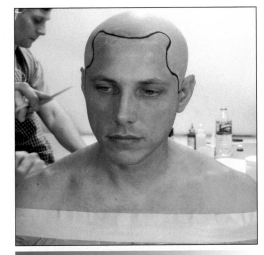

Fig. 9-195

*Gypsona Brand plaster bandages are suggested.

3. Mark the hairline with a black Sharpie. The line will transfer to the inside of the POL head cast negative.

4. Use an eyelash/eyebrow brush to coat any exposed hair (except eyelashes) with a warm liquid gelatin mixture.

Fig. 9-196

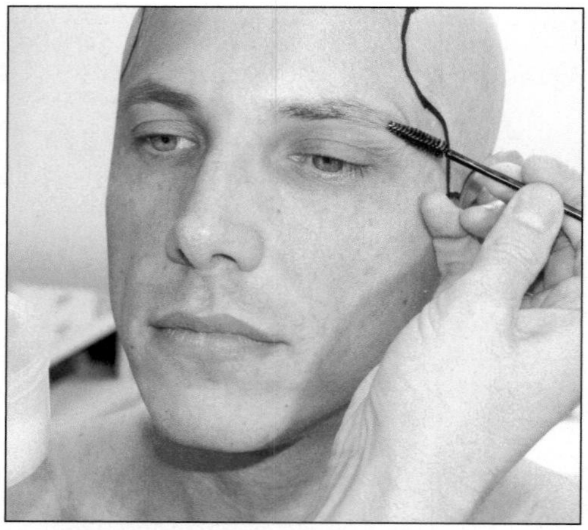

Fig. 9-197

5. Lightly coat the face, neck (including gelatin-coated hair), eyelashes, and bald cap with cholesterol/castor oil mixture.

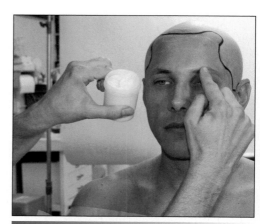

Fig. 9-198

6. Coat any lanugo hair and eyebrows/eyelashes with a very light coat of petroleum jelly.

7. Mix the first batch of POL, and fill in only the back of the ears (applied with a spatula). This step is important in order to keep the ears from dropping during casting and allow them to be easily removed from the head cast.

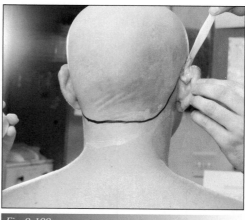

Fig. 9-199

*Gypsona Brand plaster bandages are suggested.

8. Before the first batch is set, smooth it out with petroleum jelly. This will also act as a separator for future removal of the piece.

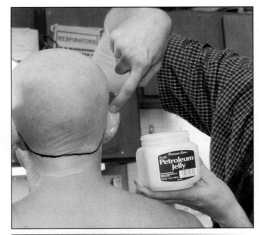

Fig. 9-200

9. Mix the second batch of POL with a spatula, and apply it to the right ear, overlapping the first batch of set POL.

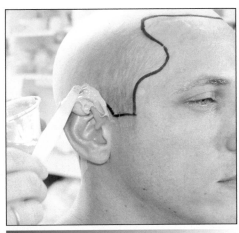

Fig. 9-201

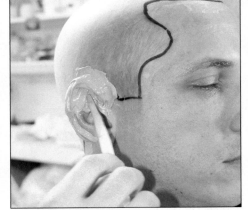

Fig. 9-202

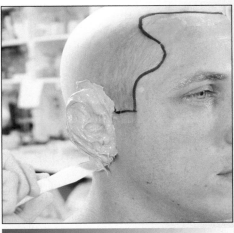

Fig. 9-203

10. Mix the third batch of POL with a spatula, and apply it to the left ear, overlapping the first batch of set POL.

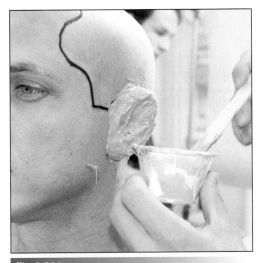

Fig. 9-204

11. Mix the fourth batch of POL, and apply it with a palette knife to the back of the head, starting in front of the crown, downward to the neck and shoulders. (DO NOT use rubber gloves.)

It is very important to let each coat set until it is tacky to the touch; otherwise, additional coats will distort previous layers.

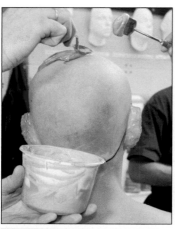

Fig. 9-205

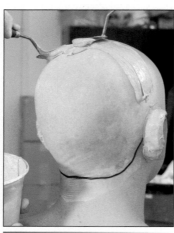

Fig. 9-206

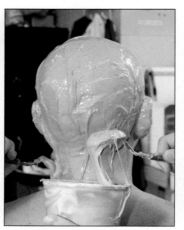

Fig. 9-207

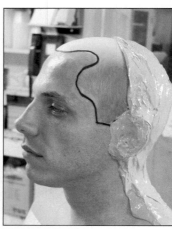

Fig. 9-208

12. Mix the fifth batch of tinted POL, and carefully apply it over the fourth batch using a spatula in an up-and-down motion. Try not to disturb the first layer of POL. The finished surface should be as smooth as possible.

Fig. 9-209

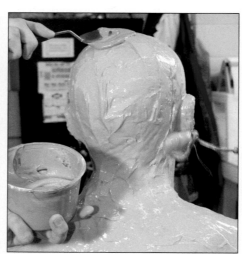

Fig. 9-210

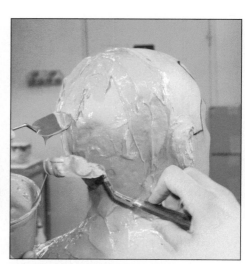

Fig. 9-211

13. Mix the sixth batch of POL, and use clean hands coated with cholesterol/castor oil mixture to apply it as follows (DO NOT use rubber gloves; apply POL in the direction of hair growth):

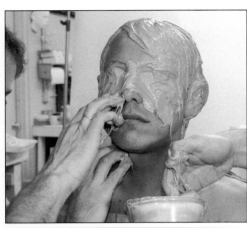

Fig. 9-212

A. Eye sockets

Fig. 9-213

B. Forehead

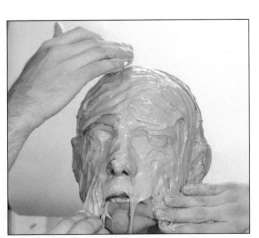

Fig. 9-214

C. Cheeks

D. Nose

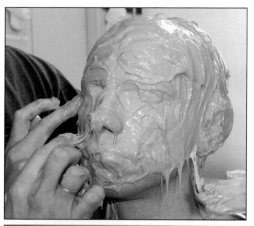

Fig. 9-215

E. Lips

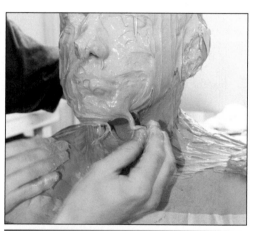

Fig. 9-216

F. Neck

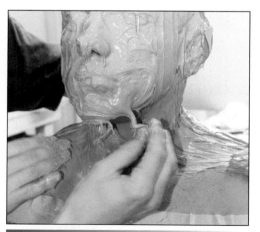

Fig. 9-217

*Gypsona Brand plaster bandages are suggested.

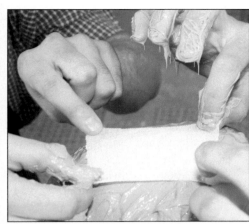

Fig. 9-218

G. Shoulders

Before the frontal coat is set, press a 4" × 2" piece of mesh material at the crown of the head where the POL will stop from splitting the back of the cast during removal.

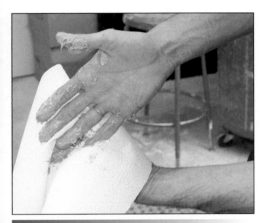

Fig. 9-219

Clean the hands with paper towels.

14. Mix the seventh batch of tinted POL, and carefully apply it over the sixth batch using a spatula in an up-and-down motion. Try not to disturb the first layer of POL. The finished surface should be as smooth as possible.

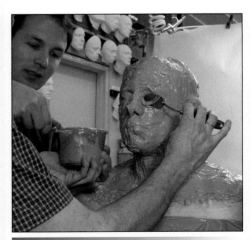

Fig. 9-220

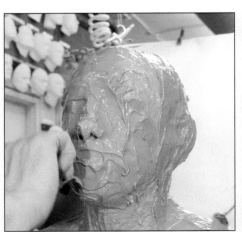

Fig. 9-221

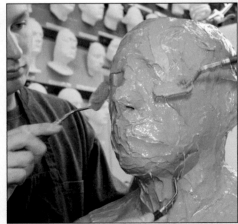

Fig. 9-222

15. Mix 2-3 tablespoons of salt into tepid water for the plaster bandages. Rubber gloves should be worn when working with plaster bandages to keep the hands from drying out and to facilitate cleanup. Dip each layer into water, and apply these in the following order:

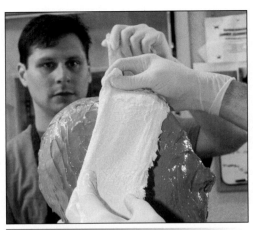

Fig. 9-223

A. #1—Triple-fold the outer edge of the bandage, and place it from the top of the head to the neck area on the right side of the head, over the alginate and touching the plaster. Kris Kobzina, A JB graduate and instructor shown assisting Matthew Mungle

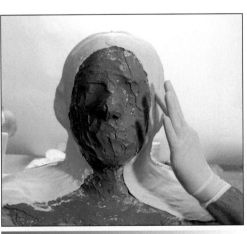

Fig. 9-224

B. #2—Triple-fold the outer edge of the bandage, and place it from the top of the head to the neck area on the left side of the head, over the alginate and touching the plaster bandage.

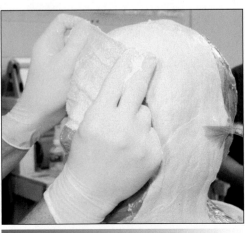

Fig. 9-225

C. #3—Over the forehead.

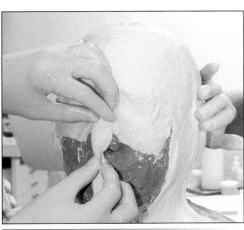

Fig. 9-226

D. #4—On the center (septum) area of the nose.

Fig. 9-227

E. #5 and #6—On the left and right sides of the nostril.

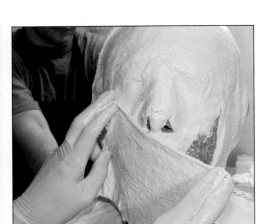

Fig. 9-228

F. #7—Under the nose and over the mouth area.

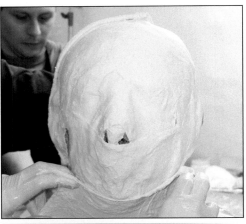

Fig. 9-229

G. #8—Under the chin area.

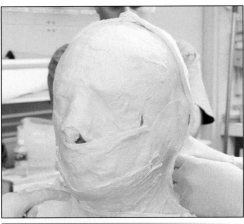

Fig. 9-230

H. #9—Triple-fold the lower edge of the bandage, and place it under the neck area in the center.

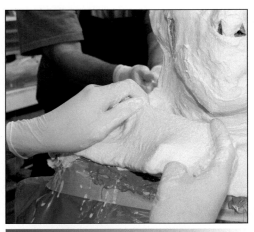

Fig. 9-231

I. #10 and #11—Triple-fold the lower edge of the bandage, and place it on the right and left sides of the shoulder area.

*Gypsona Brand plaster bandages are suggested.

Fig. 9-232

J. #12 and #13—Place on both the right and left sides of the face to strengthen the cast.

16. As soon as plaster bandage #1 and #2 in the front are applied and half-set, the second artist can apply petroleum jelly to the plaster bandage ridge in back and start the back cast. Be very careful not to get petroleum jelly onto the area where the front plaster bandage connects to #1 and #2.

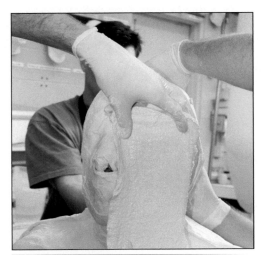

Fig. 9-233

Back plaster bandage applied as follows:

Fig. 9-234

A. #1—Triple-fold the outer edge of the bandage, and place it from the top of the head to the neck area on the right side of the head, overlapping the front plaster bandage.

Fig. 9-235

B. #2—Triple-fold the outer edge of the bandage, and place it from the top of the head to the neck area on the left side of the head, overlapping the front plaster bandage.

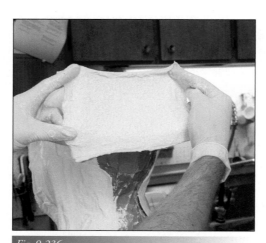

Fig. 9-236

C. #3—Place at back of head, connecting #1 and #2.

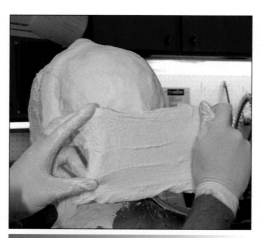

Fig. 9-237

D. #4—Back of head, overlapping #3.

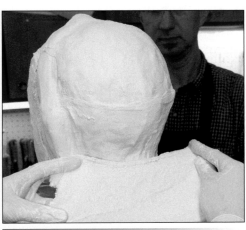

Fig. 9-238

E. #5—Nape of neck, overlapping #4.

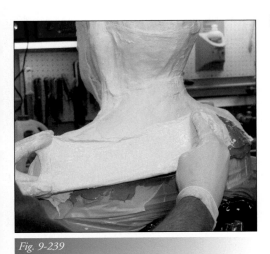

Fig. 9-239

F. #6—Triple-fold the outer edge of the bandage, and place it from the neck area to the shoulder on the left side of the head.

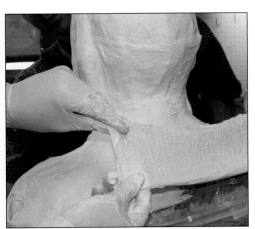

Fig. 9-240

G. #7—Triple-fold the outer edge of the bandage, and place it from the neck area to the shoulder area on the right side of the head.

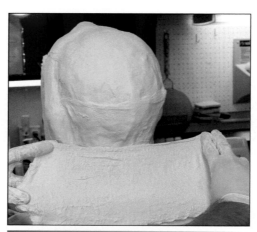

Fig. 9-241

H. #8—On the back of the head.

Fig. 9-242

I. #9—Vertically on the back of the head for reinforcement.

17. Let the last piece of plaster bandage harden (1–2 minutes). By rubbing a dry paper towel over the wet plaster bandage, it will dry faster.

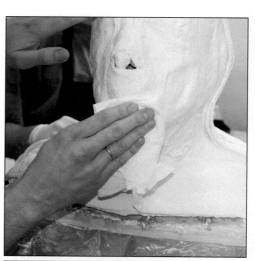

Fig. 9-243

18. Mark the join area between the front and back plaster bandages with an indelible ink pencil. Adding horizontal marks on the join area will make it easier to line up the front and back casts.

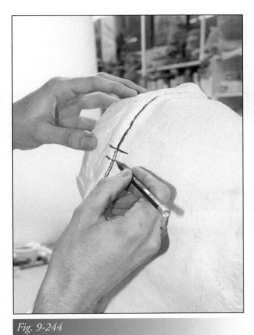
Fig. 9-244

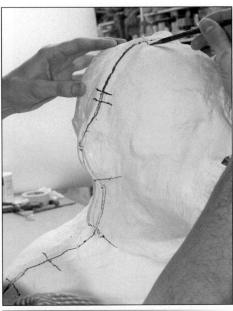
Fig. 9-245

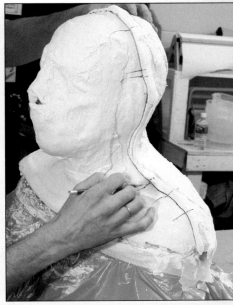
Fig. 9-246

19. Loosen the back plaster bandage, and carefully pull it off. Place it off to the side.

Fig. 9-247

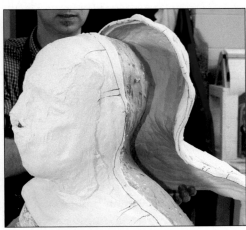
Fig. 9-248

20. Loosen the front plaster bandage, and carefully pull it off. Put the front and back together, and place these off to the side.

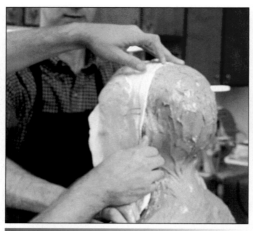

Fig. 9-249

Fig. 9-250

21. Loosen POL from the skin all around the shoulder area, both in front and back. The subject can move the head forward and backward at this point.

Fig. 9-251

Fig. 9-252

22. Ask the subject to start moving the facial muscles slightly (smile, frown, and blow air out of the mouth, for example, but do NOT wrinkle the nose excessively, as this may create a bruising effect on the bridge of the nose because of the vacuum between POL and skin).

23. Cut up the back of the POL cast to the crown of the head where the material was placed with a pair of plaster bandage scissors.

Fig. 9-253

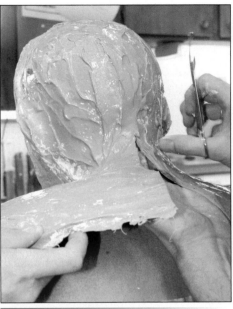

Fig. 9-254

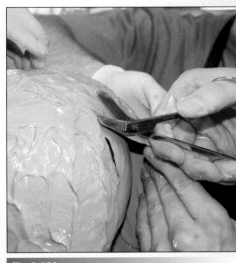

Fig. 9-255

24. Loosen the POL from the bald cap and skin in the back of the head by working the hand between the two.

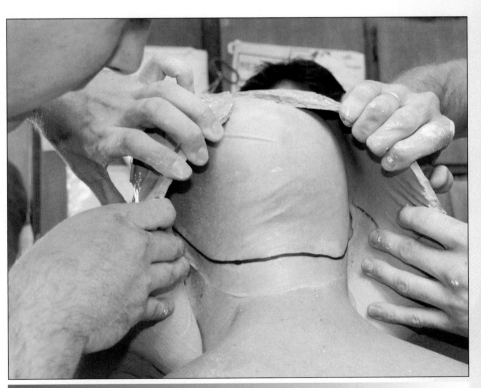

Fig. 9-256

25. Remove the back-of-ear POL plugs, which may be saved to be glued back in or tossed depending upon how thick or thin the back-of-ear areas need to be on the plaster positive cast. Plugs may be glued back in with cynoacrylate (Super Glue) or a small amount of POL after removal of the cast.

Fig. 9-257

26. Carefully peel the POL from the skin.

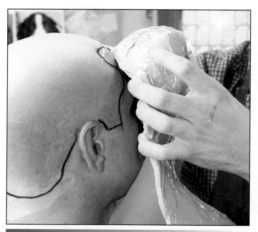

Fig. 9-258

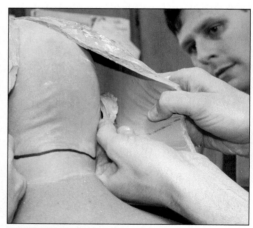

Fig. 9-259

27. Place the POL cast back into the plaster bandage mold, and ensure it is correctly seated into the mold.

Fig. 9-260

28. Remove the bald cap and adhesive with Beta Solve or isopropyl myristate. Clean the subject's skin with a warm, wet towel. *(Refer to the Alginate Face Casting section for details.)*

Fig. 9-261

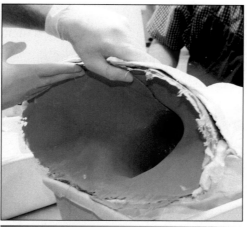

Fig. 9-262

29. The POL cast can be set aside for future castings.

Tips About Ply-O-Life

- *Do not use rubber gloves when handling POL.* (POL is a platinum-based silicone impression material and is extremely sensitive to latex rubber.) To be safe, wash the hands before handling POL, and coat them with a generous amount of cholesterol/castor oil mixture.

- If the artist is unsure about certain releases, he/she should try a test batch on his/her own skin.

- Always coat hair with gelatin, cholesterol mixture, and petroleum jelly. POL sticks to uncoated hair.

- Arm and body hair should be shaved before casting areas where it exists.

- For easy removal, do not apply plaster bandages behind the ear area.

DIGITAL RENDERINGS

Adobe Photoshop renderings have become the norm in make-up design. Directors and producers normally expect renderings of this nature to guide them in the direction of the necessary concept.

To achieve the following rendering, a digital photo was selected of the model and loaded into Photoshop on an 8″ × 10″ palette. The image was copied and placed next to a reduced version for a "before" look. A donor image, stretched and altered to fit the subject's face, was selected from a library file photo.

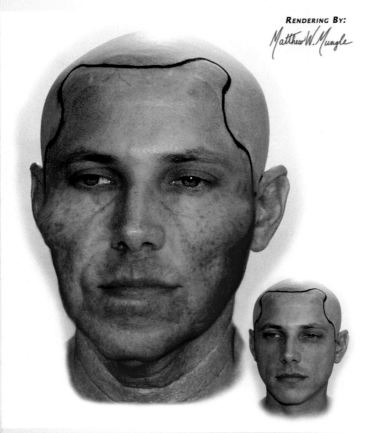

RENDERING BY:
Matthew W. Mungle

Fig. 9-263

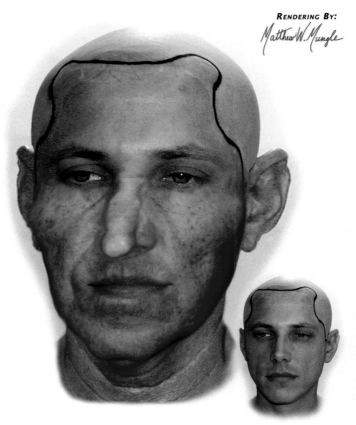

RENDERING BY:
Matthew W. Mungle

Fig. 9-264

Digital Renderings   371

RENDERING BY:
Matthew W. Mungle

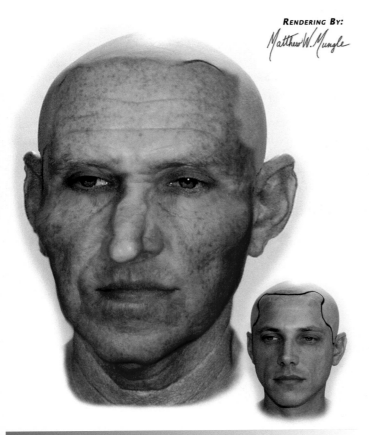

Fig. 9-265

RENDERING BY:
Matthew W. Mungle

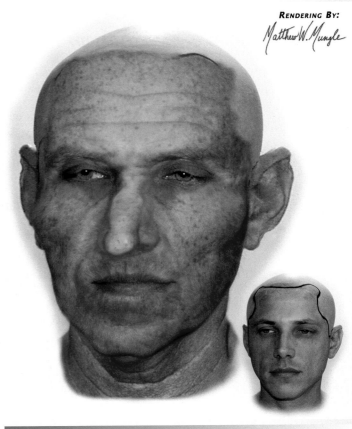

Fig. 9-266

RENDERING BY:
Matthew W. Mungle

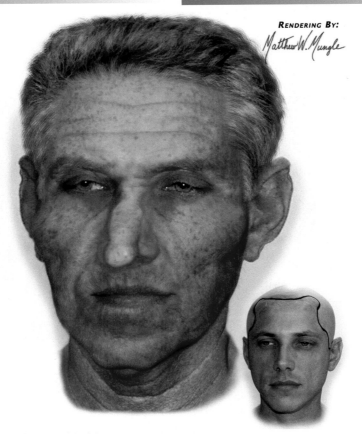

Fig. 9-267

ADDITIONAL TECHNIQUE

FLOAT-OFF TECHNIQUE

Created by Dick Smith for the old age make-up on Dustin Hoffman for *Little Big Man,* this technique is now a standard procedure used in the make-up effects industry.

This technique, for which a White Hydrocal positive must be made, is used when multiple overlapping appliances will be needed, or when a nose or other facial pieces are sculpted, and the whole face cast is necessary in order for the artist to determine how the particular appliance looks with regard to the full face.

Supply List for Float-off Technique

- White Hydrocal
- Water
- Mixing Bowl (flexible plastic)
- Palette Knife
- Rubber Gloves
- 2 Disposable 1" Brushes
- 1" or ¾" PVC Pipe—4"–5" long
- Mold-making Knife
- Alcote Separating Agent
- Stanley Planer
- Kleen Klay

White Hydrocal Positive

1. Fill in the nostril area on the Ply-O-Life face cast with Kleen Klay.

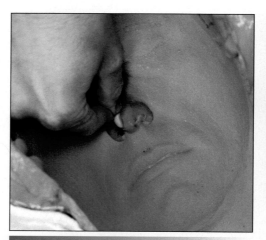
Fig. 9-265a

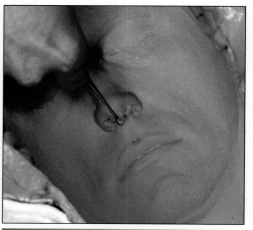
Fig. 9-265b

2. *Refer to the Mixing Plaster section of Alginate Face and Head Casting.*

3. Paint White Hydrocal (WH) into ear areas to avoid any bubbles, and continue painting until the entire surface is covered. This must be done as fast as possible to compensate for the fast setting time of WH. Pour as much WH into the negative as possible, and spatulate up on the sides and into the neck area as the material begins to thicken. Insert PVC pipe into the back of the cast before the material sets completely (usually in 4–5 minutes).

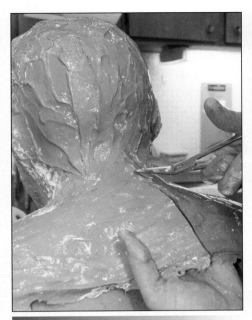

Fig. 9-265c

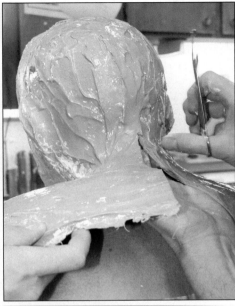

Fig. 9-265d

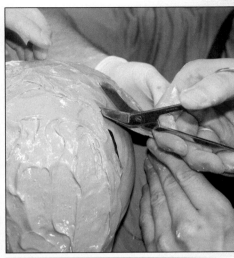

Fig. 9-266

4. Once the WH has set and cooled for 30–45 minutes, carefully pull the cast and Ply-O-Life from the plaster bandage shell. Peel Ply-O-Life from the cast.

Fig. 9-267

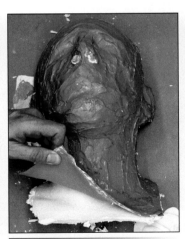

Fig. 9-268

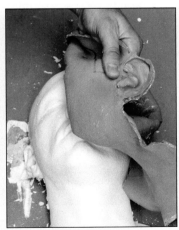

Fig. 9-269

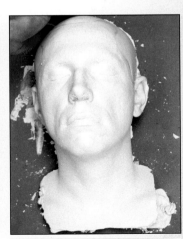

Fig. 9-270

5. Clean the plaster face cast edges with a Stanley planer.

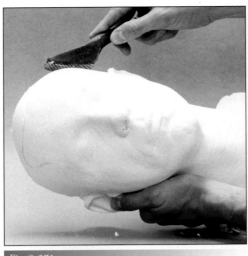

Fig. 9-271

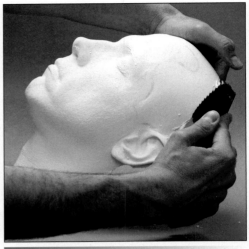

Fig. 9-272

Prepping the Face Cast for Sculpting

Paint one coat of Alcote Separating Agent over the whole face cast, and dry this with a hairdryer. Let it set for one hour to thoroughly dry.

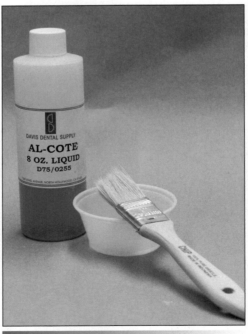

Fig. 9-273

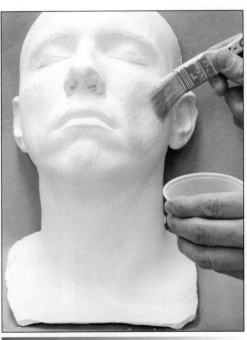

Fig. 9-274

Materials Needed for Sculpting

- Medium NSP Chavant Clay
- Sculpting Brushes
- X-Acto Knife
- Various Sculpting Tools
- 99-percent Alcohol
- Container of Cold Water

The Sculpting Procedure

1. Sculpt the desired appliance on the Alcote-coated positive with Chavant NSP Medium Clay. Kneading clay with the fingers softens it, allowing easier manipulation. Warm the positive with a hairdryer to help the clay stick more effectively.

2. Press small ½" balls of Chavant NSP Medium Clay onto the cast to build up the structure. The thickness of the clay should be from ¹⁄₁₆" to ¼".

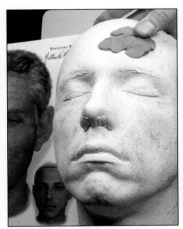

Fig. 9-275

Fig. 9-276

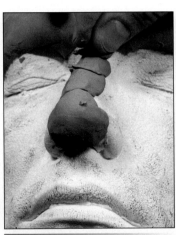

Fig. 9-277

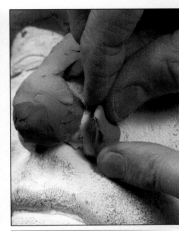

Fig. 9-278

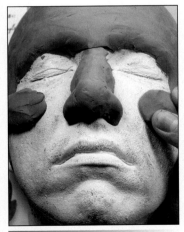

Fig. 9-279

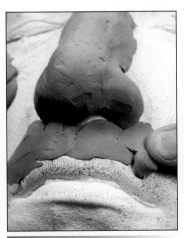

Fig. 9-280

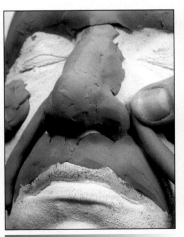

Fig. 9-281

Fig. 9-282

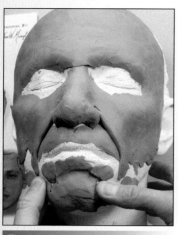

Fig. 9-283

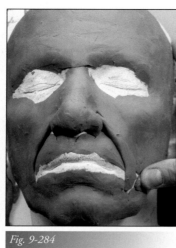

Fig. 9-284

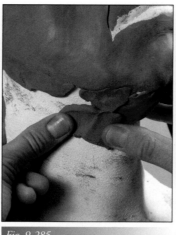

Fig. 9-285

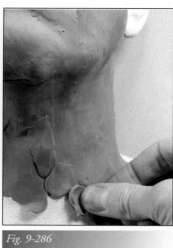

Fig. 9-286

3. Once the sculpture is blocked out, wrinkles can be carved in using a sculpture tool. Lines should be beveled and blended with the fingers in order to create natural looking skin folds.

Fig. 9-287

Fig. 9-288

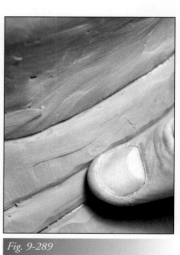

Fig. 9-289

4. Continue refining the sculpture, wrinkles, and various skin contours. Add clay wherever necessary.

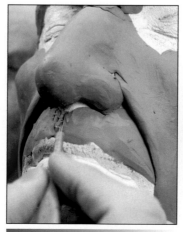

Fig. 9-290

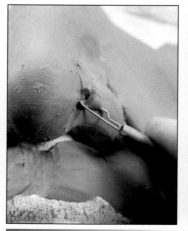

Fig. 9-291

Fig. 9-292

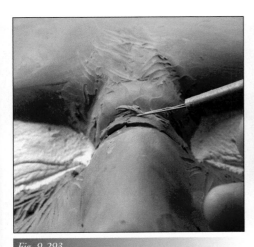

Fig. 9-293

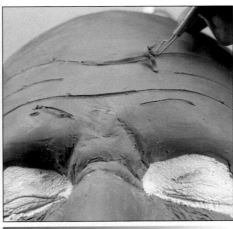

Fig. 9-294

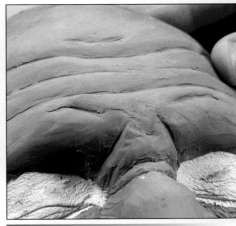

Fig. 9-295

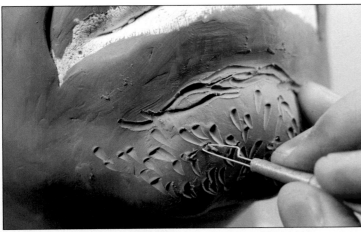

Fig. 9-296

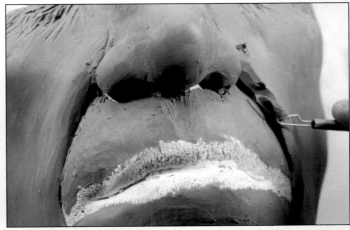

Fig. 9-297

5. Rake over the clay with a guitar bass string tool or rake tool to
   refine wrinkles and contours. Deepen wrinkles with a Kemper tool (#K21).
   Add clay to areas as necessary.

Fig. 9-298

Fig. 9-299

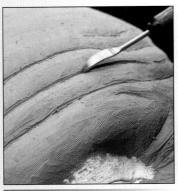

Fig. 9-300

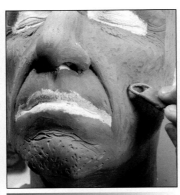

Fig. 9-301

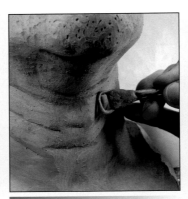

Fig. 9-302

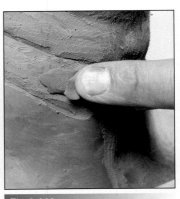

Fig. 9-303

6. Use a coarse, ½" round brush with 99-percent alcohol to brush down and refine the whole sculpture.

Only partially detail the sculpture. The final detailing will be finished after pieces are placed onto piece molds.

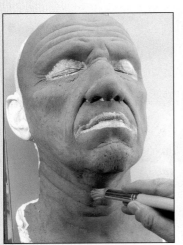

Fig. 9-304

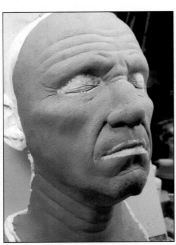

Fig. 9-305

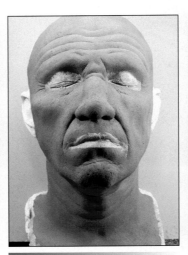

Fig. 9-306

Fig. 9-307

7. Cut the clay with an X-Acto blade, where prosthetic pieces will be divided and overlap.

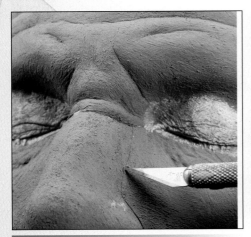

Fig. 9-308

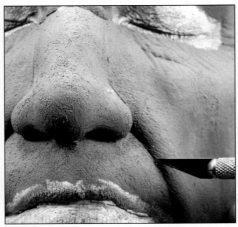

Fig. 9-309

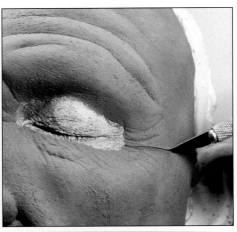

Fig. 9-310

8. Immerse the sculpture/full face cast positive into a large container of cold water for 3–4 hours AFTER PIECE MOLDS HAVE BEEN MADE. This process will loosen the clay from the WH positive, allowing the sculpted pieces to be transferred and blended onto the piece mold.

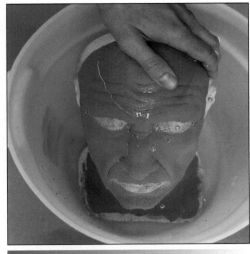

Fig. 9-311

9. *Refer to the Piece Mold-Making section for removal of clay sculptures from the positive.*

TEXTURE PADS

There are several ways of making texture pads or stamps. Fruits and vegetables such as oranges, grapefruits, lemons, and avocados all have great surface texture that may be duplicated. Paint latex, Exaflex Dental Silicone Material, or Ply-O-Life onto their surfaces, and peel off the pad. Pads may also be taken directly from casts of a hand or of an older person's face.

The following is a procedure for making texture pads from sculpted texture, which is very helpful when coarse surfaces, such as dashes or dots, are needed.

Supply List for Texture Pads

- Water
- Plastic Wrap
- Metal Palette Knife
- Rubber Gloves
- Kleen Klay
- Sculpting Tools
- Epoxy Parfilm Spray Release
- Scissors
- Die-Keen Blue Dental Stone
- Project Board
- 99-percent Alcohol
- Planer
- Mixing Bowl (preferably flexible plastic)
- Disposable ½″ Brush (with bristles cut short)
- Krylon Crystal Clear Spray

- Mold-making Knife
- Burlap Material (cut into 7″ × 6″ square)
- Metal Spline
- Two 1″ Chip (Throwaway) Brushes
- Exaflex Dental Silicone Impression Material or Ply-O-Life
- Ultracal 30
- Flat-head Screwdriver
- Disposable Paper Palette

Texture Pad Procedure

1. Sculpt out a flat surface (⅛″ thick, 6″ × 7″ square) on a project board with Kleen Klay, and smooth out the clay with a metal spline.

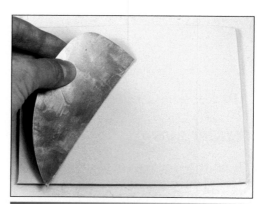

Fig. 9-312

2. Use various sculpting tools to create deep texture in the Kleen Klay. Plastic wrap may be used over clay to give a variation in texture. Texture should be as deep as possible.

Fig. 9-313

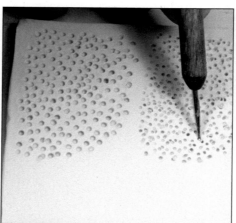

Fig. 9-314

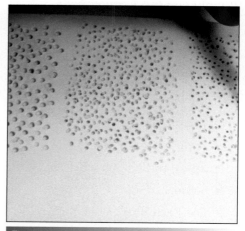

Fig. 9-315

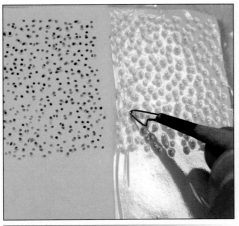

Fig. 9-316

Fig. 9-317

Fig. 9-318

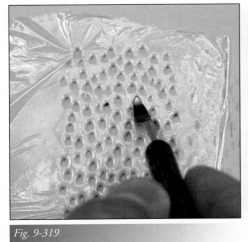

Fig. 9-319

Fig. 9-320

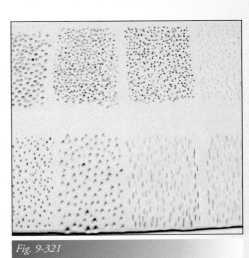

Fig. 9-321

3. Spray all of the sculpting with two light coats of Krylon Crystal Clear Spray. Let dry 15 minutes.

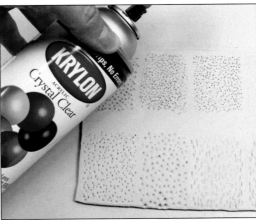

Fig. 9-322

4. Mix a batch of Stone (105 ml. of water with 500 gm. of Die-Keen Blue Stone—add 5 ml. more water if a thinner batch is needed), and paint it onto the sculpture. Stone should be used for strength and durability when casting deep crevices.

Fig. 9-323

5. Use the finger to press material into small textured areas.

Fig. 9-324

6. Smooth out the Stone, and clean the edges with a metal spline. Let the Stone set until the gloss has disappeared (1 hour).

Fig. 9-325

7. Mix a small 8 oz. batch of Ultracal (UC) 30, paint on the Blue Stone, and build the layer up to ¼″ in thickness.

Fig. 9-326

8. Lay a 6 ″ × 7″ piece of wet burlap onto the UC 30, and continue to apply the material into the burlap until the mold is at least ½″ to ¾″ thick.

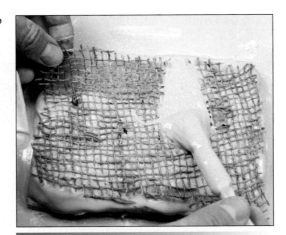

Fig. 9-327

9. Clean up the mold with a metal spatula, and let it cure overnight.

Fig. 9-328

10. Pry the stone mold from the clay with a screwdriver. The Krylon will prevent the clay from sticking to the stone.

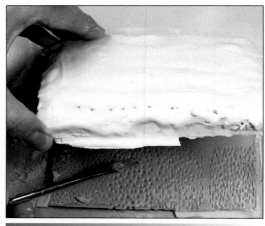

Fig. 9-329

11. Shave off any sharp edges with a mold-making knife, and clean the mold with a cut, stiff-bristled brush and 99-percent alcohol.

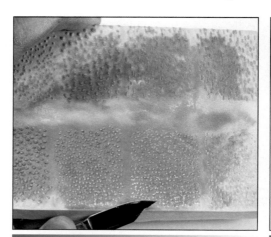

Fig. 9-330

Fig. 9-331

12. Spray the entire mold with a heavy coating of Epoxy Parfilm Release Spray.

Fig. 9-332

13. Squeeze out equal portions of Exaflex Dental Silicone on palette paper. (Ply-O-Life may also be used.)

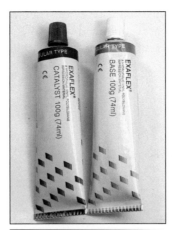

Fig. 9-333

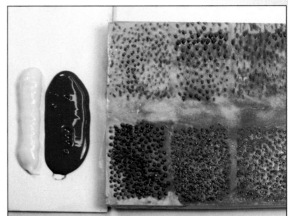

Fig. 9-334

14. After mixing the material thoroughly, use the finger to spread it evenly onto the stone mold. Exaflex has a cure time of one minute; therefore, mixing separate small quantities is advised. Cover the whole mold in small sections, and mix a second layer batch to thicken the mold. Let cure 30 minutes.

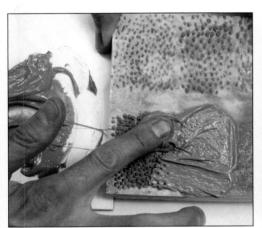

Fig. 9-335

Fig. 9-336

15. Peel the silicone mold off of the stone mold. The stone mold may be used to make additional silicone molds.

Fig. 9-337

16. Coat the mold with a heavy spray of Epoxy Parfilm, and brush the material into all the crevices, while being careful not to fill the holes.

Fig. 9-338

17. Mix a small amount of Exaflex material, and apply it onto the silicone mold. Repeat the step once more to make the texture stamp ⅛″ thick. Making the pad too thick will result in less texture pressed into the clay.

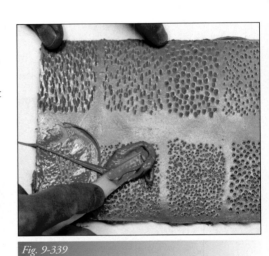

Fig. 9-339

18. Peel the pad from the mold, and cut off the rough edges with scissors.

Note: Ply-O-Life can be used in place of Exaflex material; however, both are platinum-based silicones and are affected by rubber- and sulfur-based products. For a less expensive alternative, use latex.

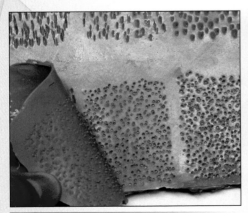

Fig. 9-340

Fig. 9-341

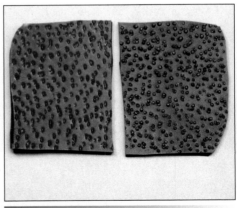

Fig. 9-342

Chapter 10

MOLDS

Chapter 10

Positive and Negative Molds

Gelatin

Chapter 10

MOLDS

POSITIVE AND NEGATIVE MOLDS

Once a face cast has been made, a positive mold will need to be produced onto which the desired facial features can be sculpted.

For normal mold-making purposes (gelatin and foam latex), Ultracal 30 should be used. If high quality, long-lasting molds are needed for gelatin, silicone, or foam appliances, make positive and negative molds out of Epoxical 415 or BJB 1630. The following sections cover all of these mold-making scenarios.

TYPES OF PLASTER, GYPSUM, AND URETHANE/EPOXY MOLDS

- White Hydrocal—A hard gypsum cement used in the float-off technique described later in this chapter, and also for the positive to enable flaring out for bucket mold techniques. Material may be poured directly into Ply-O-Life and alginate castings.

- Ultracal 30—A very hard gypsum cement used for positive and negative molds when using gelatin, silicone, or foam latex appliance materials.

- Dental Stones (Die Stone Peach or Die-Keen Blue)—These are sometimes used when an even harder stone is needed. Stones should be tested for shrinkage and expansion before use. Die-Keen Blue may be mixed with Ultracal 30 in equal proportions to produce a material harder than UC 30 alone. Die Stone Peach, which does not mix with UC 30, may be used for teeth positives.

- Epoxical 415—An extremely durable, epoxy resin-faced mold backed with Ultracal 30.

- BJB 1630 Urethane—A durable, fast-setting, non-warping urethane with low shrinkage, which sets up against alginates, clays, and silicones. Use for small molds up to 8″ × 8″, noses, chins, etc. Highly recommended.

Basic Formula for Ultracal 30

(1 × Batch)

8 oz.—Water, 24 oz.—Ultracal 30

1. Pour water into a plastic container. The water can be hot, which will make the Ultracal set faster if desired.

2. Sift the Ultracal into the water slowly and evenly.

3. Stir the Ultracal by hand or with an electric drill mixer until thoroughly mixed. Let stand 1 minute, mix, and use immediately. (Note: Mixing Ultracal 30 slightly thicker when applying it into an alginate mold makes the gypsum cement harder and less likely to chip or flake.)

Fig. 10-1

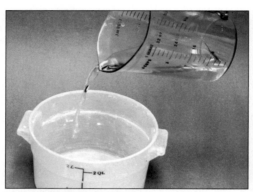

Fig. 10-2

Fig. 10-3

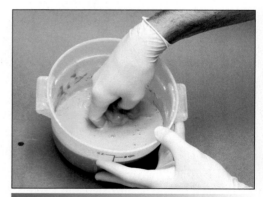

Fig. 10-4

THE FOREHEAD SCULPTURE

Supply List for Ultracal Positive Mold Duplication (The Forehead Piece)

- Water
- Palette Knives
- Rubber Gloves
- Kleen Klay
- Sculpting Tools
- Water Clay
- Scissors
- Ultracal 30
- White Hydrocal
- 8 Plaster Bandages, 10″ × 6″, 3 layers thick
- 99-percent Alcohol
- Texture Pads
- Mixing Bowls (preferably flexible plastic)
- Disposable, Soft ½″ Brush
- Krylon Crystal Clear Spray
- Mold-making Knife
- Burlap Material (cut into ten 5″ × 5″ squares and two 3″ × 8″ sections)
- Disposable 1″ Chip Brush
- 6″ Metal Conduit Pipe
- Mold Makers Sponge
- Project Board (Formica top)

Forehead Piece Procedure

1. Make a White Hydrocal piece mold of the forehead area from a Ply-O-Life negative face cast or by taking a snap from a White Hydrocal positive (*see Nose/Upper Lip Mold section*), leaving at least 1½″ around where the appliance is to be sculpted for keys and clay flashing.

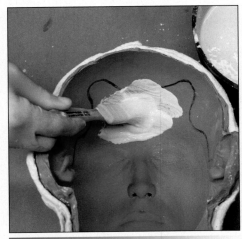

Fig. 10-5

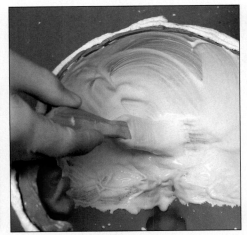

Fig. 10-5

Fig. 10-6

2. Pull the forehead piece mold from the Ply-O-Life face cast, and clean off all rough edges from the mold with a Stanley planer.

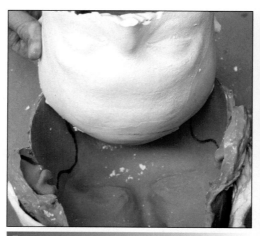

Fig. 10-7

Fig. 10-8

3. Place the forehead positive onto a project board (with Formica top), and build up around the form with water clay. In order to avoid undercuts, flare out all of them on the bottom and around the forehead area of the positive. Leave triages of ear visible for the location of where the appliance will be blended off after the Ultracal positive is made. Clean and smooth the water clay with a metal spline and wet sponge.

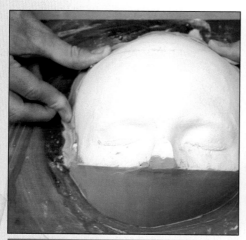

Fig. 10-9

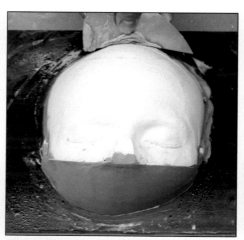

Fig. 10-10

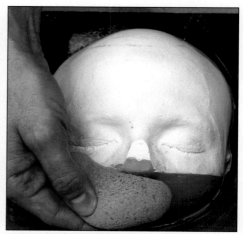

Fig. 10-11

4. Spray the form with 2 light coats of Krylon Crystal Clear.

Fig. 10-12

5. Coat the plaster forehead only with a very light coat of petroleum jelly, and remove excess with a tissue.

Fig. 10-13

Fig. 10-14

6. Mix 16 oz. of water with 14 oz. of alginate. Coat the piece mold evenly with alginate, and let set.

Fig. 10-15

Fig. 10-16

7. Trim excess alginate from the casting, remove it, and replace alginate onto the mold (facilitating removal after the plaster bandage has been formed.)

Fig. 10-17

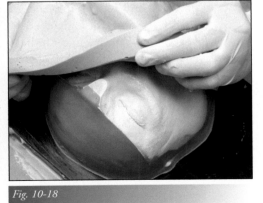

Fig. 10-18

8. Dip a single 10″, 3-layer-thick plaster bandage into warm water, and start covering the alginate at the base. Continue with multiple layers overlapping one another at least ½″ until the entire alginate is covered. Let set.

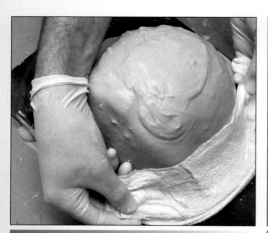

Fig. 10-19

Fig. 10-20

Fig. 10-21

9. Gently pull off the alginate and plaster bandage shell in one piece.

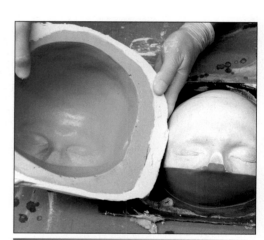

Fig. 10-22

10. Mix a half batch of Ultracal (4 oz. water and 12 oz. Ultracal), and paint this into the alginate with a 1″ chip brush. Build up the layer to ¼″ as the material thickens.

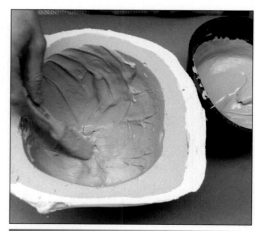

Fig. 10-23

11. After the first layer of Ultracal has lost its shine, mix a single batch of Ultracal, and paint this into the negative.

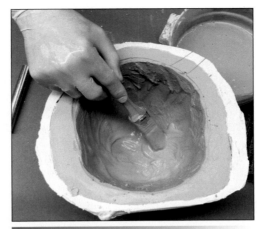

Fig. 10-24

12. Dip two layers of 5″ × 5″ square burlap into the remaining Ultracal, and gently press this into the negative mold. Continue with multiple layers, overlapping each ½″. *Be very careful* not to press too hard and crack the first set layer of Ultracal, which will result in hairline cracks in the positive mold.

Fig. 10-25

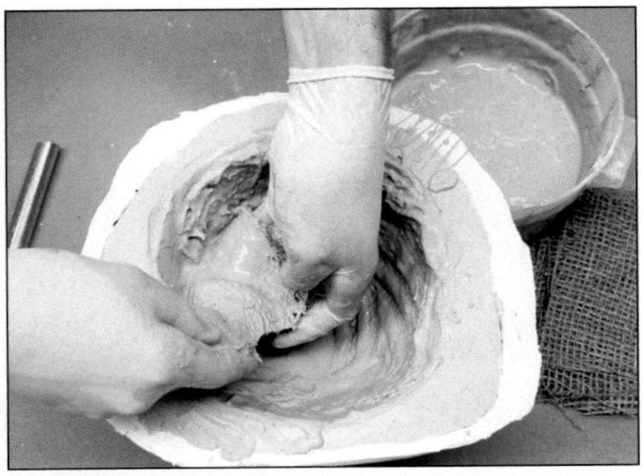

Fig. 10-26

13. Dip one layer of 3″ × 8″ burlap into the Ultracal, and reinforce the edge by making a ″snake″ out of the Ultracal-saturated burlap. Use a second layer to finish the mold edge.

Fig. 10-27

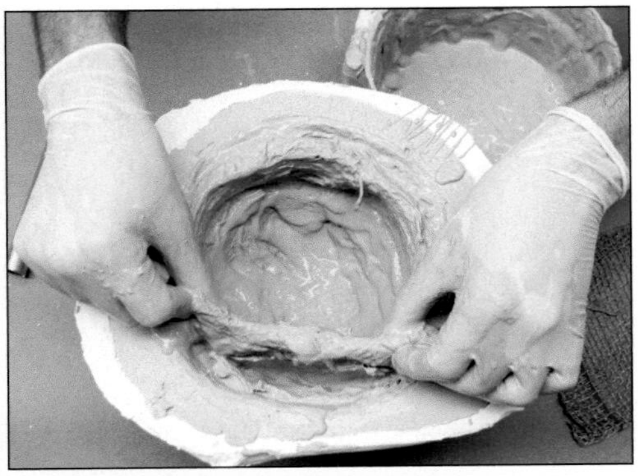

Fig. 10-28

14. Place a 6″ metal pipe in the center of the mold, and reinforce it by forming Ultracal-soaked burlap around the ends.

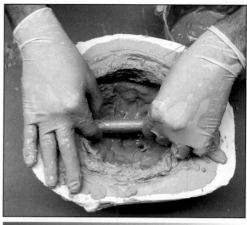

Fig. 10-29

15. Clean the edges of the alginate negative/Ultracal mold with a metal spline, and smooth out the center with a metal spatula.

Fig. 10-30

Fig. 10-31

16. Once the material begins to harden, brush the surface with a wet 1″ chip brush to smooth it. Let the mold cure for 3–4 hours.

Fig. 10-32

17. Remove the Ultracal positive from the alginate.00

Fig. 10-33

18. Clean the positive with a sculpting tool and planer. Place the mold in the oven, and cure for three hours at 180°F.

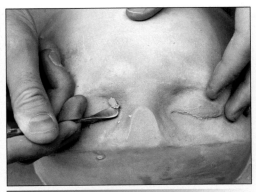

Fig. 10-34

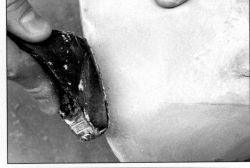

Fig. 10-35

Supply List for Sculpting the Forehead Piece

- Sculpting Tools
- 99-percent Alcohol
- Stiff Round Brush
- Soft-bristle Brush
- Krylon Crystal Clear Spray
- Texture Pads
- Hairdryer
- Plastic Wrap

Forehead Sculpting Procedure

1. Pull off the forehead from the float-off positive, and place it onto the Ultracal forehead positive.

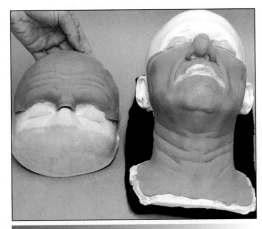

Fig. 10-36

2. Blend clay onto the Ultracal positive with sculpting tools and fingers. Warm the clay with a hairdryer if necessary.

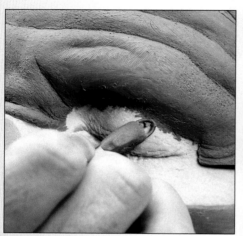

Fig. 10-37

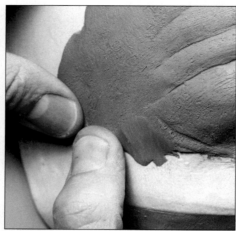

Fig. 10-38

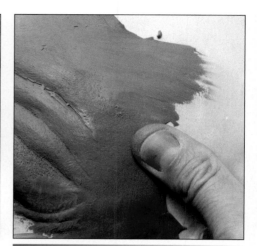

Fig. 10-39

3. Clay may be smoothed with a soft-bristle brush and 99-percent alcohol.

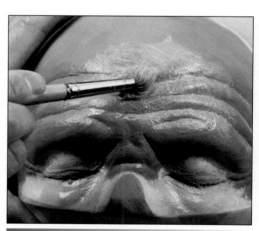

Fig. 10-40

4. Clean the edges of the sculpture with 99-percent alcohol or acetone and a soft-bristle brush.

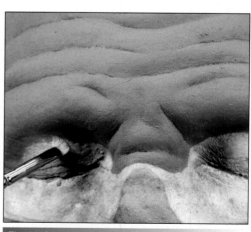

Fig. 10-41

5. Heavy texture can be achieved by carving into the clay with a curved/pointed Kemper sculpting tool and smoothing slightly with a stiff round paintbrush.

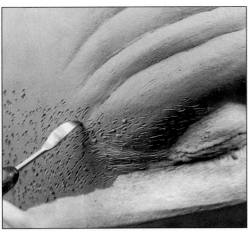

Fig. 10-42

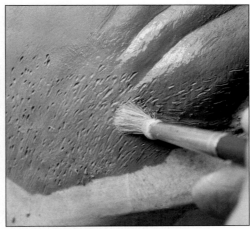

Fig. 10-43

6. Texture over all can be pressed in with texture pads.

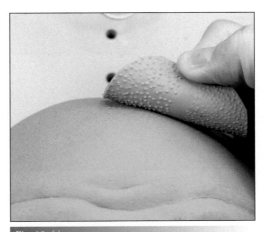

Fig. 10-44

7. Fine pore texture is applied by stretching plastic wrap tightly over sculpture and pressing the pore in with a bass guitar string, Kemper wire, and/or pin sculpting tools. Remove the plastic wrap after detailing.

Fig. 10-45

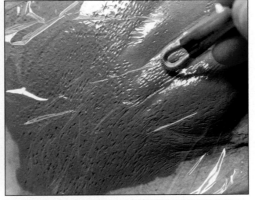

Fig. 10-46

Fig. 10-47

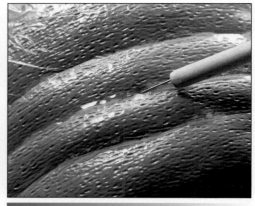

Fig. 10-48

8. Detail work, such as skin bumps, can be added with clay and refined with sculpting tools and a small, stiff-bristle brush.

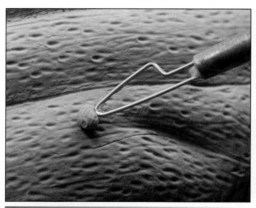

Fig. 10-49

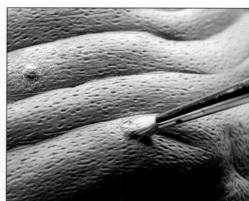

Fig. 10-50

9. The finished sculpture is now ready for flashing and molding.

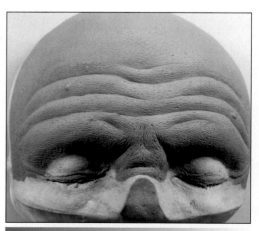

Fig. 10-51

*Gypsona Brand plaster bandages are suggested.

Supply List for Epoxical 415 Negative Mold-making

- Soft-bristle Brush
- Small Disposable Cup
- Rubber Gloves
- 12 Large Tongue Depressors
- Epoxical 415 Epoxy Coating
- Acetone
- Respirator Mask for Chemicals
- Burlap (eight of 7″ × 14″, eight of 7″ × 7″)
- Water
- 2 Project Boards with Formica top
- Small Furniture Clamp
- Hot Water
- Dishwashing Soap
- Rounded Router Bit
- Acryl 60 Liquid
- Wooden Sculpting Tool
- 99-percent Alcohol
- Partall PVA Film
- Epoxy Parfilm
- Gram Scale
- 9 Non-waxed Paper Cups
- Nylon Artist Fan Brush
- GM Foam Pigment
- Two 1″ Disposable Chip Brushes (cut short for cleaning)
- Ultracal (UC) 30
- Container (to mix UC 30)
- Mold Makers Sponge
- Metal Spline
- Two 1″ × 2″ × ½″ Boards
- One 10″ × 2″ × ½″ Board
- Black Sharpie Marker
- Electric Drill

Epoxical 415 Negative Mold-making Procedure

1. Mark three keys on the UC positive, and drill with a rounded router bit (available at hardware stores). These keys will be registered on the negative mold and keep the positive from shifting within it.

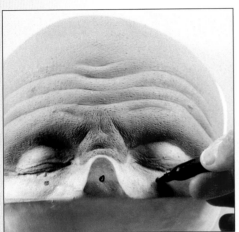

Fig. 10-52

Fig. 10-53

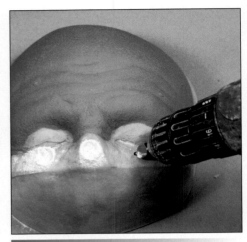
Fig. 10-54

2. Round off sharp edges of the keys with a mold-making knife.

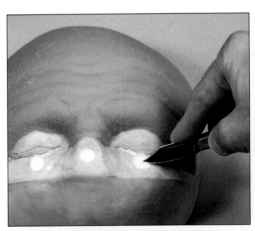
Fig. 10-55

3. Clean off all powder from the positive mold, and spray the entire sculpture with a light coat of Krylon Crystal Clear.

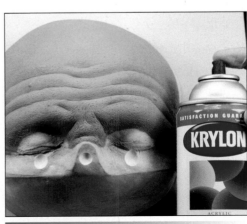
Fig. 10-56

4. Roll Kleen Klay into ¼″ round by 7″ long "snakes," and flash these around the sculpting, ⅛″ away from the edge clay (¼″ × ⅜″ high).

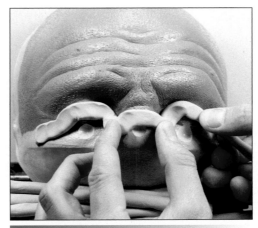
Fig. 10-57

5. Continue adding Kleen Klay snakes until the entire UC mold is covered with clay (but keys are left exposed).

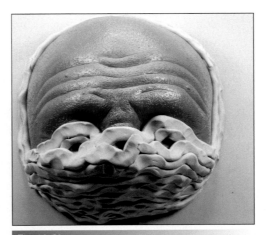
Fig. 10-58

6. Place the positive on a project board, and smooth out the clay with fingers. Lay a snake of clay around the mold, and press onto the board to help secure the mold. Clean up edges with a metal spline.

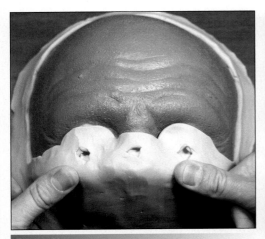
Fig. 10-59

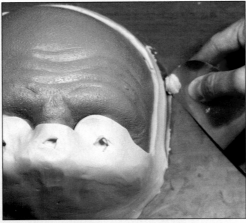
Fig. 10-60

* Gypsona Brand plaster bandages are suggested.

7. Clean out keys with a sculpting tool.

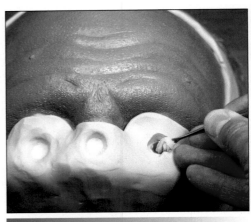

Fig. 10-61

8. Trim around the flashing, and leave ⅛″ of exposed UC mold between the sculpting and flashing in order to create a cutting edge. (Note: The cutting edge is where the casting material (gelatin or foam) is pressed out of the mold, when poured in, to create the thin tissue-like edges of the appliance. Cutting the clay too far from the sculpture may create a thicker appliance edge.)

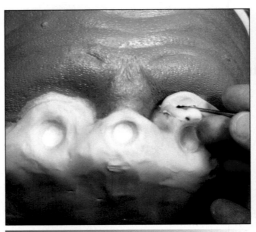

Fig. 10-62

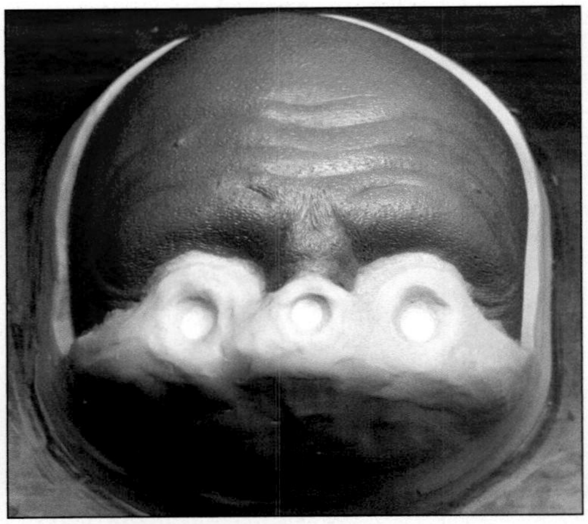

Fig. 10-63

9. Cut out clay on four points around the mold (top center, bottom center, and sides) to create surface keys, which keep the positive from rocking inside the negative mold.

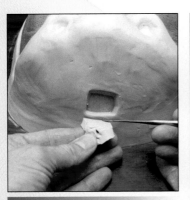

Fig. 10-64

Fig. 10-65

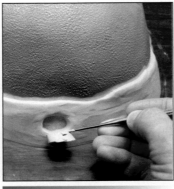

Fig. 10-66

Fig. 10-67

10. Clean all keys and cutting edges on the mold with 99-percent alcohol or acetone and a small, soft-bristle brush.

Allow 3 to 4 hours for the Epoxical mold-making procedure. Each layer must set for at least 30 minutes and up to 1½ hours depending upon atmospheric temperature. Epoxical molds should be made in a well-ventilated area or outdoors away from sunlight.

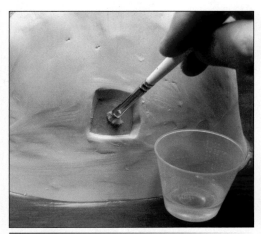

Fig. 10-68

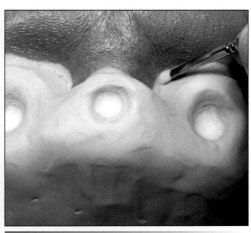

Fig. 10-69

11. Paint two coats of Partall PVA Film coating with a soft-bristle brush over the entire clay sculpture, cutting edges, and clay flashing. Let dry between coats. Paint one more coat over the clay sculpture and flashing only. Do not allow the PVA to puddle. Air-dry or dry with a hairdryer.

Fig. 10-70

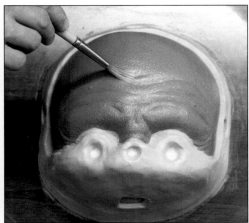

Fig. 10-71

12. After both PVA coats have dried, spray the entire mold and board with a very light coat of Epoxy Parfilm.

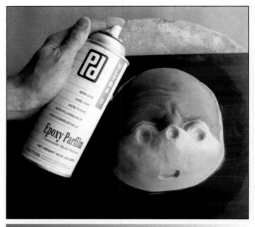

Fig. 10-72

13. Lay out Epoxical 415 components, non-waxed paper cups, tongue depressors, and gram scale. A standard mix of Epoxical 415: 6 parts B to 1 part A.

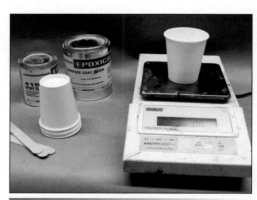

Fig. 10-73

14. While wearing a respirator and rubber gloves, weigh out 120 grams of Epoxical 415 Part B into a paper cup.

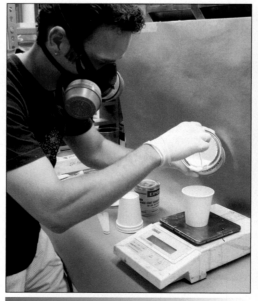

Fig. 10-74

Fig. 10-75

15. Weigh out 20 grams of Epoxical 415 Part A into the same cup.

Fig. 10-76

16. Stir both components together with a tongue depressor until thoroughly mixed.

Fig. 10-77

17. Pour the entire contents of the cup into a new, clean paper cup, and stir the components a second time.

Fig. 10-78

18. Again pour the entire contents into a clean paper cup, and stir the components a third time. This process ensures that the material is mixed thoroughly and should be done every time Epoxical is mixed for each layer.

Fig. 10-79

19. Using a nylon fan artist brush, carefully paint the first layer of Epoxical onto the sculpture, cutting edge and flashing. Paint material on in one direction, and repeat the motion in the opposite direction to make sure the sculpture texture and pores are covered (without bubbles).

Fig. 10-80

Fig. 10-81

Fig. 10-82

20. Finish painting the mold, and extend the material 1″ away from the edge of the mold. Cover the mold with a box or bucket to protect the surface from attracting dirt. Let the first layer cure until the surface is hard, but still tacky. Setting time is from approximately 30 minutes to 1 hour depending upon atmospheric temperature. (72°F is an ideal temperature in which to complete this procedure.) Clean the brush with acetone.

Fig. 10-83

Fig. 10-84

21. Mix a second batch of Epoxical 415 (120 grams of B and 20 grams of A), and add 10 drops of any color of GM Foam water-based pigment. Mix thoroughly. (Triple-cup mix the material as shown in steps 16–18.)

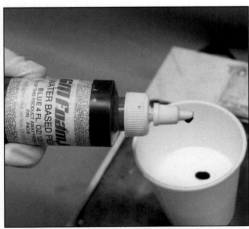

Fig. 10-85

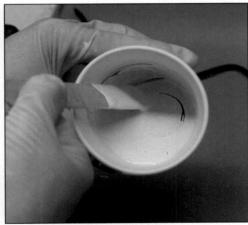

Fig. 10-86

22. Drizzle the second batch of material onto the mold, and spread it very carefully over the entire mold with the same fan brush used on the first coat (being careful not to disturb the first coat). Let cure until hard and tacky (allowing approximately the same amount of time allotted to step 20). Clean the brush with acetone.

Fig. 10-87

Fig. 10-88

23. Measure out 20 ounces of water and 20 ounces of Acryl 60 liquid into a large container, and set this aside.

Fig. 10-89

24. Mix a third batch of Epoxical 415 (120 grams of B and 20 grams of A), and add one tablespoon of Ultracal 30 into the mixture.

Fig. 10-89

25. Drizzle the mixture onto the mold, and spread it very carefully with a 1″ chip brush.

Fig. 10-89

Fig. 10-90

26. *Gently* press water-moistened, 7″ × 7″ one-layer-thick burlap pieces into the wet Epoxical material. Cover the entire mold with burlap pieces.

Fig. 10-91

27. Sift 10 cups of Ultracal 30 into a pre-measured water/Acryl 60 mix, and stir it thoroughly with the hands. (This will be a very thin mixture.)

Fig. 10-92

Fig. 10-93

28. Generously apply the Ultracal 30 mix directly to the burlap/Epoxical-coated mold using hands or a 1″ disposable brush.

Fig. 10-94

29. Dip 2-layer-thick 7″ × 14″ burlap pieces into the Ultracal mix, and form these into a snake shape. Apply the Ultracal snake around the lip of the forehead mold, and gently press it into the flange area. Repeat in order to complete a flange around the mold.

Fig. 10-95

Fig. 10-96

Fig. 10-97

Fig. 10-98

30. Dip 2 layers of 7″ × 7″ burlap into Ultracal, and cover the entire mold with several pieces, overlapping each section of burlap.

Fig. 10-99

31. Make one 2-layer-thick burlap/Ultracal snake, and form it around the top of the mold to create a ″bird's nest″ effect. This will be filled with Ultracal to make a flat bottom on the mold so that the mold will set on the counter when finished.

Fig. 10-100

32. Make two additional 1-layer-thick burlap/Ultracal snakes, and reinforce the flange on the mold to make it sturdier with less chance of warping.

Fig. 10-101

33. Cover the mold with one 7″ × 7″ layer of burlap, and lightly coat this with Ultracal in order to create a smoother outer coat to the mold.

Fig. 10-102

34. Pull the extra bits of burlap material from the Ultracal material, and place them in the bird's nest as filler.

Fig. 10-103

35. Fill the bird's nest with thickening Ultracal, and continue coating the mold with Ultracal material.

Fig. 10-104

36. As the Ultracal material thickens, spatulate it onto the mold, and place a flat project board onto the top to create a level surface.

Fig. 10-105

37. After the Ultracal has thickened additionally (5 minutes or less), remove the project board, but do not touch the flat surface of the mold.

Fig. 10-106

38. Smooth the Ultracal surface with a mold makers sponge and water. Let the mold cure for six hours (or overnight).

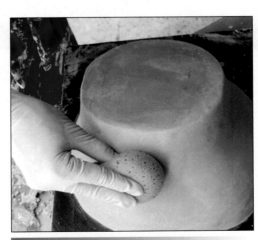

Fig. 10-107

39. Tilt the mold off of the project board, and turn it upside down.

Fig. 10-108

40. Place two small 1″ × 2″ × ½″ boards parallel with the handle of the mold, and one board over the entire width of the mold. Using a furniture clamp, carefully pry the positive from the negative mold. The mold may part more easily if the whole mold is heated in an oven for 15 minutes at 100°F.

Fig. 10-109

Fig. 10-110

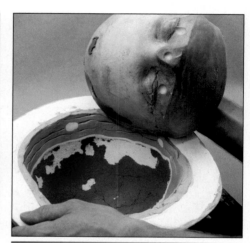

Fig. 10-111

41. Clean out the Kleen Klay and NSP sculpture clay from the negative mold with a wooden tool, as metal will scratch the surface.

Fig. 10-112

Fig. 10-113

42. Soak the negative mold in a bucket of hot water and dishwashing liquid soap for 15 minutes, and slowly scrub the clay from the mold with a cut 1″ disposable brush.

Fig. 10-114

Fig. 10-115

43. Dry the mold with a towel, and clean out the remaining clay with 99-percent alcohol and a cut 1″ brush.

Fig. 10-116

44. Scrape the clay off the forehead positive with a wooden tool, and clean off the residue of clay with 99-percent alcohol and a cut 1″ brush.

Fig. 10-117

Fig. 10-118

45. Place the clean positive into the negative, and mark registration lines onto the mold with a black Sharpie. If the mold is to be used for foam latex appliances, it will have to be *step cured* in the oven for one hour at 100°F, one hour at 150°F, and 2 hours at 200°F. This stabilizes and hardens the Epoxical. Strapping the mold together with a mold strap is highly recommended.

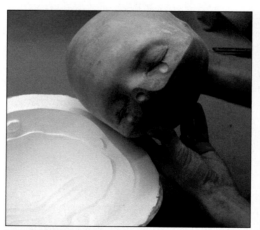

Fig. 10-119

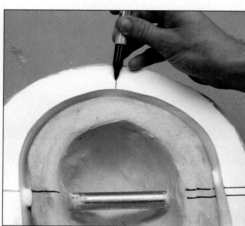

Fig. 10-120

DUPLICATING AN AREA OF THE FACE (NOSE AND UPPER LIP) FROM AN EXISTING FACE CAST

Supply List for Ultracal Positive Mold Duplication (Nose and Upper Lip Piece)

- Water
- Palette Knives
- Rubber Gloves
- Kleen Klay
- Sculpting Tools
- Water Clay
- Ultracal 30
- 5 Three-layer-thick Bandages (6″ × 6″)
- Mixing Bowls (preferably flexible plastic)
- Disposable, Soft ½″ Brush
- Krylon Crystal Clear Spray
- Mold-making Knife
- Burlap Material (cut into 4″ × 4″ squares in lengths of 3″ and 8″)
- 1″ Chip (Throwaway) Brush
- Petroleum Jelly
- Stanley Planer
- Tissues
- White Hydrocal Face Cast
- Alginate
- Clay Cutter

Nose and Upper Lip Piece Procedure

1. Coat the White Hydrocal face cast with a very light coat of petroleum jelly. Wipe excess off with a tissue.

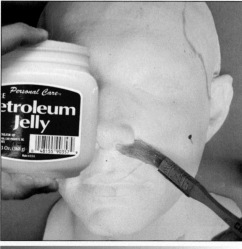

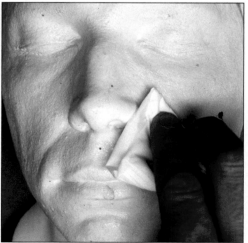

Fig. 10-121

Fig. 10-122

2. Mix a small batch of alginate, and carefully coat the area of the cast to be duplicated. avoid trapping bubbles in the cast.

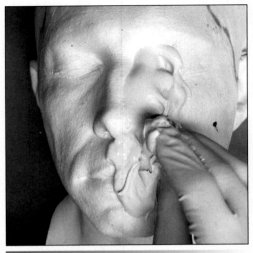

Fig. 10-123

3. After the alginate has set, carefully remove it from the face cast, and place it back (facilitating removal after the plaster bandage has been formed).

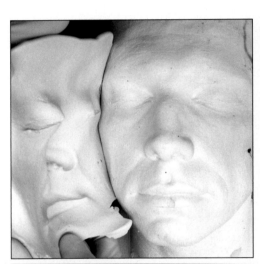

Fig. 10-124

4. Cover the alginate with plaster bandages as if taking a face cast. Allow to set.

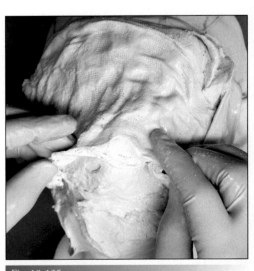

Fig. 10-125

5. Remove alginate and plaster in one piece from the positive face cast.

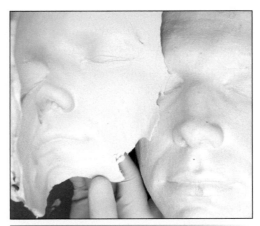

Fig. 10-126

6. Trim the excess alginate from the cast with a mold-making knife.

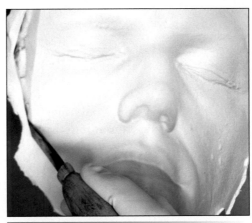

Fig. 10-127

7. Cut 2–3 pieces of water clay approximately 4″ × 10″, and press them into the alginate/plaster bandage casting to create a mold wall. Cut the top off of the water clay to create an even, level wall. Be careful not to distort the alginate when pressing the water clay into place.

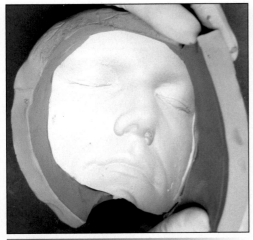

Fig. 10-128

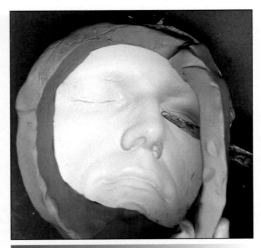

Fig. 10-129

8. Mix a half-batch of Ultracal (4 oz. water and 12 oz. Ultracal 30). Paint this into the alginate cast and up onto the water clay walls, being careful not to trap bubbles. Build this layer up to ¼″ as the Ultracal begins to set.

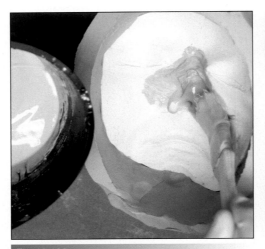

Fig. 10-130

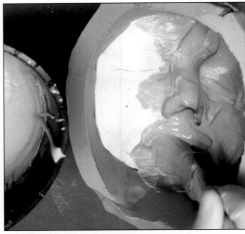

Fig. 10-131

9. After the first batch has set and lost its shine, mix a full batch of Ultracal, and paint it into the casting, being careful not to crack the first layer.

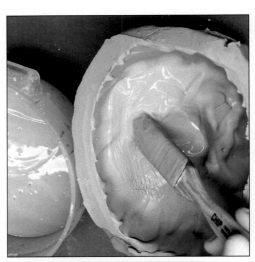

Fig. 10-132

10. Dip 4″ × 4″ square burlap pieces, two layers thick, into the Ultracal mix, and very carefully place them into the casting. (Note: Burlap-dipped Ultracal should be wet and completely saturated.)

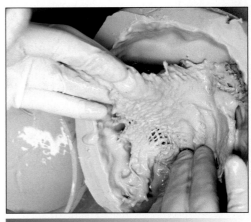

Fig. 10-133

11. Dip one 3″ × 8″ burlap piece into the Ultracal mix, and create a "snake." Work the material into the burlap. Place this piece around the edge of the mold to make a wall (1″thick) to the top of the water clay.

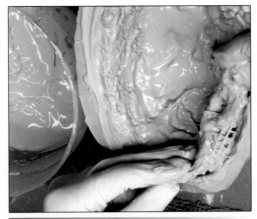

Fig. 10-134

12. As the Ultracal begins to thicken, use a palette knife to smooth and form the Ultracal into a hollow mold (1″ thick). (Note: Making the mold hollow creates a more uniform heating surface.)

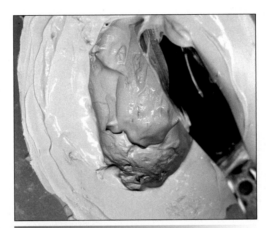

Fig. 10-135

13. Before the Ultracal sets completely, use a 1″ chip brush with water to smooth out the surface.

Fig. 10-136

14. After the Ultracal has set for at least three hours, remove the water clay walls and alginate from the piece mold.

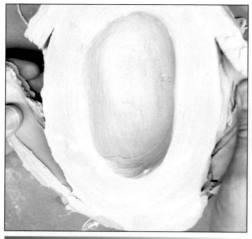

Fig. 10-137

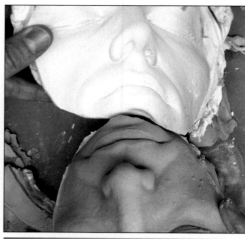

Fig. 10-138

15. Clean up the edges of the piece mold with a planer, and remove small bubbles with a mold-making knife. Place the mold in an oven at 180°F for two hours to cure out any excess moisture.

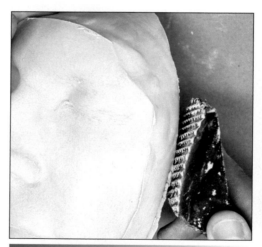

Fig. 10-139

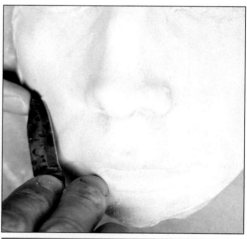

Fig. 10-140

Supply List for Sculpting the Nose and Upper Lip Piece

- Sculpting Tools
- 99-percent Alcohol
- Stiff Round Brush
- Krylon Crystal Clear Spray
- Soft-bristle Brush
- Texture Pads
- Hairdryer
- Plastic Wrap

Nose and Upper Lip Sculpting Procedure

1. Remove the nose/upper lip piece from the float-off sculpture, and press it lightly onto the piece mold.

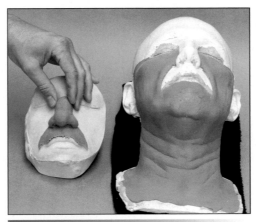

Fig. 10-141

2. Blend the edges of the clay onto the positive with fingers and sculpting tools. A hairdryer may be used to heat up the clay for easier blending.

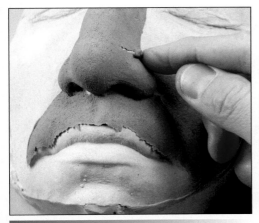

Fig. 10-142

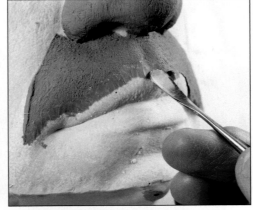

Fig. 10-143

3. Detail and refine the sculpting with the appropriate tools.

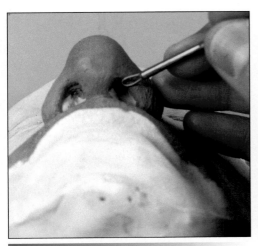

Fig. 10-144

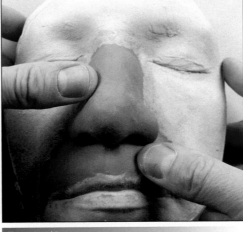

Fig. 10-145

4. After the blending and refining are finished, add pores with texture pads.

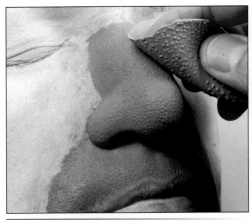

Fig. 10-146

5. Single pores may be added by stretching plastic wrap over the sculpture and tapping texture in the clay with a stylus and wire sculpting tools made by Kemper.

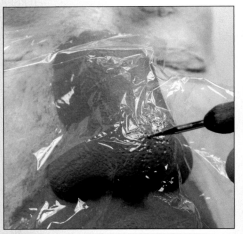

Fig. 10-147

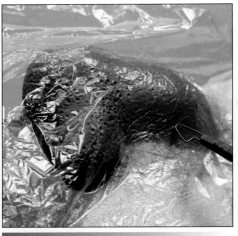

Fig. 10-148

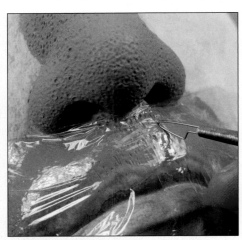

Fig. 10-149

6. The finished sculpture is now ready for flashing and molding.

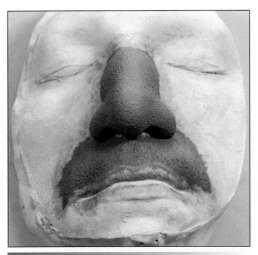

Fig. 10-150

7. Before flashing out the full appliance piece, fill the nostril area with Kleen Klay (a softer, waxy clay), and leave a slightly indented section.

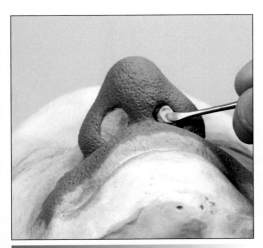

Fig. 10-151

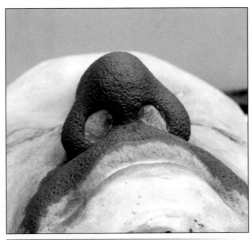

Fig. 10-152

8. When sculpting a nose, care should be taken to survey "undercut" areas where the stone curves back under and potentially prevents the negative mold from pulling straight up off of the area.

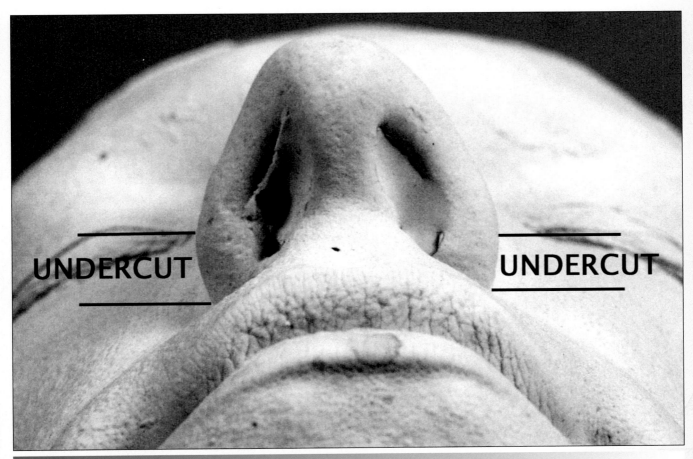

Fig. 10-153

Supply List for BJB 1630 Negative Mold-making

- BJB 1630 Urethane
- Clay Cutter
- Epoxy Parfilm Spray
- Paint Stick Stirrers
- Screwdriver
- Planer
- Wooden Sculpting Tool
- Acetone
- Kleen Clay
- Water Clay
- Non-waxed Paper Buckets
- Sculpting Tools
- ½″ Disposable Chip Brush (cut short)
- 99-percent Alcohol
- Small Nylon Brush
- Electric Drill
- Rounded Router Bit
- Black Sharpie Marker
- Petroleum Jelly
- Containers (for mixing 1630)
- 1″ Disposable Chip Brush

BJB 1630 Negative Mold-making Procedure

1. Mark four points on the positive where indented keys will need to be drilled for negative mold registration purposes.

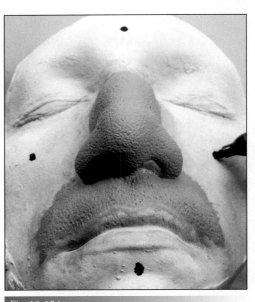

Fig. 10-154

2. Using a round-ended router bit (available in any hardware store) and a hand drill, drill keys where marked.

Fig. 10-155

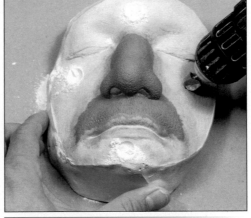

Fig. 10-156

3. Use a mold-making knife to clean up the edges of the keys.

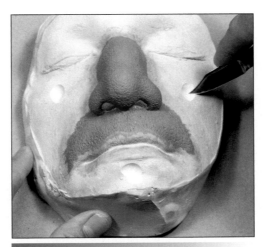

Fig. 10-157

4. Clean off all powder from the positive, and spray the entire cast with one light coat of Krylon Crystal Clear.

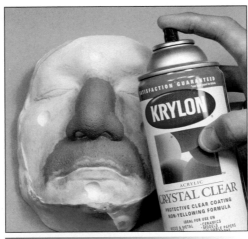

Fig. 10-158

5. Roll several Kleen Klay "snakes" (5" to 6" long, ¼" round). Start pressing each strand, one at a time, up to the edge of (but not touching) the sculpting. Continue pressing strands side by side all around the piece mold, but do not cover the indented keys.

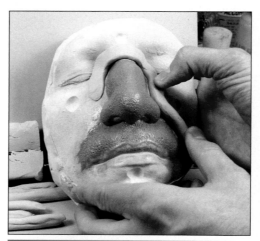

Fig. 10-159

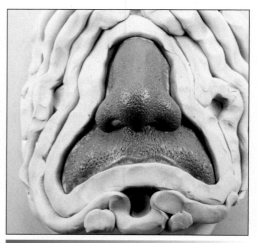

Fig. 10-160

6. Smooth out the Klay with the fingers, but do not cover the keys.

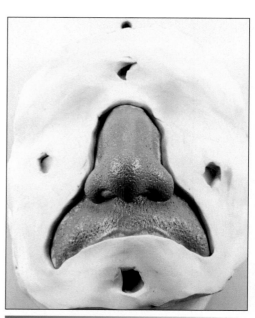

Fig. 10-161

7. Cut Kleen Klay away from the indented keys with a sculpting tool.

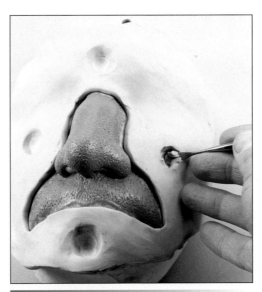

Fig. 10-162

8. Cut Kleen Klay ⅛″ away from the sculpture with a sculpting tool to create a cutting edge. (Note: The cutting edge is where the casting material, gelatin, or foam is pressed out of the mold [when poured in] to create the thin, tissue-like edges of the appliance. Cutting the Klay too far from the sculpture may create a thicker appliance edge.)

Fig. 10-163

9. Finish the flashing by smoothing all rough, sharp edges with the fingers.

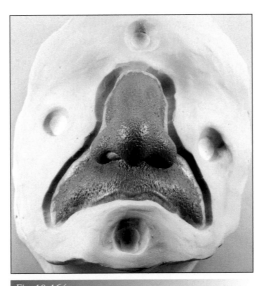

Fig. 10-164

10. Spray the entire flashed sculpture with two light coats of Krylon Crystal Clear.

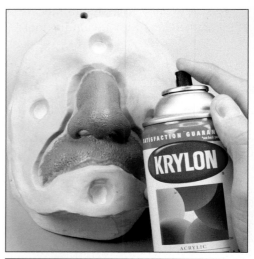

Fig. 10-165

11. Clean the cutting edge with a small nylon brush and 99-percent alcohol. Remove all clay residue without disturbing the sculpture edges. (DO NOT use acetone, as this will make the BJB 1630 stick to the Ultracal.)

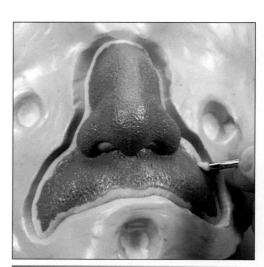

Fig. 10-166

12. Build a wall around the mold with water-based clay, ensuring that there are no gaps through which the liquid material can seep.

Fig. 10-167

13. Coat only indented keys with a very light film of petroleum jelly.

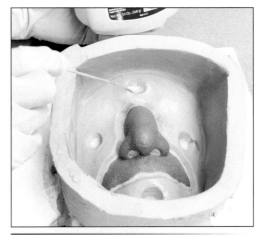

Fig. 10-168

14. Spray a very light coating of Epoxy Parfilm on the entire mold and inside the water clay walls.

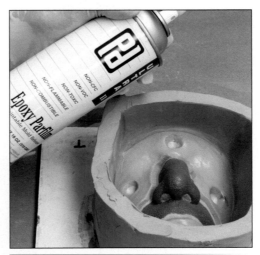

Fig. 10-169

15. Mix a 1,400-gram batch (700 gm. of A and 700 gm. of B) of BJB 1630 material (*refer to Ear Mold-making section for instructions*), and brush it onto the entire positive sculpture and flashing with a 1″ disposable brush, being careful not to trap any bubbles on the surface.

Fig. 10-170

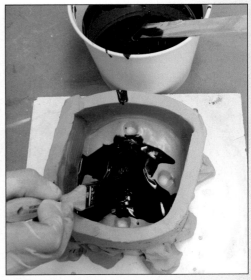

Fig. 10-171

16. Quickly pour the remaining liquid into the mold, and let it set for up to three hours until cool to the touch.

Fig. 10-172

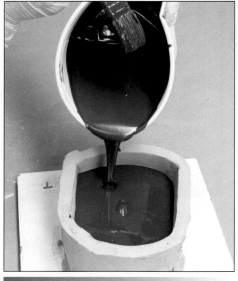

Fig. 10-173

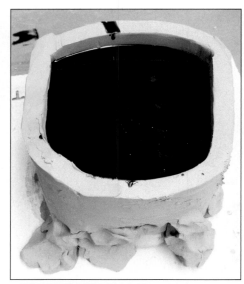

Fig. 10-174

17. Remove dried water clay from the mold.

Fig. 10-175

18. Pry the mold open with a screwdriver.

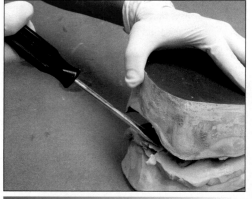

Fig. 10-176

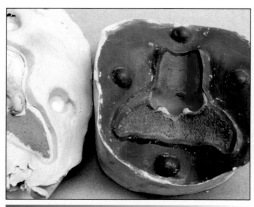

Fig. 10-177

19. Scrape off all the clay from the positive mold with a wooden sculpting tool. Clean the surface with acetone and a cut ½" disposable brush.

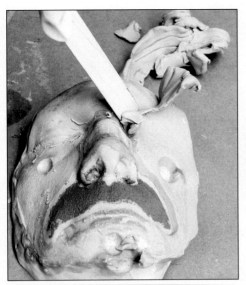

Fig. 10-178

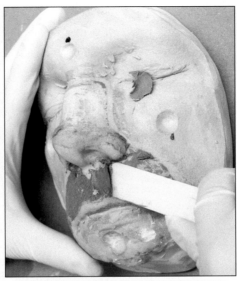

Fig. 10-179

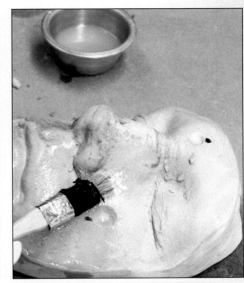

Fig. 10-180

20. Scrape out all the clay from the negative mold with a wooden sculpting tool. Clean the surface with 99-percent alcohol and a cut ½" disposable brush.

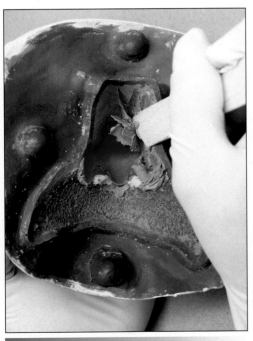

Fig. 10-181

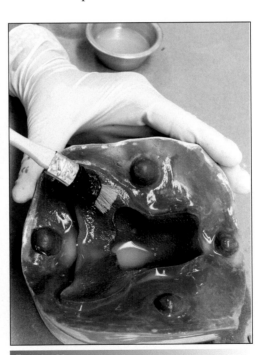

Fig. 10-182

21. Clean the sharp edges from the negative with a planer.

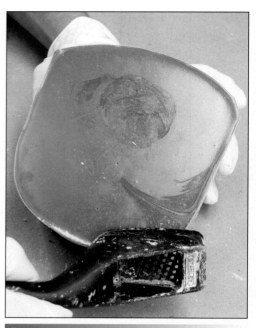

Fig. 10-183

22. Use a black Sharpie to indicate registration marks on both the front and back of the mold for easy closure.

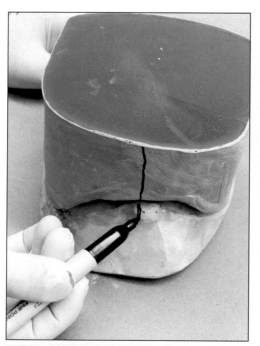

Fig. 10-184

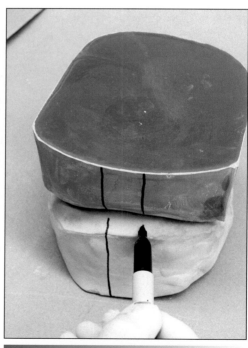

Fig. 10-185

DUPLICATING A PLASTER FACE TO MAKE A FLARED POSITIVE

Supply List for Flared Face Piece Mold-making

- Water
- Palette Knives
- Rubber Gloves
- Kleen Klay
- Metal Spline
- Water Clay
- Scissors
- Ultracal 30
- 10 to 12 Three-layer-thick Plaster Bandages (10″ × 6″)
- Two 5″ Metal Conduit Pipes
- White Hydrocal
- Mixing Bowls (preferably flexible plastic)
- Project Board (with Formica top)
- Disposable, Soft ½″ Brush
- Krylon Crystal Clear Spray
- Mold-making Knife
- Mold-making Sponge
- Burlap Material (cut into twelve 6″ × 6″ squares and six 3″ × 10″ lengths)
- 1″ Chip (Throwaway) Brush
- Petroleum Jelly
- Alginate
- Planer

Flared Face Piece Procedure

1. After determining the section of the face where an appliance is to be placed, make a White Hydrocal piece mold of the area from a Ply-O-Life negative face cast, or duplicate an area from a White Hydrocal positive, leaving at least 1½″ around where the appliance is to be sculpted for keys and clay flashing.

Fig. 10-186

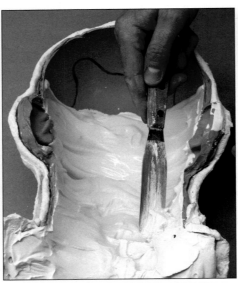

Fig. 10-187

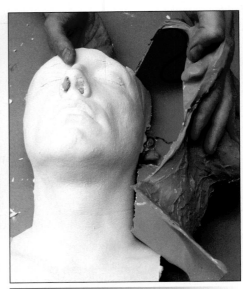

Fig. 10-188

2. Clean off all rough edges from the piece mold, and place it on a Formica-covered project board (available from any hardware store).

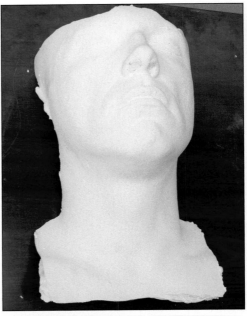

Fig. 10-189

3. Begin building up around the positive with clay, flaring out all sides to avoid under-cuts. Leave triages of ear exposed in order to create a blending area for the appliance around it. The clay on the sides of the positive should be slanted in order for the negative, when produced, to pull off without any friction or drag on the appliance.

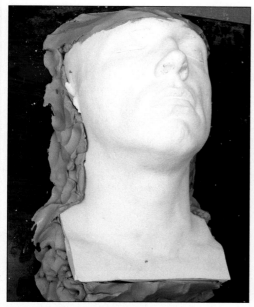

Fig. 10-190

Fig. 10-191

4. Smooth out and clean up the water clay with a metal spline and sponge moistened with water.

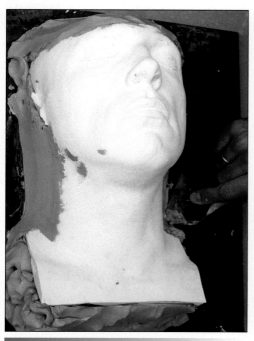

Fig. 10-192

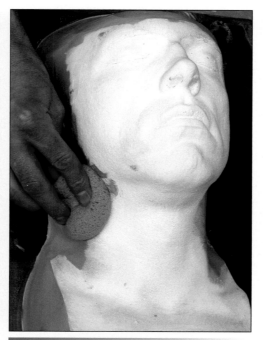

Fig. 10-193

5. Spray the positive with two light
coats of Krylon Crystal Clear.

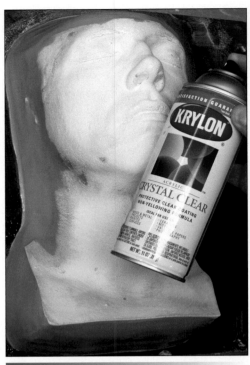

Fig. 10-194

6. Coat the plaster only with a very
light coat of petroleum jelly.

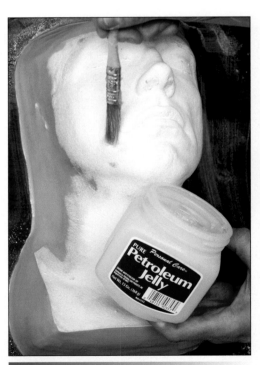

Fig. 10-195

7. Mix 24 oz. of water with 20 oz. of alginate, and mix thoroughly. Coat the piece mold evenly with alginate, and let it set.

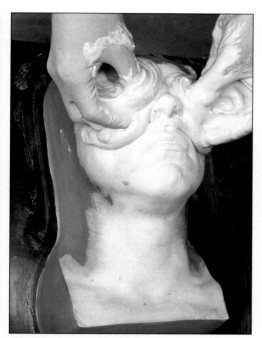

Fig. 10-196

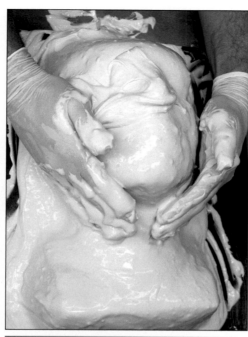

Fig. 10-197

8. Trim the edges of alginate with a mold-making knife. Remove and replace alginate onto the positive mold (facilitating removal after the plaster bandage has been formed).

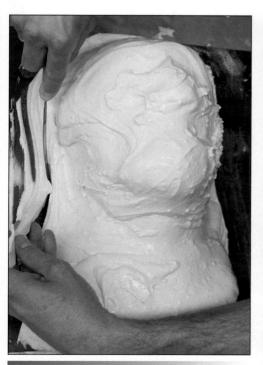

Fig. 10-198

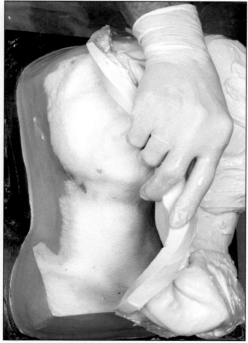

Fig. 10-199

9. Dip a 10″ three-layer-thick plaster bandage into warm water, and cover the set alginate thoroughly (encompassing the entire cast). Let it set completely.

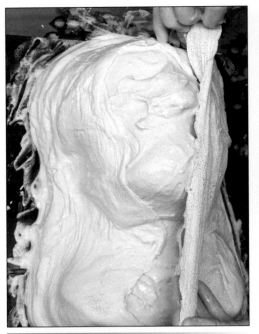

Fig. 10-200

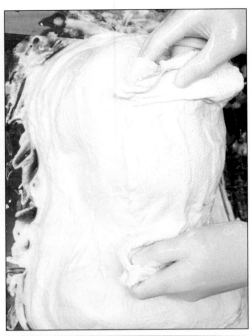

Fig. 10-201

10. Gently pull off the alginate and plaster bandage shell in one piece. Save the flared positive for reference when blending clay onto the finished Ultracal positive.

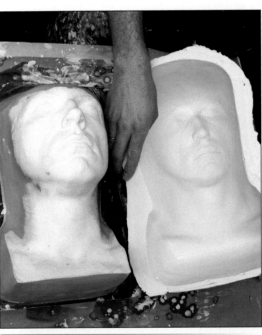

Fig. 10-202

11. Mix 4 oz. of water and 12 oz. of Ultracal 30 in a mixing bowl, and gently paint it into the alginate negative, building the coat up to at least ¼″ as the material thickens. Let this coat set until the shine has disappeared from the layer.

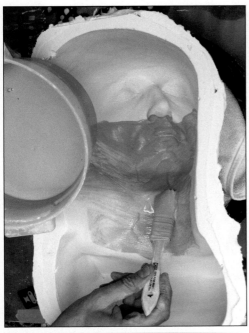

Fig. 10-203

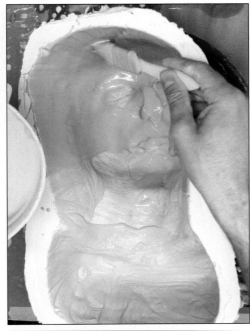

Fig. 10-204

12. Before the splash coat sets, clean the edges with a metal spline.

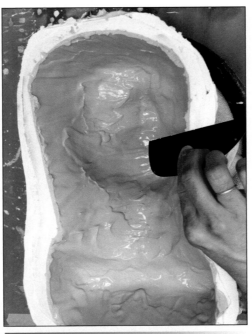

Fig. 10-205

13. Mix a double batch of Ultracal 30 (16 oz. water to 48 oz. Ultracal 30), and paint a thin coat over the first coat, being careful not to disturb or crack the layer.

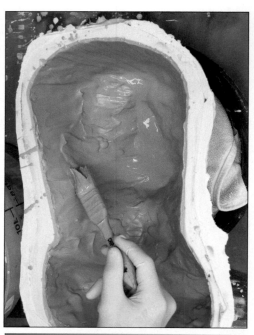

Fig. 10-206

14. Dip a double layer of 6″ × 6″ burlap into the Ultracal mix, and place this on top of the previous Ultracal coat, overlapping each burlap section at least ½″ and making sure not to trap bubbles between layers. Repeat this process until the whole negative is covered.

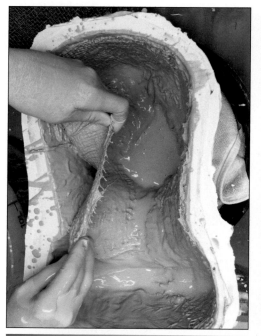

Fig. 10-207

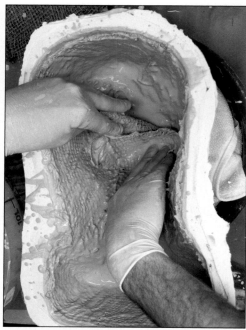

Fig. 10-208

15. Dip a double layer of 3″ × 10″ burlap into the Ultracal mix, form it into a "snake," re-dip it into the Ultracal, and place it on the edge of the mold (1″ thick). (Note: This strengthens the mold.)

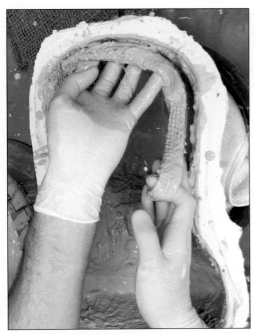

Fig. 10-209

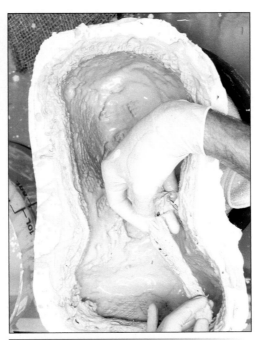

Fig. 10-210

16. Dip two separate layers of 6″ × 6″ burlap into the Ultracal mix, form this into a small snake, and re-dip it into the Ultracal. Insert a metal bar into the back of the mold near the ear area, and cover both ends with burlap/Ultracal. Placing two bars into the negative will make it easier to pull the positive from the negative when the final mold is finished.

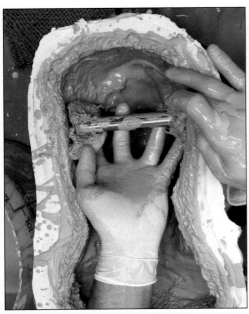

Fig. 10-211

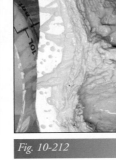

Fig. 10-212

17. Finish off the mold by smoothing the interior with a 1″ disposable brush and water

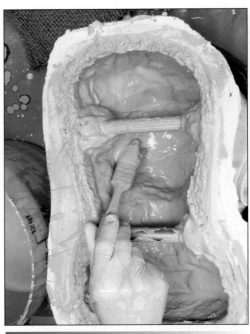

Fig. 10-213

18. When Ultracal mix thickens, spatulate onto the edge of the mold for reinforcement.

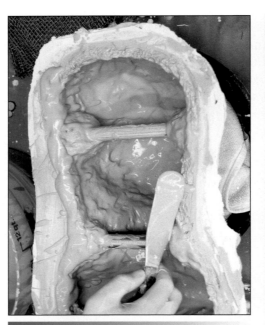

Fig. 10-214

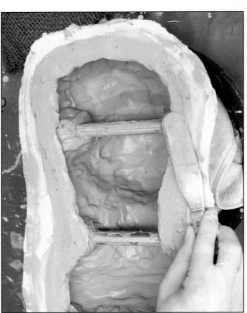

Fig. 10-215

19. Before the Ultracal sets completely, smooth the surface with a wet 1″ brush. Let Ultracal 30 set in the alginate for at least three hours.

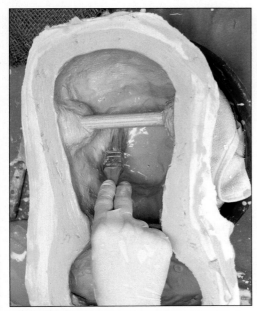

Fig. 10-216

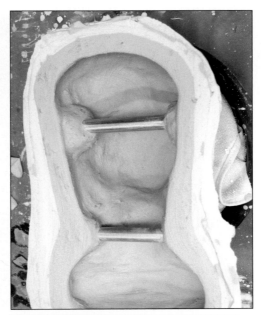

Fig. 10-217

20. Remove the piece mold from the alginate, and clean off any imperfections with a mold-making knife. Clean the edges with a planer. Place the mold in the oven at 180°F for 2 hours, face down, in order to cure out any excess moisture.

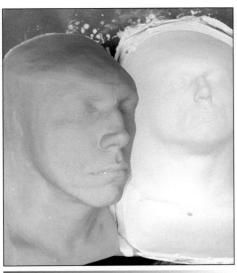

Fig. 10-218

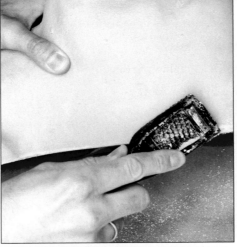

Fig. 10-219

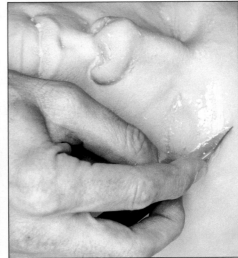

Fig. 10-220

21. After determining where the sculpture will set on the positive, plane off the nose area, and shave off the nostrils to prevent undercuts.

Fig. 10-221

Supply List for Sculpting the Face Piece

- Chavant NSP Medium Clay
- Plastic Wrap
- Kleen Klay
- Mold-making Knife
- Soft-bristle Brush (for smoothing clay)
- Acetone
- Project Board (with Formica top)
- Rounded Router Bit (for keys)
- Water Clay
- Mold-making Sponge
- Sculpting Tools
- Hairdryer
- Small Container for Liquids
- Texture Pads
- Krylon Crystal Clear Spray
- Beard Stipple Sponge
- 99-percent Alcohol
- Metal Spline
- Drill (electric or cordless)
- Clay Cutter
- Cloth Towel
- Large and Small Stiff-bristle Brushes

Face Sculpting Procedure

1. Pull clay piece from the float-off positive, and gently press it onto the cured Ultracal positive.

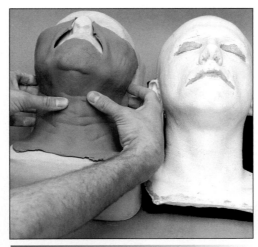

Fig. 10-222

2. Blend clay onto the positive with a metal sculpting tool and fingers. Clay may be heated with a hairdryer for easier blending.

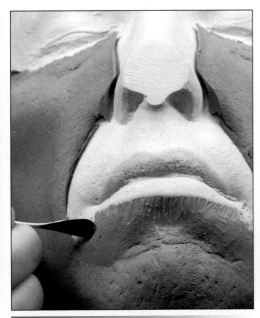

Fig. 10-223

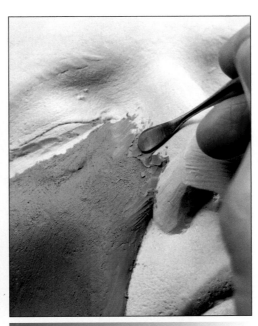

Fig. 10-224

3. Blend the outer edges of the sculpture with the fingers after heating the clay with the hairdryer.

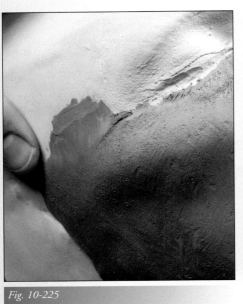

Fig. 10-225

Fig. 10-226

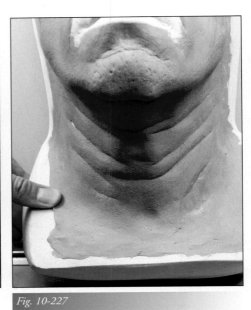

Fig. 10-227

4. Add NSP clay to areas where needed.

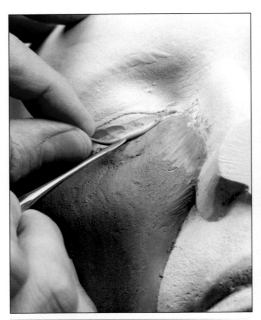

Fig. 10-228

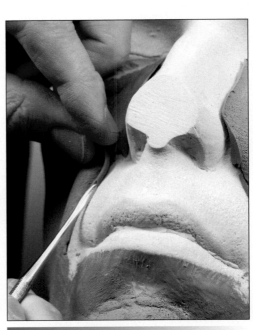

Fig. 10-229

5. Rake down the sculpture and its edges with a guitar string sculpting tool.

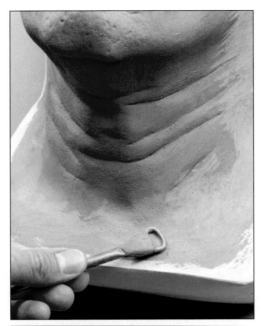

Fig. 10-230

6. The clay sculpture may be smoothed with fine drywall sandpaper and 99-percent alcohol.

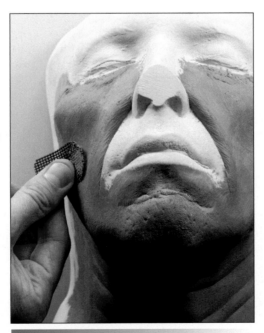

Fig. 10-231

7. Continue smoothing the clay with a soft-bristle paintbrush and 99-percent alcohol.

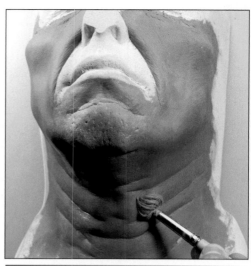

Fig. 10-232

8. Clean the edges with a cloth towel and acetone or 99-percent alcohol. Use a small brush around the nose, mouth and eye areas.

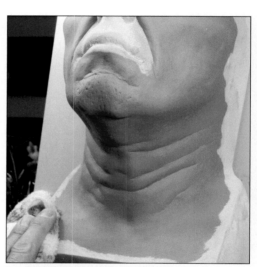

Fig. 10-233

9. Add texture to the sculpture with a pored texture pad. Heating clay with a hairdryer will make it easier to texture the surface.

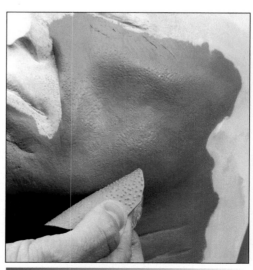

Fig. 10-234

10. Create wrinkle lines in the sculpture with a Kemper crevice tool. Smooth out these lines with a stiff, short-bristle brush and 99-percent alcohol.

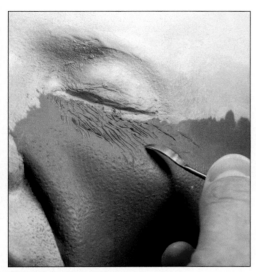

Fig. 10-235

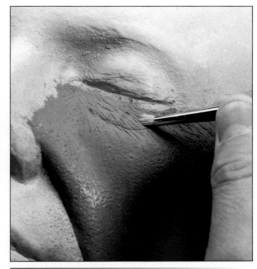

Fig. 10-236

11. Continue creating wrinkles and pore textures with a Kemper tool where needed. Smooth out lines and pores with the stiff, short-bristle brush and 99-percent alcohol.

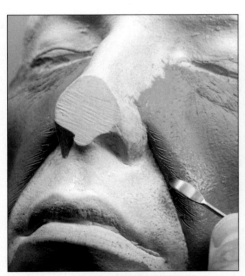

Fig. 10-237

Fig. 10-238

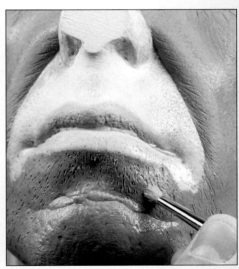

Fig. 10-239

12. Rake out deep wrinkles in the neck area with the Kemper tool, and smooth clay out with a larger, stiff-bristle brush and 99-percent alcohol.

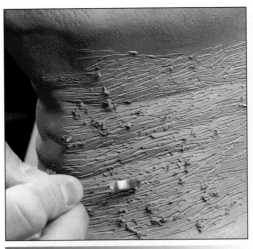

Fig. 10-240

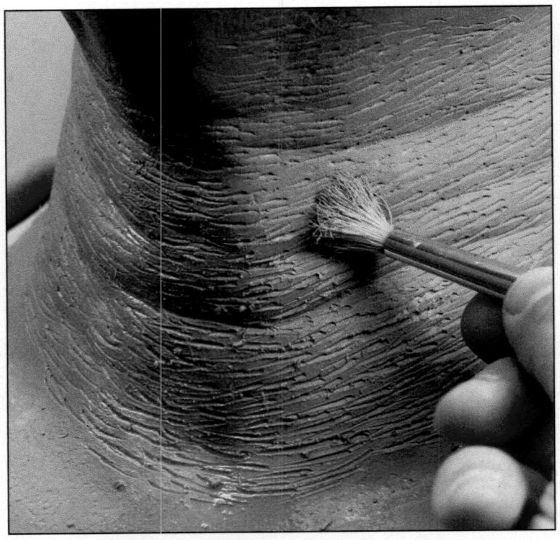

Fig. 10-241

13. Spray or brush 99-percent alcohol onto the entire sculpture, and stretch plastic wrap over the clay. Using bass guitar wire tool, press pore texture into the clay in a natural direction.

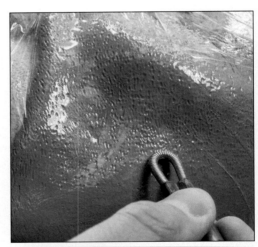

Fig. 10-242

14. Continue the pore texture over the neck area by raking a sculpting tool over plastic wrap.

Fig. 10-243

15. Using a wire Kemper tool, create dash pore texture in desired areas.

Fig. 10-244

16. After finishing the texture, remove the plastic wrap, and smooth out the texture with a pore texture pad.

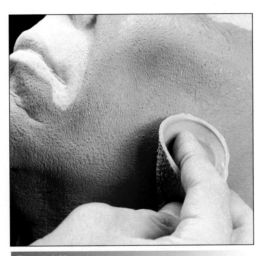
Fig. 10-245

17. Using acetone and a beard stipple sponge, rub onto a piece of clay to create clay slurry, and stipple this onto the neck area to create a small bump texture.

Fig. 10-246

Fig. 10-247

18. Lastly, add any skin bumps, etc. to the final sculpture, blend, and texture. Look over the full sculpture for areas that may need additional texture.

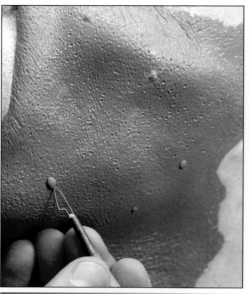

Fig. 10-248

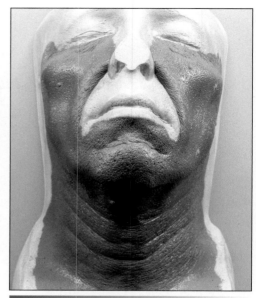

Fig. 10-249

Supply List for Ultracal 30 Negative Mold-making

- Rubber Gloves
- 1″ Disposable Chip Brush
- Burlap (14 pieces each, 7″ × 12″ and 8″ × 8″)
- Container (to mix UC 30)
- Metal Spline
- 1″ Disposable Chip Brush (cut short for cleaning mold)
- Acetone
- Ultracal 30 and Blue Die-Keen
- Water
- Mold Makers Sponge
- Wooden Sculpting Tool
- 99-percent Alcohol
- Kleen Klay
- Project Board (with Formica top)
- Krylon Crystal Clear Spray
- Water Clay
- Clay Cutter
- Black Sharpie Marker
- Small Plastic Trash Bag
- Rounded Router Bit
- Electric Drill

- Sculpting Tools
- Small Nylon Bristle Brush
- Paper Towel
- Two 2″ × 7″ × ½″ Boards
- Two 2″ × 14″ × ½″ Boards

Ultracal 30 Negative Mold-making Procedure

1. Spray the sculpture with one light coat of Krylon Crystal Clear acrylic spray coating. Let dry.

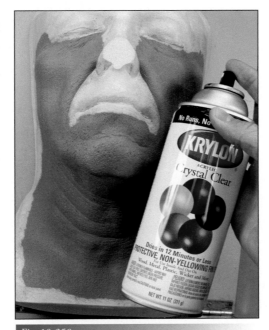

Fig. 10-250

2. Mark and drill indented keys into the positive nose, upper lip, forehead, and eye areas with a rounded router bit and drill (as explained in the previous Nose and Upper Lip Area section).

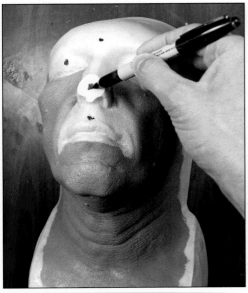

Fig. 10-251

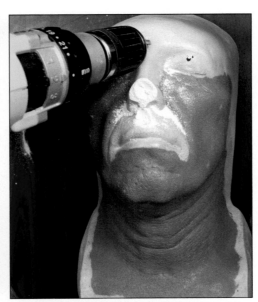

Fig. 10-252

3. Set the mold on the project board, and use Kleen Klay to flash out the mold ⅜″ high and ⅛″ away from the sculpting. Fill the entire face area except for the drilled keys, as well as the top and bottom of the mold.

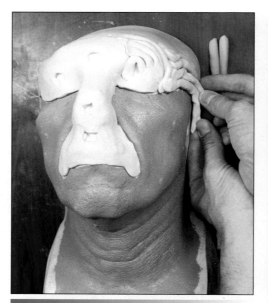

Fig. 10-253

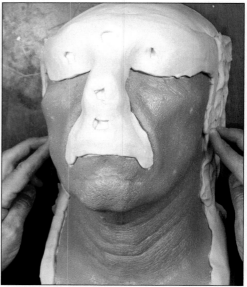

Fig. 10-254

4. Clean the edges of the flashing with a metal spline, creating a 90° angle between clay and board.

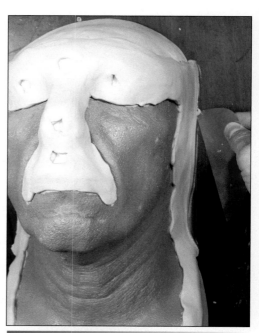

Fig. 10-255

5. Cut Kleen Klay away from the indented keys and sculpting with a metal sculpting tool. The Kleen Klay should be ⅜″ away from the Chavant sculpture.

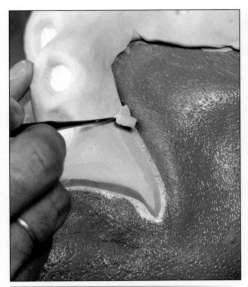

Fig. 10-256

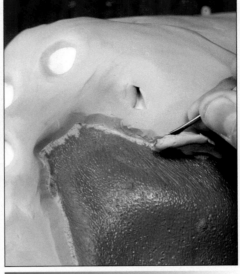

Fig. 10-257

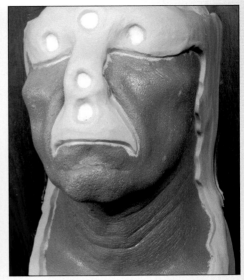

Fig. 10-258

6. Cut out Kleen Klay on the sides of the mold (where the ear would be) in order to create a contact point (surface key) whereby the negative mold keys correctly into the positive mold when made.

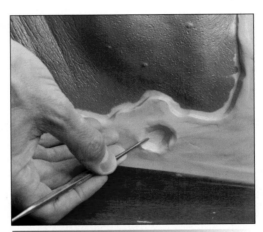

Fig. 10-259

7. Spray one more coat of Krylon acrylic spray over the entire mold.

Fig. 10-260

8. Clean the cutting edges and keys with 99-percent alcohol or acetone and a small, soft nylon-bristle brush.

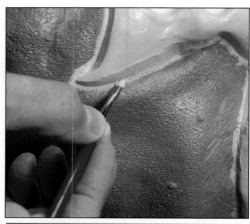

Fig. 10-261

9. Cut a 7″ × 10″ slab (⅜″ thick) of water clay, and press it into the end of the mold. Trim the excess at the top of the mold.

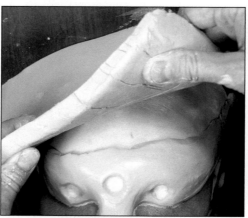

Fig. 10-262

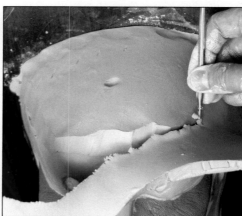

Fig. 10-263

10. Smooth out water clay with a metal spline, and remove an area in the center for a surface key (NOT an indented key).

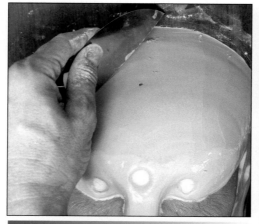

Fig. 10-264

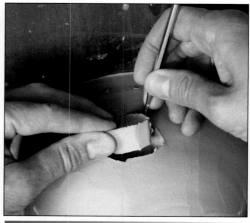

Fig. 10-265

11. Smooth out the clay with a mold makers sponge and water. A wet paper towel may be placed over the water clay in order to prevent it from drying out.

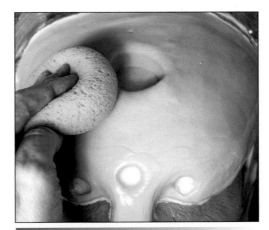

Fig. 10-266

12. Repeat step 9 on the neck end of the mold.

Fig. 10-267

13. Repeat step 10 on the neck end of the water clay.

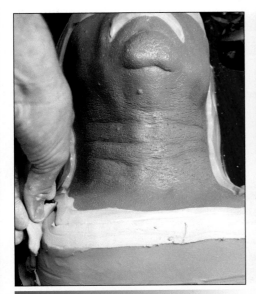

Fig. 10-268

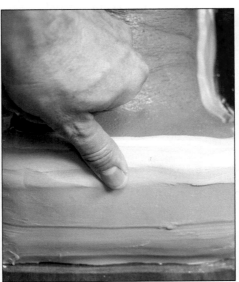

Fig. 10-269

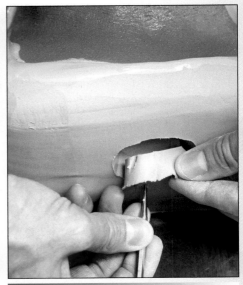

Fig. 10-270

14. Smooth the water clay with a mold makers sponge and water.

Fig. 10-271

15. Building a ⅜″ high, 1″ wide water clay border around the positive mold will result in a shorter negative mold, enabling weights to be placed onto the positive.

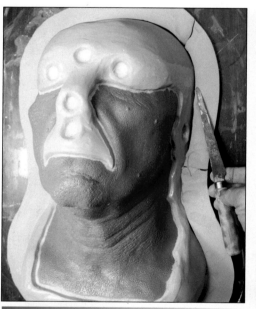

Fig. 10-272

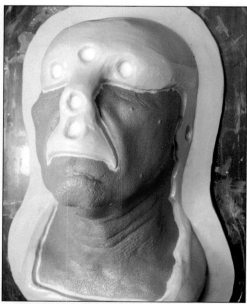

Fig. 10-273

16. Paint all keys (indented and surface) with a very light coat of petroleum jelly. DO NOT paint any petroleum jelly onto the cutting edges.

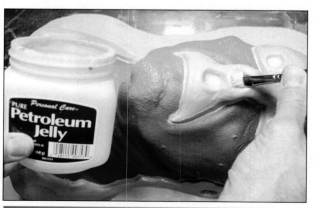

Fig. 10-274

17. Mix a double batch of Ultracal 30/Blue Die-Keen Stone mix (16 oz. water, 24 oz. Ultracal 30, and 24 oz. Die-Keen Blue Stone). Coat the sculpture with the material by using a 1″ disposable brush, being very careful not to trap any bubbles between the material and sculpture. The coat should be at least ¼″ thick. Let it set until the shine has disappeared from the Stone material layer.

Fig. 10-275

Fig. 10-276

18. Before the material has set, scrape the edges of the water clay to remove any excess or overflowing material. Wash out the brush before the material sets.

Fig. 10-277

19. Mix a large batch of Ultracal material (32 oz. water and 96 oz. Ultracal 30), and paint a thin coat over the first one, being careful not to disturb the initial layer.

Fig. 10-478

20. Dip two layers of burlap (8″ × 8″) into the Ultracal 30 mix, and place these on the side of the mold, making sure not to trap bubbles between the set Ultracal and burlap. Repeat this process until the whole mold is covered.

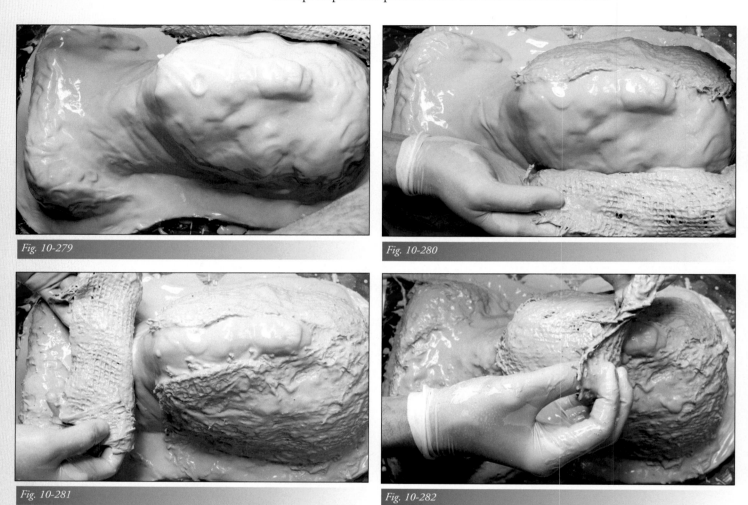

Fig. 10-279

Fig. 10-280

Fig. 10-281

Fig. 10-282

21. Dip one layer of burlap (7″ × 12″) into the Ultracal 30 mix, and place it on the edge of the mold-making, being certain not to trap any bubbles. Repeat this process until the edges of the mold are covered.

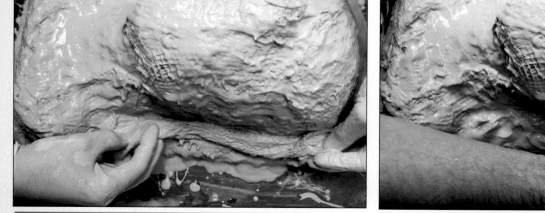

Fig. 10-283

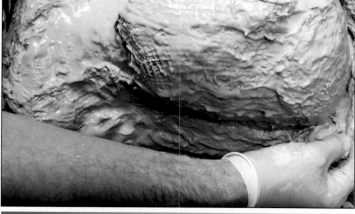

Fig. 10-284

22. Clean the outside edge of the mold with a metal spline, and smooth the mold with gloved hands.

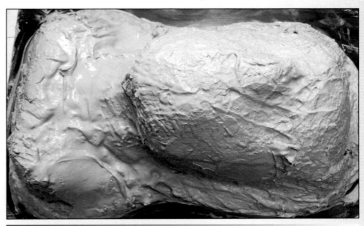

Fig. 10-285

23. Dip one layer of burlap (7″ × 12″) in the Ultracal 30 mix, and place it on the sides of the mold to reinforce the edges. Repeat this process until the edges are fully reinforced.

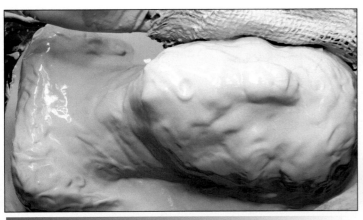

Fig. 10-286

Fig. 10-287

24. Dip a 7″ × 12″ layer of burlap into the UC (Ultracal) 30 mix, and position it on the chin area in the center of the mold. The burlap should resemble a bird's nest. Reinforce under the chin area with an 8″ × 8″ piece of UC 30/burlap.

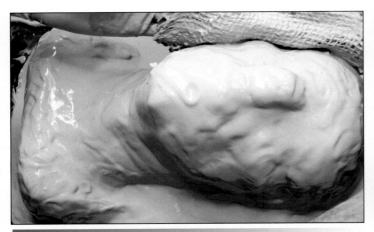

Fig. 10-288

Fig. 10-289

25. Fill the inside of the nest with UC 30, and continue pouring material over the mold to create an even finishing layer.

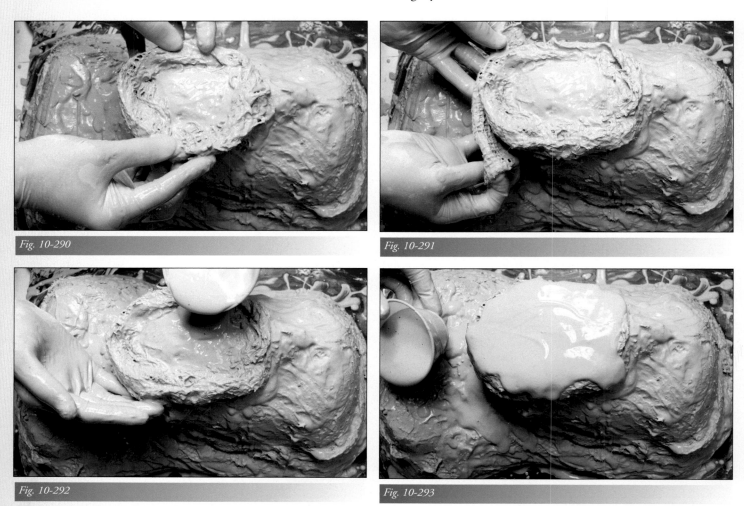

Fig. 10-290

Fig. 10-291

Fig. 10-292

Fig. 10-293

26. As the UC 30 thickens, a metal spline may be used to push the material into place and even out the mold.

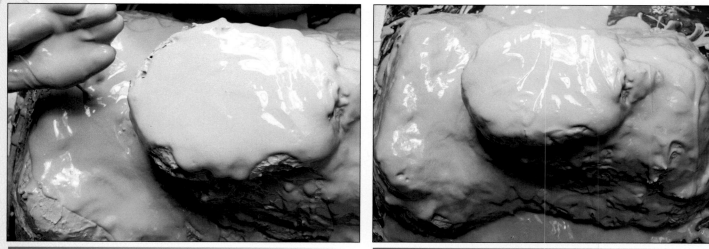

Fig. 10-294

Fig. 10-295

27. Before the material sets, place a small amount of UC 30 onto a project board, and gently press it onto the top of the mold to create a level surface. Smooth the mold with a mold makers sponge and water.

Fig. 10-296

Fig. 10-297

28. Let the mold set for 5 minutes, and remove the board by twisting it off. Continue smoothing the mold with a sponge and water.

Fig. 10-298

Fig. 10-299

29. Let the mold set overnight, wrapped in a plastic trash bag to retain moisture and prevent small cracks and warping.

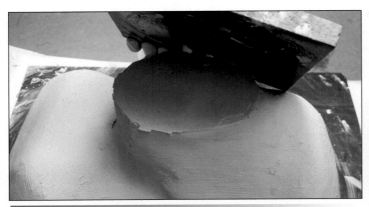

Fig. 10-300

Fig. 10-301

30. Twist the mold off of the board, and turn it over. Remove all the water and Kleen Klay from the mold's edge.

Fig. 10-302

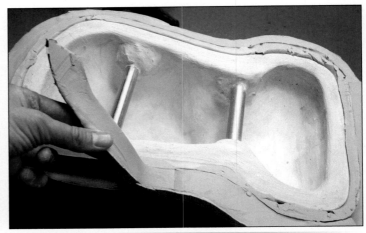

Fig. 10-303

31. Shave off the sharp edge of the mold with a planer. Place the mold into a 120ºF oven for 15 minutes, which will heat the clay in the mold and make it easier to open.

Fig. 10-304

32. Place two boards (2″ × 7″ × ½″) on each side of the mold. Then place two others (2″ × 14″ × ½″) across the top of the mold with a gap of at least 1″ between the boards and top of the mold.

Fig. 10-305

33. Secure two furniture clamps to the handles of the positive mold and the boards, and slowly tighten the clamp. The positive mold will eventually loosen from the negative.

Fig. 10-306

34. Remove the positive from the negative by pulling straight up on the mold.

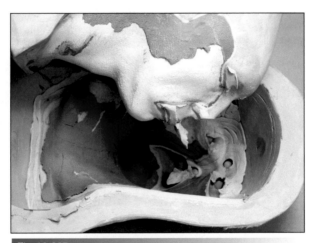

Fig. 10-307

35. Pull all the clay (Kleen and water) and Chavant from the positive and negative molds. Clean off the molds with a wooden sculpting tool *only*. Remove any residual clay with 99-percent alcohol or acetone. *Always wear a respirator when using chemicals.*

Fig. 10-308

Fig. 10-309

36. Place the positive mold back into the negative, and draw black lines on the mold with a marker in order to match the positive to the negative.

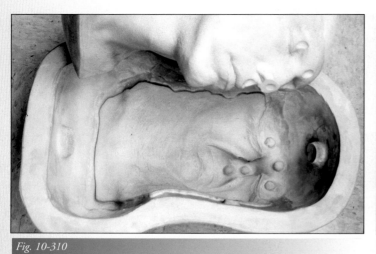

Fig. 10-310

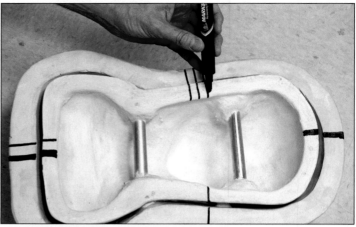

Fig. 10-311

THE EAR SCULPTURE

Supply List for Ear Piece Mold-making

- Water
- Palette Knife
- Rubber Gloves
- Krylon Crystal Clear Spray
- White Hydrocal
- Mold-making Knife
- Scissors
- Paint Stick Stirrers
- Large Plastic Deli Mixing Cups
- 6 Three-layer-thick Bandages (8″ × 6″)
- Petroleum Jelly
- Mixing Bowls (preferably flexible plastic)
- Disposable, Soft ½″ Brush
- Sculpting Tools
- Metal Spline
- Water Clay
- BJB 1630 (parts A and B)
- Gram Scale
- Large Tongue Depressors
- ½″ Chip (Throwaway) Brush
- Tissues
- Project Board (with Formica top)
- Plaster Bandages

Ear Piece Procedure

1. Make a White Hydrocal piece mold of the ear areas from a Ply-O-Life negative face cast or a duplicate from a White Hydrocal positive, leaving at least 1½″ around the appliance where it is to be sculpted for keys and clay flashing.

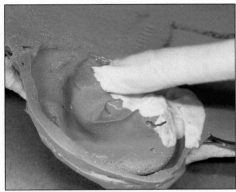
Fig. 10-312

Fig. 10-313

Fig. 10-314

2. Pull the positive from the mold, and clean off all the rough edges.

Fig. 10-315

Fig. 10-316

3. Place the ear positives onto a Formica-faced project board, and build up around the ear forms with water clay. Clean up clay with a metal spline. The middle of the ear may be filled in slightly with water clay.

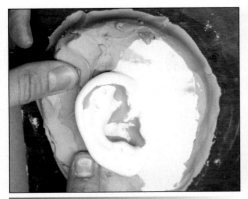
Fig. 10-317

Fig. 10-318

Fig. 10-319

4. Keep the return in the back of the
   ear visible.

Fig. 10-320

5. Spray the forms with two light coats
   of Krylon Crystal Clear. Let them
   dry, and coat only the plaster with a
   very light coat of petroleum jelly.

Fig. 10-321

6. Mix 8 oz. water with 6 oz. alginate. Coat the piece molds evenly with alginate, and
   let them set.

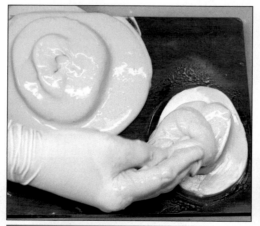

Fig. 10-322

Fig. 10-323

7. Trim excess alginate from the outside of the casting with a mold-making knife.

Fig. 10-324

8. Dip an 8″ three-layer-thick plaster bandage into warm water, and cover the set alginate thoroughly. Let it set.

Fig. 10-325

Fig. 10-326

9. Gently pull off the alginate and plaster bandage shells in one piece.

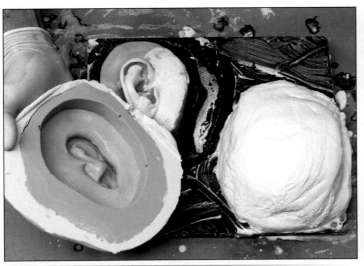

Fig. 10-327

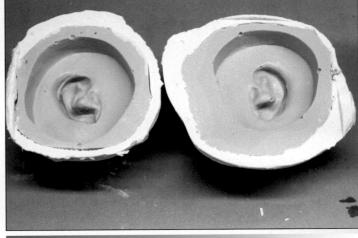

Fig. 10-328

10. Open a can of 1630, and stir each component with paint stick stirrers.

Fig. 10-329

Fig. 10-330

11. Fill both alginate negatives to the top with water, and pour the liquid back into an empty plastic cup.

Fig. 10-331

Fig. 10-332

12. Wipe out all of the water from both alginates with tissue, and place the molds on a level surface. Water clay may be used to level molds.

Fig. 10-333

13. Place the water-filled cup next to an empty cup, mark the level on the empty cup to which the water rises next to it, and then add a separate mark on the same cup halfway between the top mark and the bottom of the cup.

Fig. 10-334

14. Pour 1630 Part B up to the bottom line, ensuring the weighed amount is an even number. The material can reach slightly above the line. For these molds, the amount is 290 grams.

Fig. 10-335

Fig. 10-336

15. In a separate, smaller plastic cup, weigh the same amount of 1630 Part A, in addition to 2 extra grams to allow for excess material left in the cup when pouring this into part B.

Fig. 10-337

Fig. 10-338

16. Pour part A into part B, scraping all of the remaining material from the cup. Stir both components together until thoroughly mixed (approximately 2 minutes). (Mixed material may in fact be poured and mixed in another cup for thoroughness.)

Fig. 10-339

Fig. 10-340

Fig. 10-341

17. Paint the material into both alginates with a ½″ disposable brush to break surface tension and prevent bubbles from forming on the surface.

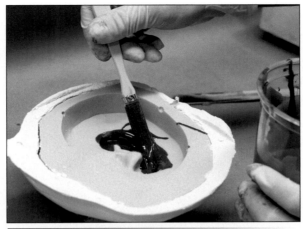

Fig. 10-342

18. Slowly pour the 1630 material into both alginates to avoid bubbles filling to the top of both alginates. Let cure for at least 1½ hours.

Fig. 10-343

Fig. 10-344

19. Remove the 1630 positives from the alginates.

Fig. 10-345

20. Plane off any sharp edges from the mold, and clean off any bubbles from the surface with a mold-making knife.

Fig. 10-346

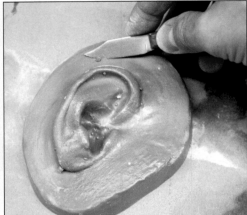

Fig. 10-347

Supply List for Sculpting the Ear Pieces

- Chavant NSP Medium Clay
- Kleen Klay
- Soft-bristle Brush
- Krylon Crystal Clear Spray
- Acetone
- Sculpting Tools
- 99-percent Alcohol

Ear Sculpting Procedure

Note: The ears were not sculpted on the float-off positive because they are too difficult to remove without damage; therefore, the ears will be sculpted separately onto 1630 positives.

1. Sculpt the ears by pressing NSP Medium Clay onto the ear positives.

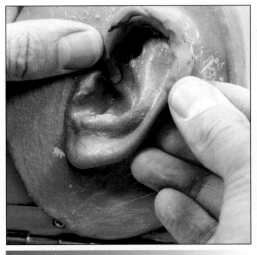

Fig. 10-348

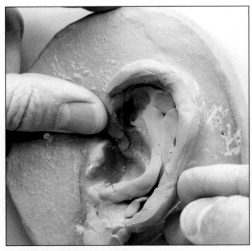

Fig. 10-349

2. After one ear has been blocked out, it is wise to block out the other in order to make them similar.

Fig. 10-350

3. Using a wire rake sculpting tool, smooth out clay to form the contours of the ears.

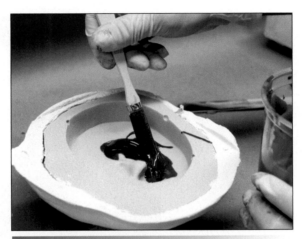

Fig. 10-351

4. Continue raking out clay to complete the sculpture.

Fig. 10-352

5. Use a stiff-bristle brush and 99-percent alcohol to smooth out the clay.

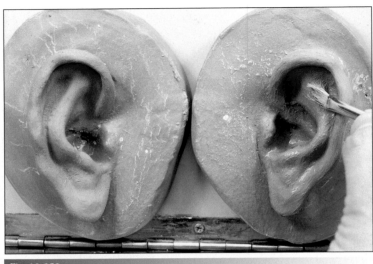

Fig. 10-353

6. Use a soft-bristle brush and 99-percent alcohol to continue smoothing the clay.

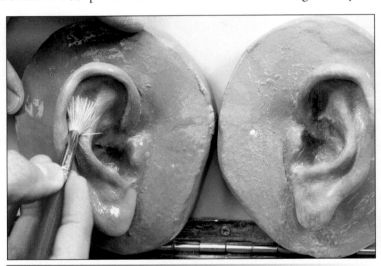

Fig. 10-354

7. Clean the blended edges of the clay with 99-percent alcohol or acetone and a small soft-bristle brush.

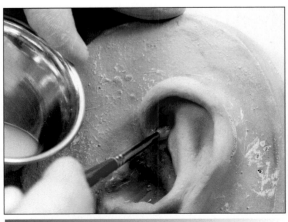

Fig. 10-355

8. Add texture to the clay sculptures by stippling the surface with a stiff-bristle brush.

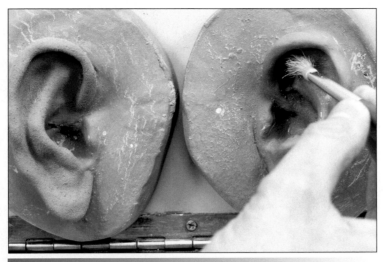

Fig. 10-356

9. Add more texture with a Kemper stylus sculpting tool.

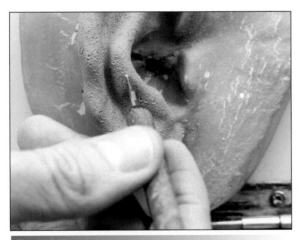

Fig. 10-357

10. Place small amounts of clay on the ear to create skin bumps. Sculpt this out with a sculpting tool.

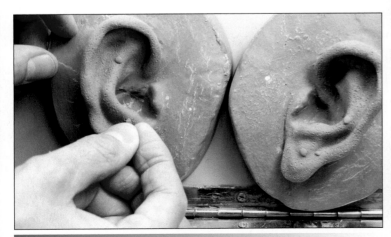

Fig. 10-358

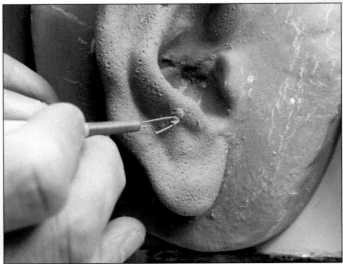

Fig. 10-359

11. Smooth and texture clay bumps with a short, stiff-bristle brush.

Fig. 10-360

Supply List for Ply-O-Life and Ultracal 30 Negative Mold-making

- Ply-O-Life Material
- Clay Cutter
- Epoxy Parfilm Spray
- Metal Spatulas
- Screwdriver
- Planer
- Wooden Sculpting Tool
- Acetone
- X-Acto Knife
- Mold-making Knife
- Water Clay
- Petroleum Jelly
- Containers (for mixing POL)
- 1″ Disposable Chip Brush
- ½″ Disposable Chip Brush (cut short)
- 99-percent Alcohol
- Ultracal 30
- GM Foam Colorants
- Burlap Pieces
- Dremel Tool
- Dremel Round-headed Bit
- Sharpie Markers (blue, red, and black)

- Electric Drill
- Round Router Bit
- Disposable Deli Cup
- Silicone Thinning Fluid

Ply-O-Life and Ultracal 30 Negative Mold-making Procedure

1. Add black marks where the keys are to be drilled for the Ply-O-Life (POL) negative mold, blue marks where the POL mold ends, and red marks for the Ultracal mother mold.

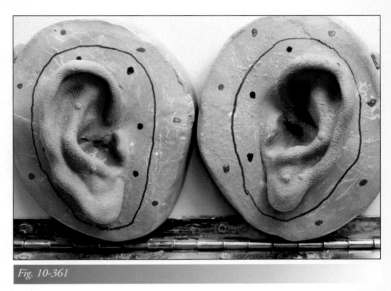

Fig. 10-361

2. Drill smaller keys for the POL mold with a Dremel tool (and round bit). Use a larger, round router bit to make outer keys.

Fig. 10-362

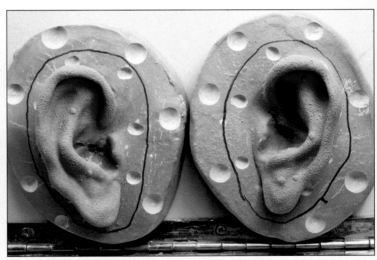

Fig. 10-363

3. Use Kleen Klay to flash out the molds around the ears, extending out to the edge of the mold. Smooth the clay, and cut the edges.

Fig. 10-364

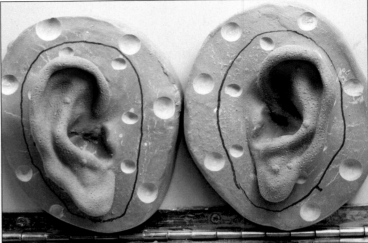

Fig. 10-365

4. Spray the mold, sculptures, and flashing with two light coats of Krylon Crystal Clear spray.

Fig. 10-366

5. Clean the edges between the flashing and the sculpture with a small, soft-bristle brush and 99-percent alcohol.

Fig. 10-367

6. Weigh out one batch of Ply-O-Life (50 gm. Base and 50 gm. Catalyst) using the instructions listed in the POL Face Casting section. Add 5 grams of silicone fluid to the mixture, and mix thoroughly. Carefully apply the POL to the ear sculpture and slightly past the blue line previously drawn on the positive mold. Use all of the mixture to cover the entire area. Repeat this process on the other ear. Let the material cure for 15 minutes.

Fig. 10-368

Fig. 10-369

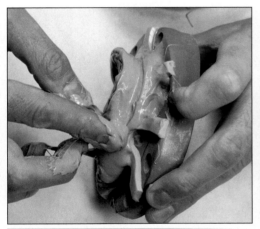
Fig. 10-370

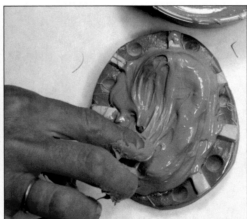
Fig. 10-371

Fig. 10-372

7. Mix a second batch (50 gm. Base and 50 gm. Catalyst) for both ears, and tint the material with GM Foam Colorants. Tinting each ear differently will help distinguish left from right. Spatulate the material onto the previous coats, and let the material cure for at least one hour.

Fig. 10-373

Fig. 10-374

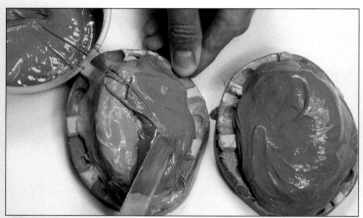

Fig. 10-375

Fig. 10-376

8. Cut off the edges of the right ear on the POL negative mold with an X-Acto knife blade, angling the cut so the mold will fit into the negative UC mother mold securely. Repeat with the left ear mold. Be careful not to cut off the flashing clay extending from the sculpture area.

Fig. 10-377

Fig. 10-378

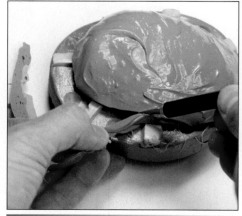

Fig. 10-379

9. Cut 3″ tall water clay walls (⅜″ thick), and press them around the ear molds, flaring the walls slightly outward.

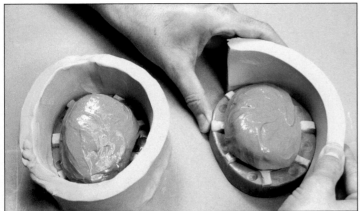

Fig. 10-380

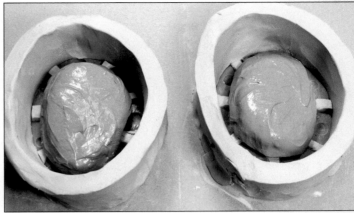

Fig. 10-381

10. Apply a very light coat of petroleum jelly to the indented keys on the positive mold.

Fig. 10-382

11. Mix a small batch of UC 30 (*refer to Ultracal 30 mixing instructions*), and paint it onto the POL mold and positive mold, while slowly building it up.

Fig. 10-383

Fig. 10-384

12. Cut burlap into a circular shape, and press it into the wet UC 30 on both molds. Top off the mold with remaining UC 30. Let this cure for two hours.

Fig. 10-385

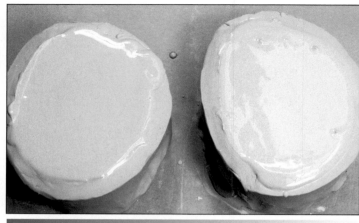

Fig. 10-386

13. Remove the dried water clay from the mold, and shave off any sharp edges.

Fig. 10-387

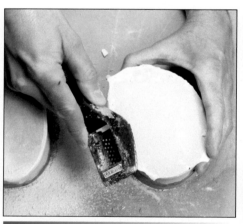

Fig. 10-388

Fig. 10-389

14. Pry the negative mold from the positive with a screwdriver, working the tool into every opening around the mold to allow for an even separation.

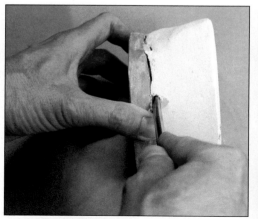

Fig. 10-390

Fig. 10-391

15. Shave off any sharp edges of the negative, being careful not to damage the registration keys. Clean out the flashing with a mold knife.

Fig. 10-392

Fig. 10-393

16. Clean clay from the negative and positive molds with a metal and wooden tool, being careful not to scratch the surface of either mold.

Fig. 10-394

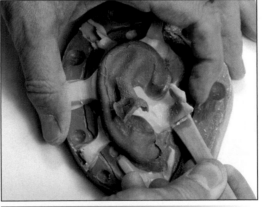

Fig. 10-395

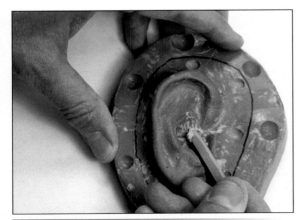

Fig. 10-396

17. Clean the positive and negative molds thoroughly with a cut, 1″ disposable brush and 99-percent alcohol.

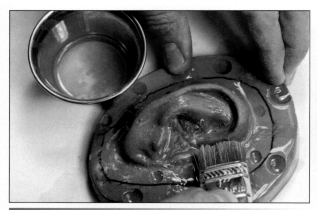

Fig. 10-397

Fig. 10-398

18. Close the molds, and make marks on the sides for lining up the positive and negative.

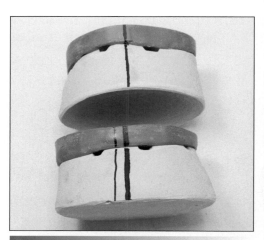

Fig. 10-399

Chapter 11

GELATIN

Chapter 11

Gelatin

Chapter 11

GELATIN

GELATIN

GELATIN INGREDIENTS

Glycerin (Glycerol)—Syrupy liquid. Sweet, warm taste. Absorbs moisture from the air. Obtained from oils and fats as a byproduct in the manufacture of soaps and fatty acids. Also, synthesis of glycerol from propylene (petroleum oils). Used as a plasticizer.

Sorbital—Syrupy liquid. Sweet taste. Decreases moisture absorption. Freely soluble in water. First found in ripe berries. Used as a plasticizer/moisture absorber.

Gelatin—Granules. Obtained by boiling skin, tendons, ligaments, bones, etc. in water. Used in jellies, adhesives, and confectioneries. Used as the coagulant in gelatin appliances.

Zinc Oxide—White odorless powder. Used as pigment in paints and cosmetics. Used as an opacifier.

Flocking—Small fibers used for internal coloration to crate a capillary look to an appliance. Rayon fibers may also be used to create a large fibrous quality to the material.

Powdered Pigment—Colored face powders or cosmetic pigments add overall coloration to a gelatin formula.

Gelatin Formula Materials

- Gelatin, 300 Bloom (250 Bloom may be used but results in a slightly weaker material)
- Sorbital (liquid)
- Glycerin
- Zinc Oxide (powder)
- Microwave-safe Container
- Microwave
- Mortar and Pestle
- Plastic Ice Trays
- Ziploc Bags
- Distilled Water
- Colored Facial Powder

- Red Flocking or Fibers
- Large Wooden Tongue Depressors
- Gram Scale (electronic or manual)
- Joe Blasco Loose Facial Powder
- Plastic Deli Cups

Basic Gelatin Formula

This formula is large and may be cut in half for smaller quantities.

Liquids

- 750 gm.—Sorbital (liquid)
- 750 gm.—Glycerin
- 10 gm.—Distilled Water

Powders

- 175 gm.—Gelatin, 300 Bloom (gelatin amount may be varied to obtain a harder or softer formula [more or less gelatin, respectively])
- 4 gm.—Zinc Oxide
- 3 gm.—Joe Blasco Ruddy Light Skin Loose Face Powder
- 2 gm.—Joe Blasco Ruddy Dark Skin Loose Face Powder
- 0.5 gm.—Factor 2 Red Flocking

1. Weigh 750 gm. of sorbital in a microwave-safe container.-

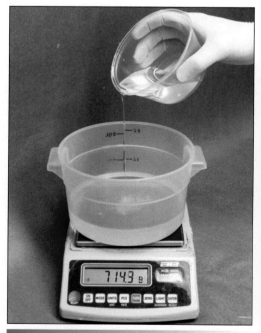

Fig. 11-1

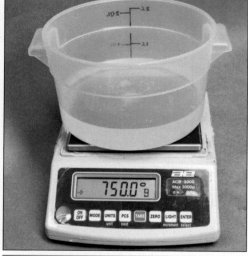

Fig. 11-2

2. Weigh 750 gm. of glycerin into the same container with sorbital to equal 1500 gm. total.

Fig. 11-3

Fig. 11-4

3. Weigh 10 gm. of distilled water into the container. The total weight should equal

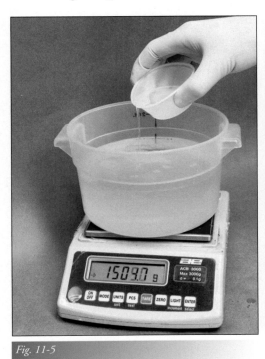

Fig. 11-5

Fig. 11-6

1510 gm. Set the liquids aside.

4. Weigh 175 gm. of gelatin granules into a plastic cup.

Fig. 11-7

Fig. 11-8

5. Weigh 4 gm. of zinc oxide into a mortar container.

Fig. 11-9

6. Weigh 3 gm. of Joe Blasco Ruddy Light Skin Loose Face Powder and 2 gm. of Joe Blasco Ruddy Dark Skin Loose Face Powder into the same mortar container.

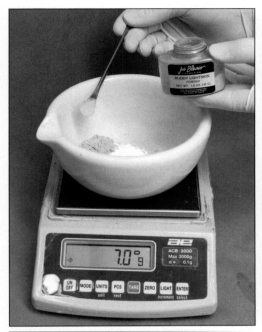

Fig. 11-10

Fig. 11-11

7. Weigh 0.5 gm. of red flocking or fiber53

Fig. 11-12

8. Pour about 3 tablespoons of gelatin granules into the mortar container with the previously weighed powder.

Fig. 11-13

9. Grind all the dry powders together with the pestle. Zinc oxide powder should be pulverized completely.

Fig. 11-14

10. Pour the ground powders into the remaining gelatin, and stir until completely mixed.

Fig. 11-15

Fig. 11-16

11. Pour the gelatin-mixed powders into the liquid mixture, and stir until completely mixed.

Fig. 11-17

Fig. 11-18

12. Let the mixture set overnight. The mixture will look thicker after setting all night because the moisture becomes absorbed into the gelatin granules.

Fig. 11-19

13. Heat in a carousel microwave oven at one-minute intervals, stirring at the end of each minute. Heat for 5 minutes total, and then set it aside for 5 minutes. Repeat this 1-minute heating cycle process until the granules have dispersed and melted completely. DO NOT LET THE MIXTURE BOIL. THIS MIXTURE IS EXTREMELY HOT, AND CARE SHOULD BE TAKEN DURING HANDLING.

Fig. 11.20

14. Pour the heated mixture into plastic ice trays, and let cool.

Fig. 11-21

Fig. 11-22

15. Remove the cubes, and place them in a Ziploc bag, facilitating future reheating in smaller quantities.

Fig. 11-23

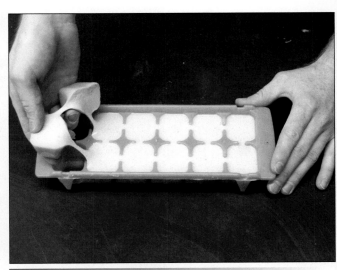
Fig. 11-24

PREPARING MOLDS TO RUN GELATIN APPLIANCES

Materials Needed

- PAM Vegetable Spray
- ¼″ Drill Bit
- Black Sharpie Marker
- Mold Knife
- Epoxy Parfilm Spray
- Portable Drill
- 1″ Disposable Brush
- Sandpaper
- Cloth Towel

Preparation

1. Mark areas where the release holes will be drilled on the face positive with a black Sharpie, and then drill holes with a portable drill and a ¼″ drill bit. Release holes should be located ⅜″ away from the appliance edge in eye areas, above the forehead, and around the neck area. No holes should be drilled where the appliance was sculpted.

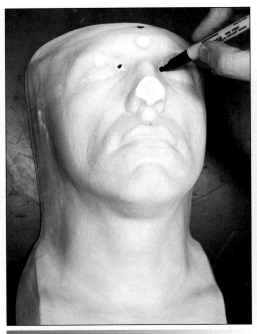

Fig. 11-25

Fig. 11-26

2. Heavily spray the positive face mold, front and back, with PAM Vegetable Spray separator or Epoxy Parfilm, and lightly scrub into the mold with a 1″ disposable brush. If using Ultracal 30 molds, let the separator soak in for at least 30 minutes before pouring the gelatin pieces. (PAM is recommended for Ultracal molds as a pickling agent before the mold is used for the first time. Epoxy Parfilm is then used as the subsequent release and as a releasing agent for 1630, Epoxical, and Ply-O-Life molds.)

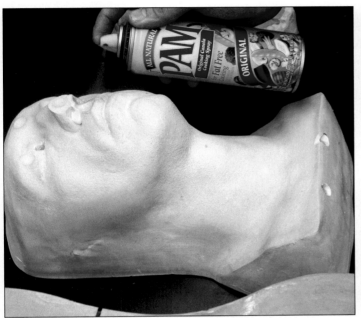

Fig. 11-27

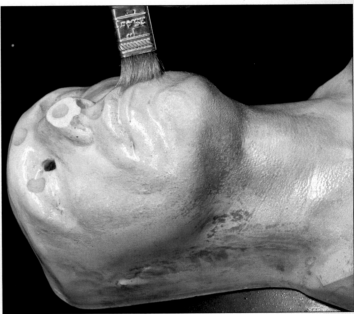

Fig. 11-28

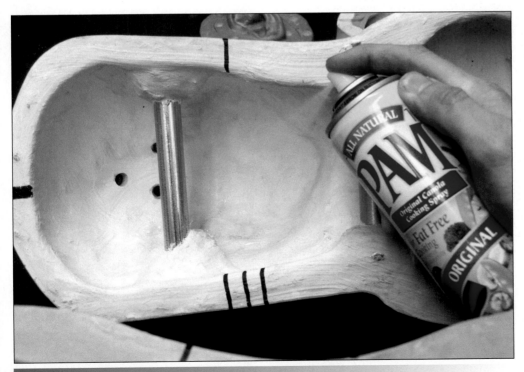

Fig. 11-29

3. Before prepping all the negative molds, trim down the top part of the negative indented keys (not the surface keys) with a mold knife or sandpaper. This step enables the positive and negative molds to fit together more tightly.

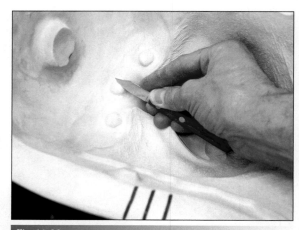

Fig. 11-30

4. Heavily spray the negative face mold with PAM Vegetable Spray separator or Epoxy Parfilm, and lightly scrub into the mold with a 1″ disposable brush. Let the separator soak in for at least 30 minutes before pouring the gelatin pieces.

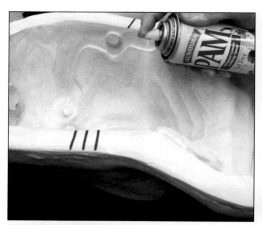

Fig. 11-31

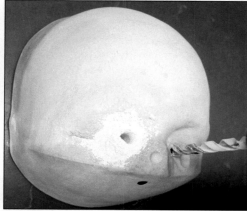

Fig. 11-32

5. Mark areas where release holes will be drilled in the forehead positive with a black Sharpie, and use a portable drill and ¼″ drill bit to drill the holes.

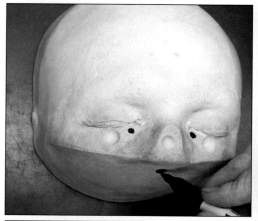

Fig. 11-33

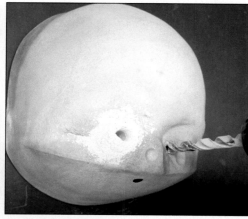

Fig. 11-34

6. Heavily spray the positive forehead mold, front and back, with PAM Vegetable Spray separator, and lightly scrub into the mold with a 1″ disposable brush. Let the separator soak in for at least 30 minutes before pouring the gelatin pieces.

Fig. 11-35

Fig. 11-36

Fig. 11-37

7. Heavily spray the negative forehead mold with Epoxy Parfilm separator, and wipe out the excess with a cloth towel.

Fig. 11-38

8. Heavily spray the positive nose/upper lip mold with PAM Vegetable Spray separator, and lightly scrub into the mold with a 1″ disposable brush. No escape holes are needed for the nose mold positive or negative.

Fig. 11-39

9. Spray the negative nose/upper lip mold with Epoxy Parfilm, and wipe out the excess with a cloth towel.

Fig. 11-40

10. Spray the negative and positive ear molds with Epoxy Parfilm, and wipe out the excess with a cloth towel.

Fig. 11-41

11. This release procedure should be repeated before every gelatin pour. Using Epoxy Parfilm as a release after the Ultracal molds have been pickled with PAM is advised.

MAKING GELATIN APPLIANCES

Materials Needed

- ¾" Soft Nylon Brush
- Pre-mixed Gelatin
- Large Wooden Tongue Depressors
- Epoxy Parfilm
- Six 25# Weights
- Furniture Clamps
- Baby Powder
- Microwave-safe Container
- Powder Puff
- Microwave

- Scissors
- Assorted Wooden Boards
- Leather Gloves
- Flat-head Screwdriver

Be very careful with hot gelatin, for it may cause severe skin burns. Gloves should be worn until the user is familiar with the gelatin procedure.

Preparation

1. Cut 10 to 15 cubed gelatin pieces in half, and place them into a microwave-safe container.

Fig. 11-42

2. Heat the gelatin cubes in a microwave oven for one-minute intervals until completely melted. DO NOT let the gelatin boil; the mixture will weaken and become discolored.

Fig. 11-43

3. Keep the 25# weights nearby. Lay them on top of the molds once the gelatin has been poured and the positive has been pressed into the negative.

Fig. 11-44

Pouring the Gelatin Face Appliance

The following process should be completed in less than 90 seconds in order to assure thin edges on the gelatin appliances. To acquire a good piece, two or three attempts at pouring a large appliance mold may be required. Heating the positive and negative molds to 100°F in a convection oven may be necessary to achieve a good cutting edge.

1. Carefully pour the hot gelatin into the negative side of the face mold from one side of the face around to the other side. Pouring the gelatin at least 5 to 6 inches from the mold will ensure that no unnecessary bubbles are trapped in the piece.

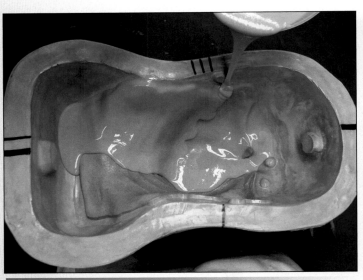

Fig. 11-45

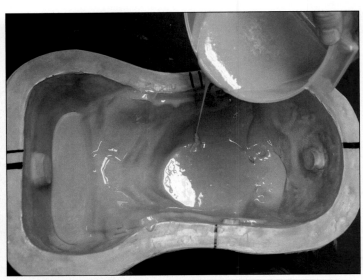

Fig. 11-46

2. Hold the mold, and tilt it to move around the gelatin material. Be very careful not to spill any of the hot gelatin onto the skin.

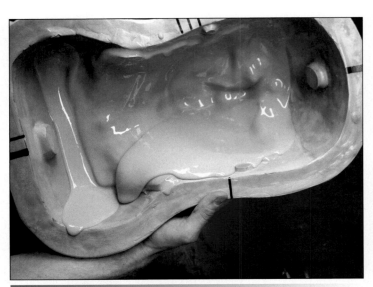

Fig. 11-47

3. Place the positive mold into the negative, and press lightly. Place two or three 25# weights onto the mold. Let the mold cool at least 45 minutes or until the gelatin is cool to the touch.

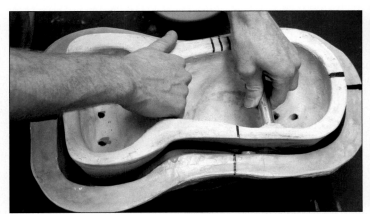

Fig. 11-48

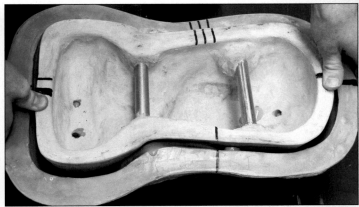

Fig. 11-49

Fig. 11-50

4. Remove the weights from the mold, and pull up the excess gelatin in the back of the positive, cutting it with scissors. This excess gelatin can be set into the cooled gelatin container to be reheated and reused at a later time.

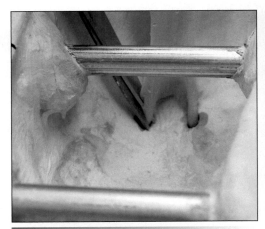

Fig. 11-51

Fig. 11-52

5. Place $1'' \times 2'' \times 8''$ boards on each side of the negative and two $1'' \times 2'' \times 14''$ boards across to connect them over the positive mold handles. Attach a furniture clamp to both of the handles and boards, and slowly tighten the clamp, which will lift the positive out of the negative mold. Remove the boards and clamps, and work a large tongue depressor in between the positive and negative molds to loosen the gelatin appliance from the positive mold.

Fig. 11-53

Fig. 11-54

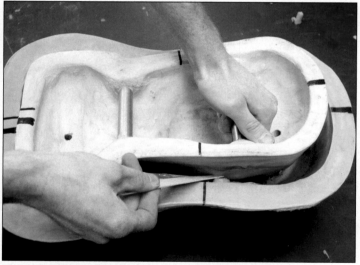

Fig. 11-55

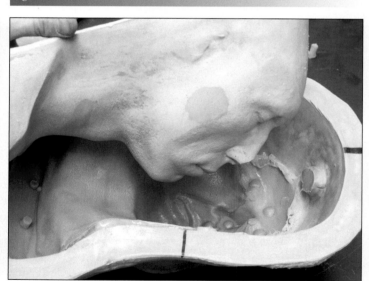

Fig. 11-56

6. Cut the excess gelatin flashing off of the appliance with scissors.

Fig. 11-57

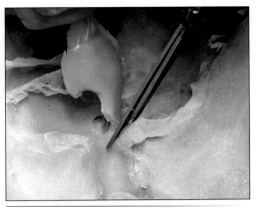

Fig. 11-58

7. Powder heavily with baby powder, as the appliance is carefully removed from the negative mold.

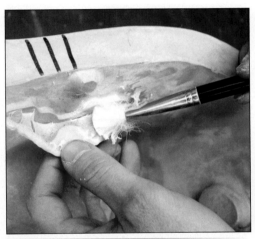

Fig. 11-59

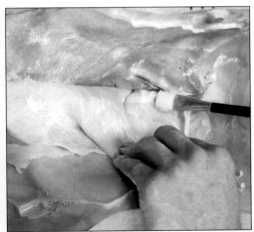

Fig. 11-60

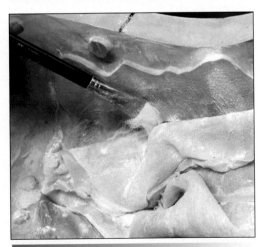

Fig. 11-61

8. Place the appliance onto the positive so the piece will not distort.

Fig. 11-62

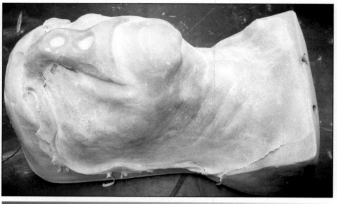

Fig. 11-63

Pouring Gelatin Forehead Appliances

1. Carefully pour the hot gelatin into the negative side of the forehead mold from one side of the forehead around to the other side. Pouring the gelatin at least 5 to 6 inches from the mold will ensure that no unnecessary bubbles are trapped in the piece.

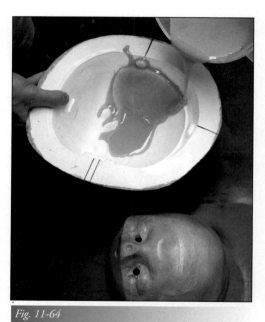

Fig. 11-64

2. Hold the mold, and tilt it to move around the gelatin material. Be very careful not to spill any of the hot gelatin onto the skin.

Fig. 11-65

3. Place the positive mold into the negative mold, and press lightly.

Fig. 11-66

4. Because the positive mold is made flush with the negative mold, it will be necessary to place a 2″ × 4″ × 6″ board (cut to fit) only onto the positive mold area. Place two or three 25# weights onto the board, while pressing only the positive mold into the negative. Let the mold cool at least 45 minutes or until the gelatin is cool to the touch.

Fig. 11-67

Fig. 11-68

5. Remove the weights and the board from the mold, and pull up the excess gelatin in the back of the positive mold, cutting it with scissors. Remember that this excess gelatin can be set into the cooled gelatin container to be reheated and reused at a later time.

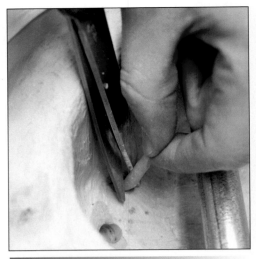

Fig. 11-69

6. Place 1″ × 2″ boards (cut 7″ long) on each side of the negative and one board (12″ long) across to connect them over the positive mold handle. Attach a furniture clamp to both the handle and the board, and slowly tighten the clamp, which will lift the positive mold out of the negative. Pull the positive mold up out of the negative slowly, while carefully loosening the gelatin appliance from the negative with a large tongue depressor.

Fig. 11-70

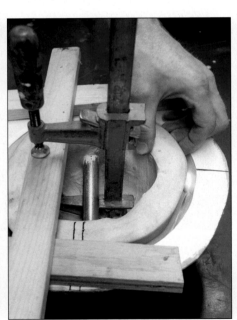

Fig. 11-71

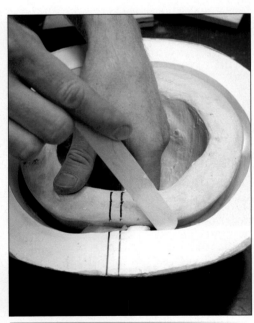

Fig. 11-72

7. Powder the appliance heavily with baby powder on both the front and back. The appliance may be left on the positive to prevent distortion of the piece.

Fig. 11-73

Pouring Gelatin Nose Appliances

1. Carefully pour the hot gelatin into the negative side of the nose mold. Pouring the gelatin at least 5 to 6 inches from the mold will ensure that no unnecessary bubbles are trapped in the piece.

Fig. 11-74

2. Hold the mold, and tilt it to move around the gelatin material. Be very careful not to spill any of the hot gelatin onto the skin.

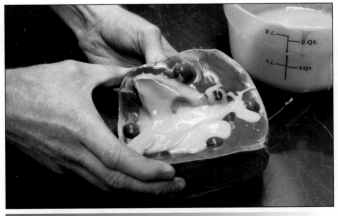

Fig. 11-75

3. Place the positive mold into the negative, and press lightly.

Fig. 11-76

4. Immediately set two 25# weights onto the positive mold. Let the mold cool at least 30 minutes or until the gelatin is cool to the touch.

Fig. 11-77

5. Remove the weights from the mold. Gently pry the positive from the negative with a flat-head screwdriver.

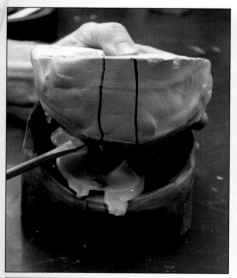

Fig. 11-78

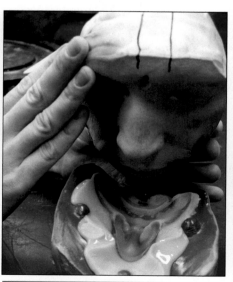

Fig. 11-79

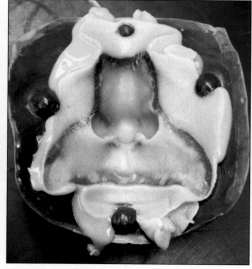

Fig. 11-80

6. Powder heavily with baby powder using a brush or a powder puff, and carefully remove the piece from the mold. Place the appliance onto the positive to prevent distortion of the piece.

Fig. 11-81

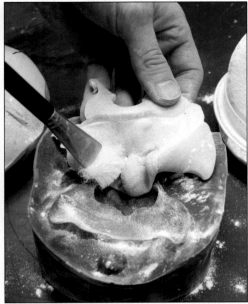

Fig. 11-82

Fig. 11-83

7. The edges on all of the gelatin appliances should appear as if they have small holes or have completely through the cutting edges of the appliance.

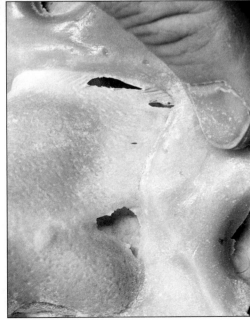

Fig. 11-84

Pouring Gelatin Ear Appliances

1. Carefully pour the hot gelatin into the negative side of the ear mold. Pour the gelatin at least 5 to 6 inches from the mold, and start at the top of the ear, tilting the mold downward to let the gelatin gradually run into the earlobe area.

Fig. 11-85

2. Place the positive mold into the negative, and press lightly.

Fig. 11-86

3. Immediately set two 25# weights onto the positive mold. Let the mold cool at least 30 minutes or until the gelatin is cool to the touch.

Fig. 11-87

4. Remove the weights from the mold, and gently pry the positive from the negative with a flat-head screwdriver.

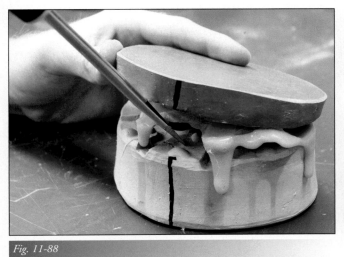

Fig. 11-88

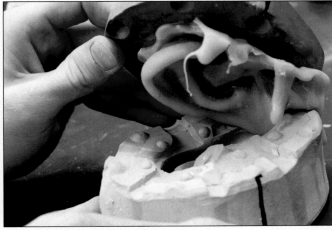

Fig. 11-89

5. Use a brush to powder the appliance heavily with baby powder. Place the appliance onto the positive to prevent distortion of the piece.

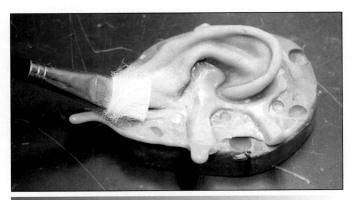

Fig. 11-90

Patching Holes in a Gelatin Appliance

When a bubble is apparent in a gelatin appliance, it is possible to patch the piece instead of running a new one.

1. Clean the area with acetone before patching-

Fig. 11-91

2. Heat a small
amount of gelatin
in a microwaveable
cup, and use a metal
tool to apply the
material to the area.

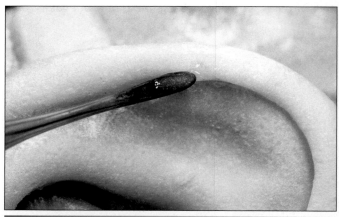

Fig. 11-92

3. After dipping the
finger into cool
water, the warm
gelatin may be
contoured to the
area of the appli-
ance. This step must
be done before the
gelatin cools.

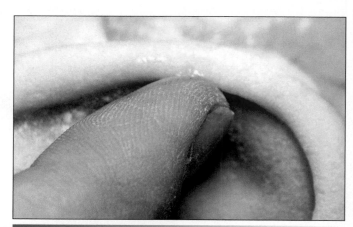

Fig. 11-93

4. Powder immediately
with a brush or
powder puff and
baby powder.

Fig. 11-94

5. On larger pieces and internal voids, open the void with a metal tool.

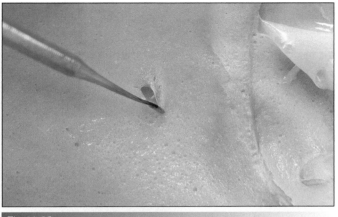

Fig. 11-95

6. Heat a small amount of gelatin in a microwaveable cup, and use a metal tool to apply the material to the area.

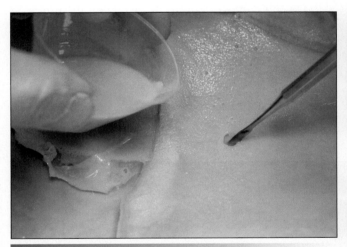

Fig. 11-96

Fig. 11-97

7. Powder immediately with a powder puff and baby powder.

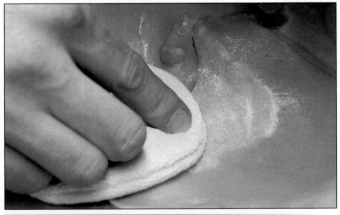

Fig. 11-98

8. For storage of the appliances, a Vacuform duplicate of the subject's face made from a plaster casting may be used.

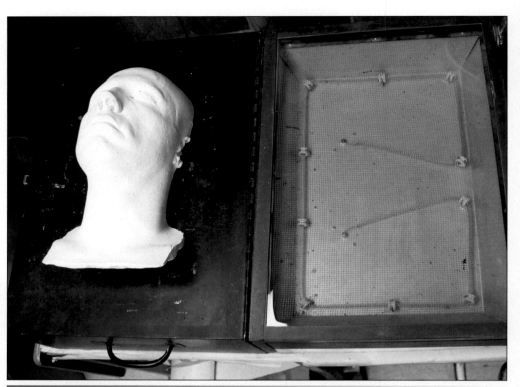

Fig. 11-99

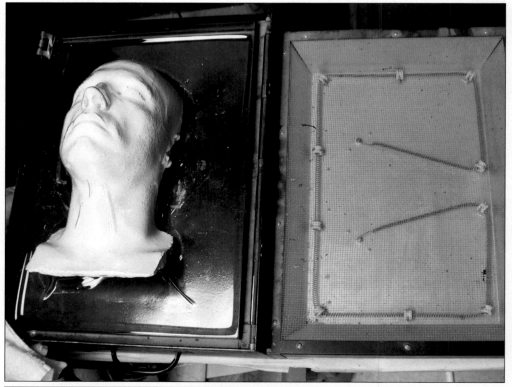

Fig. 11-100

Fig. 11-101

GELATIN PROSTHESIS APPLICATION

Materials Needed

The make-up station, with many materials from left to right:

- 9 Joe Blasco P.M. Colors (left foreground)
- Squeeze Bottles of Witch Hazel
- Acetone
- 99-percent Alcohol
- Skin-toning Liquid (which contains an antiperspirant, aluminum chloro-hydroxide)
- A Tin of No-Color Powder (foreground)
- Receptacles for Brushes and Adhesives
- Tote Bags (containing various brushes, scissors, combs, marking pencils, and metal dental spatulas, both flat and curved)
- Canister of Pointed Cotton-tipped Applicators
- Alcohol/Gafquat Solution, 2:1 (734)
- Jar of W.M. Creations Old Age Stipple B (which must be kept tightly sealed to prevent solvent evaporation)
- Squeeze Container of W.M. Creations Sealer A (typical XYXG sealer, which is excellent for creating film over various areas prior to color make-up application)
- Various Metal Containers (holding cut wedges of micro-porous, foam latex sponges, and various smaller cut sponges, which have had their ends torn to provide texture)
- Telesis Beta Bond B (modified acrylic adhesive used for the actual application of the gelatin prosthesis to the skin)

- Telesis Beta Bond Solve (an acrylic adhesive remover used only at the completion of the workday)

- JB Ozo-Kleen Brush Cleaner (featuring no isopropyl myristate or other ingredients that would leave residue on the surface of the brush and create undue problems to the gelatin formula)

- Palette of RCMA A.F. (Appliance Foundations)

- Palette of W.M. Creations Stacolor #3 (contains skin tones 1-10, including colors for lips: red, blue, yellow, green, purple, white, reddish-pink, pink-6205, black, brown, and green/black/blue [gbb] beard stipple color)

- Small Packet of Extremely Fine-tipped Cotton Applicators

- Exquisitely Handmade Lace-front Full Wig and Eyebrows (carefully pinned to a canvas block prior to use for cleaning and styling after the ventilation process)

- The Nasal and Ear Appliances (laid upon a clean white towel, while the frontal [forehead], zygomatic, and neck appliances are seated securely upon the vacuum-formed head to retain their shape until application)

- Several Powder Puffs

- Hairdryer (variable speeds)

- Several Types of Micro Brush, Super Fine Disposable Applicators (carefully bound together in groups of three to enable the simultaneous use of three applicator tips; these have unique flexibility to the extent that the tips may be manipulated in many different fashions in order to facilitate the application of age spots and other discolorations upon the appliance surface, creating an extremely natural and translucent surface appearance)

- Orange Stipple Sponges (various sizes carefully trimmed with scissors, in addition to some with a hand-ripped surface to provide an irregular area that will facilitate a mottled texture)

Preparation

Begin by removing the nasal prosthesis from the positive plastic form in order to cut the superfluous gelatin revealing the nostril holes. Once that has been completed, the prosthesis is once again placed on the plastic face form; it will thus retain its shape until it is applied to the surface of the subject's face.

The use of lightweight plastic head forms was originally developed by John Chambers for The *Planet of the Apes*, for which many facial appliances needed to be carried to location. Rather than utilize heavy stone face casts made of gypsum, Ultracal, or Hydrocal, Vacuform face forms were made *from* the stone casts, which facilitated a lightweight, fast, and convenient method of transportation.

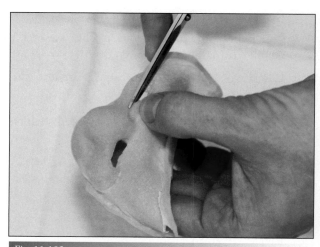

Fig. 11.102

Next, carefully clean the releasing agent (used originally in the fabrication process) from the inside of the gelatin appliances with acetone to provide a surface that will more readily accept the adhesive.

Continue by cleaning the outer surface in the exact same manner. The acetone is applied to a paper tissue and lightly rubbed over the surface of the appliance so as not to disturb its very fragile edge, but yet firmly enough to remove the agent.

During the process, very careful attention must be given to the depth of the wrinkles, and once again, the piece is turned inside out and cleaned even more precisely with a second application of acetone, all the way out to the edges of the appliance. When cleaning the thinnest portions, outward strokes are used to protect them from tearing. The ear appliances are cleaned in exactly the same manner, both inside and out.

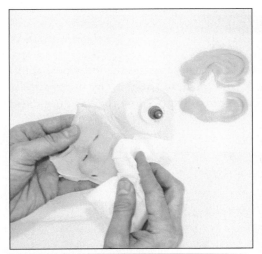

Fig. 11.103

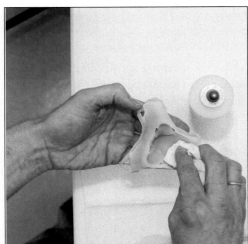

Fig. 11.104

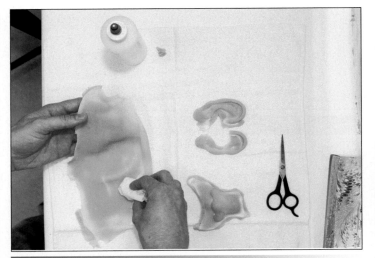

Fig. 11.105

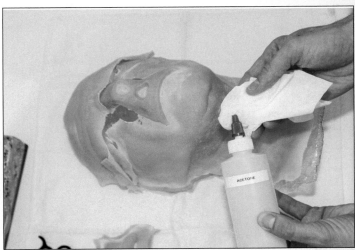

Fig. 11.106

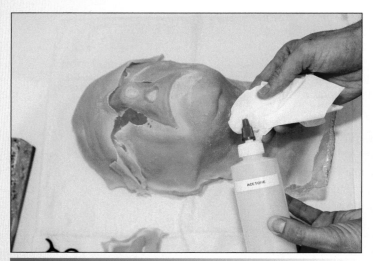

Fig. 11.107

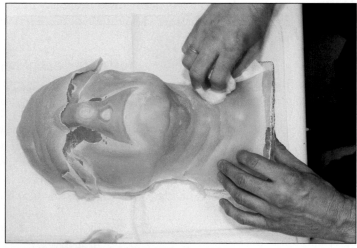

Fig. 11.108

Once the cleaning is complete, Mr. Mungle very carefully separates the individual appliance areas (nasal, zygomatic [cheekbone], neck, and forehead [frontal]) by systematically tearing at the thin edges. Then, the appliances are carefully placed on the Vacuform head form for observation.

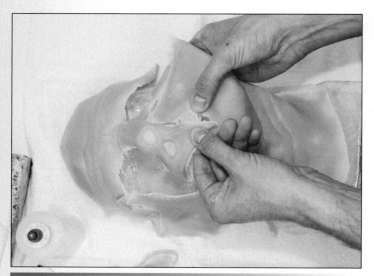

Fig. 11.109

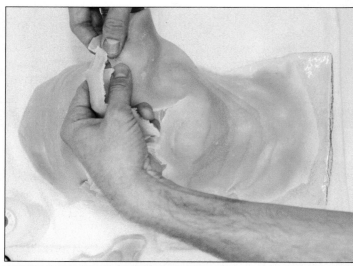

Fig. 11.10

Raise the pieces up to the light individually in order to more carefully examine their translucency and thinness, as it is the thinness of the edges that will produce an absolutely imperceptible blend onto the subject's skin surface.

Upon evaluating the surface of the appliance, Mr. Mungle is satisfied that it is ready for application. In some cases, the gelatin may not quite adapt to the surface of the negative, thereby creating imperfections. Should that be the case, a careful mixing of additional gelatin, which is then hand-applied and carefully sculpted with metal tools to affect a perfect skin surface, can quite easily alleviate the problem. As the gelatin cures, texture can be applied from stipple sponges and pointed brushes. Since the appliance here has passed the scrutiny of the artist, and its surface is deemed camera-ready, the application process begins.

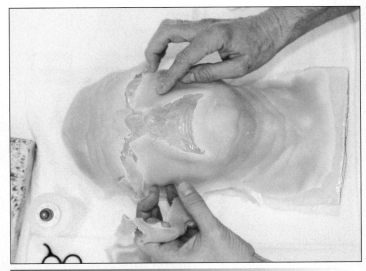
Fig. 11-111

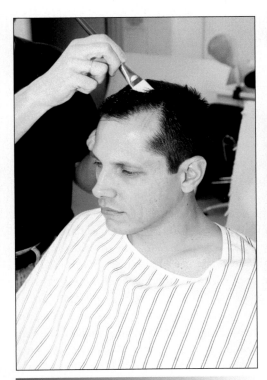
Fig. 11-112

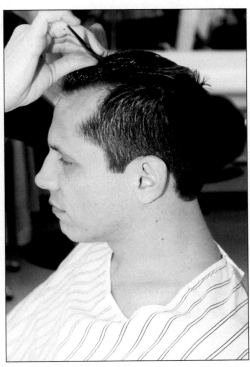
Fig. 11-113

Fig. 11-114

Matthew Mungle and Joe Blasco

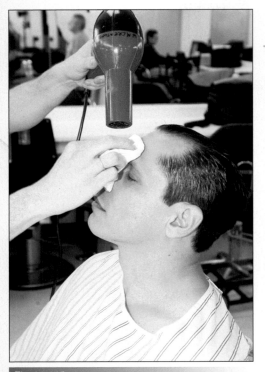

Once the subject is seated and properly covered to protect wardrobe and exposed skin, the Gafquat solution (featuring 99-percent alcohol) is painted into the hair from a disposable plastic container with a large, wide synthetic brush to flatten and prepare it for the application of the forehead appliance, which will cover the hair. Then, the hair is carefully combed into position to provide as flat a surface as possible for the acceptance of the prosthesis. Use a fine-tooth comb, and press the hair down with the hands. The use of a hairdryer will facilitate evaporation. Gafquat can be applied quite liberally with larger brushes and/or the hands if rubber or vinyl gloves are used. The Quat can be worked through the hair down to the scalp. Then the hair should be combed flat and dried simultaneously to avoid bunching that may create bulges beneath the surface of a gelatin appliance. Some artists prefer to use water to thin the Quat; however, alcohol is recommended, for it evaporates more rapidly to provide a suitable work area.

The skin is prepared by cleansing with 99-percent alcohol to remove any surface oil, which may prove to be detrimental to the adhesion process, as well as any Quat, which may have collected along the hairline. Carefully direct the alcohol fumes away from the subject's eyes. (Ask the subject to keep the eyes closed at this point.)

Fig. 11-115

Once the skin has been thoroughly cleaned, apply the astringent solution (which contains the antiperspirant) in order to retard the skin's ability to secrete perspiration that could loosen the adhesion of the appliance.

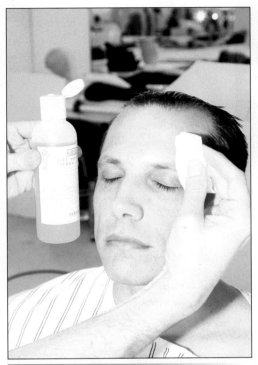

Fig. 11-116

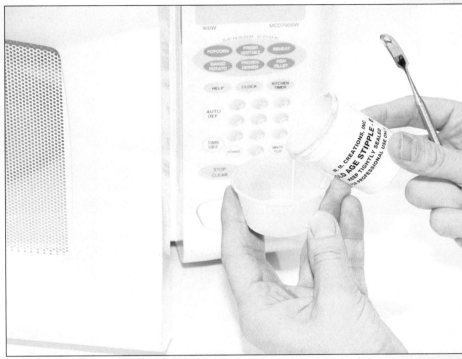

Fig. 11-117

Mr. Mungle pours W.M. Creations Old Age Stipple B into a disposable plastic container, which will then be placed into a microwave for two seconds (and never more than three) in order to heat it in preparation for application. By liquefying the formula, the artist will facilitate the process.

Affixing the Appliance

Begin with the application of stipple to the left upper eyelid using a tiny micro-porous wedge sponge while the skin is held taut. A very thin application is used, as too much stipple will provide an obvious, thick appearance.

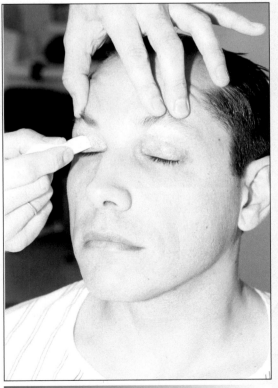

Fig. 11-118

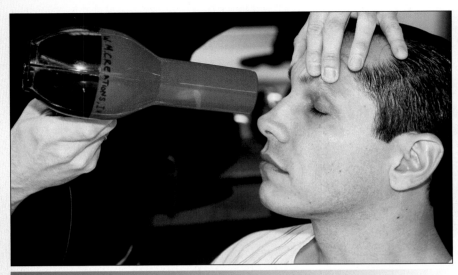

Fig. 11-119

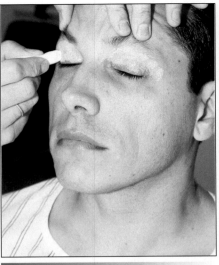

Fig. 11-120

The stipple is dried with a hairdryer on medium power while the skin is still held taut.

Once dry, another application of the stipple is applied within the parameters of the first one. Both lids can be done simultaneously by pulling the eyebrows back as the subject gently closes the eyes. (They should not be clinched tightly.)

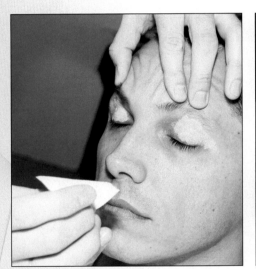

Fig. 11-121

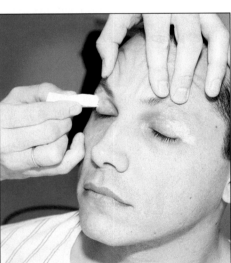

Fig. 11-122

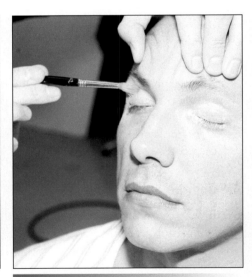

Fig. 11-123

The first two layers can be applied to the outermost edges of the application if desired, but the third layer must not reach the outer edge in order to retain the edge's thinness. The stipple is applied with one edge of the sponge and occasionally blended with the opposite edge in order to soak up any excess.

A fourth and fifth application are then added to the outermost areas of the upper eyelid for the purpose of actually creating weight in those areas that will physically enable the eyelid skin to droop dramatically as gravity exerts its effects.

Once the stipple has dried, No-Color Powder is gently brushed (very thinly) over the latex with a fine brush to prevent the latex from sticking to itself.

Once the powdering process is complete, the eyebrows are relaxed, and the wrinkles appear to form instantaneously. The excess powder is then brushed away. Any telltale whiteness from the powder will be removed throughout the remaining process of color make-up application.

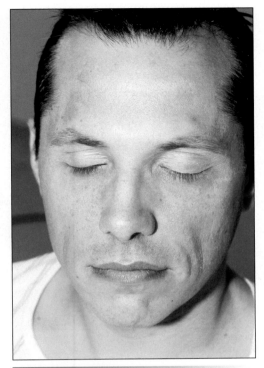

Fig. 11-124

Next, Mr. Mungle holds the nasal appliance to the subject's nose in order to observe the fit.

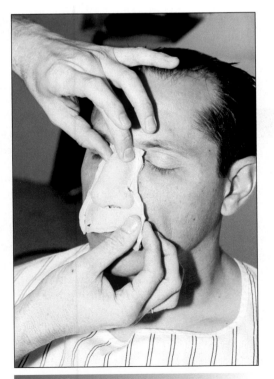

Fig. 11-125

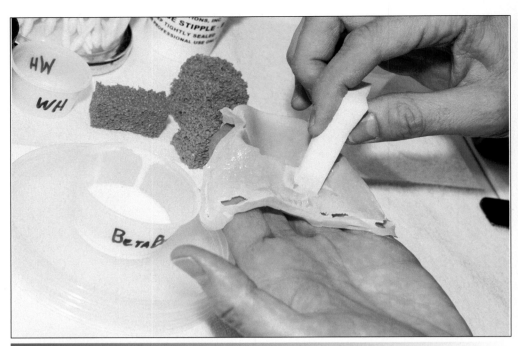

Fig. 11-126

Once satisfied, Beta Bond adhesive is applied to the entire inside of the gelatin appliance, starting from the center. He prefers to keep the flashing in place upon the appliance so that he can apply Beta Bond out to the very thinnest part of the appliance edges. If the flashing has already been removed, then the adhesive is not applied to the very edges at this time. (**Note:** Aside from the use of Beta Bond adhesive, full-strength Pros-Aide adhesive can also be used and works in exactly the same manner, as it too is a contact adhesive. Spirit gums are not recommended for this process.)

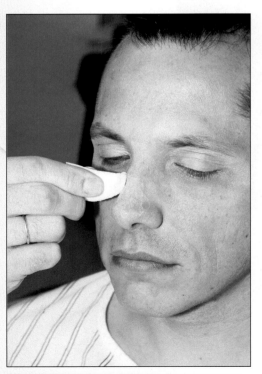

(As observed in the photos depicting the sculpting process, the pieces are floated away in a specific order, and it is that exact order that is used for the application of the finished gelatin appliance.)

While the appliance is held in the hand and the adhesive dries, he then applies the same adhesive to the entire surface of the subject's nose, noting the area where the appliance will fit. The retention of the flashing will enable the artist to hold, stretch (if necessary), and position the appliance so that its edge is perfectly placed upon the adhesive, which has just been applied to the surface of the subject's skin. (**Note:** The Beta Bond application runs slightly beyond the area where the intended edge of the piece will be adhered. Bear in mind that Beta Bond is a contact cement.)

Fig. 11-127

Once both surfaces (nose and appliance) are dry, while holding the edges away from the surface of the skin, press the tip of the appliance and the area beneath the aquiline bridge into position against the skin, before then carefully attaching areas around the nostrils. This is done through close observation and slight stretching of the piece; while pulling on the flashing, press down on the very thin edges.

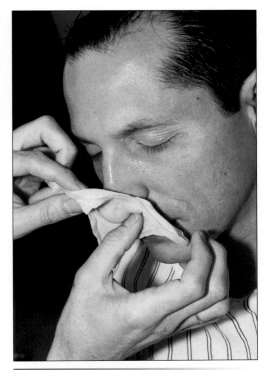

Fig. 11-128

Mr. Mungle then uses his fingers to feel around the entire edge of the piece and further press it into position, while being certain that no bubbles (nor excess stretching) will create an unusual appearance or distortion of any kind.

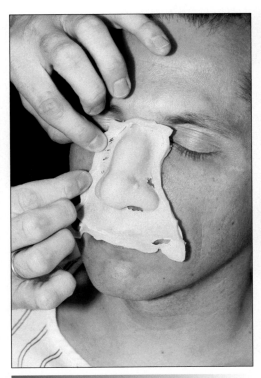

Fig. 11-129

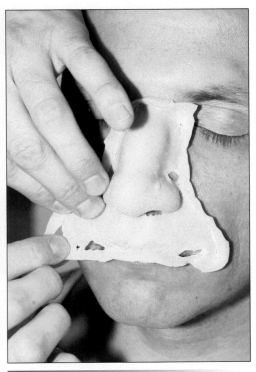

Fig. 11-130

Once the piece is firmly in place, areas that require more adhesion can be remedied through the use of Beta Bond from a tightly spun, cotton-tipped applicator of appropriate size. The flashing is kept intact throughout the entire process while the appliance (especially the edges) is continuously and effectively adhered.

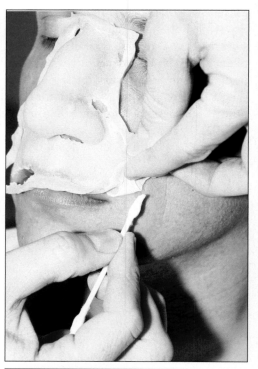

Fig. 11-131

To blend the edges, apply witch hazel with a cotton swab directly between the thinnest area and the flashing. The swab can be rolled outward towards the flashing, and as the gelatin is melted into position by the witch hazel, the flashing is gently pulled away.

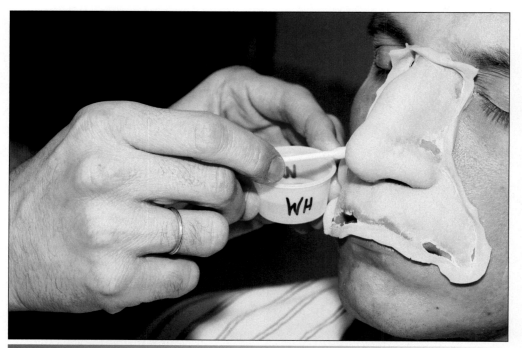

Fig. 11-132

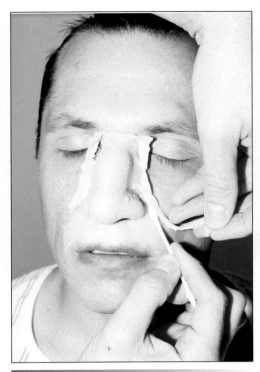

Fig. 11-133

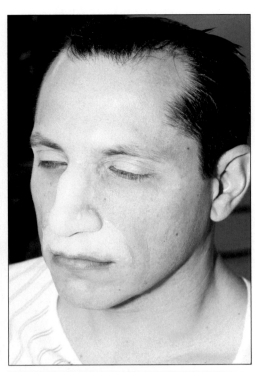

Fig. 11-134

This process is done around the entire appliance until the edges have been dissolved and the flashing removed. Swabs should be changed several times during this process, as they may accumulate material buildup, which will create adverse effects. The flashing is never pulled, but is simply allowed to fall away as the gelatin dissolves. Do not over-saturate the swabs, as too much dissolving may result. During this process, the opposite, dry end of the swab can be used to further press the appliance more tightly against the skin's surface.

Once the appliance is in position and setting, the large, one-piece combination zygomatic and neck appliance is laid flat with the inside surface forward. Apply Beta Bond to the area surrounding the subject's chin with a disposable, foam latex, micro-porous sponge. The Beta Bond is not applied out to the appliance edge.

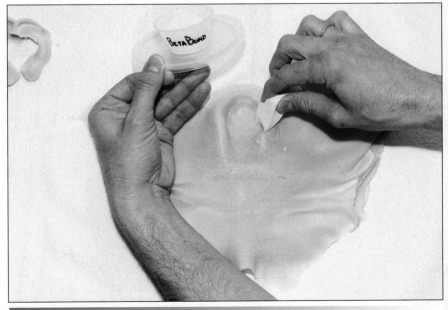

Fig. 11-135

Then, similarly, Beta Bond is applied to the subject's actual chin area, completely covering the chin, as well as out to the sides of the jaw and beneath the jaw upon the soft tissue of the neck.

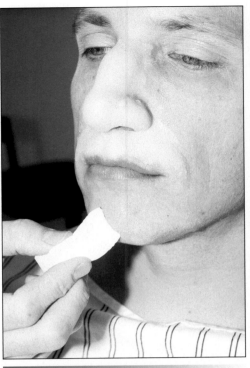

Fig. 11-136

Both the appliance and skin surface are dried to create a contact surface for application of the piece. Use the hairdryer on a tepid temperature setting to dry the application. (The hairdryer should be the type with a key that can be depressed to cool the air stream.)

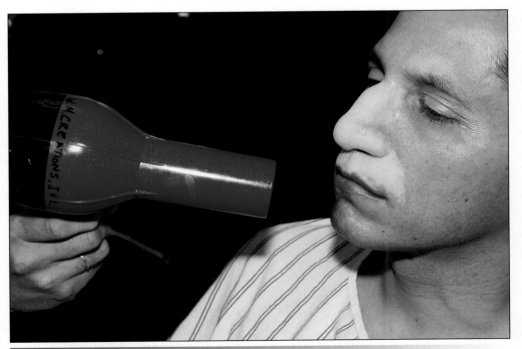

Fig. 11-137

Once both Beta Bond surfaces have dried, carefully position the piece over the chin, and delicately press it into position. An assistant or the subject may then hold both sides of the appliance while the artist continues to press the piece and further set the contact between both surfaces of Beta Bond.

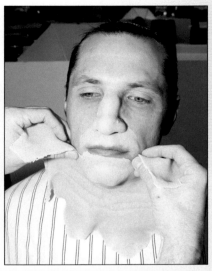

Fig. 11.139

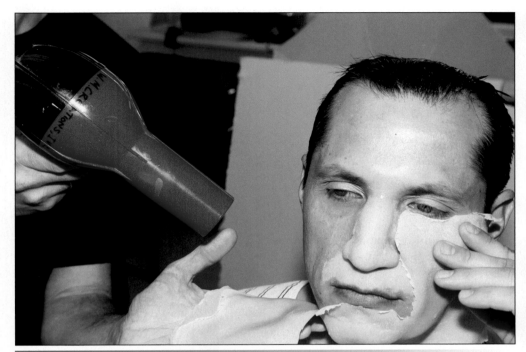

Fig. 11-138

Then the jaw line section is adhered following exactly the same procedure above. Use a hairdryer again to dry both surfaces (skin and appliance). Carefully lift the appliance, and press it (with very minimal stretching) into position against the face.

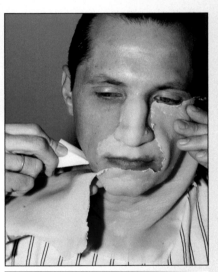

Fig. 11-140

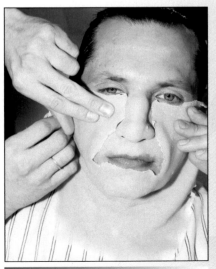

Fig. 11-141

Once the jaw section is adhered, follow with the entire cheek and under-eye areas.

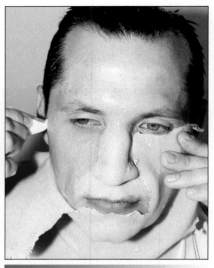

Fig. 11-142

Apply Beta Bond very carefully under the eye, as close to the lashes as possible without reaching them, and somewhat beyond the actual edges of the appliance.

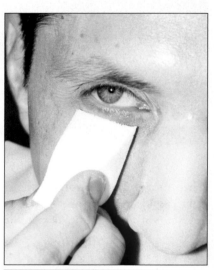

Fig. 11-143

Both skin and appliance are dried carefully before attachment.

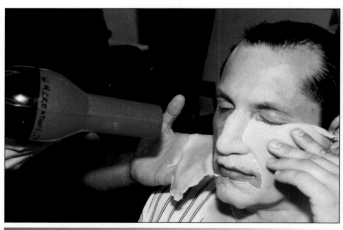

Fig. 11-144

Particular attention must be paid to the adhesion of the appliance immediately under the lower eyelash area, as this area has a tendency to show telltale signs of artificiality in extreme close-up. The artist may use a small, pointed, finely packed, cotton-tipped applicator saturated (but not overly so) in witch hazel to press the piece into position, followed by using the fingertips. The applicator can be gently rotated away from the edge and somewhat pressed against it to facilitate a finer, smoother blend.

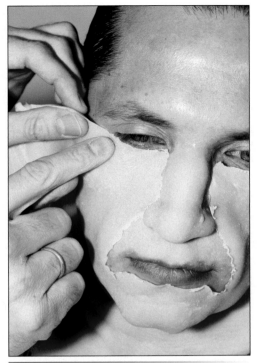

Fig. 11-145

The flashing, as with that of the nasal appliance, is left intact until Mr. Mungle is ready to dissolve the edges and complete the adhesion process. Because Beta Bond will adhere to itself, it is important that the artist not fold the appliance over itself during the application. If unwanted adhesion does occur, it can be counteracted with a swab of 99-percent alcohol, although keep in mind that the overall procedure time will increase.

Fig. 11-146

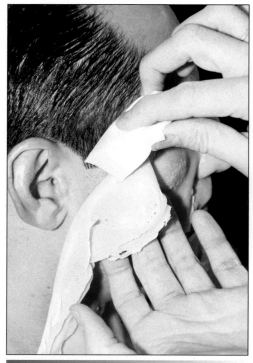

Fig. 11-147

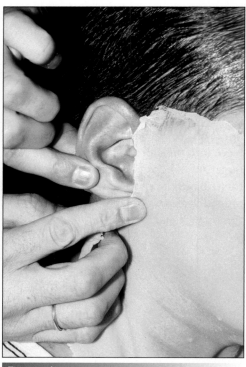

Fig. 11-148

The flashing at the outer zygomatic area is removed, and the edge of the appliance is pressed into the front of the ear and under the lobe as the ear is pulled backward to facilitate a blend directly into the actual ear opening, making the edge of the appliance absolutely imperceptible.

The exact same process is done to apply the opposite side.

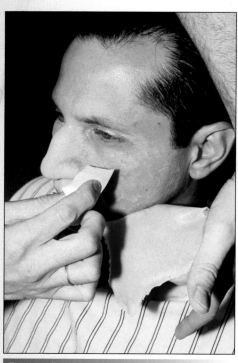

Fig. 11-149

Fig. 11-150

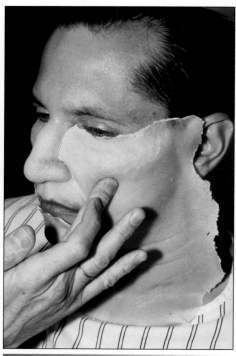

Fig. 11-151

Unlike other types of materials, gelatin lends itself quite effectively to stretching and seamless blending. The body heat throughout the wearing of the appliance will also assist in softening the appliance, so that it actually becomes more a part of the subject's actual surface anatomy as the day progresses.

Next, begin above the chin area, and apply additional Beta Bond to the underside of the appliance edge and the skin for the purpose of completing the edge application around the entire prosthetic appliance. The hairdryer should be used each time Beta Bond is applied to the skin surface and the underlying surface of the appliance throughout this process. The appliance should not be pressed against the skin until both adhesive surfaces have thoroughly dried.

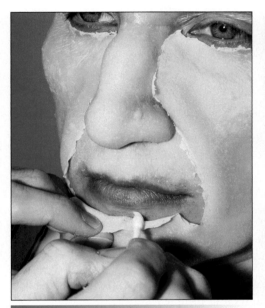

Fig. 11-152

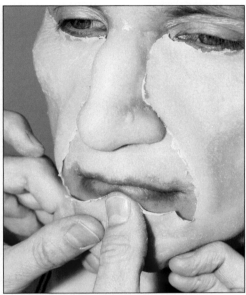

Fig. 11-153

Fig. 11-154

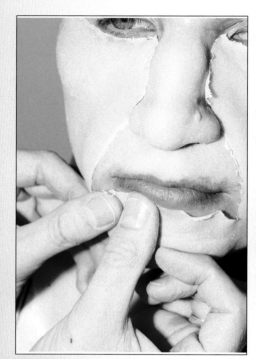

Fig. 11-155

Fig. 11-156

Fig. 11-157

Throughout the process, it is important to remember that the fingers should be periodically cleaned of material using 99-percent alcohol so that they do not inadvertently stick to the surface of any materials, tools, and/or appliances.

As the blending of the edges beneath the eyes and at the temples is in progress, the sides, bottom, and center of the neck appliance still require complete adhesion.

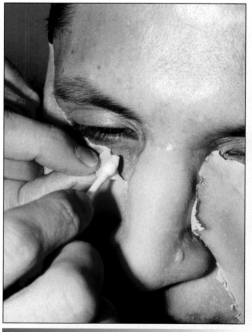

Fig. 11-158

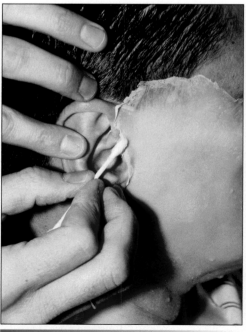

Fig. 11-159

The bottom portion of the appliance will be adhered later in the process after the remainder has been affixed to both ears and the forehead piece has been attached. This particular order of operation is due to the fact that the subject's body heat will somewhat soften the neck appliance and render it more adaptable for application to the neck, which is a much more mobile area. The softening will enable a more natural result.

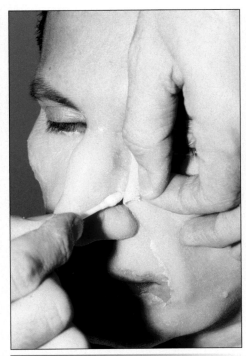

Fig. 11-160

Fig. 11-161

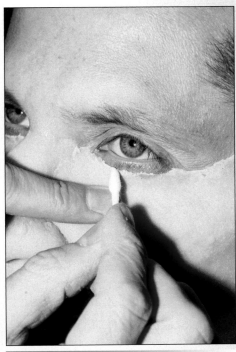

Fig. 11-162

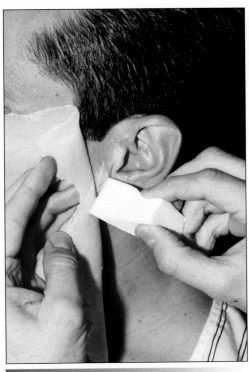

Fig. 11-163

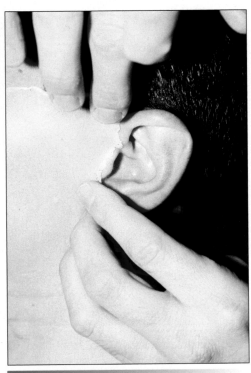

Fig. 11-164

Once all of the edges have been adhered flatly to the skin's surface, they are washed away with witch hazel. Occasionally, during the blending process, small particles of the detaching gelatin will need to be more vigorously manipulated for removal.

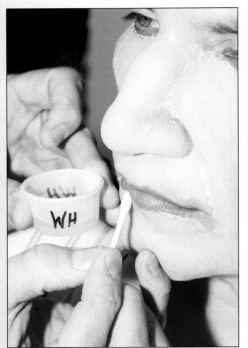

Fig. 11-165

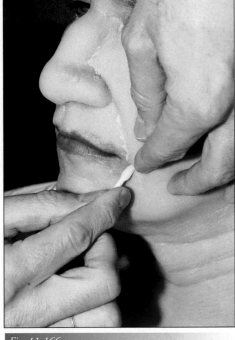

Fig. 11-166

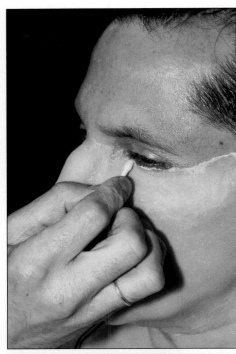

Fig. 11-167

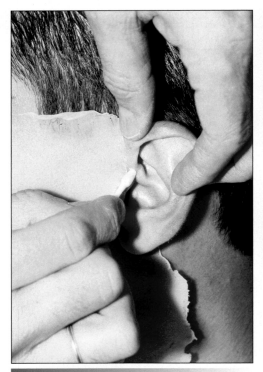

Fig. 11-168

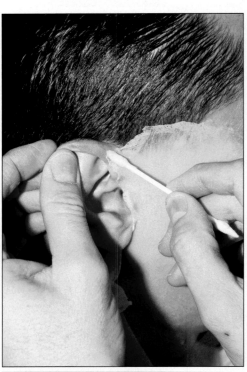

Fig. 11-169

With the neck still unattached, the forehead appliance is now prepared for application exactly as the others were. Paint adhesive in the center of the forehead piece and slightly out toward its edges.

The skin is then prepared as well, and the appliance is placed from its center against the subject's forehead once both surfaces have been properly dried. (Both the appliance and the forehead can be dried at the same time by holding the appliance near the subject's head as the hairdryer is passed back and forth across the subject's actual forehead and the interior of the appliance surface.) Flatten the eyebrows with a light application of Beta Bond, creating a surface that will accept the appliance without creating a bulge.

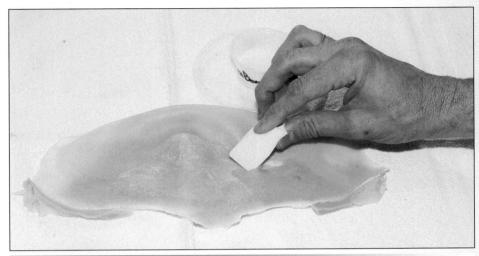
Fig. 11-170

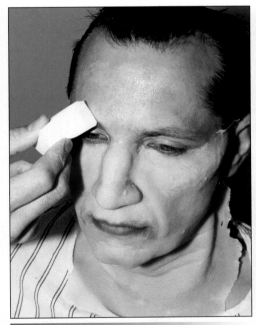
Fig. 11-171

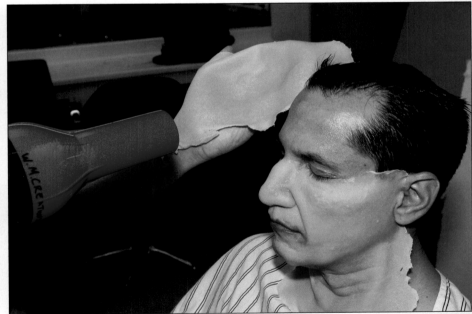
Fig. 11-172

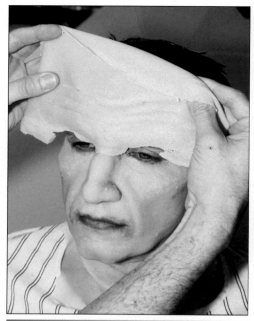

Fig. 11-173

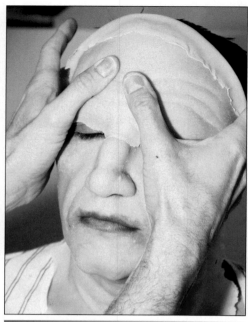

Fig. 11-174

The appliance's top edge can be folded forward, and by using a firm touch with the fingers and/or thumbs, the center, where the adhesive has been applied, is pressed snugly against the skin.

The underside edge, which attaches to the top of the nasal bone, is then lifted. Beta Bond is applied again to both surfaces and dried before the appliance is pressed firmly into place and dropped down above the nose. The edges of the appliance will perfectly blend into the already applied gelatin nasal piece.

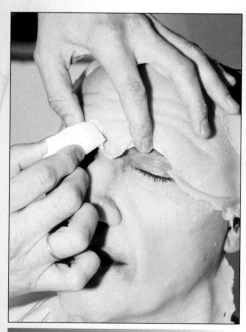

Fig. 11-175

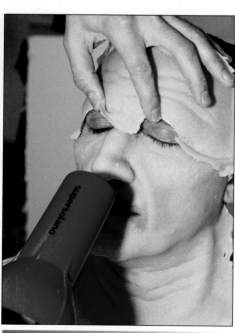

Fig. 11-176

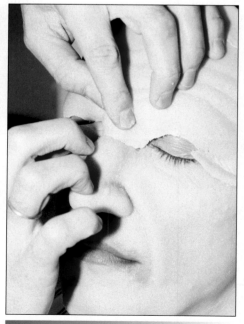

Fig. 11-177

Use a smaller wedge sponge to carefully run Beta Bond adhesive across the underside of the forehead's lower edge, which will adhere to the area directly below the subject's eyebrow.

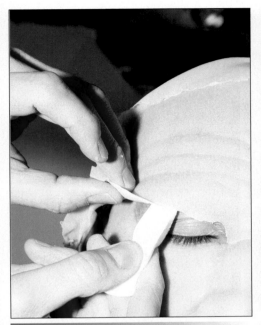

Fig. 11-178

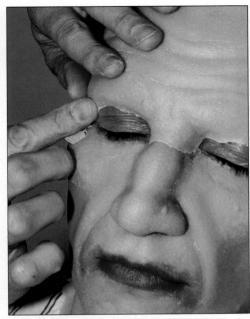

Fig. 11-179

The very same process is used to adhere the other side of the lower edge of the forehead appliance. It is important to remember that the appliance edges, which will be affixed to the inner corners of the eyes (on the sides of the nose between the eyes), must be firmly pressed against the previously applied gelatin nasal appliance.

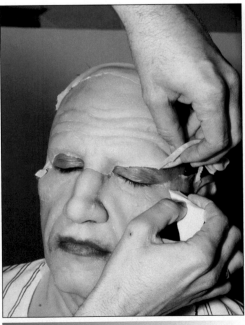

Fig. 11-180

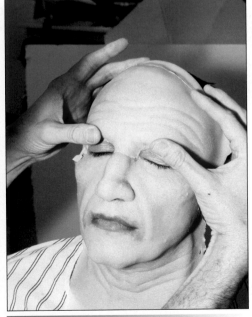

Fig. 11-181

Once the entire underside of the forehead has been adhered, the temporal area is then applied using the exact same process. The flashing is not removed until the edge is ready to be dissolved. At this point, the subject may be asked to raise the eyebrows in order for the artist to determine if any areas of the appliance have not been properly seated with adhesive.

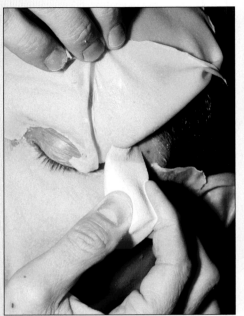

Fig. 11-182

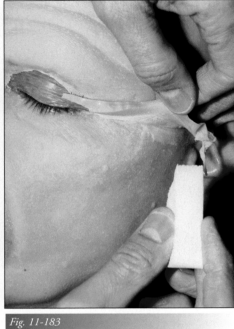

Fig. 11-183

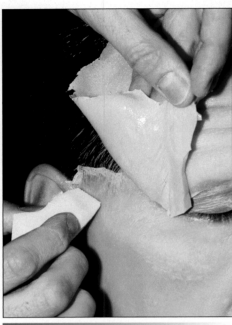

Fig. 11-184

Once both temples have been firmly secured, the process of removing the flashing and blending the temporal edges of the frontal appliance will be accomplished; however, prior to that process, the top edge of the frontal appliance is adhered by stretching it back onto the hair and pressing it firmly into position. (For ease of removal, there is an exception concerning Beta Bond adhesive; it is only applied to the underside of the appliance and not to the surface of the hair.)

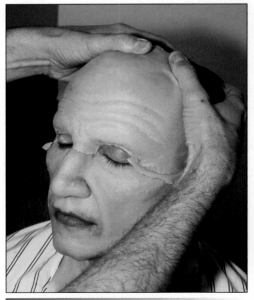

Fig. 11-186

All edges are then dissolved with witch hazel from cotton-tipped applicators as the flashing is delicately removed. It is important not to rip away the flashing, as the actual gelatin appliance may be torn in the process.

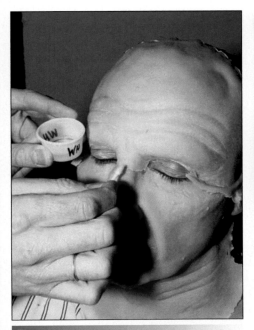

Fig. 11-187

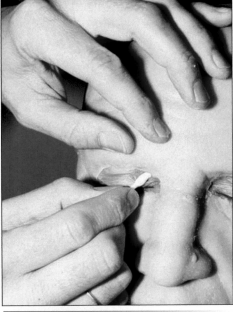

Fig. 11-188

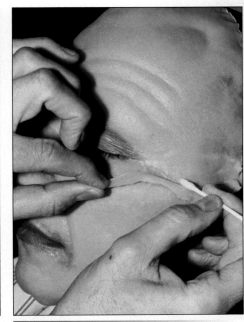

Fig. 11-189

To apply the neck section, hold the subject's head back while painting adhesive to the center of the neck, over the larynx, well down onto the breastplate, and onto the very center of the appliance, which will match up with the application on the skin.

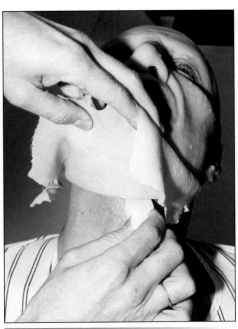

Fig. 11-190

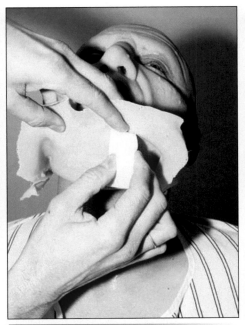

Fig. 11-191

Fig. 11-192

The head is held back during the application of the adhesive but is brought to an absolutely level position when the appliance is affixed. In fact, the subject should be required to sit up straight so that the vertebrae are perfectly in line, as most of the subject's movements will be made in an erect position.

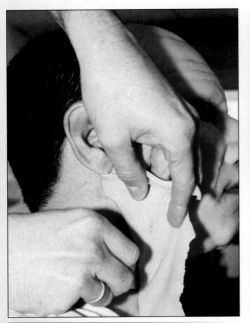

Fig. 11-193

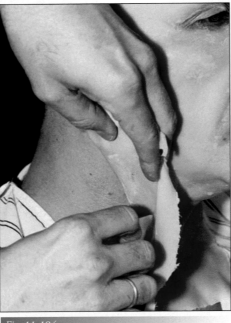

Fig. 11-194

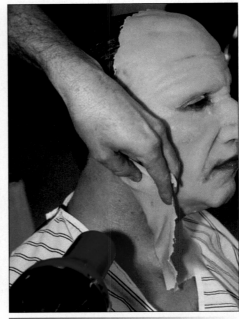

Fig. 11-195

Once the center of the appliance has been adhered, follow suit with both sides. Prior to seating the sides of the neck into position, the subject should slightly tilt the head to the side being applied; once the piece has been applied and the head returned to an erect position, the appliance will therefore become tighter and more snugly attached. The same is done for the opposite side with constant pressing to secure the underside of the appliance.

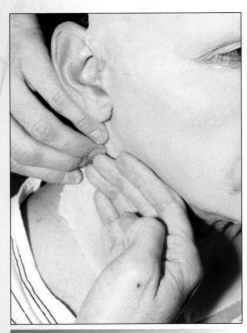

Fig. 11-196

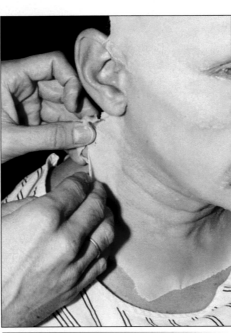

Fig. 11-197

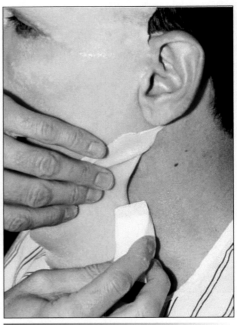

Fig. 11-198

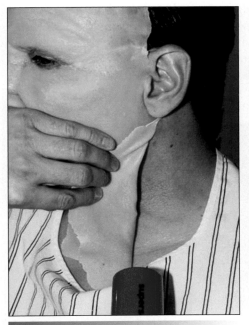

Fig. 11-199

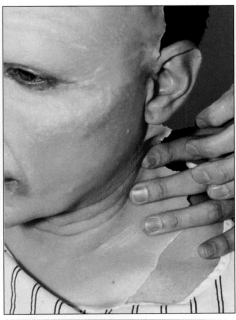

Fig. 11-200

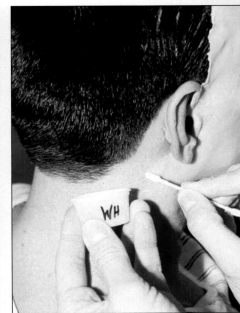

Fig. 11-201

Next, attach the ear appliances. Beta Bond is first painted within the inner surface of the ear appliances and then subsequently to the surface of the subject's actual ears. Once both surfaces are dry, the appliance is pressed into position, and its contours will readily adapt to the actual contour of the real ear.

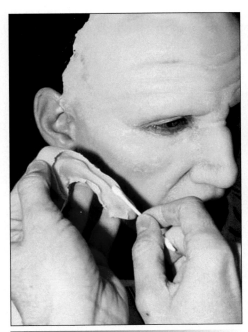

Fig. 11-202

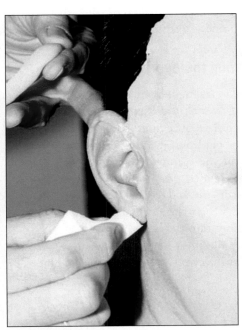

Fig. 11-203

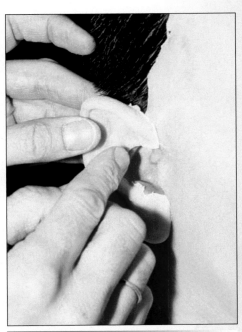

Fig. 11-204

This same process is done to both ears. The edges are also blended well with witch hazel and covered again with additional Beta Bond as a top coat. The ears are more effectively attached by beginning at the lobe and proceeding up the outer edge of the ear until the entire appliance has been adhered. Pressure must be applied within the crevices and cavities to be certain that the depressions of the ear appliance conform perfectly to the depressions of the real ear.

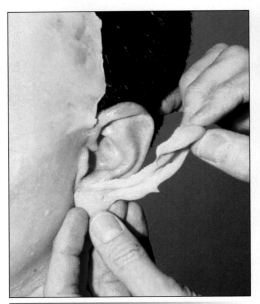

Fig. 11-205

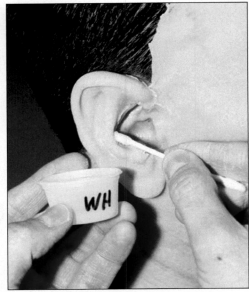

Fig. 11-206

Not until Mr. Mungle is satisfied that every edge has been perfectly blended will he begin the process of sealing the appliance (which takes place prior to coloring).

Sealing the Appliance

Prior to sealing the overall appliance, paint over all the edges and actual skin surface once more using a swab with Beta Bond, helping to further extend the blend of the appliance edge—which passes unseen to the human eye and consequently the critical eye of the camera—imperceptibly into the actual skin. (Beta Bond does not have to be painted under the eyes.)

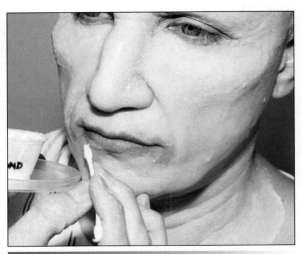

Fig. 11-207

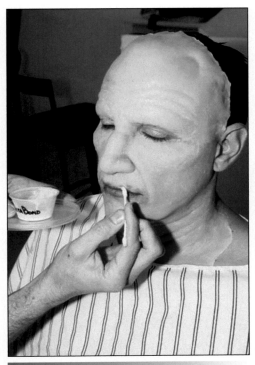

Fig. 11-208

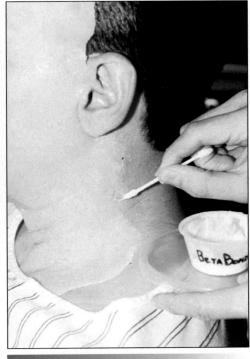

Fig. 11-209

In addition to creating an effective blend for the edges of each appliance, the Beta Bond will also create a much stronger adhesion to the sealer, which is next applied to the entire surface of the appliance. In effect, the sealer will create a second skin that is smooth and continuous, which will provide an even more accurate anatomical rendition of living tissue.

A top coat of acrylic XYXG-type adhesive known as Sealer A and manufactured by W.M. Creations will be applied. It contains a high percentage of the XYXG component, which creates a very substantial, yet flexible surface coat upon which the additional make-up colors will be painted. The sealer must be applied rapidly; otherwise, it has a tendency to string. It is recommended to apply the sealer first over all edges prior to continuing on the entire piece.

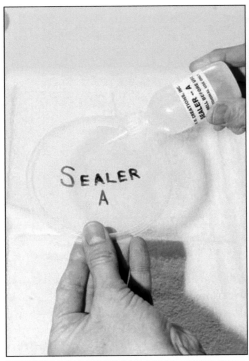

Fig. 11-210

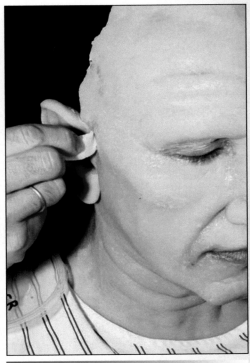

Fig. 11-211

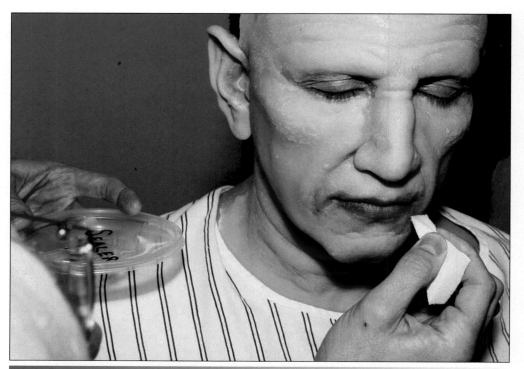

Fig. 11-212

Fig. 11-213

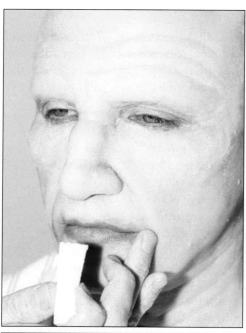

Fig. 11-214

The use of a sealer top coat enables the artist to have a number of choices of color make-up formulations, as even a make-up which is manufactured with mineral oil, in addition to the conventional Joe Blasco P.M. (Prosthetic Make-up) or RCMA A.F. (Appliance Foundation) products, can be applied to the surface. The gelatin will also accept Stacolors and tattoo ink types of color pigment products.

The sealer application can be refined by lightly pressing an index finger to areas of dried sealer to determine if any tackiness remains, which is undesirable. This also will facilitate the depression of any areas of adhesive that may have become somewhat bubbled.

Once the sealer has been applied over all of the appliance's outermost edges, as well as between the edges of each piece (where they connect), it is then applied over the entire surface. However, it is Matthew Mungle's personal preference that the sealer not be applied over the entire appliance (unless it is very small).

Color Application

The first application of color to the gelatin will feature Stacolor Pink-6205, which is somewhat spotted onto the skin using an orange stipple sponge with a serrated and/or torn surface. The color provides a realistic undertone, which overrides the grayness of the gelatin appliance. Several other colors of reddish hue are also added later, as it is important for the application of color to the appliance to be as translucent as possible in order to create a realistic light reflection. More red should be added into the ear, because the ear receives more light than other areas of the face. Any area, in fact, which the artist feels may be overly lightened, can also be adjusted via this same technique. Normally earlobes contain more red, as do certain areas of the zygomatic bone, the sides of the neck, and the nose/nostrils.

Once the translucent Stacolor has been spotted over the appliance in specific areas, apply Joe Blasco P.M. and/or RCMA A.F. Blushtone 4 (already spatulated upon wax paper) with a micro-porous, foam latex sponge (slightly moistened w/alcohol). Stacolor is applied before any cream make-up foundation because it will not be removed by the application of the cream make-up. It is especially important to remember that P.M. and/or A.F., which are normally manufactured for use upon foam rubber appliances, do not contain isopropyl myristate, as this ingredient will remove the make-up.

Fig. 11-215

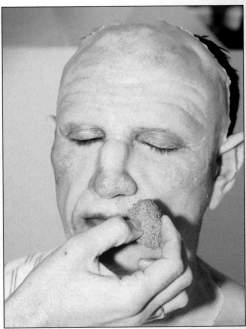

Fig. 11-216

When applying Blushtone 4, Mr. Mungle vigorously pushes the material into the sponge to create deep absorption, thereby avoiding the potential application of clumps. The make-up is then applied translucently as a stain, and not as a thick, overall rubber greasepaint, as was typical many years ago. The application of Blushtone 4 is applied back onto the natural skin to continue the coloration from the appliance for the sake of realism.

Fig. 11-217

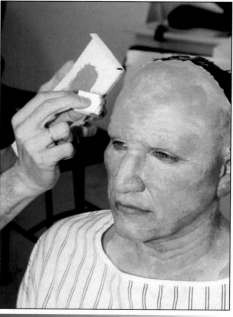

Fig. 11-218

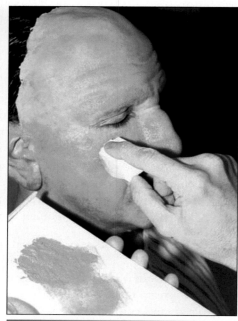

Fig. 11-219

Use a sable and/or fibrilon highlighting/ shading brush, slightly dipped in alcohol, to apply the same color to the depressions and other areas where more depth of value is desired. Various purple, maroon, and red tonalities applied into the facial shadows can enhance the overall effect of the make-up.

The step-by-step painting process rapidly brings the appliance to life. Bear in mind that this process, although quite intricate, must also be properly lit by the cinematographer to create the final visual impact on screen. Character make-ups are not usually lit flatly or with broad soft light, but are instead cross-lit and mottled with lighting to assist in the dimension-making process, as it is important to remember that the photographic process, be it filmic or electronic, is two-dimensional; it is the job of the artist to create a third dimension through the use of appliances and paint and powder accents.

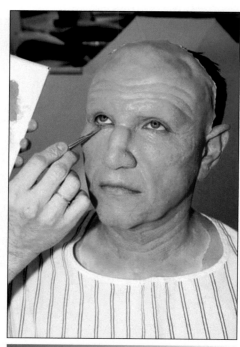

Fig. 11-220

Mr. Mungle next tears the surface of a foam latex sponge in a pattern that creates six small raised areas that will be used to deposit both darker and lighter colors for mottling and aging discolorations.

Lightly apply RCMA Gena Beige on the forehead to create light-colored areas, which will then be juxtaposed with darker tones for the purpose of having both high and low levels of light reflection and absorption, thus creating surface texture through the use of chiaroscuro.* To reiterate, this process, known as *mottling*, utilizes the illusion of high and low areas created by dark pigments that absorb light and light ones that reflect it. This technique has been used since the 1930s, not only in motion pictures and television, but onstage as well. It must be used in a much more limited manner today, as motion pictures and television processes—especially digital, Hi-Definition (HD)—and Super Hi-Definition (SHD), are extremely critical.

Fig. 11-221

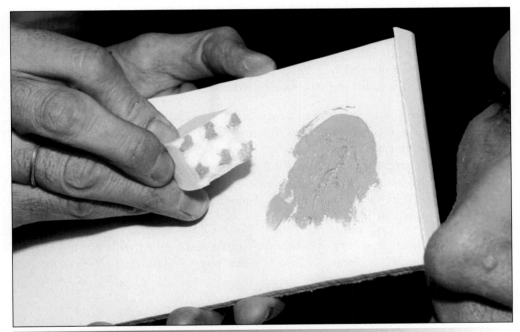

Fig. 11-222

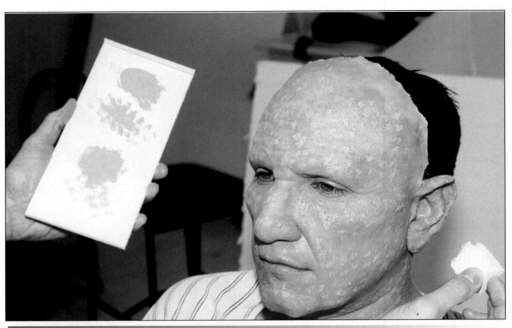

Fig. 11-223

Then add Joe Blasco Blushtone 1 to the lighter colors in an uneven, yet systematic manner that continues to accent the creation of a mottled, three-dimensional surface. As Mr. Mungle continues to apply color, he also works over particular areas and blends them into the surface. As he continues to mix more colors of varying values into the initially applied mottled effect, they gradually, if not rapidly, begin to produce what appears to be an irregular, yet realistic surface, rather than a flat surface created by old-fashioned rubber greasepaint techniques.

Continued blending is necessary with a torn, clean, foam latex sponge to further coordinate these values and remove any excess that may appear on the surface of the appliance. The artist should not be limited by the use of sponges—there are many types of brushes and other implements that can be used to facilitate identical results—although sponges are recommended because they are disposable, they fit in with the important guidelines of sanitation and sterilization (*see Volume I*). Fingers can also be used to pat and blend areas where colors may be found excessive.

As the process continues, deeper colors are chosen and applied with varying sizes of brushes to accommodate the areas of the face that require additional, yet more detailed mottling technique.

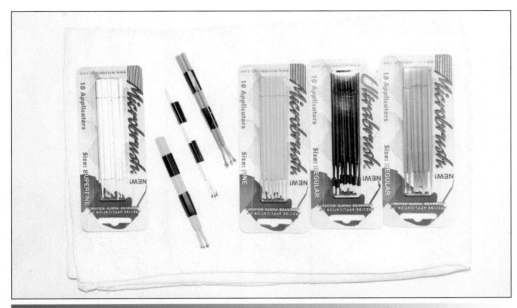

Fig. 11-224

Pictured here are Microbrush tools discovered by Mr. Mungle, which are manufactured by the Microbrush Corporation in Grafton, Wisconsin. (*See Appendix B for company listings.*) They can be taped together and used to apply more detailed mottling effects.

It is important to understand that if this make-up is to be duplicated on a daily basis for weeks or months at a time, photographs must be taken of every step of the initial make-up application process for continuity purposes. The photographs must be accompanied by detailed, written application instructions, similar to those found herein.

Fig. 11-225

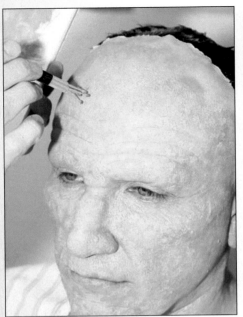

Fig. 11-226

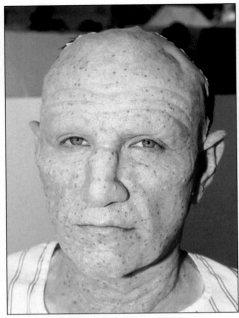

Fig. 11-227

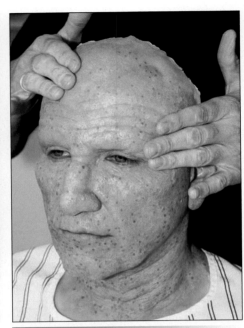

Fig. 11-228

On occasion, for specific types of aging marks, various types of templates that conform to the subject's physical anatomy can be laid over the surface while the make-up is applied through their holes in order to create identical patterns each day. In some more extreme cases, actual Vacuform faces with holes can be made, which are then placed over the subject's face, and the color is airbrushed through the holes to maintain accuracy.

The darker application of aging spots, which are quite precise and predominant in this example, are then lightly patted over—either with sponges or fingertips—to soften and blend them more realistically into the make-up surface. Depending upon the amount of light used on set, the artist must determine the degree of value to which the mottling can be applied. Darker spots may have a tendency to appear too pronounced if not blended well and softened after application.

One must remember that when applying a prosthesis, not only must the appliance itself be sculpted to perfection, but the application of surface colorants must also be applied so precisely and anatomically correct that the appliance itself becomes secondary and invisible, and appears to be the actual anatomy of the performer. Again, the mottling application and juxtapositioning of light and dark colors will provide translucency and qualities of light absorbency and reflection that create the absolutely vital anatomical illusion.

The Stacolors, tattoo inks, and Skin Illustrator types of alcohol-applied colorants are the products of choice when finishing the very detailed anatomical accents such as age marks, broken capillaries (nose/cheeks), veins (forehead/temples), and various redness and blueness. One must be cautious not to overdo the mottling, unless required by the character. Stacolors can easily be toned down by using a brush lightly dampened with alcohol. The authors recommend that all studio make-up artists familiarize themselves with the actual anatomical positioning of all veins and arteries, as well as minute capillaries found within real skin by reading and studying such books as *Gray's Anatomy*, which features vivid color photographs that can be followed.

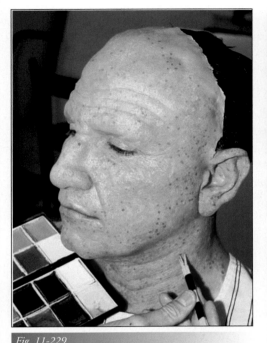

Fig. 11-229

Fig. 11-230

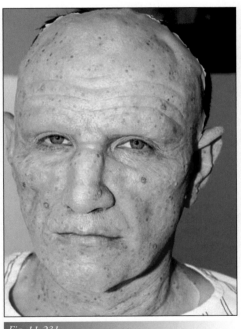

Fig. 11-231

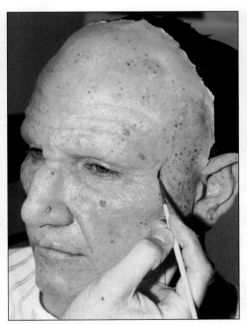

Fig. 11-232

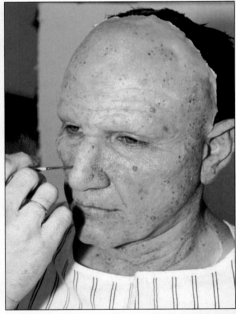

Fig. 11-233

It is important for the reader to observe every photograph throughout this entire process and become familiar with the use of each product recommended. The explanation herein of this make-up applied by Mr. Mungle is extremely detailed and should be reread several times prior to attempting such application. This gelatin formulation is specially devised by Mr. Mungle and was used for his Academy Award-nominated aging makeup applied quite expertly to James Woods in the motion picture, *Ghosts of Mississippi*. The authors highly recommend that every student of make-up view this motion picture and study the aging carefully, as it depicts one of today's most effective and realistic appliances accomplished via gelatin (rather than other prosthesis materials, which are more commonly used).

Artificial Hair Application

Mr. Mungle has chosen to begin the application of the wig and facial hair prior to finishing the minute details of skin coloring, texturing, and mottling. With the wig and facial hair in place, the artist is able to achieve a more complete image of the creation, and in doing so, is then more capable of adding details necessary to complete the project.

Following the conventional methods for application of a lace front wig (see Part I, Chapter 3). Mr. Mungle aligns the wig to the forehead appliance and manipulates it into position prior to adhering the lace with adhesive. It is important that all of the extraneous hairs be combed away from the lace prior to adhesion. The type of lace used for this custom-made wig is specially prepared and coated with a plastic film, which prevents the lace from tearing. The removal of the extraneous hairs can be done with a rattail or fine-tooth comb and then completed in a more detailed manner with fine tweezers.

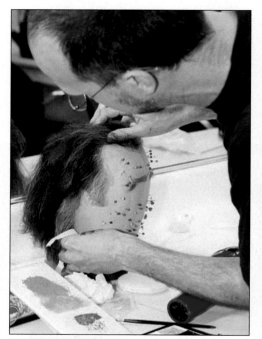

Fig. 11-234

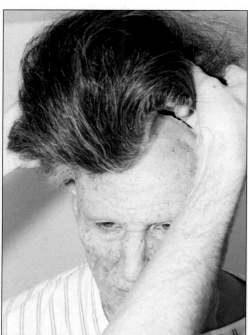

Fig. 11-235

Bear in mind that these extraneous hairs are not pulled from the lace or removed in any way—they are simply combed to avoid entanglement.

Once the lace has been adhered and the adhesive dries, the hair is then dressed and prepared according to the character's script requirements. The adhesive is a matte spirit gum, specifically formulated by W.M. Creations to dry rapidly and become invisible. It is quite strong and will hold the lace in position throughout the entire workday. During application (as shown in Part I, Chapter 3), the hair is lifted, the adhesive is applied to its underneath surface, and then the lace is gently pressed into position with a comb, orangewood stick, or any tool of choice to flatten the lace and allow the drying process to make the adhesive matte in appearance and completely invisible to the human eye. It is important not to apply too much adhesive beneath the lace, but enough for proper adhesion. Do not work beyond the edge of the lace itself.

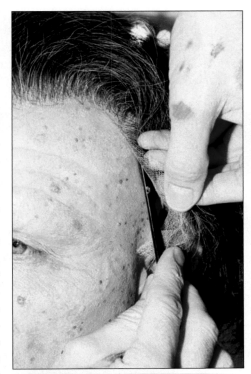

Fig. 11.236

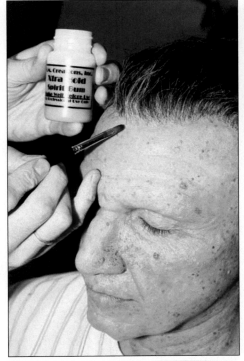

Fig. 11-237

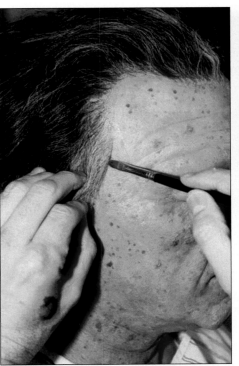

Fig. 11-238

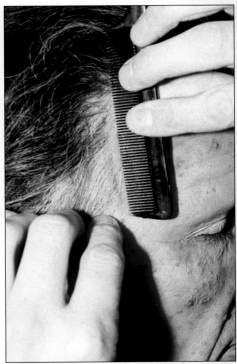

Fig. 11-239

A rattail comb can be placed down in between the hairs to further flatten the lace into position. The lace is adhered completely around the wig and to the back and sides of the neck. Any hair that would normally rise up during the performance at the nape of the neck should be glued down. There is nothing more amateurish than allowing hair to be visible at the back of a wig.

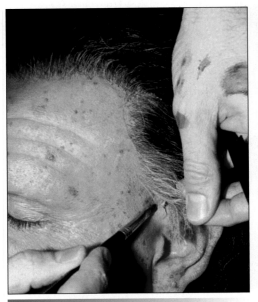

Fig. 11-240

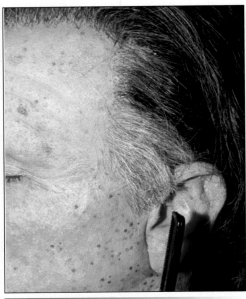

Fig. 11-241

The eyebrows are attached similarly with adhesive. Allow the surfaces to become tacky before they are gently pressed into position, with careful attention given to preventing the hairs from being flattened into the adhesive. The lace is the only area of the applied eyebrow that should be adhered; therefore, when applied correctly, the eyebrow hair can be

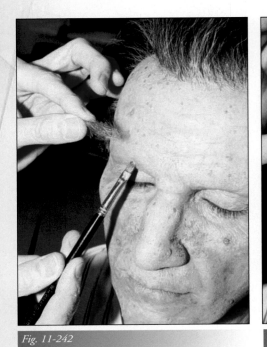

Fig. 11-242

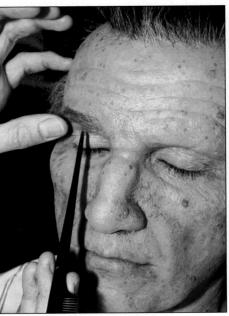

Fig. 11-243

Fig. 11-244

dressed and combed as needed.

Careful attention must be given to the underside of the eyebrow lace, as this area has a tendency to lift away from the appliance. In some cases, it is advantageous to cut away as much of the lace as possible so that no extraneous material will appear in the shot. The use of this specially manufactured and coated lace (available from W.M. Creations on special order only) enables the artist/hairdresser to trim the lace down to a minimum amount without facilitating tears, even after several uses, as the plastic coating provides reinforcement.

For the utmost effectiveness, be certain that when using W.M. Creations Extra Hold Spirit Gum, the product is well shaken and/or stirred to disperse the matting ingredient that may be retained at the container's bottom.

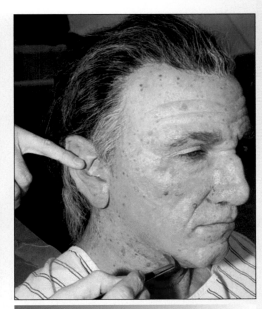

Fig. 11-245

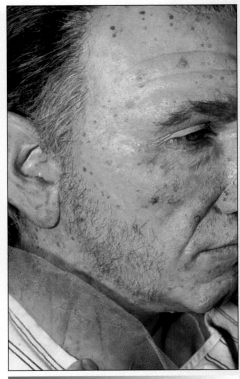

Fig. 11-246

The application of chopped hair (on the beard area) is accomplished as follows: First, apply adhesive to the surface of the appliance; second, attach lace that has extremely tiny cells (holes); and third, apply the chopped hair to the skin through this lace, which is sitting on the surface of the skin. Once Mr. Mungle is satisfied that the adhesive is dry and will hold the chopped hair in position, he then delicately removes the lace, which directs the hair to appear as though it is growing out of the skin.

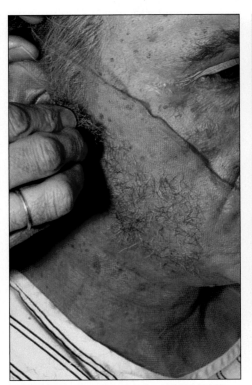

Fig. 11-247

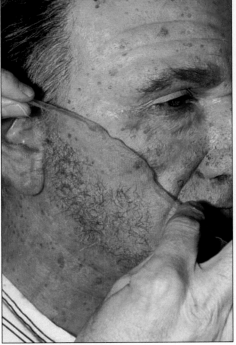

Fig. 11-248

Fig. 11-249

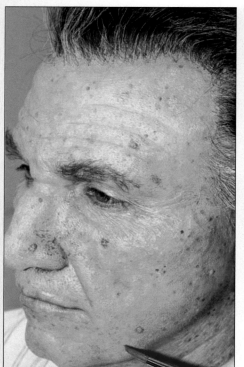

Fig. 11-250

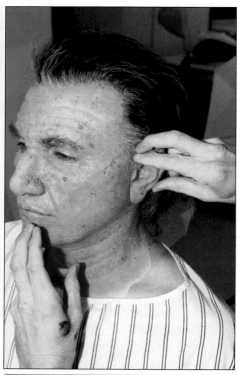

Fig. 11-251

This technique has been used by movie make-up artists for more than thirty years and has only recently become very effective for close-ups because of the fine, small cellular structure of the new lace types. In the past, the lace holes were quite large, and the clumps of hair attached would in some cases appear unnatural. This new lace will permit one hair at a time to be attached to the skin prior to its removal. This process can also be used to simulate moustache growth and any other growth required under the chin or on the sides of the neck. Any superfluous hairs veering in an unwanted direction can be pulled off by hand, with fine-pointed tweezers, or with haircutting scissors.

In some cases, the creation of eyebrows can be done with this process if lace eyebrows are unavailable. Similarly, hair can also be applied to the ears.

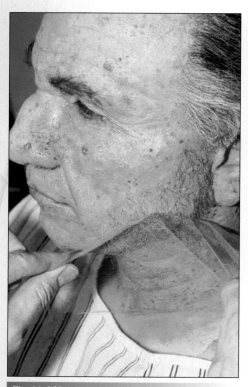

Fig. 11-252

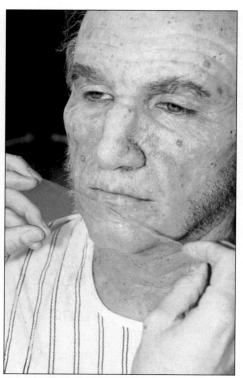

Fig. 11-253

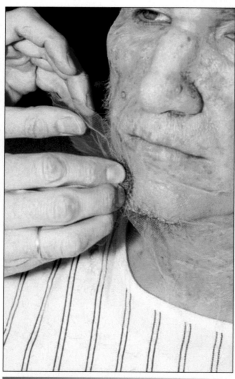

Fig. 11-254

Fig. 11-255

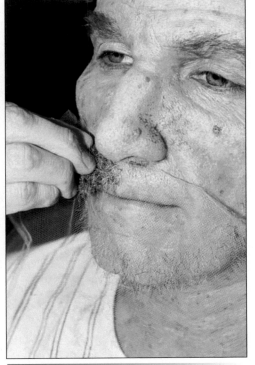

Fig. 11.256

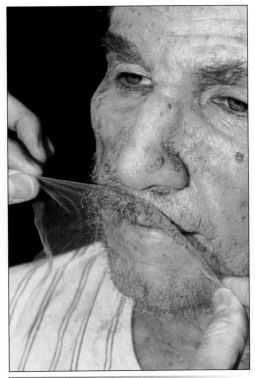

Fig. 11-257

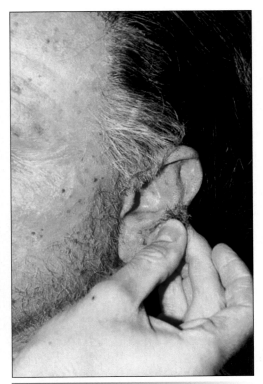

Fig. 11-258

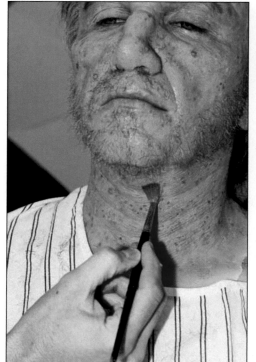

Fig. 11-259

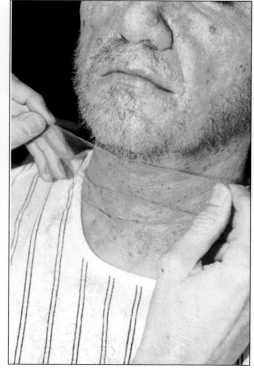

Fig. 11-260

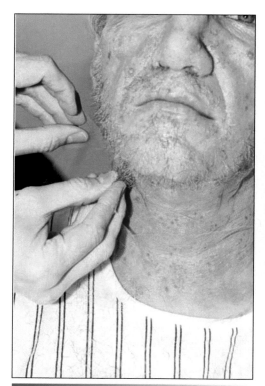

Fig. 11-261

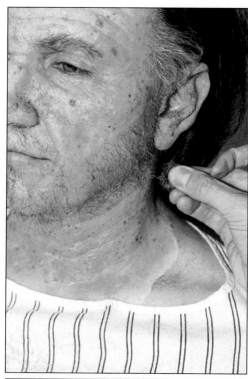

Fig. 11-262

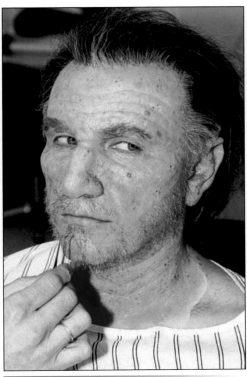

Fig. 11-263

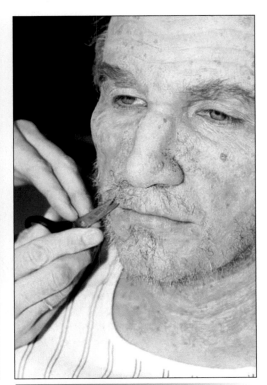

Fig. 11-264

The chopped hair can be applied by hand if desired. *(See Part I, Chapter 3, where chopped hair is rolled into a ball and pulled apart, and the ends are pressed into the adhesive.)* The adhesive must be quite tacky and almost dry, but not so dry that it fails to accept the hair. This technique is excellent for joining beard lines to the wig and neck hair, and down to the surface of the chest. Chopped hair can be cut in several lengths, and the varying lengths can be used where the artist deems appropriate. An overlay of hair may be appropriate for some areas of the lace. In some instances where the mottling may appear overly dark or dramatic, once the hair work is applied, the overall effect is reduced, resulting in an extremely anatomically correct look on camera.

To finish the project, the wig must be carefully styled and dressed by either the make-up artist or hairdresser in order to make the hair appear as realistic as all other areas of the applied work. Unless the artist is adept at styling hair, a collaboration between hairstylist and make-up artist may be necessary to

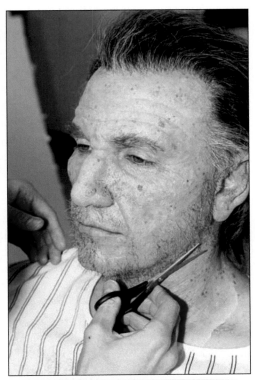

Fig. 11-265

achieve the proper results. Remember that the effectiveness of studio make-up work depends not only upon the make-up itself, but the hairstyling, wardrobe, lighting, and camera effects as well. If any one of these prove inferior, it will detract from the over-all realism, and perhaps the actor's portrayal of the character.

Wigs used for a project of this nature should be customized, especially for large budget productions. When the artist and hairdresser are using a rented wig, normally no cutting of any kind is permitted; therefore, the selection of a wig, which is rented, must be done very carefully and with great attention to the fact that once it is dressed, it will fit perfectly.

When finally dressing the lace hairpiece, do not permit the hair to appear too flat—this will make the hair look as if it is ventilated and not growing. Using a rattail comb, very carefully work around the entire lace, lifting the hair forward so that it appears to be growing directly out of the skin. Do not neglect the hands, arms, and all exposed skin, which are all integral parts of this process.

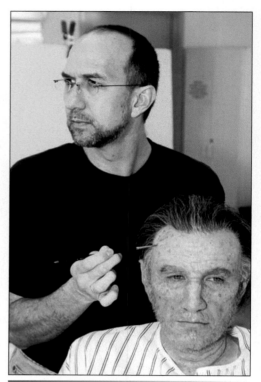
Fig. 11-266

Teeth

One must not forget to make the teeth up! Using tooth enamels of various colors, the artist can provide realistic discoloration so that the teeth are not brilliantly white and thus inappropriate for the character. If the character supposedly wears dentures, then white teeth would be in order. In this case, the teeth are being painted to look aged, and as if the character has endured a lifetime of cigarette smoking. It is important to verify with the subject that he or she is not wearing porous veneers, caps, or any other dental prosthesis that would be permanently stained and/or damaged by the application of enamel. Should this be the case, high-pigmented foundation bases, Creative Colors, P.M. and/or A.F. colors (and/or pencils), or Ultamatte colors can be used after the teeth have been dried with a tissue. These colors are applied with various brushes to accommodate either the surface of the teeth or the areas between them.

Gums can also be colored using a cotton-tipped applicator and various mixes of food coloring. When coloring the teeth, do not neglect areas down into the gums, as well as those far back within the mouth. Stacolors, tattoo colors, Skin Illustrator, and other alcohol-based colorants can also be used very effectively to more semi-permanently color the teeth.

Finishing Touches

In finishing the final details of the make-up, the artist may examine the make-up with a magnifying glass (which may in fact be appropriate for the medium), look directly at the make-up, and/or view the make-up in the mirror, which should be no further in front of the subject than three feet. For HDTV (Hi-Definition Television) and other intricate or critical processes, it is recommended that extreme attention to detail be given to every aspect of application, and that no dependency is placed upon lighting washdown.

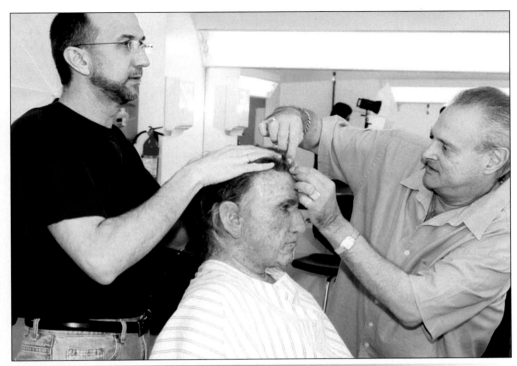

Fig. 11-267

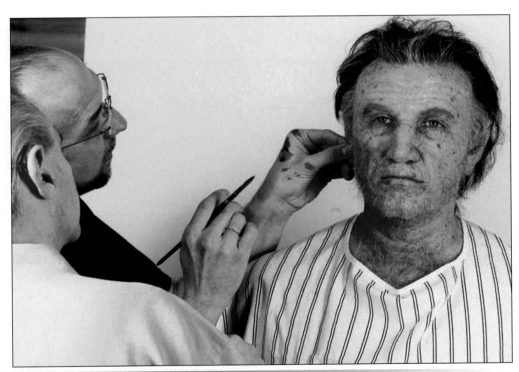

Fig. 11-268

The artist may wish to consider adding hair to any smooth areas of the ears, earlobes, the upper chest, and even the skin between the eyebrows. Obviously, all of these decisions are based on the character who in this case, as the photos clearly depict, is very unkempt and has been quite abusive to himself over the years.

The artist may also wish to utilize the advantage of contact lenses in dulling the youthful appearance of the eyes. Lenses can create a glaucoma effect, for example, and add to the realism of the portrayal.

Keep in mind the fact that when the appliance features sculpted wrinkles and expression lines, the artist need not accent or darken them, for they are already three-dimensional. It is the lighting created and directed by the cinematographer that will enable the three-dimensional wrinkles to be revealed effectively.

Gelatin is a material that produces an extremely realistic skin. But because of its inherent nature to soften as body temperature rises (and sometimes melt in certain climatic conditions), it can only be used in rare instances when the temperature of the set is controlled. Additionally, if the subject has recently consumed alcohol or perspires profusely, the gelatin will not work.

In summary, conceptualization of the character prior to make-up application is of the utmost importance, as this type of application, with its extreme detail and reliance upon realism, cannot be left to experimentation on the day of the shoot. It must be pre-designed, with all aspects determined well in advance. Creativity and knowledge go hand-in-hand; experimentation prior to the actual shooting date is certainly encouraged. Ultimately, approval from production executives will dictate the artist's final choices.

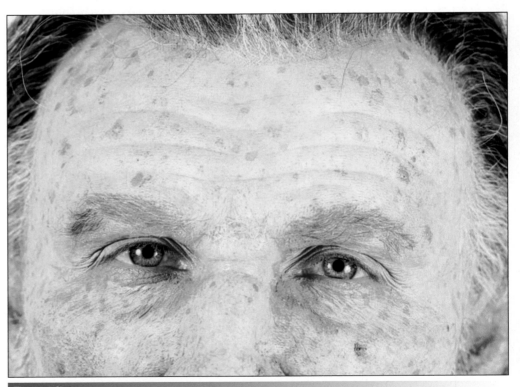

Fig. 11-269

At the very beginning of the process, Mr. Mungle designed this make-up through the use of Adobe Photoshop, a computer program. Certain changes were made during the sculpting process as can readily be seen when comparing the Photoshop (virtual) image to the actual finished make-up. Specifically, changes in the nose are quite apparent, as the Photoshop image depicts a larger, more bulbous and contorted nose than the finished result. Nevertheless, the Photoshop conceptualization is an important tool that the artist can use to show production executives a reasonable facsimile of the character's appearance once the make-up is complete. By viewing virtual images, the production personnel are able to give the make-up artist their feedback, which in turn will influence how the appliances are sculpted.

Removal

The removal process should be considered as integral as the application process insofar as the comfort of the subject is considered. Account for the time necessary for immaculate removal without pain to the performer.

Begin by removing the wig with 99-percent alcohol. The lace is carefully lifted from the prosthetic appliance with the use of a flat sable or synthetic brush. Much care is given to the shape of the lace front—avoid tearing, fraying, or disturbing it in any way. Once the wig is removed, it is reattached to the canvas wig block and pinned for more thorough cleaning. The eyebrows are also removed in exactly the same fashion and pinned to the block.

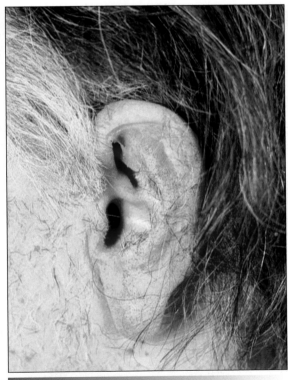

Fig. 11-270

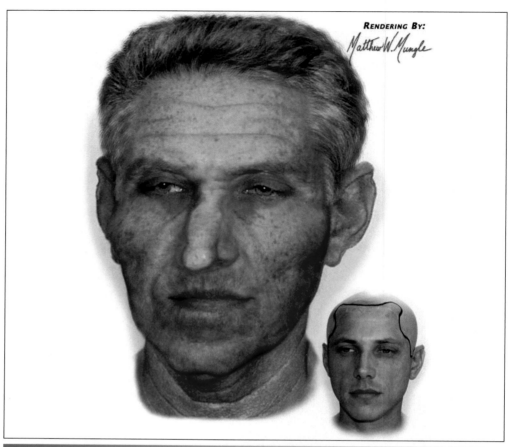

RENDERING BY:

Matthew W. Mungle

Fig. 11-271

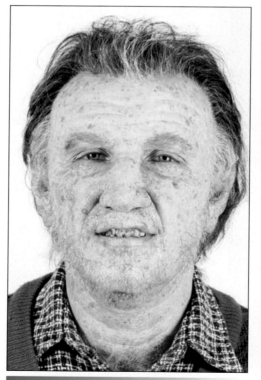

Fig. 11-272

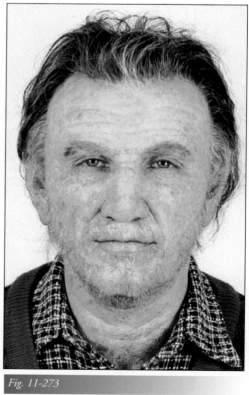

Fig. 11-273

Using a larger synthetic or sable brush, Beta Solve is applied under the edges of the appliance, and the edges are peeled away as the Solve dissolves the Beta Bond adhesive. Be careful not to apply too much, as the Solve should not run down behind the appliance and enter the eye area.

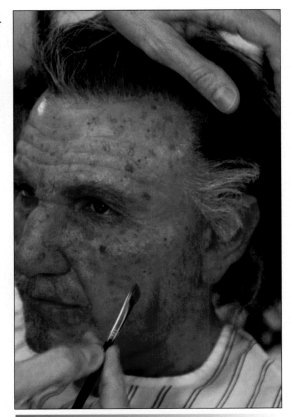

Fig. 11-274

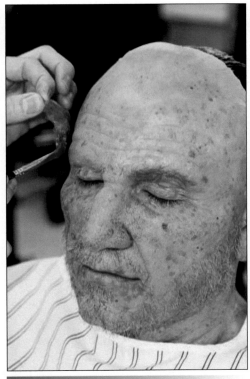

Fig. 11-275

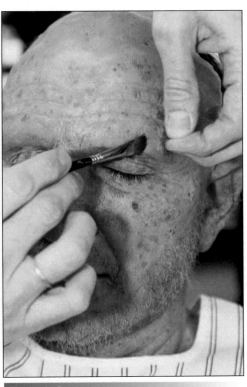

Fig. 11-276

It is imperative that the eyes be well protected either with powder puffs held in position over the eyes or several thick pieces of tissue paper. Once the entire appliance has been removed, any remnants must also be taken off with Beta Solve in exactly the same manner.

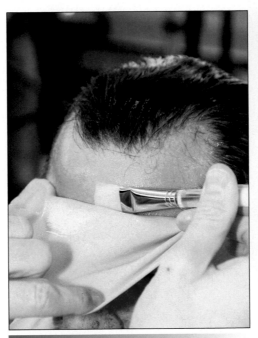

Fig. 11-277

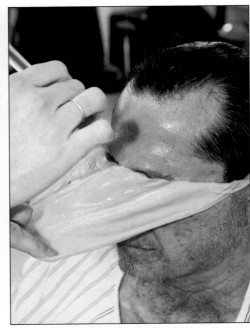

Fig. 11-278

The removal process is extremely gradual—there should be no pulling of the appliance from the skin. The appliance should simply be floated away. One side of the face is normally completed at a time. Working from top to bottom seems to be the manner that most artists prefer.

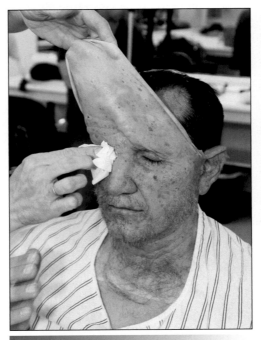

Fig. 11-279

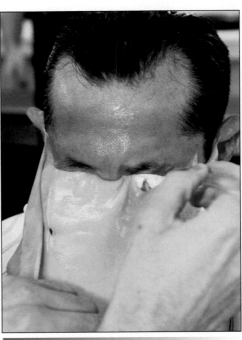

Fig. 11-280

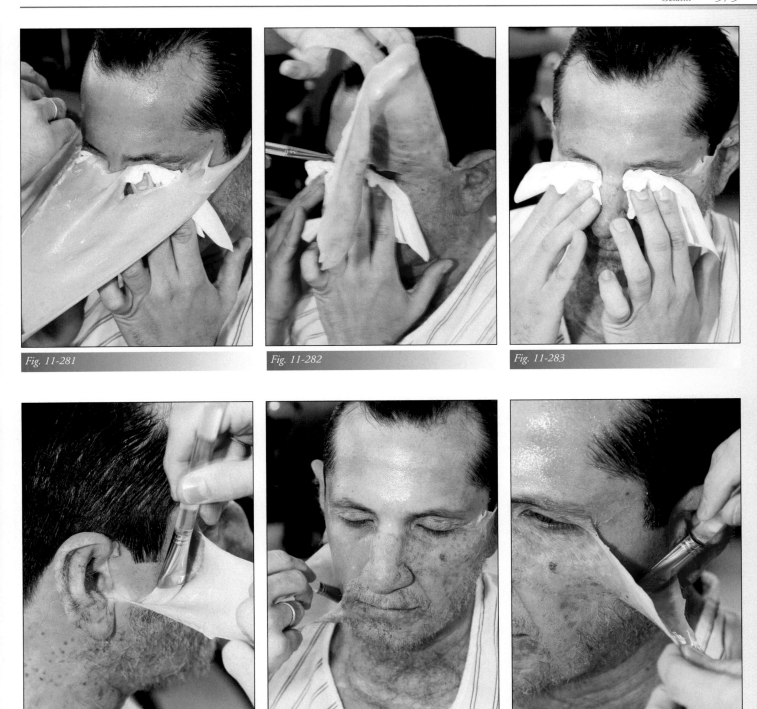

Fig. 11-281

Fig. 11-282

Fig. 11-283

Fig. 11-284

Fig. 11-285

Fig. 11-286

It is the recommendation of the authors that when working around the eyes, smaller brushes (be they flat or round, sable or synthetic) be used in place of extremely large ones, thereby eliminating the possibility of any excess Beta Solve or remover falling into the smaller orbital areas, which require more detailed work than other parts of the face.

As can be seen in the photos, the removal process is quite simple and can be accomplished rapidly in the hands of a skilled professional. Those attempting this process for the first time should work slowly to be certain that no pain is inflicted upon the subject.

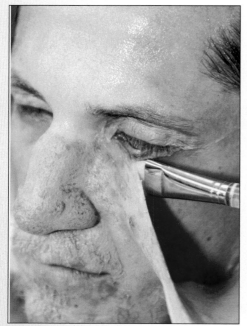

Fig. 11-287

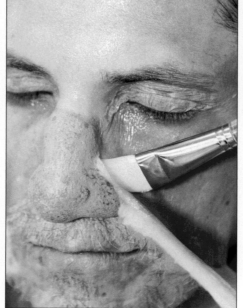

Fig. 11-288

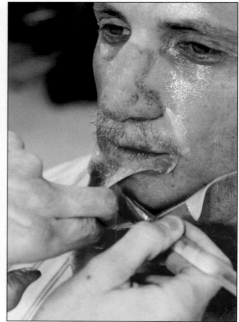

Fig. 11-289

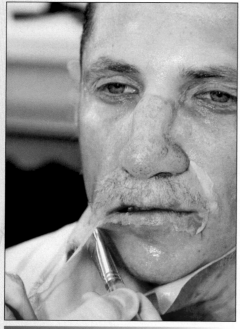

Fig. 11-290

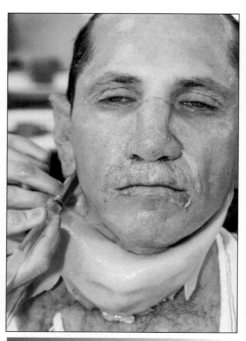

Fig. 11-291

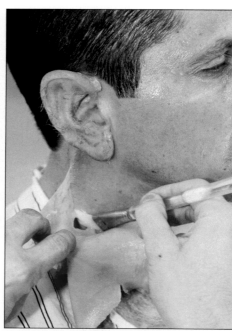

Fig. 11-292

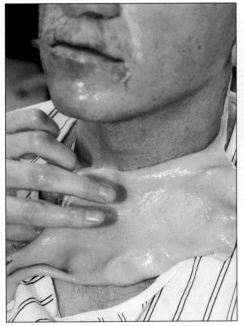

Fig. 11-293

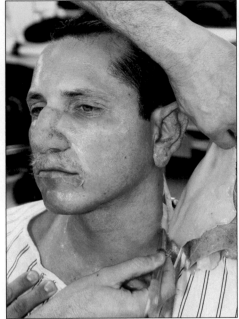

Fig. 11-294

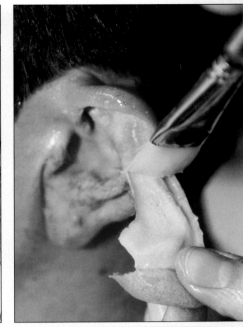

Fig. 11-295

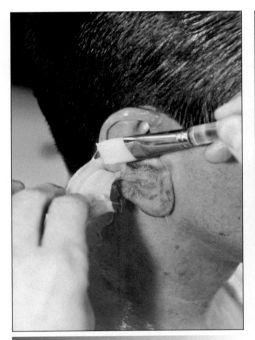

Fig. 11-296

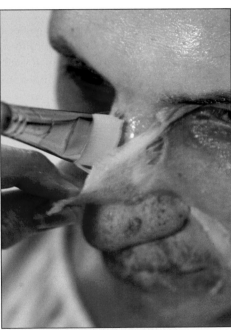

Fig. 11-297

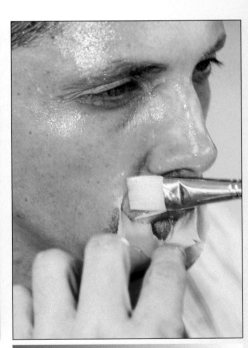

Fig. 11-298

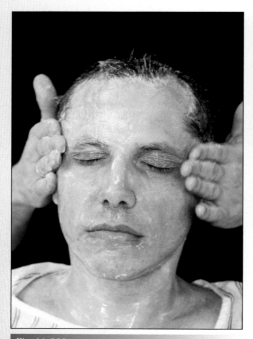

Fig. 11-299

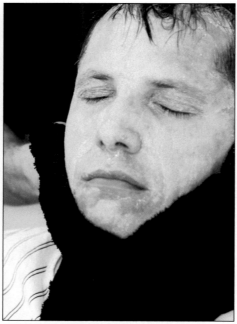

Fig. 11-300

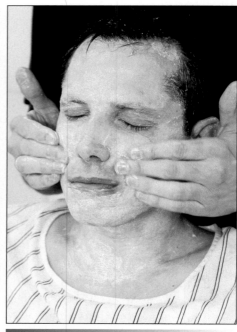

Fig. 11-301

Once all the appliances and any remnants of gelatin have been successfully removed, tepid to hot compresses consisting of terrycloth towels can be applied to the skin surface, followed by a thorough washing with a mild soap such as Dove, which will not dry the skin. As can be seen in the photos, Mr. Mungle is applying a mild, liquid hand soap (not of the detergent dish soap variety) commonly used for sensitive skin (or on babies, for example). The liquid soap and/or cream bar soap is applied to the face and gently massaged in a manner that soothes the individual and removes absolutely every remnant of make-up and adhesive.

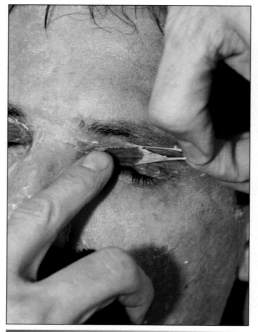

Fig. 11-302

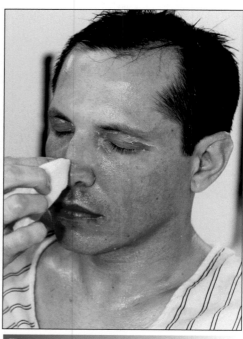

Fig. 11-303

A terrycloth towel can also be used along with the soap to more thoroughly remove remnants of gelatin and adhesive. The length of the removal process often depends upon the strength of application and the duration of the appliance's usage. The longer the appliance is used, especially in an environment in which the temperature of the stage (or the subject's body) may be somewhat higher than desired and perspiration is excreted by the subject, the easier removal may be.

When a make-up of this nature is applied continuously for many days or weeks at a time, it is important that the make-up artist recommend the subject visit a facial salon and/or dermatologist who can provide services that will eliminate any potential irritation or discomfort.

Once the soap or cleansing cream has been thoroughly applied and massaged, it should be permitted to remain on the face for approximately three to five minutes to further dissolve anything resistant to removal. Terrycloth towels can then be wetted and placed in a microwave oven for approximately three to five minutes, depending upon the number of towels. Once heated, they may be removed, unfolded, waved through the air to lightly cool them, and then applied to the face (once sufficiently cool). Press the towels firmly against the face, and hold them in position. Several towels can be used, as stated previously, until satisfied. They will act as agents for removing the soap and/or cream remover. This can be repeated several times until the face is clean.

Finally, a light moisturizer can be applied and lightly massaged into the skin. All remnants of Gafquat can be dissolved from the hair using these towels as well. The artist must pay particular attention to sensitive areas around the eyes, ears, and neck. There are many available products designed specifically for the removal of prosthetic devices. The authors recommend experimentation to determine which products are best.

Once the face has been thoroughly massaged and all the soap has been removed (in addition to Gafquat from the hair), pat the face dry, and return the hair to its original style.

The artist may wish to consider the use of a barrier cream prior to the application of prosthetics. Barrier creams, such as Aqua Cream and Derma Shield, can be applied prior to any adhesives and will protect the skin somewhat, as well as assist in the easy removal of adhesives.

The cleaning of the teeth can be accomplished simply by brushing them well with an abrasive dentifrice, which should in fact be done personally by the performer. The dentifrice and other facial creams, which are applied to relieve any possible irritation, are the responsibility of the make-up artist.

Caution with Chemicals

More difficult-to-remove pieces can be successfully eradicated with the use of a product called Mavidon. This product is specifically manufactured by Mavidon Medical Products in Lakeworth, Florida for the purpose of removing body make-up and adhesive. It was originally formulated as a solvent to remove Pros-Aide and other similar difficult-to-remove adhesives. When using this product, be certain to follow the instructions, and avoid getting any into the eyes. This material is capable of removing collodion, which, as most artists know, can normally not be removed with anything less powerful than acetone.

Considering that some products will be used that contain acetone or similar solvents, the artist must work with extreme caution, especially around the eye area. A powder puff or terrycloth towel can be used for protective purposes, and always remember to be extremely gentle, as abrasion to the skin can occur. This may not be immediately evident, but over time it will create redness and possible pain. If negative effects such as these occur, the production suffers, for the production itself may stop, and the subject will need to visit a dermatologist or other medical specialist who will be able to diagnose and properly treat the condition prior to any further make-up application.

The chemicals that are used to remove prosthetic appliances can be as volatile, if not more so than the chemicals used to manufacture them. Therefore, actors who are intending to wear prosthetic appliances—be they gelatin, silicone, or foam rubber—must be made fully aware of the dangers involved through the use of not only the product application, but the removal process as well. The subject must be explicit with the make-up artist when discussing potential allergic reactions and diseases or conditions that will be worsened or aggravated in any way by the use of adhesives, solvents, or other various chemicals. Especially important for the artist to know is whether the subject suffers from any form of liver disease or disorder, which may prove detrimental, if not fatal when the subject is exposed to chemicals such as acetone, MEK (methyl ethyl ketone), 99-percent alcohol, and various types of adhesives or solvent-based removers.

Occasionally it behooves the artist to require that the subject sign release forms that confirm the process to be harmless, thereby removing all liability from the production company, as well as the artist employed to perform the application and/or removal. These releases should be discussed with production personnel prior to the commencement of any project, and no performer should be selected who is knowingly afflicted with any form of allergy or disease with adverse effects.

SUMMARY

It is important the subject leave the make-up room as clean as during arrival. The subject should never be given the impression that he or she is being rushed or that the removal of the piece is trivial, nor should the subject feel as if any of the work needs to be removed by him or her personally, either in the make-up room or after arriving at home later in the day.

Conclusion

TO VOLUME III

This book has been a labor of love that will hopefully educate and inspire both current and aspiring make-up artists long into the future.

Aside from fulfilling the hundreds of daily operations requirements of my several corporations, every spare moment of my professional and personal life for the past five years has been dedicated to creating this comprehensive textbook. Both Vincent J-R Kehoe and I have attempted to leave no stone unturned in providing the reader with the most state-of-the-art techniques available and with information found neither in books from the past nor from ones written today.

Some make-up schools and cosmetics companies have published somewhat simple texts which only superficially present the subject of professional make-up. These books are most often nothing more than rewritten copy from beauty magazines and/or reworked material from old make-up books. Sadly, this approach to writing a book on professional make-up customarily results in a rehash of old-fashioned and outmoded methods. Some of the most poorly written books are easily recognizable by the fact that they contain absolutely no photographs of actual make-ups, but only hand-drawn sketches! Current make-up artists and serious make-up students should waste neither time nor money on books written by copycat opportunists who obviously lack the resources, talent, or understanding to properly teach the subject as evident in the lack or complete absence of step-by-step photographs.

Vincent J-R Kehoe and I have presented the reader with not only detailed written theory in text form, but also with a multitude of color photographs which, without question, emphatically present each step-by-step make-up technique in as honest and comprehensive a manner as possible without shortcuts. These are viable techniques applied by many truly talented artists who are incredibly experienced and passionate in their work, and who were not afraid to show it.

Although this volume offers current prosthetic make-up techniques and information about laboratory work, the aspiring artist must realize that a professional make-up artist needs proficiency in other aspects of the art, as emphasized in Volume I, which focuses on techniques of beauty make-up. Never before has a book on professional make-up presented the art of beauty make-up as has that text. Now, artists who have had the misconception that beauty and corrective make-up techniques are not as intricate as those of character make-up will hopefully appreciate their proper precise application and find them to be just as intriguing and challenging – if not more so, in many respects.

Similarly, books that only impart knowledge of beauty make-up are just as incomplete in providing insight and knowledge with regard to the entire scope of professional make-up artistry. Therefore, these books in combination provide the reader with a full understanding of the field, as opposed to only one interesting slice of the pie.

This series (which includes Volume II on the art of character make-up) serves as the official text of the Joe Blasco Make-up Schools and will also be made available to numerous other institutions. It is our intention, through these books, to show the current dynamics and intricacies of the techniques which permit this wonderful profession to remain healthy and constantly grow.

Since childhood, my goal has been to understand, master, and fully appreciate all aspects of make-up artistry. From decades of work through my schools, and now, with this series of books, today's and tomorrow's make-up artists may fully appreciate absolutely every area of the art.

There will always be specialists who gravitate more toward one particular aspect of the art. However, it has been our intention to provide the detailed knowledge found within these books so that all make-up artists can fully appreciate and respect the work done by all artists, regardless of their area of preference and/or expertise. It has also been my desire to help unite—if only in a small way—the entire world community of professional make-up artists, and to show how important it is that all make-up artists, regardless of specialty or level of development, respect one another and work together to create a renewed spirit of professionalism that encompasses tolerance and acceptance without negativity of any kind. Let us all embrace one another, not only for the sake of our talent, but for our profound uniqueness within the world of art. Be kind to each other, and share your knowledge . . . without fear.

Joe Blasco

Appendix A

THE MAKE-UP SCHOOL

Of the utmost importance when it comes to training acolytes today for the profession of make-up artist are the professional level make-up schools and academies. In the main employment area of Hollywood, California and its environs, the craft union no longer requires an examination, but rather determines qualification based upon the number of days worked in the field, essentially placing the cart before the horse. The New York union local, on the other hand, still bases admission on the results of a test. Yet how does one learn the profession when the Hollywood film studios no longer feature make-up departments that train apprentices to become journeymen make-up artists?

The answer is, of course, from the plethora of make-up schools that have burgeoned in both the East and West Coast production areas. Only a few, however, are well run with professional make-up artists as teachers. Others have neither the facilities nor the trained personnel to provide a necessary level of competence.

Just as the old Hollywood film studios were only as good and successful as their pictures and star performers, so are the present make-up schools only as good as their teachers, facilities, and curriculum. The best programs are not found in academic institutions where college degrees are obtained, but rather in specialized training schools for professional-level education, where instruction is given by teachers who work in film and television studios, and who are able to impart appropriate direction and work ethic.

Those who wish to attend a make-up school should first write to obtain information regarding the level of training, the identities and qualifications of the instructors, and the status of the facilities, as well as the school's environment. Carefully compare these components from different schools before selecting one. Inquire as to the status of their graduates and the positions they currently hold. Does the school have its own in-house television and film camera facilities so that the students can observe the results of their work? Does the school have adequate libraries that feature examples of make-ups, both past and present? What recommendations are made for parking and accommodation while attending class? What types of make-up kits or materials that the students can utilize in forming their own personalized kits are furnished for the class sessions? As one can readily see, there are many questions and comparisons to which a school should be ready and willing to respond.

What is the proper length of the curriculum? This depends upon the area in which the applicant is intending to seek employment. For example, if one only wishes to do make-up for weddings, perform standard beauty salon work, or prepare straight or beauty make-ups for photo studios without becoming involved in any form of character make-up, then the length of the class sessions need not be more than four to six weeks (of full days). If the applicant wishes to learn about age characteristics and other aspects of production make-up artistry (burns, scars, wounds, horror make-ups, special historical characters, hair work on beards and moustaches, etc.), twelve weeks of full-day sessions may be recommended.

The most important criterion for success, however, is an innate talent to perform the work, in addition to a deep interest and desire. Make-up is not a profession to be taken lightly or with any diffidence whatsoever. Those who prosper are strongly and deeply dedicated artists who have the gift to succeed. No good make-up artist has emerged from within a lazy person with a lack of ambition. Your final work will always be compared to that of others in the field, so you must be the best you can be—and beyond.

Listed below are but a few of the schools or academies available to prospective students. Keep in mind that one must always form one's own opinions after reviewing all the considered institutions. Invest in the best for yourself.

Due to the large number of schools, it is impossible to list all of them. The ones listed here represent the best selection of the authors:

Joe Blasco Make-Up Center West
1670 Hillhurst Avenue
Hollywood, CA 90027
Tel. (323) 467-4949, (800) 634-0008
www.joeblasco.com

Joe Blasco Make-Up Center East
5422 Carrier Drive, Suite 304
Orlando, FL 32819
Tel. (407) 363-1234, (800) 252-7261
www.joeblasco.com

Joe Blasco Broadband Make-Up Education Center
521 North Kirkman
Orlando, FL 32808
Tel. (407) 363-1232
www.broadbandmakeup.com

Blanche Macdonald Centre
100-555 West 12th Avenue
Vancouver, BC, Canada V5Z3X7
Tel. (604) 685-0347
www.blanchemacdonald.com

HOW TO SELECT A MAKE-UP SCHOOL

Just as an individual's level of education can often be deduced by those whose learning processes are more developed, either through academic study and/or actual life experience, so can a make-up artist's level of understanding and competency be recognized by artists who have already attained a level of expertise that the neophyte strives so diligently to achieve.

It is unfortunate that so many uninformed prospective students of make-up believe there is only one way to accomplish any make-up application process, and that all schools are the same! That is why it is vitally important that those seeking a school of make-up artistry be certain they choose one with only experienced artists as teachers, and not ex-real estate agents or actors who have recently graduated themselves and are perhaps not experienced or well-versed enough in the art's intricacies to instruct. Many so-called make-up schools will harbor these inexperienced people who do not fully understand the art, or who simply misinterpret it and subsequently pass on an unacceptable level of comprehension to their unknowing students.

Therefore, it is of vital importance that the prospective student fully investigate all schools before making a decision. The best schools are owned by highly experienced, qualified, and respected studio make-up artists who hire neither novices nor individuals who are unsuitable and unable to work in the real entertainment industry. One should seriously examine whether a school has a set, unchanging faculty. This is the first red flag that indicates the education may be stagnant, not current, and sadly, inaccurate. Unfortunately, even some schools that boast professional ownership are often undesirable. Certain name professionals have not kept up with modern techniques, and more pathetically, are not innovators. They either do not possess or have long lost the innate passion, talent, and vision to create new methods that are so vital to constantly advancing the art. Prospective students who wish to obtain the finest education must thoroughly inspect the facility when on tour in order to determine the school's level of professionalism, especially where cleanliness is concerned. A dirty, unkempt, unsanitary facility is a definite indication that you should take your valuable time and money elsewhere.

But, perhaps the greatest indicator of all is the behavior of the administration. Slovenly dressed, rude, and unsophisticated-appearing individuals should make it crystal clear that you have entered the wrong door. Locate the exit immediately!

A professional make-up school worth attending is one wherein none of the above negative indicators exist, and one at which the enrollment director or school director never denigrates other schools in an effort to sway your financial contribution that will support a waning cause. It is vital that future make-up artists not waste their time and money on schools where the only claim to fame is that their instructors were trained or worked at another school.

If that is the case, then the student, by enrolling at the spin-off school, may be reliving a second generation of incorrect interpretation from instruction given years and years ago, with the only updates coming from what the instructors may have learned from fashion magazine ads meant to promote trends and temporary styles of make-up technique.

So, then how does a future student of make-up choose the correct make-up school? Do so by not only understanding and following the few and relatively simple guidelines offered in the above text, but also by being honest with yourself concerning the degree of passion, dedication and love of the art you possess. Individuals with a strong desire to succeed in make-up will recognize a commensurate level of passion for make-up (or a lack thereof) in prospective institutions.

Visit in person, and listen intently. Look deeply into the eyes of all persons with whom you meet while interviewing and touring all potential facilities. If you feel that the representatives of these schools possess your same level of desire to be the best, then you have found your make-up school. Remember: Never enroll until you have seen all schools!

JOE BLASCO

Fig. App-1

Fig. App-2

Fig. App-3

Fig. App-4

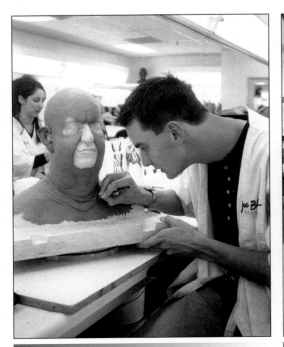

Fig. App-5

Fig. App-6

Fig. App-7

Teaching The World The Fine Art of Make–Up

Fig. App-8

Fig. App-9

Make-up artist Kelcey Fry instructing at Joe Blasco Make-up Center.

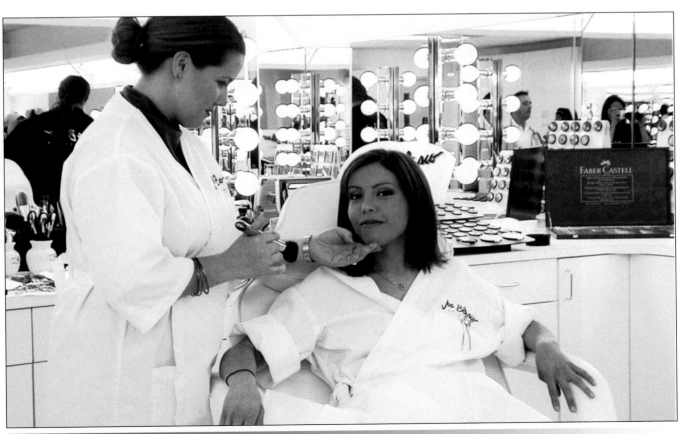

Fig. App-10

Fig. App-11

Fig. App-12

Fig. App-13

Fig. App-14

Fig. App-15

Fig. App-16

Make-up artist Gil Mosko guest instructing at Joe Blasco Make-up Center.

Fig. App-17

Fig. App-18

Student make-up materials. What's inside the box? The Joe Blasco Student Make-up Kits contain products that have been personally selected by Mr. Blasco and his team of working professional instructors.

Fig. App-19

Fig. App-20

Fig. App-21

The Hollywood facility includes:

1. *The Make-up Department Application Area Classrooms*

2. *Hair Work Classroom*

3. *Special Make-up Effects Lab*

4. *School Administrators' Offices*

5. *Restrooms and Break Areas*

6. *Joe Blasco Cosmetics Facility Store*

7. *Joe Blasco Cosmetics Offices*

8. *Video Bay*

9. *Make-up Museum*

10. *1st Floor Photo Gallery*

11. *MUATV Studio*

12. *Viewing Theatre*

13. *Professional Make-up Demonstration/Lecture Halls*

14. *Cosmetics Laboratory*

15. *Portfolio Stage*

Fig. App-22

Fig. App-23

Fig. App-24

Fig. App-25

Fig. App-26

Fig. App-27

Once students apply make-up in the classroom, they are taken to the portfolio stage, where they begin to feel and see what it is like to be on a television set. A videotape and/or CD-ROM containing digital still images is created, and the best work is recorded. This allows the student to show the best work to prospective employers the way it was meant to be seen.

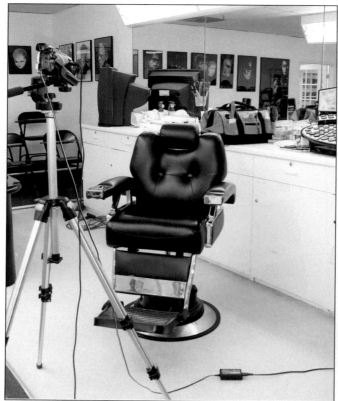

Fig. App-28

Fig. App-29

Fig. H-30

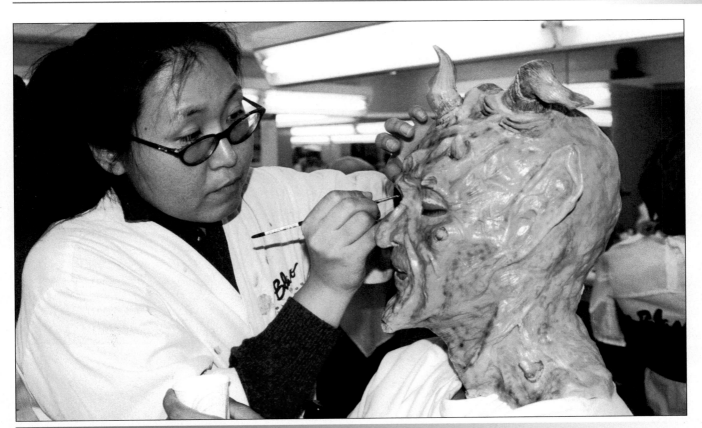

Fig. App-31

Fig. H-32

Make-up artist Larry Bones instructing at Joe Blasco Make-up Center.

Make-up artist Jill Rockow instructing at Joe Blasco Make-up Center.

Fig. App-36

Joe Blasco receives the 2004 Distinguished Achievement Award in Make-up from the United States Institute for Theatre Technology. Mr. Forrest J. Ackerman, founder of Famous Monsters of Filmland *magazine, Mr. Joe Blasco, and Mr. Vincent J-R Kehoe, founder of RCMA Make-up.*

Fig. App-37

Fig. App-38

Fig. App-39

Fig. App-40

Fig. App-41

Fig. App-42

Joe Blasco also enumerates a sage and sincere list of manners and recommendations that follow to those who attend his outstanding make-up academies in Hollywood and in Florida. I fully endorse these work ethics for those who wish to become, or even currently are studio make-up artists in today's very competitive and knowledgeable world.

VINCENT KEHOE

ATTENDING A MAKE-UP SCHOOL

- As this field of endeavor is to be your life's work, treat it with care and diligence.

- Collect photos of your work for a portfolio that can be shown to agents or prospective clients. Make one of stills, videotape, and DVD if possible. Gain permission to shoot in class while in school and on various sets when working professionally. Students should be very critical of the photographs placed in their final collection, as they will be judged. Never have to make any excuse for an image that is displayed, and never include any photos (or printed illustrations) of your own work, which do not serve as good representations of your make-up. Do not include images that fail to show your work in close-up form, even if they have appeared in magazines or other media.

- Subscribe to all the trade papers and magazines to familiarize yourself with what is happening in the business.

- Secure a reliable car for transportation, and keep it well maintained.

- Buy yourself a dependable cell phone and pager, but turn these off while in class and when at work onstage.

- Keep in touch with your classmates for job leads or assistant positions after you graduate.

- Stay sharp with your craft by using the free, lifetime alumni workshop facilities. Practice, practice, practice—and watch any available videos often.

- Attend all Saturday seminars, and take extensive notes. These special sessions are designed for you, so take advantage of them.

- Browse bookstores—both old and new—for reference materials on stage and screen make-up. Start a reference collection. Also utilize amazon.com or other similar resources on the Internet, and search under make-up for the subject.

- If you change your address or telephone number, whether you are in school or in business, notify everyone. Remember: If people can't find you, they can't hire you.

- Be on time—always! Be early if possible.

- Admit when you are wrong.

- Sanitation is a necessity. Keep your nails and body clean. Use breath mints and de-odorants, and do not smoke. Wash your hands with soap that won't dry the skin, and do so before every make-up in front of the subject. If there is no sink in the make-up area, you can employ gel hand sanitizer, Seabreeze, witch hazel, or alcohol to sanitize your hands. Always keep your station clean. Always keep your kit and case immaculate. Your cleanliness will be judged in school and in the future at work.

- Instructors will always observe how you look in class, just as a performer will judge your appearance when you are working. If you are a woman and wear garish make-up, the actress will be apt to think, "Am I going to look like that?" And as a male make-up artist, avoid using strong after-shave lotions and colognes, or wearing sloppy clothing. You are in a designer clothes-conscious business; don't imitate the poorly clad masses.

AFTER GRADUATION AND STARTING OUT IN BUSINESS

- Start and maintain a list of production managers and companies.

- Print a business card and a résumé of your education that you can easily distribute. An accompanying photo may be helpful to clients.

- Search the Yellow Pages and Internet for photographers to whom you can send your résumé, and compose a letter showing your availability.

- Work on student films. Be compensated if possible. Is a film or tape copy available? Are screen credits/meals provided? Leave your business cards and résumés at costume and wig shops, community theatre groups, and at film and stage departments at local schools and colleges. Almost all of these will have some budget for make-up to at least cover your expenses; but work, and get credit for it in programs, etc.

- Do not lie to anyone about your work. Do not undercut anyone else's salary. Find out the minimum price range from the union, and never go below it.

- Never assume anything! Always verify everything. Get a call-sheet from the assistant director for the next day's plans.

- Do not borrow money from anyone.

- Try to avoid cliques and questionable groups.

- Communicate with the school concerning any information of which you might be in doubt.

- Learn proper nutrition. Stay healthy, and avoid drugs and alcohol.

- Join a make-up agency, and contact the local make-up artist's union for membership. Place an ad in production directories.

- Never be pompous or arrogant about your work. Stay humble!

- Use a reliable alarm clock or wake-up service on workdays.

- Show up one hour prior to call time. Meet crewmembers.

WHEN YOU ARE WORKING

- Introduce yourself and get to know your production manager, assistant directors, lighting director, cameramen, wardrobe people, and craft services personnel.

- Have a firm handshake, a warm smile, and look directly into people's eyes when you speak. Always be sincere.

- Develop a pleasant, harmonious personality! Be professional. Have fun, but remember: Make-up is a job—your job! If you take a job and a better one comes along, keep the old one, or find someone as competent as you to replace you. It's hard to lose a reputation for laxness or unreliability.

- Have pre-production meetings with the principal players before shooting commences. Do test make-ups if possible, on-camera, so others can see and approve them.

- Never speak badly about other make-up artists; it is not good business.

- Never retouch another make-up artist's work without permission. When onstage or on location, always be aware of what is known as a hot-set. This term refers specifically to either entire sets or sections of sets that have been designated as areas that absolutely should not be walked upon or changed in any way. A hot-set is usually a set that requires more shooting and must be left as is on-camera for production continuity.

- It is your responsibility to keep the talent looking good at all times. Ask for "last looks" before the camera rolls. Always carry what you require for retouching so there are no delays. Do not ruin a shot by standing in an inappropriate place. Do touch-ups between takes.

- Do not make noise during a take (beeper, phone, laughter, talking, shuffling feet, jingling coins or keys, etc.). Don't bump into light stands; you may make it necessary for a shot to be relit.

- Always recommend hiring a hairdresser. Never touch a hairdresser's work without permission.

- Never leave work early without notification from the make-up department head, production manager, and talent.

- Never start a job without a contract or deal memo, which should contain all the hours, salary information, and all duties that you will be required and obligated to perform.

- Try to eat in the studio commissary or at the craft service setup during lunch, dinner, and break times. Leaving the studio can create inadvertent and unexpected problems, which can lead to a late arrival back at the studio or location. Never be late returning from any meal break.

- Attend all production meetings, and always take notes. See rushes if you can.

In the end, what makes a good make-up artist?

Many things, all of which must be extremely positive in nature. To cite only a few:

One who is able to improvise! One who has a strong desire for excellence. One who is able to employ one product for a number of purposes. One who is a well-rounded craftsman, able to excel in all facets of one's specialty and profession.

How should a good make-up artist work?

An attribute that immediately comes to mind is speed. Always work fast. Remember: Time is equal to production money.

An artist should always work with grace and gentility, and make all the assigned performers comfortable. A make-up artist should always treat a performer with respect. When doing make-up, never place your hands on top of the performer's head. It is rude and uncomfortable for the subject. It also disturbs the hairstyle and upsets the hairdresser. Never lean on the performer. Keep a proper distance from the performer while working, and when finished with the make-up, stand behind the person and look in the mirror to see that everything is properly set and balanced. As a make-up artist, you are there to provide a service to the performer and the production. Do your best to shine in everyone's eyes.

Always apply products with brushes, sponges, puffs, and other professional tools. Do not use your fingers. Remember: You are a professional.

As a final note: Try writing down both your personal and professional goals, and review them often. Remember: At every moment, you will be confronted with situations that require decisions. Therefore, take the time to stop and think prior to acting. Correct decisions will keep you firmly on your path toward both personal and professional success. Most importantly, never lose sight of your dream.

WHAT MAKES JOE BLASCO
MAKE-UP ARTIST TRAINING UNIQUE

What makes the Joe Blasco schools so unique is based upon their long history. Joe Blasco Make-up Center West in Hollywood, California was the second professional make-up school personally designed and created by Joe Blasco. Although several make-up artists and groups of make-up artists in the past would independently teach various aspects of professional make-up artistry at which they were proficient, all of the instruction was in the form of seminars that were not state-approved, and could therefore not be classified as schools for professional make-up artistry. Many cosmetics companies in the past provided seminars for the purpose of promoting and selling their products, but these could also not be classified in this way. Other seminars taught by union make-up artists for the purpose of training individuals to pass the union test and/or to provide them with information that would permit them to pass specific areas of the test were also not state-approved, could only be considered private seminars, and were thus not schools.

Considering all of the above, once the apprentice program had been dissolved, there was no place where an individual who wished to become a make-up artist could go to learn all phases of professional make-up artistry in an organized, systematic, and comprehensive manner until 1968, when Joe Blasco designed a curriculum and acquired state-approved status for a small salon located at 1313 Westwood Boulevard in Los Angeles that was owned by Linda and Stewart Haines. Blasco had been working at the *Los Angeles Times* when an advertisement for that salon piqued his interest and helped generate in him the idea that a professional school for make-up artistry was needed. He convinced the owners that the salon, which up until that time had sold private label cosmetics and only instructed mature women in self-applied hairstyling techniques, application of eyelashes, and other society make-up artistry, could be transformed, under his guidance, into a full-fledged, state-approved school for professional make-up. The owners agreed and took a chance on Blasco's idea by hiring him immediately. Under Blasco's direction and efforts, the school became state-approved and successful enough that a new, larger location was needed, and the company moved to the Wilshire district. At this school, Joe Blasco created the first extremely comprehensive syllabus that taught professional make-up artistry from beauty make-up to detailed foam latex prosthesis fabrication and application, and was assisted by the likes of Ben Nye, Sr. and Rudy Horvatich, both of whom Blasco invited to teach as guest instructors at the school from time to time, and from whom Blasco would later learn a tremendous amount. Two years later, Blasco left the school, which he did not own, to accept a job as an independent apprentice/employee with Ben Nye, Sr. at Ben's first make-up studio on Santa Monica Boulevard where Ben taught him the intricacies of film make-up artistry, in addition to cosmetics chemistry, which would prove valuable when Blasco embarked on his own line of cosmetics over a decade later.

Up until the time when Blasco implemented the school at the salon owned and operated by the Haines, there was no state school of any kind which taught professional make-up in an organized and structured system. Aspiring make-up artists – once the apprenticeship program had been dissolved – would have to knock on the doors of many make-up artists and convince them to train them in various aspects of make-up artistry. Unfortunately, these artists were not always proficient in every aspect of the art and therefore did not have the credibility to teach a complete course that covered all aspects of studio make-up artistry. The first school which Blasco created did exactly that.

Blasco actually began teaching professional make-up artistry at the Mason Felix School. A small cosmetology school in Pittsburgh, Pennsylvania. He created and taught classes that encompassed all phases of professional make-up in the year 1965. The curriculum he created at the Mason Felix School served as a template for the first California state-approved school which he would later create in Los Angeles during 1968 at the afore-mentioned salon-turned-make-up school.

While working sporadically with Rudy Horvatich at ABC Television in the early '70s, Blasco pioneered many of the blood and gore effects, including the invention of the make-up bladder technique, a special make-up effect which would be used for years to come throughout the industry, for the early films of David Cronenberg. In 1976, he decided to open a new school, under his ownership, where he taught private classes. This school was the first Joe Blasco Make-up Center, and its success was predicated upon his original entrepreneurial ideas that he had honed and improved upon in creating an all-encompassing make-up program for aspiring artists. The school became incorporated the very next year. While operating the school, he continued to work as both a make-up artist and as a department head on thousands of shows for ABC during the 1970s, as well as into the 1980s and throughout the 1990s.

All professional schools today in the United States and Canada, as well as throughout Europe, were created after Blasco's successful pioneering efforts. Joe Blasco deeply under-stood the difficulty that prospective make-up artists were having in learning professional make-up techniques, especially women who wished to enter into the field. The Blasco Schools were the first to train women in a field that was predominately male-oriented. Today, the majority of make-up artists worldwide are in fact women, and the Blasco Schools were the first to initiate this trend.

The uniqueness of the Joe Blasco Schools and the high degree of sophistication of their curriculum can readily be seen when visiting the Hollywood School, the Orlando School (which was opened in 1991 and marked the first time that an institution such as his main-tained two major locations), and the new Joe Blasco Broadband Make-up Education Fa-cility in Orlando, which teaches live classes over the internet to many subscribers throughout the world. This system permits live classes taught personally by Joe Blasco and many other talented make-up artists, whom Blasco selects from the United States and Eu-rope, to be shown to students simultaneously at the Orlando and Hollywood Schools, as well as to the new licensed affiliate Joe Blasco Schools. These classes are not taped, but are in fact live HDTV broadcasts which are completely interactive during which students are able to ask questions and be given answers by Mr. Blasco and other artists who will be con-ducting the live broadcasts. The broadcasts are viewed on large HDTV plasma screens where live make-up application is seen in extreme detail and in true, full color. No other school offers this Joe Blasco, worldwide live interactive system. This is another example of Joe Blasco's innovative efforts to raise the standards and change the playing field of make-up education as it is currently known. To do this, Joe Blasco has actually purchased a build-ing near Universal Studios in Orlando, Florida that has been completely adapted into a television studio with lecture halls, classrooms, a large television stage, and a control room, as well as state-of-the-art equipment with which the broadband broadcast can be transmit-ted worldwide via T-1, T-2, and T-3 fiber optic lines.

The education offered at all Joe Blasco Make-up Centers is not solely derived from tech-niques originated by Joe Blasco, but is in fact a compilation of techniques taught to Mr. Blasco by such fine artists as George and Gordon Bau, John Chambers, Mr. Giles (Rome), Lee Greenway, Abe Haberman, Kiva Hoffman, Rudy Horvatich, Vincent J-R Kehoe, Hal King, Ben Nye, Sr., Lou Philippi, and many other master make-up artists too numerous to mention who were Mr. Blasco's original teachers. Mr. Blasco's curriculum encompasses not only their many techniques, but also his interpretations and revisions of them, which modernizes and systematically combines them all into make-up application methods which are unique to the Joe Blasco Schools.

All other make-up schools which are in existence today were created after the Blasco Schools. Also, many of them are operated by Joe Blasco graduates and/or individuals who were one-time employees of the Blasco organization. The Joe Blasco Schools, being the first state-approved institutions to teach professional make-up artistry, have actually become the template which others have followed in an attempt to duplicate Blasco's success in the field of make-up education.

ADDITIONAL JOE BLASCO MAKE-UP SCHOOL INFORMATION

- The first to initiate the use of television cameras so that students could actually see their work as it would appear on television, as well as being the first to include photography of the student's work utilizing motion picture film in full camera format for students to see their make-up when photographed with various Eastman Kodak color negative film stock.

- The first to create the video portfolio which enables students to create videotapes, and now DVD's which allow students to show their work to prospective employers. Joe Blasco created this system in the late '70s by offering his students video portfolios in addition to their still photographic ones, and this offering now includes the latest state-of-the-art DVD technology.

- Blasco was the first to become a union signatory to the Make-up Artists and Hairstylists Local 798 I.A.T.S.E. Aside from his many past innovations, his idea to become a signatory was extremely unique and enabled him to pick from the cream of the crop of union make-up artists, allowing him to offer his students the finest union make-up education possible, as well as to financially contribute to the health, welfare, and pension plans of Local 798 make-up artists and hairstylists who teach at his Orlando facility.

- All Local 706 and 798 make-up artists who teach at either the Hollywood facility or the Orlando facility are paid key make-up and hairstyling union rates, which enables them to maintain the same quality of life they have while working at the major film and television studios. Blasco is now in the process of finalizing the unionization of his Hollywood, California School as a signatory to Make-up Artists and Hairstylists Local 706 I.A.T.S.E. for the purpose of being able to also contribute to the health, welfare, and pension plans of those fine Local 706 make-up artists who work at that facility.

- The school is subsidized financially by the multi-million dollar Joe Blasco Cosmetics Company, permitting the school to pay the highest salaries to its teachers and therefore enabling the schools to attract the most prestigious and renowned make-up artists as instructors.

- Mr. Blasco is the innovator of the Lifetime Student Enrollment Program (L.S.E.P.), which other schools are now beginning to adapt by following in his footsteps. This unique program, which Blasco pioneered, enables all students to attend class for the duration of their lifetimes once they have successfully obtained the Joe Blasco diploma. Once students graduate, they may continue to attend the Joe Blasco Schools at any time they wish in the future for the duration of their lifetime, thus constantly keeping abreast of new techniques, new products, and having the great advantage of attending many classes with varied and numerous teachers, all of which will provide the students with greatly diversified knowledge in all aspects of make-up artistry, and all of which is free of charge after graduating from the initial beauty and/or professional program.

- The only government-approved schools owned by a seasoned, veteran artist and cosmetics chemist who designed and developed many innovations in cosmetics products, including natural red neutralizers, Dermaceal, and Ultamatte, in addition to being the first to invent airbrush make-up, originally called Aeroflow, as confirmed by Dinair®, the leading airbrush make-up used extensively at all Joe Blasco Make-up Schools.

- The Joe Blasco Make-up Schools do not charge their students a fee for lab time (also known as workshop hours). It is important for prospective make-up students to understand that lab hours should be part of the actual program, and as Joe Blasco believes, they should not be charged extra for their time in lab. It was also Joe Blasco who first created the workshop hours as an addition to the actual class time, enabling students to work free of charge for an additional two hours each day while being supervised by an instructor.

- Any student who is enrolled in the professional daytime class can also attend the night class free of charge, while nighttime students, when able, can attend the daytime class free of charge.

- The schools have been in existence longer than any others and are celebrating their 30th anniversary this coming year on July 19th (the anniversary of the passing of Jack Pierce, an artist who provided Mr. Blasco with great inspiration). Mr. Blasco wanted to bring to life—on the same day of the year—something that would give back to the industry what had been taken away with Mr. Pierce's passing, and he conceptualized the opening as a tribute to Mr. Pierce's lifetime in make-up and his innovative genius which influenced and inspired make-up artists past and present, and will continue to do so into the future.

- The Blasco School has the largest facility and contains the most modern equipment of all make-up schools internationally. Maintaining large classes requires the Blasco organization to have from two to four instructors in every class, depending upon class size and its one-on-one teacher-to-student requirements. Joe Blasco was the first to implement more than one teacher per class into his educational program. It was also Joe Blasco who first implemented the "on-set" hairdressing classes that serve as hairdressing appreciation for interested make-up artists, as well as advanced hairstyling classes for set use by licensed cosmetologists who wish to learn hairdressing for the entertainment industry.

- Mr. Blasco personally supervises all of the classes and is very involved in booking the professional make-up artists who teach at all of his facilities. He makes special appearances at both the East and West Coast Schools to teach advanced techniques in all phases of the art from beauty make-up to prosthesis application. Because the schools bear the Joe Blasco name, the syllabus must adhere to his strict requirements of excellence and the credibility that Mr. Blasco has personally established as the pioneer of all professional government-approved make-up schools.

- The schools maintain student stores which sell not only Joe Blasco Cosmetics®, but also products from Kryolan®, Mehron®, Graftobian®, Premiere Products®, Dinair®, Air Craft®, Cinema Secrets®, La Femme®, and RCMA® among others, many of which are featured in the complete professional make-up case that students receive.

- Mr. Blasco is the only make-up school proprietor to receive a prestigious Lifetime Distinguished Make-up Achievement Award for his work in make-up artistry, make-up education, and cosmetics manufacturing—bestowed upon him in 2004—from the U.S.I.T.T. (United States Institute of Theatre Technology).

- More award-winning and prominent make-up artists have graduated from the Joe Blasco Make-up Schools than from any others. There are currently more Joe Blasco graduates entering the Make-up Artist Trade Unions (Local 706 and 798)

Fig. App-43

Joe Blasco, Bill Corso, and Vincent J-R Kehoe. Mr. Corso, a graduate of the Hollywood Joe Blasco Make-up School, poses proudly with the Oscar® he was awarded for best make-up for his work in the motion picture Lemony Snicket's A Series of Unfortunate Events.

than graduates from any other schools. The schools have graduated more artists since 1968 than any other make-up schools in the history of make-up education.

- Aside from scores of Emmys that his students have received, both graduates Matthew Mungle and Bill Corso have won Academy Awards® for their work in *Bram Stoker's Dracula* and *Lemony Snicket's A Series of Unfortunate Events*, respectively.

- In addition to the above, this book, *The Professional Make-up Artist*, co-written by Mr. Vincent J-R Kehoe, serves as the official textbook of the Joe Blasco Make-up Schools. As you have seen, this book is the most detailed and comprehensive ever written to date on the art of professional make-up. This book is divided into two volumes: The first, which you are now reading, covers the history of make-up, all aspects of video and film picturization, and all extremely detailed and comprehensive beauty make-up artistry techniques; the second teaches all aspects of character make-up and laboratory procedures. These hardbound volumes, printed in full color, each with over 1,000 pages and more than 2,500 color illustrations and photographs, feature the work of numerous fine artists. These most comprehensive textbooks are unique to the Joe Blasco Schools and are only sold to other make-up institutions, colleges, and universities upon Mr. Blasco's approval of the quality of their instruction and the rate of their students' success in the field of make-up education. No other make-up schools aside from the Joe Blasco Schools, except those which also use these books as their formal texts, offer their students such a comprehensive and complete work of this magnitude.

- Joe Blasco personally continues to organize an association of the world's finest make-up schools (the Joe Blasco Association of International Make-up Schools, or A.I.M.S.), which meet his stringent educational standards and guidelines as established by this book. Aside from professional make-up schools, Joe Blasco will also accept state-approved cosmetology schools, high school and college drama departments, film schools, acting schools, medical make-up institutions, mortuary schools, and other such institutions, which will benefit from the high-quality education only available through Joe Blasco and the Joe Blasco Broadband Make-up Broadcast System, into the new association.

For information on how your school or institution can become part of this worldwide make-up educational system, visit www.broadbandmakeup.com and/or call (407) 363-1232.

Much of the Joe Blasco Make-up School uniqueness can be seen daily at muatv.com.

Appendix B

CURRENT SUPPLIERS AND MANUFACTURERS

A&S Case
5260 Vineland Avenue
North Hollywood, CA 91601
Tel. (800) 394-6181
www.ascase.com

A.D.M. Tronics, Inc.
224 S. Pegasus Avenue
Northvale, NJ 07647
Tel. (201) 767-6040
www.admtronics.com

Pros-Aide 1 and 2, Pros-Aide Cream,
Aqua Cream, and Cast-Aide

Alan Gordon Enterprises
5625 Melrose Avenue
Los Angeles, CA 90038
Tel. (323) 466-3561
www.alangordon.com

**Alcone, Inc.
(A New York beauty supply legend)**
5–45 49th Street
Long Island City, NY 11101
Tel. (800) 466-7446
www.alconeco.com

Art Molds
18 Bank Street
Summit, NJ 07901
Tel. (908) 273-5401
www.artmolds.com

Alginates and Mold Making Materials

Ball Beauty Supply
416 N. Fairfax Avenue
Los Angeles, CA 90036
Tel. (800) 588-0244
www.ballbeauty.com

BJB Enterprises
14791 Franklin Avenue
Tustin, CA 92780
Tel. (714) 734-8450
www.bjbenterprises.com

Epoxies, Urethanes, and TC-1630

Boneyard FX
511 S. First Avenue #116
Arcadia, CA 91006
Tel. (800) 878-0566
www.boneyardfx.com

Burman Industries
13536 Saticoy Street
Van Nuys, CA 91402
Tel. (818) 782-9833
www.burmanfoam.com

Alginates (Accu-cast), BJB Products,
Plasters, Sculpting Tools, Gelatin,
Gelatin Components, Urethanes,
Silicones, All Make-Up Effects Needs,
and Lab Supplies

Cinema FX/Davis Dental
7347 Ethel Avenue
North Hollywood, CA 91605
Tel. (818) 765-4994
www.cinemafx.com

Lab Supplies

Circle K Products
Mailing: P.O. Box 909
Temecula, CA 92593
Physical: 47825 De Luz Rd.
Temecula, CA 92590
Tel. (909) 695-1955,
Fax (909) 695-0605

Silicone Products
(Tin- and Platinum-based)

Coast Airbrush
312 N. Anaheim Boulevard
Anaheim, CA 92805
Tel. (714) 635-5557
www.coastairbrush.com

Eco-House, Inc.
P.O. Box 220, Station A
Fredericton, New Brunswick E3B 4Y9 –
Canada
Tel. (506) 366-3529,
Fax (506) 366-3577
www.eco-house.com

Edward French, Inc.
Special Makeup FX Studio
9209 Lakeview Terrace
Chatsworth, CA 91311
Tel. (818) 340-4852
Fax (818) 340-4837
www.edwardfrench.com

Frends Beauty Supply
(A Hollywood beauty supply legend)
5270 Laurel Canyon Boulevard
N. Hollywood, CA 91607
Tel. (888) 7-FRENDS
www.frendsbeautysupply.com

Frends FX Supply
5270 Laurel Canyon Boulevard
North Hollywood, CA 91607
Tel. (818) 769-3834,
Fax (818) 769-8124
www.frendsbeautysupply.com

Alginates, Plasters, Sculpting Tools, Gelatin
Components, All Make-Up Effects Needs,
and Lab Supplies

Gable's Beauty Supply
117 Northwest 9th Terrace
Hallendale, FL 33009
Tel. (800) 565-3233
www.equilibrix.com/gbs/gbs05_04.html

Graftobian
510 Tasman Street
Madison, WI 53714
Tel. (608) 222-7849
www.graftobian.com

Fine Theatrical and Specialty Make-Up
Products

*The following products are available from
Graftobian:*

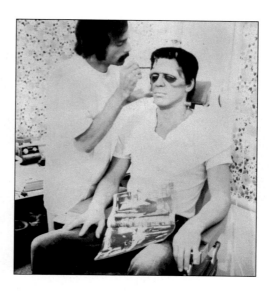

Joe Blasco spraying black nestles "streak and tips" temporary hair color to the "construction makeup" head piece, after removal from the actors head. The entire head piece was "constructed" by hand in two and a half hours from cardboard, cotton, lepages glue, liquid latex, creped wool and prosthetic makeup base. The "piece" could then be used again and again with only minor touchups.

A faded vintage photo of Joe Blasco applying a Frankenstein monster makeup to Craig Littler for the Dove production "Shasta Cola" commercial in 1971.

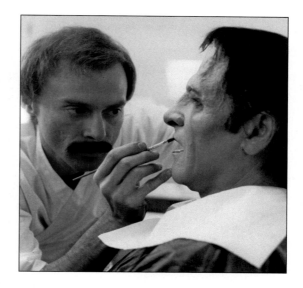

With the head piece in place, Joe Blasco applies cotton with "burn cloth" tissue "over-lay" to facilitate a blended edge from the piece on to the actor's skin. The construction "bender" is then covered with"prosthetic" coloring called P.M. (Prosthetic Makeup)

Joe Blasco applying the Frankenstein monster makeup. Mr. Blasco created scores of "monster" make-ups using only construction makeup techniques and not prosthetics. Forrey J. Ackerman, the creator and editor of "Famous Monsters of Filmland Magazine" called Mr. Blasco "the new Jack Pierce". The actor is Christopher Weeks.

Joe Blasco applies the famous shadow depression originally designed by Jack Pierce for the 1931 Boris Karloff version of the Frankenstein monster.

Christopher Weeks in another construction Frankenstein monster makeup by Joe Blasco prior to wardrobe.

Joe Blasco applying "The Monster" makeup to Christopher Weeks, who played the monster several times in the 1970's.

Christopher Weeks and Joe Blasco

Joe Blasco creates another version of The Frankenstein Monster.

Blasco doing some last minute touch-ups on the set of "Shasta Cola's Igor."
called the monster "Igor" …the camera man on the shoot, Haskel Wexler,
Mr. Blasco should have been cast as the "Mad Doctor" – this photo cer-
y illustrates his reason why.

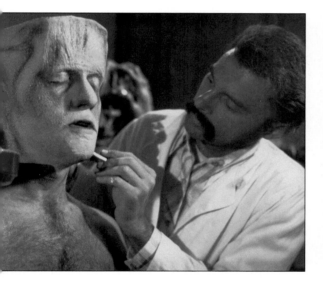

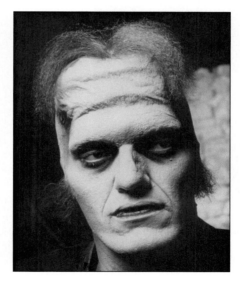

her Frankenstein type construction monster makeup being applied
e Blasco.

A close up of Richard Kiel in "construction" monster makeup by Joe Blasco.

Richard Kiel in "construction" monster makeup. Another of Blasco's many Frankenstein's monsters.

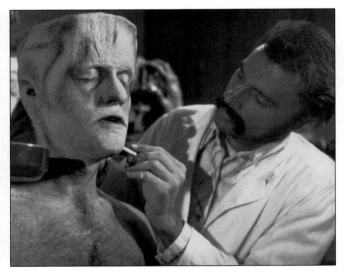

Side angle of another Joe Blasco "construction" monster, staring actor Richard Kiel.

Image Exclusives
8020 Melrose Avenue
West Hollywood, CA 90046
Tel. (323) 651-4678

Joe Blasco
Professional Make-up Store
521 N. Kirkman
Orlando, Fl 32808
Tel. (800) 252-7261,
Fax (407) 352-5190
www.joeblasco.com

Select brands of professional make-up,
including Joe Blasco and RCMA Cosmetics

Joe Blasco
Professional Make-up Store
1670 Hillhurst
Los Angeles, CA 90027
Tel. (800) 634-0008,
Fax (323) 664-7142
www.joeblasco.com

Select brands of professional make-up,
including Joe Blasco and RCMA Cosmetics

Julie Hewett
Tel. (800) 761-6647
www.juliehewett.net

Krylon
www.krylon.com

Makeup Guru
www.makeupguru.com

Motion Picture F/X Company
123 S. Victory Boulevard
Burbank, CA 91502
Tel. (818) 563-2366
Fax (818) 563-2389
www.makeupkits.com

Alginates, BJB Products, Plasters, Sculpting Tools, Silicones, Gelatin Components,
All Make-Up Effects Needs, and
Lab Supplies

Naimie's Beauty Center
(A Hollywood beauty supply legend)
12640 Riverside Drive, (Valley Village)
North Hollywood, CA 91607
Tel. (818) 655-9922
www.naimies.com

Paasche Airbrush Company
7440 W. Lawrence Avenue
Harwood Heights, IL 60706-3412
Tel. (708) 867-9191
Fax (708) 867-9198

Premiere Products, Inc.
P.O. Box 12422
La Crescenta, CA 91224
Tel. (818) 897-2440
www.ppi.cc

Beta Bond, Beta Solv, Super Solv, and Telesis Adhesives (New Silicone Adhesives)

Robinson Beautilities
12320 Venice Boulevard
Los Angeles, CA 90066
Tel. (310) 398-5757

Smooth-On
2000 Saint John Street
Easton, PA 18042
Tel. (610) 252-5800, (800) 762-0744
www.smoothon.com

Body Double Silicone Casting Material, Urethanes, and Epoxies

Spectrum Chemicals
14422 S. San Pedro Street
Gardena, CA 90248
Tel. (800) 772-8786
Fax (310) 516-6118

Studioworks
814 N. Hollywood Way
Burbank, CA 91505
Tel. (818) 848-1838

Tinsley Transfers, Inc.
P.O. Box 10011
Burbank, CA 91510
www.tinsleytransfers.com

Vapon, Inc.
299-B Fairfield Avenue
Fairfield, NJ 07004
Tel. (800) 443-8856
Fax (973) 575-6164

Ve's Favorite Brushes
30625 Hasley Canyon Road
Castaic, CA 91384
Tel. (661) 294-3900
www.favoritebrushes.com

W.M. Creations, Inc.
5755 Tujunga Avenue
North Hollywood, CA 91601
Tel. (818) 763-6692
Fax (818) 763-6693
www.matthewwmungle.com

Old Age Stipples, Stacolors (Liquids and Palette Forms), X-Tra Hold Spirit Gums, Scar Material, Scab Materials, Brush Holders, Adhesive Holders, Liquid Plastic Material, and Sealers

Wilshire Sterling Beauty Supplies
1244 Vine Street
Los Angeles, CA 90038
Tel. (323) 463-6801

MANUFACTURERS
(That have provided us with information):

Dremel
4915 21st Street
Racine, WI 53406
Tel. (800) 437-3635
www.dremel.com

Burman Industries
13536 Saticoy Street
Van Nuys, CA 91402
Tel. (818) 782-9833
www.burmanfoam.com

The following products are available from Burman Industries:

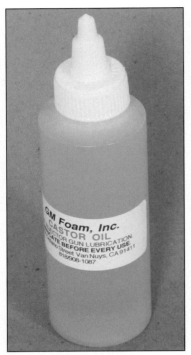

Fig. App. B13

Castor oil

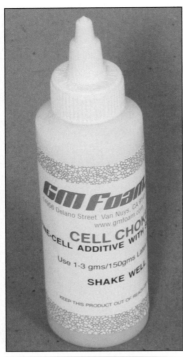

Fig. App. B14

Cell choke

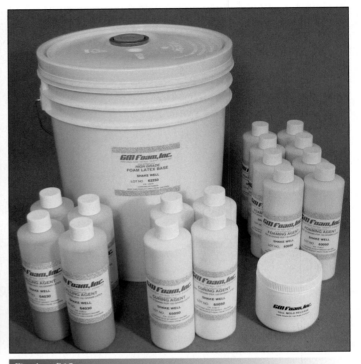

Fig. App. B15

Five-gallon foam kit.

Fig. App. B16

Foam Increaser

Fig. App. B17

Injector

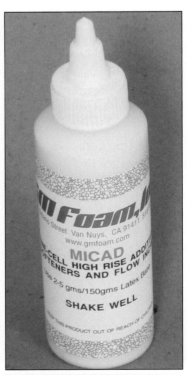

Fig. App. B18

Micad

Fig. App. B19

One-gallon foam kit.

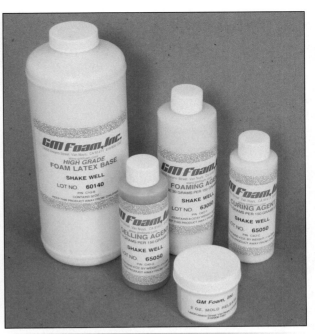

Fig. App. B20

One-quart foam kit.

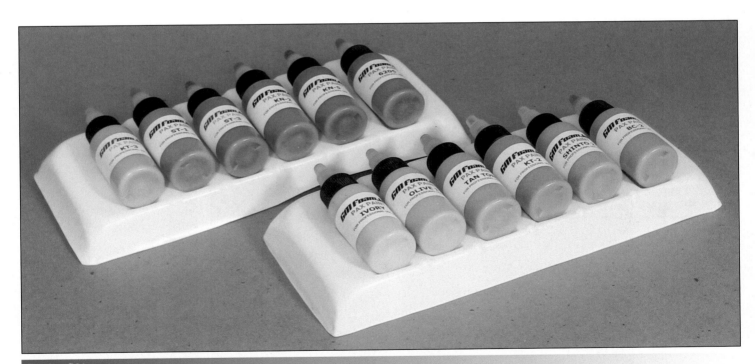

Fig. App. B21

Pax paints

Burman Industries
13536 Saticoy Street
Van Nuys, CA 91402
Tel. (818) 782-9833
www.burmanfoam.com

All GM Foam products are available from Burman's

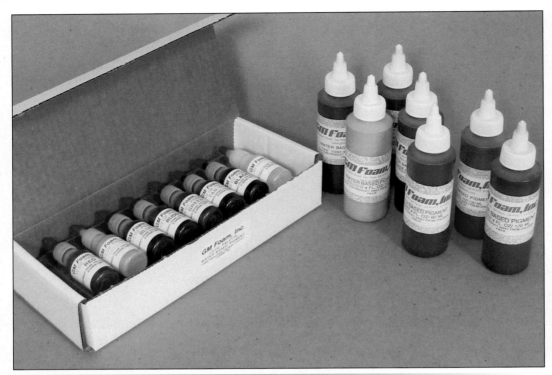

Fig. App. B22

Pigments

Fig. App. B23

Foam Stabilizer

Fig. App. B24

A Larger Size of Foam Stabilizer

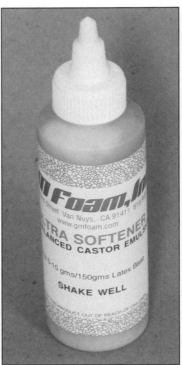

Fig. App. B25

Ultra Softener

Fig. App. B26

Water-based Primer

Joe Blasco Cosmetics
1670 Hillhurst Avenue
Hollywood, CA 90027
Tel. (323) 671-1092
(407) 297-1449
(800) 553-1580
Fax (407) 522-9916
www.joeblasco.com

Mavidon
1820 2nd Avenue North
Lake Worth, FL 33461
Tel. (800) 654-0385
www.mavidon.com

Medical Quality Disposables by QOSMEDIX
150-Q Executive Drive
Edgewood, NY 11717
Tel. (631) 242-3270
www.qosmedix.com

Mehron, Inc.
100 Red Schoolhouse Road
Chestnut Ridge, NY 10977
Tel. (845) 426-1700
www.mehron.com

Microbrush International
1376 Cheyenne Avenue
Grafton, WI 53024
Tel. (866) 866-8698
www.microbrush.com

RCMA
P.O. Box 850
Somis, CA 93066
Tel. (805) 386-4744

Reel Creations, Inc. (Fred Blau)
7831 Alabama Avenue, Suite 21
Canoga Park, CA 91304
Tel. (818) 346-7335
www.reelcreations.com

BRITISH MAKE-UP SUPPLIERS

The following list, provided by Christopher Tucker, is comprised of British businesses. Currently, all these suppliers will provide make-up brushes, cosmetics, foam latex kits,

and other prosthetic supplies.

Screenface
20–24 Powis Terrace
Westbourne Park Road
Notting Hill, London W11 1JH
Tel: 020 7221 8289
Fax: 020 7836 3955

Screenface
48 Monmouth Street
Covent Garden
London WC2 9EP

Make-Up Artist Provisions
6 Goldhawk Mews
Shepherds Bush
London W12 8PA
Tel: 020 8740 0808
Fax: 020 8740 0802

Charles H Fox Ltd
22 Tavistock Street
Covent Garden
London WC2E 7PY
Tel: 020 7379 3111
Fax: 020 7379 34

HAIR/WIG SUPPLIERS

For wigs and hairpieces:

Angels Wigs
1 Garrick Road
London NW9 6AA
Tel: 020 8202 2244
Fax: 020 8202 1820

BBC Resources
Freepost BBC Resources
London W12
Tel: 08700 100883
www.bbcresources.com

Banbury Postiche Ltd
Little Bourton House
Southam Road
Banbury Oxfordshire OX16 1 SR
Tel: 01295 757400
Fax: 01295 757401

Pam Foster Associates Ltd
Unit 009, The Chandlery,
50 Westminster Bridge Road
London SE1 7QY
Tel: 020 7721 7641

Fax: 020 7721 7409

Hairaisers
105 Cleveland Street
London W1T 6PR
Tel: 020 7580 7666
Fax: 020 7436 5766

London & New York Wig Co.
Unit107, Blackfriars Foundry,
156 Blackfriars Road
London SE1 8EN
Tel: 020 7721 7095
Fax: 020 7721 7026

Ray Marston Wig Studio Ltd
No4 Charlotte Road
London EC2A 3DH
Tel: 020 7739 3900
Fax: 020 7739 8100

Sarah Phillips & Co
Unit 11, Tottenham Green
Co-Operative Workshop,
2 Somerset Road
London N17 9ED
Tel: 020 8808 2171
Fax: 020 8808 2157

Wig Specialities Ltd
173 Seymour Place
London W1H 4PW
Tel: 020 7262 6565
Fax: 020 7723 1566

PROSTHETICS MATERIALS SILICONE/POLYURETHANE/ ALGINATE/CHEMICALS

W.P. Notcutt Ltd
Homewood Farm
Newark Lane
Ripley, Surrey GU23 6DJ
Tel: 01483 223311
Fax: 01483-479594

Jacobson Chemicals
Jacobson House
The Crossways, Churt
Farnham, Surrey GU10 2JD
Tel: 01428 713637

Fax: 01428 712835

Bentley Chemicals Ltd
Rowland Way
Hoo Farm Industrial Estate
Kidderminster
Worcestershire DY11 7RA
Tel: 01562 515121
Fax: 01562 515847

FOAM LATEX CHEMICALS
(Processing chemicals in bulk only)

Aquaspersions Ltd
Tel: 01422 386200
Fax: 01422 386239

DENTAL/TEETH

Fangs FX Ltd
The Studio
Sheepcote Dell Road
Beamond End
Amersham Bucks HP7 OQS
Tel/Fax: 0870 747 3337

ACRYLIC EYES

Cantor-Nissel
Nissel House
Fensomes Close
Hemel Hemstead
Herts HP2 5DH
Tel/Fax: 01442 254553

CONTACT LENSES

The Reel Eye Company
365–367 Watling Street
Radlett
Herts WD7 7LB
Tel: 01923 850207
Fax: 01923 850738

SCULPTORS' TOOLS AND MATERIALS SUPPLIERS

Alec Tiranti Ltd
Shop & Mail Order

(for alginate, silicone rubber, polyurethanes, plasters, dental & sculptors tools, etc.)

70 High Street
Theale, Reading
Berkshire RG7 5AR
Tel: 0118 9302775
Fax: 0118 9323487

London Shop:
27 Warren Street
London W1T 5NB
Tel: 020 7636 8565

LIGHTING

Duro-Test Lighting, Inc.
123 N. Union Avenue, Suite #104
Cranford, NJ 07016
Tel. (800) BUY-DURO
www.duro-test.com

Sylvania
100 Endicott Street
Danvers, MA 01923
Tel. (978) 777-1900
www.sylvania.com

General Electric
www.ge.com

COSMETIC DENTISTRY

Dr. Michael S. Bjornbak, DDS
5644 Van Nuys Boulevard, Suite 2
Sherman Oaks, CA 91401
Tel. (818) 781-3411
www.shermanoaksdental.com

Dr. Gary O'Brien, DDS
411 N. Central Avenue, #225
Glendale, CA 91203
Tel. (818) 956-0639

Sirona Dental Systems (CEREC)
www.cereconline.com

Dr. Keith Eskanos, DDS
436 N. Roxbury Drive
Beverly Hills, CA 90210
Tel. (310) 890-2702

CONTACT LENSES

Professional Vision Care Associates
Dr. Mort Greenspoon
Dr. Stacey Sumner
14607 Ventura Boulevard
Sherman Oaks, CA 91403
Tel. (818) 789-3311

Dr. D. Wes Wheadon
San Robertson Square
8955 Santa Monica Boulevard
West Hollywood, CA 90069
Tel. (310) 273-7136

PHYSICIANS

Dr. Irving Posalski, MD
(Internal Medicine/
Infectious Diseases)
Cedars-Sinai Medical Office Towers
8635 W. Third Street, Suite 1185W
Los Angeles, CA
Tel. (310) 855-0976
www.healthyworldtraveler.com
iposalsk@ucla.edu

Dr. Dale A. Prokupek, MD
(Internal Medicine)
8641 Wilshire Boulevard, Suite 100
Beverly Hills, CA 90211
Tel. (310) 659-9572
(310) 659-4740

Dr. George H. Semel, MD
(Cosmetic Surgery)
450 S. Beverly Drive
Beverly Hills, CA 90212
Tel. (310) 277-0222
www.drsemel.com

Dr. Millard Zisser, MD
(Dermatology)
8635 W. 3rd Street #1060W
Los Angeles, CA 90048
Tel. (310) 659-2770

Fig. App. B26

Joe Blasco, Matthew Mungle create a full head cast with then student Bob Arrollo, who went on to become the makeup department head for the popular T.V. show "E.R." Mr. Blasco personally taught both Matthew Mungle and Bob Arrollo.

Appendix N

HOLLYWOOD SUPPLY HOUSE HISTORY AND LEGENDS, THE TRUE STORY

INTRODUCTION

For many years, perhaps starting as far back as the early 1920s, make-up artists have had to invent not only the techniques, but also the many products and tools which were necessary to satisfy the ever-changing industry within which they worked. First for stage, and then for motion pictures, still photography, and finally television, make-up artists have been required to be extremely creative and innovative in a manner in keeping with the many other artisans who were also pioneers during the golden era of film and television.

As strange as it may seem today, beauty supply stores of the past only sold products to licensed cosmetologists and were not originally designed to be supply houses for the beauty make-up artists and special make-up effects artists. In fact, most professional make-up was sold through drugstores in Los Angeles, such as Lee's Drugs, which was located on the southwest corner of Hollywood and Highland, Schwab's Pharmacy, which was located at Sunset and Laurel Canyon, and Columbia Cosmetics, which was located at Gower Gulch and was physically part of the Columbia Pictures complex on the southeast corner of Gower and Sunset.

FRENDS BEAUTY SUPPLY

In the early days, Frends Beauty Supply, Atlas Beauty Supply, Mercury Beauty Supply, and Jack Sperling were among the first cosmetology supply houses to begin selling to professional make-up artists. Mr. Sig Frends, who also catered to cosmetologists, began to understand – through his association with a new, young, and enthusiastic employee by the name of Naimie Ojeil – that make-up artists required better outlets for their needs.

Sig Frends and Eddie Nave were originally partners in Atlas Beauty Supply. Sig and his wife Ethel decided to start Frends as a retirement store, which he opened up in order to keep busy and earn an income. (Mercury Beauty Supply was opened by Eddie Nave when he decided to go his separate way, but has just recently gone out of business.) Frends Beauty Supply grew from a small store into one of the premiere suppliers for the Hollywood motion picture and television industry.

In the mid-1980s, Frends closed temporarily. As told to us by current manager Mr. Nigel Dare, who hails from Georgetown, Guyana in South America, Mr. Emad Esper, a developer who currently owns Frends, had suffered a back injury and wanted to invest in something new. When the opportunity to purchase Frends came along, he took it. At the time, he had no knowledge of beauty supplies, and for a few years, running the business proved difficult.

Fig. N-1

Frends Beauty Supply.

Fig. N-2

Fig. N-3

An inside view of Frends Beauty Supply.

Fig. N-4

Fig. N-5

Fig. N-6

Nigel, who migrated seventeen years ago with his family to the United States, landed his first job at Frends in 1988 in the shipping and receiving department. Growing up in Guyana, Nigel had never encountered many of the products he came across at the store, so out of curiosity, he began to study their labels and acquire product knowledge. A few years later, the then-manager of Frends, Mr. Hashem Jaffar, who knew all of the inner workings of the company, decided to leave. Because Nigel had spent time in the warehouse and had become well-acquainted with all the company's products, he was promoted to the job of purchaser, and a year or so after that, after being with the company for only four years, was appointed manager.

After managing Frends for a few years, Nigel started his own beauty supply close to CBS Television, but things failed to develop as well as he had hoped, and he headed to New York City to begin a new business. Disenchanted with the climate, and having made so many friends in Los Angeles, he decided to return when he heard that Frends was looking for someone to run the store. Mr. Esper, the owner of Frends, has been very supportive over the years, and the two of them have succeeded in making a mark in the industry and returning Frends Beauty Supply to its original glory.

The individuals who now comprise the workforce at Frends are very happy to be a part of making movies! Nigel stated in conversation with the authors that it is his job to acquire anything that make-up artists and hairdressers may need, and to do so from all over the world in a timely manner. He went on to state that the beauty supply business is a business of providing constant satisfaction, and Frends will do whatever it takes to deliver to professional make-up artists not only in Hollywood, but also throughout the United States, Canada, South America, Europe, and Asia…worldwide!

Fig. N-7

The staff of Frends Beauty Supply.

NAIMIE'S BEAUTY CENTER

The name Naimie Ojeil has become legendary in the Hollywood beauty supply industry! Now as owner of Naimie's Beauty Center with partner Mr. Sam Bekerian, Mr. Ojeil has worked diligently to supply many specialty items that artists would normally be unable to locate. The company's distribution is worldwide, and the center is quite unique inasmuch as it does not have the look of a beauty supply store, but rather that of a very refined and upscale department store, make-up boutique, and spa combined.

Naimie started his career at the original Frends Beauty Supply. Originally working as a salesman, he later became known as one of the most knowledgeable and influential individuals of the beauty supply profession. He credits Sig Frends as his mentor and states openly that Sig was like a father to him. Sig taught Naimie to succeed in the make-up supply business, and few people actually knew how very close the two of them were. Naimie claims that Sig always protected him from the politics of the business, and when he first started, he helped develop his awareness and strength, both in business and in his personal life. When Naimie decided to leave Frends and open Naimie's Beauty Center, he at first had great difficulty, and as any good father figure would, Sig took him back to work until he got up on his feet. Naimie is proud to say that when he finally opened his own store, Sig gave him his blessing and actually continued to help him along the way, even after Naimie had become independent. Naimie has reiterated several times to the authors that he will always cherish Sig and speak of him with love and appreciation.

Fig. N-8

Naimie's Beauty Center.

Fig. N-9

Fig. N-10

An inside view of Naimie's Beauty Center.

Back in the early days, beauty supply stores mostly catered to hairdressers. Sig Frends, who was a close friend of the owner of Kay-De Powder Puff, acquired the company's puffs and sponges, and for make-up artists, sold professional pencils from La Femme. Those pencils may have been the very first products to be sold directly to make-up artists, according to many of the pioneers in the beauty make-up profession. The La Femme Company, one of the very first make-up companies to sell specialty-type products to make-up artists through the beauty suppliers, was founded by Abe Balaban and is run today by his son, Gary.

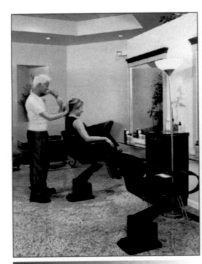

Fig. N-11

Naimie's Beauty Salon.

Fig. N-12

The entrance of Naimie's Spa.

Fig. N-13

Naimie's Wig Salon.

Naimie, realizing that make-up artists in the past were having to purchase their products from drugstores, started to research where he could get products that make-up artists needed, and after many meetings with the Max Factor Company and with Sig Frends, was successful in purchasing specialty products, not only from Factor and La Femme, but from many other specialty make-up companies from around the world. Naimie brought this business to Frends. With his innovative ideas and the approval of Sig, he personally provided a pivotal point in the make-up industry by understanding that beauty supply companies were failing to reach their potential when it came to supplying the artists. The evolution of the beauty supply business into what we see today is in large part a result of the many ideas which Naimie refined from others, and in many cases, actually developed on his own while collaborating with Sig. As stated earlier, beauty supply houses were originally for hairdressers, and it was impossible to shop within those stores without a cosmetology license. It was Naimie who approached Sig Frends and prompted him to expand his horizons by opening his doors not only to licensed cosmetologists, but also to professional make-up artists and the general public. Many beauty supply stores throughout the world have followed in the footsteps originally created by these two men. As Sig taught Naimie to believe in himself and not be afraid to take chances, Naimie began to push the envelope by providing innovations in marketing, distribution, and product development for professionals.

It was Naimie who noticed that make-up artists were using unsanitary upholstery sponge to apply make-up. Sig permitted him to create a line of wedge-cut sponges, which were a synthetic blend and stiffer than the upholstery version that crumbled easily when brushed across a man's beard area. These wedge-cut sponges were actually a Naimie Ojeil innovation.

Naimie also emphasized the fact that make-up artists were using professional oil painting brushes, which were a very high-quality sable and in fact much more sophisticated than the only make-up brushes (made by Max Factor) available to make-up artists at that time. Naimie, seeing the need for better artist's brushes, approached Sig with the idea of making copies of the most popular brushes that make-up artists bought from art supply stores. These brushes actually became the first high-quality professional brushes specifically intended for make-up use. Today, there are thousands of brands of brushes in specific sizes and shapes for make-up application, and few make-up artists know how pivotal Naimie Ojeil was in this development.

Much of Naimie's success came from collaborating with many expert make-up artists and hairstylists who would share their knowledge and provide him with a level of understanding for the products they needed and the importance of getting them quickly. During those early days, Naimie faced many opponents who did not like the changes and who actually, in many respects, did not want to see him or Sig Frends succeed. But Sig interceded and taught Naimie how to endure, and Naimie's appreciation of the make-up and hair profession gave Naimie the inspiration to be unrelenting in his desire to create one of the best professional beauty supply centers in the world – first at Frends, and now at his own store on Riverside Drive in North Hollywood.

Naimie's Beauty Center, which is actually a mini professional department store, as well as a cosmetics and hair center, is a one-stop shop! Today, Naimie's Beauty Center is one of the best known names in the professional beauty make-up supply business.

Fig. N-14

Fig. N-15

Burman Industries, now part of the Naimie Ojeil and Samuel Bekerian Conpanies.

Fig. N-16

Fig. N-17

Fig. N-18

OTHER HOLLYWOOD SUPPLY HOUSES

Robinson's Beautilities, a company that has been around as long as the authors can recall, and which began as a costume supply company, now offers many professional make-up and hair products to both the film and television industries.

Another fine professional beauty supply house in Hollywood, California is Image Exclusives, located in the very trendy area of Melrose Avenue in West Hollywood, just east of Fairfax, near CBS Television. Image Exclusives, owned by Monet and Dee Mansano, has become one of the most popular supply houses within the actual geographical area of Hollywood.

The Ball Beauty Supply is a longtime and historic beauty supply on Fairfax Avenue that has catered to professional make-up artists for many years.

EAST COAST SUPPLY HOUSES

One of the early suppliers on the East Coast was Paramount Drug Store, at the corner of 53rd and Broadway in New York City, operated by Frank Kalen and his son, Marshall. In 1950, Paramount Theatrical Enterprises, which began by selling eyelashes to showgirls out of a pharmacy in Times Square in New York City, became one of the first supply houses of professional products for the live stage and television arenas. The authors can remember the early days, when practically every professional product for make-up artistry use was obtained from this company.

Shortly thereafter, the company moved to a larger space, changed its name to Alcone (after its founder, Alvin Cohen), and expanded into mail order, which still remains its mainstay of business. Alcone's owner today, Vincent Mallardi, like Naimie Ojeil, Emad "Ed" Esper, Sig Frends, Jack Sperling, and Helen Cohen, has carried on the evolution of the professional make-up supply house and has enabled professionals throughout the East Coast, and in fact, the world to purchase the same high quality products found in Hollywood, as well as additional professional products manufactured on the East Coast, many of which were not available to Hollywood make-up artists.

Also on the East Coast in Florida is the very well-known Gable's Beauty Supply, which has grown considerably into several locations during the past few years and stands as one of the region's largest suppliers.

CONCLUSION

Many make-up artists of the past can fondly remember entering the doors of Columbia Cosmetics, Frends Beauty Supply, Lee's Drugs, and the Schwab Pharmacy on Sunset to purchase all of the specialized products that enabled them to express their love for the art. Therefore, aside from the many innovative make-up artists and hairstylists, we must not forget those individuals who created the beauty supply business and in doing so, also helped to further the education and knowledge of aspiring and currently working make-up artists both yesterday and today.

(For contact information, please see Appendix B.)

Dedications

Joe Blasco at ABC-TV's General Hospital *make-up room, captured during a rare quiet moment in 1974 by a friend, Richard A. Rivas.*

Joe Blasco

I gratefully dedicate both volumes of this book to my first teachers,
Richard Corson and Vincent J-R Kehoe.

And to my other teachers: Ben Nye, Sr., Hollis Bane, Jack Barron, George Bau,
Gordon Bau, John Chambers, Larry Darr, Alberto De Rossi, George Dibie,
Giles Gilbert, Lee Greenway, Aida Grey, Abe Haberman, Gene Hibbs,
Kiva Hoffman, Rudy Horvatich, Mary Keats, Hal King, Ben Lane,
June Miggins, Charles Nash, Charles Parker, Lou Phillippe, Don Post, Sr.,
Bob Salvatore, Peter Saxby, Bob Schiffer, Bud Sweeney, Ted Tetzlaff,
Harry Thomas, and Claude Thompson.

Also: Barbara Steele, Miss Rona Barrett, Carol Burnett, Nancy Centi,
Dick Clark, Katherine Gavatorta, and Steven Lockwood.

To my mother,
Margaret "Margo" Wast

. . . I thank you all.

Joe Blasco

From Small Town Beginnings . . .

The entrance to the small borough of North Irwin, the area of Western Pennsylvania where Joe Blasco's make-up career began—a testament to the fact that you do not have to have been born or raised in Hollywood, nor have family there, in order to succeed in the world of professional make-up!

Mr. Blasco's Mother: Margaret "Margo" Wast

Mr. Kehoe's mother, Bertha F. Kehoe, nee Roux.

Vincent J-R Kehoe

When my first make-up book was published in 1958, I dedicated it to my mother, as she had been a great inspiration and always a supporter of all my efforts at success. Now, some forty-seven years and over fifteen books on different subjects (with many printings in various languages) later, I am most proud of this current new set of books, and I rededicate my contribution to them to her.

Over the years, since I first started as a professional make-up artist, as well as many other professional endeavors which I have pursued as a writer, photographer, filmmaker, lecturer, and so forth, there have been others who have contributed, encouraged, and aided me in my life's work in so many subjects. First, I should like to mention Charles Sampas, City Editor and columnist for the Lowell Sun Newspaper; Arthur Seelig of the Jerome Cargill Producing Company; Russell Neale of Hastings House, publisher of my first work; Albert McCleery of NBC Television, director/producer of the Hallmark Hall of Fame *original productions, with whom I worked for almost three years; Dick Smith, who headed the NBC-TV make-up department during its beginning years in black-and-white and who developed color television make-up for them for Compatible Color; and Major General Sir Christopher Welby-Everard, KBE, CB, DL, of the 10th Foot Royal Lincolnshire Regimental Association for his help and encouragement in forming and leading, as Honorary Colonel, the American Contingent of this famous British Regiment for the American Bicentennial, crowned by my being appointed the Commander of the Guard of Honor for Her Majesty Queen Elizabeth II during her visit to Boston, Massachusetts in July of 1976.*

There are many, many others who have supported my endeavors, but none so faithfully as my friend, Bradford Bigham of Concord, Massachusetts, whom I have been privileged to know for many years.

And finally, and dearly, my lovely wife, Gena, who has put up with me for these many years.

Vincent J-R Kehoe

July 2005

Just one last word in closing from the authors:

We would like to thank Mr. Naimie Ojeil for bringing us together, and Mr. Ronald Jason Palmieri for finalizing the agreement which made this book become a reality.

Joe Blasco paints the head which he created for the film "Track of the Moon Beast." In this film Mr. Blasco designed and constructed the complete "body-suit" worn by Chase Cordel as the "Moon Beast." Blasco also sculpted and applied all of the various "transformation" appliances which were photographed in time-lapse photography to change the actor into the "Moon Beast." During the process, Mr. Blasco injured his hand and could not complete the sculpting of the hands and feet. John Chambers recommended that Blasco call a very young, but talented boy to finish the sculpting...his name was Rick Baker!

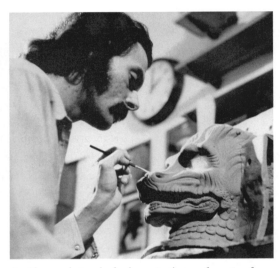

Joe Blasco sculpting the final stage in the transformation from man to "Moon Beast."

Joe Blasco sculpting one of the earlier stages of the "Moon Beast" transformation process.